Real World
Microeconomics

Second Edition

Edited by David Moglen

cognella
San Diego, CA

Bassim Hamadeh, CEO and Publisher
Michael Simpson, Vice President of Acquisitions
Jamie Giganti, Managing Editor
Jess Busch, Senior Graphic Designer
Kristina Stolte, Acquisitions Editor
Michelle Piehl, Project Editor
Alexa Lucido, Licensing Coordinator

First published in the United States of America in 2015 by Cognella, Inc.

Printed in the United States of America

ISBN: 978-1-63487-011-5 (pbk) / 978-1-63487-012-2 (br)

cognella™

www.cognella.com 800.200.3908

CONTENTS

Introduction

By David Moglen

Economics. The economy. An economist. These words provoke images of factories churning out merchandise, money changing hands, or financial people on Wall Street, all of which is perfectly accurate. The idea of what is economics may seem somehow distant when you start, but it is all around you. You may well find as you go on that you have long ago internalized most concepts in economics. For example, most people make choices in life in an ongoing effort to make themselves as happy as possible. Businesses try to make as much money in profit as they can. Microeconomics formalizes these and other intuitive concepts into a toolbox of standard graphs, formulas, and reasoning to interpret, apply, and predict reality.

Major decisions are based on economics. How much should a company charge for their goods? How much output should they produce? How many workers should they hire? Microeconomics provides the tools to most profitably answer these questions, vital if you plan to have a role in running a company. Microeconomics explains the full implications of what happens when an industry is competitive, versus when it is monopolized, as well as market structures which fall in between those extremes.

This book contains several special features to enhance your learning and link the theory the real world.

In-Class Project

Numerous activities designed for small groups (up to five students per group) to apply concepts in a real-world context. Any of the in-class projects can be assigned as homework.

Unlocking the Mysteries

Discover the hidden answers to make your understanding of the model on a real-world level much more concrete; the story behind the graph. If rent control hurts some renters, why might they still support it? How exactly can minimum wage be modeled as causing unemployment when a doctor or a lawyer, or even someone making twenty dollars an hour, is not directly affected by an eight dollar minimum hourly wage? Why did mortgage lenders provide home loans if their professional expertise ensured them that the borrowers would default?

Discussion Questions

Open-ended inquiries to illuminate topics which can initiate discussion for the whole class, or be assigned for short-answer responses. Many of these question sets will follow incisive articles or excerpts on issues that profoundly resonate for people in their everyday lives.

Experiments

Economic experiences which involve everyone's simultaneous participation to simulate a real market. Thus, experiments must be held in class.

These frequently interspersed features will reinforce your knowledge, as will the contributing authors' question sets available for your practice at the end of each chapter.

The * ("star" or "asterisk") symbol indicates that particular question is somewhat more difficult or requires deeper analysis. It is up to the teacher whether starred questions will be required along with non-starred questions in a given problem set, offered as bonus questions, or discussion topics for the class as a whole.

You will cultivate a skill in reading between the lines when analyzing news stories, current events, and important real-world situations. You will develop the tools to work with the economic forces behind the choices and conflicts faced by yourself and your community.

CHAPTER 1
Modern Economics

1 Modern Economics

By Joseph E. Stiglitz and Carl E. Walsh

The past decade has seen tremendous changes in the world economy. Many of these changes are linked to new technological advances that have transformed what the global economy produces, the ways in which many goods and services are produced, where they are produced, and how goods and services are transferred from the firms that produce them to the households, governments, and other firms that buy them. New technologies are transforming everything, from how airlines sell tickets to how automobiles are produced, from how we buy books to how we communicate with one another.

Like the industrial revolution of the eighteenth and nineteenth centuries that transformed first Britain and then other countries from agricultural to manufacturing based economies, the information revolution of the late twentieth and early twenty first centuries promises to transform almost all aspects of our daily lives. In 1999, in recognition of the growing importance of new, high-tech firms, Microsoft and Intel the producer of the Windows computer operating system and the major producer of the microprocessors at the heart of personal computers, respectively, were added to the Dow-Jones Industrial Average, the most widely followed index of prices on U.S. stock markets. Though the booming stock market of the late 1990s that was driven in part by enthusiasm for new technologies came to an end in 2000, innovation continues to be a critical force in the economy.

But the old economy is still alive and kicking. Four of the five largest United States corporations in *Fortune* magazine's top 500 list for 2003 were traditional industrial firms—General Motors, Exxon, Ford, and General Electric. IBM at number 8 and Verizon Communications at number 10 were the only information or "tech" firms in the top 10. Hewlett-Packard was number 14 and Dell Computers was 36, but Microsoft managed to make it no higher than number 47.

So the old economy and the new economy coexist side by side. But it is not just the emergence of new software and Internet companies that represents the effects of new technologies. The way all firms do business is being changed, and their customers are being affected too. Assembly lines now rely on robots aided and controlled by computers. Car repair shops with grease-stained floors have been replaced by clean, quiet garages where computers diagnose a car's problems. The way we buy things is also changing. Whether an individual purchases a car, book, or CD over the Web; books a hotel or plane reservation; or even applies to a college through the Internet, the relationship between people and firms is evolving. New technologies are changing the way courses are taught, too—textbooks like this one have Web sites that provide students with help, with interactive exercises, and with links to news, policy debates, and the latest economic information. The address of the home page for this text is www.wwnorton.com/stiglitzwalsh4.

With such far-reaching changes, what insights and understanding does the study of economics have to offer? After all, the field usually looks to Adam Smith, an eighteenth-century Scottish professor of moral philosophy, as its founder. Smith published his most famous book, *The Wealth of Nations,* in 1776, a time when today's industrial economies were still overwhelmingly agriculture-based. It might seem unlikely that a theory developed to understand the factors that determine the price of wheat would have much to say about today's modern economy.

But, in fact, study of economics continues to provide a critical understanding of today's global economy. As Carl Shapiro and Hal Varian of the University of California, Berkeley, put it, "Technology changes. Economic laws do not."[1] The way we produce things, what we produce, and how goods are exchanged have altered tremendously since Smith wrote. Yet the same fundamental laws of economics that explained agricultural prices in the eighteenth century can help us understand how economies function in the twenty-first century The foundation laid by Adam Smith and built upon by generations of economists has yielded insights that will continue to offer guidance to anyone wishing to make sense of the modern economy.

Over the past two hundred years, economists have refined and expanded our understanding of economic behavior. By incorporating the role of information and technological change, they are now able to explain much more than was possible just twenty years ago, offering new insights into topics that range from why car dealers build fancy showrooms to how the factors important for encouraging the production of new ideas differ from those that encourage the production of new cars.

But what are these insights? What do economists study? And what can we learn from looking at things from the perspective of economics? How can economics help us understand why we need to worry about the extinction of salmon but not of sheep, why auto manufacturers advertise but wheat farmers don't, why countries that rely on uncoordinated markets have done better than countries that rely on government planners, and why letting a single firm dominate an industry is bad?

The headlines from some recent news stories involving the computer industry and the Internet illustrate some of the key issues that a study of economics can help illuminate.

---

[1]Carl Shapiro and Hal R. Varian, *Information Rules: A Strategic Guide to the Network Economy* (Boston: Harvard Business School Press, 1999), p. 2.

- **"Bill to Curb Online Piracy Is Challenged as Too Broad,"** *New York Times,* June 24, 2004. A bill recently introduced in the U.S. Senate aims to restrict the illegal online sharing of music and other files. This proposed legislation represents just the latest development in the running battle between the companies that own the rights to the music and consumers who want to freely share music files. After all, it doesn't cost the music company any more to have a file shared by a thousand people than it does to have it shared by two. So why, many ask, should they have to pay for music files? The advent of digital music has made it possible for listeners to exchange copies indistinguishable from the originals. But if the producers of the music cannot earn a profit, they have less incentive to seek out and record new artists. Property rights in this case, the legal right of the music company to charge for the use of its property, play an important role in market economics, and disputes over property rights aren't new. But the new information technologies have made trading this property much easier and raised new questions. As we will see, economics can tell us a great deal about the issues involved in these disputes.

- "**Internet Drug Trade Proves Bitter Pill for Canada**," *Financial Times,* April 21, 2004. The Internet has changed the nature of the market for goods such as prescription drugs. Buyers in Florida can as easily have their prescriptions filled by a pharmacy based in California, or Canada, as by one in Florida. But why has this led to shortages of some popular prescription drugs in Canada? What will be the likely consequences for drug prices in Canada and the United States?

- **"Intel Cancels 2 Chip Projects,"** *San Jose Mercury News,* May 8, 2004. After spending as much as $2 billion on a new line of computer chips called the Itanium, Intel pulled the plug on the project. As the company decided whether to go ahead with the project, was the money already invested a factor? Firms are always concerned about costs, but economics gives critical insights that help us understand which costs are important and whether some costs, such as the $2 billion Intel had already sunk into the Itanium project, aren't.

- **"EBay Bids and Buys Baazee,"** *The Economic Times,* June 23, 2004. According to a story on economictimes.indiatimes.com, the online auction company eBay purchased Baazee.com, an Indian online shopping company, for $50 million. The purchase extends eBay's network throughout Asia, adding to its current ventures in Hong Kong, Singapore, and China. By linking online buyers and sellers globally, eBay will enable a consumer in Sioux City, Iowa, to trade with someone in Bangalore, India.

- **"Oracle's Bid for PeopleSoft to Be Tested in Court,"** *New York Times,* June 7, 2004. In early 2004, the software giant Oracle announced that it was making a hostile bid to buy PeopleSoft, another software company. The U.S. Justice Department initially filed a lawsuit to block this takeover, arguing that it would reduce competition in the market for business software. Oracle was eventually allowed to take over PeopleSoft, but why does the government try to ensure that there is competition? What are the advantages of competition? What tools does the government use to promote competition?

- **"FASB Holds Meeting on Expensing Stock Options,"** *San Jose Mercury News,* June 24, 2004. Many tech companies, particularly those located in California's Silicon Valley, have used stock options to reward their employees.

This mechanism grants the employee the opportunity to purchase shares in the company at a set price. If the company does well and its shares go up in value, the employee can sell the stock for a profit—a prospect that creates an incentive to work hard and help the company succeed. The Federal Accounting Standards Board (FASB) proposed new accounting rules requiring firms that offer stock options to report these as an expense, thereby reducing the firm's reported profits. The FASB argues that to do so would present investors with a more accurate picture of the firm's profits, enabling investors to make better decisions about buying stock in the company.

News headlines frequently focus on economic issues, and these six point to some of the key topics that economists study: the role of incentives and information, globalization and exchange, competition and government regulation, costs and business decisions. The study of economics will give you new insights into the news stories you see in the paper, it will give you insights into the world of business, and it will help you understand the world of economics you participate in every day.

Internet Connection

TRACKING THE DIGITAL ECONOMY

Since 1998 the U.S. department of Commerce has issued an annual report on the digital economy. You can find the latest, report at www.esa.doc.gov/reports.cfm.

What Is Economics?

Headlines can illustrate many of the important issues with which economics deals, but now a definition of our subject is in order. *Economics* studies how individuals, firms, government, and other organizations within our society make *choices,* and how these choices determine society's use of its resources. Why did consumers choose to buy small, energy-efficient cars in the 1970s and large sports utility vehicles in the 1990s? What determines how many individuals work in health care industries and how many work in the computer industry? Why did the income gap between rich and poor rise in the 1980s? To understand how choices are made and how these choices affect the use of society's resources, we must examine five concepts that play an important role: trade-offs, incentives, exchange, information, and distribution.

1. Choice involves **trade-offs**—deciding to spend more on one thing leaves less to spend on something else; devoting more time to studying economics leaves less time to study physics.
2. In making choices, individuals respond to **incentives**. If the price of Zen MP3 players falls relative to the price of iPods, there is a greater incentive to buy a Zen. If the salaries for engineers rise relative to the salaries of people with an MBA, there is an increased incentive to choose to study for an engineering degree rather than a business degree.
3. When we **exchange** with others, our range of choices becomes larger.
4. Making intelligent choices requires that we have, and utilize, **informatio**n.
5. Finally, the choices we make, about how much education to get, what occupation to enter, and what goods and service to buy, determine the **distribution** of wealth and income in our society.

These five concepts define the core ideas that are critical to understanding economics. They also guide the way economists think about issues and problems. Learning to "think like an economist" means learning how to discover the trade-offs and incentives faced, the implications of exchange, the role of information, and the consequences for distribution. These key concepts are emphasized throughout the text in "Thinking Like an Economist" boxes.

TRADE-OFFS

Each of us is constantly making choices—students decide to study at the library rather than in the dorm, to have pizza rather than sushi, to go to college rather than work full-time. Societies, too, make choices—to preserve open spaces rather than provide more housing, to produce computers and import televisions rather than produce televisions and import computers, to cut taxes rather than increase government expenditures. In some cases, individuals or governments explicitly make these choices. You decided to study economics rather than some other subject. The government decides each year whether to cut taxes or to increase spending. In other cases, however, the choices were the result of the uncoordinated actions of millions of individuals. Neither the government nor any one individual decided that the United States would import cars from Japan and export wheat to India. But in each case, choice involves trade-offs—to get more of one thing involves having less of something else. We are forced to make trade-offs because of **scarcity.**

Scarcity figures prominently in economics; choices matter because resources are scarce. For most of us, our limited income forces us to make choices. We cannot afford everything we might want. Spending more on rent leaves less available for clothes and entertainment. Getting a sunroof on a new car may mean forgoing leather seats to stay within a fixed budget. Limited income is not the only reason we are forced to make trade-offs. Time is also a scarce resource, and even the wealthiest individual must decide what expensive toy to play with each day. When we take time into account, we realize scarcity is a fact of life for everyone.

One of the most important points on which economists agree concerns the critical role of scarcity. We can summarize this point as follows:

There is no free lunch. Having more of one thing requires giving up something else. Scarcity means that trade-offs *are a basic, fact of life.*

INCENTIVES

It is one thing to say we all face trade-offs in the choices we make. It is quite another to understand how individuals and firms make choices and how those choices might change as economic circumstances change. If new technologies are developed, will firms decide to increase or decrease the amount of labor they employ? If the price of gasoline rises, will individuals decide to buy different types of automobiles?

When faced with a choice, people evaluate the pros and cons of the different options. In deciding what to eat for dinner tonight, you and your roommates might weigh the advantages and disadvantages of having a frozen pizza again over going out for sushi. Similarly, a firm evaluates the pros and cons of its alternatives in terms of the effects different choices will have on its profits. For example, a retail chain deciding on the location for a new store must weigh the relative advantages of different locations. One location might have more foot traffic but also higher rent. Another location might be less desirable but have lower rent.

When decision makers systematically weigh the pros and cons of the alternatives they face, we can predict how they will respond to changing economic conditions. Higher gas prices raise the cost of driving, but the cost of driving a fuel-efficient car rises less than the cost of driving a sports utility vehicle. Therefore, households weighing a car purchase have a greater incentive to choose the fuel-efficient car. If a firm starts selling more of its goods through the Internet, it will rely less on foot traffic into its retail store. This shift reduces its incentive to pay a high rent for a good location.

Economists analyze choices by focusing on incentives. In an economic context, incentives are benefits (including reduced costs) that motivate a decision maker in favor of a particular choice. Many things can affect incentives, but among the most important are *prices.* If the price of gasoline rises, people have a greater incentive to drive less. If the price of MP3 players falls, people have a greater incentive to buy one. When the price of a good rises, firms are induced to produce more of that good, in order to increase their profits. If a resource used in production, such as labor or equipment, becomes more expensive, firms have an incentive to find new methods of production that economize on that resource. Incentives also are affected by the return people expect to earn from different activities. If the income of college graduates rises relative to that of people with only a high school diploma, people have a greater incentive to attend college.

When economists study the behavior of people or firms, they look at the incentives being faced. Sometimes these incentives are straightforward. Increasing the number of courses required to major in biology reduces the incentive to pick that major. In other circumstances, they may not be so obvious. For example, building safer cars may create incentives to drive faster. Identifying the incentives, and disincentives, to take different actions is one of the first things economists do when they want to understand the choices individuals or firms make.

Decision makers respond to incentives; for understanding choices, incentives matter.

Trade-offs and Incentives in Practice: Online Music Sharing

Since 1999, when Napster introduced the first file-sharing program that allowed users to swap music files over the Internet, the practice has been embroiled in controversy. On one side is the music industry, which views the sharing of music files as an illegal activity, and on the other side are the companies producing the software that allows file sharing and the millions of music lovers who do not want to pay for music. The debates now also encompass the movie industry, as digitized movies can be shared as easily as music files. The legal battle between MGM and Grokster, a distributor of peer-to-peer file-sharing software, reached the United States Supreme Court in 2005.

Incentives are at the heart of the case against file sharing. Record companies make money by selling CDs. They, or the artists who create the music, hold copyrights that give them the right to charge others for its use. Copyrighted material, which includes books like this text as well as music, cannot be distributed or sold without the permission of the copyright holder. In that way, the holder of the copyright—the book publisher, author, artist, composer, or record company—is able to limit access to the material and charge a fee for its use. When music could only be copied by physically duplicating a tape recording or burning a CD, it was costly to make illegal copies. While people might burn a CD to use in the car or give to a friend, this type of sharing was relatively minor, and something the music industry tolerated.

The advent of digital music changed the situation dramatically. Now, a music file can be shared with millions of other listeners. In 1999, Napster introduced a filesharing service that focused exclusively on music. In the process, Napster helped to popularize the MP3 format; by February 2001 the service had over 26 million users worldwide. Napster also quickly attracted the attention of the record companies, who sued Napster for distributing copyrighted music without paying royalties to the copyright holders. In 2001, Napster settled the lawsuit, agreeing to pay $26 million to the music copyright holders. Faced with paying this huge fee, Napster declared bankruptcy in 2002. It has recently converted itself to a subscription service for downloading music legally.

Napster's place has been taken by services such as Grokster and Morpheus that offer peer-to-peer (p2p) file sharing. In their legal battles with the music industry, these services have argued that they should not be held liable simply becuse their products might be used to duplicate copyrighted materials illegally. However, in July 2005, the U.S. Supreme Court ruled that the services could be found liable because they knowingly promoted products that were designed to infringe on the rights of copyright holders and did nothing to disourage this illegal activity.

So how does all this relate to the concept of incentives? First, free music clearly creates an incentive for music lovers to download songs rather than pay for them by buying a CD. This is at the heart of the music industry's opposition to p2p file sharing. Second, if record companies cannot charge for their music because it can be downloaded for free, they have less of an incentive to record new music. According to the record industry, by reducing the incentive to produce new music, file sharing will ultimately reduce the opportunities for new musicians to record with major record labels.

While the effects of free, online file sharing on incentives are clear, the magnitude of those effects is open to debate. The music industry points to a decline in CD sales, from 942.5 million CDs in 2000 to 766.9 in 2004, as evidence that the availability of free downloads has hurt their business. However, critics of the music industry argue that this decline in sales is simply a reflection of the economic slowdown and rise in unemployment that began in 2001. Some studies have argued that the availability of free music downloads might actually increase CD sales. Listening to music online can actually increase interest in new music and individuals who are able to listen to music online before buying an album may actually be more likely to purchase CDs. A study by economists at the University of North Carolina and the Harvard Business School was unable to find any effect of online access to music on subsequent CD sales.

Whatever the ultimate outcome of this battle might be, incentives are essential to understanding the issues. The incentive to avoid paying

Thinking Like an Economist

INCENTIVES AND THE PRICE OF AOL

Today, most online services such as AOL charge their customers a fixed monthly fee for Internet access. In the earlier days of the Internet, the access charge was commonly based on how many minutes the member was connected to the Internet. In 1997, AOL announced that it would change its pricing policy and move to a flat monthly fee with unlimited minutes of connect time. AOL's servers were quickly overwhelmed and members found it almost impossible to log on.

Why? Because charges were no longer based on the number of minutes a member was logged on, many customers never logged off. Once connected, they simply left AOL running, typing up its modem capacity. When members had to pay on a per-minute basis, they had an incentive to log off when the service was not being used. The flat fee left no incentive to economize on connect time. The flat fee left no incentive would have shown AOL that it need to greatly increase its modem capacity before announcing the new pricing plan.

for music provided by low-cost or free access reduces the incentive of record companies to discover, record, and promote new musical talents.

EXCHANGE

Somehow, decisions that are made by individuals, households, firms, and government as they face trade-offs and respond to incentives, together determine how the economy's limited resources, including its land, labor, machines, oil, and other natural resources, are used. The key to understanding how this happens lies in the role of *voluntary* exchange in *markets.*

Long before the rise of modern industrial societies, the benefits of exchange were well understood. Coastal societies with access to fishing resources, for example, would trade some of their fish to inland societies in return for meat and furs. The coastal group sought meat and furs that were worth more to them than the fish they gave up; the inland group likewise exchanged meat and furs for fish. Both groups benefited from voluntary exchange.

In modern societies, millions of exchanges take place. Few individuals produce any of the goods and services they themselves want to consume. Instead, teachers, police officers, lawyers, and construction workers sell their labor services to a school district, a city, a client, or a homebuilder and then exchange the income they earn for all the various goods and services they wish to consume that are produced by others. An important insight in economics is the recognition that *both* parties in a voluntary exchange gain. Whether it takes place between two individuals, between an individual and a firm, or between residents of two different countries, exchange can improve the well-being of both parties.

Economists describe any situation in which exchange takes place as *a market.* For thousands of years, societies have established physical locations such as village markets or periodic trading fairs where people have brought their products, haggled over terms of exchange, and reaped the benefits of trade. The economic concept of markets covers any situation in which exchange takes place, though this exchange may not necessarily resemble a traditional village market or a modern stock exchange. In department stores and shopping malls, customers rarely haggle over the price. When manufacturers purchase the materials they need for production, they give in exchange money, not other goods. Most goods, from cameras to clothes, are not sold directly from producers to consumers. Instead they are sold from producers to distributors, from distributors to retailers, and from retailers to consumers. All of these transactions are embraced by the concept of markets and a **market economy**.

In a market economy like that of the United States, most exchanges take place through markets, and these exchanges are guided by the prices of the goods and services involved. The goods and services that are scarcer, or require more resources for their production, come at a higher price. Automobiles are more expensive than paper cups; lawyers charge more than janitors. As a result, markets enable consumers and firms to make choices that reflect scarcity, and therefore lead to efficient uses of resources.

Internet Connection

AUCTION SITES

An auction is one form of market that used to require potential buyers to be physically present in a single location. Now, auctions are held over the Internet and can involve participants from around the world. Some sites, such as eBay (www.ebay.com), offer just about everything for sale. Other sites specialize. For instance, Heritage Coins (www.heritagecoins.com) provides an auction site for rare coins. Even the U.S. government has gotten into the act. The U.S. Treasury does not actually auction items online, but it uses the Web to publicize the locations at which confiscated property will be auctioned (www.treas.gov/auctions/customs.)

Market economies thus rely primarily on market exchanges to resolve the most basic economic questions: What and how much is produced? How is it produced? For whom is it produced? And who makes the economic decisions? Individuals and firms make the decisions. Individuals make decisions that reflect their own desires as they respond to the incentives they face. Firms make decisions that maximize their profits, and to do so they strive to produce the goods that consumers want at the lowest possible cost. This process determines what is produced, how it is produced, and for whom. As firms compete in the quest for profits, consumers benefit, both from the kinds of goods produced and from the prices at which they are supplied. On the whole, markets ensure that society's resources are used efficiently.

In some areas, however, markets lead to outcomes that society may find inadequate. There may be too much pollution, too much inequality, and too little concern about education, health, and safety. When the market is not perceived to be working well, people often turn to government. An economy such as in the United States is often called *a mixed economy*—one that relies primarily but not exclusively on the free interaction of producers and consumers to determine what is produced, how, and for whom. In some areas, the government makes the decisions, in others it imposes regulations that affect the incentives firms and households face; and in many areas, both the *private sector* (households and businesses) and the *public sector* (local, state, and federal governments) are involved (education is a good example).

Governments play a critical role in all market economies. For example, governments provide the legal structure within which private firms and individuals operate. No one would open a store if others could simply steal things off the shelf with impunity; the store owner needs to know there is a legal system that he can use to prosecute theft. No bank would lend money to a family to buy a home if it could not legally require the family to repay the loan. Governments also regulate businesses in many ways. There are regulations to ensure firms do not discriminate by race or sex, do not mislead consumers, and are careful about the safety of their workers. In some industries, such as education and mail service, the government is a major supplier of services. In other industries, such as the defense industry, government is the major purchaser. The government also supplies goods and services that the private sector does not, such as the national defense, roads, and currency. Government programs provide for the elderly through Social Security (which pays income to retired individuals) and Medicare (which funds the medical needs of the aged). The government helps those who have suffered economic dislocation, through unemployment insurance for those temporarily unemployed and disability insurance for those who are no longer able to work. The government also provides a safety net of support for the poor, particularly children, through various welfare programs.

One can easily imagine the government controlling the economy more directly. In countries where decision making is centralized and concentrated in the government, government bureaucrats might decide what and how much a factory should produce and set the wages that should be paid. At least until recently, governments in countries such as the former Soviet Union and China attempted to control practically all major decisions regarding resource allocation. Even in Europe, not long ago many governments ran oil companies, coal mines, and the telephone system. Increasingly, however, governments have sold these enterprises to the private sector, a process called *privatization.*

Market economies in which individuals and firms make the decisions about what to produce and how much to pay have proven adept at developing new technologies and products. It is hard to imagine government bureaucrats developing MP3 players or iMacs in neon colors. Markets also generally ensure that resources are used efficiently.

Exchange in markets is *a key to understanding how resources are allocated, what is produced, and who earns what.*

INFORMATION

Making informed choices requires information. After all, it is hard to weigh the costs and benefits of alternative choices if you do not know what they are! A firm that is contemplating the purchase of a new software system needs to know not only the costs of the various alternatives but also the capabilities and limitations of each. Information is, in many ways, like other goods and services. Firms and individuals are willing to purchase information, and specialized institutions develop to sell it. In many areas, separate organizations are designed solely to provide information to consumers. *Consumer Reports* is a prime example. The Internet also now serves as a major source of independent information for buyers. But there are some fundamental ways in which information differs from other goods. A car seller will let you test-drive a vehicle, but a seller of information cannot let you see the information before you buy. Once you have seen the information, you have no incentive to pay for it. Another way information differs from other goods is that unlike a can of soda or a bagel, information can be freely shared. When I tell you something, it does not subtract from what I know (though it may subtract from the profits I might earn from that information).

In some key areas of the economy, the role of information is so critical that it affects the nature of the market. In the used-car market, buyers and sellers negotiating over the price of a vehicle may have quite different information about its quality. The seller may have better information about the quality of the car but also has an incentive to misrepresent its condition, since better-quality cars command higher prices. As a result, the buyer will be reluctant to trust claims that the car is in perfect shape.

When consumers lack adequate information to make informed choices, governments frequently intervene to require that firms provide information. In the United States, we are all familiar with the mandatory nutritional information placed on food products. The Securities and Exchange Commission (SEC) that oversees American stock markets compels firms to meet certain reporting requirements before their stock can be listed on exchanges such as the New York Stock Exchange. Such reporting helps ensure that private investors have reliable information on which to base their investment decisions. Often, however, these regulations do not work adequately, as the Enron scandal in 2001 clearly illustrates. The oil trading company Enron had cooked its books to overstate its profitability in its mandated reports. One outcome of Enron's subsequent financial collapse was the introduction of new regulations designed to improve the reliability of the information that companies must provide to the public. Governments also regulate the safety of products. In the United States, the Food and Drug Administration (FDA) must approve new pharmaceuticals before they can be sold. The need for such oversight was driven home in 2005 when the drug manufacturer Merck had to pull its pain relief drug Vioxx off the market after studies suggested it increased the risk of heart attacks and strokes. Critics of the FDA argued that the agency is not adequately monitoring the safety of drugs once they are approved, and proposals have been made to establish a new government review board whose job it will be to decide when new information warrants removing a drug from the market.

Even in the absence of regulation, firms have incentives to signal to buyers that their products are of high quality. One way they do this is to offer guarantees that a producer of low-quality goods could not afford to offer.

Imperfect information also can interfere with incentives. Employers want to create incentives for employees to work hard. One way to do this is to base pay on a measure of how productive each worker is. Often, however, it is difficult to measure a worker's productivity. Under such conditions, it is difficult to link pay to performance. For example, a major debate in the United States concerns tying teacher salaries to performance. Because it is hard to measure teaching performance, the pay of most teachers is based primarily on how long they have been teaching.

Information, or its absence, plays a key role in determining the shape of markets and the ability of private markets to ensure that the economy's scarce resources are used efficiently.

DISTRIBUTION

The market economy determines not only what goods are produced and how they are produced but also for whom they are produced. Many people find unacceptable the way the market distributes goods among households. "While recognizing the efficacy of capitalism to produce wealth, there remains considerable unease among some segments about the way markets distribute that wealth and about the effects of raw competition on society."[2] Like bidders at an auction, what market participants are willing and able to pay depends on their income. Incomes differ markedly across occupations. Some groups of individuals—including those without skills that are valued by the market—may receive such a low income that they cannot feed and educate their children without outside assistance. Government provides the assistance by taking steps to increase income equality.

[2]Alan Greenspan, speech at the Federal Reserve Bank of Kansas City Jackson Hole Conference, August 25, 2000.

Steps that soften the distributional impact of markets may blunt economic incentives. While welfare payments provide an important safety net for the poor, the taxation required to finance them may discourage people from working and saving. If the government takes one out of every two or three dollars that an individual earns, that individual may not be inclined to work as much. And if the government takes one out of every two or three dollars a person earns from interest on savings, the person may decide to spend more and save less. Thus, efforts by the government to redistribute income may come at the cost of reduced economic efficiency.

The primary reliance on private decision making in the United States reflects economists' beliefs that this reliance is appropriate and necessary for economic efficiency. However, economists also believe that certain interventions by government are desirable. Like the appropriate balance between public and private sectors, the appropriate balance between concerns about equality (often referred to as *equity concerns)* and efficiency is a central issue of modern economies. As elsewhere, trade-offs must be made.

Wrap-up

FIVE CORE IDEAS

1. *Trade-offs:* resources are scarce, so trade-offs are a basic fact of life.
2. *Incentives:* in making choices, decision makers respond to incentives.
3. *Exchange:* people benefit from voluntary exchange, and in market economies, market exchanges lead to the efficient use of resources.
4. *Information:* the structure that markets take and how well they can function depend critically on the information available to decision makers.
5. *Distribution:* markets determine how the goods and services produced by the economy are allocated to members of society.

The Three Major Markets

The market economy revolves around exchange between individuals (or households) who buy goods and services from firms, and firms, which take *inputs,* the various materials of production, and produce *outputs,* the goods and services that they sell. In thinking about a market economy, economists focus their attention on three broad categories of markets in which individuals and firms interact. The markets in which firms sell their outputs to households are referred to collectively as the **product market**. Many firms also sell goods to other firms; the output of the first firm becomes the input of the second. These transactions too are said to occur in the product market.

On the input side, firms need (besides the materials they buy in the product market) some combination of labor and machinery to produce their output. They purchase the services of workers in the **labor market**. They raise funds to buy inputs in the **capital market**. Traditionally, economists also have highlighted the importance of a third input, land, but in modern industrial economies land is of secondary importance. For most purposes, it suffices to focus attention on the three major markets—products, labor, and capital—and this text will follow that pattern.

As Figure 1.1 shows, individuals participate in all three markets. When individuals buy goods and services, they act as *consumers* in the product market. When people act as *workers,* economists say they "sell their labor services" in the labor market. When people buy shares of stock in a firm, deposit money in a savings account, or lend money to a business, they are participating in the capital market as *investors.*

KEEPING TRACK OF TRICKY TERMS

Terms in economics often are similar to terms in ordinary usage, but they can have special meanings. The terms *markets* and *capital* illustrate this problem.

Though the term *market* is used to conjure up an image of a busy *marketplace,* there is no formal marketplace for most goods and services. There are buyers and sellers, and economists analyze the outcomes *as if* there were a single marketplace in which all transactions occur. For example, economists analyze the "market for books," even though the buyers and sellers in the market for books interact in thousands of individual bookstores and online selling locations.

Moreover, economists often talk about the "market for labor" as if all workers were identical. But workers differ in countless ways. In some cases, these differences are important. We might then talk about the "market for skilled workers" or the "market for computer engineers." In other cases—such as when we are talking about the overall state of the

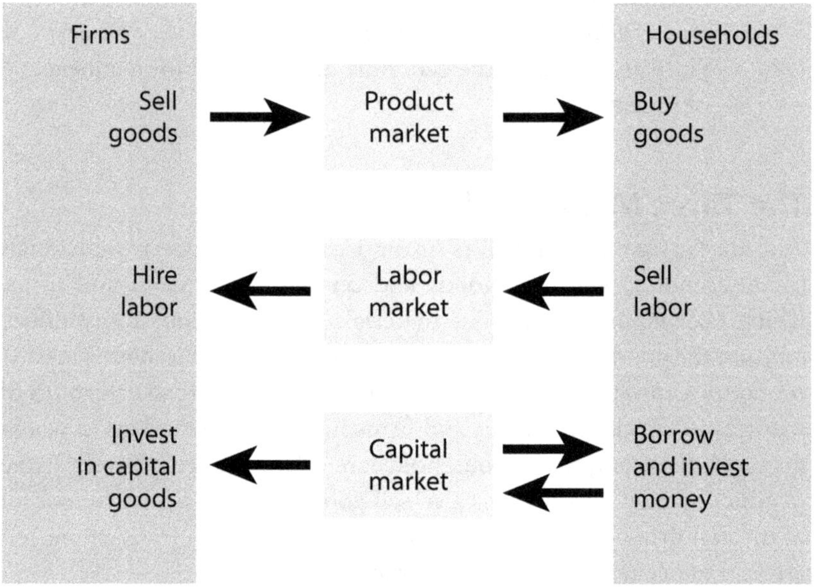

FIGURE 1.1
The Three Markets
To economists, people wear different hats. They are usually consumers in the product market, workers in the labor market, and borrowers or lenders in the capital market.

economy and focusing on the overall unemployment rate (the proportion of workers who are looking for jobs but cannot find them)-these differences can be ignored.

When newspapers refer to the *capital market,* they mean the bond traders and stockbrokers and the companies they work for on Wall Street and in other financial districts. When economists use the term *capital market,* they have in mind, a broader concept that includes all the institutions concerned with raising funds (and, as we will see later, sharing and insuring risk), including banks and insurance companies.

The term *capital* is used in still another way—to refer to the machines and buildings used in production. To distinguish this particular usage, in this book we refer to machines and buildings as **capital goods**. The term *capital markets* thus refers to the markets in which funds are raised, borrowed, and lent. *Capital goods markets* refers to the markets in which capital goods are bought and sold.

Wrap-up

THE THREE MAJOR MARKETS

1. *The product market:* the markets in which firms sell the goods they produce.
2. *The labor market:* the market in which households sell labor services and firms buy labor services.
3. *The capital market:* the market in which funds are borrowed and lent.

Microeconomics and Macroeconomics: The Two Branches of Economics

Economists have developed two different ways to look at the economy. The detailed study of the decisions of firms and households, and of prices and production in specific industries is called **microeconomics**. Microeconomics *(micro* is derived from the Greek word meaning "small") focuses on the behavior of the units—the firms, households, and individuals—that make up the economy. It is concerned with how the individual units make decisions and what affects those decisions.

By contrast, **macroeconomics** *(macro* is derived from the Greek word meaning "large") looks at the behavior of the economy as a whole, in particular the behavior of such aggregate measures as the overall rates of unemployment, inflation, and economic growth and the balance of trade. The aggregate numbers do not tell us what any one firm or household is doing. They tell us what is happening in total, or on average. In a dynamic economy, there are always some industries expanding and others contracting. For instance, the economic expansion of the late 1990s saw rapid growth in Internet-related industries, while oil firms in Texas contracted. But there are times when overall growth in an economy slows and times when the level of economic activity actually declines, not just in an isolated industry but seemingly across all or almost all industries.

In macroeconomics, we also look at the behavior of the general level of prices, interest rates, and exchange rates. Why do prices of almost all goods and services seem to rise at rapid rates during some periods, while at other times they remain stable? Why do interest rates fluctuate? And what determines the value of the dollar relative to other currencies?

In approaching these questions, it is important to remember that the behavior of the economy as a whole is dependent on the decisions made by the millions of households and firms in the economy, as well as the decisions made by the government. Micro and macro perspectives are simply two ways of looking at the same thing. Microeconomics is the bottom-up view of the economy; macroeconomics is the top-down view.

Wrap-up

THE BRANCHES OF ECONOMICS

- **Microeconomics**: focuses on the decisions of households and firms and the detailed study of prices and production in specific industries.
- **Macroeconomics**: focuses on the behavior of the economy as a whole and the behavior of aggregate variables such as overall employment, output, economic growth, the price level, and inflation.

The Science of Economics

Economics is *a social science.* It studies the social problem of choice from a scientific viewpoint, which means that it is built on a systematic exploration of the problem of choice. This systematic exploration involves both the formulation of theories and the examination of data.

A **theory** consists of a set of assumptions (or hypotheses) and conclusions derived from those assumptions. Theories are logical exercises: *if* the assumptions are correct, *then* the results follow. If all college graduates have a better chance of getting jobs and Ellen is a college graduate, then Ellen has a better chance of getting a job than a nongraduate. Economists make predictions with their theories. They might use their theory to predict what would happen if a tax is increased or if imports of foreign cars are limited. The predictions of a theory are of the form, "If a tax is increased and if the market is competitive, then output will decrease and prices will increase."

In developing their theories, economists use *models.* To understand how models are used in economics, consider a modern car manufacturer trying to design a new automobile. It is extremely expensive to construct a new car. Rather than creating a separate, fully developed car for every conception of what engineers or designers would like the new car to be, the company uses models. The designers might use a plastic model to study the general shape of the vehicle and to assess reactions to the car's aesthetics. The engineers might use a computer model to study air resistance, from which they can calculate fuel consumption.

Just as engineers construct different models to study particular features of a car, economists construct different models of the economy—in words or equations—to depict particular features of the economy. An economic model might describe a general relationship ("When incomes rise, the number of cars purchased increases"), describe a quantitative relationship ("When incomes rise by 10 percent, the number of cars purchased rises, on average, by 12 percent"), or make a general prediction ("An increase in the tax on gasoline will decrease the demand for cars").

The theory of the market economy traces back to the Scottish economist Adam Smith (1723–1790) and the publication of *Inquiry into the Nature and Causes of the Wealth of Nations* in 1776. Considered by many to be the most influential economics book ever written, it articulates the powerful and wonderfully democratic ideal of a self-organizing economy that creates an equitable and socially optimal allocation of a society's productive resources through the interaction of small buyers and sellers making decisions based on their individual needs and interests.

Market theory, as articulated by Smith and those who subsequently elaborated on his ideas, developed into an elegant and coherent intellectual construction grounded in carefully articulated assumptions regarding the conditions under which such self-organizing processes would indeed lead to socially optimal outcomes. For example:

- Buyers and sellers must be too small to influence the market price.
- Complete information must be available to all participants and there are no trade secrets.
- Sellers must bear the full cost of the products they sell and pass them on in the sale price.
- Investment capital must remain within national borders and trade between countries must be balanced.
- Savings must be invested in the creation of productive capital.

There is, however, a critical problem, as international financier George Soros has observed: "Economic theory is an axiomatic system: as long as the basic assumptions hold, the conclusions follow. But when we examine the assumptions closely, we find that they do not apply to the real world. Herein lies the catch: the conditions of what we currently call a capitalist economy directly contradict the assumptions of market theory in every instance."

In summary, the market system will result in socially optimal outcomes if certain assumptions are true. Soros' point is we can't expect efficient outcomes let alone equitable outcomes since some or all of the basic assumptions are not being achieved. Some sectors might adhere to the assumptions completely. There is some extent to which the economy in many sectors will fail to achieve the basic assumptions. When the economy is not productively efficient, unable to make the most output (total goods produced) for the given amount of inputs (such as quantity of available labor) that it can, that's a result of failing to achieve the basic assumptions.

DISCOVERING AND INTERPRETING RELATIONSHIPS

A variable is any item that can be measured and that changes. Prices, wages, interest rates, and quantities bought and sold are variables. What interests economists is the connection between variables. When economists see what appears to be a systematic relationship among variables, they ask, could it have arisen by chance or is there indeed a relationship? This is the question of *correlation*.

Economists use statistical tests to measure and test correlations. Consider the problem of deciding whether a coin is biased. If you flip the coin 10 times and get 6 heads and 4 tails, is the coin a fair one? Or is it weighted toward heads? Statistical tests will show that the result of 6 heads and 4 tails easily could have happened by chance, so the evidence does not prove that the coin is weighted. It also does not prove that the coin is *not* weighted. The evidence is not strong enough for either conclusion. But if you flip the coin 100 times and get 80 heads, statistical tests will tell you that the possibility of this happening by blind chance with a fair coin is extremely small. The evidence supports the assertion that the coin is weighted.

A similar logic can be used on correlations among economic variables. People with more education tend to earn higher wages. Is the connection merely chance? Statistical tests support the existence of a systematic relationship between education and wages.

CAUSATION AND CORRELATION

Economists want to accomplish more than just asserting that different variables are indeed correlated. They would like to conclude that changes in one variable *cause* the changes in another variable. This distinction between correlation and causation is important. If one variable "causes" the other, then changing the first variable necessarily will change the other. If the relationship is just a correlation, this may not be true.

During the 1970s, imports of Japanese cars into the United States increased while sales of U.S.-produced cars decreased. The two variables were negatively correlated. But did increased Japanese car sales *cause* the decrease in sales of American-made cars? Perhaps both were responding to a common factor that was the true cause of both the rise in Japanese car sales and the decline in sales of American cars. In fact, that is what was happening—the huge increase in oil prices after 1973 caused consumers to shift their purchases away from gas-guzzling American cars and toward more fuel-efficient Japanese cars.

Why Economists Disagree

Economists are frequently called on to make judgments on matters of public policy. Should the government cut taxes? How should Social Security be reformed? Should Internet commerce be taxed? In these public policy discussions, economists often disagree. These disagreements

IN-CLASS PROJECT

Graduating Into a Recession

By David Moglen

This article illustrates how the personal decisions you make as an individual are connected to economic forces. It also provides practice writing good responses for all written work in this economics class and in your future academic career. Just like any written response, a good answer should go back and forth between quotes (using "quote marks") and your own analysis/ interpretation—in your own words.

Directions

As a group activity, each group (as always, up to five students per group) is given a number from one to four, and answers that number below after reading the article. As a set of Discussion Questions, the whole class has read the article and is ready to respond to all four questions collectively.

For all these questions: Imagine the economy is clearly in a deep recession.

1. If you are about to graduate with a bachelor's degree (BA), how should the economic situation influence your decision of what to do next as an individual in this economy? Start by asking yourself, what are the main options people have when they are about to complete or just finished with their BA?
2. What does the research by Columbia University economist Mr. von Wachter mean for your decisions about where you should apply to college, what your major should be, and the type of job you should try to get as a recent graduate?
3. If the economy is not in a recession, would that guarantee that average real wages would rise? What do you think are the major factors that explain this?
4. Which aspects of this article and the issues it raises macroeconomic, and in which way are they microeconomic?

THE CURSE OF THE CLASS OF 2009

For college grads lucky enough to get work this year, low wages are likely to haunt them for a decade or more

By Sara Murray

The bad news for this spring's college graduates is that they're entering the toughest labor market in at least 25 years.

The worse news: Even those who land jobs will likely suffer lower wages for a decade or more compared to those lucky enough to graduate in better times, studies show.

Andrew Friedson graduated last year from the University of Maryland with a degree in government and politics and a stint as student-body president on his résumé. After working on Barack Obama's presidential campaign for a few months, Mr. Friedson hoped to get a position in the new administration. When that didn't pan out he looked for jobs on Capitol Hill. No luck there, either.

So now, instead of learning about policymaking and legislation, he's earning about $1,250 a month as a high school tutor and a part-time fundraiser for Hillel, a Jewish campus organization. To save money, he's living with his parents.

If asked a year ago whether he'd be tutoring now, Mr. Friedson says, "I would have laughed in your face."

Trading down to a lower-skilled job isn't just a hit to Mr. Friedson's ego. It could also hurt his bank account for years to come. Economic research shows that the consequences of graduating in a downturn are long-lasting. They include lower earnings, a slower climb up the occupational ladder and a widening gap between the least-and most-successful grads.

In short, luck matters. The damage can linger up to 15 years, says Lisa Kahn, a Yale School of Management economist. She used the National Longitudinal Survey of Youth, a government data base, to track wages of white men who graduated before, during and after the deep 1980s recession.

Ms. Kahn found that for each percentage-point increase in the unemployment rate, those with the misfortune to graduate during the recession earned 7% to 8% less in their first year out than comparable workers who graduated in better times. The effect persisted over many years, with recession-era grads earning 4% to 5% less by their 12th year out of college, and 2% less by their 18th year out.

For example, a man who graduated in December 1982 when unemployment was at 10.8% made, on average, 23% less his first year out of college and 6.6% less 18 years out than one who graduated in May 1981 when the unemployment rate was 7.5%. For a typical worker, that would mean earning $100,000 less over the 18-year period.

The impact on wages could be just as severe this time around, says Ms. Kahn. That's because of the depth of this recession and the possibility that the unemployment rate may approach the 10.8% level not seen since the early 1980s. The rate hit 8.9% in April, the Labor Department reported Friday.

One reason behind declining wage potential, economists say: The caliber of jobs available in a recession, and their accompanying wages, tend to suffer. High-end firms hire fewer people and drive down salaries because jobs are in such demand.

That means many graduates end up with lower-wage, lower-skill jobs at less-prestigious firms or in firms outside their field of interest. Once the economy picks up and they try for better jobs, these workers have to learn skills they should have been developing immediately out of college. In the meantime, colleagues who graduated in a better economy have already developed these skills and progressed much further.

For Brad Dechter, a 24-year-old who majored in graphic design, this could mean starting at the bottom when and if he gets a job at an advertising agency. He studied at the Art Institute of Colorado partly because the Denver school advertises that 86% of alumni get a job within six months of graduation. So far, no dice.

Eight months after graduation, Mr. Dechter is making just $500 a month freelancing for bands, designing flyers and album covers. When he runs short of cash, he borrows from his friends. He spends his days on Craigslist searching for job openings instead of learning the marketing and design skills he would have picked up in his first year at an agency.

"I've pretty much given up on trying to find my dream job," says Mr. Dechter.

Christine Pacheco, director of career services at the Art Institute, acknowledges that graduates face a struggle now. "They may need to take two part-time jobs and do some freelance rather than get a full-time job," she says.

College graduates remain better off than those with only high-school diplomas, in good times and bad. The unemployment rate in April among four-year college graduates between 20 and 24 years old was 6.1%; among those the same age with only high-school diplomas, it was 19.6%.

But a college degree isn't an automatic ticket to upward mobility, either. Even before the recession began, graduates were seeing their wages shrink. Between 2002 and 2007, according to government data, the inflation-adjusted hourly wage for men ages 25 to 35 with bachelor's degrees (and no graduate degrees) fell 4.5%. For the typical woman, inflation-adjusted wages fell 4.8%.

This year, employers say they'll hire 22% fewer college graduates than last year, according to the National Association of Colleges and Employers, an organization of career counselors. At the same time, colleges are expected to see the highest number of graduates in a decade. The average starting salary for graduates who do get jobs, meanwhile, dropped to $48,515 this spring, down 2.2% from the same time last year, according to NACE.

Plenty of recent graduates are making far less than the average. Between her business marketing degree and numerous New York City contacts, Nicole Buckley, 21, figured she would find a marketing job after graduating in December from Siena College, a small Catholic liberal arts college near Albany, N.Y. She didn't expect to be working the jobs she has now, five months after graduation: As a full-time receptionist with a part-time gig as a model, promoting Bacardi rum and Grey Goose vodka to patrons at bars. But after doing two interviews a day and applying to more than 50 jobs, she had to do something to pay the bills.

"I don't think anyone went to college and said, 'I want to graduate and make $25,000 a year,' " says Ms. Buckley. She estimates her earnings at a little less than $30,000 between the two jobs.

Sarah Veilleux, 22, one of Ms. Buckley's two roommates in a $1,125-a-month Brooklyn apartment, graduated in May 2008 from the University of New Hampshire with a communications degree. For a few months, she worked selling band merchandise at a music venue. Then she found her ideal job: doing promotions for Sirius Satellite Radio. But they need her only 20 hours a week.

"As soon as I saw the offer for Sirius," she says, "it didn't matter how many hours a week." She spends the other half of her week doing administrative tasks for a staffing company, earning $1,500 a month—$18,000 a year—between the two jobs.

Still, Ms. Veilleux probably will be better off than those who take low-wage jobs outside their fields, says Till Marco von Wachter, a Columbia University economist. Mr. von Wachter, with a couple of colleagues, has looked at wage data covering 70% of all Canadians who graduated from college between 1976 and 1995, a span encompassing two recessions. His work indicates that graduates who get jobs in their fields—even low-paying jobs—are able to learn the right skills, and thus have an edge when the economy rebounds.

Mr. von Wachter also found that what recession-era graduates studied, and where they went to school, made a big difference in how quickly they caught up to workers who graduated in boom times. People who majored in fields that lead to high-paying jobs, such as chemistry, biology, physics and engineering, tended to catch up to other graduates more quickly, primarily by switching jobs during the economic recovery and landing at better firms. In contrast, says Mr. von Wachter, the wages of humanities majors at less prestigious schools were less likely to catch up to the wages of their peers who graduated in healthier times.

For some graduates, the recession has had an unintended upside: a career path they never thought they wanted.

Diane Hempe, 24, planned to be a teacher. But after graduating from the University of Maryland last year with an elementary education degree, she failed to find a job at a school. So she settled for working at a day-care center, where the $12 an hour she brought in felt like an affront.

In December, Ms. Hempe went in an entirely new direction. She took a job in the customer-service department at a Wells Fargo call center in Frederick, Md. "I definitely know I can move up," she says. "I can be in customer service; I can be in collections; I can be in so many different departments."

And in the meantime she's shifting her long-term goals. Instead of getting a master's degree in education like she once thought she would, Ms. Hempe says eventually she plans to get her master's in business.

Others are opting to ride out the slump doing public service. At AmeriCorps, a nationwide community-service network, applications more than tripled to about 48,500 between November 2008 and March 2009 compared to the same time period a year earlier. Teach for America received 35,000 applications this year—42% more than last year. About 70% of those were recent college graduates. Among the most common reasons people cited for applying, according to Teach for America, were poor job conditions and President Barack Obama's call to public service.

Another alternative to unemployment or a low-paying job: Stay in school.

Graduate applications for 2007–2008 were up 8% nationwide compared to the year before, according to the most recent numbers from the Council of Graduate Schools. Schools such as Northwestern University and Harvard are already tracking double-digit increases this year.

College grads who went to graduate school instead of the job market during the early '80s recession didn't suffer the same wage losses, says Ms. Kahn, the Yale economist.

That's the approach John Bence is taking. A 2008 graduate of Kenyon College in Ohio, the history major worked with a temp agency and did a six-month stint at an international consulting company. After repeatedly losing out on jobs—at museums, universities, consulting firms—to more-qualified candidates with master's degrees, he'll head to New York University to get a master's degree in history, specializing in archival management.

"I wasn't surprised I didn't get those jobs in, like, museums," Mr. Bence says. "But I was surprised that no one was willing to hire me to do anything."

arise for two reasons. First, economists can differ in their views on the consequences of a proposed policy. Second, they can differ in how they evaluate those consequences.

When economists describe the economy and construct models that predict how the economy will be affected by different policies, they are engaged in what is called **positive economics**. When they evaluate alternative policies, weighing the various benefits and costs, they are engaged in **normative economics**.

Consider the positive and normative aspects of a proposal to restrict imports of textiles produced in developing countries. Positive economics would describe the consequences: the increased prices American consumers would have to pay for clothes, the increased sales of American textiles, the increased employment and profits of U.S. textile manufacturers, and the reduced employment among textile workers in developing countries. Economists might disagree over the consequences of restricting imports because they disagree over the magnitude of the effects, perhaps agreeing that prices to consumers would rise but disagreeing over the size of that rise.

Joseph Stiglitz and Carl Walsh, "Modern Economics," *Principles of Microeconomics*, pp. 3–22.

In the end, though, the policy question is, *Should there be restraints on textile imports?* This is a normative question. Normative economics would weigh these various effects—the losses to consumers, the gains to U.S. textile workers, the increased profits—to reach an overall judgment. Normative economics develops frameworks within which these complicated judgments can be systematically made. Good normative economics also tries to be explicit about precisely which values or objectives it is incorporating. It tries to couch its statements in the form "If these are your values, then this is the best policy."

Economists, like members of any other profession, often have different values. Two economists might agree that a particular tax change would increase saving but would benefit the wealthy more than the poor. However, they might reach different conclusions about the desirability of that tax change. One might oppose it because it increases income inequality; the other might support it because it promotes saving. They differ in the values they place on the effects of the policy change, so they reach different conclusions even when they agree on the positive analysis of the proposed policy.

While economists may often seem to differ greatly among themselves, in fact they agree more than they disagree. When they do disagree, economists try to be clear about the source of their disagreement: (1) to what extent does it arise out of differences in models, (2) to what extent does it arise out of differences in estimates of quantitative relationships, and (3) to what extent does it arise out of differences in values? Clarifying the source of and reasons for disagreement can be a very productive way of learning more about an issue.

Summary

1. Economics is the study of how individuals, firms, and governments within our society make choices. Choices, and therefore trade-offs are unavoidable because desired goods, services, and resources are inevitably scarce.
2. Economists study how individuals, firms, and governments within our society make choices by focusing on incentives. People respond to changes in incentives by altering the decisions they make.
3. Exchange occurs in markets. Voluntary exchange can cause the other party to change. Additional outside factors may be influencing both.
4. Making choices requires information. Limited or imperfect information can interfere with incentives and affect the ability of the private market to ensure an efficient use of society's scarce resources.
5. The incomes people receive are determined by the market economy. Concerns over the equitable distribution of wealth and income in the economy lead to government programs that increase income equality.
6. The United States has a mixed economy, one in which there is a mix of public and private decision making. The economy relies primarily on the private interaction of individuals and firms to determine how resources are allocated, but government plays a large role as

well. A central question for any mixed economy is the balance between the private and public sectors.

7. The term *market* is used to describe any situation where exchange takes place. In the U.S. market economy, individuals, firms, and government interact in product markets, labor markets, and capital markets.
8. The two major branches of economics are microeconomics and macroeconomics. Microeconomics focuses on the behaviour of the firms, households, and individuals that make up the economy. Macroeconomics focuses on the behaviour of the economy as a whole.
9. Economists use models to study how the economy works and to make predictions about what will happen if something is changed. A model can be expressed in words or equations and is designed to mirror the essential characteristics of the particular phenomena under study.
10. A correlation exists when two variables tend to change together in a predictable way. However, the simple existence of a correlation does not prove that one factor causes the other to change. Additional outside factors may be influencing both.
11. Positive economics is the study of how the economy works. Disagreements in positive economics center on the appropriate model of the economy or market and the quantitative magnitudes characterizing the models.
12. Normative economics deals with the desirability of various actions. Disagreements in normative economics center on differences in the values placed on the various costs and benefits of different actions.

Key Terms

trade-offs
incentives
exchange
information
distribution
scarcity
market economy
product market
labor market
capital market
capital goods
microeconomics
macroeconomics
theory
correlation
causation
positive economics
normative economics

Review Questions

1. Why are trade-offs unavoidable? Why are incentives important in understanding choices?
2. After a voluntary exchange, why are both parties better off?
3. As a commodity, how does information differ from standard goods? How do information imperfections affect markets?
4. Why might there be a trade-off between equity and efficiency?
5. What is a mixed, economy? Describe some of the roles government might play, or not play, in a mixed economy.
6. Name the three main economic markets, and describe how an individual might participate in each one as a buyer or a seller.
7. Give two examples of economic issues that are primarily microeconornic and two examples that are primarily macroeconomic. What is the general difference between microeconomics and macroeconomics?
8. What is a model? Why do economists use models?
9. Give two examples of variables that you would expect to be positively correlated. For each example, explain whether a causal relationship exists between the two variables.
10. How does each of the following affect the incentive to go to college?
    a. An increase in tuition costs
    b. A fall in the interest rate on student loans
    c. A rise in wages for unskilled jobs
    d. An increase in incomes of college graduates
11. Characterize the following events as microeconomic, macroeconomic, or both.
    a. Unemployment increases this month.
    b. A drug company invents and begins to market a new medicine.
    c. A bank lends money to a large company but turns down a small business.
    d. Interest rates decline for all borrowers.
    e. A union negotiates for higher pay and better health insurance.
    f. The price of oil increases.
12. Characterize the following events as part of the labor market, the capital market, or the product market.
    a. An investor tries to decide which company to invest in.
    b. With practice, the workers on an assembly line become more efficient.
    c. The opening up of economies in Eastern Europe offers new markets for American products.
    d. A big company that is losing money decides to offer its workers special incentives to retire early, hoping to reduce its costs.
    e. A consumer roams around a shopping mall looking for birthday gifts.
    f. The federal government uses a surplus to pay off some of its debt.
13. The back of a bag of cat litter claims, "cats that use cat litter live three years longer than cats that don't." Do you think that cat

litter actually causes an increased life expectancy for cats, or can you think of some other factors to explain this correlation? What evidence might you collect to test your explanation?

14. Life expectancy in Sweden is almost eighty years. Does this prove that if an Indian moved to Sweden, he would live longer? That is, does this prove that living in Sweden causes an increase in life expectancy, or can you think of some other factors to explain these faces? What evidence might you collect to test your explanation?
15. During 2004, some economists argued that the federal Reserve should undertake policies to slow the economic expansion in the United States in order to ensure low inflation. Other economists opposed such policies, arguing that the dangers of inflation were exaggerated and attempts by the Federal Reserve to slow the economy would lead to higher unemployment. Is this a disagreement about positive economics, or about normative economics? Explain.

CHAPTER 2

Tradeoffs, Efficiency and Global Trade

2 Tradeoffs, Efficiency and Global Trade

By Timothy Taylor

In November 1968, the Rolling Stones recorded a song called: "You Can't Always Get What You Want." But economists had already been singing a similar tune for many years. For example, an English economist named Lionel Robbins (1898–1984) wrote *An Essay on the Nature and Significance of Economic Science* in 1932, in which he described the problem of not always getting what you want in this way:

> The time at our disposal is limited. There are only twenty-four hours in the day. We have to choose between the different uses to which they may be put. The services which others put at our disposal are limited. The material means of achieving ends are limited. We have been turned out of Paradise. We have neither eternal life nor unlimited means of gratification. Everywhere we turn, if we choose one thing we must relinquish others which, in different circumstances, we would wish not to have relinquished. Scarcity of means to satisfy given ends is an almost ubiquitous condition of human nature. Here then, is the unity of subject of Economic Science, the forms assumed by human behavior in disposing of scarce means.

Economics studies how every person, every firm, and every society must make choices, because none of them can have everything that they desire.

This chapter begins with a discussion of three broad categories of choices made by individuals and households: choices about which goods to consume, how many hours to work, and how much to borrow or save. Not coincidentally, these three categories of choices match the three main markets of microeconomics discussed in the circular flow diagram in Chapter 1: the markets for goods, labor, and financial capital. The discussion then introduces a framework for thinking about society's choices. Finally, the chapter discusses some concerns over whether the economic approach to facing scarcity and making choices describes accurately either how choices *are* actually made or how choices *should* be made.

Choosing What to Consume

People live in a world of scarcity: that is, they can't have all the time, money, possessions, and experiences they wish. Since people must choose, they inevitably face trade-offs, in which they have to give up things that

budget constraint: A diagram which shows what choices are possible, given the prices.

opportunity set: Another name for the budget constraint.

they desire to get other things that they desire more. When economists analyze how individuals make these choices, they divide the decision process into two steps. The first step is to consider what choices are possible for individuals. The second step is to think about which choices individuals actually make, based on their individual preferences. The model that economists use for illustrating the process of individual choice in a situation of scarcity is the **budget constraint**, sometimes also called the **opportunity set**, a diagram which shows what choices are possible.

A CONSUMPTION CHOICE BUDGET CONSTRAINT

To illustrate how the budget constraint model applies to choices about how much of each good to consume, consider the case of Alphonso, illustrated in Exhibit 2-1. Each graph in Exhibit 2-1 shows a different combination of Alphonso's income and the prices for two goods, burgers and bus tickets. In Exhibit 2-1a, Alphonso has $10 in spending money each week that he can allocate between bus tickets for getting to work and the burgers that he eats for lunch. Burgers cost $2 each, and bus tickets in Alphonso's town are 50 cents. Different combinations of choices that are possible for Alphonso are shown in the table and also depicted graphically in the accompanying budget constraint. Each combination of burgers and bus tickets shown in the table and the budget constraint adds up to exactly $10. Thus, the points along the budget constraint represent what consumption opportunities are possible for Alphonso.

HOW CHANGES IN INCOME AND PRICES AFFECT THE BUDGET CONSTRAINT

Changes in income will alter the budget constraint. For example, say that Alphonso's spending money increases to $12 per week. Exhibit 2-1b shows both his original budget constraint and his new budget constraint. In the new budget constraint, each combination of burgers and bus tickets at the given prices now adds up to $12. A higher income level means that the budget constraint will be to the right of the original budget constraint; conversely, a lower income level means that the budget constraint will lie to the left of the original budget constraint.

Now suppose Alphonso's income remains the same, but the price of one of the goods increases. Changes in the price of goods will affect Alphonso's budget constraint. In other words, his income level stays at $10 per week, but the price of bus tickets rises to $1 each, while the price of burgers remains at $2. Exhibit 2-1c shows how this change in price alters the budget constraint. A higher price for one good causes the budget constraint to shift inward; more specifically, the budget constraint swings inward as if on a hinge attached to the vertical axis or the horizontal axis—depending on which good's price has risen. Conversely, a lower price for one good would lead to an outward shift of the budget constraint.

A change in income causes the budget constraint to shift so that the new budget constraint is parallel to the original. However, a change in prices causes the slope of the budget constraint to change so that the budget constraint is steeper or flatter. Why are the effects different?

Exhibit 2-1 Alphonso's Consumption Choice Opportunity Set

(a) Each point on the opportunity set represents a combination of burgers and bus tickets whose total cost adds up to Alphonso's income of $10. The slope of the budget line is determined by the relative price of burgers and bus tickets. All along the budget set, giving up a burger means gaining four bus tickets.

(b) If Alphonso's income increases from $10 to $12, his opportunity set shifts to the right of the original budget set. The lower line is the original budget set, and the upper line is the new budget set. On the new budget set, each combination of burgers and bus tickets now adds up to a total cost of $12. However, because the trade-off of burgers for bus tickets is unchanged—still one burger for every four bus tickets—the slope of the budget line is unchanged.

(c) Alphonso's income remains at $10, as in *(a)*, but the cost of bus tickets rises from 50 cents to $1. This change causes the budget set to swing inward, as if on a hinge at the upper left. If Alphonso wishes to purchase only burgers, the change in price of bus tickets doesn't alter how many he can buy. However, giving up a burger now adds only two bus tickets, not four. The budget line slopes more steeply as a result.

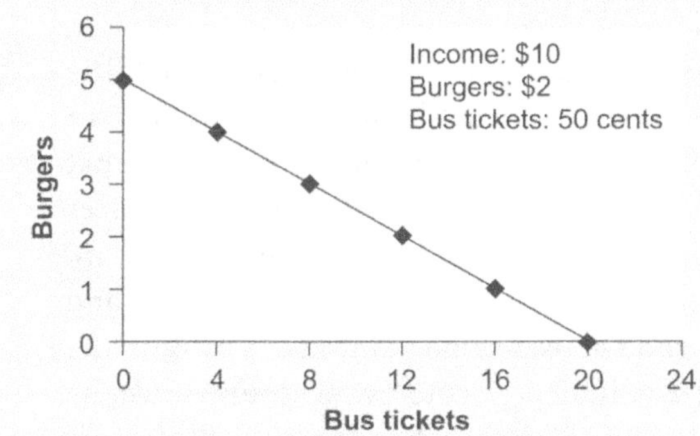

Quantity of Burgers (at $2)	Quantity of Bus Tickets (at 50 cents)
0	20
1	16
2	12
3	8
4	4
5	0

(a) First set of choices: Total income $10.

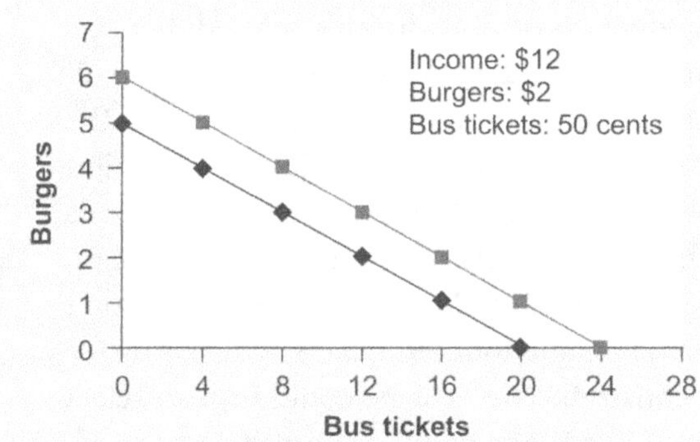

Quantity of Burgers (at $2)	Quantity of Bus Tickets (at 50 cents)
0	24
1	20
2	16
3	12
4	8
5	4
6	0

(b) Second set of choices: Total income $12.

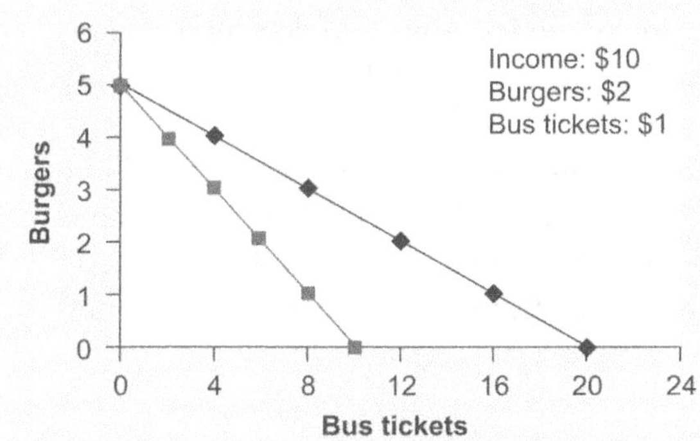

Quantity of Burgers (at $2)	Quantity of Bus Tickets (at $1)
0	10
1	8
2	6
3	4
4	2
5	0

(c) Third set of choices: Total income $10.

The slope of the budget constraint is determined by the relative price of the two goods, which is calculated by taking the price of one good and dividing it by the price of the other good. The *relative* price conveys the trade-off between the two goods, in this case burgers and bus rides. In Alphonso's first budget constraint in Exhibit 2-1a, if he gives up one burger, he can take four additional bus trips because the price of a burger is four times the price of a bus trip (that is, $2 versus 50 cents). The slope of this budget constraint shows that a loss of 1 burger equals a gain of 4 bus tickets. In Exhibit 2-1b, income changes but the relative prices of the two goods don't change, and so the slope of the budget constraint doesn't change either. In Exhibit 2-1c, however, giving up one burger means gaining only two bus trips (that is, $2 versus $1), and so the slope of the budget constraint changes to a loss of 1 burger means a gain of only 2 bus tickets.

Clearing It Up: Sketching Budget Constraints:

As an economics student, you will need to know how to sketch budget constraints quickly and accurately. Here's a suggestion: Start by calculating, based on income and the prices of the two goods, how much of each good each person could buy if that person were not buying any of the other good. These calculations will determine the points on the two axes of the budget constraint. Then the other points form a straight line between these endpoints.

PERSONAL PREFERENCES DETERMINE SPECIFIC CHOICES

What choice will Alphonso make along his budget constraint? The answer is simple: Alphonso will choose what he personally prefers. In economics, **utility** refers to the level of satisfaction or pleasure that people receive from their choices. Thus, when people make the choices that provide the highest level of satisfaction, economists say that they are "maximizing utility." In Alphonso's case, if he prefers to sit at home and eat, he buys a lot of burgers and chooses some point like A or B on the budget constraint in Exhibit 2-2. If he prefers to travel around town, he buys lots of bus tickets and chooses some point like D or E on the budget constraint. It's Alphonso's choice.

However, the logic of the budget constraint dictates that Alphonso's choice will be a point on the actual budget constraint itself: choice B with four burgers and four bus tickets—not a choice that is above the budget set or below it. Alphonso might desire a point like H in Exhibit 2-2 with five burgers and 16 bus tickets, offering more of both goods than choice B. However, choice H is outside the budget constraint, which means that Alphonso can't afford it. Conversely, Alphonso won't choose a point like J with two burger and four bus tickets, which is inside the boundary of the budget constraint, because he could instead select a choice on the budget set itself like B that would have at least as much of one good and more of the other—or a choice that would offer even more of both goods. In this simple model, Alphonso doesn't have any other goods on which to spend his money, and so if he doesn't spend his money, it is wasted.

utility:
The level of satisfaction or pleasure that people receive from their choices.

The budget constraint diagram shows what choices are possible, but it does not specify which choice is made. If two people have the same income and face the same prices, then they have identical budget constraints; but if those two people have different personal preferences, they will make different choices.

The Origins of Economic Utility

In the late eighteenth century, a philosopher and occasional economist named Jeremy Bentham (1748–1832) constructed a philosophy called "utilitarianism," which was based on the "happiness principle" that all of society's decisions ought to be made according to the amount of pleasure and pain that they cause individuals. Bentham wrote: "The greatest happiness of the greatest number is the foundation of morals and legislation."

Utilitarianism may not sound very radical, but consider some of its implications for the world of the late eighteenth and early nineteenth century. The utilitarian philosophy did not say that the happiness of a king, queen, or member of the nobility was more important than the happiness of an average person. It did not place the happiness of men above the happiness of women. It did not say that the happiness of the unemployed, criminals, children, or the poor was any less important than the happiness of anyone else.

Bentham was the unofficial leader of a group called the Philosophical Radicals, who favored voting rights for all with a secret ballot, government programs to provide jobs for the unemployed, government-run banks to help the poor save money, better conditions in prisons, limits on child labor, and—important to economists—market competition and free trade among countries. The Philosophical Radicals weren't always right, but at least by modern standards, they were on the side of the angels more often than not. Egeridius? Intri terfecu lartum me hori peconves aretem. Nos vivehena, menatiu speropu blintil inatum esimus hordiem pervidi cestra, qua Senica re consulesses C. Opim quam etid restimus atqui iderfec maio Cast pulius clemo cerebem habit. Upienti ngulus suam te nostorehem iam interit.

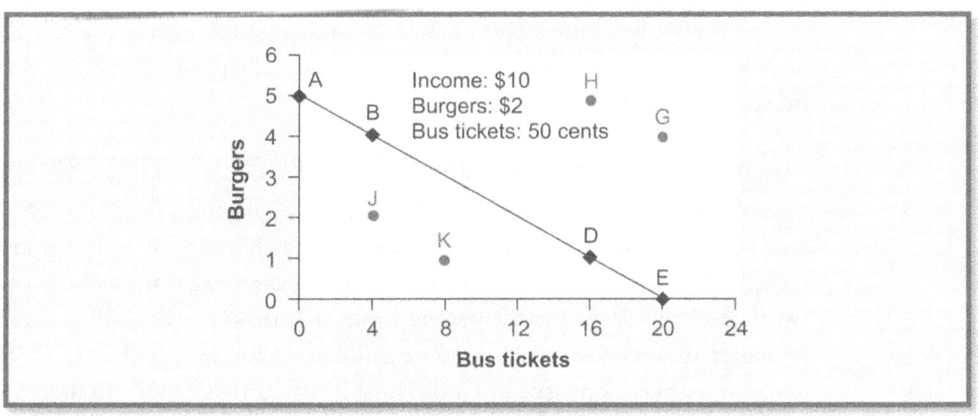

Exhibit 2-2 Personal Preferences Determine the Actual Choice:

If Alphonso likes burgers a lot, he will probably choose points A or B. If he likes bus tickets a lot, he will probably choose points D or E. Points H and G beyond the opportunity set are unattainable, given his level of income, no matter how much Alphonso might like them. Points J and K would be wasteful. For example, rather than choosing point J, he could have both more burgers and the same number of bus tickets at point B. Similarly, instead of choosing point K, he could have the same number of burgers but many more bus tickets at point D.

FROM A MODEL WITH TWO GOODS TO THE REAL WORLD OF MANY GOODS

The budget constraint diagram containing just two goods may seem so simple as to be simple-minded. In a modern economy, people choose from thousands of goods, not just two.

However, thinking about a model with many goods is straightforward. Instead of drawing just one budget constraint, showing the trade-off between two goods, you can draw multiple budget constraints, showing the possible trade-offs between many different pairs of goods. Or in more advanced classes in economics, you would use mathematical equations that include many possible goods and services that can be purchased, together with their quantities and prices, and show how the total spending adds up to the overall amount of money available. However, the graph with two goods clearly illustrates three basic concepts: (1) how the budget constraint is determined by income and prices; (2) how changes in income or relative prices cause a budget constraint to shift; and (3) how the personal preferences of an individual are represented by the point that is chosen on the budget constraint.

Choosing Between Labor and Leisure

The budget constraint applies to the labor-leisure choice just as it does to the decision of what quantity of goods to consume. But in the labor-leisure budget constraint, the decision isn't about what quantities of goods to buy, given their prices a limited amount of income; instead, it's about what number of hours to work, given the wage that can be earned and the limited number of hours in a day. Again, the first step is to use the budget constraint to show what is possible, while the second step is for each individual to make their personally preferred choice that maximizes utility.

AN EXAMPLE OF A LABOR-LEISURE BUDGET CONSTRAINT

Beulah has a job as an assistant manager of a fast-food restaurant. She can work as many as 60 hours per week if she chooses. Of course, most people don't have jobs that let them choose exactly how many hours to work each week; but most people have at least some flexibility about whether to look for a part-time or a full-time job or whether to work overtime or take on a second job. Thus, it isn't unreasonable to imagine people making choices about the number of hours they work. Exhibit 2-3 shows two of Beulah's labor-leisure budget constraints.

In Exhibit 2-3a, Beulah's wage is $9 per hour. The table and the budget constraint show the trade-off that she faces between income and leisure. Because Beulah receives an hourly wage, the more hours she works, the more her income rises and her leisure diminishes. The horizontal axis of the exhibit measures both labor hours and leisure hours at the same time, but in opposite directions. The quantity of hours of leisure is measured from left to right, while the quantity of hours of labor is measured from right to left. Since Beulah has a total of 60 hours available that she could work, the horizontal axis shows how she divides up this time between leisure and work.

HOW A CHANGE IN WAGES AFFECTS THE LABOR-LEISURE BUDGET CONSTRAINT

A change in the wage will shift Beulah's budget constraint. If her wage rises to $11 per hour, perhaps because she has gained more experience or training, then the trade-offs that she faces change as well. Both her original budget constraint and her new set of tradeoffs are shown in Exhibit 2-3b. A new wage changes the slope of the budget constraint because a new wage means a different trade-off between hours of leisure and income.

MAKING A CHOICE ALONG THE LABOR-LEISURE BUDGET CONSTRAINT

Living in a world of scarcity—no one has more than 24 hours in a day—requires that people must make choices about how to spend their time, but the fact of scarcity doesn't dictate what choices they make. In deciding how many hours to work, Beulah will make a choice that maximizes her utility; that is, she will choose according to her preferences for leisure time and income. If she chooses to work 60 hours per week, she will have more income to spend on food, rent, clothing, cars, vacations, or other material goods. However, if she prefers leisure time over material satisfactions, she may choose to work fewer hours so that she has more time for family, friends, and low-cost hobbies such as reading or yoga. Exhibit 2-4 illustrates both possibilities. If Beulah prefers a relatively high level of income, then she will choose a point close to A, with $540 of income, 60 hours of work and no leisure. If she prefers instead a relatively high level of leisure, she might choose a point like C with 50 hours of leisure, 10 hours of work, and $90 in income.

Clearing It Up: Measuring Labor and Leisure on the Same Axis

The labor-leisure budget constraint involves illustrating three factors—hours of labor, hours of leisure, and dollars of income—on only two axes. This illustration only works because the hours of both labor and leisure appear on the horizontal axis. After all, all leisure means no labor, and all labor means no leisure. On the horizontal axis, hours of leisure are measured from left to right, but hours of labor are measured from right to left. The trade-off here is between the two goods of leisure and income because labor is not a "good" in itself, but instead a mechanism for earning income.

Exhibit 2-3 Beulah's Labor-Leisure Opportunity Set

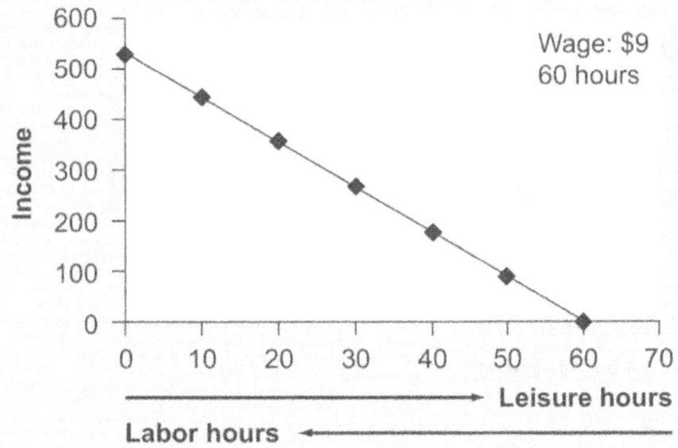

Hours worked	Leisure time	Income
0	60	$0
10	50	$90
20	40	$180
30	30	$270
40	20	$360
50	10	$450
60	0	$540

(a) First set of choices: Wage $9 per hour. The points on the opportunity set show what combinations of leisure and income that Beulah can have with her 60 hours of time, given that she can earn a wage of $9 per hour. The trade-off between leisure and income, which is the wage $9 per hour, determines the slope of the line.

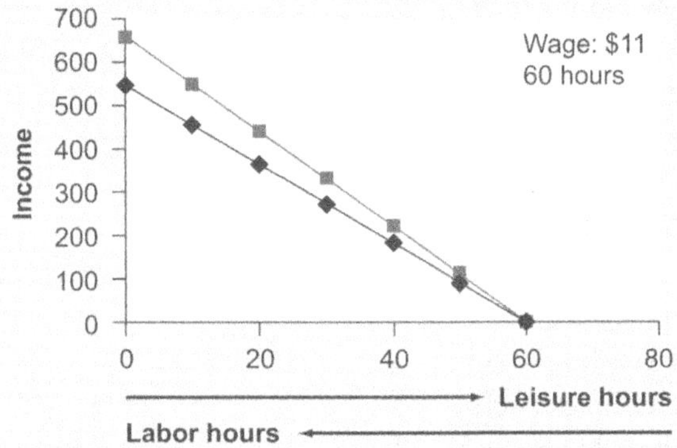

Hours worked	Leisure time	Income
0	60	$0
10	50	$110
20	40	$220
30	30	$330
40	20	$440
50	10	$550
60	*0*	*$660*

(b) Second set of choices: Wage $11 per hour. If Beulah's wage increases from $9 per hour to $11 per hour, her 60 hours of time has not changed, but the trade-off that she faces between leisure and income has changed. With the higher wage, giving up a certain number of hours of leisure brings a higher income, so the budget set rotates upward.

Beulah might desire a combination of income and leisure that is outside her budget constraint; for example, she would probably like to have both 60 hours of leisure and $540 of income, which is the choice shown at point S. However, the budget constraint shows the limits of what choices are possible, given the wage and hours available, and choices beyond the budget constraint are not possible. Moreover, Beulah will not choose a point inside the budget constraint like T, which is 50 hours of labor, 10 hours of leisure, and $200 of income. In effect, a choice like T would mean that Beulah was working for only $4 per hour (that is, $200 of income divided by 50 hours of work), when she can actually earn a wage of $9 per hour. Thus, the labor-leisure budget constraint illustrates: (1) how the budget set of possible choices for leisure and income are determined by the wage rate and the total quantity of hours that can be worked; (2) how changes in the wage rate cause the budget constraint to shift; and (3) how the personal preferences of an individual for choosing between leisure and income are represented by the point that is chosen on the budget constraint.

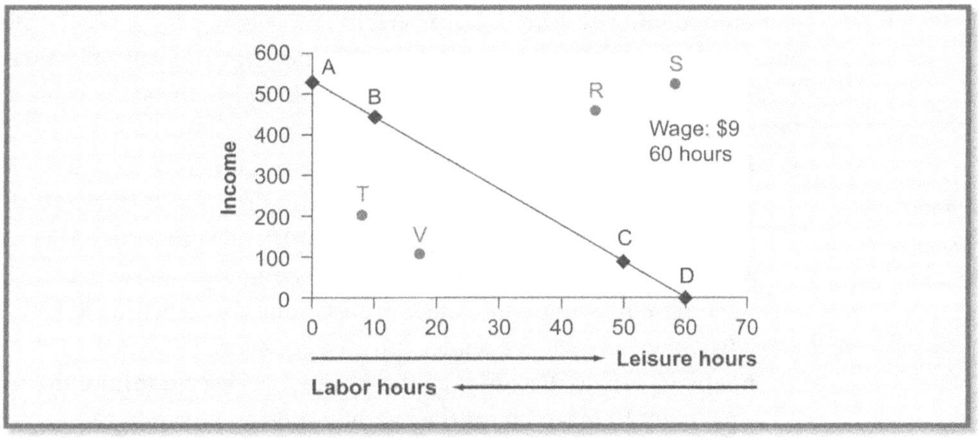

Exhibit 2-4 Beulah's Personal Choice on a Labor-Leisure Opportunity Set

If Beulah strongly prefers income, she will work a lot of hours and choose a point like A or B. If she strongly prefers leisure, she will work few hours and make a choice like C or D. Given that she has 60 hours of time and a wage of $9 per hour, she cannot choose points like R or S that are outside her budget set. Points like T or V inside her budget set would be wasteful; they would be like giving up hours of leisure but not being paid.

Choosing Between Present and Future Consumption

An intertemporal choice reaches across time. Borrowing money is an intertemporal choice, because it involves borrowing money to spend in the present but promising to repay in the future. Saving money is also an intertemporal choice, because it involves less consumption in the present, but the ability to consume more in the future. The intertemporal choice budget constraint shows the trade-off between present and future consumption.

INTEREST RATES: THE PRICE OF INTERTEMPORAL CHOICE

In the consumption choice budget constraint presented earlier, the trade-off between goods is determined by the relative prices of the two goods. In the labor-leisure budget constraint, the trade-off between leisure and income is based on the wage. In the intertemporal choice budget constraint, the trade-off between present consumption and future consumption is based on the interest rate or the rate of return. The price of borrowing money is the interest that you pay on the loan. The reward for saving money is the interest that you receive. Interest rates are worth more discussion, because they may seem less familiar than other prices.

The key to understanding the economic function of interest rates is to recognize that $100 you will receive in the future has less economic value than $100 you receive today. Imagine that a friend owes you $100, and when the time comes to pay, the friend says: "Hey, no problem, I'll have the money for you in five years." You protest, and your supposed friend says, "Hey, you are still getting repaid your full $100, so what are you complaining about?" You probably aren't going to persuade this loser, your former friend, to repay you sooner, but you can offer three arguments as to why $100 in the future doesn't have the same value as $100 today:

risk premium: A payment to make up for the risk of not being repaid in full.

inflation: Rise in the overall level of prices.

time value of money: The cost of having to wait for repayment.

1. *Risk of not being repaid.* The future is uncertain. Your friend could get hit by a bus. You could get hit by a bus. (The way this friendship is going, you could run over your former friend with a bus.) Having $100 in your pocket is a sure thing. Having a promise of $100 is uncertain. Anytime someone borrows money, whether the lender is a friend or a bank, the lender must be concerned about the risk of not being repaid. Part of the interest rate is a **risk premium**, that is, a payment to make up for the risk of not being repaid in full.
2. *Inflation.* In most years, there is a rise in the price level called **inflation.** In recent U.S. history, this increase has typically been 1-3% per year, but in some other countries the rate of inflation has been much higher. If the overall level of prices rises by 3% then on average a dollar will buy 3% less in terms of goods and services at the end of the year. If that 3% is being subtracted each year from the buying power of the currency, then being repaid $100 in the future will provide less buying power than receiving the money immediately. A lender demands an interest rate in part to compensate for any expected inflation, so that the money that is repaid in the future will have at least as much buying power as the money that was originally loaned. (The concept of inflation, along with its underlying causes and policy solutions, is discussed at length in the macroeconomics section of the book.)
3. *Time value of money.* Even if you knew with complete certainty that the $100 will be repaid in the future, and even if the rate of inflation is zero, it is still annoying to wait several years for repayment. If you have the money now, you can spend it on something now if you wish to do so and receive benefits from that spending. Being forced to wait is an intangible cost, but still a cost. This cost of having to wait is referred to as the **time value of money**.

Thus, when explaining to your friend why you should receive interest payments if you need to wait five years for your money, you can point out that an interest rate has three components:

Interest rate = Risk premium + Expected rate of inflation
+ Time value of money.

In effect, interest payments are a compensation for the risk of not being repaid, the fact that inflation tends to reduce the buying power of money over time, and the unpleasantness of having to wait to have money available.

Thinking about these three components of interest rates helps to explain why interest rates differ across times and places. At times and places when inflation is high, interest rates will also be high. Differences in interest rates at a point in time can usually be traced to the different risk premiums involved. For example, when the U.S. government borrows money the interest rate is quite low, perhaps an annual rate of 3–4%, because the chance that the federal government will not repay what it has borrowed is quite low. A large corporation might pay an annual interest rate of 6–7% because, although the firm is still unlikely not to pay back the loan, the risk is greater than with a federal government. A medium-size or small firm would pay a still higher interest rate because it has a greater risk of not repaying the loan. Individuals pay a relatively low interest rate when they borrow money from a bank to purchase a home because the bank (the lender) does a credit check before lending any money in the first place. The credit check is supposed to ensure that a home buyer has the financial means to cover the cost; if the buyer is unable to meet the payments, the bank can take the house and sell it. However, individuals pay a higher interest rate on credit card borrowing because there is a greater risk that such loans will not be repaid.

THE POWER OF COMPOUND INTEREST

Interest rates are usually expressed in annual terms. For example, an annual interest rate of 7% means that if you borrow \$100 you will need to repay \$107 a year from now, or if you save \$100 you will receive \$7 in interest payments a year from now. But what if you are planning to save money for a period of many years, allowing the interest to accumulate over time? The formula for starting with a certain amount of money in the present, and a certain interest rate or rate of return, and figuring how much it would be worth at a date in the future is:

$$(\text{Amount at present}) \times (1 + \text{interest rate})^{\text{number of years}} = \text{Amount at future time}$$

For example, Christopher is planning to make a financial investment of \$500. He will put this money in a savings account that pays an interest rate of 6% annually and leave it in the account for some years as the interest accumulates.

Exhibit 2-5 applies this formula for Christopher and shows what his financial investment would be worth at various dates in the future. Notice that if he leaves the financial investment alone for 20 years, the original \$500 will more than triple in value to \$1,603; if he leaves the financial investment alone for 40 years, it will increase more than 10-fold to \$5,143. How can a seemingly moderate interest rate like 6% per year produce such large increases? The answer lies in the power of **compound interest**, which refers to the situation when interest payments are allowed to accumulate, so that in later time periods, the interest rate is paid not only on the original amount, but also on the interest that has accumulated in previous years. In the equation for how a financial investment increases in value over time, the number of years is an exponent. When quantities are raised to high exponential powers, they will eventually expand very quickly. The exponent represents the power of compound interest—as time goes by, Christopher is not just earning interest on his original \$500, but also on the earlier interest he earned. If

compound interest: When interest payments accumulate, so that in later time periods, the interest rate is paid on the interest that has been earned and reinvested in previous years.

interest rates are relatively low, compound interest doesn't make much of a practical difference over a short time period of a few years. But over several decades, even a relatively low interest rate will compound in a way that yields significant returns on the initial financial investment.

AN EXAMPLE OF INTERTEMPORAL CHOICE

Consider the case of Desdemona, who is lucky enough to receive a gift of $10,000 from a wealthy aunt. She faces a choice: how much money should she consume now, and how much should she save for future consumption? Again, the first step is to use the budget constraint to show the range of possible choices, while the second step is to illustrate the individually preferred choice that maximizes her utility.

Exhibit 2-5
Christopher's Potential Savings

Starting with $500, interest rate of 6%

After 1 year	$\$500\,(1 + .06)^{1} = \$530$	After 10 years	$\$500\,(1 + .06)^{10} = \$895$
After 2 years	$\$500\,(1 + .06)^{2} = \$562$	After 20 years	$\$500\,(1 + .06)^{20} = \$1{,}603$
After 5 years	$\$500\,(1 + .06)^{5} = \$669$	After 40 years	$\$500\,(1 + .06)^{40} = \$5{,}143$

Exhibit 2-6 Desdemona's Intertemporal Budget Constraint

The points along the budget set represent the combinations of present and future consumption that are available to Desdemona, based on her inheritance of $10,000 and an interest rate of 9% per year. The trade-off between present consumption and future consumption—and thus the slope of the budget line—is determined by the interest rate. Choices like Q or P are unavailable to Desdemona, even if she would like them. She will not make choices like R or S because they give up present consumption without taking future consumption, which would be wasteful. Thus, she will choose among points like A through F, based on her personal preferences.

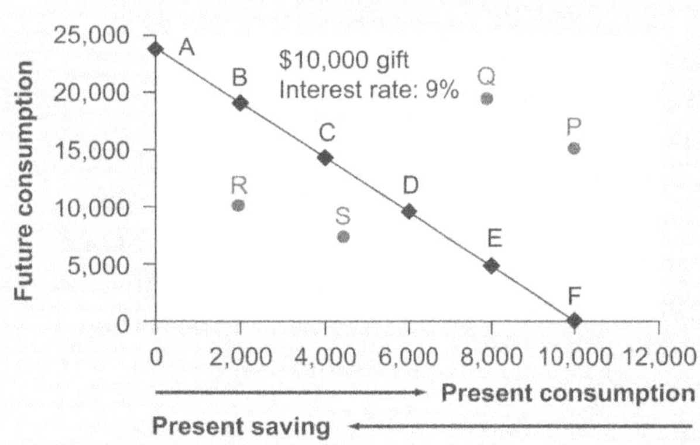

Consume in present	Save in present	Consume in future
0	$10,000	$23,673
$2,000	$8,000	$18,939
$4,000	$6,000	$14,204
$6,000	$4,000	$9,469
$8,000	$2,000	$4,734
$10,000	$0	$0

In the intertemporal choice budget constraint, the two axes represent consumption in the present and consumption in the future. Let's assume that if Desdemona saves some of the money, she can earn an annual interest rate of 9% for the next 10 years. Exhibit 2-6 shows Desdemona's choices in both a table and a budget constraint. The levels of future consumption that are available to her 10 years from now are calculated by using the formula for compound interest. At one extreme, she can consume all of the $10,000 in the present and have nothing left in the future. At the other extreme, she can save the entire $10,000, consume none of it in the present, and have $23,673 to spend 10 years from now. In Exhibit 2-6, both present consumption and present savings are shown on the horizontal axis. Consumption is measured from left to right; saving is measured from right to left. In effect, the horizontal axis shows how the income that is available in the present is divided into either consumption or savings. (This approach applies the same logic as the way in which hours of labor and leisure were both shown on the horizontal axis in the labor-leisure budget constraint.) If the interest rate rises, then the budget constraint has a steeper slope; a lower interest rate causes the budget constraint to shift downward to a flatter slope.

Desdemona will seek to maximize her utility and choose the option that brings her the greatest degree of satisfaction. Inevitably, this choice will be one of the points on the budget constraint such as A, B, C, D, E, or F. Even if Desdemona wants to choose a point like Q, with $8,000 of consumption in the present, $2,000 of savings, and $20,000 of future consumption, she can't have it because choice Q is outside her budget constraint. Moreover, Desdemona will not choose a point inside the budget constraint like R, with $2,000 in present consumption and $10,000 in future consumption because such a choice would be like throwing away money. Instead of choosing R, Desdemona would certainly prefer a choice like C with more consumption in both the present and the future.

In the real world, the trade-off between present and future consumption is considerably more complex than the basic intertemporal budget constraint shown here. Instead of making one decision in the present about whether to consume now or save for 10 years from now, people receive income in many different years and make decisions about how much to save over different periods of time. Moreover, financial investments usually don't pay a guaranteed rate of return, so people need take into account the risk and uncertainty of investments. Later chapters will take up the details of financial investing in greater detail. But the basic intertemporal budget constraint here illustrates three themes: (1) how the budget constraint of possible choices for present and future consumption are determined by the quantity of income in the present and the interest rate; (2) how changes in the interest rate will cause the intertemporal budget constraint to shift; and (3) how the personal preferences of an individual for present and future consumption are represented by the point that is chosen on the intertemporal budget constraint.

Three Implications of Budget Constraints: Opportunity Cost, Marginal Decision-Making, and Sunk Costs

The budget constraint framework has some possibly unexpected implications for how a sensible utility-maximizing individual will make decisions. Let's now draw out three of those implications, involving *opportunity cost, marginal decision making,* and *sunk costs.*

OPPORTUNITY COST

opportunity cost: Whatever must be given up to obtain something that is desired.

When most people want to know the cost of an item or a service, they look for a price tag. When economists want to determine cost, they go one step further. They use the idea of **opportunity cost**, which is whatever must be given up to obtain something that is desired. In the examples discussed earlier, if Alphonso wants more burgers, the opportunity cost is measured in bus tickets; if he wants more bus tickets, the opportunity cost is measured in burgers. In Beulah's labor-leisure choice, if she wants more income, the opportunity cost is hours of leisure; if she wants more leisure time, the opportunity cost is dollars of income. In Desdemona's intertemporal choice, the opportunity cost of greater consumption in the present is less consumption in the future and vice versa. The idea of opportunity cost, as its name implies, is that the cost of one item is the lost opportunity to do or consume something else.

Opportunity Costs

By David Moglen

Economic Actor	Nearly Always Trying to Maximize	Basic Action/ Choice	Opportunity Cost
Consumers	Utility	Buying a good yielding the most utility	Lost utility from second-best good
Businesses	Profit	Producing the good yielding the most profit	Lost profit from second most profitable good the business could make
Government	Unknown; no one agreed-upon target	Spending money in a certain way, change a certain tax, change or introduce a law or regulation	Unknown; no one agreed-upon second-best option
Country (as shown in a PPC graph)	Output/ efficiency	Produce more of one good	Lost output of second good
Labor	Wages + net nonmonetary advatages	Choose to work one hour	Lost utility from an hour of leisure time (the leisure trade-off)

Opportunity Cost in the Airport

After the terrorist plane hijackings on September 11, 2001, many steps were proposed to improve air travel safety. For example, the federal government could provide armed "sky marshals" who would travel inconspicuously with the rest of the passengers. The cost of having a sky marshal on every flight would be roughly $3 billion per year. Retrofitting all U.S. planes with reinforced cockpit doors to make it harder for terrorists to take over the plane would have a price tag of $450 million. Buying more sophisticated security equipment for airports, like three-dimensional baggage scanners and cameras linked to face recognition software, could cost another $2 billion.

But the single biggest cost of greater airline security doesn't involve spending money. It's the opportunity cost of additional waiting time at the airport. About 750 million passengers took plane trips in the United States in 2008. Since the 9/11 hijackings, security screening has become more intensive, and consequently, the procedure takes longer than in the past. Say that, on average, each air passenger spends one extra hour in the airport per trip. Economists commonly place a value on time to convert an opportunity cost in time into a monetary figure. Because many air travelers are relatively high-paid business people, conservative estimates set the average price of time for air travelers at $20 per hour. By these estimates, the opportunity cost of delay in airports is 750 million hours × 20 dollars/ hour, or $15 billion per year. Clearly, the opportunity costs of waiting time can be just as important as costs that involve direct spending.

In many cases, it is reasonable to refer to the opportunity cost as the price. If your cousin buys a new bicycle for $300, then $300 measures the amount of "other consumption" that he has given up. For practical purposes, there may be no special need to identify the specific alternative product or products that could have been bought with that $300, but sometimes the price as measured in dollars may not accurately capture the true opportunity cost. This problem can loom especially large when costs of time are involved. For example, consider a boss who decides that all employees will attend a two-day retreat to "build team spirit." The out-of-pocket monetary cost of the event may involve hiring an outside consulting firm to run the retreat. But an opportunity cost exists as well: during the two days of the retreat, none of the employees are doing any other work. Attending college is another case where the opportunity cost exceeds the monetary cost. The out-of-pocket costs of attending college include tuition, books, room and board, and other expenses. But in addition, during the hours that you are attending class and studying, it is impossible to work at a paying job. Thus, college imposes both an out-of-pocket cost and an opportunity cost of lost earnings—and both costs should be taken into account.

In some cases, making the opportunity cost explicit can alter behavior. Imagine, for example, that you are an employee who goes out to lunch every day and spends $8 at a local restaurant. You may know perfectly well that bringing a lunch from home would only cost $3 a day, but somehow referring to the opportunity cost of buying lunch at the restaurant as $5 each day (that is, the $8 it costs minus the $3 your lunch from home would cost) doesn't seem to matter much. However, if you work

Can Economics Take Pride in Being the "Dismal Science"?

Economics is often called the dismal science. Yet few people would toss that phrase around so easily if they knew its origin. The "dismal science" phrase originated with British essayist Thomas Carlyle (1795-1881). In an 1849 article, Carlyle described the study of "political economy," as economics was then called, as a "dreary, desolate and indeed quite abject and distressing one; what we might call, by way of eminence, the *dismal science*."

This put-down has echoed through time. But not many people know why Carlyle disliked economics. The "dismal science" comment appeared in his essay "Occasional Discourse on the Negro Question." In that essay, Carlyle made the racist argument that white landowners should compel black people in the West Indies to give up their natural laziness and instead to work hard and have some purpose in their otherwise meaningless lives. Carlyle didn't just believe that black people should be ordered around by whites; he believed that all the "weak" people, black and white alike, should be compelled by the strong to do "the work they were appointed for," as he put it.

Carlyle thought economics was the "dismal science" because it rested on the assumption that people, regardless of race and social status, were best suited to make their own decisions about their own lives. Carlyle's insult is one that economists can wear with pride.

250 days a year, that $5 per day adds up to $1,250 for a year—which is the cost of a decent vacation. If the opportunity cost is described as "a nice vacation" instead of "$5 a day," you might make different choices.

MARGINAL DECISION-MAKING AND DIMINISHING MARGINAL UTILITY

The budget constraint framework helps to emphasize that most choices in the real world aren't about getting all of one thing or all of another; that is, they aren't about choosing either the point at one end of the budget constraint or else the point all the way at the other end. Instead, most choices involve **marginal analysis**, which involves comparing the benefits and costs of choosing a little more or a little less of a good.

marginal analysis: Comparing the benefits and costs of choosing a little more or a little less of a good.

The utility that a person receives from consuming the first unit of a good is typically more than the utility received from consuming the fifth or the tenth unit of that same good. When Alphonso makes his choice between burgers and bus tickets, for example, the first few bus rides that he chooses might provide him with a great deal of utility— perhaps they help him get to a job interview or a doctor's appointment. But later bus rides might provide much less utility—they may only serve to kill time on a rainy day. Similarly, the first burger that Alphonso chooses to buy may be on a day when he missed breakfast and is ravenously hungry. However, if Alphonso has a burger every single day, the last few burgers may taste pretty boring. Similarly, if Beulah is working 60 hours per week and thinking about whether to take a few hours of leisure, that break may provide her with a great deal of utility. But if she is working only 10 hours a week, with 50 hours of leisure already, then taking a few more hours of leisure seems likely to provide much less utility.

The general pattern that consumption of the first few units of any good tends to bring a higher level of utility to a person than consumption of later units is a common pattern. Economists refer to this pattern the **law of diminishing marginal utility**, which means that as a person receives more of a good, the additional or marginal utility from each additional unit of the good declines.

law of diminishing marginal utility: As a person receives more of a good, the marginal utility from each additional unit of the good is smaller than from the previous unit.

The law of diminishing marginal utility explains why people and societies rarely make all-or-nothing choices. You wouldn't say, "My favorite food is (say) ice cream, so I will eat nothing but ice cream from now on." Instead, even if you get a very high level of utility from your favorite food, if you ate it exclusively, the additional or marginal utility from those last few servings would not be very high. Similarly, most workers don't say: "I enjoy leisure, so I'll never work." Instead, workers recognize that even though some leisure is very nice, a combination of all leisure and no income isn't so attractive. Thus, the budget constraint framework suggests that when people make choices in a world of scarcity, they will use marginal analysis and think about whether they would prefer a little more or a little less.

sunk cost: Costs that were incurred in the past and cannot be recovered, and thus should not affect current decisions.

SUNK COSTS

In the budget constraint framework, all decisions involve what will happen next: that is, what quantities of goods will be consumed, how many hours will be worked, or how much will be saved. These decisions do not look back to past choices. Thus, the budget constraint framework assumes that **sunk costs**, which are costs that were incurred in the past and cannot be recovered, should not affect the current decision.

Consider the case of Edgar who pays $8 to see a movie, but after watching the film for 30 minutes he knows that it's truly terrible. Should he stay and watch the rest of the movie because he paid $8, or should he leave? The money he spent is a sunk cost and unless the theater manager is feeling kindly, Edgar won't get a refund. But staying in the movie still means paying an opportunity cost in time. Thus, Edgar's choice is whether to spend the next 90 minutes suffering through a cinematic disaster or to do something—anything—else. The lesson of sunk costs is to forget about the money that's irretrievably gone and instead to focus on the marginal costs and benefits of future options.

production possibilities frontier: A diagram that shows the combinations of output that are possible for an economy to produce.

For people and firms alike, dealing with sunk costs can be frustrating. It often means admitting an earlier error in judgment. Many firms, for example, find it hard to give up on a new product that is doing poorly because they spent so much money in creating and launching the product. But the lesson of sunk costs is to ignore them and make decisions based on what will happen in the future.

The budget constraint or opportunity set framework provides a framework for thinking about how individuals make economic decisions like what to consume, how much to work, and how much to save. The purpose of this model is not to tell utility-maximizing individuals what they *should* do, but only to convey the range of available choices for what individuals *could* do, and to provide a way of showing what choices people actually make.

The Production Possibilities Frontier and Social Choices

In a world of scarcity, individuals cannot have everything they want and must instead make a choice along a budget constraint. Firms cannot have all the profits they want and must struggle to come up with new ways of pleasing customers. Society as a whole cannot have everything it might want, either. A production possibilities frontier is a graph that shows the combinations of output that are possible for an economy to produce. In effect, a **production possibilities frontier** is a budget constraint for the economy as a whole.

An example of a production possibilities frontier faced by every economy is the macroeconomic choice between consumption and real investment. Consumption refers to goods and services that are used up this year. Real investment (as opposed to financial investment) refers to expenditures on equipment (like machinery) that can be used to produce goods or services for some years into the future. Thus, expenditures on consumption often serve a more immediate need or desire, but expenditures on investment typically help to increase the economy's level of output in the future.

A production possibilities frontier for the choice between consumption and investment is shown in Exhibit 2-7 by the line labeled PPF_1. At point A, the economy is devoting all of its resources to producing goods for current consumption and nothing to investment. At points B, C, and D, the economy is gradually shifting toward lower levels of consumption and higher levels of investment. At point E, at the other end of the production possibilities frontier, the economy is devoting all of its resources to producing goods for real investment and no resources to current consumption. In a market-oriented economy, the choice between consumption and real investment is not made by the government or by any single organization, but rather is the result of many decisions made by households and firms. However, government policies can use taxes, regulations and other policies to influence the choices of individuals as to how much they should consume or save, and also to influence the eagerness with which firms will make real investments. Just as different people will make different choices along a budget constraint, according to their personal preferences, different societies will make choices about how much to consume and to invest.

Over time, societies that invest a greater share of GDP will tend to expand their ability to produce output. Therefore, a society that chooses

Exhibit 2-7 The Consumption and Investment Trade-Off

A production possibilities frontier shows the possible combinations of output that a society can produce. Points A, B, C, and D illustrate some possible choices along PPF_1, moving from all consumption at A to greater investment at B, C, and D. PPF_2 and PPF_3 show an outward shift of the frontier, which would happen as an economy grows and can afford more of both consumption and investment.

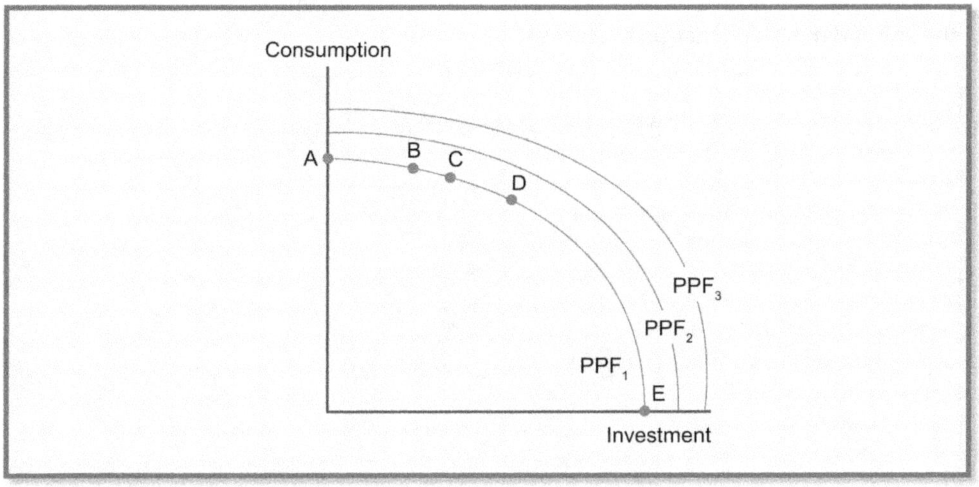

a high level of consumption and low level of investment, like point B, will find that in the future its production possibilities frontier shifts outward only a bit, perhaps from PPF_1 to PPF_2. However, a society that consumes relatively less in the present and invests more, like point D, will find that in the future its production possibilities frontier has shifted outward more dramatically, from PPF_1 to PPF_3. Thus, a consumption-investment production possibilities frontier shows the range of choices available to society, illustrates which choice will happen, and even has implications for how the PPF will shift in the future.

THE SHAPE OF THE PRODUCTION POSSIBILITIES FRONTIER AND DIMINISHING MARGINAL RETURNS

The budget constraints presented earlier in this chapter, showing individual choices about what quantities of goods to consume, how much to work and how much to save, were all straight lines. The reason for these straight lines was that the slope of the budget constraint was determined by relative prices of the two goods in the consumption budget constraint, by the wage in the labor-leisure budget constraint, and by the interest rate in the intertemporal budget constraint. However, the production possibilities frontier for consumption and investment was drawn as a curved line. Why does the PPF have a different shape?

Consider another example of a production possibilities frontier that arises when government decision makers must decide how much money to spend on competing government priorities, like education and improving health. Exhibit 2-8 shows a production possibilities frontier for this trade-off. In this diagram there are no specific numbers on the axes because there is no single way to measure levels of education

Exhibit 2-8 A Health vs. Education Production Possibilities Frontier

This production possibilities frontier shows a trade-off between devoting social resources to health and devoting them to education. At choices like A and B, most social resources go to health. At choices like D and E, most go to education. The curvature of the PPF shows that when a large share of resources is already devoted to health (as at point B), devoting still more resources to health and moving to point A produces only a small gain in health but a substantial loss in education. Thus, the curvature of the PPF demonstrates the law of diminishing marginal returns.

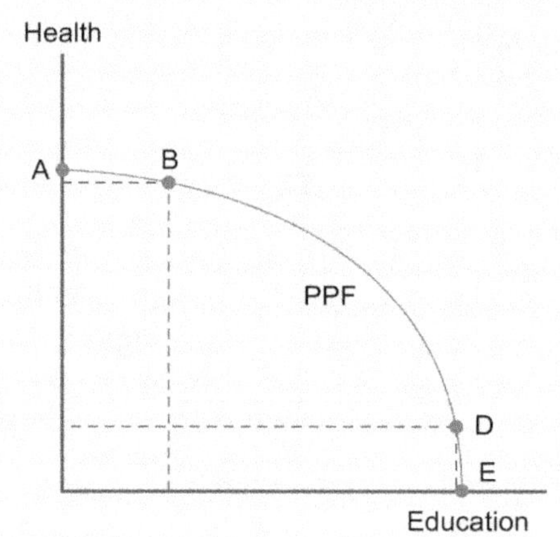

and health. However, when you think of improvements in education, you can think of accomplishments like more years of school completed, fewer high-school dropouts, and higher scores on standardized tests. When you think of improvements in health, you can think of longer life expectancies, lower levels of infant mortality, and fewer outbreaks of disease. At choice A, the government is committing all of its resources to producing health and none to education; at choice D, the government is committing all resources to education and none to health. As the economy grows over time this production possibilities frontier will shift to the right, making it possible for society to have more of both education and health. But in the immediate present, choosing more of one means choosing less of the other.

To understand why the PPF is curved, start by considering point A at the top left-hand side of the PPF. At point A, literally all of the available resources are being devoted to health and literally none to education. This situation would be extreme and even ridiculous. For example, children are seeing a doctor every day, whether they are sick or not, but not attending school. People are having cosmetic surgery on every part of their bodies, but no high school or college education exists. Now imagine that some of these resources are diverted from health to education, so that the economy is at point B instead of point A. Diverting some marginal resources away from A to B causes relatively little reduction in health because the last few marginal dollars going into health care services aren't producing much additional gain in health. However, putting those marginal dollars into education, which is

the law of diminishing returns: As additional increments of resources are added to producing a good or service, the marginal benefit from those additional increments will decline.

IN-CLASS PROJECT

The Production Possibilities Curve (PPC)

By David Moglen

Directions:

Graph—You will be assigned a group number from 1-5. Take the first country (on the left) associated with the same number (above) as the question number you are assigned (below). In other words, Shock 1 (Movement from on to inside the curve) goes with Country 1 (Argentina), Shock 2 goes with country 2 and so on.

Alternatively, your instructor may mix and match the shocks with the country data, for example shock 3 (growth in the economy) could be matched with country #5, or any other country for that matter.

Once you have been assigned a group number, draw the graph with points A (before the shock) and B (after the shock) as described. Fully label the graph including estimated numeric values on x and y axes for points A and B. Label the axes according to the good and units of that good specified in the data.

Your points A or B could be a variety of different places & you must choose only one. Assume all examples start and end with output at potential—on the curve—unless otherwise indicated.

You should use k for thousand and m for million. Use a curved PPC since this is a single-country example.

***Explanation**—Say what is happening to the Land, Labor or Capital in your example to cause the change described. Be specific to the industry, e.g. if the factor you want to say is causing the shock you are given (below) is *Labor*, and the good is mechanical, maybe you say something (be specific) is happening to affect employment of *factory workers* (or whatever would correctly reflect the situation described).

Or as another example, if you wanted to use *capital* and the good is some kind of clothing, you would say what's happening with the *sewing machines.*

If you wanted to talk about the labor used to make clothes, you could be specific by saying what is happening to the *seamstresses, tailors,* or *clothing designers.* If you wanted to talk about the land resources for clothing, you could talk about *cotton, silk,* or *textiles.* In other words, as you describe the shock to result in the graph you have drawn, you are being specific to the good in question when you mention any input, and never just say land, labor or capital, or even simply machine or worker, as those terms alone are not specific to the product you are diagramming.

Use a curved PPC. In other words name at least one *input*—one thing you would need to produce this good—and say what is happening to it to cause the shock you are assigned (below).

Questions (Shocks):

1. Movement from inside to on the curve
2. Movement from on to inside the curve
3. Growth in the economy
4. Negative Growth in the economy
5. Potential output for one of the goods triples

Data:

Countries and Their Maximum Output of Two Goods
(All data are before the shock has occurred.)

1. Argentina
(Weekly)
32,000 barrels of wine
4,800 lawnmowers

2. Germany
(Yearly)
2.4 million hours of accounting services
140 helicopters

3. Norway
(Daily)
23,000 square yards of carpeting
1,900 hours of business consulting services

4. Cape Verde
(Monthly)
350,000 wigs
400 clay sculptures

5. Canada
(Hourly)
2,050 gallons of maple syrup
980 hockey sticks

The Budget Constraint and the Production Possibilities Frontier

When you study economics, you may feel buried under an avalanche of diagrams: diagrams in the text, diagrams in the lectures, diagrams in the problems, diagrams on exams. Your goal should be to recognize the common underlying logic and pattern of the diagrams, not to memorize each of the individual diagrams.

This chapter uses only one basic diagram, although it is presented with different sets of labels. The consumption choice budget constraint, the labor-leisure budget constraint, and the intertemporal choice budget constraint for individuals, along with the production possibilities frontier for society as a whole, are all the same basic diagram. The exhibit shows an individual budget constraint and a production possibilities frontier for two goods, Good 1 and Good 2. The trade-off diagram always illustrates three basic themes: scarcity, trade-offs, and economic efficiency.

The first theme is scarcity. It is not feasible to have unlimited amounts of both goods. Budget constraints can shift, either as a result of movements of income or of prices. Production possibilities frontiers can shift, too, either as a national economy expands or as the trade-offs between the two goods shift. But even if the budget constraint or a PPF shifts, scarcity remains—just at a different level.

The second theme is trade-offs. As depicted in the budget constraint or the production possibilities frontier, it is necessary to give up some of one good to gain more of the other good. The details of this trade-off vary. In a budget constraint, the trade-off is determined by the relative prices of the goods: that is, the relative price of two goods in the consumption choice budget constraint; the relative price of labor and leisure (the wage) in the labor-leisure budget constraint; and the relative price of present and future consumption (the principal saved plus the interest rate or rate of return) in the intertemporal choice budget constraint. These trade-offs appear as a straight line. However, the trade-offs in many production possibilities frontiers are represented by a curved line because the law of diminishing returns holds that as resources are added to an area, the marginal gains tend to diminish. But regardless of the specific shape, trade-offs remain.

The third theme is economic efficiency or getting the most benefit from scarce resources. All choices on the production possibilities frontier show productive efficiency because in such cases, there is no way to increase the quantity of one good without decreasing the quantity of the other. Similarly, when an individual makes a choice along a budget constraint, there is no way to increase the quantity of one good without decreasing the quantity of the other. The choice on a production possibilities set that is socially preferred, or the choice on an individual's budget constraint that is personally preferred, will display allocative efficiency.

The basic budget constraint/production possibilities frontier diagram will recur throughout this book. Some examples include using these trade-off diagrams to analyze one source of the gains from international trade and to examine the trade-offs between environmental protection and economic output, between equality of incomes and economic output, and the macroeconomic trade-off between consumption and investment. Don't be confused by the different labels. The budget constraint/production possibilities frontier diagram is always just a tool for thinking carefully about scarcity, trade-offs, and efficiency in a particular situation.

The Trade-Off Diagram

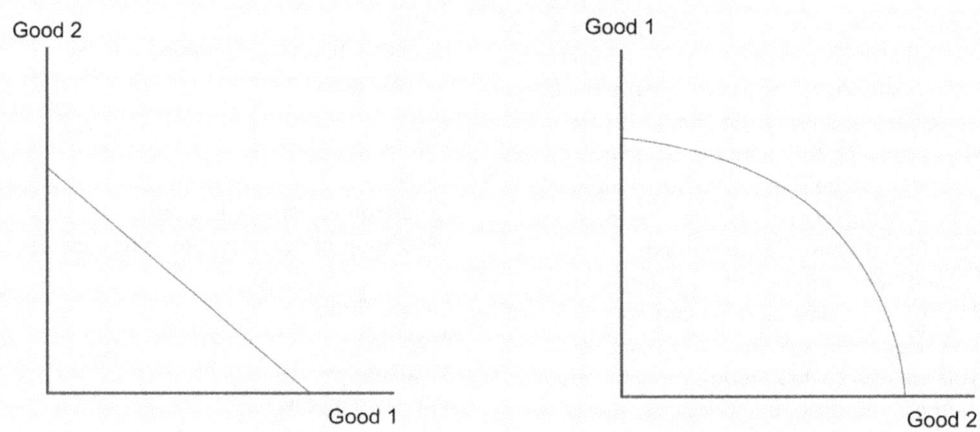

(a) An individual opportunity set.

(b) A social production possibilities frontier.

completely without resources at point A, can produce relatively large gains. For this reason, the shape of the PPF from A to B is relatively flat, representing a relatively small drop-off in health and a relatively large gain in education.

Now consider the other end, at the lower right, of the production possibilities frontier. Imagine that society starts at choice D, which is devoting nearly all resources to education and very few on health, and moves to point E, which is devoting all spending to education and none to health. For the sake of concreteness, you can imagine in the movement from D to E, the last few doctors must become high school science teachers, the last few nurses must become school librarians rather than dispensers of vaccinations, and the last few emergency rooms are turned into kindergartens. The gains to education from adding these last few resources to education are very small. However, the opportunity cost loss to health will be fairly large, and thus the slope of the PPF between D and E is steep, showing a small gain in education and a large drop in health.

The lesson here is not that society is likely to make an extreme choice like devoting no resources to education at point A or no resources to health at point E. Instead, the lesson is that the gains from committing additional marginal resources to education depend on how much is already being spent. If very few resources are currently committed to education, then an increase of a certain amount can bring relatively large gains; on the other side, if a large number of resources are already being committed to education, then an increase of a certain amount will bring relatively smaller gains. This pattern is common enough that it has been given a name: **the law of diminishing returns**, which holds that as additional increments of resources are added to a certain purpose, the marginal benefit from those additional increments will decline. This pattern is common. When government spends a certain amount more on reducing crime, for example, the original gains in reducing crime could be relatively large. But additional increases typically cause relatively smaller reductions in crime, and paying for enough police and security to reduce crime to nothing at all would be tremendously expensive.

The curvature of the production possibilities frontier shows that as additional resources are added to education, moving from left to right along the horizontal axis, the original gains are fairly large, but gradually diminish. Similarly, as additional resources are added to health, moving from bottom to top on the vertical axis, the original gains are fairly large, but again gradually diminish. In this way, the law of diminishing returns produces the outward-bending shape of the production possibilities frontier.

efficiency:
When it is impossible to get more of something without experiencing a trade-off of less of something else.

productive efficiency:
When it is impossible to produce more of one good without decreasing the quantity produced of another good.

PRODUCTIVE EFFICIENCY AND ALLOCATIVE EFFICIENCY

The study of economics does not presume to tell a society what choice it should make along its production possibilities frontier. In a market-oriented economy with a democratic government, the choice will involve a mixture of decisions by individuals, firms, and government. However, economics can point out that some choices are unambiguously better

Exhibit 2-9 Productive and Allocative Efficiency

Productive efficiency means it is impossible to produce more of one good without decreasing the quantity that is produced of another good. Thus, all choices along a given PPF like B, C, and D display productive efficiency, but R does not. Allocative efficiency means that the particular mix of goods being produced—that is, the specific choice along the production possibilities frontier—represents the allocation that society most desires.

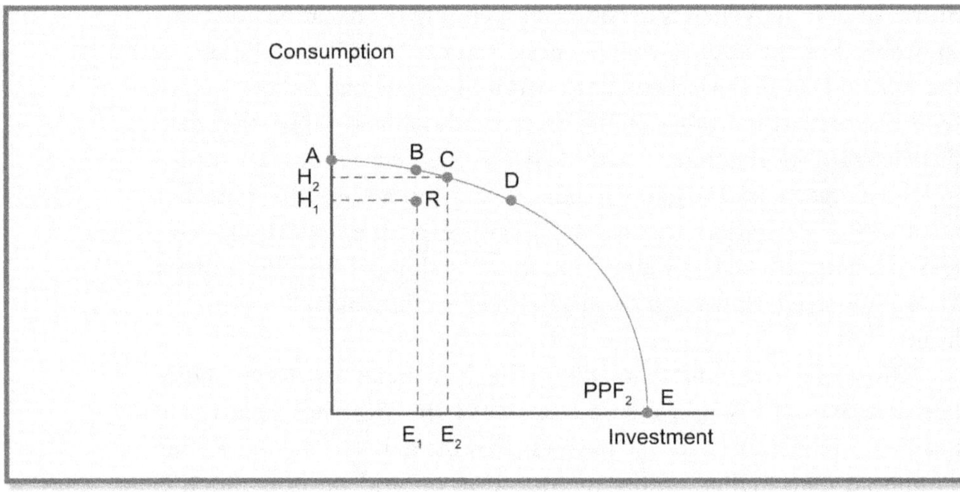

allocative efficiency: When the mix of goods being produced represents the allocation that society most desires.

than others. In everyday usage, the concept of efficiency refers to lack of waste. An inefficient machine operates at high cost, while an efficient machine produces without wasting energy or materials. An inefficient organization operates with long delays and high costs, while an efficient organization meets schedules, is focused, and performs within budget.

To an economist, **efficiency** refers to the situation in which it is impossible to get more of one thing without experiencing a trade-off of less of something else. The production possibilities frontier can illustrate two kinds of efficiency: *productive efficiency* and *allocative efficiency.* Exhibit 2-9 illustrates these ideas using a production possibilities frontier between consumption and investment.

Productive efficiency means that, given the available inputs and technology, it is impossible to produce more of one good without decreasing the quantity that is produced of another good. Thus, all choices on the PPF in Exhibit 2-9, including A, B, C, D, and E, display productive efficiency. As a firm moves from any one of these choices to any other, either consumption increases and investment declines or vice versa. However, any choice inside the production possibilities frontier is productively inefficient and wasteful because it is possible to produce more of one good, the other good, or some combination of both goods. For example, point R is productively inefficient because it is possible at choice C to have more of both goods: investment on the horizontal axis is higher at point C than point R (E_2 is greater than E_1) and consumption on the vertical axis is also higher at point C than point R (H_2 is greater than H_1).

Allocative efficiency means that the particular mix of goods being produced—that is, the specific choice along the production possibilities frontier—represents the allocation that society most desires. How to determine what a society desires can be a controversial question, and it will be addressed in political science, sociology and philosophy classes as well as in economics. Only one of the productively efficient choices will be the allocatively efficient choice for society as a whole.

WHY SOCIETY MUST CHOOSE

Every economy faces two situations in which it may be able to expand consumption of all goods. In the first case, a society may discover that it has been using its resources inefficiently, in which case by improving efficiency and moving to the production possibilities frontier it can have more of some or all goods. In the second case, as an economy grows over a period of years, the production possibilities frontier for a society will tend to shift outward and society will be able to afford more of all goods. But improvements in productive efficiency take time to discover and implement, and economic growth happens only gradually. Thus, a society must face scarcity and choose between tradeoffs in the present. For government, this process often involves trying to identify where additional spending could do the most good and where reductions in spending would do the least harm. At the individual and firm level, the market economy coordinates a process in which firms seek to produce goods and services in the quantity, quality, and price that people want. But for both the government and the market economy in the short term, increases in production of one good typically mean offsetting decreases somewhere else in the economy.

Confronting Objections to the Economic Approach

It's one thing to understand the economic approach to decision-making and another thing to feel comfortable applying it. The sources of discomfort typically fall into two categories: that people don't act in the way that fits the economics model, and that even if people did act that way, they should try not to. Let's consider these arguments in turn.

A FIRST OBJECTION: PEOPLE, FIRMS, AND SOCIETY DON'T ACT LIKE THIS

The economic approach to decision-making seems to require more information than most individuals possess and more careful decision-making than most individuals actually display. After all, do you or any of your friends draw a budget constraint and mutter to yourself about maximizing utility before you head to the shopping mall? Do members of the U.S. Congress contemplate production possibilities frontiers before they vote on the annual budget? The messy ways in which people and societies operate somehow doesn't look much like neat budget constraints or smoothly curving production possibilities frontiers.

However, the economics approach can be a useful way to analyze and understand the trade-offs of economic decisions even if it doesn't describe how those decisions are actually made. To appreciate this point, imagine for a moment that you are playing basketball, dribbling to the right, and throwing a bounce-pass to the left to a teammate who is running toward the basket. A physicist or engineer could work out the correct speed and trajectory for the pass, given the different movements involved and the weight and bounciness of the ball. But when you're playing basketball, you don't perform any of these calculations. You just pass the ball, and if you're a good player, you will do so with high accuracy. Someone might argue: "The scientist's formula of the bounce-pass requires a far greater knowledge of physics and far more specific information about speeds of movement and weights than the basketball player actually has, so it must be an unrealistic description of how basketball passes are actually made." This reaction would be wrongheaded. The fact that a good player can throw the ball accurately because of practice and skill, without making a physics calculation, doesn't mean that the physics calculation is wrong.

Similarly, from an economic point of view, someone who goes shopping for groceries every week has a great deal of practice with how to purchase the combination of goods that will provide that person with utility, even if the shopper doesn't phrase decisions in terms of a budget constraint. Government institutions may work imperfectly and slowly, but in general, a democratic form of government feels pressure from voters and social institutions to make the choices that are most widely preferred by people in that society. Thus, when thinking about the economic actions of groups of people, firms, and society, it is reasonable as a first approximation to analyze them with the tools of economic analysis.

A SECOND OBJECTION: PEOPLE, FIRMS, AND SOCIETY SHOULDN'T DO THIS

The economics approach portrays people as self-interested. For some critics of this approach, even if self-interest is an accurate description of how people behave, these behaviors are not moral. Instead, the critics argue that people should be taught to care more deeply about others. Economists offer several answers to this concerns.

First, economics is not a form of moral instruction. Rather, it seeks to describe economic behavior as it actually exists. Philosophers draw a distinction between **positive statements**, which describe the world as it is, and **normative statements**, which describe how the world should be. In the study of economics, positive and normative arguments often blend into each other: for example, if an economist analyzes a proposal for building a subway system in a certain city and finds that the benefits are higher than the costs, then is this study a positive analysis that merely states what *will* happen or a normative analysis which describes what *should* happen? But even if the line between positive and normative statements isn't always crystal clear, economic analysis does try to remain rooted in the study of the actual people who inhabit the actual economy. Yes, if the world were populated by saints, the economy would look different. But it isn't.

Second, self-interested behavior and profit-seeking can be labeled with other names, such as personal choice and freedom. The ability to make personal choices about buying, working, and saving is an important personal freedom. Some people may choose high-pressure, high-paying jobs so that they can earn and spend a lot of money. Others may earn a lot of money and give it to charity or spend it on their friends and family. Others may devote themselves to a career that can require a great deal of time, energy and expertise but does not offer high financial rewards, like being an elementary school teacher or a social worker. Still others may choose a job that does not take lots of their time or provide a high level of income, but still leaves time for family, friends, and contemplation. Some people may prefer to work for a large company; others might want to start their own business. People's freedom to make their own economic choices has a moral value worth respecting.

Third, self-interested behavior can lead to positive social results. For example, when people work hard to make a living, they create economic output. Consumers who are looking for the best deals will encourage businesses to offer goods and services that meet their needs. Adam Smith, writing in the *Wealth of Nations*, christened this property the "invisible hand." In describing how consumers and producers interact in a market economy, Smith wrote:

> Every individual ... generally neither intends to promote the public interest, nor knows how much he is promoting it. He intends only his own security, only his own gain. And he is in this led by an invisible hand to promote an end which was no part of his intention. By pursuing his own interest he frequently promotes that of society more effectually than when he really intends to promote it.

The metaphor of the invisible hand suggests the remarkable possibility that broader social good can emerge from selfish individual actions.

Fourth, even people who focus on their own self-interest in the economic part of their life often set aside their own narrow self-interest in other parts of life. For example, you might focus on your own self-interest when asking your employer for a raise or negotiating to buy a car. But then you might turn around and focus on other people when you volunteer to read stories at the local library, help a friend move to a new apartment, or donate money to a charity. Thus, self-interest is a reasonable starting point for analyzing many economic decisions, without needing to imply that people never do anything that is not in their own immediate self-interest.

Facing Scarcity and Making Trade-offs

The study of economics is rooted in a fundamental insight about the human condition. The world we live in is a place of scarcity, whether measured in terms of time, money, natural resources, or material goods. As a result, people must face trade-offs and make choices. The main economic trade-offs for individuals are their decisions about what to consume, how much to work, and how much to save. For society as a whole and for government decision-makers, the task is to use scarce resources as efficiently as possible to meet people's needs. Economics delves into the questions of how individuals, firms and government will interact, and thus into the decisions that society will make about what to produce, how to produce, and for whom to produce.

Key Concepts and Summary

1. The real world is one of scarcity: that is, a world in which people's desires exceed what is possible. As a result, economic behavior involves trade-offs in which individuals, firms, government and society must give up one thing that they desire to obtain things that they desire more.
2. Individuals face three main categories of trade-offs: the consumption choice of what quantities of goods to consume, the labor-leisure choice of what quantity of hours to work, and the intertemporal choices that involve costs in the present and benefits in the future, or benefits in the present and costs in the future.
3. The **budget constraint**, sometimes called the **opportunity set**, illustrates the range of choices available. The slope of the budget constraint is determined by the relative price of the choices. Choices beyond the budget constraint are impossible. Choices inside the budget constraint are wasteful.
4. People will choose along their budget constraints in a way that maximizes their satisfaction or **utility**, which is based on their own distinctive personal preferences.
5. An interest rate has three components: the **risk premium** to cover the risk of not being repaid, the rate of expected **inflation**, and the **time value of money.** The formula for how **compound interest** accumulates over time is:

   $(\text{Amount at present}) * (1 + \text{Interest rate})^{\text{number of years}} = \text{Amount at future time}$

6. **Opportunity cost** measures cost by what is given up in exchange. Sometimes opportunity cost can be measured in money, but it is often useful to consider whether time should be included as well, or to measure it in terms of the actual resources that must be given up.
7. Most economic decisions and trade-offs are not all-or-nothing. Instead, they involve **marginal analysis**, which means they are about decisions on the margin, involving a little more or a little less.
8. The **law of diminishing marginal utility** points out that as a person receives more of something—whether it is a specific good or another resource—the additional marginal gains tend to become smaller.
9. Because **sunk costs** occurred in the past and cannot be recovered, they should be disregarded in making current decisions.
10. A **production possibilities frontier** defines a set of choices faced by society as a whole. The shape of the PPF is typically curved outward, rather than straight. Choices outside the PPF are unattainable and choices inside the PPF are wasteful. Over time, a growing economy will tend to shift the PPF outwards.

11. The **law of diminishing returns** holds that as increments of additional resources are devoted to producing something, the marginal increase in output will become smaller and smaller.
12. All choices along a production possibilities frontier display **productive efficiency**; that is, it is impossible to use society's resources to produce more of one good without decreasing production of the other good. The specific choice along a production possibilities frontier that reflects the mix of goods that society prefers is the choice with **allocative efficiency**.

Vocabulary Terms

Absolute advantage
Allocative efficiency
Comparative advantage
Future value
Opportunity Costs
Present value
Productive efficiency
Specialization

Review Questions

1. Explain why scarcity leads to trade-offs.
2. Name the three main categories of economic tradeoffs that individuals face.
3. What determines the slope of the consumption choice budget constraint? The labor-leisure budget constraint? The intertemporal budget constraint?
4. Explain why individuals make choices that are directly on the budget constraint, rather than inside the budget constraint or outside it.
5. Does the economic approach specify what choices people should make? Why or why not?
6. What does it mean to "maximize utility"?
7. What are the three components of the interest rate?
8. What is the formula for how compound interest accumulates over time?
9. What is opportunity cost?
10. What is the law of diminishing marginal utility?
11. What are sunk costs?
12. What does a production possibilities frontier illustrate?
13. Why is a production possibilities frontier typically drawn as a curve, rather than a straight line?
14. Explain why societies cannot make a choice above their production possibilities frontier and should not make a choice below it.
15. What are diminishing marginal returns?
16. What is productive efficiency? Allocative efficiency?
17. Is the economic model of decision-making intended as a literal description of how individuals, firms, and the government actually make decisions?

IN-CLASS PROJECT

Steps for International Trade Using the PPC Graph

By David Moglen

Directions:

When an example has one country, the PPC is modeled as curved—which is more accurate? When two countries are trading, it is a useful simplification that improves the model to draw all lines straight.

1. Use the data to draw two straight-line PPCs in one, fully-labeled, X-Y space.

(Daily)	Trinidad = T	Sicily = S
Milk (in gallons) = M	5,000	100,000
Cell Phones = C	30,000	40,000

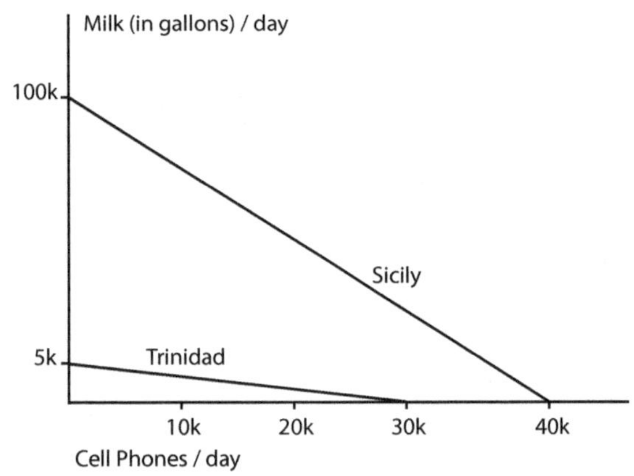

2. Set up tradeoff ratios. Change the numbers below Trinidad into a fraction.

	Trinidad	Now, do the same for Sicily:	Sicily
M (Milk)	5,000		100,000
C (Cell Phones)	30,000		40,000

Now, do the same for Sicily. Now, reduce the numerator to 1.

	Trinidad	Now, do the same for Sicily:	Sicily
M (Milk)	1		1
C (Cell Phones)	6		.4

3. Draw a "Combined PPC without Trade" line. This is just a straight line between the points where both countries have hypothetically put all their resources into producing one good. Go back to the original data. If

both Trinidad and Sicily produce milk, up to 5,000 gallons can come from Trinidad and up to 100,000 Sicily. So, combined they can make up to 105,000. Mark the quantity of 105,000 on the Milk axis. Similarly for cell phones, 30,000 (from Trinidad) + 40,000 (from Sicily) = 70,000. Mark this quantity on the Cell Phones axis. Now draw a straight line between 70,000 phones and 105,000 gallons, and label it "Combined PPC without Trade."

4. Determine Specialization and draw a "Combined PPC with Trade" line. The tradeoff ratio fractions ask the question, how much does it cost to produce milk (the good in the numerator, the top of the fraction) in each country. In Trinidad the opportunity cost of a gallon of milk is 6 cell phones. In Sicily the cost to make the gallon of milk is 0.4 cell phones. Sicily has lower opportunity cost in the production of milk (their denominator is lower; 0.4 is less than 6) so they have comparative advantage in milk and should specialize in dairy. Trinidad should specialize in cell phones. Draw the point that would indicate both nations have gone 100% into their specialty. Trinidad produces 30,000 cell phones and Sicily produces 100,000 gallons of milk. That (30,000, 100,000) point is labeled "C." Draw lines to connect point C to the same axes intercepts (70,000 phones and 105,000 gallons) you found in Step 3. Label this line "Combined PPC with Trade."

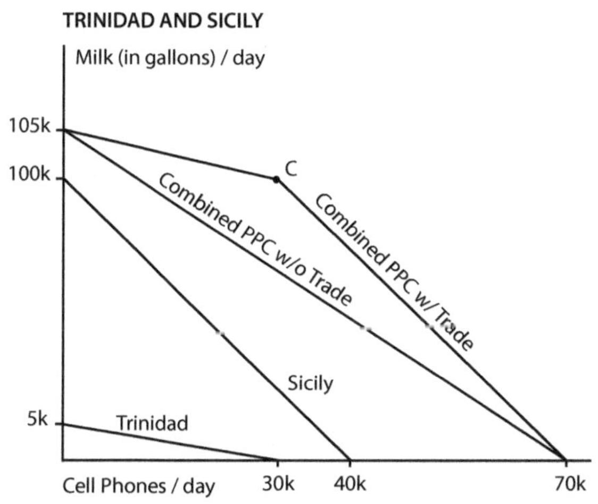

5. Write Terms of Trade Statements. Without more information (which is usually never given) we can't say exactly how many of Trinidad's cell phones will trade for a gallon of Sicilian milk, but we can state it as a range. Take the two denominators from the above fraction you had in Step 2 once you had already equalized the numerators to 1.

Terms of Trade Statement 1

One gallon of milk will trade for between _________ and _________ cell phones.
Insert the two denominators in the blanks. It is customary to put the smaller number first.

Terms of Trade Statement 1

One gallon of milk will trade for between 0.4 and 6 cell phones.

To do the same thing for one cell phone, you should go back to the original data. Flip the tradeoff ratios so that you are now looking at not Milk/Cell phones (M/C) but C/M for both countries. Now, do the same for Sicily, as in:

	Trinidad	Now, do the same for Sicily:	Sicily
C (Cell Phones)	30,000		40,000
M (Milk)	5,000		100,000

The fractions reduce to:

	Trinidad	Now, do the same for Sicily:	Sicily
C (Cell Phones)	1		1
M (Milk)	.167		2.5

Sicily = S (daily):	
Cell phones (C)	1
Milk (M)	2.5

And the Terms of Trade Statement is:

Terms of Trade Statement 2

One cell phone will trade for between 0.167 and 2.5 gallons of milk.

IN-CLASS PROJECT

Terms of Trade

By David Moglen

Directions

You will be assigned in class one of the *pairs* of nations (from 1–5) in the data section. In other words, since this is the trade example, now you are using the data from both countries in a given question.

The Answer has two parts: draw four PPC "curves" (made up of all straight lines) on one graph. For example, the PPC for France, PPC for China, PPC for combined w/o trade, PPC for combined w/ trade. Clearly label all four lines and the axes, The heading above the graph should say France + China.

The second part is to give terms of trade statements for the two different goods. This means you will have two separate sentences, using the exact wording of correct terms of trade statements—one statement for each good. Round partial numbers to two digits after the decimal. This completes your answer.

Assume straight-line PPCs.

Data

Countries and Their Maximum Output of Two Goods

1. **Argentina (weekly)**
   32,000 barrels of wine
   4,800 lawnmowers

   Brazil (weekly)
   46,600 barrels of wine
   2,700 lawnmowers

2. **Germany (yearly)**
   2.4 million hours of accounting services
   140 helicopters

   Italy (yearly)
   1.3 m hrs of accounting services
   120 helicopters

3. **Norway (daily)**
   23,000 sq. yards of carpeting
   1,900 hours of business consulting services

   Finland (daily)
   17,000 sq. yards of carpeting
   600 hours of business consulting services

4. **Cape Verde (monthly)**
   350,000 wigs
   400 clay sculptures

   Portugal (monthly)
   840,000 wigs
   720 clay sculptures

5. **Canada (hourly)**
   2,050 gallons of maple syrup
   980 hockey sticks

   Iceland (hourly)
   230 gallons of maple syrup
   440 hockey sticks

CHAPTER 3
Business Organization

3 Business Organization

By David Moglen

ORGANIZATION OF THE ECONOMY

The U.S. economy, like other nations, has three domestic sources of spending, and a fourth in its international trading partners. Together, the spending of these four economic actors adds up to GDP. The organization of these economic actors is the result of an evolving set of decisions by policymakers in government and the public at large.

Figure 1

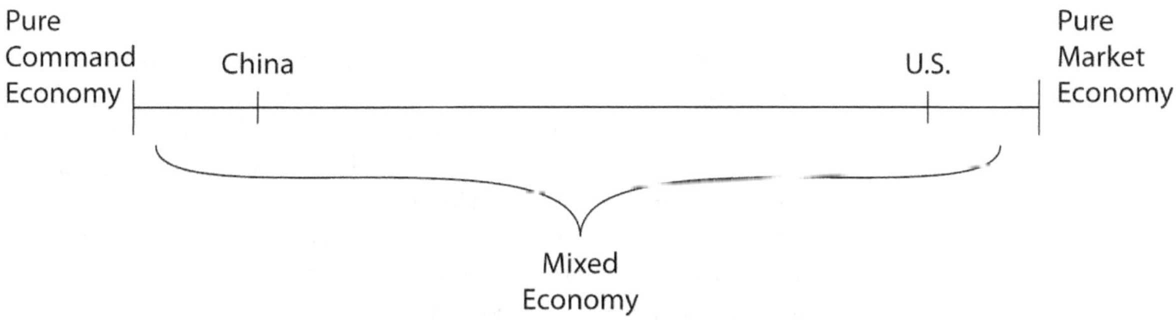

As you can see from the spectrum shown in Figure 1, the different possible types of economies range between two extremes – those of *pure market economies* and *pure command economies*. The latter are also known as *centrally planned economies*. The U.S. puts enough economic activity in the private sphere that it is routinely referred to as a market economy. However, strictly speaking, all modern national economies are *mixed economies* because they all contain at least some elements of *private sector* (consumers and business firms) ownership and control as well as some *public sector* (government) ownership and control. Additionally, historical economies and some regions in today's economies could be described as *traditional economies*, in that occupations, decisions about where to live, decisions about what to buy, and the bounds of social mobility are determined by heredity. In other words, if society says the son of a shoemaker will also be a shoemaker, and the daughter of a clothing designer will also be a clothing designer, that is called a *traditional economy*.

While the degree of public sector relative to private sector control determines where on the above spectrum we should place any specific country, the below relationship (shown in the *Simple Circular Flow Diagram*) applies to all types of economies.

Figure 2: Simple Circular Flow Diagram:

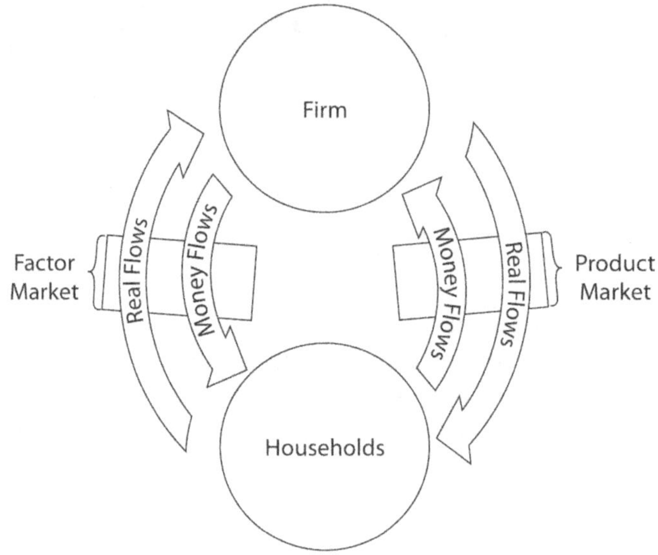

As you can see above in Figure 2, the firms buy inputs in the economy in the *factor market*. Households (as well as businesses, and government) buy output (produced by firms) in the *product market*. In other words, firms are the supply and households are the demand in the retail (product) market. Households are the supply and firms are the demand in the resource (factor) market. For example, you as an individual member of your household sell your labor to the company so you are a supplier in the labor market.

While this circular flow is universal, it is not the only universal aspect that applies to all economies worldwide. Another attribute common to all national economies is that they must answer the three *key economic questions*:

- What is produced
- How is it produced
- Who consumes it

Notice that even the extremes in the above spectrum, the pure market or the pure command economy, were they to exist in reality (recall it is better to call all real economies "mixed") would have to answer the above key economic questions in some way. So to would any (realistic) economies between those two poles. Other economic questions may go unanswered by some nations, such as how to maximize equity or how to maximize competition.

Another universal aspect common to all economies is that the private sector and public sector can both engage in *market activities* and *nonmarket activities*. Some examples are given in the chart below. The distinction is that market activities are exchanges in which both sides give something and both sides get something, such as in a purchase. In most cases, one side is giving up some money and the other side gives a good, service, or resource for that money. Nonmarket implies that one side gives and the other side does not provide anything in return, such as a subsidy, volunteering, or charity.

Sector	Market Activities	Nonmarket Activities
Private Sector	People buy goods Firms make and sell goods Firms pay workers	People give to charity People volunteer Firms establish charities
Public Sector	Federal government pays for roads and military County government sells permits and certificates	Federal government provides corporate and farm subsidies, welfare, food stamps, and foreign development assistance

As you can see from the chart above, while it may be tempting to draw a firewall between market and nonmarket activities, and to say that private sector is solely in the market and the public sector is strictly in the nonmarket activities, the reality is quite different. The guiding slogan for this structure should be "both can do both." Both the public and private sectors engage in both types of activities, the monetized market exchanges as well as nonmarket giving.

As we saw in Chapter Two, ("Opportunity Costs") consumers seek to nearly always maximize utility and their opportunity cost is the lost utility from the foregone (next best) purchase. Business firms seek to nearly always maximize profit and their opportunity cost is the lost profit from the foregone (next best) business venture. Opportunity cost and a goal as to what should be maximized are both undefined and ambiguous for government. Before we get to the main focus of Chapter Three, the attributes of three main business types, let's briefly cover the functions of government as understood by modern economists.

GOVERNMENT

The actions of the government can be broadly divided into two categories: *Actor* or *Referee*. The actor role for government is when it buys or sells anything. Any appropriation, or change in the budget (even a decrease in spending) is an example of the actor role. When the school district pays a fifth-grade teacher, or the state government builds a new university, the government is being an actor in the economy. The referee role means new laws or regulations are being passed or rolled back/ repealed. The speed limit increasing from 55 to 65 miles per hour is an example of the referee role. So to is the decision made by European governments to ban pharmaceutical advertising on TV.

The following six roles of government are all up for debate, and often form the basis for the national debate raging in media, society and voting booths every election year. While some would like to see an expansion of government power in some or all of the following functions, others would like to see the function curtailed (reduced) or eliminated altogether, in favor of a privatized solution. That said, there is the most agreement about the first governmental function. Providing certain economic institutions is a role of government that is virtually universally accepted.

Roles of Government:

1. Promote Economic Institutions

Institutions are also referred to as social fabric, fabric of society, or social capital.

- Freedom of Contract
- Private Property

Enforcement of property laws also applies to intellectual property such as patented goods.

- A legal system that protects contracts, property rights, and other safeguards for business activity
- The corporate form or alternative mechanism to spread out risk and encourage risk-taking like starting a big business with a significant required investment
- Policies that promote the health and education (e.g. social capital) of the public

2. Promote Optimal Competition

Agencies like the Department of Justice, headed by the Attorney General, and the Federal Trade Commission (FTC) have the power to sanction monopolies and take them to court, where remedies up to and including the breaking up of the company can occur. These court cases against monopolies and cartels are part of Antitrust Law, and they are a major focus later in Chapter 15. Also theories like Joseph Schumpeter's "Creative Destruction" hold that a more laissez-faire approach is often better since monopoly power is an incentive to others to provide consumers the same utility in a way that circumvents (and partly or wholly) destroys the incumbent/ established monopoly's hold on the market. This logic says the government usually can let the market work out competition issues.

3. Correct for Externalities

Remember back to the assumptions of market theory. "Atomistic market participants" (e.g. many small producers) were assumed to be competing – not a monopoly. If there is a market failure in that bad effects from monopolies occur, as you see above, there are ways to correct for that. Similarly, inaccurate prices were an assumption of market theory – i.e. when there are negative externalities – third parties (not the buyer or seller) are negatively impacted. Air and water Pollution are major examples, but others are harmful products like alcohol, cigarettes and weapons. The government has agencies empowered to compel firms to internalize these social costs into the offending producer's costs - then there is no more externality.

4. Promote Economic Growth and Stability

Many (but not all) economists hold that the government has a responsibility to enact policies to counter economic fluctuations. This is called countercyclical fiscal policy. Also many of these same economists believe the government should promote growth. In the U.S., ideal growth and stability is approximately 5% unemployment, 2-3% annual GDP growth, and 2-3% inflation.

5. Identify and Provide Public Goods

What is an inherently *public good* and what is an inherently (i.e. by definition) *private good* is a serious, continual debate in every country. Many countries have their energy sector like oil and gas companies in the public sector. In the U.S., it is beyond imagination that Exxon and Chevron and other oil companies would be owned by the government (but if they were they would probably be merged – i.e. the provider of the public good is often a government-owned monopoly). All developed countries (also known as the industrialized, or rich countries) provide health care as a public good except the U.S.

Transportation infrastructure (roads, highways, bridges, shipping ports and airports) is considered a public good. American public goods also include K-12 public education, community colleges, disaster relief, food, drug, and consumer product safety standards, libraries, shipping ports, airports, military, homeland security, courts, jails, prisons, Social Security, Medicare, Medicaid, the University of California and California State University systems, the majority of grants for basic research including the National Institutes of Health and their twenty-seven institutes and centers (see http://www.nih.gov/icd/) to name a few.

6. Correct Market Failures

One situation that has been evidently long-viewed as a market failure would be a completely free market in labor. So to avoid what are perceived as negative results from a free market in labor, tight immigration restrictions are in place. In particular, high-skilled labor enters on a very limited basis through the H1-B visa. A free market would put more American technology sector workers out of work in the short-run. Whether it's worth it due to other gains in the long-run is up for debate, although most economists agree that efficiency results from the free market rather than from barriers and "protectionism" like visa quotas.

Yet another situation that has been viewed as a market failure would be a free market in human organs, for example when someone needs a kidney. Such a market is illegal. It is the same with adoptions (no market exists legally).

Business Firms

The three main business types should be understood in terms of their advantages and disadvantages. While these are the only three you need to study, if you were to start a business you should learn about the hybrids – several additional business types that exist. A great starting point to survey this topic is provided by the article (link is provided) in the section entitled "Beyond the Three Basic Business Types: LLPs, LLCs, and S Corporations" which appears later in this chapter.

Sole proprietorships are the most simple business type to set up. One individual or a married couple ("mom and pop") sets this up to run their small business. There is no separation between business and personal income for tax purposes, nor is there separation of business and personal assets for liability purposes. This is called *unlimited liability*

Partnerships are set up by two or more partners. They also lack separation between business and personal income and assets.

Corporations, referring specifically to publicly traded corporations, do have a line between business assets and the personal assets of their owners (the stockholders), referred to *limited liability.* Taxes are assessed first on corporate profits and second on earnings when they are received by stockholders in the form of dividends and/or capital gains. This two-stage assessment of taxes is called *double taxation.*

Managers are separate from owners, which is called *absentee ownership.* This quality confers advantages (such as ability to hire the most specialized managers) as well as disadvantages to the corporation. For example, the principal-agent problem covers a variety of ways in which managers (executives) diverge from the goals of the owners (stockholders) who only want to maximize profits.

Figure 3: Breakdown of firms and sales by business type

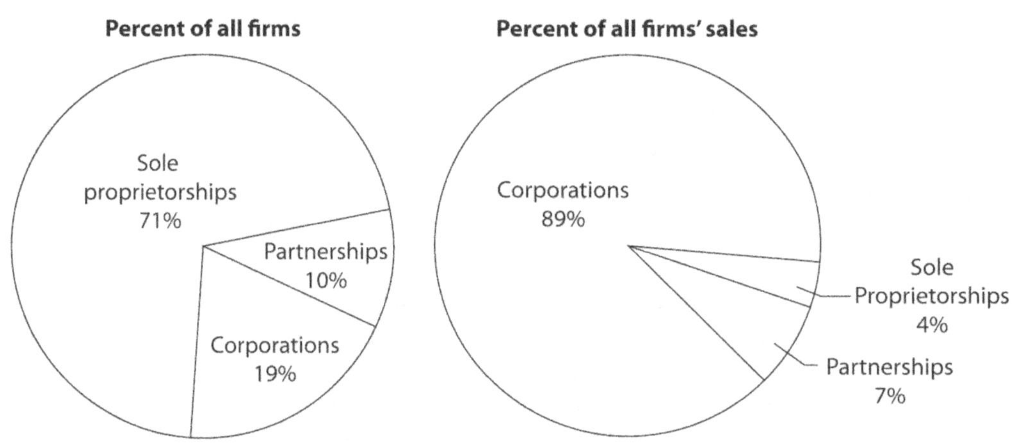

As you can see above in Figure 3 (from 2008, www.irs.ustreas.gov/taxstats) corporations only make up 19% of all registered business firms, but earn 89% of the sales revenue nationwide. While corporations are not in the majority if you add how many business firms of all types (mostly sole proprietorships) exist in the U.S., the majority of the profits made by all businesses are earned by corporations. This is because any larger firm is most likely to be a corporation. Furthermore, any publicly firm traded is most likely to be a corporation. The exception is a business organization called a Master Limited Partnership (MLP), which is a partnership that is allowed to sell stock shares to the public.

BUSINESS TYPE	ADVANTAGES	DISADVANTAGES
Sole Proprietorships (SP)	Inexpensive and simple to start	Limited life
	Best incentives for efficiency=best accountability	Unlimited liability
		Can't hire the most specialized managers (therefore lack potential ability to achieve maximum efficiency)
		Limited access to capital
Partnerships	Compared to SP, more specialized managers	Compared to corporations, less specialized managers
	Compared to SP, access to capital is better	Compared to corporations, less access to capital
	Accountability is better than in corporations	Limited life
		Unlimited liability
		Accountability is worse than in SP
Corporations	Limited liability	More expensive to start and more complicated paperwork
	Corporate personhood	Principal-Agent Problems
	Unlimited life	Double Taxation
	Best access to capital	More complicated and frequent financial reporting requirements

To clarify, access to capital refers to the amount of money and range of options to raise money available to the firm. In other words, it is financial capital – money the firm might need to spend on expansion, remodeling, or other non-recurring expenses. What are the firm's options to raise this money, beyond the fact they sell some product as part of their business?

The sole proprietor can only borrow from the bank, and the amount of their business loan is not very much. The partnership can do the same, although with greater borrowing power due to the partners' combined credit. But access to capital is most advantageous for the corporation; both the amount of funds they can access and the varieties available to them exceed that of the other two business types.

Besides the basic bank loan or credit line (short-term bank loan) that sole proprietors and partnerships can access (corporations can do that too), the corporate form enables a different type of *debt financing*. The corporation can issue *bonds*, which are loans from individual savers like yourself to the firm. For example, you could lend $1,000 today, with interest, to almost any firm you could name, from Coca Cola to Ford Motor Corporation, simply by buying one of their corporate bonds. Your stockbroker or online stock trading account would be the means to do this.

Even more significant than the varieties of debt financing which are available to it, the corporation can raise money by issuing *stock* shares, which is called *equity financing*. Each share is a very small percentage ownership of the actual firm. The first time a firm offers shares for sale to investors (i.e. the firm "goes public") it is called an IPO – initial public offering. They also can release more shares for sale later – even years later – in secondary offerings.

The *Principal-Agent Problem* is a huge area of study in economics and occurs anytime there is an agent (manager) in some control other than the real owner. For the firm the primary manager is the CEO (Chief Executive Officer). Others in the Agent category are the other executives, the board of directors, upper management/ supervisors, and even, to a much lesser extent, regular employees. The Principal is the owner – in this case, the stockholders. These shareholders have one primary goal: profit maximization. But the executives may want something else. Examples of the principal-agent problem, executives acting in their own interest more than the stockholders' interests, can be filed into one of four categories: "low and insufficient effort, inefficient or extravagant investments, entrenchment strategies or self dealing actions."[1]

Corporate Personhood

It sounds like a strange concept if you have never heard of this. What are the key court decisions that enable corporations to back political causes, officeholders, and ballot measures or initiatives?

1 http://www.cer.ethz.ch/research/wp_07_63.pdf

YEAR	CASE NAME	BASIC MEANING
1886	Santa Clara County v. Southern Pacific Railroad	Corporations are legally people for most purposes
1976	Buckley v. Valeo	Money is a form of speech, and therefore entitled to First Amendment protections
2010	Citizens United v. FEC (Federal Elections Commission)	Strikes down laws limiting direct corporate contributions to Federal campaigns and requiring disclosure and transparency in political corporate spending. How complete this deregulation of campaign finance law will go remains to be seen as future cases work their way through the courts.

Summary

All economies on the spectrum from pure market to pure command must answer key economic questions such as what to produce and how to make it. In the predominantly market-based economies, these key questions are mainly answered by the price system. All modern economies can be described using a circular-flow diagram. Government has a variety of roles, although the extent of its engagement in each fuels political debates and power struggles, and the assertiveness of the state varies widely in different countries. Firms, or businesses, fall into three categories. Each can be described and compared to the others through their unique advantages and disadvantages.

Competition and cooperation between firms, the balance of power between the private and public sectors, and the role of corporate money in politics: these are the open questions over which policy wars are waged and corporate strategies are formed. These tensions and conflicts determine if you will get a good price or not for your car, your house, your education, whether there will be plenty of good jobs in the future, and the quality and availability of services from child care to medical care, from mail delivery to internet broadband (e.g. for watching videos on the web). The key actor besides business and government is the consumer: you. Collectively, you as consumers determine the fate of firms, the priorities of your policymakers, and the health of the economy.

Key Terms

Actor
Bonds
Centrally planned economy
Circular flow model
Corporate personhood
Corporation
Debt financing
Double taxation
Economic Institutions
Equity financing
Externality
Factor market
Key economic questions
Limited liability/ unlimited liability
Limited life/ unlimited life
Market activity
Market failures
Mixed economy
Nonmarket activity
Partnership
Principal-agent problem
Private sector
Product market
Public good
Public sector
Pure command economy
Pure market economy
Referee
Sole proprietorship
Stocks
Traditional economy

Study Questions

1. If you are setting up a dog-walking business, which of the three main business types would you select and why?
2. Firms sometimes engage in stock buybacks where they use cash to buy their own stock. Explain when this would be a good idea and when it would be a bad idea. How does this plan compare with returning money to shareholders as a dividend?
3. What are the economic incentives and goals of the competing parties in a hostile takeover? Make sure to mention management,

shareholders, and the corporate takeover specialist (individual or private equity company) in this process.

4. Firms sometimes "spinoff" part of their company (see ITT, Motorola, Marathon, and AT&T). What are the circumstances where this is a good idea for original company? How can an investor tell if the parent or the spinoff company is the better investment in the stock market?
5. Which type of economy is more likely to seek the following goals (answer for each one separately):
   a. Maximum competition
   b. Maximum income equality
   c. Maximum adherence to dominant culture
   d. Maximum entrepreneurship
6. How does a corporation reduce risk for those who invest their money in its activities? Are there some specific companies or sectors who help corporations or others in the economy to reduce negative impacts of certain risks?
7. What are some specific examples of actions by executives that would fit into each of the four categories stated in the principal-agent problem section? Describe a policy (either corporate or governmental) solution to the principal-agent problem.

IN-CLASS PROJECT

Mervyn's and Private Equity

By David Moglen

As you gain familiarity with the three basic business types discussed in this chapter, it will aid your knowledge of the modern economy to certain very influential classes of firms, Private Equity (PE) companies. PE's are somewhat like another group of firms that may sound familiar, venture capital (VC) firms. While VC firms provide seed money and guidance to early stage startups (Google, Facebook, just about every internet company or Web 2.0 social networking company are examples of firms aided by VC's), Private Equity companies buyout established firms, some of which may have a reputation spanning decades as you see in this case study about the retailer, Mervyn's.

Directions

Read the article from Businessweek article below, because it has the most content and places this specific case in a broader, national context. Then, either a class discussion can be held to answer the questions below, or your teacher can assign you a group number (from 1–5) and then your group will write their answer to the same numbered question as your assigned group number.

Notice there is a lot of data on the right-hand side of this article's text. A lot of the sidebar content indicates the relevance of this issue to hundreds of other firms in the economy besides Mervyn's.

Here are some additional articles on this case study:

http://www.startribune.com/business/27838769.html?elr=KArks:DCiU1OiP:DiiUiacyKUnciaec8O7EyU

http://www.bloggingbuyouts.com/2008/09/08/mervyns-says-private-equity-owners-wrecked-company/

http://en.wikipedia.org/wiki/Mervyns

http://www.reuters.com/article/marketsNews/id USBNG19007920080904

As always, *a good answer includes* (1) "quotes" with in-text citations (author's last name, paragraph number or page number for multi-page articles, in parenthesis after each quote, and (2) your own *analysis*.

As in all sets of word questions, it is a good idea to read all questions before you start answering any of them, and before you read the article(s).

Questions

1. Why did Mervyn's go bankrupt? (Mervyn's perspective)
2. What did Private Equity (PE) companies get from owning Mervyn's? (PE's perspective)
3. How are PE companies and corporate buyout specialists different from most firms in the economy? In other words, how are their practices and goals different from other business owners like Mervyn's founder Mervin G. Morris?

Consider

"Of the 105 big U.S. companies that have filed for bankruptcy this year, 66 have been owned by buyout shops or been spun off by "them" (Business Week 1). So, over half of the major corporate bankruptcies in the US were firms that went through the same sort of Private Equity restructuring as Mervyn's. Hint: If you buy a company that is reasonably healthy (e.g. worth $1.2 BILLION as Mervyn's was in 2004), and when you are done with it a few years later it is essentially or totally bankrupt, then it's hard to say all these PE companies do is buy a firm at a low price and sell at a higher price; there must be more to it than that. It is hard to sell a bankrupt company at a high price.

4. Detail the ideal policies (propose new laws or regulations) that would have led to a better outcome, e.g., one in which Mervyn's could have avoided bankruptcy?
5. What do you think Cerberus would argue for why there shouldn't be any new law or policy reducing its ability to operate as they have been, or any new rules or penalties as a result of Mervyn's current lawsuit against Cerberus or from any other lawsuit against any PE firm?

HOW PRIVATE EQUITY STRANGLED MERVYNS

Cerberus, Sun Capital, and Lubert-Adler stripped the 59-year-old retailer of its assets and threw 30,000 people out of work

By Emily Thornton
BusinessWeek 10/20/10

On the morning of Oct. 23, Mervin G. Morris went to the Hayward (Calif.) headquarters of Mervyns department stores one last time. As the retail chain's founder walked into the rust-colored concrete building, scores of shell-shocked employees were shuffling out with boxes full of their personal effects. Dozens rushed up to tell Morris, 88, how much they had enjoyed working at Mervyns. One woman told him she had been there 42 years. "It was a horrible scene," he says. As Morris walked past a lunch room, some 70 workers rose to give him a standing ovation. He later walked out in tears.

The grief is understandable. Mervyns, the chain that Morris founded six decades ago with $25,000 and two employees, is about to disappear. Its 149 remaining stores are being liquidated. More than 18,000 people have been thrown out of work—without severance and, in many cases, weeks of vacation pay—amid the toughest job market in a generation.

It didn't have to be this way. Mervyns, a midrange seller of apparel, housewares, and other department-store fare, might have weathered the economic storm that's battering so many of its rivals. Much of the blame for its demise lies with three private equitytitans: Cerberus Capital Management, Sun Capital Partners, and Lubert-Adler.

When those firms bought Mervyns from Target (TGT) for $1.2 billion in 2004, they promised to revive the limping West Coast retailer. Then they stripped it of real estate assets, nearly doubled its rent, and saddled it with $800 million in debt while sucking out more than $400 million in cash for themselves, according to the company. The moves left Mervyns so weak it couldn't survive.

Mervyns' collapse reveals dangerous flaws in the private equity playbook. It shows how investors with risky business plans, unrealistic financial assumptions, and competing agendas can deliver a death blow to companies that otherwise could have survived. And it offers a glimpse into the human suffering wrought by owners looking to turn a quick profit above all else.

Buyout Shops Gone Wild

Private equity firms buy companies with the goal of improving them and then selling them for a profit. To pay for their deals, they often take on debt, hence the term leveraged buyout. In recent years the buyout shops went wild, taking advantage of unusually low interest rates and easy borrowing terms. At their peak in 2006 they acquired 667 companies worth $372 billion. But debt levels soared: From 2005 through the third quarter of 2008, private equity firms loaded a staggering $741 billion of debt onto their companies' balance sheets, according to Standard & Poor's/LCD Group, which, like BusinessWeek, is owned by The McGraw-Hill Companies (MHP).

When the credit crunch hit, lenders pulled back and dealmaking ground to a halt. Debt-heavy companies were left unable to refinance just as the economy was slowing. The optimism and confidence of the buyout boom gave way to fear—and massive layoffs.

What's happening at Mervyns is happening elsewhere at an alarming rate. While private equity firms control just a tiny fraction of U.S. corporations, their companies are disproportionately troubled. Of the 105 big U.S. companies that have filed for bankruptcy this year, 66 have been owned by buyout shops or been spun off by them, according to Capital IQ, another unit of McGraw-Hill. Investors, meanwhile, remain skeptical of many of the recent buyouts that haven't yet blown up but soon could. Loans made for those deals are now trading for as little as 33 cents on the dollar. Video on buying stakes in Private Equity.

Mervyns, to be sure, had been in decline for years. Founded by Morris in San Lorenzo, Calif., in 1949, the company grew over the next several decades into a midsize chain with more than 50 stores in three states. In 1978, Morris sold the company to Dayton Hudson (now Target) for $300 million. Retail analysts say Dayton neglected the brand as it focused on building the Target franchise (funded, in part, by Mervyns' earnings). Over time it opened fewer new Mervyns stores; existing ones took on a shabby look. By the time Target sold the chain in August 2004, the company, with 257 stores and some 30,000 employees, appeared ripe for improvement. "At first, there was total excitement," says Kathi Finley, a former information systems specialist and 34-year veteran laid off in October. "It was like, 'Yahoo! We're on our own!' "

But while the buyout firms wanted to fix up Mervyns, an obsession with real estate got in the way. Mervyns' new owners were eager to turn the company's real estate into gold. When the acquisition closed, they split the company into two main pieces—the retail operation and a much more valuable entity that held the real estate. Over time the owners would shut down 90 underperforming stores and close two of its four distribution centers in order to sell some of the land they owned. They also sold the decades-old property leases on many other stores to outside companies—and then turned around and rented the property back at current market rates. The owners kept the proceeds from the land and lease sales for themselves.

But the real estate strategy had a glitch: According to court documents, the rent payments to the new landlords were practically double what the old payments were, since many of the original leases had been negotiated back

THE BUYOUT BUST | As retail buyouts go bankrupt...

COMPANY	BUYERS	DATE PURCHASED*	BANKRUPTCY DATE
Linens Holding	Apollo Silver Point Capital Tri-Artisan Capital NRDC Equity	February 2006	May 2008
Mervyns	Cerberus Capital Sun Capital Lubert-Adler	August 2004	July 2008
Sharper Image	Sun Capital Windsong Brands	May 2007	February 2008
Goody's Family Clothing	Prentice Capital GMM Capital	October 2005	June 2008
Value City Department Stores	Emerald Capital Crystal Capital	January 2008	October 2008
Home Interiors and Gifts	HM Capital	April 1998	April 2008

Data: Capital IQ *Closing date

...The debt of other buyouts is trading at distressed levels	
COMPANY	LOAN PRICE (CENTS ON THE DOLLAR)
Tribune	33
Univision Communications	49
Michaels Stores	57
Hexion Specialty Chemicals	61
Realogy	63
Freescale Semiconductor	65
First Data	71

Data. Markit.com

in the 1980s. To prevent big losses, Mervyns' new owners had to cut other costs—drastically.

"We Can't Even Have Water?"

Slashing expenses, it seems, was always baked into the plan. Soon after Mervyns' new owners took control, they laid off scores of people at company headquarters. They canceled some charity efforts and training programs and outsourced some human resources and marketing services. Even though sales were solid, the owners told managers to clamp down on spending for supplies, and they downsized the annual Christmas party. At headquarters, they took away water coolers. For recently laid-off employee Cindy Fajardo, that was a signal of doom: "People thought, 'we can't even have water?' "

It appeared to some outsiders that the real estate plan, rather than a desire to revive the brand, was driving the restructuring. One executive approached by Cerberus to run Mervyns says he declined the job because the buyout firms seemed "more focused on closing the first 50 to 75 stores than anything else."

But former J.C. Penney (JCP) executive Vanessa Castagna, recruited to be Mervyns' first chief after the buyout and given an equity stake, believed the owners wanted to turn Mervyns around. She was comfortable with the real estate strategy. "The owners," she says, "wanted to maximize the value of the transaction and to monetize the real estate value."

Early on, there were some positive signs. Even amid the closures, Mervyns opened 11 stores in Hispanic neighborhoods to tap what it saw as an underserved market. It invested $200 million in a new information technology system—a necessity to separate the chain from Target's system—and held a barbecue in its headquarters' parking lot to celebrate the launch. Morris, who kept close ties at the company over the years, made an appearance at the event.

But Mervyns' operating income slipped right away, from $160 million in 2003 (the last full year of results at Target) to around $100 million in 2005 and the same in 2006. During those years, the private equity firms took a total of $137 million in "distributions" directly from company coffers, according to people familiar with the finances.

The higher lease costs and distribution fees came back to bite. As the California economy softened, Castagna found it more difficult to maneuver financially. She says she tried to persuade the owners to renegotiate lease payments but was told "those were the going market rates." In February 2007, when her two-year contract ended, Castagna left. Now she's a director at Levi Strauss.

Mervyns' owners replaced Castagna with Richard B. Leto, a former Kohl's (KSS) executive who had been brought in as Mervyns' president after the buyout. Leto says he promptly advised his bosses to sell the chain to another retailer. "Because of the age of the company, the age of our stores, and the condition of our physical plants [as well as] the intrusion in the West by Kohl's and Penney's," Leto says, "I felt the best thing to do, given the appropriate opportunity, was to sell the business."

But the owners were rarely on the same page, many insiders say. The messy structure of their deal created competing agendas from the start. Cerberus, the $27 billion private equity behemoth that owns Chrysler and many other corporations, had equal stakes in both the Mervyns chain and the separate real estate company. Lubert-Adler, a Philadelphia firm specializing in real estate, had a larger stake in the real estate entity. Sun Capital, a $10 billion owner of 90 companies, held a bigger stake in Mervyns' department store operation. "I could never figure out how they planned on running the company when there was this natural fight built into the structure," says a former Mervyns executive. "And the answer is, it didn't work very well."

In late 2007, having soured on the prospect of further profits, Cerberus sold its stake to Sun, which assumed majority control. Sun in turn promised to buy out Lubert-Adler, too, for an additional $20 million.

Mervyns' 2006 profit turned into a $64 million loss for 2007 as sales fell by 7.4%. Leto says Sun executives fired him shortly before Christmas. He was replaced on an interim basis by Vice-President Chuck Kurth. Then, in March 2008, Sun brought in the fourth CEO in 12 months: John Goodman, a highly regarded former president of the Dockers brand at Levi Strauss.

Just weeks into the job, Goodman found himself in crisis. Mervyns relied heavily on CIT Group (CIT), the big corporate lender, to guarantee transactions with vendors. By March, CIT grew so worried about Mervyns' creditworthiness that it started cutting back on new deals. That sparked fears among other creditors and vendors that Mervyns couldn't pay its bills. Suppliers began refusing to ship merchandise unless Mervyns agreed to tougher payment terms. Stores posted signs announcing they didn't have advertised merchandise. Out of desperation, Goodman started circulating Mervyns' balance sheet to vendors and some of his own managers to show that the retailer had ample financing. "That scared me even more," says former Mervyns manager Yasmin Zialcita.

Sun, meanwhile, reneged on its promise to buy the Lubert-Adler stake, a sign that it, too, might not have been interested in sticking with Mervyns for the long term. It didn't offer to make further investments to stabilize the company, either—a disappointment to some creditors. One of them charges that "the Sun people acted like the classic short-term-oriented Wall Street guys: 'I want to get my money and run.'"

Pep Talk

With losses mounting, Sun and Lubert-Adler decided to take Mervyns into bankruptcy. On July 29, 59 years to the day after the company was founded, Goodman addressed the troops at headquarters. Although the owners were closing 26 more stores, Goodman said, Mervyns could pull through as a leaner retailer or as part of another company. "He told us to hang in there. Be strong. We're going to make it," recalls former employee-relations representative Michelle Diaz.

Creditors soon approached Goodman with an odd idea: On behalf of Mervyns he should sue the private equity owners who had seemingly run the company into the ground. As the CEO, they reminded him, it was his fiduciary responsibility to preserve as much of the company's value as possible. Normally creditors do the litigating in such situations, but the four-year statute of limitations to bring suit against the buyout was about to expire, and they couldn't get organized in time to file a complaint of their own. Goodman was being asked to sue the very people who had hired him five months earlier.

On Sept. 2, Goodman announced in a memo to staff that the company was planning to file suit. In the memo he alleged that the buyout firms had used financial engineering to acquire Mervyns' "considerable real estate holdings, and then leased back properties to the company at substantially increased rates," moves that helped force the company into Chapter 11. The complaint, filed in Delaware bankruptcy court, alleges that Mervyns' private equity owners deliberately rendered the company insolvent.

About 1,000 employees at headquarters were summoned to separate rooms at 10 a.m. on Oct. 7. Most were told they had been selected to "take the company to a higher level." At least 100 were told they had to be out of the building by noon. They would be paid for the day, but that was it—no severance. "There were a lot of people in tears," recalls 19-year vet Steve Sunyog. He says the treatment "was a slap in the face." Loretta Robinson, a former merchandise coordinator with 32 years at the company, was fortunate to find another job at an office-furnishings store. But the new job is a 50-mile commute and pays less. She says she's borrowing money from her parents and adding ham and beans to pots of soup to stretch them further. "I need every dime," she says.

At the time of the firings, Goodman was furiously shopping Mervyns to potential buyers. But there was a deal-breaker: the new rent payments. Mervyns' landlords wouldn't agree to lower them enough to attract a buyer. Absent cheaper rents, no suitor thought the chain could survive the recession.

Soon rumors began to circulate that no deal would transpire. Executives started packing up their things and walking out. As fears of liquidation spread, "there was mass panic," says Zialcita, 37, the former manager. Employees lined up to hand in their resignations on the belief that it would give them a better chance of getting paid for unused vacation days. "There weren't enough hands in human resources to handle all of the people," says a former executive.

Their worst fears were realized days later when Sun and Lubert-Adler, unable to dig themselves out of their mess, decided that liquidation was the only option. Says Sun Capital Partners in a written statement to BusinessWeek: "When it was acquired, Mervyns was struggling. Significant improvements were achieved, but financial headwinds and the challenging retail environment proved insurmountable." (Lubert-Adler didn't return phone calls or e-mails seeking comment.)

The move rippled through Mervyns' supplier network. Ben Coons, CEO of Advanced Wireless in Lakeville, Minn., is out a major customer and as much as $30,000 for unpaid services: "That's about a third of the biweekly payroll. That stings."

Goodman, for one, has landed on his feet, starting a new job as CEO of mall-based specialty retailer Charlotte Russe (CHIC) in November. But most of the thousands thrown out of work are faring much worse. A bankruptcy court recently ruled that some creditors must be paid before employees, meaning many former workers may not receive vacation pay.

"There Is No Money"

Those people are scrambling. Former communications analyst Jeff Rainey, a 28-year veteran, says he feels "powerless" and may have to file for bankruptcy. Numerous others say they're asking their families for help—from single mother Barbara Durden, who's leaning on her brothers, to marketing veteran Katherine Begley, who may have to move herself and her husband (who suffers from Alzheimer's) into the home of her 93-year-old father. David Magallon, a former security manager and father of three girls, says he has cut off his family's cable TV and turned off the heat. "There is no money," he laments. Christmas this year will be "stuff that we make, and cards."

On Nov. 20, employees filed a suit against Mervyns seeking class action status, alleging the company violated the law by not giving them 60 days notice that they would be terminated. Mervyns declined to comment on pending litigation.

The collapse has prompted many Mervyns lifers to rue the day the company was sold to private equity. "I feel like we were robbed," says Zialcita. Private equity "is so nasty." Devastated by her experience, she vows never to work for a company again. Zialcita now hopes to start a wedding floral business.

Morris, meanwhile, is heartbroken to see the chain he built crumble. "There was no way it could survive," he says. On Oct. 23, having gotten a call from Goodman's assistant asking if he wanted to pick up some old pictures, he stumbled into the company's final day of existence before liquidation. "I couldn't believe it," he says. His wife, he says, had one thought when she heard about the bankruptcy: "Maybe you shouldn't have sold the company."

CHAPTER 4
Demand and Supply

4 Demand and Supply

Timothy Taylor

When people talk about prices, the discussion often takes a judgmental tone. A bidder in an auction pays thousands of dollars for a dress once worn by Diana, Princess of Wales. A collector spends thousands of dollars for some drawings by John Lennon of the Beatles. Mouths gape. Surely such purchases are a waste of money? But when economists talk about prices, they are less interested in making judgments than in gaining a practical understanding of what determines prices and why prices change. In 1933, the great British economist Joan Robinson (1903–1983) explained how economists perceive price:

> The point may be put like this: You see two men, one of whom is giving a banana to the other, and is taking a penny from him. You ask, How is it that a banana costs a penny rather than any other sum? The most obvious line of attack on this question is to break it up into two fresh questions: How does it happen that the one man will take a penny for a banana? and: How does it happen that the other man will give a penny for a banana? In short, the natural thing is to divide up the problem under two heads: Supply and Demand.

As a contemporary example, consider a price often listed on large signs beside well-traveled roads: the price of a gallon of gasoline. Why was the average price of gasoline in the United States $3.15 per gallon in January 2011? Why did the price for gasoline rise to $3.75 per gallon six months later by June 2011? To explain why prices are at a certain level and why that level changes over time, economic analysis focuses on the determinants of what gasoline buyers are willing to pay and what gasoline sellers are willing to accept. For example, the price of a gallon of gasoline in June of a given year is nearly always higher than the price in January of that year; over recent decades, gasoline prices in midsummer have averaged about 10 cents per gallon more than their midwinter low. The likely reason is that people want to drive more in the summer, and thus they are willing to pay more for gas at that time. However, in 2011, gasoline prices rose by much more than the average winter-to-summer rise, which suggests that other factors related to those who buy gasoline and firms that sell it changed during those six months, too.

This chapter introduces the economic model of demand and supply. The discussion begins by examining how demand and supply determine the price and the quantity sold in markets for goods and services, and how changes in demand and supply lead to changes in prices and quantities. In Chapter 5, the same demand and supply model is applied to markets for labor and financial capital. In Chapter 6, the same supply and demand model is applied to international trade. In situation after situation, in different places around the world, across different cultures, even reaching back into history, the demand and supply model offers a useful framework for thinking about what determines the prices and quantities of what is bought and sold.

Demand, Supply, and Equilibrium in Markets for Goods and Services

Markets for goods and services include everything from accounting services, air travel, and apples to zinc, zinfandel wine, and zucchini. Let's first focus on what economists mean by demand, what they mean by supply, and then how demand and supply interact in an economic model of the market.

DEMAND FOR GOODS AND SERVICES

demand: A relationship between price and the quantity demanded of a certain good or service.

quantity demanded: The total number of units of a good or service purchased at a certain price.

Economists use the term **demand** to refer to a relationship between price and the quantity demanded. Price is what a buyer pays (or the seller receives) for a unit of the specific good or service. **Quantity demanded** refers to the total number of units that are purchased at a given price. A rise in price of a good or service almost always decreases the quantity demanded of that good or service; conversely, a fall in price will increase the quantity demanded. When the price of a gallon of gasoline goes up, for example, people look for ways to reduce their purchases of gasoline by combining several errands, commuting by carpool or mass transit, or taking weekend or vacation trips by car close to home. Economists refer to the relationship that a higher price leads to a lower quantity demanded as the **law of demand**.

law of demand: The common relationship that a higher price leads to a lower quantity demanded of a certain good or service.

demand schedule: A table that shows a range of prices for a certain good or service and the quantity demanded at each price.

demand curve: A line that shows the relationship between price and quantity demanded of a certain good or service on a graph, with quantity on the horizontal axis and the price on the vertical axis.

Exhibit 4-1 gives a hypothetical example in the market for gasoline. The table that shows the quantity demanded at each price is called a **demand schedule**. Price in this case is measured per gallon of gasoline. The quantity demanded is measured in millions of gallons. A **demand curve** shows the relationship between price and quantity demanded on a graph, with quantity on the horizontal axis and the price per gallon on the vertical axis. The demand schedule shown by the table and the demand curve shown on the graph are two ways of describing the same relationship between price and quantity demanded.

Each individual good or service needs to be graphed on its own demand curve, because it wouldn't make sense to graph the quantity of apples and the quantity of oranges on the same diagram. Demand curves will appear somewhat different for each product; for example, they may appear relatively steep or flat, or they may be straight or curved. But

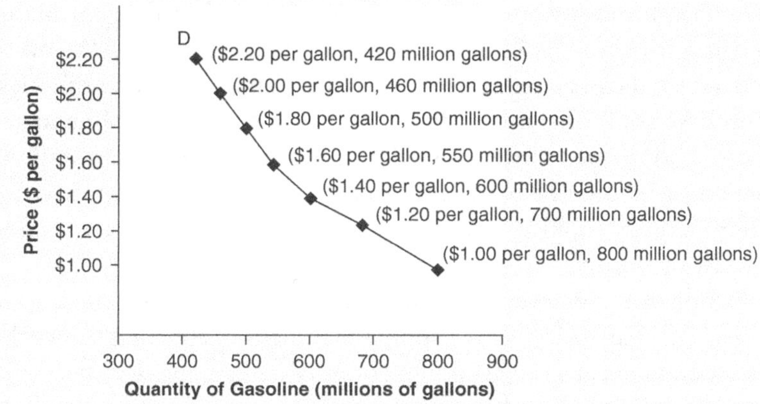

Price (per gallon)	Quantity demanded (in millions of gallons)
$1.00	800
$1.20	700
$1.40	600
$1.60	550
$1.80	500
$2.00	460
$2.20	420

Exhibit 4-1 A Demand Curve for Gasoline

The table that shows quantity demanded of gasoline at each price is called a demand schedule. The demand schedule shows that as price rises, quantity demanded decreases. These points are then graphed on the figure, and the line connecting them is the demand curve D. The downward slope of the demand curve again illustrates the pattern that as price rises, quantity demanded decreases. This pattern is called the law of demand.

CLEARING IT UP
Demand Is Not Quantity Demanded

In economic terminology, demand is not the same as quantity demanded. When economists refer to demand, they mean the relationship between a range of prices and the quantities demanded at those prices, as illustrated by a demand curve or a demand schedule. When economists refer to quantity demanded, they often mean only a certain point on the demand curve, or perhaps the horizontal axis of the demand curve or one column of the demand schedule.

nearly all demand curves share the fundamental similarity that they slope down from left to right. In this way, demand curves embody the law of demand; as the price increases, the quantity demanded decreases, and conversely, as the price decreases, the quantity demanded increases.

SUPPLY OF GOODS AND SERVICES

When economists talk about **supply**, they are referring to a relationship between price received for each unit sold and the **quantity supplied**, which is the total number of units sold in the market at a certain price. A rise in price of a good or service almost always leads to an increase in the quantity supplied of that good or service, while a fall in price will decrease the quantity supplied. When the price of gasoline

supply: A relationship between price and the quantity supplied of a certain good or service.

quantity supplied: The total number of units of a good or service sold at a certain price.

rises, for example, profit-seeking firms are encouraged to expand exploration for oil reserves; to carry out additional drilling for oil; to make new investments in pipelines and oil tankers to bring the oil to plants where it can be refined into gasoline; to build new oil refineries; to purchase additional pipelines and trucks to ship the gasoline to gas stations; and to open more gas stations or to keep existing gas stations open longer hours. The pattern that a higher price is associated with a greater quantity supplied is so common that economists have named it the **law of supply**.

law of supply: The common relationship that a higher price is associated with a greater quantity supplied.

supply schedule: A table that shows a range of prices for a good or service and the quantity supplied at each price.

supply curve: A line that shows the relationship between price and quantity supplied on a graph, with quantity supplied on the horizontal axis and price on the vertical axis.

Exhibit 4-2 illustrates the law of supply, again using the market for gasoline as an example. A **supply schedule** is a table that shows the quantity supplied at a range of different prices. Again, price is measured per gallon of gasoline and quantity supplied is measured in millions of gallons. A **supply curve** is a graphical illustration of the relationship between price, shown on the vertical axis, and quantity, shown on the horizontal axis. The supply schedule and the supply curve are just two different ways of showing the same information. Notice that the horizontal and vertical axes on the graph for the supply curve are the same as for the demand curve.

Just as each product has its own demand curve, each product has its own supply curve. The shape of supply curves will vary somewhat according to the product: steeper, flatter, straighter, or curved. But nearly all supply curves share a basic similarity: they slope up from left to right. In that way, the supply curve illustrates the law of supply: as the price rises, the quantity supplied increases, and conversely, as the price falls, the quantity supplied decreases.

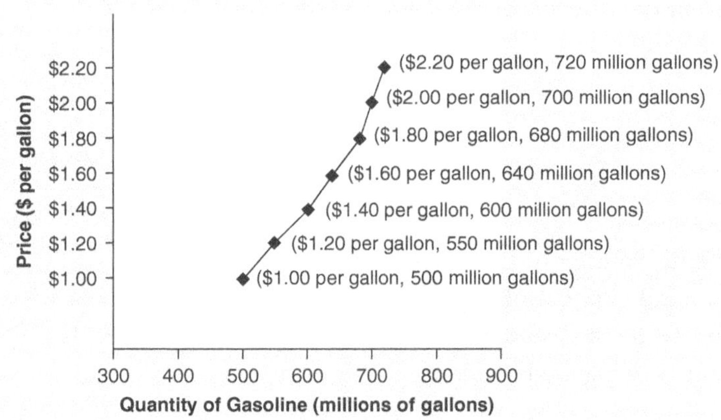

Price (per gallon)	Quantity supplied (millions of gallons)
$1.00	500
$1.20	550
$1.40	600
$1.60	640
$1.80	680
$2.00	700
$2.20	720

Exhibit 4-2 A Supply Curve for Gasoline

The supply schedule is the table that shows quantity supplied of gasoline at each price. As price rises, quantity supplied also increases. The supply curve S is created by graphing the points from the supply schedule and then connecting them. The upward slope of the supply curve illustrates the pattern that a higher price leads to a higher quantity supplied—a pattern that is common enough to be called the law of supply.

CLEARING IT UP

Supply Is Not the Same as Quantity Supplied

In economic terminology, supply is not the same as quantity supplied. When economists refer to supply, they mean the relationship between a range of prices and the quantities supplied at those prices, a relationship that can be illustrated with a supply curve or a supply schedule. When economists refer to quantity supplied, they often mean only a certain point on the supply curve, or sometimes, they are referring to the horizontal axis of the supply curve or one column of the supply schedule.

EQUILIBRIUM—WHERE DEMAND AND SUPPLY CROSS

Because the graphs for demand and supply curves both have price on the vertical axis and quantity on the horizontal axis, the demand curve and supply curve for a particular good or service can appear on the same graph. Together, demand and supply determine the price and the quantity that will be bought and sold in a market.

Exhibit 4-3 illustrates the interaction of demand and supply in the market for gasoline. The demand curve D is identical to Exhibit 4-1. The supply curve S is identical to Exhibit 4-2. When one curve slopes down, like demand, and another curve slopes up, like supply, the curves intersect at some point.

In every economics course you will ever take, when two lines on a diagram cross, this intersection means something! The point where the supply curve S and the demand curve D cross, designated by point E in Exhibit 4-3, is called the equilibrium. The **equilibrium price** is defined as the price where quantity demanded is equal to quantity supplied. The **equilibrium quantity** is the quantity where quantity demanded and quantity supplied are equal at a certain price. In Exhibit 4-3, the equilibrium price is $1.40 per gallon of gasoline and the equilibrium quantity is 600 million gallons. If you had only the demand and supply schedules, and not the graph, it would be easy to find the equilibrium by looking for the price level on the tables where the quantity demanded and the quantity supplied are equal.

equilibrium price: The price where quantity demanded is equal to quantity supplied.

equilibrium quantity: The quantity at which quantity demanded and quantity supplied are equal at a certain price.

The word equilibrium means "balance." If a market is balanced at its **equilibrium** price and quantity, then it has no reason to move away from that point. However, if a market is not balanced at equilibrium, then economic pressures arise to move toward the equilibrium price and the equilibrium quantity.

equilibrium: The combination of price and quantity where there is no economic pressure from surpluses or shortages that would cause price or quantity to shift.

Imagine, for example, that the price of a gallon of gasoline was above the equilibrium price; that is, instead of $1.40 per gallon, the price is $1.80 per gallon. This above-equilibrium price is illustrated by the dashed horizontal line at the price of $1.80 in Exhibit 4-3. At this higher price of $1.80, the quantity demanded drops from the equilibrium quantity of 600 to 500 million gallons. This decline in quantity reflects how people and businesses react to the higher price by seeking out ways to use less gasoline, like sharing rides to work, taking mass transit, and avoiding

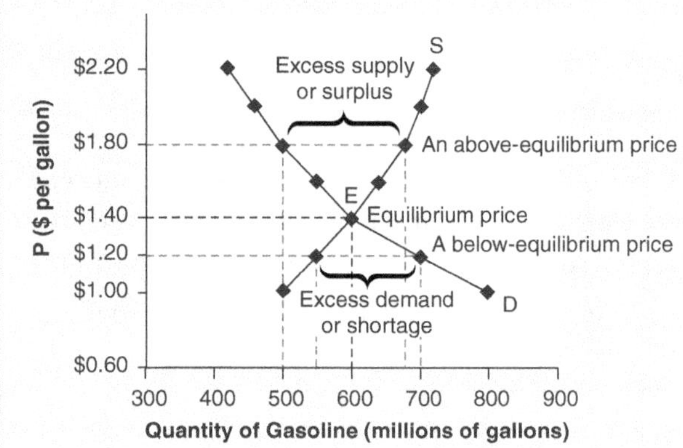

Price (per gallon)	Quantity demanded	Quantity supplied
$1.00	800	500
$1.20	700	550
$1.40	600	600
$1.60	550	640
$1.80	500	680
$2.00	460	700
$2.20	420	720

Exhibit 4-3 Demand and Supply for Gasoline

The demand curve D and the supply curve S intersect at the equilibrium point E, with a price of $1.40 and a quantity of 600. The equilibrium is the only price where quantity demanded is equal to quantity supplied. At a price above equilibrium like $1.80, quantity supplied of 680 exceeds the quantity demanded of 500, so there is excess supply or a surplus. At a price below equilibrium such as $1.20, quantity demanded of 700 exceeds quantity supplied of 550, so there is excess demand or a shortage.

faraway vacation destinations. Moreover, at this higher price of $1.80, the quantity supplied of gasoline rises from the 600 to 680 million gallons, as the higher price provides incentives for gasoline producers to expand their output. At this above-equilibrium price, there is **excess supply**, or a **surplus**; that is, the quantity supplied exceeds the quantity demanded at the given price. With a surplus, gasoline accumulates at gas stations, in tanker trucks, in pipelines, and at oil refineries. This accumulation puts pressure on gasoline sellers. If a surplus of gasoline remains unsold, those firms involved in making and selling gasoline are not receiving enough cash to pay their workers and to cover their expenses. In this situation, at least some gasoline producers and sellers will be tempted to cut prices, because it's better to sell at a lower price than not to sell at all. Once some sellers start cutting gasoline prices, others will follow so that they won't lose sales to the earlier price-cutters. These price reductions in turn will stimulate a higher quantity demanded. In this way, if the price is above the equilibrium level, incentives built into the structure of demand and supply will create pressures for the price to fall toward the equilibrium.

Now suppose that the price is below its equilibrium level at $1.20 per gallon, as shown by the dashed horizontal line at this price in Exhibit 4-3. At this lower price, the quantity demanded increases from 600 to 700 million gallons as drivers take longer trips, spend more minutes warming up their car in the driveway in wintertime, stop sharing rides to work, and purchase cars that get fewer miles to the gallon. However, the below-equilibrium price reduces gasoline producers' incentives to produce and sell gasoline, and the quantity supplied of gasoline falls from 600 to 550 million gallons. When the price is below equilibrium, there is **excess demand**, or a **shortage**; that is, at the given price the quantity demanded, which has been stimulated by the lower price, now

excess supply: When at the existing price, quantity supplied exceeds the quantity demanded; also called a "surplus."

surplus: When at the existing price, quantity supplied exceeds the quantity demanded; also called "excess supply."

excess demand: At the existing price, the quantity demanded exceeds the quantity supplied, also called "shortage."

shortage: At the existing price, the quantity demanded exceeds the quantity supplied, also called "excess demand."

exceeds the quantity supplied, which had been depressed by the lower price. In this situation, eager gasoline buyers mob the gas stations, only to find many stations running short of fuel. Oil companies and gas stations recognize that they have an opportunity to make higher profits by selling what gasoline they have at a higher price. As a result, the price rises toward the equilibrium level.

SHIFTS IN DEMAND AND SUPPLY FOR GOODS AND SERVICES

A demand curve shows how quantity demanded changes as the price rises or falls. A supply curve shows how quantity supplied changes as the price rises or falls. But what happens when factors other than price influence quantity demanded and quantity supplied? For example, what if demand for, say, vegetarian food becomes popular with more consumers? Or what if the supply of, say, diamonds rises not because of any change in price, but because companies discover several new diamond mines? A change in price leads to a different point on a specific demand curve or a supply curve, but a shift in some economic factor other than price can cause the entire demand curve or supply curve to shift.

THE *CETERIS PARIBUS* ASSUMPTION

A demand curve or a supply curve is a relationship between two and only two variables: quantity on the horizontal axis and price on the vertical axis. Thus, the implicit assumption behind a demand curve or a supply curve is that no other relevant economic factors are changing. Economists refer to this assumption as ***ceteris paribus***, a Latin phrase meaning "other things being equal." Any given demand or supply curve is based on the being equal. *ceteris paribus* assumption that all else is held equal. If all else is not held equal, then the demand or supply curve itself can shift.

AN EXAMPLE OF A SHIFTING DEMAND CURVE

The original demand curve D_0 in Exhibit 4-4 shows at point Q that at a price of $20,000 per car, the quantity of cars demanded would be 18 million. The original demand curve also shows how the quantity of cars demanded would change as a result of a higher D_0 or lower price; for example, if the price of a car rose to $22,000, the quantity demanded would decrease to 17 million, as at point R.

ceteris paribus: Other things being equal.

The original demand curve D_0, like every demand curve, is based on the *ceteris paribus* assumption that no other economically relevant factors change. But now imagine that the economy expands in a way that raises the incomes of many people. As a result of the higher income levels, a **shift in demand** occurs, which means that compared to the original demand curve D_0, a different quantity of cars will now be demanded at every price. On the original demand curve, a price of $20,000 means a quantity demanded of 18 million, but after higher incomes cause an

shift in demand: When a change in some economic factor related to demand causes a different quantity to be demanded at every price.

Exhibit 4-4 Shifts in Demand: A Car Example

Increased demand means that at every given price, the quantity demanded is higher, so that the demand curve shifts to the right from D_0 to D_1. Decreased demand means that at every given price, the quantity demand is lower, so that the demand curve shifts to the left from D_0 to D_2.

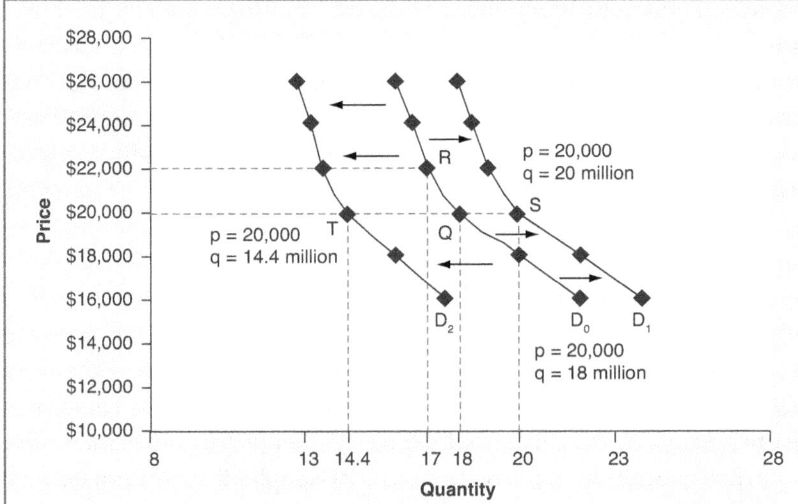

Price	Decrease to D_2	Original Quantity Demanded D_0	Increase to D_1
$16,000	17.6 million	22.0 million	24.0 million
$18,000	16.0 million	20.0 million	22.0 million
$20,000	14.4 million	18.0 million	20.0 million
$22,000	13.6 million	17.0 million	19.0 million
$24,000	13.2 million	16.5 million	18.5 million
$26,000	12.8 million	16.0 million	18.0 million

increase in demand, a price of $20,000 leads to a quantity demanded of 20 million, at point S. Exhibit 4-4 illustrates the shift in demand as a result of higher income levels with the shift of the original demand curve D_0 to the right to the new demand curve D_1.

This logic works in reverse, too. Imagine that the economy slows down so that many people lose their jobs or work fewer hours and thus suffer reductions in income. In this case, the shift in demand would lead to a lower quantity of cars demanded at every given price, and the original demand curve D_0 would shift left to D_2. The shift from D_0 to D_2 represents a decrease in demand; that is, at any given price level, the quantity demanded is now lower. In this example, a price of $20,000 means 18 million cars sold along the original demand curve, but only 14.4 million cars sold after demand has decreased.

When a demand curve shifts, it does not mean that the quantity demanded by every individual buyer changes by the same amount. In this example, not everyone would have higher or lower income, and not everyone would buy or not buy an additional car. Instead, a shift in a demand captures an overall pattern for the market as a whole.

FACTORS THAT SHIFT DEMAND CURVES

A change in any one of the underlying factors that determine what quantity people are willing to buy at a given price will cause a shift in demand. Graphically, the new demand curve lies either to the right or to the left of the original demand curve. Various factors may cause a demand curve to shift: changes in income, change in population, changes in taste, changes in expectations, and changes in the prices of closely related goods. Let's consider these factors in turn.

A *change in income* will often move demand curves. A household with a higher income level will tend to demand a greater quantity of goods at every price than a household with a lower income level. For some luxury goods and services, such as expensive cars, exotic spa vacations, and fine jewelry, the effect of a rise in income can be especially pronounced. However, a few exceptions to this pattern do exist. As incomes rise, many people will buy fewer popsicles and more ice cream, less chicken and more steak; they will be less likely to rent an apartment and more likely to own a home; and so on. **Normal goods** are defined as those where the quantity demanded rises as income rises, which is the most common case; **inferior goods** are defined as those where the quantity demanded falls as income rises.

normal goods: Goods where the quantity demanded rises as income rises.

inferior goods: Goods where the quantity demanded falls as income rises.

Changes in the composition of the population can also shift demand curves for certain goods and services. The proportion of elderly citizens in the U.S. population is rising, from 9% in 1960, to 13% in 2000, and to a projected (by the U.S. Census Bureau) 20% of the population by 2030. A society with relatively more children, like the United States in the 1960s, will have greater demand for goods and services like tricycles and day care facilities. A society with relatively more elderly persons, as the United States is projected to have by 2030, has a higher demand for nursing homes and hearing aids.

Changing tastes can also shift demand curves. In demand for music, for example, 50% of sound recordings sold in 1990 were in the rock or pop music categories. By 2008, rock and pop had fallen to 41% of the total, while sales of rap/hip-hop, religious, and country categories had increased. Tastes in food and drink have changed, too. From 1970 to 2011, the per person consumption of chicken by Americans rose from 40 pounds per year to 84 pounds per year, and consumption of cheese rose from 11 pounds per year to 33 pounds per year. Changes like these are largely due to movements in taste, which change the quantity of a good demanded at every price: that is, they shift the demand curve for that good.

Changes in expectations about future conditions and prices can also shift the demand curve for a good or service. For example, if people hear that a hurricane is coming, they may rush to the store to buy flashlight batteries and bottled water. If people learn that the price of a good like coffee is likely to rise in the future, they may head for the store to stock up on coffee now.

The demand curve for one good or service can be affected by *changes in the prices of related goods.* Some goods and services are **substitutes** for others, which means that they can replace the other good to some extent. For example, if the price of cotton rises, driving up the price of clothing, sheets, and other items made from cotton, then some people will shift to comparable goods made from fabrics like wool, silk, linen, and polyester. A higher price for a substitute good shifts the demand curve to the right; for example, a higher price for tea encourages buying more coffee. Conversely, a lower price for a substitute good has the reverse effect.

substitutes: Goods that can replace each other to some extent, so that a rise in the price of one good leads to a lower quantity consumed of another good, and vice versa.

Other goods are **complements** for each other, meaning that the goods are often used together, so that consumption of one good tends to increase consumption of the other. Examples include breakfast cereal and milk; golf balls and golf clubs; gasoline and sports utility vehicles; and the five-way combination of bacon, lettuce, tomato, mayonnaise, and bread. If the price of golf clubs rises, demand for a complement good like golf balls decreases. A higher price for skis would shift the demand curve for a complement good like ski resort trips to the left, while a lower price for a complement has the reverse effect.

complements: Goods that are often used together, so that a rise in the price of one good tends to decrease the quantity consumed of the other good, and vice versa.

SUMMING UP FACTORS THAT CHANGE DEMAND

Six factors that can shift demand curves are summarized in Exhibit 4-5. The direction of the arrows indicates whether the demand curve shifts represent an increase in demand or a decrease in demand based on the six factors we just considered. Notice that a change in the price of the good or service itself is not listed among the factors that can shift a demand curve. A change in the price of a good or service causes a movement along a specific demand curve, and it typically leads to some change in the quantity demanded, but it doesn't shift the demand curve. Notice also that in these diagrams, the demand curves are drawn without numerical quantities and prices on the horizontal and vertical axes. The demand and supply model can often be a useful conceptual tool even without attaching specific numbers.

When a demand curve shifts, it will then intersect with a given supply curve at a different equilibrium price and quantity. But we are getting ahead of our story. Before discussing how changes in demand can affect equilibrium price and quantity, we first need to discuss shifts in supply curves.

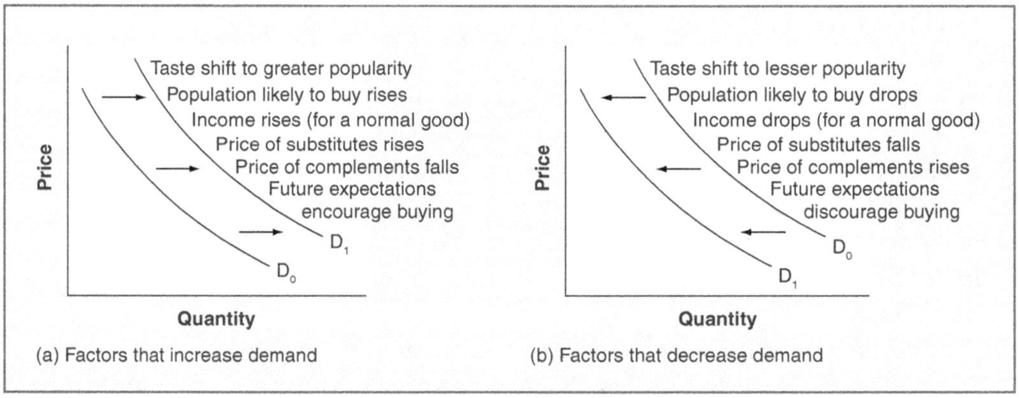

Exhibit 4-5 Some Factors That Shift Demand Curves

The left-hand panel *(a)* offers a list of factors that can cause an increase in demand from D_0 to D_1. The right-hand panel *(b)* shows how the same factors, if their direction is reversed, can cause a decrease in demand from D_0 to D_1. For example, greater popularity of a good or service increases demand, causing a shift in the demand curve to the right, while lesser popularity of a good or service reduces demand, causing a shift of the demand curve to the left.

AN EXAMPLE OF A SHIFT IN A SUPPLY CURVE

A supply curve shows how quantity supplied will change as the price rises and falls, based on the *ceteris paribus* assumption that no other economically relevant factors are changing. But if other factors relevant to supply do change, then the entire supply curve can shift. Just as a shift in demand is represented by a change in the quantity demanded at every price, a **shift in supply** means a change in the quantity supplied at every price. In thinking about the factors that affect supply, remember the basic motivation of firms: to earn profits. If a firm faces lower costs of production, while the prices for the output the firm produces remain unchanged, a firm's profits will increase. Thus, when costs of production fall, a firm will supply a higher quantity at any given price for its output, and the supply curve will shift to the right. Conversely, if a firm faces an increased cost of production, then it will earn lower profits at any given selling price for its products. As a result, a higher cost of production typically causes a firm to supply a smaller quantity at any given price. In this case, the supply curve shifts to the left

shift in supply: When a change in some economic factor related to supply causes a different quantity to be supplied at every price.

As an example, imagine that supply in the market for cars is represented by S_0 in Exhibit 4-6. The original supply curve, S_0, includes a point with a price of $20,000 and a quantity supplied of 18 million cars, labeled as point J, which represents the current market equilibrium price and quantity. If the price rises to $22,000 per car, *ceteris paribus,* the quantity supplied will rise to 20 million cars, as shown by point K on the S_0 curve.

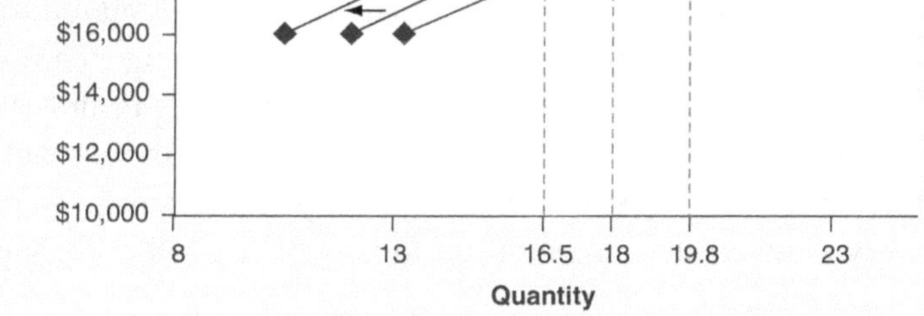

Price	Decrease to S_1	Original Quantity Supplied S_0	Increase to S_2
$16,000	10.5 million	12.0 million	13.2 million
$18,000	13.5 million	15.0 million	16.5 million
$20,000	16.5 million	18.0 million	19.8 million
$22,000	18.5 million	20.0 million	22.0 million
$24,000	19.5 million	21.0 million	23.1 million
$26,000	20.5 million	22.0 million	24.2 million

Exhibit 4-6 Shifts in Supply: A Car Example

Increased supply means that at every given price, the quantity supplied is higher, so that the supply curve shifts to the right from S_0 to S_2. Decreased supply means that at every given price, quantity supplied of cars is lower, so that the supply curve shifts to the left from S_0 to S_1.

Now imagine that the price of steel, an important material input in manufacturing cars, rises, so that producing a car has now become more expensive. At any given price for selling cars, car manufacturers will react by supplying a lower quantity. The shift of supply from S_0 to S_1 shows that at any given price, the quantity supplied decreases. In this example, at a price of $20,000, the quantity supplied decreases from 18 million on the original supply curve S_0 to 16.5 million on the supply curve S_1, which is labeled as point L.

Conversely, imagine that the price of steel decreases, so that producing a car becomes less expensive. At any given price for selling cars, car manufacturers can now expect to earn higher profits and so will supply a higher quantity. The shift of supply to the right from S_0 to S_2 means that at all prices, the quantity supplied has increased. In this example, at a price of $20,000, the quantity supplied increases from 18 million on the original supply curve S_0 to 19.8 million on the supply curve S_2, which is labeled M.

FACTORS THAT SHIFT SUPPLY CURVES

A change in any factor that determines what quantity firms are willing to sell at a given price will cause a change in supply. Some factors that can cause a supply curve to shift include: changes in natural conditions, altered prices for inputs to production, new technologies for production, and government policies that affect production costs.

The cost of production for many agricultural products will be affected by *changes in natural conditions.* For example, the area of northern China that typically grows about 60% of the country's wheat output experienced its worst drought in at least 50 years in the second half of 2009. The U.S. agricultural sector experienced a severe drought in 2012. A drought decreases the supply of agricultural products, which means that at any given price, a lower quantity will be supplied; conversely, exceptionally good weather would shift the supply curve to the right.

Goods and services are produced using combinations of labor, materials, and machinery. When *the price of a key input to production changes*, the supply curve is affected. For example, a messenger company that delivers packages around a city may find that buying gasoline is one of its main costs. If the price of gasoline falls, then in the market for messenger services, a higher quantity will be supplied at any given price per delivery. Conversely, a higher price for key inputs will cause supply to shift to the left.

When a firm discovers a *new technology*, so that it can produce at a lower cost, the supply curve will shift as well. For example, in the 1960s a major scientific effort nicknamed the Green Revolution focused on breeding improved seeds for basic crops like wheat and rice. By the early 1990s, more than two-thirds of the wheat and rice in low- income countries around the world was grown with these Green Revolution seeds—and the harvest was twice as high per acre. A technological improvement that reduces costs of production will shift supply to the right, so that a greater quantity will be produced at any given price.

Government policies can affect the cost of production and the supply curve through taxes, regulations, and subsidies. For example, the U.S. government imposes a tax on alcoholic beverages that collects about $8 billion per year from producers. There is a wide array of government regulations that require firms to spend money to provide a cleaner environment or a safer workplace. A government subsidy, on the other hand, occurs when the government sends money to a firm directly or when the government reduces the firm's taxes if the firm carries out certain actions. For example, the U.S. government pays more than $20 billion per year directly to firms to support research and development. From the perspective of a firm, taxes or regulations are an additional cost of production that shifts supply to the left, leading the firm to produce a lower quantity at every given price. However, government subsidies reduce the cost of production and increase supply.

SUMMING UP FACTORS THAT CHANGE SUPPLY

Natural disasters, changes in the cost of inputs, new technologies, and the impact of government decisions all affect the cost of production for firms. In turn, these factors affect firms' willingness to supply at a given price. Exhibit 4-7 summarizes factors that change the supply of goods and services. Notice that a change in the price of the product itself is *not* among the factors that shift the supply curve. Although a change in price of a good or service typically causes a change in quantity supplied along the supply curve for that specific good or service, it does not cause the supply curve itself to shift.

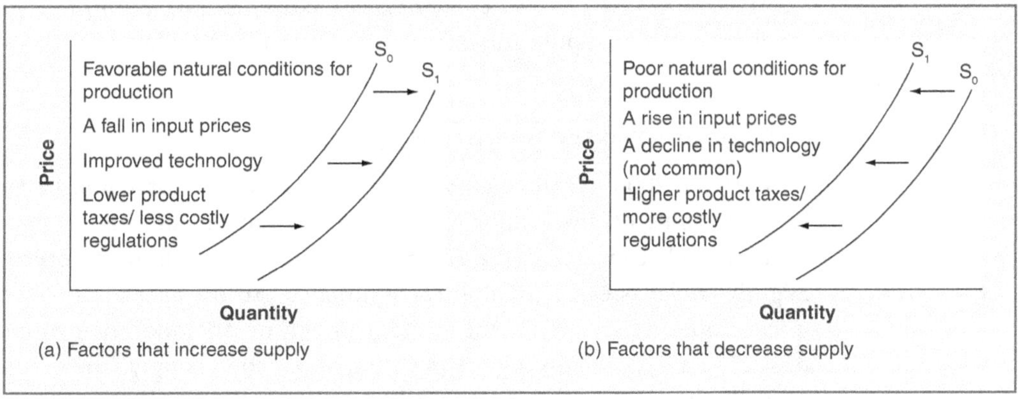

Exhibit 4-7 Some Factors That Shift Supply Curves

The left-hand panel *(a)* offers a list of factors that can cause an increase in supply from S_0 to S_1. The right-hand panel *(b)* shows that the same factors, if their direction is reversed, can cause a decrease in supply from S_0 to S_1.

Shifts in Equilibrium Price and Quantity: The Four-Step Process

Because demand and supply curves appear on a two-dimensional diagram with only price and quantity on the axes, an unwary visitor to the land of economics might be fooled into believing that economics is only about four topics: demand, supply, price, and quantity. However, demand and supply are really "umbrella" concepts: demand covers all of the factors that affect demand, and supply covers all of the factors that affect supply. The factors other than price that affect demand and supply are included by using shifts in the demand or the supply curve. In this way, the two-dimensional demand and supply model becomes a powerful tool for analyzing a wide range of economic circumstances.

To understand how this works, let's begin with a single economic event. It might be an event that affects demand, like a change in income, population, tastes, prices of substitutes or complements, or expectations about future prices. It might be an event that affects supply, like a change in natural conditions, input prices, or technology, or government policies that affect production. How does this economic event affect equilibrium price and quantity? We can analyze this question using a four-step process.

> Step 1: Think about what the demand and supply curves in this market looked like before the economic change occurred. Sketch the curves.
> Step 2: Decide whether the economic change being analyzed affects demand or supply.
> Step 3: Decide whether the effect on demand or supply causes the curve to shift to the right or to the left, and sketch the new demand or supply curve on the diagram.
> Step 4: Compare the original equilibrium price and quantity to the new equilibrium price and quantity.

To make this process concrete, let's consider one example that involves a shift in supply and one that involves a shift in demand.

GOOD WEATHER FOR SALMON FISHING

In summer 2000, weather conditions were excellent for commercial salmon fishing off the California coast. Heavy rains meant higher than normal levels of water in the rivers, which helps the salmon to breed. Slightly cooler ocean temperatures stimulated growth of plankton, the microscopic organisms at the bottom of the ocean food chain, thus providing everything in the ocean with a hearty food supply. The ocean stayed calm during fishing season, so commercial fishing operations didn't lose many days to bad weather. How did these weather conditions affect the quantity and price of salmon? Exhibit 4-8 uses the four-step approach to work through this problem.

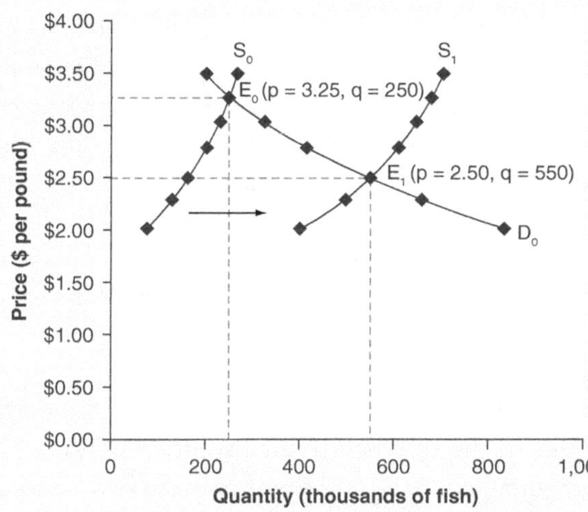

Price per Pound	Quantity Supplied in 1999	Quantity Supplied in 2000	Quantity Demanded
$2.00	80	400	840
$2.25	120	480	680
$2.50	160	550	550
$2.75	200	600	450
$3.00	230	640	350
$3.25	250	670	250
$3.50	270	700	200

Exhibit 4-8 Good Weather for Salmon Fishing: The Four-Step Process

Step 1: Draw a demand and supply diagram to illustrate what the market for salmon looked like in the year before the good weather arrived. The demand curve D_0 and the supply curve S_0 show that the original equilibrium price is $3.25 per pound and the original equilibrium quantity is 250,000 fish.

Step 2: Will the change described affect supply or demand? Good weather is an example of a natural condition that affects supply.

Step 3: Will the effect on supply be an increase or decrease? Good weather is a change in natural conditions that increases the quantity supplied at any given price. The supply curve shifts to the right, moving from the original supply curve S_0 to the new supply curve S_1, which is shown in both the schedule and the figure.

Step 4: Compare the new equilibrium price and quantity to the original equilibrium. At the new equilibrium E_1, the equilibrium price falls from $3.25 to $2.50, but the equilibrium quantity increases from 250,000 to 550,000 salmon.

1. Draw a demand and supply diagram to show what the market for salmon looked like before the good weather arrived. The original equilibrium E_0 was $3.25 per pound, and the original equilibrium quantity was 250,000 fish. (This price per pound is what commercial buyers pay at the fishing docks; what consumers pay at the grocery is higher.)
2. Did the economic event affect supply or demand? Good weather is a natural condition that affects supply.
3. Was the effect on supply an increase or a decrease? Good weather increases the quantity that will be supplied at any given price. The supply curve shifts to the right from S_0 to S_1.
4. Compare the new equilibrium price and quantity to the original equilibrium. At the new equilibrium, E_1, the equilibrium price fell from $3.25 to $2.50, but the equilibrium quantity increased from 250,000 to 550,000 salmon. Notice that the equilibrium quantity demanded increased, even though the demand curve did not move.

In short, good weather conditions increased supply for the California commercial salmon fishing industry. The result was a higher equilibrium quantity of salmon bought and sold in the market at a lower price.

SEAL HUNTING AND NEW DRUGS

In the late 1990s, about 280,000 Canadian seals were killed each year. In 2000, the number dropped to 90,000 seals. What happened? One major use of seals was that some of their body parts were used as ingredients in traditional medications in China and other Asian nations that promised to treat male impotence. However, pharmaceutical companies—led by Pfizer Inc., which invented the drug Viagra—developed some alternative and medically proven treatments for male impotence. How could the invention of Viagra and other drugs to treat male impotence affect the harvest of seals? Exhibit 4-9 illustrates the four-step analysis.

1. Draw a demand and supply diagram to illustrate what the market for seals looked like in the year before the invention of Viagra. In Exhibit 4-9, the demand curve D_0 and the supply curve S_0 show the original relationships. In this case, the analysis is performed without specific numbers on the price and quantity axes. (Not surprisingly, detailed annual data on quantities and prices of the body parts of seals are not readily available.)

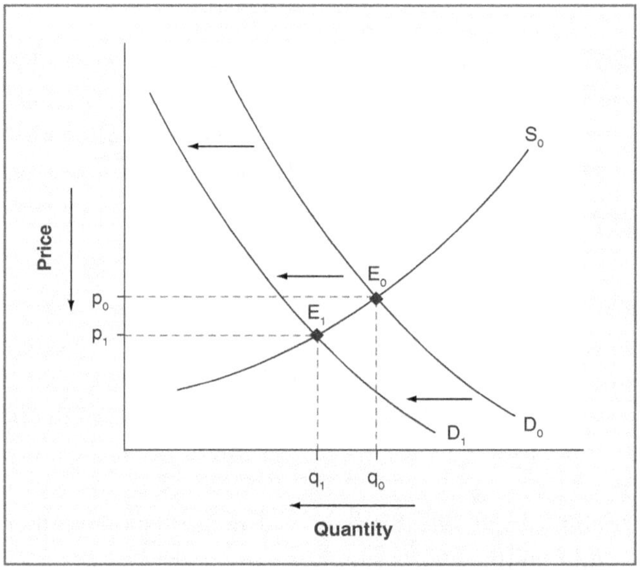

Exhibit 4-9 The Seal Market: A Four-Step Analysis

Step 1: Draw a demand and supply diagram to illustrate what the market for seals looked like in the year before the invention of Viagra. The demand curve D_0 and the supply curve S_0 show the original relationships.

Step 2: Will the change described affect supply or demand? A newly available substitute good, like Viagra, will affect demand for the original product, seals.

Step 3: Will the effect on demand be positive or negative? A less expensive substitute product will tend to mean a lower quantity demanded of the original product, seal, at every given price, causing the demand curve for seal to shift to the left from D_0 to D_1.

Step 4: Compare the new equilibrium price and quantity to the original equilibrium price. The new equilibrium E_1 occurs at a lower quantity and a lower price than the original equilibrium E_0.

2. Did the change described affect supply or demand? A newly available substitute good, like Viagra, will affect demand for the original product, seal body parts.
3. Was the effect on demand an increase or a decrease? An effective substitute product for male impotence means a lower quantity demanded of the original product at every given price, causing the demand curve for seals to shift left to the new demand curve D_1.
4. Compare the new equilibrium price and quantity at E_1 to the original equilibrium price and quantity at E_0. The new equilibrium E_1 occurs at a lower quantity and a lower price than the original equilibrium E_0.

The extremely sharp decline in the number of Canadian seals killed in the late 1990s, together with anecdotal evidence that the price of seal body parts dropped sharply at this time, suggests that the invention of drugs to treat male impotence helped reduce the number of seals killed. In fact, some environmentalists are hoping that such drugs may reduce demand for other common ingredients for traditional male potency medicines, including tiger bones and monkey heads.

THE INTERCONNECTIONS AND SPEED OF ADJUSTMENT IN REAL MARKETS

In the real world, many factors that affect demand and supply can change all at once. For example, the demand for cars might increase because of rising incomes and population, and it might decrease because of rising gasoline prices (a complementary good). Likewise, the supply of cars might increase because of innovative new technologies that reduce the cost of car production, and it might decrease as a result of new government regulations requiring the installation of costly pollution-control technology. Moreover, rising incomes and population or changes in gasoline prices will affect many markets, not just cars. How can an economist sort out all of these interconnected events? The answer lies in the *ceteris paribus* assumption. Look at how each economic event affects each market, one event at a time, holding all else constant.

In the four-step analysis of how economic events affect equilibrium price and quantity, the movement from the old to the new equilibrium seems immediate. But as a practical matter, prices and quantities often do not zoom straight to equilibrium. More realistically, when an economic event causes demand or supply to shift, prices and quantities set off in the general direction of equilibrium. Indeed, even as they are moving toward one new equilibrium, prices are often then pushed by another change in demand or supply toward another equilibrium.

CLEARING IT UP

Shifts of Demand or Supply versus Movements along a Demand or Supply Curve

One common mistake in applying the demand and supply framework is to confuse the shift of a demand or a supply curve with the movement along a demand or supply curve. As an example, consider a problem that asks whether a drought will increase or decrease the equilibrium quantity and equilibrium price of wheat. Lee, a student in an introductory economics class, might reason:

"Well, it's clear that a drought reduces supply, so I'll shift back the supply curve, as in the shift from the original supply curve S_0 to S_1 shown on the diagram (call this Shift 1). So the equilibrium moves from E_0 to E_1, the equilibrium quantity is lower and the equilibrium price is higher. Then, a higher price makes farmers more likely to supply the good, so the supply curve shifts right, as shown by the shift from S_1 to S_2 on the diagram (shown as Shift 2), so that the equilibrium now moves from E_1 to E_2. But the higher price also reduces demand and so causes demand to shift back, like the shift from the original demand curve D_0 to D_1 on the diagram (labeled Shift 3), and the equilibrium moves from E_2 to E_3."

At about this point, Lee suspects that this answer is headed down the wrong path. Think about what might be wrong with Lee's logic, and then read the answer that follows.

Answer: Lee's first step is correct: that is, a drought shifts back the supply curve of wheat and leads to a prediction of a lower equilibrium quantity and a higherequilibrium price. The rest of Lee's argument is wrong because it mixes up shifts in supply with quantity supplied, and shifts in demand with quantity demanded. A higher or lower price never shifts the supply curve, as suggested by the shift in supply from S_1 to S_2. Instead, a price change leads to a movement along a given supply curve. Similarly, a higher or lower price never shifts a demand curve, as suggested in the shift from D_0 to D_1. Instead, a price change leads to a movement along a given demand curve. Remember, a change in the price of a good never causes the demand or supply curve for that good to shift.

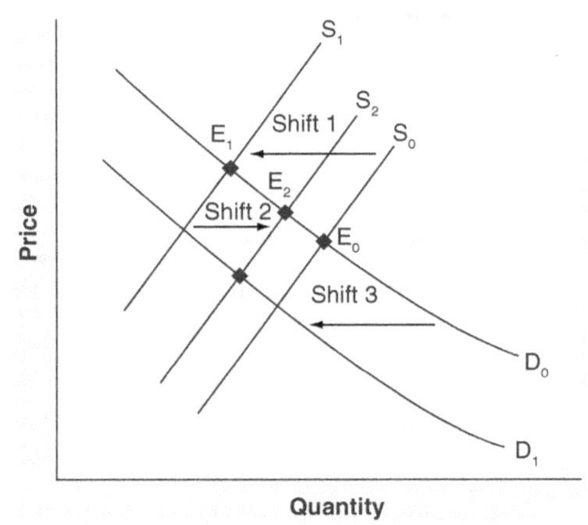

Demand and Supply Shifters

By David Moglen

Demand Shifters

Price is not a demand shifter. Like a shift in supply, price changes will not shift or change demand, they will cause movement along the demand curve, a change in quantity demanded (change in Qd).

1. Buyers' income
   - Level of GDP per capita aka PCI, or
   - A change in Distribution of income can shift Demand. While level of PCI would be assumed unchanged, if you were given: "Income becomes more unequal" as the shock, and the good in question is private helicopters, your response would be . . . demand increases.
   - But if you were given: "Income becomes more unequal" (same shock as above) but the good is: bargain retail (all shopping at Wal-Mart, Ross, K-Mart, the Dollar Store), your answer is . . . demand decreases.
2. Buyers' taste and preferences

   Any medical advice to eat or consume a certain product (or to avoid any food or consumable item), advertising, fads/trends, religious or cultural changes that impact the consumption of a good all fall under "tastes". In the market for bread, pasta, and ceral (carbohydrates), what would the increasing popularity of the Atkins Diet do to demand?
3. Price of complements and substitutes
4. Buyers' expectations of future market conditions (especially the good's future price) but could more generally be their outlook on the economy, jobs, income, and sense of personal economic stability captured by a survey called consumer confidence (CC).
5. Number of buyers in the market (aka size of the market)

   For number of buyers, it could be described as a population (pop) increase (or decrease). If US population increases, then demand goes up for all goods, including, say, software.

   Also, it does not have to be the level of population—it could be the makeup of the population. If you are told that a demographic has changed (you then have to assume level of pop—as anything else in the economy—is unchanged and held constant).

   Example: If the shock is "population is aging" and the good is health care, the result is an increase in demand.

   If the shock is "population is aging" and the good is video games, the result is decrease in demand.

Supply Shifters

Price is not a supply shifter. Like a shift in demand, price changes will not shift or change Supply, they will cause movement along the supply curve, a change in quantity supplied (change in Qs).

1. Level of Productivity, Technology, or Human Capital used in production
2. Input prices (raw or intermediate materials that are needed to make output are called "inputs"). This also refers to the cost associated with any of the four "factors of production". Also called resource prices. Usually would be specific such as a change in the price of oil, employees' wages, the cost of buying or running a machine or factory, or rental costs.
3. Prices of other goods (specifically, the price of another goods the firm could produce instead).
4. Expectations about future prices for the good. Can also be firms generalized expectations about the economy, captured by a survey called business confidence (BC).
5. Number of firms in the industry; also might best be described as any of the following-Number of Suppliers/Producers/Resources
6. The firm's objective: e.g. profit maximizing or something else? This shifter is extremely rare, and generally means an industry has gone from public to private (privatized) or private to public (nationalized). A subtler shift would be industry becomes deregulated or more regulated.

Key Concepts and Summary

1. A **demand schedule** is a table that shows the **quantity demanded** at different prices in the market. A demand curve shows the relationship between quantity demanded and price in a given market on a graph. The **law of demand** points out that a higher price typically leads to a lower quantity demanded.
2. A **supply schedule** is a table that shows the **quantity supplied** at different prices in the market. A **supply curve** shows the relationship between quantity supplied and price on a graph. The **law of supply** points out that a higher price typically leads to a higher quantity supplied.
3. The **equilibrium price** and **equilibrium quantity** occur where the supply and demand curves cross. The **equilibrium** occurs where the quantity demanded is equal to the quantity supplied.
4. Economists often use the ***ceteris paribus*** or "other things being equal" assumption, that while examining the economic impact of one event, all other factors remain unchanged for the purpose of the analysis.
5. Factors that can shift the demand curve for goods and services, causing a different quantity to be demanded at any given price, include changes in tastes, population, income, prices of **substitute** or **complement** goods, and expectations about future conditions and prices.
6. Factors that can shift the supply curve for goods and services, causing a different quantity to be supplied at any given price, include natural conditions, input prices, changes in technology, and government taxes, regulations, or subsidies.
7. When using the supply and demand framework to think about how an event will affect the equilibrium price and quantity, proceed through four steps: (a) sketch a supply and demand diagram to think about what the market looked like before the event; (b) decide whether the event will affect supply or demand; (c) decide whether the effect on supply or demand is negative or positive, and draw the appropriate shifted supply or demand curve; (d) compare the new equilibrium price and quantity to the original ones.

Vocabulary Terms

Ceteris Paribus
Complements
Demand
Demand Schedule
Equilibrium
Input Costs
Quantity demanded
Quantity supplied
Shifts

Substitutes
Supply
Supply Schedule
Tastes

Review Questions

1. In the economic view, what determines the level of prices?
2. What does a downward-sloping demand curve mean about how buyers in a market will react to a higher price?
3. Will demand curves have the same exact shape in all markets?
4. What does an upward-sloping supply curve mean about how sellers in a market will react to a higher price?
5. Will supply curves have the same shape in all markets?
6. What is the relationship between quantity demanded and quantity supplied at equilibrium?
7. How can you locate the equilibrium point on a demand and supply graph?
8. When analyzing a market, how do economists deal with the problem that many factors that affect the market are changing at the same time?
9. If the price is above the equilibrium level, would you predict excess supply or excess demand? If the price is below the equilibrium level, would you predict a shortage or a surplus?
10. Explain why a price that is above the equilibrium level will tend to fall toward equilibrium. Explain why a price that is below the equilibrium level will tend to rise toward the equilibrium.
11. Name some factors that can cause a shift in the demand curve in markets for goods and services.
12. What's the difference between demand and quantity demanded?
13. Name some factors that can cause a shift in the supply curve in markets for goods and services.
14. Is supply the same thing as quantity supplied? Explain.

IN-CLASS PROJECT

Demand and Supply

By David Moglen

Directions

Draw the Demand-Supply diagram with correctly labeled axes and the name of the market at the top.

The market you are drawing is the good in **bold**, which (in most of the questions) is the end-user, retail, "product" market (think about this when labeling axes) in the United States, unless otherwise indicated.

Show Equilibrium points A (before the shock) and B (after the shock) and **estimate numerical coordinates** on X and Y axes.

The one thing you write outside of the graph: **Categorize the shifter—choose the entry from the list of Demand or Supply shifters that most closely describes the shock.** No explanation is necessary.

1. The market for Cashmere Sweaters in the month of November was impacted because shoppers started to think there would be unusually steep price increases coming up in January.
2. Rare earth metals are vital to produce **cell phones**. Show how the cell phone market is impacted when China shuts off exports of rare earth metals (which then skyrocket in price) due to a dispute with Japan.
3. Show how the September 11th attack impacts the market for **airport body scanners** in 2002.
4. A tsunami in Japan sharply reduces the flow of auto parts to **car** factories all over the world.
5. Hurricane Katrina greatly impacted tourism (market: "**New Orleans Souvenirs**") in New Orleans even though the tourist section of the city ("The French Quarter") was essentially unharmed.
6. In the market for **bodyguards in war zones**, private military companies (PMCs) have to react when the demand for their prison interrogators skyrockets during wartime.
7. **Nokia's Smartphone** business has suffered due to popularity of iPhones and Android phones.
8. Due to the extremely low price of natural gas, the **coal** industry is in decline. Note—power plants can run on either coal or natural gas.
9. **Malaysian home** prices are up 10% this year due to foreigners buying.
10. As the **flat screen TV** industry matured, factories were able to improve production machinery enough to produce twice as many TV's as before.
11. In the market for small business conventional **bank loans in Africa**, borrowers are now able to get crowdsourced micro-finance (micro-loans) for a lower interest rate than they could last year. Note—the microloan from an NGO/nonprofit such as Kiva and the bank loan are different products offered by different lenders.
12. Companies like Sony produce both laptops and **stereos**. When consumer buy fewer laptops as they shift instead to smartphones and tablets, show how the stereo market is impacted.
13. Due in part to U.S. tariffs (import sales tax) on steel imports, **U.S.-made appliances** went into decline.
14. Two Shocks: Private for-profit universities must now disclose their low graduation rates in their advertising; UC's cut classes due to budget cuts. Market: **UC Education**, annually.

EXPERIMENT

Producers and Consumers

By David Moglen

Supplies

3X5 cards, any color, enough for every group of 4–5 students to get one. So a 40–student class should have about 10 cards.

Directions

Form your usual group. You will receive one 3X5 card per group. Write the name of a good your group will sell to the rest of the class. Imagine it's the month of December and the groups can be shopping for themselves, friends, or family. The time period is one month and people shop a lot in December. All groups have to spend $3,000 to $5,000.

But for now just take a minute or two to think of what good your group will produce and sell. It could be a good or a service, real or imagined, or a known major brand. There are no costs and winning is determined solely on revenue, not profits, so don't worry that the good you select will cost too much to produce. But do think about the $3,000 to $5,000 spending limit per group; you can't expect anyone to buy something from you for $5,000 per unit or more, or even anywhere close to that price because they will be over-budget.

Which brings us to the price. Determine your price, write it small on the card, and don't tell anyone outside of your group. Your teacher will come around within two-three minutes and write down on their own card the name of the good and your stated price for each group in the class.

During the shopping phase, groups will get to name their price for your good, in addition to the quantity of your good they will buy at that price. They will enter their shopping request in the space your teacher will have written on the board, like so:

T T T T

Where number of T's = number of groups in the class.

As soon as even one group is ready, they should walk up to the board and write above one of the T's the name of their good. If they want to include any details, features, brand, etc., they can write it there as well. Also, before shopping starts, the teacher should ask each group to verbally announce to the class any pitch they have for their good (briefly-takes 5–10 seconds per group). The left column of the T is labeled Q for the quantity the shopping group wants to buy. The right column of the T is labeled P for price per unit the group wants to pay for that good.

A sale has only gone through if the shoppers state a price equal or greater to your price. Let's say you write down (on the card and on the board) that your good is glass kitchen tables, and you write on the card (and keep it secret) that your price is $400. Then a group comes up to the board during the shopping phase and writes under your good that they will buy 2 for $600, then you made a sale, two in fact, at your price of $400. So that is $800 of revenue.

If they offer even as low as $400, that would be a sale. But if they want to buy, say, 5 tables for $180 each, then you didn't make any sale. These offers did not "go through". You should, however write down on a sheet of paper every entry shoppers put on the board – even prices that are too low for you - under your good as you will need this data to draw your demand curve at the end of this experiment.

Winning

The group with the highest Total Revenue (=Sales) will win bonus points (or participation credits). To avoid collusion, there should not be second-place points on this project. There is one caveat: for the winning group to receive their bonus points, **they must have at least $1000 of their purchases actually go through**. So if they lowballed everyone and offered fifty cents for all their purchases, they cannot win. They have to have written on the board purchases totaling at least $1000 that have been accepted by the other groups.

Each group will turn in at the end of the exercise. (**Bold** indicates a specific item you are turning in:)

1. Producing Phase: The 3X5 card with the **name of the good** and your price written on it. This is also a good place to write your total revenue where **TR=your price quantity of units you sold**. This number is the sole basis on which the winning group is decided.

2. Shopping Phase: Send one or two members to the board and write under the goods on the board: quantities (in the Q column) and prices per unit (in the P column) that your group wants to buy. Your spending, using these prices you as a shopper are willing to pay, are used to show that you spent $3,000 to $5,000. **Show the math to indicate you are within these spending limits on a separate sheet of paper.** You do not need to buy every good, and you cannot buy your own good.

3. Demand-Supply Graph: **Write down on your paper all the shoppers' quantities and prices written on the board under your good.** Draw a demand curve for your good based on the data shoppers have given you for your good. For help on this, see the text on adding up individual's demand curves to get a market demand curve (you are only drawing the market demand curve). Draw your supply curve as a horizontal line, with a vertical value = your stated price. As always with any graph, fully label your axes, show point A as the intersection of D and S, and the time period should be per month.

Staple the sheet of paper to your 3X5 card and make sure all group members' names are written on either the paper or the card, or both if a stapler is unavailable.

Appendix 4-A: Currency

CAUTION

What is customary for Americans need not be customary for foreigners. The Japanese, naturally, think of prices in terms of yen, the British think of them in terms of pounds, the Germans in terms of marks. When it comes to exchange rates, therefore, different customs prevail. Americans may talk of a rate of 1ø per yen; the Japanese may refer to the same reality as ¥100 per dollar. Americans may talk of a rate of $1.63 per British pound; the British may call the same thing £61 per dollar. To make matters worse, banks, newspapers, television stations, and even text books differ in their handling of this matter. Nothing but extreme vigilance, therefore, can save us from confusion when talking about the foreign-exchange market.

Figure 4-10 illustrates how an exchange rate is determined. At some high rate, such as $.015 per yen, the quantity of yen demanded may be zero (point *A*). Every American may find every good cheaper in the United States, so why buy yen to purchase goods in Japan? Apply this exchange rate, for example, to Table 3 and note how a unit of Japanese steel would cost $.015 per yen times ¥10,000 = $150, while a unit of Japanese rice would cost $.015 per yen times €4,000 = $60. At successively lower exchange rates, however, more and more Japanese goods would become attractive to Americans and the quantity of yen demanded might rise along line *AB*. (Can you see, looking at Table 3, that Japanese steel would be cheaper than U.S. steel below a rate of $100 per ¥10,000, or $.01 per yen? Can you see that even Japanese rice would be cheaper than U.S. rice below a rate of $10 per ¥4,000, or $.0025 per yen?)

We can tell a similar story about supply. At some high exchange rate, such as $.015 per yen, the quantity of yen supplied would be large (point *C*). Every Japanese would find every good cheaper in the United States and would offer to sell yen to get the dollars needed to buy American goods. Apply This exchange rate to Table 3 and note how a Japanese would then picture the U.S. price of a unit of steel at $100/$.015 per yen, or ¥6,666.66, while a unit of U.S. rice would be seen to cost a mere $10/$.015 per yen, or ¥666.66. At successively lower exchange rates, however, fewer and fewer American goods would look attractive to the Japanese; at some very low rate, their appetite for American goods and their supply of yen would vanish altogether (point *D*).

Looking at Figure 4-10, we can instantly see that the only viable exchange rate is the one corresponding to point *E*, or $.007 per yen. At any higher rate (such as $.015 per yen) a surplus of yen (such as *AC*) would appear and the rate would fall. At any lower rate (such as $.002 per yen) a shortage of yen (such as *FG*) would exist and the rate would rise. Incidentally, as Figure 4-10 shows, when the exchange rate is expressed as so many dollars per yen, any fall in the rate is

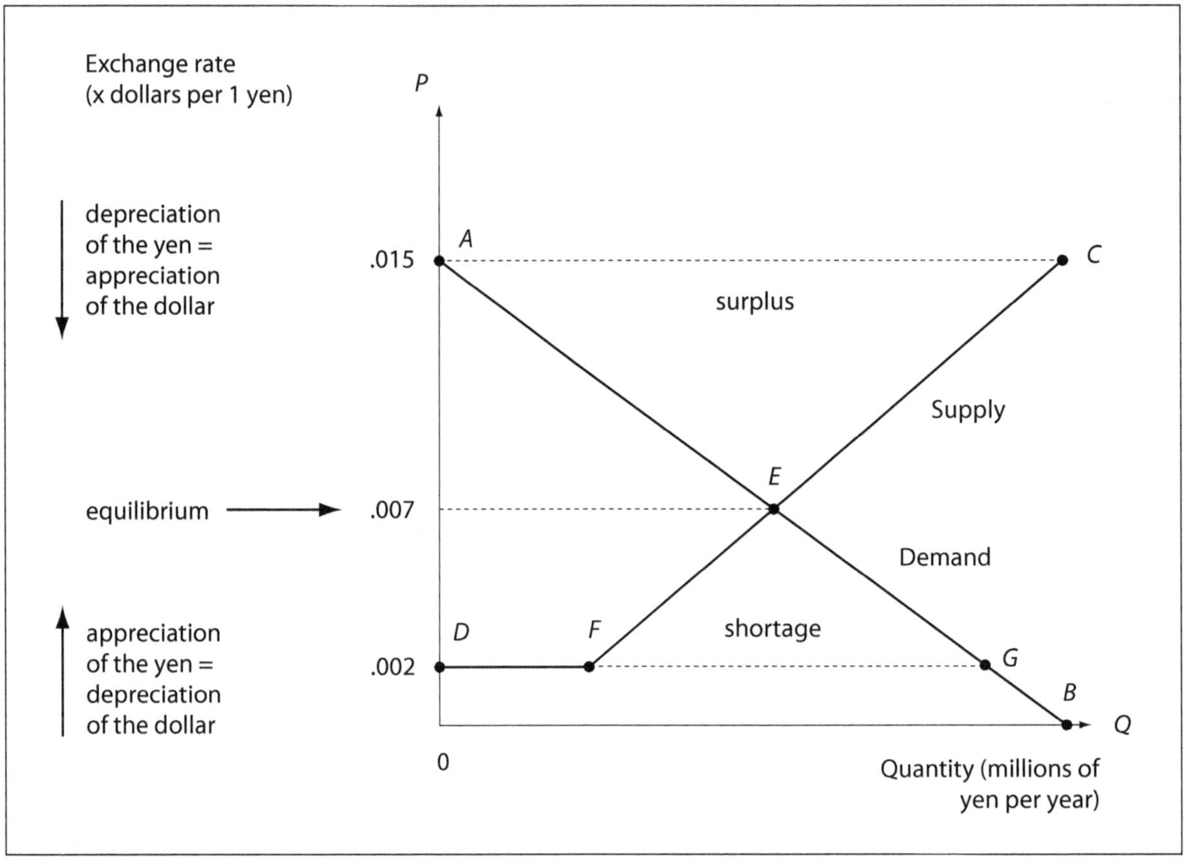

FIGURE 4-10
The Market for Japanese Yen
A competitive market for foreign money works just like the market for an ordinary good: The price, now called the *exchange rate,* falls in the face of surpluses and rises in the face of shortages, until equilibrium is reached.

referred to as a **depreciation** of the yen and, by implication, as an **appreciation** of the dollar. (You can see why: *A* yen is then worth fewer dollars, but a dollar is worth more yen.) Analogously, any rise in the rate as defined here is an appreciation of the yen and a depreciation of the dollar.

CAUTION

If an exchange rate is expressed as x units of foreign money per dollar, all of the statements made in the text and in Figure 3 about depreciation and appreciation have to be reversed. Under those circumstances, a rise in the exchange rate, for example, denotes an appreciation of the dollar and a simultaneous depreciation of the foreign money.

Having introduced the foreign-exchange market, we are ready to see how the capitalist market economy encourages people to trade in accordance with comparative advantages. Review Table 3, given our Figure 4-10 equilibrium exchange rate of $.007 per yen. At this rate, the Japanese price of steel comes to $.007 per yen times ¥10,000 = $70 per unit, which is cheaper than the U.S. price. On the other hand, the American price per unit of rice comes to $10/$.007 per yen, or ¥1,428.57, which is cheaper than the Japanese price. Accordingly, Americans will buy Japanese steel and Japanese will buy American rice, just as pictured in Figure 2. Indeed, this result is not an accident. As long as relative goods prices in each country reflect the goods' opportunity costs (as in our Table 3), and as long as free markets for foreign exchange are allowed to establish equilibrium rates of exchange, the country with comparative advantage will also have the absolutely lower price, and trade in accordance with comparative advantage will occur spontaneously. Ricardo's promise will be realized; scarcity in each country will be less intense than before.

IN-CLASS PROJECT

Currency: The U.S. Dollar

By David Moglen

Directions:

As a Group Work, groups are assigned a number from 1–4 and then answer both A and B accordingly. For example, Group 3 would answer #3 from Part A and #3 from Part B. Bonus points for all groups for Part A, #5.

As a homework, everyone answers all questions.

Part A:

Questions where appreciation or depreciation of the currency is the endogenous effect/result:

All of these Three Questions will be answered by your graph of this shift in the market for the US Dollar. (This means you do not need a statement in response to these questions): What will shift (D or S), will D or S increase or decrease in the Market for the U.S. Dollar and is the result appreciation or depreciation of the dollar?

For all of these, draw the fully-labeled graph showing this one shift for the E/$1 market.

1. U.S. consumers buy more Chinese-made consumer goods like flat-panel televisions and computers, household appliances, toys and clothing.
2. A growing Chinese middleclass buys more Ford and GM-made cars.
3. U.S. shifts from energy independence/ being a net oil exporter to foreign oil dependence/ being a net importer.
4. Asian Central Banks and Middle Eastern Kingdoms buy U.S. T-bills (i.e. loan money to the U.S. government) This is part of the dollar's role as a reserve currency for the entire world.
5. Oil stops being denominated—sold/traded in petrodollars and instead oil trades and is priced in Euros (which would then in this context start being referred to as petroeuros)

Part B:

Questions where appreciation or depreciation of the currency is the exogenous shock

1. How will depreciation of the dollar affect (quantity of) U.S. imports?
2. How will depreciation of the dollar affect (quantity of) U.S. exports?
3. How will appreciation of the dollar affect (quantity) purchases of U.S. financial instruments e.g. stocks bonds and mutual funds? Investors view the currency change as an ongoing trend into the foreseeable future.
4. How will appreciation of the dollar affect (quantity) purchases of foreign financial instruments e.g. stocks bonds and mutual funds? Investors view the currency change as an ongoing trend into the foreseeable future.

CHAPTER 5
Price Controls

5 Price Controls

By William Baumol

A CASE STUDY: Rent Controls in New York City

New York is the only major city in the United States that has had rent controls continuously since World War II. The objective of rent control is, of course, to protect the consumer from high rents. But most economists believe that rent control does not help the cities or their inhabitants and that, in the long run, it makes almost everyone worse off. Elementary supply-demand analysis shows us what actually happens.

Figure 5-1 is a supply–demand diagram for rental units in New York. Curve *DD* is the demand curve and curve *SS* is the supply curve. Without controls, equilibrium would be at point *E*, where rents average $1200 per month and 3 million units are occupied. If rent controls are effective, they must set a ceiling price *below* the equilibrium price of $1200. But with a low rent ceiling, such as $800, the quantity of housing demanded will be 3.5 million (point *B*) while the quantity supplied will be only 2.5 million (point *C*).

The diagram shows a shortage of 1,000,000 apartments. This theoretical concept of a "shortage" manifests itself in New York City as an abnormally low vacancy rate—typically about half the national urban average.

As we expect, rent controls have spawned a lively black market in New York. The black market raises the effective price of rent-controlled apartments in many ways, including bribes, "key money" paid to move up on the waiting list, and requiring prospective tenants to purchase worthless furniture at inflated prices.

According to the diagram, rent controls reduce the quantity supplied from 3 million to 2.5 million apartments. How does this show up in New York? First, some property owners, discouraged by the low rents, have converted apartment buildings into office space or other uses. Second, some apartments have been inadequately maintained. After all, rent controls create a shortage which makes even dilapidated apartments easy to rent. Third, some landlords have actually abandoned their buildings rather than pay rising tax and fuel bills. These abandoned buildings rapidly become eyesores and eventually pose threats to public health and safety.

FIGURE 5-1
Supply–Demand Diagram for Rental Housing
When market forces are permitted to set rents, the quantity of dwellings supplied will equal the quantity demanded. But when a rent ceiling forces rent below the market level, the number of dwellings supplied (point *C*) will be less than the number demanded (point *B*). Thus, rent ceilings induce housing shortages.

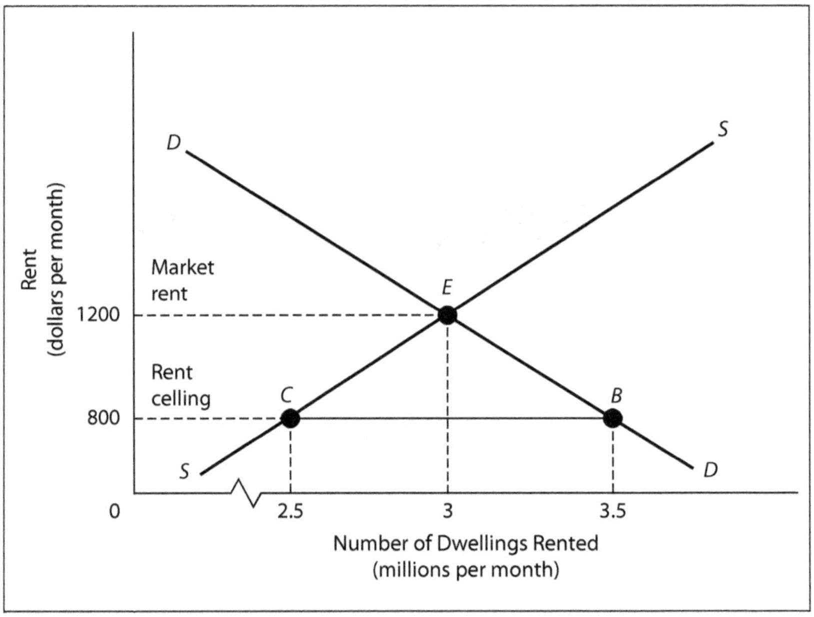

With all these problems, why do rent controls persist in New York City? And why are some other cities moving in the same direction? Part of the explanation is that most people simply do not understand the problems that rent controls create. Another part is that landlords are unpopular politically. But a third, and important, part of the explanation is that not everyone is hurt by rent controls. Those who benefit from controls fight hard to preserve them. In New York, for example, many tenants pay rents that are only a fraction of what their apartments would fetch on the open market. They are, naturally enough, quite happy with, this situation. This last point illustrates another very general phenomenon:

Virtually every price ceiling or floor creates a class of people with a vested interest in preserving the regulations because they benefit from them. These people naturally use their political influence to protect their gains, which is one reason why it is so hard to eliminate price ceilings or floors.

Restraining the Market Mechanism: Price Floors

A **Price Floor** is a legal minimum on the price that may be charged for a commodity.

Interferences with the market mechanism are not always designed to keep prices *low*. Agricultural price supports and minimum wages are two notable examples in which the law keeps prices *above* free-market levels. **Price floors** are typically accompanied by a standard set of symptoms:'

1. A surplus develops as sellers cannot find enough buyers. *Example:* Surpluses of various agricultural products have been a persistent, and costly, problem for the U.S. government. The problem is even more severe in the European Community, where the so-called common agricultural policy holds prices even higher.
2. Where goods, rather than services, are involved, the surplus creates a problem of disposal. Something must be done about the excess of quantity supplied over quantity demanded.

Example: The government has often been forced to purchase, store, and then dispose of large amounts of surplus agricultural commodities.

3. To get around the regulations, sellers may offer discounts in disguised and often unwanted-forms. *Example:* When airline fares were regulated by the government, airlines offered more and better food and stylish uniforms for flight attendants instead of lowering fares. Today, the food is worse but tickets cost much less.
4. Regulations that keep prices artificially high encourage overinvestment in the industry. Even inefficient businesses whose high operating costs would doom them in an unrestricted market can survive beneath the shelter of a generous price floor. *Example:* This is why the airline and trucking industries both went through painful "shake outs" of the weaker companies in the 1980s.

Once again, a specific example is useful.

A CASE STUDY: Milk Price Supports

America's extensive program of farm price supports began in 1933 as "a temporary method of dealing with an emergency"—farmers were going broke in droves. It is with us still today, even though the farm population of the United States is less than a sixth of what it was then.

One of the more absurd legacies of that "temporary emergency" is a maze of milk-marketing orders covering the pricing and distribution of milk in 44 milk producing regions of the country. By setting the prices of milk, butter, and cheese as high as three times those on world markets, the government ensures that America will suffer from chronic overproduction—as Figure 5-2 shows.

In the diagram, the equilibrium price for milk is 70¢ per quart, but we assume that the government sets *a price floor* at 90¢. At this high price, farmers produce 80 billion quarts per year—20 billion above the equilibrium quantity. But consumers want to purchase only 50 billion—10 billion below the equilibrium quantity. The result is a huge *surplus* of milk—30 billion quarts per year in the example.

In a market economy like ours, Congress cannot simply set prices by decree; it must do something to enforce the price floor. Normally, that "something" is buying up the surplus, that is, adding 30 billion quarts per year in *government demand* to the private demand shown in Figure 5-2.[1] That, of course, requires a lot of the taxpayers' money. In addition, all the surplus milk must be stored somewhere—usually as cheese—for milk does not keep well. That creates another bill for the taxpayer to pick up. But there is more. We pay again as consumers in the form of higher prices for milk—90¢ rather than 70¢ in the example. According

[1]Draw a new demand curve into Figure 5-2 which includes this government demand. It must be parallel to DD but 30 billion quarts farther to the right. If you draw it accurately, it will pass exactly through point *B*.

FIGURE 5-2
Analysis of Milk Price Supports
In this diagram, which repeats the supply and demand curves from Figure 5-3, the support price for milk (90¢ per quart) exceeds the equilibrium price (which is 70¢. Quantity supplied at the support price is 80 billion quarts per year (point *B*) while quantity demanded is only 50 billion (point *A*). To keep the price at 90¢, the government must buy up the 30-billion-quart surplus each year.

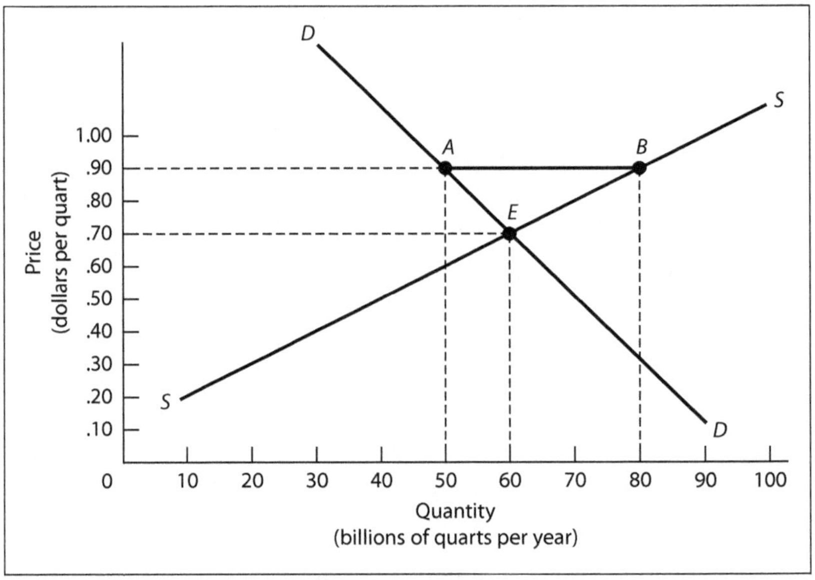

to current estimates, milk price supports cost American taxpayers and consumers together about $10–$12 billion a year.

Sometimes the government tires of all this and tries something else. For example, in 1986 it offered to pay dairy farmers to slaughter 1.6 million cows. The result? An uproar from beef raisers as meat prices collapsed.[2] As we said earlier, those who would flaunt the will of the market had better be prepared for unforeseen consequences.

A Can of Worms

Our two case studies—rent controls and milk price supports—illustrate some of the major side effects of price floors and ceilings, but barely hint at others. There are difficulties that we have not even mentioned, for the market mechanism is a tough bird that imposes suitable retribution on those who seek to circumvent it by legislative decree. Here is a partial list of other problems that may arise when prices are controlled.

FAVORITISM AND CORRUPTION

When price ceilings or floors create shortages or surpluses, someone must decide who gets to buy or sell the limited quantity that is available. This can lead to discrimination along racial or religious lines, political favoritism, or corruption in government. For example, it has been argued that the high U.S. support price for sugar has led to widespread corruption in Caribbean nations, as foreign producers vie for the valuable right to export sugar cane to the United States.

[2]See Review Question 8 at the end of the chapter.

UNENFORCEABILITY

Attempts to limit prices are almost certain to fail in industries with numerous suppliers, simply because the regulating agency must monitor the behavior of so many sellers. Ways will be found to evade or violate the law, and something akin to the free-market price will generally reemerge. But there is an important difference: since the evasion mechanism, whatever its form, will have some operating costs, those costs must be borne by someone. Normally, that someone is the consumer.

AUXILIARY RESTRICTIONS

Fears that a system of price controls will break down invariably lead to regulations designed to shore up the shaky edifice. Consumers may be told when and from whom they are permitted to buy. The powers of the police and the courts may be used to prevent the entry of new suppliers. Occasionally, an intricate system of market subdivision is imposed, giving each class of firms a protected sphere in which others are not permitted to operate. Laws banning conversion of rent controlled apartments to condominiums are one example. Milk-marketing orders are another. A few years ago, milk cost so much less in New Jersey than in New York that people were actually smuggling milk into New York State!

LIMITATION OF VOLUME OF TRANSACTIONS

To the extent that controls succeed in affecting prices, they can be expected to reduce the volume of transactions. Curiously, this is true regardless of whether the regulated price is *above* or *below* the free-market equilibrium price. If it is set above the equilibrium price, quantity demanded will be below the equilibrium quantity. On the other hand, if the imposed price is set below the free-market level, quantity supplied will be cut down. Since sales volume cannot exceed either the quantity supplied or the quantity demanded, a reduction in the volume of transactions is the result.[3]

MISALLOCATION OF RESOURCES

Departures from free-market prices are likely to produce misuse of the economy's resources because the connection between production costs and prices is broken. For example, Russian farmers used to feed their farm animals bread, instead of unprocessed grains, because price ceilings kept the price of bread ludicrously low. In addition, just as more complex locks lead to more sophisticated burglary tools, more complex regulations lead to the use of yet more resources for their avoidance. New jobs are created for executives, lawyers, and economists. It may well be conjectured that at least some of these expensive professionals could be put to better use elsewhere.

[3]See Review Question 9 at the end of the chapter.

Policy Debate

ECONOMIC ASPECTS OF THE WAR ON DRUGS

For years now, the U.S government has engaged in a highly publicized "war on drugs." At part of this effort, billions of dollars have been spent on trying to stop illegal drugs at the border. In some sense, interdiction has succeeded: literally tons of cocaine and other drugs have been seized by federal agents. Yet all these efforts have made barely a difference to America's city streets. Simple economic reasoning explains why.

When drug interdiction works, it shifts the supply curve of drugs to the left, thereby driving up street prices. But that, in turn, raises the rewards for potential smugglers and attracts more criminals in to the "industry", which shifts the supply curve back to the right. The net result is that increased shipments of drugs to our shores replace much of what the authorities confiscate. This is why many economics believe that any successful anti-drug program must concentrate on reducing *demand* which would lower the street price of drugs, not on reducing *supply* which can only raise it.

Some economists-and some noneconomists as well-would go even further and advocate *legalization* of many drugs. While this remains a highly controversial position which few are ready to endorse, the reasoning behind it is straightforward. A stunningly high number of crimes committed in America—especially robberies and murders—are drug-related. One major reason is that street prices of drugs are so high that addicts must steal to get the money and drug traffickers are all too willing to kill to protect their highly profitable "businesses".

How would things differ if drugs were legal? Since Colombian farmers earn pennies for drugs that sell for hundreds of dollars on the streets of Los Angeles and New York, we may safely assume that drugs would be vastly cheaper under legalization. And that, proponents pointed out, would reduce drug-related crimes dramatically. When, for example, was the last time you heard of a gang killing connected with the distribution of cigarettes or alcoholic beverages?

The argument against legalization of drugs is largely moral: Should the state sanction potential lethal substances? But there is also an economic aspect. The vastly lower street prices of drugs that would increase drug use. Thus, while legalization would almost certainly reduce crime, it would also produce more addicts. The key question here-to which no one has a good answer-is: How many more addicts? If you think the increase in quantity demanded would be large, you are unlikely to find legalization an attractive option.

Economists put it this way. Free markets are capable of dealing with the three basic coordination tasks: deciding *what* to produce, *how* to produce it, and *to whom* the goods should be distributed. Price controls throw a monkey wrench into the market mechanism. Though the market is surely not flawless, and government interferences often have praiseworthy goals, good intentions are not enough. Any government that sets out to repair what it sees as a defect in the market mechanism must take care lest it cause even more serious damage elsewhere. As a prominent economist once quipped, societies that are too willing to interfere with the operation of free markets soon find that the invisible hand is nowhere to be seen-a point that the formerly communist nations grew to understand in a very painful way.

A Simple But Powerful Lesson

The lessons you have learned in this chapter may seem elementary, even obvious. In many respects, they are. But they are also very important, indeed, indispensable. Although the law of supply and demand is one of the simplest principles in economics, it is also one of the most powerful. Astonishing as it may seem, many people in authority, even highly intelligent people, fail to understand the law of supply and demand or cannot apply it to concrete situations.

For example, a few years ago the *New York Times* carried a dramatic front page picture of the president of Kenya setting fire to a large pile of elephant tusks that had been confiscated from poachers. The accompanying story explained that the burning was intended as a symbolic act to persuade the world to halt the ivory trade.[4] Economists claim no expertise on the likely psychological effect of burning elephant tusks, though one may doubt that it touched the hearts of criminal poachers. However, one economic effect was clear. By reducing the supply of ivory on the world market, the burning of tusks forced up the price of ivory, which raised the illicit rewards reaped by those who slaughter elephants. That could only encourage more poaching-precisely the opposite of what the Kenyan government sought to accomplish.

[4]The *New York Times*, July 19, 1989.

FIGURE 5-3

Dealing with the Surplus

This graph illustrates two of many approaches open to a government that has legislated an above-equilibrium minimum price (here of $3 per bushel) and has to deal with the ensuing surplus problem as well. First, as pane (a) demonstrates, regular consumers can buy whatever they are willing to take at the minimum price (point *a*). Subsequently, the government can use the taxpayers' money to buy up the surplus (*ab*). In this example, regular consumers end up spending $1,500 million per year (shaded area) and the government spends an additional $3,000 million per year (crosshatched area).

Second, as panel (b) demonstrates regular consumers can be given the *entire* crop (*de*), which farmers supply when promised the "target" price of $3 per bushel. As point *f* indicates, these consumers will buy that crop, but only for $1 per bushel. Subsequently, the government can use the taxpayers' money to pay farmers a subsidy equal to the difference between the promised "target" price of $3 and the realize market price of $1. In this example, regular consumers end up spending $1,500 million per year (shaded area), and the government spends another $3,000 million per year (crosshatched area).

Note: It is only a coincidence that the shaded areas in the two panels and the cross-hatched areas in the two panels and the crosshatched areas in the two panels are equal to each other.

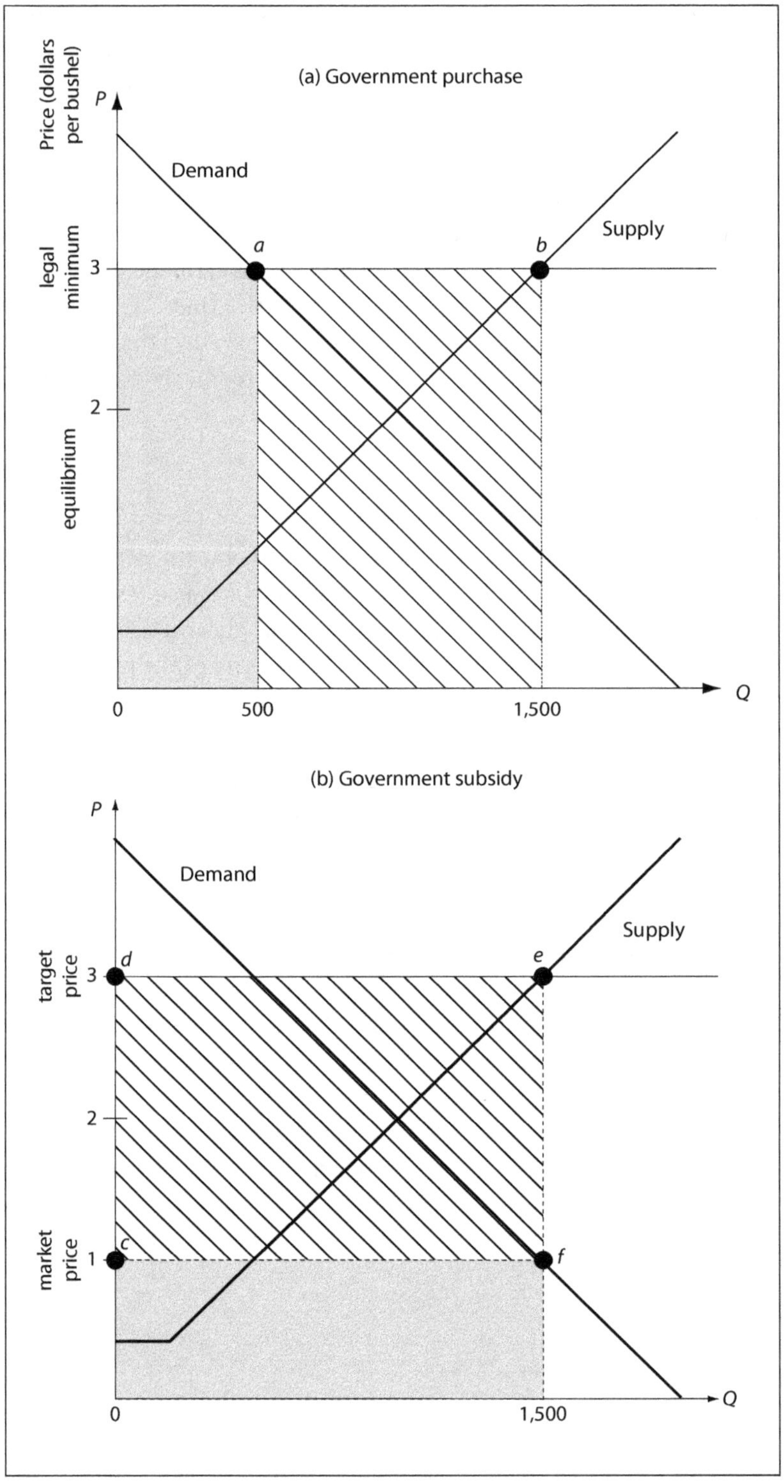

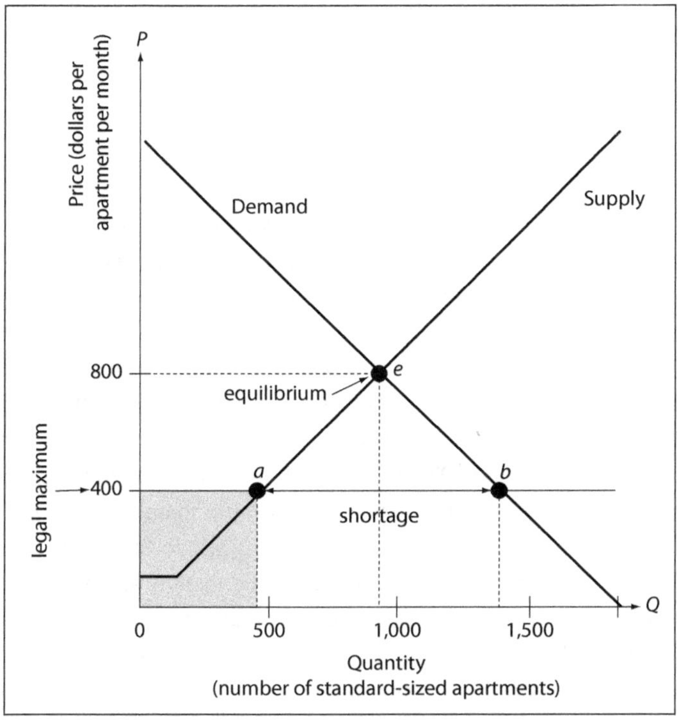

FIGURE 5-4

Setting a Maximum Price for Apartment Rental

In this apartment-rental market, free competition among sellers or buyers would establish an equilibrium at *e*, corresponding to a monthly rent of $800 per apartment and the renting of 1,000 apartments. If government, however, intervenes by setting a legal maximum rent of $400, a shortage of *ab* emerges. As price falls from the equilibrium level to the legal maximum, quantity demanded increases along *eb* while quantity supplied decreases along *ea*. A shortage of ab emerges. In this example, only 500 apartments are actually rented, for a total monthly payment of $400 per apartment times 500 apartments, or $200,000 (shaded). Yet would-be renters of another 1,000 apartments (distance ab) fail to find any that are available. To them the low rent is nothing but a cruel mockery.

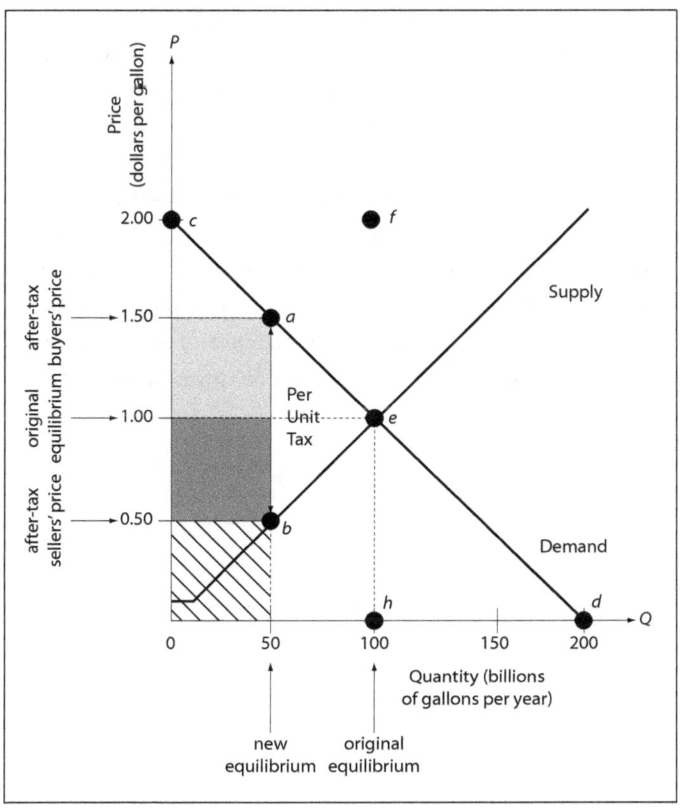

FIGURE 5-5

Imposing an Excise Tax on Gasoline

Equilibrium occurs at e, corresponding to a price of $1 per gallon per year. If government intervenes by imposing an excise tax of $1 per gallon, a $1 wedge appears between the price buyers pay (point a) and the price sellers ultimately receive (point b). A new and lower equilibrium quantity emerges (corresponding to the location of the wedge).

In this example, buyers ultimately pay $1.50 per gallon times 50 billion gallons, or $75 billion per year (the sum of the shaded plus dotted plus crosshatched areas). Sellers pass on to the government $1 per gallon times 50 billion gallons, or $50 billion per year (the sum of the shaded plus dotted areas). Thus the sellers' after-tax receipts only equal 50¢ per gallon times 50 billion gallons, or $25 billion per year (the crosshatched area). Compared to the original equilibrium price, buyers pay 50¢ more per gallon; sellers get 50¢ less. Thus, the tax burden, by coincidence, is equally shared.

Example 1

THE STORY OF RENT CONTROL

The story depicted by Figure 11 has been confirmed by the experience of renters in many cities throughout the world. In the United States, rent control was introduced in New York in 1943 and has since spread to many other cities, ranging from Boston and Washington, D.C., to Los Angeles and San Francisco, and to well over 200 smaller towns. At the time of their enactment, rent-control laws are typically justified as a long-overdue means of putting greedy, villainous landlords in their place and of helping their innocent, overcharged victims.

Inevitably, the kind of shortage depicted by distance *ab* in Figure 11 develops and tends to grow worse over time. The short-run decrease in quantity supplied (along *ea*) as landlords quickly convert rent-controlled apartments to uncontrolled office space, private condominiums, and similar alternative uses is followed by decreases in long-run supply (not shown in Figure 11). Such a leftward shift of the entire supply line occurs when new construction comes to a halt and existing rental units disappear. At first, landlords skimp on maintenance as their profits are squeezed between fixed revenues and rising costs. A vicious circle is set up. Poor maintenance of electrical wiring turns buildings into firetraps and causes accidents, so insurance rates go up. So do city taxes for fire protection. Lack of janitorial services forces people to share water facilities. Before long, tenants end up living in vermin-infested, badly ventilated quarters. Children get lead poisoning from eating peeling paint. Everyone gets sick from breathing garbage processed by inefficient incinerators. Everyone freezes in winter when old furnaces break down and go untended. In anger, residents turn to vandalism. Insurance rates go up some more, as do city taxes for police protection.

Eventually, the rental units become so dilapidated as to be unlivable. Finally, instead of paying taxes on useless buildings, landlords abandon them, as happened to 200,000 units in New York between 1965 and 1975. In due time, most abandoned buildings fall victim to vandals who strip them of heating, plumbing, electrical installations, windows, paneling, flooring, and stairways. Before long, they are littered with garbage, blackened by arsonists, and damaged beyond repair. The charred rubble becomes inhabited by homeless people. Thus entire slums are born, and what remains are eyesores and threats to public health and safety.

In the meantime, a black market develops in which people on waiting lists attempt to acquire scarce rental units at above-ceiling prices. A million different methods are in common use. They range from outright bribes to paying "key money" to requiring any new tenant to buy worthless furniture at incredibly inflated prices.

As with so many price-fixing programs, there is no certainty that this program truly helps the poor. In New York City, for example, many tenants in rent-controlled apartments (who recently paid a median rent of $330 a month) are middle and upper income families. Many landlords are small investors of moderate income.

DISCUSSION QUESTIONS

Farm Subsidies / Agricultural Price Supports

By David Moglen

Read the two article excerpts below and answer the questions that follow.

From page two of "Cornucopia Blues" by Brent Cunningham, online at http://www.thenation.com/article/cornucopia-blues:

"In *Enough*, Thurow and Kilman relay an anecdote about Ethiopia during the 2003 famine that shows the grim consequences of the Iron Triangle's stranglehold on food aid. As trucks laden with 1 million tons of US corn, wheat, peas, beans and lentils rolled into Nazareth, a city of around 230,000 people in central Ethiopia, they passed warehouses stuffed with 100,000 metric tons of Ethiopian grains, beans and peas—the surplus from a bumper crop two years earlier that had failed to sell when prices collapsed. (Here again was the legacy of structural adjustment: the dearth of storage facilities meant that farmers had no choice but to dump their grain on the market at the same time; and the stunted internal markets and an ancient transportation network that still relied heavily on donkeys meant that there was no way to move the glut of grain to the parts of the country that needed it.) The market was undermined further by the arrival of international food aid. "American farmers have a market in Ethiopia, but we don't have a market in Ethiopia," huffed Kadir Geleto, who managed a grain-trading operation in Nazareth."

Geleto understood that Ethiopian-grown grain alone couldn't feed the hungry when the rains failed, but he also knew that the deluge of American food aid had created a cycle of dependency that sapped the incentive of many of his countrymen to work to feed their families. Why, Geleto wondered, didn't America provide cash aid to buy up the local surplus and then send food aid to cover the rest of the shortage?

During the 2003 famine, Andrew Natsios, the administrator of the US Agency for International Development, asked the same question. He knew that if he had the flexibility to buy surplus grain in Ethiopia, food aid would be cheaper and made available to the hungry faster than food shipped from the United States. As Thurow and Kilman write in Enough, Natsios also knew that the Iron Triangle had consistently quashed efforts to allow for such flexibility in American food policy. But by 2005, with the reverberations from the 2003 famine keeping world leaders nominally focused on ending hunger in Africa, Natsios convinced President Bush that "reforming the...food-aid program would complement his initiative to end famine in the Horn of Africa." Bush's budget that year included a proposal that one-quarter of the $1.2 billion in food-aid money be used to buy African crops. But when Natsios presented the idea in April of that year to the annual food-aid industry conference in Kansas City, he was nearly run out of town. Robert Zachritz of World Vision, a Christian aid group, described the reception Natsios received as "hostile." The law governing food aid didn't change. As Ó Gráda notes in Famine, "Public Law 480 has allowed U.S. food producers to match philanthropy with self-interest for over half a century."

1. What does the author mean when he links these problems to "structural adjustment"?
2. What happened when Mr. Nastios said that farm subsidies would be better spent buying from Ethiopian rather than American farmers?
3. Can you guess what might explain this reaction?

From "Another Year at the Federal Trough: Farm Subsidies for the Rich, Famous, and Elected

IN-CLASS PROJECT

Price Controls

By David Moglen

Directions

You will be given a group number from 1–3. Answer the corresponding questions. Your fully labeled graphs should have the name of the market at the top and axes labeled specifically to that good or service, complete with relevant units on the Price and Quantity axes as well as a time period on the Quantity axis.. You need to make up numbers for equilibrium (point A) in addition to points B and possibly a point C if any of those numbers are not given.

1. Draw graph showing a quota of 7 million foreign-made cars per year when the equilibrium is 14 million auto imports per year. (Graph)

Categorize as winners or losers from the quota policy each of the following groups: consumers, domestic producers, foreign producers able to sell under the quota, the government (budgetary impact), and foreign producers unable to sell under the quota. Explain why each is in that category.(List)

*Why might this policy succeed; in other words, why might the "winners" beat the "losers" in getting this policy implemented and upheld? Mention the governing body who passes the law; what is that federal, state, or local government body called, where certain elected officials gathered in a room to pass this law? Now what exactly, in detail, is going on during the one-month period these lawmakers are considering a law that would require this price control. Describe as many activities as you can for what the winners will do to try to get the price control passed, so they can win, and what, if anything the losers do to counter-act this and fight for their goals. If you say the losers do nothing then explain why.(3-7 sentences)

2. Graph a subsidy to stabilize farmers' incomes by creating a binding price floor of $700 per ton of soybeans when equilibrium price is $400 per ton. (Graph)

Categorize as winners or losers from the price control policy each of the following groups: consumers, producers, foreign farmers whose countries receive the distributed excess output, and the government (budgetary impact). Explain why each is in that category. (List)

*Why might this policy succeed; in other words, why might the "winners" beat the "losers" in getting this policy implemented and upheld? Mention the governing body who passes the law; what is that federal, state, or local government body called, where certain elected officials gathered in a room to pass this law? Now what exactly, in detail, is going on during the one-month period these lawmakers are considering a law that would require this price control. Describe as many activities as you can for what the winners will do to try to get the price control passed, so they can win, and what, if anything the losers do to counter-act this and fight for their goals. If you say the losers do nothing then explain why. (3-7 sentences)

3. Graph the market for Berkeley two-bedroom apartment units when equilibrium is $1,900 per month and the rent control limit is $900 per month. At the equilibrium rental price, 300,000 units are rented. Assume one renter per unit. (Graph)

Categorize as winners or losers from the price control policy each of the following groups: current renters, potential renters (in the long run), landlords, and the government (budgetary impact). Explain why each is in that category.

(List)

*Why might this policy succeed; in other words, why might the "winners" beat the "losers" in getting this policy implemented and upheld? Mention the governing body who passes the law; what is that federal, state, or local government body called, where certain elected officials gathered in a room to pass this law? Now what exactly, in detail, is going on during the one-month period these lawmakers are considering a law that would require this price control. Describe as many activities as you can for what the winners will do to try to get the price control passed, so they can win, and what, if anything the losers do to counter-act this and fight for their goals. If you say the losers do nothing then explain why. (3–7 sentences)

4. Draw the same market described in Question 1, with the same starting and ending quantities, but instead of a quota causing the change from A to B, make it a $7,500 tariff on imported cars that causes the change.

5. Draw the market for H1-B (high-skilled foreign) workers when the number of H1-B visas is controlled by a quota system that begins at 65,000 per year and then increase to 120,000 per year. Both these numbers are quota quantities – the number of visas for the year. You need to make up numbers for equilibrium (point A) in addition to points B and C. All these points should have vertical and horizontal numerical values clearly shown.

Who are the primary winners and losers in this situation, and why?

6. Show a Third-Party payer market where the surgery is costing patients $150 while the total payment to the hospital for the surgery (including payment to the doctor and all other staff) is $1,000. Who pays the third-party payment in this market?

UNLOCKING THE MYSTERIES

Rent Control

By David Moglen

Mystery #1: How do landlords reduce the number of units rented out?

Take a look at this model below of a $700 rent control in Boston, Massachusetts, when the free market rental rate would have been $1,200.

Remember, renters are the demand and landlords are the supply. Notice this graph includes a line labeled SSR, or short run supply. Short run supply is vertical at the equilibrium quantity of two million units rented out at point A. Imagine that the city of Boston has just yesterday implemented rent-control, so you are still in the short run. While we know from where the $700 rent control price meets their SLR that landlords want to reduce the number of apartment units they provide to 1.3 million, in the short run they have to continue renting the same two million units to their current renters.

Why can't landlords immediately kick out 700,000 renters and get down to suppliers' ideal quantity of 1.3 million?

Think about it for a minute.

There are laws against evicting someone who has been on time with their rent. Even someone who missed their payment can't be kicked out the next day. Renters are on a lease, and while some leases will run out within the month, others may take about a full year for their lease to run out. Then, after a year, you are in the long run in this market and the landlords can reduce the number of units they rent out and force the 700,000 renters between Qs and Qe to go look for somewhere else to live.

While they can't reduce supply in the short run, how do the landlords reduce their units in the short run? In the graph, how do they go from point b' on their short run supply curve to point b on the long run supply curve?

A lot of these options for the landlords rely on whether the rent control law, and other city laws allow them. If there are no loopholes, and the landlord has no other options, they will most likely pursue the last choice on the list.

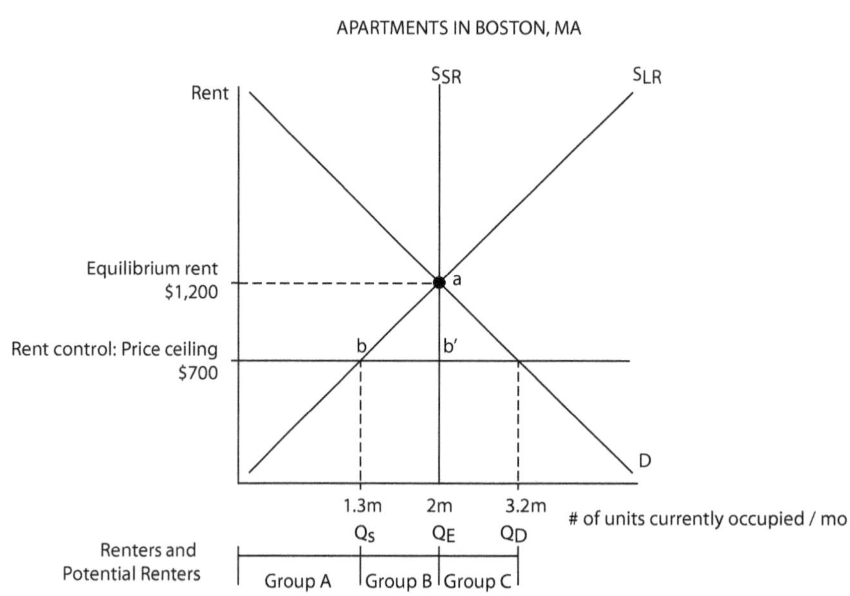

a. Convert to condominiums: a condo is simply their apartment unit sold off like a house or any other real estate. They have removed the 700,000 units from the market because they are not being rented out anymore because they have sold it to an owner-occupant.
b. Convert to luxury or furnished apartment.
c. Rezone property to business or mixed-use.
d. Abandon property, provide zero maintenance, and let it become a slum. Renters or squatters may remain there until city building inspectors condemn the property and remove any people inside.

Mystery #2: Alternative allocative mechanisms

Had Boston apartments been left to the free market, the price system would have determined who will get to buy this good. You would be at point A, with two million units rented at the price of $1,200. In other words, whoever had the money and was willing to rent would have gotten a unit.

Under rent control, not everyone willing to pay the $700 rent gets a unit. In fact, 3.2 million wish to rent and only 1.3 million actually get a place. So it is not the price system determining who gets what; price controls require an Alternative Allocative Mechanism:

a. Lottery
b. Waiting in line/first come, first served
c. Rationing
d. Seller's Preference

Mystery #3: Renter's who lose their apartment—are they for or against rent control?

If rent control leads to a shortage, and many renters eventually lose their homes, why do the renters support and even aggressively advocate for such a law?

If the renter is in the group who gets to keep their apartment and just pay the decreased rent, of course they are in favor of rent control. But what about the renters in the graph who lose their apartment due to the landlord converting it to a condo or leaving it without maintenance, abandoning the property for city building inspector to condemn and expel any squatters or remaining renters? Why would the person who loses their place to live advocate for the very rent control law that caused their effective eviction?

The answer primarily is that before the law is passed and leases have time to expire/abandoned buildings have time to become blighted, individual renters don't know if they are in the lucky group who gets to stay in their place with lower rent (Group A in the graph), or the unlucky group who loses their apartment (Group B). Everyone hears there is a possibility of a law mandating lower rent, and thinks they will benefit. Refer to Mystery 1, above; all renters continue to think they will be winners until a year passes.

Another reason most renters will support rent control proposals are the normative aspects. In Berkeley, rent control can be rationalized as essential for students and employees of UC Berkeley. In New York City and San Francisco, the argument can be made that maintaining an artistic population rather than being a white collar, Wall Street-only city requires some relief from the city's unaffordable rents. At many mobile-home parks, space rentals are rent-controlled in the interest of the mostly elderly and/or low-income residents.

Directions

Break into your small groups. Whichever group finishes all questions with 100% accuracy gets bonus points but must, when asked by the teacher, write out how you got your answer on the board for the class.

1. There is rent control. Demand decreases. Will the shortage increase or decrease?
2. There is rent control. The price ceiling decreases. Will the shortage increase or decrease?
3. There is an agricultural price support (Price Floor) for wheat. Supply decreases. Will the surplus increase or decrease?
4. There is an agricultural price support (Price Floor) for wheat. The price floor decreases. Will the surplus increase or decrease?

UNLOCKING THE MYSTERIES

Minimum Wage

By David Moglen

Minimum wage is a price control; specifically, as a wage floor, it should be modeled the same way as a price floor. As we know from the price floor example in the chapter, price floors cause a surplus. The market we are analyzing with a minimum wage is the Labor Market. So basic theory says a surplus will occur, which in the Labor Market is called unemployment. Supply of workers exceeds businesses' demand at the artificially high wage. While there is debate among economists as to whether there are any unemployment effects of miniumum wage,[1] part of the lack of an effect is readily apparent: how can changing the minimum wage from, say, $6.55 to $7.25 (the most recent increase) have any direct effect on a doctor making $200 per hour, or a mechanic making $50 per hour, or a factory worker making $15 per hour? In other words, it is a non-binding price control for most workers.

In the Labor market, the horizontal (quantity) axis is labeled L for number of workers, and the vertical (price) axis is labeled Wage. For a realistic equilibrium quantity (where number of workers the labor force supplies equals the number businesses demand-in other words, the intersection of supply and demand) we'll estimate L=150 million.

What should be our estimate for the equilibrium wage, in other words, the vertical measure of point A, equilibrium, where supply and demand cross? What is a wage that represents all 150 million workers in the economy, when some are paid very little, others get incredibly high salaries, and everyone else is somewhere in between? The wage that would represent all workers is the *average* hourly wage. It's been about $19 per hour in the most recent data.[2] So our estimate of equilibrium wage on the vertical axis reads $19. (*see* Panel A)

Now let's draw the minimum wage: a binding price floor at $7.25 per hour. Do you notice anything wrong with this picture? (*see* Panel B)

Right! The only way to draw a binding price floor—one that will have any impact of number of workers employed or their wage, is to draw it above equilibirum wage. But $7.25 is not above $19. For this market showing *all* U.S. workers, the horizontal price floor/ minimum wage line would have to be drawn well below equilibrium–a non-binding price floor.

Panel A

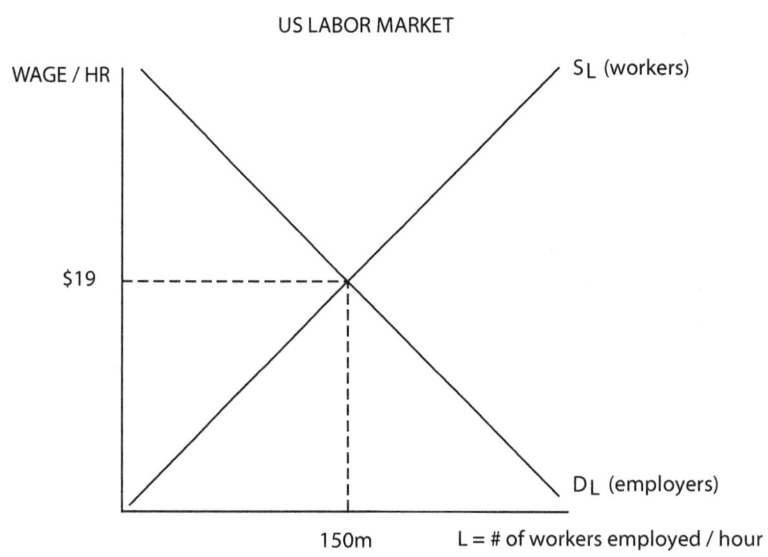

The only way to have a market where a minimum wage of $7.25 would have any impact is if we remove from the picture almost all workers, and leave in only the entry-level/ unskilled workforce. Now we have a model that at least makes sense when it says minimum wage causes unemployment, at least for this limited category of workers. We can leave it to economists to debate whether minimum wage induces unemployment for even the entry-level workers.[3] (*see* Panel C)

Panel B

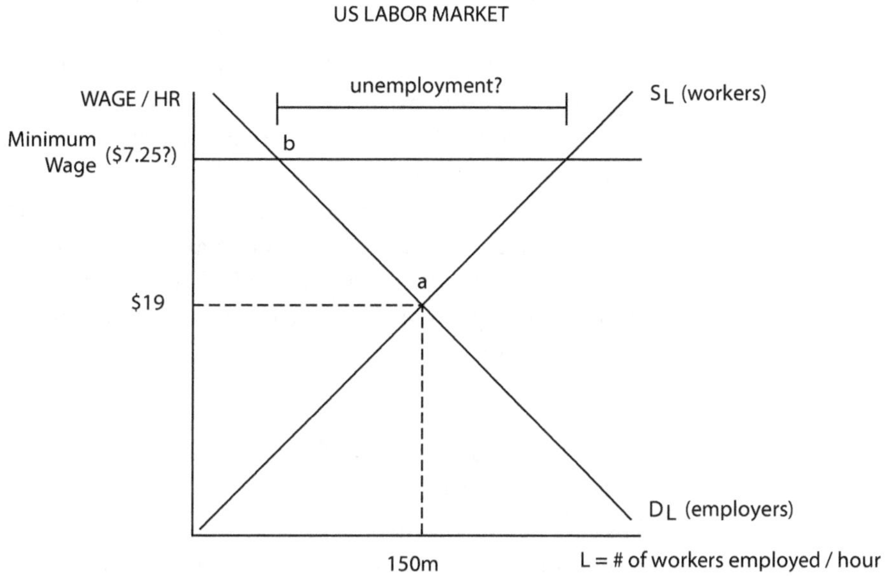

Panel C

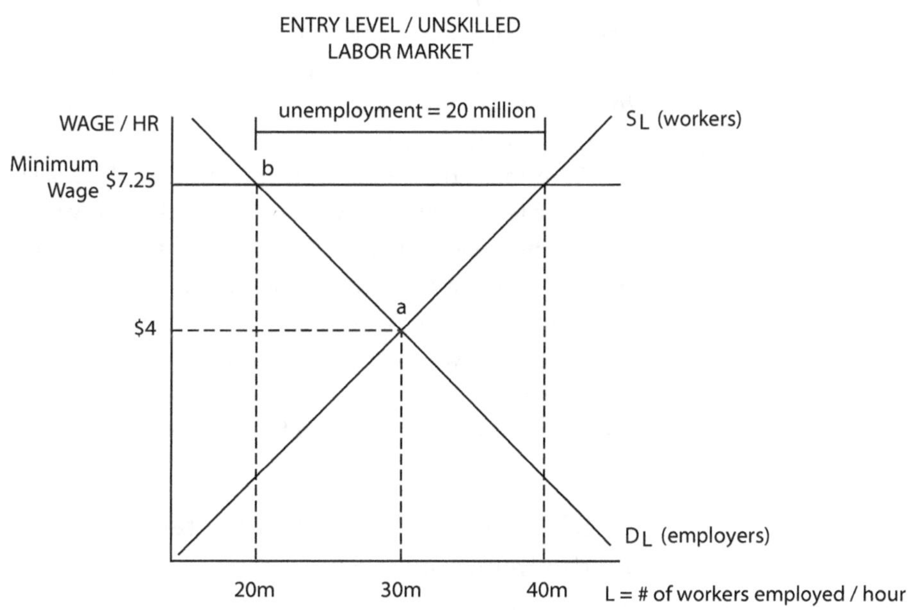

[1] http://en.wikipedia.org/wiki/minimum_wage.
[2] http://www.bls.gov/news.release/empsit.t24.htm
[3] http://en.wikipedia.org/wiki/minimum_wage.

The Minimum Wage

The Fair Labor Standards Act of 1938 set a minimum wage of 25 cents an hour, covering 43% of the nonagricultural labor force. By early 1989, the minimum wage had been increased 13 times, and its coverage more than doubled. Some workers do not receive the minimum wage because their industries are still not included; even in those that are, some firms do not comply with this law, because there are inadequate penalties for breaking it. By 1989, the minimum wage had become a heated issue because it had not been raised since 1981 and had therefore been eroded by inflation. It was still $3.35 an hour, even though the average U.S. wage had increased by more than 32%, from $7.25 to $9.60. Congress wanted the rate raised to $4.55 to compensate for inflation. President Bush opposed any increase above $4.25.

To analyze the minimum wage in the United States where some industries are covered by it and some are not, consider two cases. (1) Suppose the minimum wage is applied to only one industry; and (2) suppose it is applied to all industries. The U.S. economy is between these two polar cases.

CASE 1: Only One Industry is Covered by the Minimum Wage

This case can be described in panel *c* Unlocking the Mysteries: Minimum Wage. Suppose that there is initially a perfectly competitive, free-market wage of W_1, where supply equals demand for labor. Then the government imposes a minimum wage W_3, above W_1. Because of the higher wage, employers hire fewer workers. Equilibrium moves back up the demand curve from E_1 to E_3, with the number of workers employed falling from N_1 to N_3. As a result, there is the red efficiency loss because too few workers are hired in this industry.

Why then does the government introduce this policy? The answer is to provide a fairer, equitable wage and thus help to solve the poverty problem. In fact, this policy can indeed be expected to redistribute income, but not necessarily in the way intended, since some workers lose while others gain. The winners are the N_3 workers who still have a job in this industry and who enjoy a wage increase from W_1 to W_3. The losers are the N_3N_1 workers who lose their jobs in this industry or are not hired in the first place. They are left in lower productivity jobs paying lower wages elsewhere.

CASE 2: All Industries Are Covered by the Minimum Wage

The result in this case is the same in many respects. The winners are those who retain their jobs, where—as the losers are those who do not. There is now one important difference, however. Those who lose their jobs do not get jobs elsewhere. Because the whole economy is covered, there are no other jobs for them to get. Because they become unemployed, they lose far more than they do in case 1. Moreover, the overall efficiency loss to the economy is greater because their lost output is no longer partially offset by their output in other, lower productivity jobs. They don't get another job. The result is a large gap between the income of those who still have a job (whose wage has increased) and those who no longer have a job (whose wage has disappeared).

Since much, but not all, of U.S. employment is subject to the minimum wage, the world in which we live lies somewhere between case 1 and case 2. It is likely that some workers who lose their jobs because of a minimum wage will get lower productivity jobs elsewhere, but some will not. For those who obtain jobs elsewhere, there is an efficiency loss because they produce less. For those who remain unemployed, there is an even greater efficiency loss because they produce nothing.

THE MINIMUM WAGE AND TEENAGE UNEMPLOYMENT

Who are the workers who lose their jobs? The answer is often teenagers. Because they lack work experience and seniority, they tend to be the "last hired, first fired." Consequently, their unemployment rate is more than double the national average. *Minority* teenagers get the worst of both worlds; their unemployment rate is more than four times the national average. The University of Michigan's Charles Brown estimates that an increase in the minimum wage to $4.55 would result in 150,000 fewer jobs for teenagers over three years, with black teenagers suffering most.

One way to reduce the teenage unemployment problem is to institute a "two-tiered system," with a lower minimum wage for teenagers than for adults. Numerous such proposals have come before Congress. Indeed, since 1961 employers in higher education, retailing, and other services have been allowed to pay students 15% less than the minimum wage for part-time or summer work.[5] In 1989, President Bush proposed a lower minimum wage for new workers—many of whom are teenagers—during a six-month training period. Such proposals for a two-tiered minimum wage have been opposed by labor unions on the grounds that they are not fair. Employers might lay off adults with families to support in order to hire teenagers at a lower wage.

THE MINIMUM WAGE: Concluding Observation

The minimum wage can affect not only the wage of the unskilled, but it can also have a "ripple effect" in raising the wage of skilled workers who are above the minimum. The reason is that employers have sometimes regarded it as only fair to maintain a gap between the two wage levels, and workers have tried hard to maintain this gap by bargaining for increases in skilled wages whenever the minimum wage has been increased.

On the other hand, there are several reasons for believing that the minimum wage is less important than is often supposed.

1. *It has not been very effective in reducing inequality.* The reason is that it has raised the income, not just of the working poor, but of the non-poor as well. One estimate indicates that less than 20% of the benefits from an increased minimum wage would go to households living below the poverty line for a family of four. At the same time, over 60% of the benefits would go to households with incomes at least double the poverty level. (In many such cases, it would be teenage children still holding jobs who would benefit.)
2. *The minimum wage may* be less *damaging to efficiency than Figure* 21-6*c suggests.* It is true that, in perfect competition, the minimum wage does lead to the efficiency loss shown in that diagram. However, in the imperfectly competitive labor markets, it may lead to an efficiency gain.
3. *There are fewer clear winners and clear losers than the standard analysis implies.* It is frequently difficult to distinguish between the winners who get the minimum wage jobs and the losers who do, not. The reason is that, in minimum wage jobs, there is a high turnover rate (according to one estimate, over 12% *per month).* Therefore workers share these jobs to some extent. Accordingly, many individuals are both part-time winners (when they have one of the minimum wage jobs) *and* part-time losers (when they do not). This means that the concern about clear losers who end up without any jobs at all is sometimes exaggerated. It also means that there are fewer clear winners. Moreover, even for a "winner" who still has a job and has gotten a wage increase, part of this increase may be an illusion if employers who have to pay the higher wage cover this additional cost by cutting back or other benefits to labor such as on-the-job training.

Summary

This chapter covers price controls and the more accurately described situations that take a market away from the free market equilibrium outcome. For the most part, the government is the force capable of mandating a price and quantity far different from what the market is naturally gravitating towards (equilibrium price and equilibrium quantity). However, in the case of the third-party payer markets. The cause of the non-equilibrium result can be a corporate policy as well. Inefficiencies can be seen in the graph and found in many other real-world, often unintended consequences of these policies

Vocabulary Terms

Alternative allocative Methods
Copayment
Price Ceiling
Price Floor
Protectionism
Quota
Rent Control
Shortage

Subsidy

Surplus

Tariff

Third-Party Payer Market

Review Questions

1. Summarize what you think are the feelings of Ethiopian farmers on subsidized crops from the rich countries after reading the Discussion Questions on Farm Subsidies in this chapter.
2. What do alternative allocative methods do? Name five of them. Which of these would you recommend for rent control, and why? Which of these would you recommend (and why) for the distribution of a limited number of import quotas?
3. What are the arguments for and against minimum wage? What is the key insight communicated by Panels A, B and C in the minimum wage section?

IN-CLASS PROJECT

Immigrant Labor Market

By David Moglen

This project further applies your skills with price controls by taking the market for (legal and illegal) immigrant labor as an example of a market with both a quota (the limited number of immigration visas) and a minimum wage that is actually a binding price floor.

Notice the market is specified as entry-level immigrant labor. Highly-skilled or moderately skilled workers are not subject to a binding minimum wage, as explained the Unlocking the Mysteries: Minimum Wage feature.

Directions:

Everyone should answer all four questions.

1. If the visa quota and the minimum wage are both enforced, what is the wage and number of workers employed?
2. If only the visa quota is enforced, what is the wage and number of workers employed?
3. If only the minimum wage is enforced, what is the wage and number of workers employed?
4. If neither visa quota nor minimum wage are enforced, what is the wage and number of workers employed?

Legal and Illegal Entry Level Immigrant Labor Market

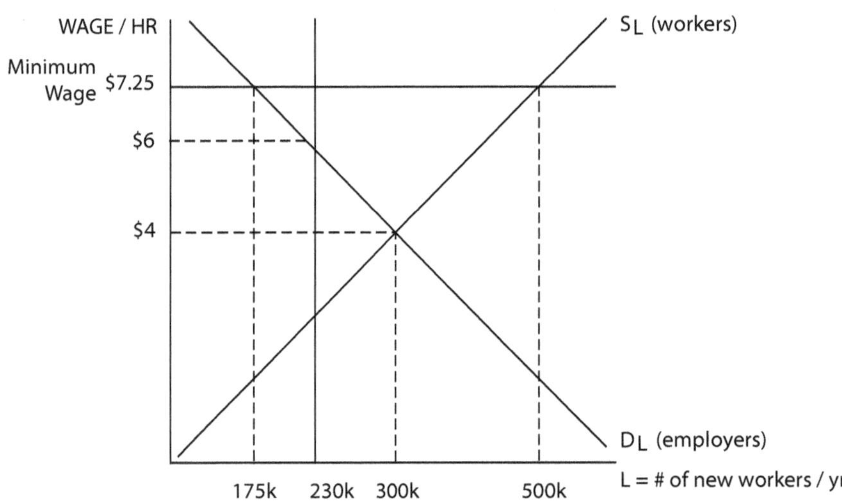

CHAPTER 6
Elasticity

6 Elasticity

By Timothy Taylor

A demand curve shows that a higher price will lead to a lower quantity demanded. But how much lower? A supply curve shows that a higher price will lead to a higher quantity supplied. But how much higher?

Whether a change in price will affect quantity demanded or quantity supplied by a relatively large or a small amount, often has real practical significance. For example, the typical U.S. state imposed a tax of $1 per pack of cigarettes at the start of 2008, and in 2009 the federal tax on cigarettes was raised to $1 per pack. Taxes on cigarettes serve two purposes: to raise tax revenue for government and to discourage consumption of cigarettes. But if a higher cigarette tax discourages cigarette consumption by quite a lot, then because a greatly reduced quantity of cigarettes is sold, the cigarette tax on each pack won't raise much revenue for the government. Alternatively, a higher cigarette tax that doesn't discourage cigarette consumption by much will actually raise more tax revenue for the government. Thus, when a government agency tries to calculate the effects of altering its cigarette tax, it must analyze how much the tax affects the quantity of cigarettes consumed.

This issue reaches beyond governments and taxes; every firm faces a similar issue. Every time a firm considers raising the price that it charges, it must consider how much a price increase will reduce the quantity demanded of what it sells. Conversely, when a firm offers a special reduction in sales price, it must expect (or hope) that the lower price will lead to a higher quantity demanded of its product.

This chapter introduces the concept of **elasticity**, which measures how much a percentage change in price leads to a percentage change in quantity demanded or quantity supplied. The chapter begins with the price elasticity of demand, which looks at the responsiveness of quantity demanded to a change in price, and then examines the price elasticity of supply, which looks at the responsiveness of quantity supplied to a change in price. The concept of elasticity is then applied to a number of real-world situations, including ticket prices at concerts, cigarette taxes, airline ticket prices, changes in world oil prices, and others.

elasticity:
How much a percentage change in price leads to a percentage change in quantity demanded or quantity supplied.

Exhibit 6-1 Same Data for Demand Curve, Different Appearance

These two demand curves present exactly the same data on price and quantity. The only difference is that (a) is drawn with the vertical axis relatively long, while (b) is drawn with the horizontal axis relatively long. Both demand curves still slope down, but whether the slope appears steep or flat is determined by how the curve is drawn, not by the data.

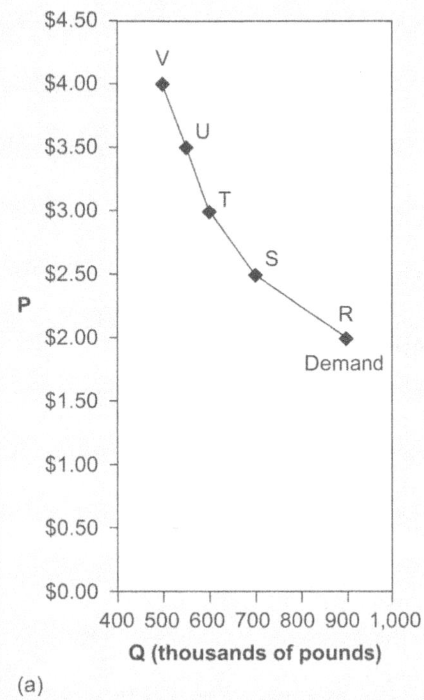

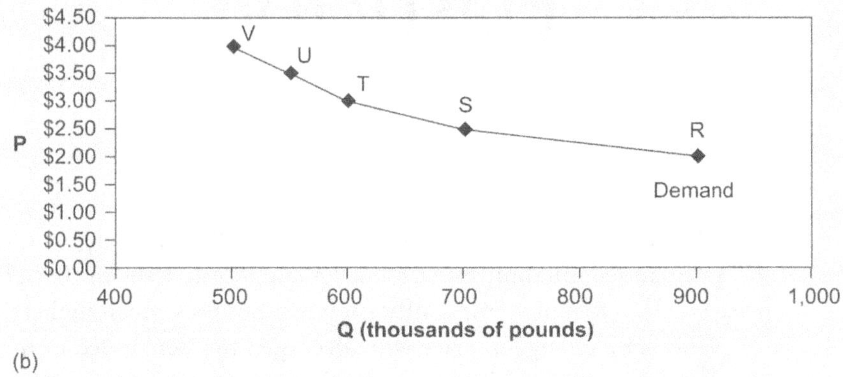

Price per Pound	Quantity Demanded in Pounds
$2.00	900,000
$2.50	700,000
$3.00	600,000
$3.50	550,000
$4.00	500,000

Price Elasticity of Demand

When investigating how sensitive the quantity demanded is to a change in price, looking at the demand curve might seem like an obvious starting point. But the visual appearance of demand curves can be misleading. Exhibit 6-1 illustrates the problem. The data on price and quantity demanded of cheese for Exhibit 6-1a and 6-1b is identical. But in Exhibit 6-1a, the demand curve for cheese is graphed with a tall vertical axis and narrow horizontal axis, so that the demand curve appears to slope down steeply. In Exhibit 6-1b, the identical data is graphed with a short vertical axis and a wide horizontal axis, so that the demand curve appears to slope down in a relatively flat way. Remember, the data behind these two demand curves is exactly the same! In both Exhibit 6-1a and 6-1b, the demand curve slopes down, but should the shape of the demand curve for cheese be described as "steep" or "flat"? Answering this question with "it depends on how you draw it" is not very useful.

The vocabulary of elasticity offers a method of discussing how quantity demanded responds to changes in price that doesn't depend on whether the axes are drawn relatively longer or shorter. It doesn't even depend on what units are used to measure price and quantity. Instead of trying to discuss the steepness or flatness of supply and demand curves based on their visual appearance, which can be misleading, elasticity discusses the shape of demand and supply curves with numerical calculations of percentage changes.

CALCULATING THE ELASTICITY OF DEMAND

The numerical example of a demand curve D for small television sets presented in Exhibit 6-2 can help to illustrate the issues. In this case, this demand curve for small television sets is a straight line. Let's calculate the elasticity from G to H. [. . .]

$$\frac{[1{,}600 - 1{,}800] \,/\, [(1{,}600 + 1{,}800) \,/\, 2]}{[130 - 120] \,/\, [(130 + 120) \,/\, 2]} = \frac{-2/17}{2/25} = \frac{-0.1176}{0.08}$$

Therefore, the elasticity of demand from G to H is = –0.1176/0.08 = –1.47. An elasticity number is not followed by any units. Elasticity is a ratio of one percentage change to another percentage change—nothing more.

Calculations of elasticity are all arithmetic, so what is the intuitive meaning of the number that emerges from the calculation? Hark back to the original meaning of elasticity: that is, the change in quantity demanded that results from a percentage change in price. Thus, if the price started off at 65—midway between the price at points A and B in the example—then a 10% increase in price of small televisions would cause a 4.5% reduction in quantity demanded, or conversely, a 10% fall in price would cause a 4.5% increase in the quantity demanded of small televisions. However, if the price started off in the range between 120 and 130—that is, midway between prices at points G and H in the example—then a 10% percent increase in price would cause a 14.7% decline in quantity demanded of small televisions, or conversely, a 10% fall in price would cause a 14.7% rise in the quantity demanded.

The word "elasticity," in its everyday use, refers to stretchiness: more elastic stretches more, while less elastic stretches less. The elasticity of demand has the same general meaning, except that in this case the stretchiness refers to how much the quantity demanded stretches or contracts in response to a change in price. Exhibit 6-3 shows a selection of demand elasticities for different goods and services drawn from a variety of different studies by economists. A typical practice in these studies is to calculate the elasticity of demand using the current market equilibrium as the starting point.

Exhibit 6-2 Calculating the Price Elasticity of Demand

The price elasticity of demand is calculated as the percentage change in quantity divided by the percentage change in price. Between two points like A and B, or between G and H, the formula is:

$$\text{Elasticity} = \frac{\text{(change in quantity)/[(sum of the two quantities/2)]}}{\text{(change in price)/[(sum of prices/2)]}}$$

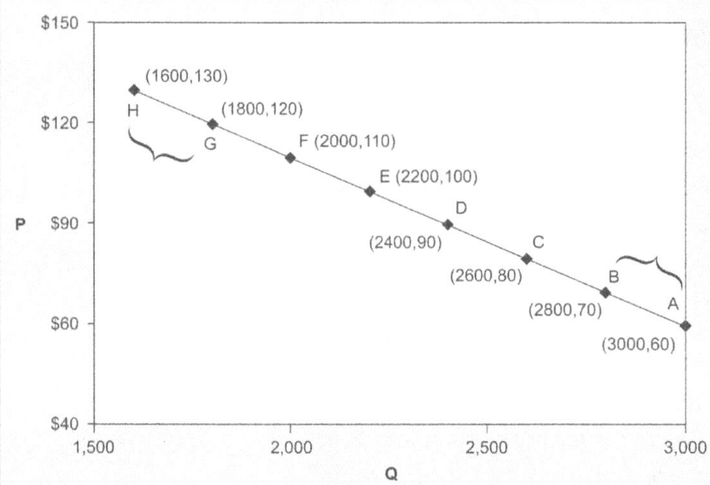

Points	P	Q
A	60	3,000
B	70	2,800
C	80	2,600
D	90	2,400
E	100	2,200
F	110	2,000
G	120	1,800
H	130	1,600

Elasticity in the Vending Machine

America has 1.5 million vending machines that sell snacks and candy. Tens of millions of Americans are overweight. Could vending machines be used to nudge people toward a healthier diet?

Several years ago, researchers in the School of Public Health at the University of Minnesota decided to study how to encourage people to eat low-fat snacks from vending machines, including low-fat pretzels, chips, cookies, candy, and fruit snacks. Working with a company that refills vending machines, they found 12 worksites and 12 schools to participate. At these vending machines, they offered a range of price cuts for low-fat snacks. On some of the machines, they also posted signs identifying the low-fat snacks and encouraging people to buy them.

The signs encouraging people to eat low-fat foods had little effect. But lower prices for low-fat snacks offered a real incentive. The study found that elasticity of demand for low-fat snacks is about 2. That is, a 10% cut in the price of low-fat snacks led to an increase of 20% in the quantity of such snacks consumed, and a 50% cut in the price of such snacks led to an increase of 100% in sales of low-fat snacks. As it turned out, the price cuts for low-fat snacks didn't even cause the average profits per vending machine to decline, because an increase in the volume sold was enough to compensate for the lower prices.

Clearing It Up: Elasticity Is Not Slope

Although the elasticity of a supply or demand curve is obviously related to the shape of the curve, it isn't the same as what the mathematicians call "slope." Not even close. Slope, you may remember from a high school mathematics class (or from the Appendix to Chapter 1), is rise divided by run (sometimes teachers say "rise over run"); that is, the change on the vertical axis (the rise) divided by the change on the horizontal axis (the run). This calculation differs from elasticity in two ways. First, elasticity is the change in what is on the horizontal axis (quantity) divided by the change in what is on the vertical axis (price). Thus, elasticity involves run/rise, not rise/run. Second, elasticity is the percentage change, which is a different calculation from slope. A straight line has only one slope, but as the example in the chapter shows, a straight-line demand curve has a different elasticity at every point.

A POSSIBLE CONFUSION, A CLARIFICATION, AND A WARNING

The most common confusion about elasticity is to think that it measures the slope of the demand curve. Elasticity is not the slope of the demand curve! The examples above have shown that whether a demand curve appears to have a steep or a flat slope depends on how it is drawn. Even when the demand curve is a straight line, with the same mathematical slope at all points, the elasticity will differ quite substantially in different parts of that line. The calculation of elasticity is based on percentage change, which is not the same as the calculation for slope.

Many students who are confronted with the elasticity formula wonder why, in the numerator and denominator, the formula divides by the average value of either the two quantities (in the numerator) or the two prices (in the denominator). The reason is to avoid a situation where in calculating the elasticity between points A and B, one person divides the change in quantity by the quantity level at A while another divides it by the quantity level at B—thus leading to two different answers for the same question. By using the average quantity and average price between A and B, this possible confusion is eliminated. At a more advanced level of economics, using the tools of calculus, elasticity can be calculated at a specific point—in which case the need to divide by the average quantity and price at two different points doesn't arise.

Exhibit 6-3 Some Selected Elasticities of Demand

Housing	0.12	Coal	0.66
Electricity	0.2	Soft drinks	0.70
Taxi cabs	0.22	Coffee	0.72
Gasoline	0.35	Beer	0.7 to 0.9
North Atlantic air travel (first class, business, economy)	0.4, 0.62, 0.12	New vehicle	0.87
Long-distance telephone	0.5	Intercity rail travel (peak, off-peak)	0.15, 1.0
Wine	0.55	Computer	1.44
Beef	0.59	Cable TV (basic rural, basic urban, premium)	0.69, 1.51, 1.77
Kitchen and household appliances	0.63	Restaurant meals	2.27
Chicken	0.64	Lamb	2.71

Finally, here's a warning: Since demand curves slope down, the percentage change in quantity demanded in response to a percentage change in price will be a negative number—that is, either a higher price leads to a lower quantity demanded, or a lower price leads to a higher quantity demanded. However, economists have often dropped the negative sign on the elasticity of demand for decades now. After all, economists know that demand curves generally slope downward, so they don't need the reminder of the negative sign. So when you are reading or listening to something about economics and run across an elasticity of demand that has no negative sign, don't be surprised.

Price Elasticity of Supply

Just as the price elasticity of demand reveals how a percentage change in price will lead to a percentage change in quantity demanded, the price elasticity of supply measures how a percentage change in price will lead to a percentage change in quantity supplied. Again, the elasticity cannot be easily inferred from glancing at the appearance of a supply curve. Instead, elasticity requires a numerical calculation.

CALCULATING THE ELASTICITY OF SUPPLY

Assume that you are renting an apartment in the Philadelphia metropolitan area, where the cost of housing for renters is $650 per month. Say that your neighborhood has 10,000 rental units. This situation is illustrated in both Exhibit 6-4a and Exhibit 6-4b, where the original equilibrium in both graphs is at a price of $650 and a quantity of 10,000 rental apartments. Now imagine that your neighborhood suddenly becomes a more popular and fashionable place to live—that is, demand for rental housing in your neighborhood shifts to the right. Both Exhibit 6-4a and Exhibit 6-4b show an identical shift of a demand curve for rental housing out to the right from D_0 to D_1. However, the shape of the supply curve for rental housing differs in the two graphs. As a result, in Exhibit 6-4a, the new equilibrium E_1 in your neighborhood occurs at a higher rental price of $900 per month and a slightly higher equilibrium quantity of 11,000 rental units, while in Exhibit 6-4b, the new equilibrium E1 results in a slightly higher rental price of $700 per month and a substantially higher equilibrium quantity of 13,000 rental units in your neighborhood. The elasticity of supply is a useful tool for explaining the different outcomes in these two situations.

elasticity of supply: The percentage change in quantity supplied divided by the percentage change in price.

Let's begin with the calculations. The **elasticity of supply** is defined as the percentage change in quantity supplied divided by the percentage change in price. Again, the percentage change between two quantities is calculated by taking the change between the two quantities and dividing by the average of the two quantities. Similarly, the percentage change between two prices is calculated by taking the change between the two prices and dividing by the average of the two prices. Thus, the formula for elasticity of supply is:

$$\text{Elasticity of supply} = \frac{\%\text{ change in quantity supplied}}{\%\text{ change in price}}$$

$$= \frac{(\text{change in quantity / average of original quantities})}{(\text{change in price / average of original prices})}$$

First, apply this formula to the elasticity of supply between E0 and E1 in Exhibit 6-4a.

$$\frac{[11{,}000 - 10{,}000] / [(11{,}000 + 10{,}000) / 2]}{[900 - 650] / [(900 + 650) / 2]} = \frac{1{,}000/10{,}500}{250/775} = \frac{.095}{.322}$$

The elasticity of supply in this example is .095/.322 = .295. Now apply the same formula for elasticity of supply to the change between E_0 and E_1 in Exhibit 6-4b.

$$\frac{[13{,}000 - 10{,}000] / [(13{,}000 + 10{,}000) / 2]}{[700 - 650] / [(700 + 650) / 2]} = \frac{3{,}000/11{,}500}{50/675} = \frac{.261}{.074}$$

The elasticity of supply in this case is .261/.074 = 3.53.

Exhibit 6-4 How a Shift in Demand Can Affect Price or Quantity More

The intersection E_0 between supply curve S and demand curve D_0 is the same in both (a) and (b). The increase in demand from D_0 to D_1 is the same in both (a) and (b). The new equilibrium E_1 has a higher price and quantity than the original equilibrium E_0 in both (a) and (b). However, the shape of supply differs in (a) and (b). As a result, in (a), the new equilibrium E_1 happens at a much higher price but only a small increase in quantity, while in (b), the new equilibrium happens at only a small increase in price but a relatively large increase in quantity.

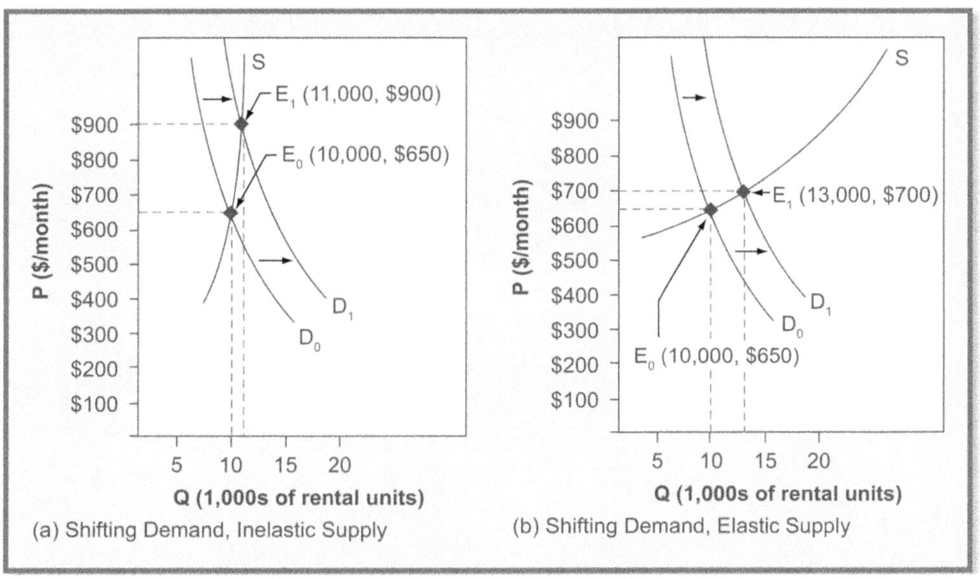

(a) Shifting Demand, Inelastic Supply (b) Shifting Demand, Elastic Supply

Again, as with the elasticity of demand, the elasticity of supply is not followed by any units. Elasticity is a ratio of one percentage change to another percentage change—nothing more.

What is the intuitive meaning of these calculations? The elasticity of supply in Exhibit 6-4a is relatively small. A 10% rise in price causes only a 2.9% rise in the quantity supplied in Exhibit 6-4a. The elasticity of supply in Exhibit 6-4b is relatively large. In this case, a 10% rise in price would bring an increase in supply of 35%. The much greater elasticity of supply in Exhibit 6-4b means that quantity supplied will react much more to a certain percentage change in price.

In situations like this one, the supply curve in Exhibit 6-4a often reflects the situation in the short-term, when the quantity supplied of rental housing cannot increase much in the short term of a year or two. As a result, the elasticity of supply is fairly low and the increase in demand is primarily reflected in higher prices. However, the supply curve in Exhibit 6-4b makes more sense from the longer run perspective of several years, when the quantity supplied of housing has time to rise more substantially. As a result, in the long run the very same rise in demand is reflected more in a rise in the quantity of housing and less in a rise in price.

Exhibit 6-5 Elastic, Unitary, and Inelastic: Three Cases of Elasticity

If . . .	Then . . .	And It's Called . . .
% change in quantity > % change in price	$\frac{\text{\% change in quantity}}{\text{\% change in price}} > 1$	Elastic
% change in quantity = % change in price	$\frac{\text{\% change in quantity}}{\text{\% change in price}} = 1$	Unitary elasticity
% change in quantity < % change in price	$\frac{\text{\% change in quantity}}{\text{\% change in price}} < 1$	Inelastic

Elastic, Inelastic, and Unitary Elasticity

Numerical measures of elasticity can be usefully divided into three broad categories: elastic, inelastic, and unitary elasticity. The categories are summarized in Exhibit 6-5. When quantity demanded or supplied is highly sensitive to changes in price, it is said to be elastic. Specifically, an elastic demand refers to a situation in which a certain percentage change in price leads to a larger percentage change in quantity demanded or quantity supplied. For example, a 10% rise in the price would cause a decline of more than 10%—perhaps 20%—in the quantity demanded of a good. Since elasticity refers to the percentage change in quantity divided by the percentage change in price, saying that a demand curve or supply curve is **elastic** means that the elasticity calculated from the formula is greater than 1.

elastic:

The elasticity calculated from the appropriate formula has an absolute value greater than 1.

Demand will be elastic when consumers find it easy to shift back and forth between goods and services. For example, if the price of lamb rises, many consumers will shift to other meats and foods. Supply will be elastic when it is relatively easy to expand or contract production. For example, at a time when most of the factories in an industry are running at only about half of their full production level, it will be relatively easy to ramp up production higher.

Infinite elasticity refers to the extremely elastic situation where quantity changes by an infinite amount in response to any change in price at all. A demand curve with infinite elasticity appears in Exhibit 6-6a and a supply curve with infinite elasticity appears in Exhibit 6-6b. Infinite elasticity creates horizontal demand and supply curves.

infinite elasticity:

The extremely elastic situation where quantity changes by an infinite amount in response to any change in price.

Exhibit 6-6 Infinite Elasticity

The horizontal lines in (a) and (b) show that an infinite quantity will be demanded (a) or supplied (b) at a specific price. This illustrates the cases of a perfectly elastic or infinitely elastic demand and supply curve.

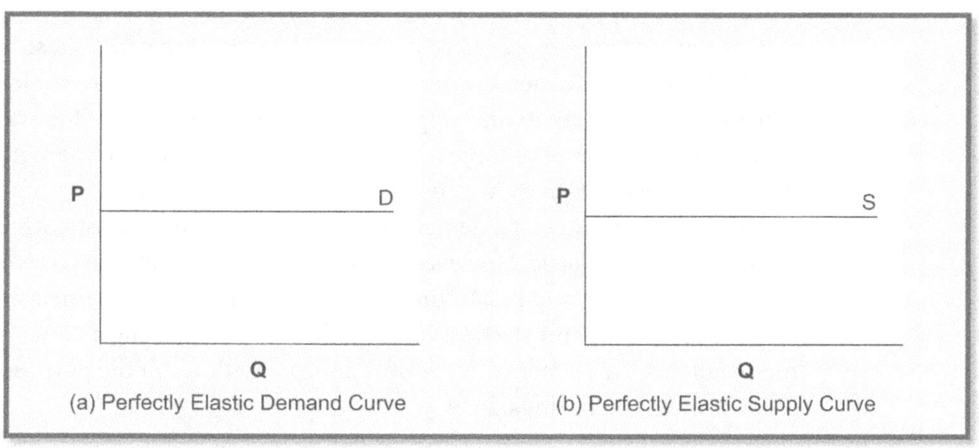

inelastic:
the elasticity calculated from the appropriate formula has an absolute value less than 1.

At the other extreme from elastic is **inelastic**—the situation where a certain percentage change in the price will cause a smaller percentage change in the quantity demanded or supplied. For example, when demand is inelastic a 10% rise in the price would cause a decline of less than 10%—say, only 3%—in the quantity demanded of a good. Since elasticity is calculated as the percentage change in quantity divided by the percentage change in price, inelastic means that the level of elasticity will be less than 1.

Demand will be inelastic when consumers find it difficult to shift back and forth between goods and services. For example, if you have an illness that requires a certain drug to reduce your pain or to keep you alive, and the price of that drug rises, you may not have to cut back very much, if at all, on consumption of that drug, but instead you have to find a way to save money elsewhere in your budget. Supply is often inelastic in the short run, because over a time period of a few months or even a year or two, businesses often have a limited ability to expand their quantity supplied in a dramatic way, given that they have only so many factories and workers on hand.

zero elasticity:
The highly inelastic case in which a percentage change in price, no matter how large, results in zero change in the quantity.

Zero elasticity refers to the highly inelastic case in which a percentage change in price, no matter how large, results in zero change in quantity. A demand curve with zero elasticity appears in Exhibit 6-7a; a supply curve with zero elasticity of zero appears in Exhibit 6-7b. Zero elasticity refers to curves that are vertical.

On the borderline between elastic and inelastic, the percentage change in quantity demanded is equal to the percentage change in quantity supplied, which is the case of unitary elasticity. In this case, a rise of, say, 10% in price would lead to a decline of 10% in the quantity demanded, or a fall of, say 5% in price would lead to a fall of 5% in the quantity supplied.

When economists are sketching examples of demand and supply, it is common to sketch a demand or supply curve that is close to vertical, and then to refer to that curve as "inelastic." It is also common to sketch a demand or supply curve that is close to horizontal, and then to refer to that demand or supply curve as "elastic." Such statements must be handled with care. Remember, a close-to-horizontal or close-to-vertical demand or supply curve may appear that way because of how the axes are drawn, not because of some inherent characteristic of the underlying data. Moreover, elasticity will usually vary along a demand or supply curve, so that one zone of a demand or supply curve can be elastic while another zone is inelastic. However, it is often convenient for purposes of sketching diagrams and illustrating economic intuition to treat inelastic as close to vertical and elastic as close to horizontal. As long as one remembers that such statements are only approximations for the purposes of illustration, no harm is done.

Exhibit 6-7 Zero Elasticity

The (a) vertical demand and (b) vertical supply curves show that there will be zero percentage change in quantity demanded or supplied, regardless of the price. This illustrates the case of zero or perfect inelasticity.

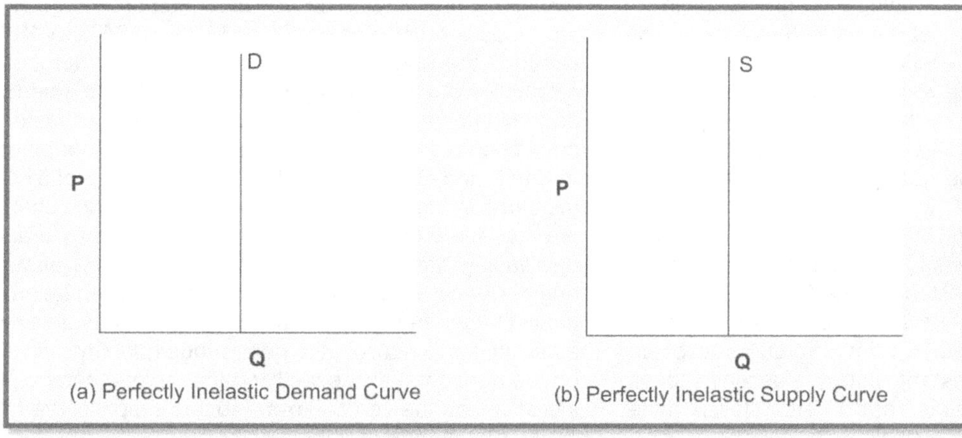

Applications of Elasticity

Elasticities are useful in a wide range of circumstances. Even knowing only that a demand or supply curve is elastic or inelastic can lead to interesting insights.

DOES RAISING PRICE BRING IN MORE REVENUE?

Imagine that a band on tour is playing in an indoor arena with 15,000 seats. To keep this example simple, assume that the band keeps all the money from ticket sales. (For example, you can imagine that the owners of the arena make their money from parking and concessions.) Assume further that the band pays the costs for its appearance, but that these costs like travel, setting up the stage, and so on, are the same regardless of how many people gather in the audience. Finally, assume that all the tickets have the same price. (The same insights apply if ticket prices are more expensive for some seats than for others, but the calculations become more complicated.) The band knows that it faces a downward-sloping demand curve; that is, if the band raises the price of tickets it will sell fewer tickets. How should the band set the price for tickets to bring in the most total revenue, which in this example, because costs are fixed, will also mean the highest profits for the band? Should the band sell more tickets at a higher price or fewer tickets at a lower price?

The key concept in thinking about collecting the most revenue is the elasticity of demand. Total revenue is price times the quantity of tickets sold. Imagine that the band starts off thinking about a certain price, which will result in the sale of a certain quantity of tickets. The three possibilities are laid out in Exhibit 6-8. If demand is elastic at that price level, then the band should cut the price, because the percentage drop in price will result in an even larger percentage increase in the quantity sold—thus raising total revenue. However, if demand is inelastic at that

What Does a Unitary Elasticity of Demand or Supply Look Like?

A demand curve with unitary elasticity at all points is a curved line, but a supply curve with unitary price elasticity at all points is a straight line running through the origin.

To gain some intuition about why this is true, first consider the demand curve with a unitary price elasticity of demand at all points. As you move down the demand curve from A to B, the price falls by 33% and quantity demanded rises by 33%; as you move from B to C, the price falls by 25% and the quantity demanded rises by 25%; as you move from C to D, the price falls by 16% and the quantity rises by 16%. Notice that in absolute value, the declines in price, as you step down the demand curve, are not identical. Instead, price falls by $3 from A to B, by a smaller amount of $1.50 from B to C, and by a still smaller amount of $0.75 from C to D. As a result, a demand curve with constant unitary elasticity moves from a steeper slope on the left and a flatter slope on the right—and a curved shape overall.

In moving up the supply curve from left to right, each increase in quantity of 30, from 90 to 120 to 150 to 180, is equal in absolute value. However, in percentage value, the steps are decreasing, from 33.3% to 25% to 16.7%, because the original quantity points in each percentage calculation are getting larger and larger, which expands the denominator in the elasticity calculation. Next consider the price changes moving up the supply curve. From points D to E to F and G on the supply curve, each step of $1.50 is the same in absolute value. However, if the price changes are measured in percentage change terms, they are also decreasing, from 33.3% to 25% to 16.7%, because the original price points in each percentage calculation are getting larger and larger in value. Along the constant unitary elasticity supply curve, the percentage quantity increases on the horizontal axis exactly match the percentage price increases on the vertical axis—so this supply curve has a constant unitary elasticity at all points.

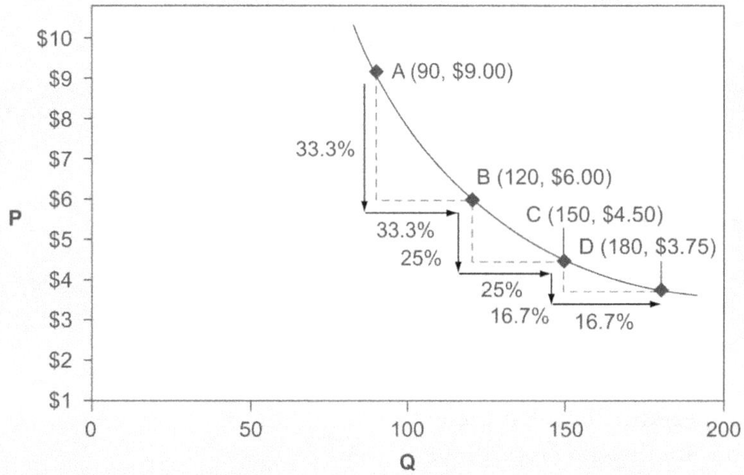

A Constant Unitary Elasticity Demand Curve

A demand curve with constant unitary elasticity will be a curved line. Notice how each step down the demand curve has an identical change in quantity demanded and in price.

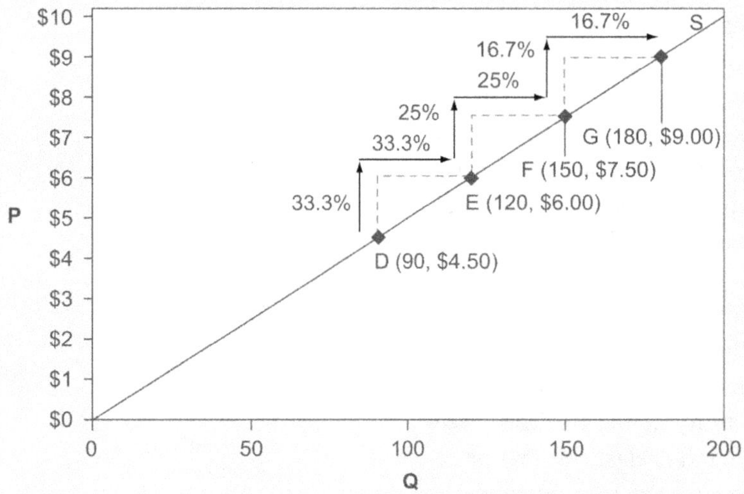

A Constant Unitary Elasticity Supply Curve

A constant unitary elasticity supply curve is a straight line reaching up from the origin. Between each point, the percentage increase in quantity demanded is the same as the percentage increase in price.

original quantity level, then the band should raise the price of tickets, because a certain percentage increase in price will result in a smaller percentage decrease in the quantity sold—and total revenue will rise. If demand has a unitary elasticity at that quantity, then a moderate percentage change in the price will be offset by an equal percentage change in quantity—so the band will earn the same revenue whether it (moderately) increases or decreases the price of tickets.

Exhibit 6-8 Will the Band Earn More Revenue by Changing Ticket Prices?

If Demand Is . . .	Then . . .	Therefore . . .
Elastic	% change in Q > % change in P	A given % rise in P will be more than offset by a larger % fall in Q, so that total revenue P × Q falls
Unitary	% change in Q = % change in P	A given % rise in P will be exactly offset by an equal % fall in Q, so that total revenue P × Q is unchanged
Inelastic	% change in Q < % change in P	A given % rise in P will cause a smaller % fall in Q, so that total revenue P × Q rises

What if the band keeps cutting price, because demand is elastic, until it reaches a level where all 15,000 seats in the available arena are sold? If demand remains elastic at that quantity, the band might try to move to a bigger arena, so that it could cut ticket prices further and see a larger percentage increase in the quantity of ticket sold. Of course, if the 15,000 seat arena is all that's available or if a larger arena would add substantially to costs, then this option may not work.

Conversely, a few bands are so famous, or have such fanatical followings, that demand for tickets may be inelastic right up to the point where the arena is full. These bands can, if they wish, keep raising the price of tickets. Ironically, some of the most popular bands could make more revenue by setting prices so high that the arena is not filled—but those who buy the tickets would have to pay very high prices. However, bands sometimes choose to sell tickets for less than the absolute maximum they might be able to charge, often in the hope that fans will feel happier and spend more on recordings, T-shirts, and other paraphernalia.

PASSING ON COSTS TO CONSUMERS?

Most businesses face a day-to-day struggle to figure out ways to produce at a lower cost, as one pathway to their goal of earning higher profits. However, in some cases, the price of a key input over which the firm has no control may rise. For example, many chemical companies use petroleum as a key input, but they have no control over the world market price for crude oil. Coffee shops use coffee as a key input, but they have no control over the world market price of coffee. If the cost of a key input rises, can the firm pass those higher costs along to consumers in the form of higher prices? Conversely, if new and less expensive ways of producing are invented, can the firm keep the benefits in the form of higher profits or will the market pressure them to pass the gains along to consumers in the form of lower prices? The elasticity of demand plays a key role in answering these questions.

Imagine that as a consumer of legal pharmaceutical products, you read a newspaper story that a technological breakthrough in the production of aspirin has occurred, so that every aspirin factory can now make aspirin more cheaply than it did before. What does this discovery mean to you? Exhibit 6-9 illustrates two possibilities. In Exhibit 6-9a, the demand curve is drawn as highly inelastic. In this case, a technological breakthrough that shifts supply to the right from S0 to S1, so that the equilibrium shifts from E0 to E1, creates a substantially lower price for the product with relatively little impact on the quantity sold. In Exhibit 6-9b, the demand curve is drawn as highly elastic. In this case, the technological breakthrough leads to a much greater quantity being sold in the market at very close to the original price. If you already consume large amounts of aspirin, then you tend to benefit more from a lower price than a greater quantity sold in the market; if you are not yet an aspirin consumer, but a small decrease in price makes you willing to purchase them, you benefit more from the expanded quantity sold in the market.

Producers of aspirin may find themselves in a nasty bind here. The situation shown in Exhibit 6-9a, with extremely inelastic demand, means that a new invention may cause the price to drop dramatically while quantity changes little. As a result, the new production technology can lead to a drop in the revenue that firm's earn from sales of aspirin! However, if strong competition exists between producers of aspirin, each producer may have little choice but to search for and implement any breakthrough that allows it to reduce production costs. After all, if one firm decides not to implement such a cost-saving technology, it can be driven out of business by other firms that do. Since demand for food is generally inelastic, farmers may often face the situation in Exhibit 6-9a. That is, a surge in production leads to a severe drop in price that can actually decrease the total revenue received by farmers. Conversely,

Fluctuating Coffee Prices

Coffee is an international crop. The top five coffee-exporting nations are Brazil, Vietnam, Colombia, Indonesia, and Guatemala. In these nations and others, 20 million families depend on selling coffee beans as their main source of income. These families are exposed to enormous risk, because world price of coffee bounces up and down. For example, in 1993, the world price of coffee was about 50 cents per pound; in 1995 it was four times as high, at $2.00 per pound. By 1997 it had fallen by half to $1.00 per pound. In 1998 it leaped back up to $2.00 per pound. By 2002 it had fallen back to 50 cents a pound; by the end of 2005 it went back up to about $1.00 per pound. By 2009, the price had fallen back to about 65 cents per pound. The reason for these price bounces lies in a combination of inelastic demand and shifts in supply. The elasticity of coffee demand is only about 0.3; that is, a 10% rise in the price of coffee leads to a decline of about 3% in the quantity of coffee consumed. When a major frost hit the Brazilian coffee crop in 1994, coffee supply shifted to the left with an inelastic demand curve, leading to much higher prices. Conversely, when Vietnam entered the world coffee market as a major producer in the late 1990s, the supply curve shifted out to the right. With a highly inelastic demand curve, coffee prices fell dramatically.

poor weather or other conditions that cause a lousy year for farm production can sharply raise prices so that the total revenue received by farmers rises—at least for those farmers who have something to sell.

Elasticity also reveals whether firms can pass higher costs that they incur to consumers. In this case, some of the most vivid applications involve addictive substances. For example, the demand for cigarettes is relatively inelastic among regular smokers who are somewhat addicted; economic research suggests that increasing the price of cigarettes by 10% leads to about a 3% reduction in the quantity of cigarettes smoked by adults, so the elasticity of demand for cigarettes is 0.3. If society increases taxes on companies that make cigarettes, the result, as in Exhibit 6-10a, the supply curve shifts from S0 to S1. However, as the equilibrium moves from E0 to E1, these taxes are mainly passed along to consumers in the form of higher prices. These higher taxes on cigarettes will raise tax revenue for the government, but they won't much affect the quantity of smoking. If the goal is to reduce the quantity of cigarettes demanded, this must be achieved by shifting this inelastic demand back to the left, perhaps with public programs to discourage the use of cigarettes or to help people to quit. For example, anti-smoking advertising campaigns have shown some ability to reduce smoking. However, if demand for cigarettes was more elastic, as in Exhibit 6-10b, then an increase in taxes that shifts supply from S0 to S1 and equilibrium from E0 to E1 would reduce the quantity of cigarettes smoked substantially. Youth smoking seems to be more elastic than adult smoking—that is, the quantity of

Exhibit 6-9 Passing along Cost Savings to Consumers

Cost-saving gains cause supply to shift out to the right from S0 to S1; that is, at any given price, firms will be willing to supply a greater quantity. If demand is inelastic, as in (a), the result of this cost-saving technological improvement will be substantially lower prices. If demand is elastic, as in (b), the result will be only slightly lower prices. Consumers benefit in either case, from a greater quantity at a lower price. But the benefit takes different forms, depending on the elasticity of demand.

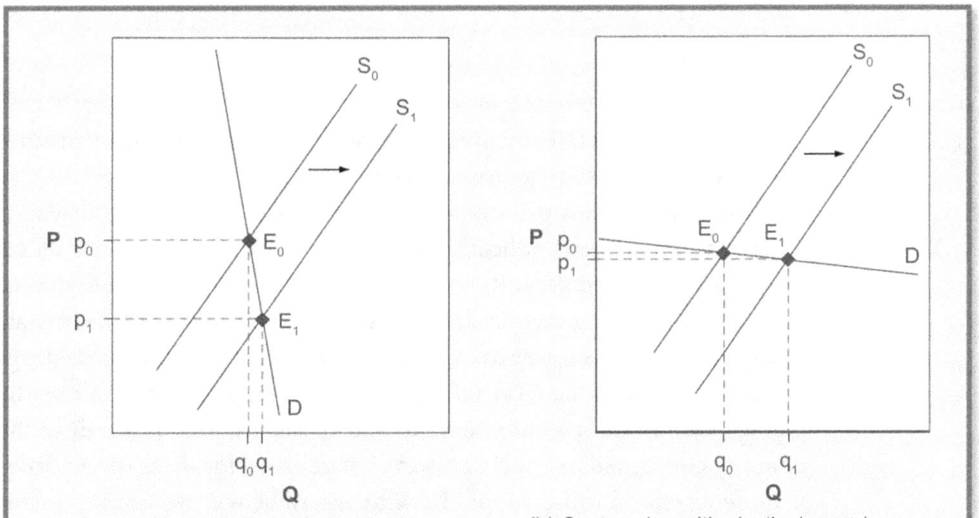

(a) Cost-saving with inelastic demand

(b) Cost-saving with elastic demand

Clearing It Up: For Supply Shifts, Check Elasticity of Demand, and Vice Versa

If the question is whether a shift in supply will have a greater effect on equilibrium price or quantity, the answer lies not with the elasticity of supply, but with the elasticity of demand. That's because the shifting supply curve is moving along a fixed demand curve—and the shape of that demand curve will determine the eventual outcome. Similarly, if the question is whether a shift in demand will have a greater effect on equilibrium price or quantity, the answer lies not with the elasticity of demand, but with the elasticity of supply. After all, when a shifting demand curve moves along a fixed supply curve, the shape of that supply curve will determine the eventual outcome.

Exhibit 6-10 Passing along Higher Costs to Consumers

Higher costs, like a higher tax on cigarette companies for the example given in the text, lead supply to shift back to the left. This shift is identical in (a) and (b). However, in (a), demand is inelastic, and so the cost increase can largely be passed along to consumers in the form of higher prices, without much of a decline in equilibrium quantity. In (b), demand is elastic, so the shift in supply results primarily in a lower equilibrium quantity. Consumers suffer in either case, but in (a), they suffer from paying a higher price for the same quantity, while in (b), they suffer from buying a lower quantity (and presumably needing to shift their consumption elsewhere).

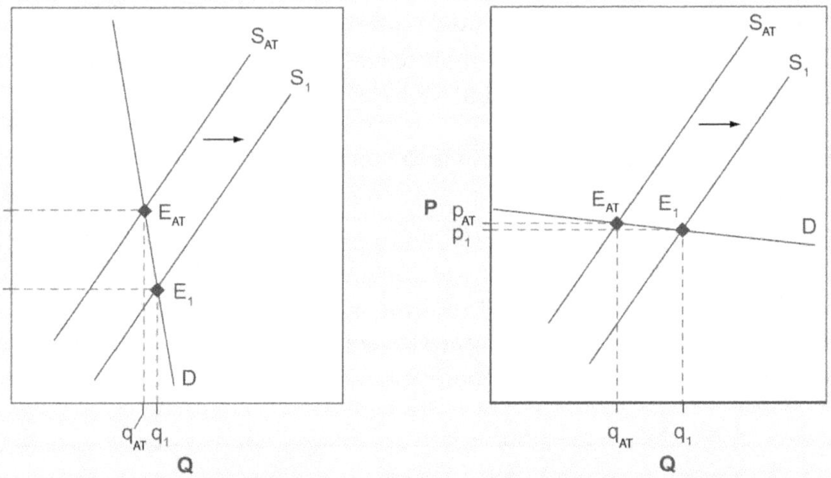

(a) Cost-saving with inelastic demand (b) Cost-saving with elastic demand

youth smoking will fall by a greater percentage than the quantity of adult smoking in response to a given percentage increase in price.

The enforcement of laws against the production or sale of illegal drugs offers another application of this scenario. Laws against illegal drugs can be viewed as shifting the supply curve back to the left; that is, as a result of making certain drugs illegal, the quantity available for sale at any given price is lower than it was before. If demand for these drugs is inelastic, then producers of illegal drugs can essentially pass along the higher price from law enforcement, and these laws will not reduce the quantity consumed by much. However, if demand for these illegal drugs is quite elastic, shifting supply back to the right will reduce the quantity consumed dramatically. Many of the arguments over legalization of drugs—"Strict enforcement will cut drug use!" "No, it will only put more money in the pockets of drug dealers!"—are really assertions about whether enforcement will have a greater impact on quantity or on price, and thus are really claims about the elasticities of demand and supply. But the truth is that we lack evidence on elasticities of supply and demand for illegal drugs. In 2001, the prestigious National Research Council published a report by a Committee on Data and Research for Policy on Illegal Drugs. The committee, which included several economists, concluded: "Viewing the unending public debate about drug policy, the committee became painfully aware that what we don't know keeps hurting us."

Exhibit 6-11 How a Shift in Supply Can Affect Price or Quantity More

The intersection E_0 between demand curve D and supply curve S_0 is the same in both (a) and (b). The shift of supply to the left from S_0 to S_1 is identical in both (a) and (b). The new equilibrium E_1 has a higher price and a lower quantity than the original equilibrium E_0 in both (a) and (b). However, the shape of the demand curve D is different in (a) and (b). As a result, the shift in supply can result either in a new equilibrium with a much higher price and an only slightly smaller quantity, as in (a), or in a new equilibrium with only a small increase in price and a relatively larger reduction in quantity, as in (b).

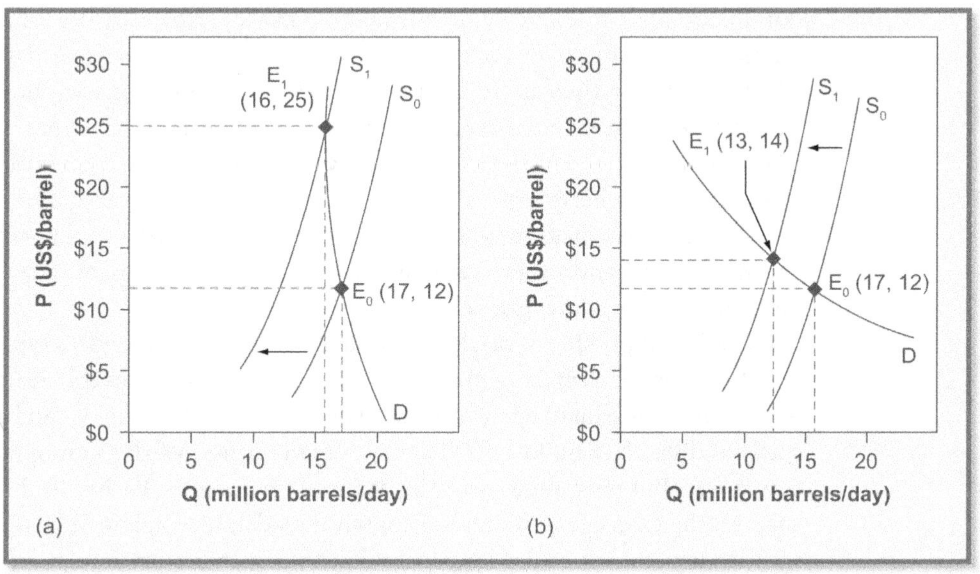

LONG-RUN VS. SHORT-RUN IMPACT

Elasticities are often lower in the short run than in the long run. On the demand side of the market, it can sometimes be difficult to change quantity demanded in the short run, but easier in the long run. Consumption of energy is a vivid example. In the short run, it's not easy for a person to make substantial changes in the energy consumption. Maybe you can carpool to work sometimes or adjust your home thermostat by a few degrees if the cost of energy rises, but that's about all. However, in the long-run you can purchase a car that gets more miles to the gallon, or choose a job that is closer to where you live, or buy more energy-efficient home appliances, or install more insulation in your home. As a result, the elasticity of demand for energy is somewhat inelastic in the short run, but much more elastic in the long run.

Exhibit 6-11 is an example, based roughly on historical experience, for the responsiveness of quantity demanded to price changes. In 1973, the price of crude oil was $12 per barrel and total consumption in the U.S. economy was 17 million barrels per day. That year, the nations who were members of the Organization of Petroleum Exporting Countries cut off oil exports to the United States for six months and did not bring exports back to their earlier levels until 1975—a policy that can be interpreted as a shift of the supply curve to the left in the U.S. petroleum market. Exhibit 6-11a and Exhibit 6-11b show the same original equilibrium point and the same identical shift of a supply curve to the left from S_0 to S_1.

However, Exhibit 6-11a and Exhibit 6-11b show two different possible shapes for the demand curve for oil. Exhibit 6-11a shows inelastic demand for oil in the short run, while Exhibit 6-11b shows more elastic demand for oil in the long run. In Exhibit 6-11a, the new equilibrium E1 occurs at a price of $25 per barrel and an equilibrium quantity of 16 million barrels per day. In Exhibit 6-11b, the new equilibrium E1 results in a smaller price increase to $14 per barrel and larger reduction in equilibrium quantity to 13 million barrels per day. In 1983, for example, U.S. petroleum consumption was 15.3 million barrels a day, which was lower than in 1973 or 1975. U.S. petroleum consumption was down even though the U.S. economy was about one-fourth larger in 1983 than it had been in 1973. The primary reason for the lower quantity was that higher energy prices spurred conservation efforts, and after a decade of home insulation, lower mileage cars, more efficient appliances and machinery, and other fuel-conserving choices, the demand curve for energy had become more elastic.

On the supply side of markets, producers of goods and services typically find it easier to expand production in the long-term of several years than in the short run of a few months. After all, in the short run it can be costly or difficult to build a new factory, hire many new workers, or open new stores. But over a few years, all of these are possible. Earlier in this chapter, the example of rental housing in Philadelphia explained how a shift in demand for rental housing is likely to increase price relatively more than quantity in the short run, because it's difficult for the quantity of rental housing to adjust dramatically in the short run. However, in the long run that same shift in demand will be reflected more in a rise in equilibrium quantity than a rise in equilibrium price.

Indeed, in most markets for goods and services, prices bounce up and down more than quantities in the short run, but quantities often move more than prices in the long run. The underlying reason for this pattern is that supply and demand are often inelastic in the short run, therefore shifts in either demand or supply can cause a relatively greater change in prices. But since supply and demand are more elastic in the long run, the long-run movements in prices are more muted, while quantity adjusts more easily in the long run.

Elasticity as a General Concept

The basic idea of elasticity—how a percentage change in one variable causes a percentage change in another variable—doesn't just apply to supply and demand curves in the markets for goods and services, but can also apply to many economic relationships. In these ways, the idea of elasticity can be used to clarify and re-explain some concepts introduced earlier in this book, like normal and inferior goods, substitute and complement goods, and others. Indeed, the concept of elasticity can also be applied to factors other than price that affect quantity.

INCOME ELASTICITY OF DEMAND

The income elasticity of demand is the percentage change in quantity demanded divided by the percentage change in income.

$$\text{Elasticity of savings} = \frac{\text{\% change in quantity of financial savings}}{\text{\% change in interest rate}}$$

For most products, most of the time, the income elasticity of demand is positive: that is, a rise in income will cause an increase in the quantity demanded. This pattern is common enough that these goods are referred to as **normal goods**. However, for a few goods, an increase in income means that one might purchase less of the good; for example, a person with a higher income might buy fewer hamburgers, because they are buying more steak instead, or a person with a higher income might buy less cheap wine and more imported beer. When the income elasticity of demand is negative, the good is called an **inferior good**.

normal good:
A good where the quantity demanded rises when income rises.

inferior good:
A good where the quantity demanded declines as income increases.

The concepts of normal and inferior goods were introduced in Chapter 4, in the discussion of supply and demand. A higher level of income causes a demand curve to shift to the right for a normal good, which means that the income elasticity of demand is positive. However, for an inferior good, that is, when the income elasticity of demand is negative, a higher level of income would cause the demand curve for that good to shift to the left.

CROSS-PRICE ELASTICITY OF DEMAND

A change in the price of one good can shift the quantity demanded for another good. If the two goods are complements, like bread and peanut butter, then a drop in the price of one good will lead to an increase in the quantity demanded of the other good. However, if the two goods are substitutes, like plane tickets and train tickets, then a drop in the price of one good will cause people to substitute toward that good, and to reduce consumption of the other good. Cheaper plane tickets lead to fewer train tickets, and vice versa.

The **cross-price elasticity of demand** puts some meat on the bones of these ideas. The term "cross-price" refers to the idea that the price of one good is affecting the quantity demanded of a different good.

cross-price elasticity of demand:
The percentage change in the quantity of good A that is demanded as a result of a percentage change in good B.

Specifically, the cross-price elasticity of demand is the percentage change in the quantity of good A that is demanded as a result of a percentage change in the price of good B.

$$\text{Cross-price elasticity of demand} = \frac{\text{\% change in quantity demanded of good A}}{\text{\% change in price of good B}}$$

If good A is a substitute for good B, like coffee and tea, then a higher price for B will mean a greater quantity consumed of good A. But if good A is a complement for good B, like coffee and sugar, then a higher price for good B will mean a lower quantity consumed of good A.

ELASTICITY IN LABOR AND FINANCIAL CAPITAL MARKETS

elasticity of labor supply: The percentage change in hours worked divided by the percentage change in wages.

The concept of elasticity also applies in labor markets and financial capital markets. In the labor market, for example, the **elasticity of labor supply**—that is, the percentage change in hours worked divided by the percentage change in wages—will determine the shape of the labor supply curve. Specifically:

$$\text{Elasticity of labor supply} = \frac{\text{\% change in quantity of labor supplied}}{\text{\% change in wage}}$$

The wage elasticity of labor supply for teenage workers is generally thought to be fairly elastic: that is a certain percentage change in wages will lead to a larger percentage change in the quantity of hours worked. Conversely, the wage elasticity of labor supply for adult workers in their 30s and 40s is thought to be fairly inelastic. When wages move up or down by a certain percentage amount, the quantity of hours that adults in their prime earning years are willing to supply changes but by a lesser percentage amount.

elasticity of savings: The percentage change in the quantity of savings divided by the percentage change in interest rates.

In markets for financial capital, the **elasticity of savings**—that is, the percentage change in the quantity of savings divided by the percentage change in interest rates—will describe the shape of the supply curve for financial capital. That is:

$$\text{Elasticity of savings} = \frac{\text{\% change in quantity of financial savings}}{\text{\% change in interest rate}}$$

Sometimes laws are proposed that seek to increase the quantity of savings by offering tax breaks so that the return on savings is higher. Such a policy will increase the quantity if the supply curve for financial capital is elastic, because then a given percentage increase in the return to savings will cause a higher percentage increase in the quantity of savings. However, if the supply curve for financial capital is highly inelastic, then a percentage increase in the return to savings will cause only a small increase in the quantity of savings. The evidence on the supply curve of financial capital is controversial, but at least in the short run, the elasticity of savings with respect to the interest rate appears fairly inelastic.

STRETCHING THE CONCEPT OF ELASTICITY

The elasticity concept doesn't even need to relate to a typical supply or demand curve at all. For example, imagine that you are studying whether the Internal Revenue Service should spend more money on auditing tax returns. The question can be framed in terms of the elasticity of tax collections with respect to spending on tax enforcement; that is, what is the percentage change in tax collections derived from a percentage change in spending on tax enforcement? Or imagine that you are interested in a policy that trims back on Social Security payments in a way that might encourage some elderly people to work rather than retire. The question can be framed in terms of the elasticity of hours of work with respect to Social Security payments; that is, what is the percentage change in work hours that will result from a certain percentage change in Social Security payments? With all of the elasticity concepts that have just been described, some of which are listed in Exhibit 6-12, the possibility of confusion arises. When you hear the phrases "elasticity of demand" or "elasticity of supply," they refer to the elasticity with respect to price. Sometimes, either to be extremely clear or because a wide variety of elasticities are being discussed, the elasticity of demand or the demand elasticity will be called the **price elasticity of demand** or the "elasticity of demand with respect to price." Similarly, elasticity of supply or the supply elasticity is sometimes called, to avoid any possibility of confusion, the **price elasticity of supply** or "the elasticity of supply with respect to price." But in whatever context elasticity is invoked, the idea always refers to percentage change in one variable, almost always a price or money variable, and how it causes a percentage change in another variable, typically a quantity variable of some kind.

price elasticity of demand: Same as elasticity of demand.

price elasticity of supply: Same as elasticity of supply.

Exhibit 6-12 Some Applications of the Income Elasticity Concept

$$\text{Income elasticity of demand} = \frac{\%\text{ change in quantity demanded}}{\%\text{ change in income}}$$

$$\text{Cross-price elasticity of demand} = \frac{\%\text{ change in quantity demanded of good A}}{\%\text{ change in price of good B}}$$

$$\text{Wage elasticity of labor supply} = \frac{\%\text{ change in quantity of labor supplied}}{\%\text{ change in wage}}$$

$$\text{Wage elasticity of labor demand} = \frac{\%\text{ change in quantity of labor demanded}}{\%\text{ change in wage}}$$

$$\text{Interest rate elasticity of savings} = \frac{\%\text{ change in quantity of savings}}{\%\text{ change in interest rate}}$$

$$\text{Interest rate elasticity of borrowing} = \frac{\%\text{ change in quantity of borrowing}}{\%\text{ change in interest rate}}$$

Conclusion

Framing a question in terms of elasticity is often a very useful step. When summarizing or comparing the results of a number of different studies, which are often done using different data sources, time periods, or statistical methods, it is a great help if the studies are trying to estimate a single common concept. The concept of elasticity takes the shape of demand and supply curves out of the realm of guesswork based on appearance, depending on how the curves happen to be drawn. In this way, the concept of elasticity nails down the idea of how quantity changes in response to changes in price in a way that provides a shorthand for discussion and an engine for analysis.

EXHIBIT 6-13

Passing Along a Tax to Consumers

A tax on the output of an industry shifts the supply curve up by the amount of the tax. Panel A shows that if the demand curve is relatively inelastic, as it is for cigarettes, then most of the tax will be passed on to consumers in higher prices. Panel B shows that if the demand curve is relatively elastic, as it is for cheddar cheese, then most of the tax cannot be passed along to consumers in higher prices, and must instead be absorbed by producers.

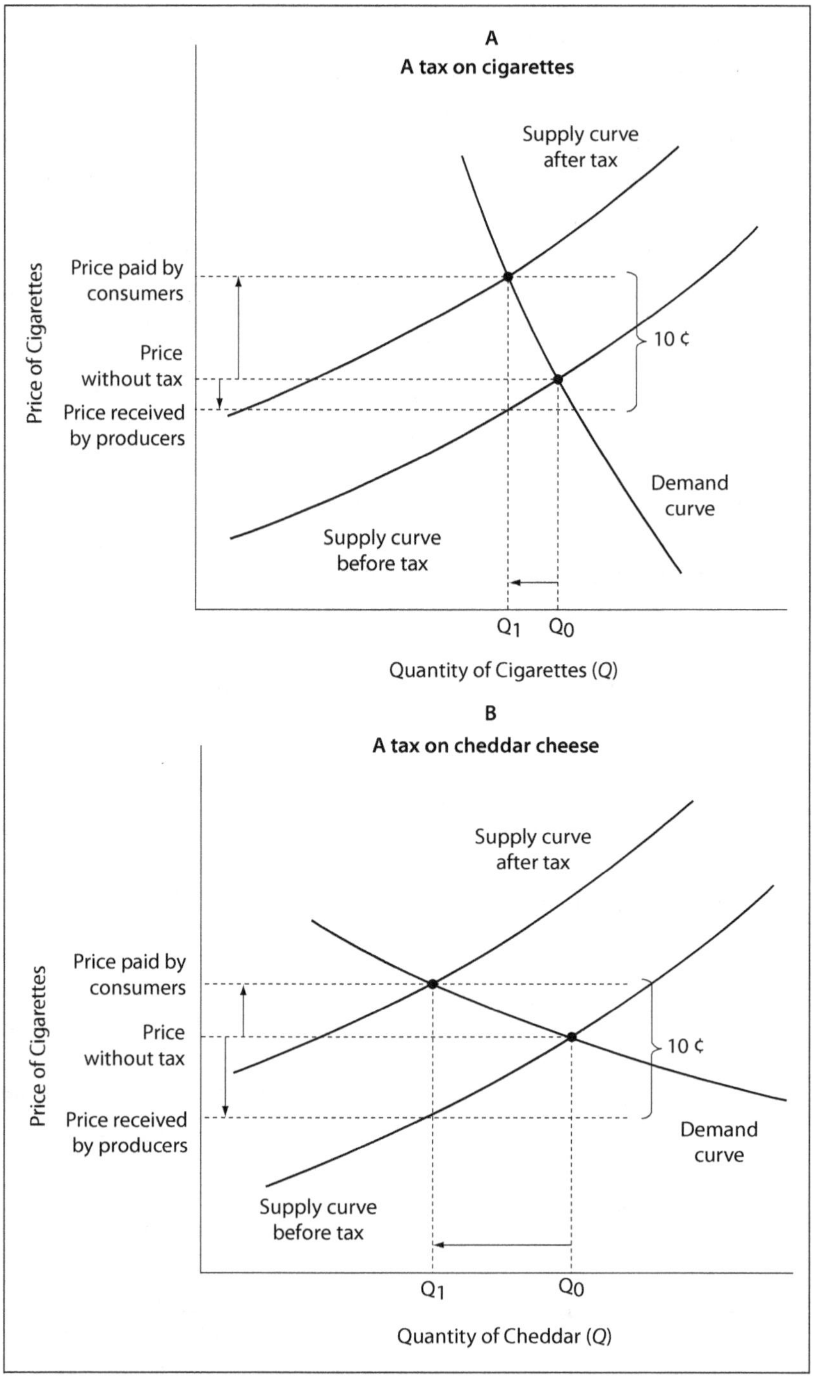

Calculating the exact percent that buyer and seller are paying of a given tax is easy. For the percent buyers pay, find

$$\frac{E_s}{E_s + E_d} * 100$$

For the percent sellers pay, find

$$\frac{E_d}{E_s + E_d} * 100$$

This is how you calculate the exact "burden of a tax," also know known as "tax incidence."

Key Concepts and Summary

1. Elasticity is a tool for measuring how much a percentage change in price causes a percentage change in quantity demanded, quantity supplied or other economic variables.
2. The **elasticity of demand** is the percentage change in quantity demanded divided by the percentage change in price. The elasticity of supply is defined as the percentage change in quantity supplied divided by the percentage change in price.
3. An **elastic** demand or supply curve is one for which a given percentage change in price leads to a larger percentage change in quantity demanded or supplied, so that the percentage change in quantity divided by the percentage change in price will be greater than 1. An **inelastic** demand or supply curve is one where a given percentage change in price will cause a smaller percentage change in quantity demanded or supplied, so that the percentage change in quantity divided by the percentage change in price will be less than one. A **unitary elasticity** means that a given percentage change in price leads to an equal percentage change in quantity demanded or supplied, so that the percentage change in quantity divided by the percentage change in price will be equal to one.
4. A demand or supply curve with **zero elasticity** would be extremely inelastic, or vertical in appearance. A demand or supply curve with **infinite elasticity** would be extremely elastic, or horizontal in appearance.
5. The elasticity of supply and demand determines whether a shift in supply or demand will have a larger affect on quantity or price. If demand is elastic, then shifts in supply will have a larger effect on quantity than on price. If demand is inelastic, then shifts in supply will have a larger effect on price than on quantity. If supply is elastic, then shifts in demand will have a larger effect on quantity than on price. If supply is inelastic, then shifts in demand will have a larger effect on price than on quantity.
6. In the market for goods and services, quantity supplied and quantity demanded are often relatively slow to react to changes in price in the short run but react more substantially in the long run. As a

result, demand and supply often (but not always) tend to be relatively inelastic in the short run and relatively elastic in the long run.

7. Elasticity is a general term, referring to percentage change divided by percentage change that can be applied to many economic connections. For instance, the **income elasticity of demand** is the percentage change in quantity demanded divided by the percentage change in income. The **cross-price elasticity** of demand is the percentage change in the quantity demanded of a good divided by the percentage change in the price of another good.
8. Elasticity applies in labor markets and financial capital markets just as it applied in markets for goods and services. The wage elasticity of labor supply is the percentage change in the quantity of hours supplied divided by the percentage change in the wage. The elasticity of savings with respect to interest rates is the percentage change in the quantity of savings divided by the percentage change in interest rates.

Vocabulary Terms

Burden of a tax
Cross-price elasticity
Demand elasticity
Income elasticity
Price elasticity
Supply elasticity
Tax incidence

Review Questions

1. If you wanted to make a demand or supply curve appear relatively steep, would you stretch out the horizontal or the vertical axis? What about if you wanted it to make it appear relatively flat?
2. What is the formula for calculating the elasticity of demand?
3. What is the formula for calculating the elasticity of supply?
4. If demand or supply is elastic, is the response of quantity to changes in price relatively large or small?
5. If demand or supply is elastic, what is the range of the possible numerical values it can have?
6. If demand or supply is inelastic, is the response of quantity to changes in price relatively large or small?
7. If demand or supply is inelastic, what is the range of the possible numerical values it can have?
8. What is the numerical value of a unitary elasticity?
9. What units of measurement, if any, are used with elasticity?
10. Describe the general appearance of a demand or a supply curve with zero elasticity.
11. Describe the general appearance of a demand or a supply curve with infinite elasticity.
12. If demand is elastic, will shifts in supply have a larger effect on equilibrium quantity or on price?

13. If demand is inelastic, will shifts in supply have a larger effect on equilibrium price or on quantity?
14. If supply is elastic, will shifts in demand have a larger effect on equilibrium quantity or on price?
15. If supply is inelastic, will shifts in demand have a larger effect on equilibrium price or on quantity?
16. Would you usually expect elasticity of demand or supply to be higher in the short run or in the long run? Why?
17. What is the formula for the income elasticity of demand?
18. What is the formula for the cross-price elasticity of demand?
19. What is the formula for the wage elasticity of labor supply?
20. What is the formula for elasticity of savings with respect to interest rates?

APPLY YOUR SKILLS

Elasticity

By David Moglen

Directions:

Break into your small groups. Whichever group finishes all questions with 100% accuracy gets bonus points but must, when asked by the teacher, write out how you got your answer on the board for the class.

Note:

Whenever calculating percent change is needed, use (new-old)/old*100=% change. For example, if original quantity Q1 is 50 shoelaces and new quantity Q2 is 75 shoelaces, (75-50)/50*100=50%. From 50 to 75 you have a 50% increase in the number of shoelaces sold. Round figures to two decimal places.

This simple percent change equation is easier than the one shown earlier in the book.

1. For the iPad: P1=$700, P2= $800. Q1=11 million IPads sold per year and demand elasticity – 1.8. Solve for the new quantity Q2.
2. For stereo equipment: Q1=4/ year for one person. Q2=12. Y2 (their new income level) = $65,000. Income Elasticity=3. Solve for Y1 (original income level).
3. Demand is inelastic. Price goes down. Will total revenue increase or decrease?
4. Demand elasticity=1.9. Price increases. Will total revenue increase or decrease?
5. Supply elasticity=2.5. Demand elasticity=0.8 Now there is a 15% sales tax. Who is primarily bearing the burden of this tax, the good's buyers or sellers?
6. There is a 9% sales tax. Supply elasticity=1.1. Demand elasticity=1.7. Calculate the percent suppliers pay.

IN-CLASS PROJECT

Elasticity Group Work

By David Moglen

Directions:

After you are assigned a group number from 1-3, answer the same question as the group number you are given.

1. (Demand Elasticity): Draw the demand curve based on the following points A and B. Hamburgers: P1=\$4, P2=\$5, Q1=100, Q2=90, time period: per week. Hint: draw the points (A, B) based on numbers above first, then connect the dots. That is your demand curve. Calculate demand elasticity from point A to B. Is this Elastic, Inelastic, or Unit Elastic?

   Draw in separate graphs for comparison: demand for coal in one week, one month, one year and one decade. Use example numbers for points A and B for any two of the four graphs. Then use those example vertical and horizontal coordinates for A and B to calculate demand elasticity for any two of the four graphs. Label axes on all 4 graphs.

   You should start by drawing on 4 blank, unlabeled X/Y spaces (i.e. draw 4 really big L's. Those are your X/Y spaces –graphs- on which to draw one elasticity line each). Have demand in one graph be relatively flat, then in the next steeper, the next steeper, and the next steepest. Now ask yourself, is it the 1-week or the 1-decade graph that is supposed to be most or least elastic and fill in graphs accordingly.

2. (Cross-Price Elasticity and Demand Elasticity): What might be the cross elasticity of demand for Tacos and Hamburgers? What might be the cross elasticity of demand for Soda and Hamburgers? Use example numbers for the numerator and denominator in both elasticity equations. No graph needed.

   Draw in separate graphs for comparison: the demand curve for Tacos at Mexican fast food restaurants, for meals at all fast food restaurants, for food at all restaurants, and demand for all food items (grocery store, restaurants, all food). Use example numbers for points A and B for any two of the four graphs. Then use those example vertical and horizontal coordinates for A and B to calculate demand elasticity for any two of the four graphs. Label axes on all 4 graphs.

   You should start by drawing on 4 blank, unlabeled X/Y spaces (i.e. draw 4 really big L's. Those are your X/Y spaces –graphs- on which to draw one elasticity line each). Have demand in one graph be relatively flat, then in the next steeper, the next steeper, and the next steepest. Now ask yourself, is it the tacos or all food graph that is supposed to be most or least elastic and fill in graphs accordingly.

3. (Income Elasticity): Draw and fully label the graphs of income elasticity for both of the following two goods: poultry (frozen or refrigerated chicken in the grocery store) has income elasticity of .3 and restaurant meals have income elasticity of 2.4. Your description of each should include specifically whether the good is income inelastic or income elastic. Your graphs should be fully labeled and include example numbers for points A and B that conform to the numbers given above. Hint: Come up with the example numbers first that conform to the income elasticity numbers

in the question. Plot those two (Before and after/ A and B) points on the graph and then connect those dots.

Those are the real elasticity numbers for poultry and restaurant meals in the U.S. **Explain**, without using any variation of the word (in) elastic(ity), what is the logical reason why poultry has income elasticity of .3 and restaurant meals have income elasticity of 2.4. Imagine the person you are explaining it to has never taken an econ class and has just said to you, "Why would the quantity change be anything other than exactly in proportion to the income change. In other words, if their income has gone up 50%, then I think their quantities of both poultry and restaurant meals should also go up by exactly 50%. Why is that not correct?" (1–2 sentences for each good).

For Practice Only (Supply Elasticity):

4. Explain why elasticity of supply is elastic or inelastic, draw the graph, and give an example of a likely number for the elasticity of supply for fish in a coastal town where most of the people can spend some time fishing if the Price of Fish rises, but have other forms of income to which they can also devote all (or some of) their time.
5. Explain why elasticity of supply is elastic or inelastic, draw the graph, and give an example of a likely number for the elasticity of supply for agricultural goods when factors cannot easily be shifted in (or out) of the industry.

CHAPTER 7
Consumer Behavior and Utility

7 Consumer Behavior and Utility

By Timothy Taylor

Everyone has their own personal tastes and preferences. The French say: "Chacun à son goût," or "Each to his own taste." An old Latin saying states, "De gustibus non est disputandum," or "There's no disputing about taste." But if people's decisions are based on their own tastes and personal preferences, then how can economists hope to analyze such decisions?

An economic explanation for why people make different choices begins with accepting the proverbial wisdom that tastes are a matter of personal preference. But economists also believe that the choices people make are influenced by their incomes, by the prices of goods, and by factors like climate or natural setting. This chapter will introduce the economic theory of how households make choices about what to buy, how much to work, and how much to save. The analysis in this chapter will build upon the three budget constraints introduced in Chapter 2: the consumption choice budget constraint, the labor-leisure budget constraint, and the intertemporal budget constraint. This chapter will also illustrate how economic theory offers a systematic way of thinking about the full range of possible events and responses, which can prevent jumping to possibly misguided conclusions about how households will respond to changes in prices or incomes.

Consumption Choices

Information on the consumption choices of Americans is available from the Consumer Expenditure Survey that is carried out by the U.S. Bureau of Labor Statistics. Exhibit 8-1 shows spending patterns for the average U.S. household. The first row shows income, and after taxes and personal savings are subtracted, it shows that the average U.S. household spent $49,279 on consumption. The table then breaks down consumption into various categories. The average U.S. household spent roughly one-third of its consumption on shelter and other housing expenses, another one-third of its income on food and vehicle expenses, and the rest on the items shown. Of course, these patterns will vary for specific households by differing levels of family income, by geography, and by preferences.

Timothy Taylor, "Household Decision Making," *Principles of Macroeconomics*, pp. 149–168.

Exhibit 7-1 U.S. Consumption Choices in 2006–2007

Average U.S. household income before taxes	$61,820		
Average annual expenditure	$49,279		
Major Categories of Spending			
Food at home	$3,441 (7%)	Healthcare	$2,810 (6%)
Food away from home	$2,681 (5%)	Entertainment	$2,637 (5%)
Housing	$16,684 (34%)	Education	$917 (2%)
Apparel and services	$1,893 (4%)	Personal insurance and pensions	$5,305 (11%)
Transportation	$8,737 (18%)	All else: alcohol, tobacco, reading, personal care, cash contributions, miscellaneous	$4,177 (8%)

Total Utility and Diminishing Marginal Utility

To understand how a household will make its consumption choices, economists turn to the budget constraint model introduced in Chapter 2. That model uses a graph to illustrate the choice between two goods. The quantity of one good was measured on the horizontal axis and the quantity of the other good was measured on the vertical axis. The budget constraint line shows the various combinations of goods that it is possible to buy given a certain level of income. For example, consider the situation of Jose, shown in Exhibit 7-2. Jose likes to collects T-shirts and watch movies. In Exhibit 7-2a, the quantity of T-shirts that Jose purchases is shown on the horizontal axis, while the quantity of movies that he attends is shown on the vertical axis. If Jose had unlimited income or goods were free, then he could consume without limit. But Jose must face a consumption choice budget constraint. Jose has a total of $56 to spend. The price of T-shirts is $14 and the price of movies is $7. Five specific choices along the budget constraint, combinations of T-shirts and movies, are listed in the table and on the graph.

utility:
The level of satisfaction or pleasure that people receive from their choices.

marginal utility:
The additional utility provided by one additional unit of consumption.

Jose wishes to choose the point that will provide him with the greatest **utility**, which is the term that economists use to describe a person's level of satisfaction or happiness. Let's begin with an assumption, which will be discussed in more detail later, that Jose can measure his own utility with a measurement called "utils." Exhibit 7-2b presents two tables showing how Jose's utility is connected with his consumption of T-shirts or movies. The first column of the table shows the quantity of T-shirts consumed. The second column shows the total utility, or total amount of satisfaction, that Jose receives from consuming that number of T-shirts. The most common pattern of total utility, as shown here, is that consuming additional goods leads to greater total utility. The third column shows **marginal utility**, which is the additional utility provided by one additional unit of consumption. The most common pattern for marginal utility is **diminishing marginal utility**, which means that each marginal unit of a good consumed provides less of an addition to utility than the previous unit. For example, the first T-shirt Jose picks is his favorite. The fourth T-shirt is just to something to wear when all his other clothes are in the wash.

diminishing marginal utility:
The common pattern that each marginal unit of a good consumed provides less of an addition to utility than the previous unit.

Exhibit 7-2 A Choice between Consumption Goods

(a) Jose has income of $56. Movies cost $7 and T-shirts cost $14. The points on the budget constraint show his possible choices. (b) The table shows total utility and marginal utility from consumption of T-shirts and movies. The typical pattern, illustrated here, is that total utility rises as the quantity consumed rises, but marginal utility falls as the quantity consumed rises. (c) The table shows total utility at each point along Jose's consumption choice budget set. The maximum level of utility occurs at choice S.

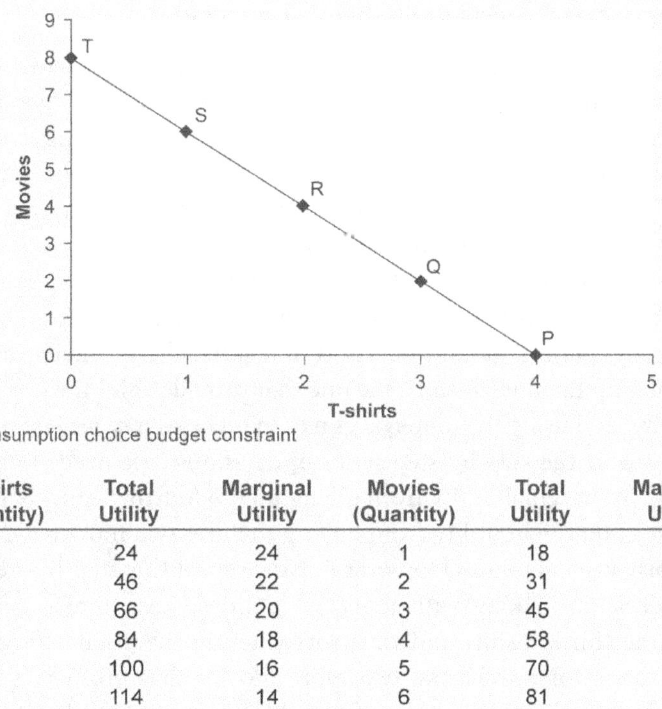

(a) A consumption choice budget constraint

T-Shirts (Quantity)	Total Utility	Marginal Utility	Movies (Quantity)	Total Utility	Marginal Utility
1	24	24	1	18	16
2	46	22	2	31	15
3	66	20	3	45	14
4	84	18	4	58	13
5	100	16	5	70	12
6	114	14	6	81	11
7	126	12	7	91	10
8	136	10	8	100	9

(b) Total and marginal utility

Point	T-Shirts	Movies	Total Utility
P	4	0	84 + 0 = 84
Q	3	2	66 + 31 = 97
R	2	4	46 + 58 = 104
S	1	6	24 + 81 = 105
T	0	8	0 + 100 = 100

(c) Finding the choice with the highest utiltiy

The rest of Exhibit 7-2b shows the quantity of movies that Jose attends, his total utility from consuming each quantity of movies, and his marginal utility from attending each additional movie. Total utility follows the expected pattern: it increases as the quantity of movies rises. Marginal utility also follows the expected pattern: each additional movie brings a smaller gain in utility than the previous one. The first movie Jose attends is the one he wanted to see the most, and thus provides him with the highest level of utility or satisfaction. The fifth movie he attends is just to kill time. Once Jose has defined in his own mind how much utility he will receive from consuming different quantities of T-shirts and movies, he is ready to make the choice that will give him the maximum amount of utility. Exhibit 7-2c looks at each point on the budget constraint in Exhibit 7-2a, adds up Jose's total utility numbers from Exhibit 7-2b for consuming T-shirts and movies, and calculates the total utility for each of Jose's possible choices. For Jose, the highest total utility for the possible combinations of goods occurs at point S, with a total utility of 105 from consuming 1 T-shirt and 6 movies.

CHOOSING WITH MARGINAL UTILITY

People are unlikely to carry around in their heads a mental picture of their total utility for every quantity consumed of every good. Instead, most people probably approach their utility-maximizing combination of choices in a step-by-step way. This step-by-step approach is based on looking at the trade-offs, measured in terms of marginal utility, of consuming less of one good and more of another.

For example, say that Jose starts off thinking about spending all his money on T-shirts and choosing point P in Exhibit 7-2. Jose chooses this starting point randomly; he has to start somewhere. Then Jose considers giving up the final T-shirt, the one that provides him the least marginal utility, and using the money he saves to buy two movies instead. Exhibit 7-3 tracks the step-by-step series of decisions Jose needs to make. The drop in marginal utility from giving up the fourth T-shirt is 18, but the gain in marginal utility from buying the first two movies is 31. So Jose clearly prefers point Q to point P. Now repeat this step-by-step process of decision-making with marginal utilities. Jose thinks about giving up the third T-shirt and thus surrendering marginal utility of 20, in exchange for purchasing two more movies that promise a combined marginal utility of 27. Jose prefers point R to point Q. What if Jose thinks about going beyond R to point S? Giving up the second T-shirt means a marginal utility loss of 22, and the marginal utility gain from the fifth and sixth movies would combine to make a marginal utility gain of 23, so Jose prefers point S to R.

However, if Jose seeks to go beyond point S to point T, he finds that the loss of marginal utility from giving up the first T-shirt is 24, while the marginal utility gain from the last two movies is only a total of 19. Through these stages of thinking about marginal trade-offs, Jose again concludes that S, with 1 T-shirt and 6 movies, is the choice that will provide him with the highest level of total utility. This step-by-step approach will reach the same conclusion regardless of Jose's original starting point.

A RULE FOR MAXIMIZING UTILITY

This process of decision making suggests a rule to follow when maximizing utility. Since the price of T-shirts is twice as high in this example, the marginal T-shirt needs to provide twice the marginal utility of a marginal movie. If the marginal T-shirt provides less than twice the marginal utility of the marginal movie, then the marginal T-shirt isn't providing enough utility to justify its relative price and Jose should attend more movies. If the marginal T-shirt provides more than twice the marginal utility of the marginal movie, then Jose should buy more T-shirts. Notice that at Jose's optimal choice of point S, the marginal utility from the second T-shirt, of 22, is exactly twice the marginal utility of the sixth movie, which is 11. At this choice, the marginal utility per dollar is the same for both goods. This is a tell-tale signal that Jose has found the point with highest total utility.

Exhibit 7-3 A Step-by- Step Approach to Maximizing Utility

T-shirts are $14, movies are $7, and income is $56.

Try	Which Has	Total Utility	Marginal Gain and Loss of Utility, Compared with Previous Choice	Conclusion
Choice 1: P	4 T-shirts and 0 movies	84 from 4 T-shirts + 0 from 0 movies = 84	—	—
Choice 2: Q	3 T-shirts and 2 movies	66 from 3 T-shirts + 31 from 0 movies = 97	Loss of 18 from 1 less T-shirt, but gain of 31 from 2 more movies, for a marginal utility gain of 14	Q is preferred over P
Choice 3: R	2 T-shirts and 4 movies	46 from 2 T-shirts + 58 from 4 movies = 104	Loss of 20 from 1 less T-shirt, but gain of 27 from two more movies for a marginal utility gain of 7	R is preferred over Q
Choice 4: S	1 T-shirt and 6 movies	24 from 1 T-shirt + 81 from 6 movies = 105	Loss of 22 from 1 less T-shirt, but gain of 23 from two more movies, for a marginal utility gain of 1	S is preferred over R
Choice 5: T	0 T-shirts and 8 movies	0 from 0 T-shirts + 100 from 8 movies = 100	Loss of 24 from 1 less T-shirt, but gain of 19 from two more movies, for a marginal utility loss of 5	S is preferred over T

This argument can be written as a general rule: the utility-maximizing choice between consumption goods occurs where the ratio of the prices of the two goods is equal to the ratio of the marginal utilities. When the price of good 1 is divided by the price of good 2, at the utility-maximizing point this will equal the marginal utility of good 1 divided by the marginal utility of good 2. This rule can be written in algebraic form:

$$\frac{P_1}{P_2} = \frac{MU_1}{MU_2}$$

Along the budget constraint, the prices of the two goods remain the same, so the ratio of the prices doesn't change. However, the marginal utility of the two goods changes with the quantities consumed. At the optimal choice of 1 T-shirt and 6 movies, point S, the price ratio of 2:1 matches the marginal utility trade-off of 22:11. A sensible economizer will only pay twice as much for something if, in the marginal comparison, the item confers twice as much utility.

MEASURING UTILITY WITH NUMBERS

This discussion of utility started off with an assumption that it is possible to place numerical values on utility, an assumption that may smell questionable. You can buy a thermometer for measuring temperature at the hardware store, but what store sells a "utilimometer" for measuring utility? However, while measuring utility with numbers is a convenient assumption to clarify the explanation, the key assumption is not that utility can be measured by an outside party, but only that individuals can decide what they prefer.

To understand this point, think back to the step-by-step process of finding the choice with highest total utility by comparing the marginal utility that is gained and lost from different choices along the budget constraint. As Jose compares each choice along his budget constraint to the previous choice, what matters is not the specific numbers that he places on his utility—or whether he uses any numbers at all—but only that he personally can identify which choices he prefers. In this way, the step-by-step process of choosing the highest level of utility resembles rather closely how many people make consumption decisions. We think about what will make us the happiest; we think about what things cost; we think about buying a little more of one item and giving up a little of something else; we choose what provides us with the greatest level of satisfaction. The vocabulary of comparing the points along a budget constraint and total and marginal utility is just a set of tools for discussing this everyday process in a clear and specific manner. It's welcome news that specific utility numbers aren't central to the argument, since a good utilimometer is hard to find.

How Changes in Income and Prices Affect Consumption

Choices Just as utility and marginal utility can be used to discuss making consumer choices along a budget constraint, these ideas can also be used to think about how consumer choices change when the budget constraint shifts in response to changes in income or price. Indeed, because the budget constraint framework can be used to analyze how quantities demanded change because of price movements, the budget constraint model can illustrate the underlying logic behind demand curves.

How Changes in Income Affect Consumer Choices

Let's begin with a concrete example illustrating how changes in income level affect consumer choices. Exhibit 7-4 shows a budget constraint that represents Kimberly's choice between concert tickets at $50 each and getting away overnight to a bed-andbreakfast for $200 per night. Kimberly has $1,000 per year to spend between these two choices. After thinking about her personal utility and marginal utility and applying the decision rule that the ratio of the prices should be equal to the ratio of marginal utilities, Kimberly chooses point M, with 6 concerts and 3 overnight getaways as her utility-maximizing choice.

Now assume that the income that Kimberly has to spend on these two items rises to $2,000 per year, causing her budget constraint to shift to the right. How does this rise in income alter Kimberly's utility-maximizing choice? Kimberly will again consider the utility and marginal utility that she receives from concert tickets and overnight getaways and seek her utility-maximizing choice on the new budget line. But how will her new choice relate to her original choice?

The possible choices along the new budget constraint can be divided into three groups, which are divided up by the dashed horizontal and vertical lines that pass through the original choice M in the figure. All choices on the upper left of the new budget constraint that are to the left of the vertical dashed line, like choice P with 2 concert tickets and 32 concerts, involve less of the good on the horizontal axis but much more of the good on the vertical axis. All choices to the right of the vertical dashed line and above the horizontal dashed line—like choice N with 5 overnight getaways and 20 concert tickets—have more consumption of both goods. Finally, all choices that are to the right of the vertical dashed line but below the horizontal dashed line, like choice Q with 4 concerts and 9 overnight getaways, involve less of the good on the vertical axis but much more of the good on the horizontal axis.

All of these possibilities are theoretically possible, depending on Kimberly's personal preferences as expressed through the total and marginal utility she would receive from consuming these two goods. When income rises, the most common reaction is to purchase more of both goods like choice N, which is to the upper right relative to Kimberly's original choice M, although exactly how much more of each good will vary according to personal taste. Conversely, when income falls, the

Exhibit 7-4 How a Change in Income Affects Consumption Choices

The utility-maximizing choice on the original budget constraint is M. The dashed horizontal and vertical lines extending through point M allow you to see at a glance whether the quantity consumed of goods on the new budget constraint is higher or lower than on the original budget constraint. On the new budget constraint, a choice like N will be made if both goods are normal goods. If overnight stays is an inferior good, a choice like P will be made. If concert tickets are an inferior good, a choice like Q will be made.

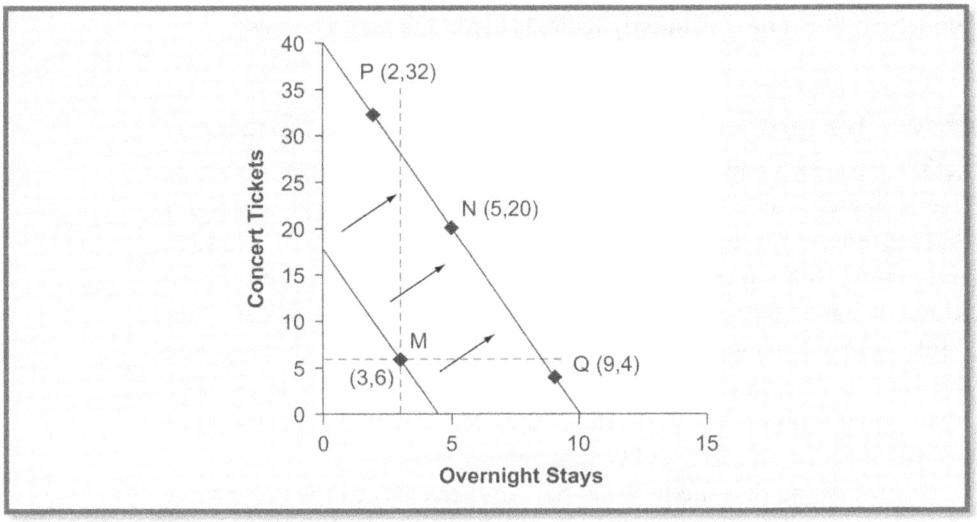

most typical reaction is to purchase less of both goods. As defined earlier in Chapter 4, goods and services are called "normal goods" when a rise in income leads to a rise in the quantity consumed of that good and a fall in income leads to a fall in quantity consumed.

However, depending on Kimberly's preferences, a rise in income could cause consumption of one good to increase while consumption of the other good declines. For example, a choice like P means that a rise in income caused her quantity consumed of overnight stays to decline, while a choice like Q would mean that a rise in income caused her quantity of concerts to decline. Goods where the quantity demanded declines as income rises (or conversely, where the quantity demanded rises as income falls) are called "inferior goods." An inferior good occurs when people trim back on a good as income rises, because they can now afford the more expensive choices that they prefer. For example, a higher-income household might eat less hamburger or be less likely to buy a used car, and instead eat more steak and buy a new car.

HOW PRICE CHANGES AFFECT CONSUMER CHOICES

For analyzing the possible effect of a change in price on consumption, let's again use a concrete example. Exhibit 7-5 represents the consumer choice of Ichiro, who chooses between purchasing baseball bats and cameras. A price increase for baseball bats, the good on the horizontal axis, causes the budget constraint to move inward, as if on a hinge from the vertical axis. As in the previous section, the point labeled M represents the originally preferred point on the original budget constraint, which Ichiro has chosen after contemplating his personal utility and marginal utility and the trade-offs involved along the budget constraint. In this example, the units along the horizontal and vertical axis are not numbered, so the discussion must focus on whether more or less of certain goods will be consumed, not on numerical amounts.

After the price increase, Ichiro will make a choice along the new budget constraint. Again, his choices along the new budget constraint can be divided into three segments by the dashed vertical and horizontal lines. In the upper left portion of the new budget constraint, at a choice like H, Ichiro consumes more cameras and fewer bats; in the central portion of the new budget constraint, at a choice like J, he consumes less of both goods; at the right-hand end, at a choice like L, he consumes more bats but fewer cameras.

The typical response to higher prices is that a person chooses to consume less of the product with the higher price. This effect occurs for two reasons, which occur simultaneously. The **substitution effect** is that when a price changes, consumers have an incentive to consume less of the good with a relatively higher price and more of the good with a relatively lower price. The **income effect** is that a higher price means that, in effect, the buying power of income has been reduced (even though actual income has not changed), which lead to buying less of the good. In this example, the higher price for baseball bats would cause Ichiro to consume a lower quantity of bats because the substitution effect will encourage him to substitute consumption away from the relatively higher-priced bats and the income effect of a higher price reduces his buying power and also encourages reduced consumption of bats.

substitution effect:
When a price changes, consumers have an incentive to consume less of the good with a relatively higher price and more of the good with a relatively lower price; always happens simultaneously with an income effect.

income effect:
A higher price means that, in effect, the buying power of income has been reduced, even though actual income has not changed; always happens simultaneously with a substitution effect.

Exactly how much will a higher price for bats cause Ichiro's consumption of bats to fall? Exhibit 7-5 suggests a range of possibilities. Ichiro might react to a higher price for baseball bats by purchasing the same quantity of bats, but cutting his consumption of cameras. This choice is the point K on the new budget constraint straight below the original choice M. Alternatively, Ichiro might react by dramatically reducing his purchases of bats, and instead buying more cameras, at a choice that represents buying fewer of both goods. The key conclusion is that it would be imprudent to assume that a change in the price of baseball bats will only or primarily affect the good whose price is changed, while the quantity consumed of other goods remains the same. A change in the price of one good can also have a range of effects, either positive or negative, on the quantity consumed of other goods.

What about a choice like point L in the lower right of the new budget constraint? In this case, Ichiro responds to a higher price for baseball bats by purchasing more bats. A good where a higher price leads to a higher quantity demanded for a good (or a lower price leads to a lower quantity demanded for a good) is a theoretical possibility, discovered more than a century ago, and called a **Giffen good**. The demand curve for a Giffen good would slope up, rather than down! However, Giffen goods should be considered a theoretical possibility rather than a likely event. A famous economist named Francis Ysidro Edgeworth (1845–1926)

Giffen good:
The theoretical but unrealistic possibility that a higher price for a good could lead to a higher quantity demanded (or a lower price leads to a lesser quantity demanded).

Exhibit 7-5 How a Change in Price Affects Consumption Choices

The original utility-maximizing choice is M. When the price rises, the budget constraint shifts in to the left. The dashed lines make it possible to see at a glance whether the new consumption choice involves less of both goods, or less of one good and more of the other. The new possible choices would be less baseball bats and more cameras, like point H, or less of both goods, as at point J. Choice K would mean that the higher price of bats led to exactly the same quantity of bats being consumed, but fewer cameras. Choices like L are ruled out as theoretically possible but highly unlikely in the real world, because they would mean that a higher price for baseball bats means a greater quantity consumed of baseball bats.

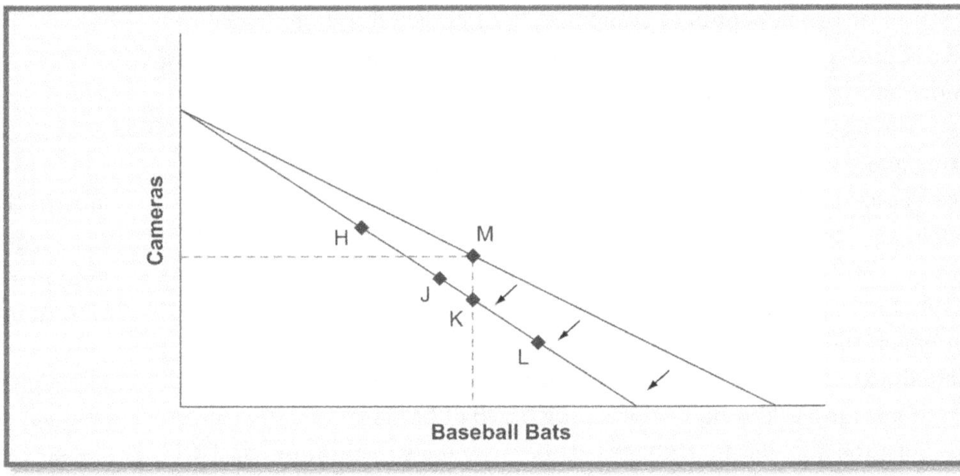

summed up the situation regarding Giffen goods in this way in 1914: "Only a very clever man would discover that exceptional case; only a very foolish man would take it as the basis of a rule for general practice."

THE FOUNDATIONS OF DEMAND CURVES

Changes in the price of a good lead the budget constraint to shift. A shift in the budget constraint means that when individuals are seeking their highest utility, the quantity that is demanded of that good will change. In this way, the logical foundations of demand curves—which show a connection between prices and quantity demanded—are based on the underlying idea of individuals seeking utility. Exhibit 7-6a shows a budget constraint with a choice between housing and "everything else." (Putting "everything else" on the vertical axis can be a useful approach in some cases, especially when the focus of the analysis is on one particular good.) The preferred choice on the original budget constraint that provides the highest possible utility is labeled M_0. The other three budget constraints represent successively higher prices for housing of P_1, P_2, and P_3. As the budget constraint shifts in, and in, and in again, the utility-maximizing choice are labeled M_1, M_2, and M_3, and the quantity demanded of housing falls from Q_0 to Q_1 to Q_2 to Q_3.

Thus, as the price of housing rises, the budget constraint shifts to the left, and the quantity consumed of housing falls. This relationship—the

Preferences Inside the Household?

In the mid-1970s, the United Kingdom made an interesting policy change in its "child allowance" policy. This program provides a fixed amount of money per child to every family, regardless of family income. Traditionally, the child allowance had been distributed to families by withholding less in taxes from the paycheck of the family wage earner— typically the father in this time period. The new policy instead provided the child allowance as a cash payment to the mother. As a result of this change, households have the same level of income and face the same prices in the market, but the money is more likely to be in the purse of the mother than in the wallet of the father.

Should this change in policy alter household consumption patterns? Basic models of consumption decisions, of the sort examined in this chapter, assume that it doesn't matter whether the mother or the father receives the money, because both parents seek to maximize the utility of the family as a whole. In effect, this model assumes that everyone in the family has the same preferences.

In reality, the share of income controlled by the father or the mother does affect what the household consumes. When the mother controls a larger share of family income, a number of studies in the United Kingdom and in a wide variety of other countries have found that the family tends to spend more on restaurant meals, child care, and women's clothing, and less on alcohol and tobacco. As the mother controls a larger share of household resources, children's health improves, too. These findings suggest that when providing assistance to poor families, in high-income countries and low-income countries alike, the monetary amount of assistance isn't all that matters: it also matters which member of the family actually receives the money.

price of housing rising from P_0 to P_1 to P_2 to P_3, while the quantity of housing demanded falls from Q_0 to Q_1 to Q_2 to Q_3—is graphed on the demand curve in Exhibit 7-6b. Indeed, the vertical dashed lines stretching between the top and bottom of Exhibit 7-6 show that the quantity of housing demanded at each point is the same in both (a) and (b). Thus, the shape of a demand curve is ultimately determined by the underlying choices about maximizing utility subject to a budget constraint.

APPLICATIONS IN BUSINESS AND GOVERNMENT

The budget constraint framework for making utility-maximizing choices offers a reminder that people can react to a change in price or income in a range of different ways. For example, in the winter months of 2005, costs for heating homes skyrocketed in many parts of the country as prices for natural gas and electricity soared. Many people reacted by reducing the quantity demanded of energy; for example, by turning down the thermostats in their homes by a few degrees and or wearing a heavier sweater inside. Even so, many home heating bills rose as much as $200 dollars per month or even more, so people adjusted their consumption in other ways, too. Each household cut back on what it valued least on the margin; for some it might have been some dinners out, or a vacation, or postponing buying a new refrigerator or a new car. Indeed, sharply higher energy prices can have effects beyond the energy

Exhibit 7-6 The Foundations of a Demand Curve: An Example of Housing

(a) As the price increases from P_0 to P_1 to P_2 to P_3, the budget constraint on the upper part of the diagram shifts to the left. The utilitymaximizing choice changes from M_0 to M_1 to M_2 to M_3. As a result, the quantity demanded of housing shifts from Q_0 to Q_1 to Q_2 to Q_3. (b) The demand curve graphs each combination of the price of housing and the quantity of housing demanded. Indeed, the quantities of housing are the same at the points on both (a) and (b). Thus, the original price of housing P_0 and the original quantity of housing Q_0 appear on the demand curve as point E_0. The higher price of housing P_1 and the corresponding lower quantity demanded of housing Q_1 appear on the demand curve as point E_1.

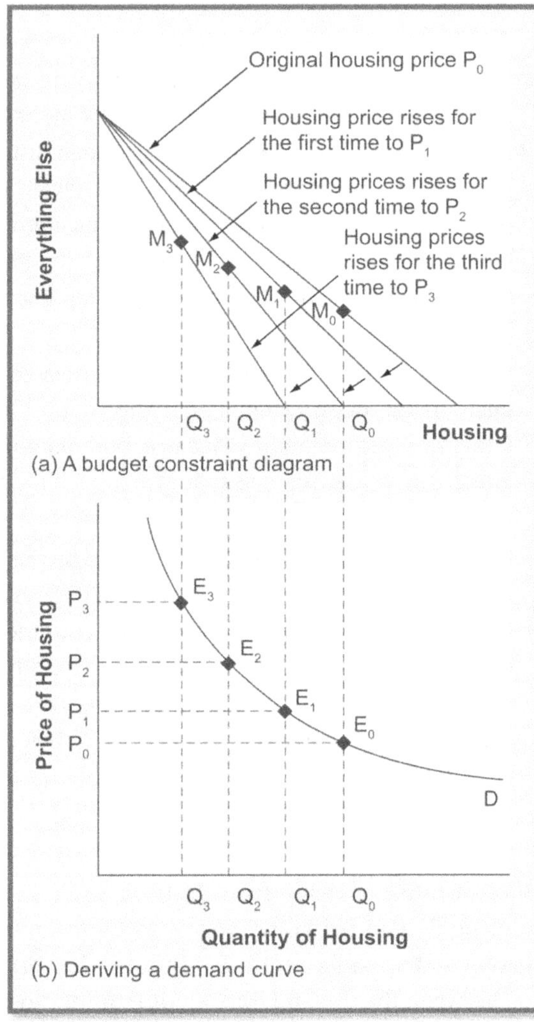

market, leading to a widespread reduction in purchasing throughout the rest of the economy.

A similar issue arises when the government imposes taxes on certain products, like it does on gasoline, cigarettes, and alcohol. Say that a tax on alcohol leads to a higher price at the liquor store, the higher price of alcohol causes the budget constraint to pivot left, and consumption of alcoholic beverages is likely to decrease. However, people may also react to the higher price of alcoholic beverages by cutting back on other purchases; for example, they might cut back on snacks at restaurants like chicken wings and nachos. It would be unwise to assume that the alcoholic beverage industry is the only industry affected by the tax on alcoholic beverages.

As a final example of the range of possible reactions, consider a proposal that came up in the aftermath of the terrorist airplane hijackings on September 11, 2001. Congress believed that it was necessary to provide some financial assistance to airlines. One possible method of providing that assistance was in the form of coupons for airline tickets that would be distributed to all Americans, thus providing assistance to ordinary Americans as well as to the airline companies. But what happens if Americans spend their coupons on airplane trips they would have taken anyway, and then use the money they saved to purchase something else? Since airline coupons free up income to spend in other ways, they are very similar to receiving additional income in the form of cash. The result may be that air travel coupons don't give any special assistance to the airline industry—at least no more assistance than a distribution of government checks would have provided. Of course, this argument doesn't prove that the $15 billion package of government assistance to airlines passed in October 2001 was sensible, or the right amount of money. But at least handing the money directly to the airlines made sure that the airlines actually received the money, rather than opening up the possibility that the main impact of an attempt to assist the airlines would be felt in other markets. The budget constraint framework serves as a constant reminder to think about the full range of effects that can arise from changes in income or price, not just effects on the one product that might seem most immediately affected.

Labor-Leisure Choices

The decision-making process of a utility-maximizing household applies to decisions about what quantity of hours to work in much the same way that it applies to purchases of goods and services. Choices made along the labor-leisure budget constraint, as wages shift, provide the logical underpinning for the labor supply curve. The discussion also offers some insights about the range of possible reactions when people receive higher wages, and specifically about the claim that if people are paid higher wages, they will work a greater quantity of hours.

U.S. workers averaged 39.2 hours per week on the job in 2007. This average includes part-timers; for full-time workers only, the average was

Hours Worked per Week	Number of Workers	Percentage of Workforce
1–14 hours	6.4 million	4.6%
15–34 hours	25.9 million	18.5%
35–40 hours	69.3 million	49.4%
41–48 hours	13.6 million	9.7%
49–59 hours	14.5 million	10.3%
60 hours and over	10.4 million	7.4%

Exhibit 7-7

Persons at Work, by Average Hours Worked per Week in 2007 (Total number of workers: 140.1 million)

Total compensation per hour	$26.42
Wages and salaries	$18.67
Vacation and holiday pay	$1.50
Sick leave and other leave	$0.28
Bonuses and premium pay	$0.79
Employee insurance (mainly health)	$1.87
Company retirement plans	$0.95
Employer payments to Social Security	$1.25
Unemployment and worker's compensation insurance	$0.66
Other benefits (Medicare)	$0.31

Exhibit 7-8

Total Compensation: Wages, Benefits, and Taxes in 2007

42.9 hours per week. Exhibit 7-7 shows that more than half of all workers are on the job 35–48 hours per week of work, but significant proportions work less or more than this amount. Exhibit 8-8 breaks down the average compensation received by private industry workers, including wages and benefits. Wages and salaries are about three-quarters of total compensation received by workers; the rest is in the form of health insurance, vacation pay, and other benefits. The compensation received by workers differs for many reasons, including experience, education, skill, talent, membership in a labor union, and the presence of discrimination against certain groups in the labor market. Issues surrounding the inequality of incomes in a market-oriented economy are explored in Chapters 16 and 17.

THE LABOR-LEISURE BUDGET CONSTRAINT

How do workers make their decisions about the quantity of hours to work? Again, let's proceed with a concrete example. The economic logic is precisely the same as in the case of a consumption choice budget constraint, but the labels are different on a labor-leisure budget constraint.

Vivian has 70 hours per week that she could devote either to working or leisure, and her wage is $10/hour. The lower budget constraint in Exhibit 7-9 shows Vivian's possible choices. As discussed in Chapter 2, the horizontal axis of this diagram measures both leisure and labor, by showing how Vivian's time is divided between leisure and labor. Hours of leisure are measured from left to right on the horizontal axis, while hours of labor are measured from right to left. Vivian will compare choices along this budget constraint, ranging from 70 hours of leisure and no income at point S to zero hours of leisure and $700 of income at point L. She will choose the point which provides her with the highest total utility. For this example, let's assume that Vivian's utility-maximizing choice occurs at O, with 30 hours of leisure, 40 hours of work, and $400 in weekly income.

For Vivian to discover the labor-leisure choice that will maximize her utility, she doesn't have to place numerical values on the total and marginal utility that she would receive from every level of income and leisure. All that really matters is that Vivian can compare, in her own mind, whether she would prefer more leisure or more income, given the trade-offs she faces. If Vivian can say to herself: "You know, I'd really rather work a little less and have more leisure, even if it means less income," or "You know, I'd be willing to work more hours to make some extra income," then as she gradually moves in the direction of her preferences, she will seek out the utility-maximizing choice on her labor-leisure budget constraint.

Now imagine that Vivian's wage level increases to $12/hour. A higher wage will mean a new budget constraint that tilts up more steeply; conversely, a lower wage would have led to a new budget constraint that was flatter. How will a change in the wage and the corresponding shift in the budget constraint affect Vivian's decisions about how many hours to work? Vivian's choices of quantity of hours to work and income along

Exhibit 7-9 How a Rise in Wages Alters the Utility-Maximizing Choice

Vivian's original choice is point O on the lower opportunity set. A rise in her wage causes her opportunity set to swing upward. In response to the increase in wages, Vivian can make a range of different choices available to her: a choice like D, which involves less work; and a choice like B, which involves the same amount of work but more income; or a choice like A, which involves more work and considerably more income. Vivian's personal preferences will determine which choice she makes.

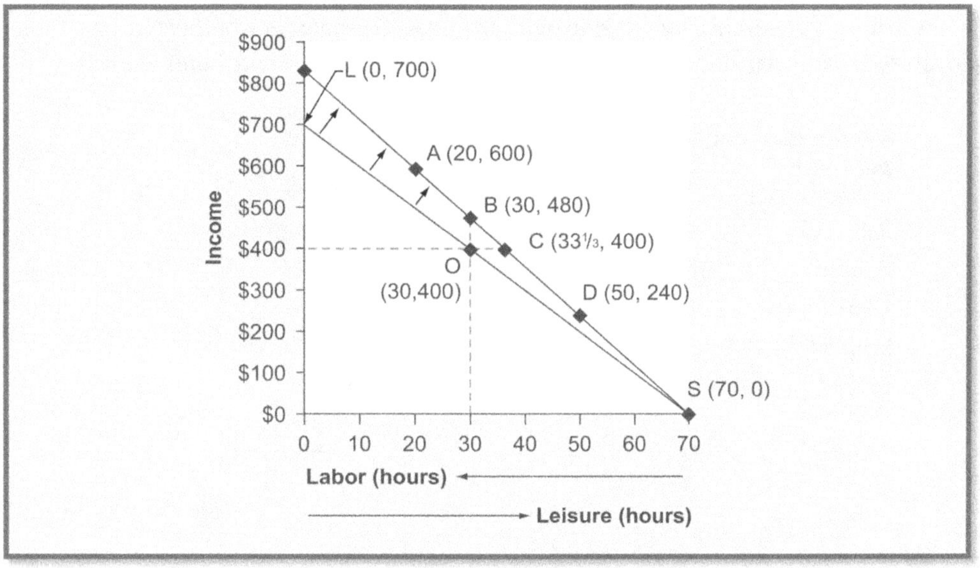

her new budget constraint can be divided into several categories, using the dashed horizontal and vertical lines in Exhibit 7-9 that go through her original choice O. One set of choices in the upper-left portion of the new budget constraint involve more hours of work (that is, less leisure) and more income, at a point like A with 20 hours of leisure, 50 hours of work, and $600 of income (that is, 50 hours of work multiplied by the new wage of $12 per hour). A second choice would be to work exactly the same 40 hours, and to take the benefits of the higher wage in the form of income that would now be $480, at choice B. A third choice would involve more leisure and income at point C (that is, 33-1/3 hours of work multiplied by the new wage of $12 per hour equals $400 of total income). A fourth choice would involve less income and more much more leisure at point like D, with a choice like 50 hours of leisure, 20 hours of work, and $240 in income.

In effect, Vivian can choose whether to receive the benefits of her wage increase in the form of more income, or more leisure, or some mixture of these two. With this range of possibilities, it would be unwise to assume that Vivian (or anyone else) will necessarily react to a wage increase by working substantially more hours. Maybe they will; maybe they won't.

Is America a Nation of Workaholics?

Americans work a lot. The table shows average hours worked per year in the United States, Canada, Japan, and several European countries, with most of the data from 2008. To get a perspective on these numbers, someone who works 40 hours per week for 50 weeks per year, with two weeks off, would work 2,000 hours per year. The gap in hours worked is a little astonishing; the 250-300 hour gap between how much Americans work and how much Germans or the French work amounts to roughly 6-7 weeks less of work per year! Economists who study these international patterns debate the extent to whether average Americans and Japanese have a preference for working more than, say, Germans, or whether German workers and employers face particular kinds of taxes and regulations that lead to fewer hours worked.

Average annual hours actually worked per employed person	
United States	1,824
Japan	1,759
Spain	1,799
Canada	1,751
United Kingdom	1,669
France	1,441
Germany	1,443
Sweden	1,585

APPLICATIONS OF UTILITY MAXIMIZING WITH THE LABOR-LEISURE BUDGET CONSTRAINT

The theoretical insight that higher wages will sometimes cause an increase in hours worked, sometimes cause hours worked not to change by much, and sometimes cause hours worked to decline, has led to labor supply curves that look like the one in Exhibit 7-10. The bottom-left portion of the labor supply curve slopes upward, which reflects the situation of a person who reacts to a higher wage by supplying a greater quantity of labor. The middle, close-to-vertical portion of the labor supply curve reflects of labor. The very top portion of the labor supply curve is called a **backward-bending supply curve for labor**, which is the situation of high-wage people who can earn so much that they respond to a still-higher wage by working fewer hours.

backward-bending supply curve for labor: The situation when high-wage people can earn so much that they respond to a still-higher wage by working fewer hours.

The different responses to a rise in wages—more hours worked, the same hours worked, or fewer hours worked—are patterns exhibited by different groups of workers in the U.S. economy. Many full-time workers have jobs where the number of hours is held relatively fixed, partly by their own choice and partly by their employer's practices. These workers don't much change their hours worked as wages rise or fall, so their supply curve of labor is inelastic. However, part-time workers and younger workers tend to be more flexible in their hours, and more ready to increase hours worked when wages are high or cut back when wages fall.

The backward-bending supply curve for labor, when workers react to higher wages by working fewer hours and having more income, is not

Exhibit 7-10 A Backward-Bending Supply Curve of Labor

The bottom upward-sloping portion of the labor supply curve shows that as wages increase over this range, the quantity of hours worked also increases. The middle, nearly vertical portion of the labor supply curve shows that as wages increase over this range, the quantity of hours worked changes very little. The backward-bending portion of the labor supply curve at the top shows that as wages increase over this range, the quantity of hours worked actually decreases. All three of these possibilities can be derived from the how a change in wages causes movement in the labor-leisure budget constraint, and thus different choices by individuals.

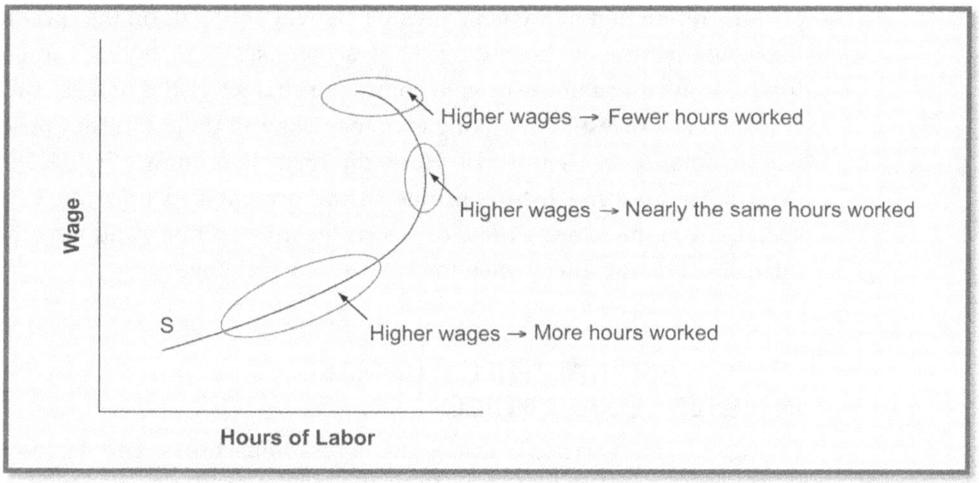

observed often in the short run. However, some well-paid professionals, like dentists or accountants, may react to higher wages by choosing to limit the number of hours, perhaps by taking especially long vacations, or taking every other Friday off. Over a long-term perspective, the backward-bending supply curve for labor is common. Over the last century, Americans have reacted to gradually rising wages by working fewer hours; for example, the length of the average work-week has fallen from about 60 hours per week back in 1900 to the present average of less than 40 hours per week.

Recognizing that workers have a range of possible reactions to a change in wages casts some fresh insight on a perennial political debate: the claim that a reduction in income taxes—which would, in effect, allow people to earn more per hour—will encourage people to work more. The leisure-income budget set points out that this connection will not hold true for all workers. Some people, especially part-timers, probably will react to higher wages by working more. Many will work the same number of hours. Some people, especially those whose incomes are already high, may react to the tax cut by working fewer hours. Of course, cutting taxes may be a good or a bad idea for a variety of reasons, not just because of its impact on work incentives, but the specific claim that that tax cuts will lead people to work more hours is only likely to hold for specific groups of workers and will depend on how and for whom taxes are cut.

Intertemporal Choices in Financial Capital Markets

Rates of saving in America have never been especially high, but they seem to have dipped even lower in recent years, as shown in Exhibit 7-11. A decision about how much to save can be represented on the intertemporal budget constraint that was introduced in Chapter 2. Household decisions about the quantity of financial savings show the same underlying pattern of logic as the consumption choice decision and the labor-leisure decision.

The discussion of financial saving here will not focus on the specific financial investment choices, like bank accounts, stocks, bonds, mutual funds, or owning a house or gold coins. The characteristics of these specific financial investments, along with the risks and trade-offs they pose, will be detailed in Chapter 19. Here, the focus is on how a household determines how much to consume in the present and how much to spend, given the expected rate of return (or interest rate), and how the quantity of saving alters when the rate of return changes.

USING MARGINAL UTILITY TO MAKE INTERTEMPORAL CHOICES

Savings behavior varies considerably across households. One factor is that households with higher incomes tend to save a larger percentage of their income. This pattern makes intuitive sense; a well-to-do family has the flexibility in its budget to save 20–25% of income, while a poor family struggling to keep food on the table will find it harder to put money aside.

life-cycle theory of savings: The common pattern that many people save little or borrow heavily early in life, save more in the middle of life, and then draw upon their accumulated savings later in life.

A second key factor is linked to age. The **life-cycle theory of savings** points out a common pattern that many people save little or borrow heavily early in life, so that they can pay for a college education and buy a first home; save more in the middle of life, to pay off college and home loans and to prepare for retirement; and then draw upon their accumulated savings later in life after retirement. A third factor that causes personal saving to vary is personal preferences. Some people may prefer to consume more now, and let the future look after itself. Others may wish to enjoy a lavish retirement, complete with expensive vacations, or to pile up money that they can pass along to their grandchildren. There are savers and spendthrifts among the young, middle-aged and old, and among those with high, middle, and low income levels. Yelberton is a young man starting off at his first job. He thinks of the "present" as his working life and the "future" as after retirement.

Yelberton's plan is to save money from ages 30–55, retire at age 60, and then live off his retirement money from ages 60–85. On average, therefore, he will be saving for 30 years. If the rate of return that he can receive is 6% per year, then $1 saved in the present would build up to $5.74 after 30 years (using the formula for compound interest, $1(1+.06)30 = $5.74). Say that Yelberton will earn $1,000,000 over the 25 years from age 30 to age 55 (this amount is an annual salary of $40,000

Exhibit 7-11 Personal Savings as a Percentage of Personal Income

Personal savings were about 7–11% of personal income for most of the years from the late 1950s up to the early 1990s. Since then, the rate of personal savings has fallen substantially, although it seems to have bounced back a bit in 2008.

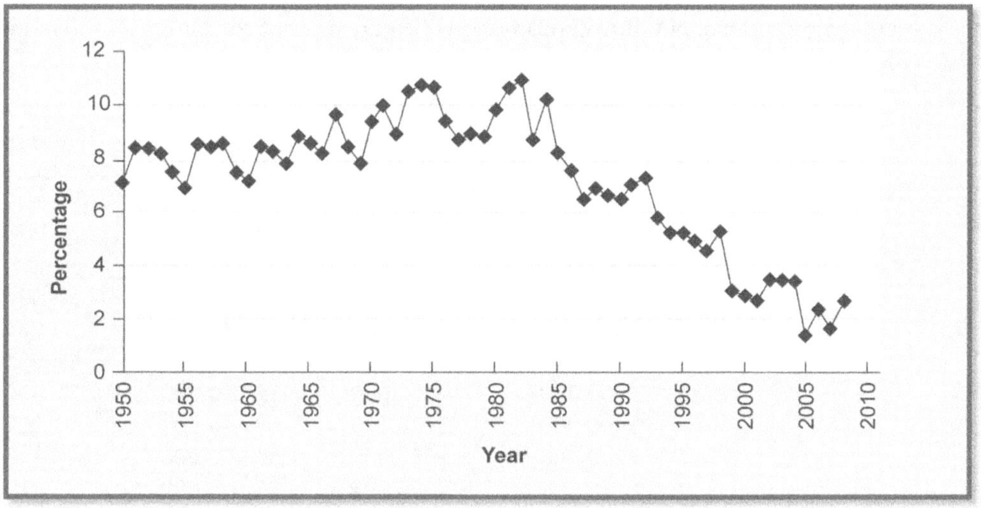

multiplied by 25 years). Thus, the question for Yelberton is how much of those lifetime earnings to consume during his working life, and how much to put aside until after retirement. This example is obviously built on simplifying assumptions, but it does convey the basic life-cycle choice of saving during working life for future consumption after retirement.

Exhibit 7-12 shows Yelberton's intertemporal budget constraint. Yelberton's choice involves comparing the utility of present consumption during his working life and future consumption after retirement. The rate of return that determines the slope of the intertemporal budget line between present consumption and future consumption in this example is the annual interest rate compounded over 30 years, not just one year. Thus, in the lower budget constraint line on the exhibit, future consumption in this table grows by increments of $574,000, because each time $100,000 is saved in the present, it compounds to $574,000 after 30 years at a 6% interest rate. If some of the numbers on the future consumption axis look bizarrely large, remember that this occurs because of the power of compound interest over substantial periods of time, and because the figure is grouping together all of Yelberton's saving for retirement over his lifetime.

Yelberton will compare the different choices along the budget constraint and choose the one that provides him with the highest utility. For example, he will compare the utility he would receive from a choice like point A, with consumption of $1 million in the present, zero savings, and zero future consumption; point B, with present consumption of $800,000, savings of $200,000, and future consumption of $1,148,000; point C, with present consumption of $600,000, savings of $400,000, and future consumption of $2,296,000; or even choice D, with present

Exhibit 7-12 Yelberton's Choice: The Intertemporal Budget Set

Yelberton will make a choice between present and future consumption. With an annual rate of return of 6%, he decides that his utility will be highest at point B, which represents a choice of $800,000 in present consumption and $1,148,000 in future consumption. When the annual rate of return rises to 9%, the intertemporal budget constraint pivots up. Yelberton could choose to take the gains from this higher rate of return in several forms: more present saving and much higher future consumption (J), the same present saving and higher future consumption (K), more present consumption and more future consumption (L), or more present consumption and the same future consumption (M).

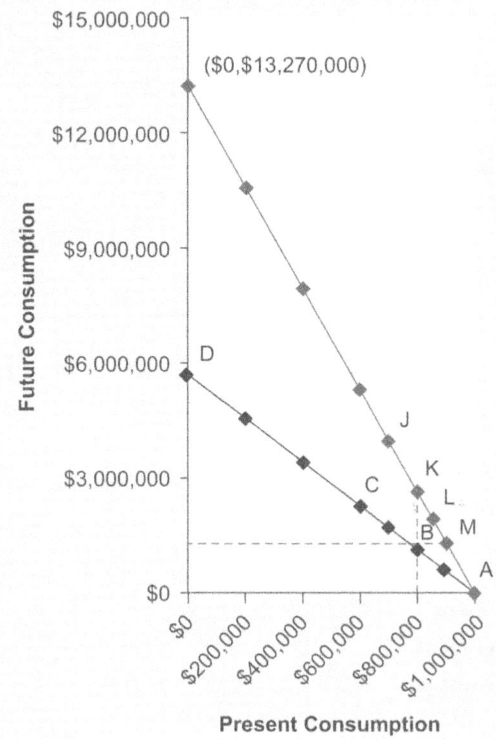

Present Consumption	Savings	Future Consumption (6% annual return)	Future Consumption (9% annual return)
$1,000,000	0	0	0
$900,000	$100,000	$574,000	$1,327,000
$800,000	$200,000	$1,148,000	$2,654,000
$700,000	$300,000	$1,722,000	$3,981,000
$600,000	$400,000	$2,296,000	$5,308,000
$400,000	$600,000	$3,444,000	$7,962,000
$200,000	$800,000	$4,592,000	$10,616,000
0	$1,000,000	$5,740,000	$13,270,000

consumption of zero, savings of $1,000,000, and future consumption of $5,740,000. Yelberton will also ask himself questions like:

"Would I prefer to consume a little less in the present, save more, and have more future consumption?" or "Would I prefer to consume a little more in the present, save less, and have less future consumption?" In this way, by considering marginal changes toward more or less consumption, he can seek out the choice that will provide him with the highest level of utility. Let's say that Yelberton's preferred choice is B.

Imagine that Yelberton's annual rate of return rises from 6% to 9%. In this case, each time he saves $100,000 in the present, it will be worth $1,327,000 30 years from now (using the formula for compound interest that $100,000 (1 + .09)30 = $1,327,000). A change in rate of return alters the slope of the intertemporal budget constraint: a higher rate of return or interest rate will cause the budget line to pivot upwards, while a lower rate of return will cause it to swing downwards. If Yelberton were to consume nothing in the present and save all $1,000,000, with a 9% rate of return, his future consumption would be $13,270,000, as shown on Exhibit 7-12.

As the rate of return rises, Yelberton considers a range of choices on the new intertemporal budget constraint. The dashed vertical and horizontal lines running through the original choice B help to illustrate his range of options. One choice is to reduce present consumption (that is, to save more) and to have considerably higher future consumption at a point like J above and to the left of his original choice B. A second choice would be to keep the level of present consumption and savings the same, and to receive the benefits of the higher rate of return entirely in the form of higher future consumption, which would be choice K. A third choice would be that Yelberton could have both more present consumption—that is, less savings—but still have higher future consumption because of the higher interest rate, which would be choice like L, above and to the right of his original choice B. Thus, the higher rate of return might cause Yelberton to save more, or less, or the same amount, depending on his own preferences. A fourth choice would be that Yelberton could react to the higher rate of return by increasing his current consumption and leaving his future consumption unchanged, as at point M directly to the right of his original choice B. The actual choice of what quantity to save and how saving will respond to changes in the rate of return will vary from person to person, according to the choice that will maximize each person's utility.

APPLICATIONS OF THE MODEL OF INTERTEMPORAL CHOICE

The theoretical model of the intertemporal budget constraint suggests that when the rate of return rises, the quantity of saving may rise, fall, or remain the same, depending on the preferences of individuals. For the U.S. economy as a whole, the most common pattern seems to be that the quantity of savings doesn't adjust much to changes in the rate of return. As a practical matter, many households either save at a fairly steady pace, by putting regular contributions into a retirement account or by making regular payments as they buy a house, or they don't save much at all. Of course, some people will have preferences that cause them to react to a higher rate of return by increasing their quantity of saving; others who will react to a higher rate of return by noticing that with a higher rate of return, they can save less in the present and still have higher future consumption. One prominent example in which a higher rate of return leads to a lower savings rate occurs when firms save money because they have promised to pay workers a certain fixed level of pension benefits after retirement. When rates of return rise, those companies can save less money in the present in their pension fund and still have enough to pay the promised retirement benefits in the future.

This insight suggests some skepticism about political proposals to encourage higher savings by providing savers with a higher rate of return. For example, Individual Retirement Accounts (IRAs) and 401(k) accounts are special savings accounts where the money going into the account is not taxed until it is taken out many years later, after retirement. The main difference between these accounts is that an IRA is usually set up by an individual while a 401(k) needs to be set up through an employer. By not taxing saving in the present, the effect of an IRA or a 401(k) is to increase the return to saving in these accounts. IRA and 401(k) accounts have attracted a large quantity of savings since they became common in the late 1980s and early 1990s. For example, the amount in IRAs rose from $239 billion in 1992 to $3,667 billion by 2005. However, overall U.S. personal savings, as discussed earlier, actually dropped from low to lower in the late 1990s and into the 2000s. Evidently, the larger amounts in these retirement accounts are being offset, in the economy as a whole, either by less savings in other kinds of accounts, or by a larger amount of borrowing (that is, negative savings).

A rise in interest rates makes it easier for people to enjoy higher future consumption. But it also allows them to enjoy higher present consumption, if that is what individuals desire. Again, a change in prices—in this case, in interest rates—leads to a range of possible outcomes.

The Unifying Power of the Utility-Maximizing Budget Set Framework

The choices of households are determined by an interaction between prices, budget constraints, and personal preferences. The flexible and powerful terminology of utility-maximizing gives economists a vocabulary for bringing these elements together. Not even economists believe that people walk around mumbling about their marginal utilities before they walk into a shopping mall, accept a job, or make a deposit in a savings account. However, economists do believe that individuals seek their own satisfaction or utility and that people often decide to try a little less of one thing and a little more of another. If these gentle assumptions are accepted, then idea of utility-maximizing households facing budget constraints becomes highly plausible, too.

Key Concepts and Summary

1. Economic analysis of household behavior is based on the assumption that people seek the highest level of **utility** or satisfaction. Individuals are the only judge of their own utility.
2. In general, greater consumption of a good brings higher *total utility*. However, the additional utility received from each unit of greater consumption tends to decline in a pattern of **diminishing marginal utility**.
3. The utility-maximizing choice on a consumption budget constraint can be found in several ways. You can add up total utility of each choice on the budget-line and choose the highest total. You can choose a starting point at random and compare the marginal utility gains and losses of moving to neighboring points—and thus eventually seek out the preferred choice. Alternatively, you can compare the ratio of the prices of goods 1 and 2 to the ratio of the

marginal utilities of goods 1 and 2 and apply the rule that at the optimal choice, the ratio of prices must equal the ratio of marginal utilities: $P_1/P_2 = MU_1/MU_2$.

4. The budget constraint framework suggest that when income or price changes, a range of responses are possible. When income rises, households will demand a higher quantity of normal goods, but a lower quantity of inferior goods. When the price of a good rises, households will typically demand less of that good—but whether they will demand a much lower quantity or only a slightly lower quantity will depend on personal preferences. Also, a higher price for one good can lead to more or less of the other good being demanded.
5. When making a choice along the labor-leisure budget constraint, a household will choose the combination of labor, leisure, and income that provides the most utility. The result of a change in wage levels can be higher work effort, the same work effort, or lower work effort.
6. When making a choice along the intertemporal budget constraint, a household will choose the combination of present consumption, savings, and future consumption that provides the most utility. The result of a higher rate of return (or higher interest rates) can be a higher quantity of saving, the same quantity of saving, or a lower quantity of saving, depending on preferences about present and future consumption.

Vocabulary Terms

(note: some of these are in the Chapter 7 Appendix, which immediately follows this chapter)

Budget constraint
Giffen good
Income effect
Indifference Curves
Marginal utility
Substitution effect
Total utility
Utility maximization equation

Review Questions

1. Who makes the decision about how much utility an individual will receive from consuming a good?
2. Would you expect total utility to rise or fall with additional consumption of a good? Why?
3. Would you expect marginal utility to rise or fall with additional consumption of a good? Why?

4. Is it possible for total utility to increase while marginal utility diminishes? Explain.
5. If a person does not have a complete mental picture of his or her total utility for every level of consumption, how can they find their utility-maximizing consumption choice?
6. What is the rule relating the ratio of prices of two goods and the ratio of marginal utilities of those goods at the optimal choice? Explain why, if this rule does not hold, the choice cannot be utility-maximizing.
7. As a general rule, is it safe to assume that a change in the price of a good will always have its most significant impact on the quantity demanded of that good, rather than on the quantity demanded of other goods? Explain.
8. How will a utility-maximizer find the choice of leisure and income that provides the greatest utility?
9. As a general rule, is it safe to assume that a higher wage will encourage significantly more hours worked for all individuals? Explain.
10. How will a utility-maximizer find the choice of present and future consumption that provides the greatest utility?
11. As a general rule, is it safe to assume that a lower interest rate will encourage significantly lower financial savings for all individuals? Explain.

APPENDIX A

Indifference Curves and the Consumption Decision

This chapter explained the consumption decision in terms of the budget constraint facing the individual and the individual's choice of her most preferred point on the budget constraint. Effects of changes in prices on the quantity demanded were analyzed in terms of income and substitution effects.

To help them more rigorously analyze choices and the consequences of changes in prices, economists have developed an extremely useful tool called **indifference curves**. Indifference curves give the combinations of goods among which an individual has no preference (that is, is indifferent) or which yield the same level of utility. This appendix shows how indifference curves can be used to derive the demand curve and to separate more precisely changes in consumption into income and substitution effects.

USING INDIFFERENCE CURVES TO ILLUSTRATE CONSUMER CHOICES

In this chapter solutions to consumer choice problems were characterized as having two stages: first, identify the opportunity set, and second, find the most preferred point in the opportunity set. The budget constraint defines the opportunity set for consumers with a given income to spend on goods. Figure 7-4 repeats the budget constraint for Fran, who must divide her income between candy bars and CDs. In the chapter, we simply said that Fran would choose the most preferred point along the

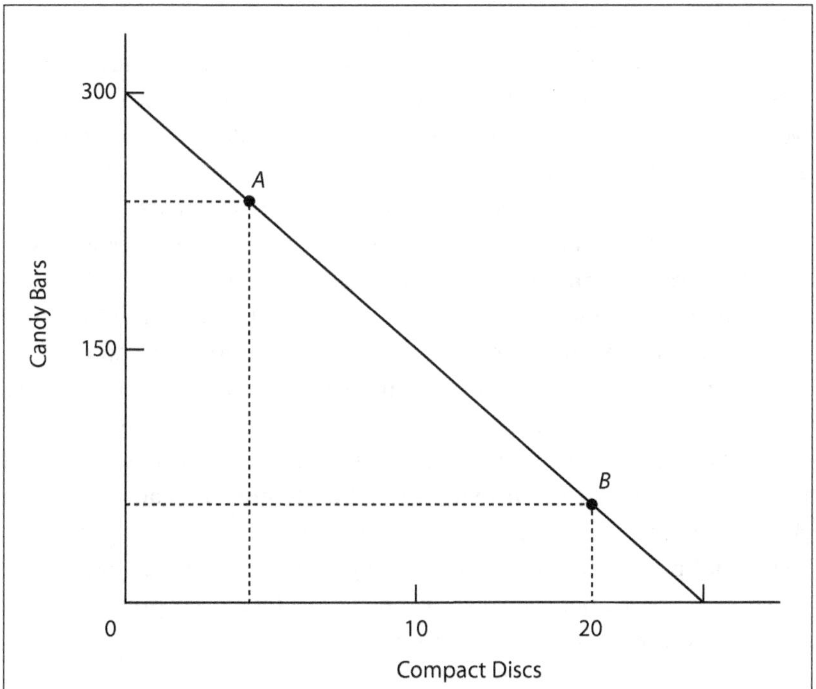

FIGURE 7-4
Budget Constraint
The budget constraint defines the opportunity set. Fran can choose any point on or below the budget constraint. If she has strong preferences for CDs, she might choose *B*; if she has strong preferences for candy bars, she might choose point *A*.

budget constraint. If she likes CDs a lot, she might choose point *B*; if she has a stronger preference for candy, she might choose point *A*.

The concept of the indifference curve can help us see which of these points she chooses.

The indifference curve shows the various combinations of goods that make a person equally happy. For example, in Figure 7-5, the indifference curve I_0 gives all those combinations of candy bars and compact discs that Fran finds just as attractive as 150 candy bars and 10 CDs (point *A* on the curve). At *B*, for instance, she has 12 CDs but only 130 candy bars-not so much candy, but in her mind the extra CDs make up for the loss. The fact that *B* and *A* are on the same indifference curve means that Fran is indifferent to the choice between them. That is, if you asked her whether she preferred *A* to *B* or *B* to *A*, she would answer that she couldn't care less.

Indifference curves simply reflect preferences between pairs of goods. Unlike demand curves, they have nothing to do with budget constraints or prices. The different combinations of goods along the indifference curve cost different amounts of money. The indifference curves are drawn by asking an individual which he prefers: 10 candy bars and 2 CDs or 15 candy bars and 1 CD? or 11 candy bars and 2 CDs or 15 candy bars and 1 CD? or 12 candy bars and 2 CDs or 15 candy bars and 1 CD? When he answers, "Given those options, I am indifferent," the two points that represent those choices are on the same indifference curve.

Moving along the curve in one direction, Fran is willing to accept more CDs in exchange for fewer candy bars; moving in the other direction, she is willing to accept more candy bars in exchange for fewer CDs. Any point on the same indifference curve, by definition, makes her just as happy as any other-whether it is point *A* or *C* or an extreme point like *D*, where she has many candy bars and very few CDs, or *F*, where she has relatively few candy bars but more CDs.

However, if Fran were to receive the same number of candy bars but more CDs than at *A*-say 150 candy bars and 15 CDs (point *E*)-then she would be better off, on the principle that "more is better." The new indifference curve I_1 illustrates all those combinations of candy bars and CDs that make her just as well-off as the combination of 150 candy bars and 15 CDs.

Figure 7-5 shows two indifference curves for Fran. Because more is better, Fran (or any individual) will prefer a choice on the indifference curve that is higher than another curve. On the higher indifference curve, she can have more of both items. By definition, we can draw an indifference curve for *any* point in the space of an indifference curve diagram. Also by definition, indifference curves cannot cross, as Figure 7-6 makes clear. Assume that the indifference curves I_0 and I_1 cross at point *A*. That would mean that Fran is indifferent to a choice between *A* and all points on I_0 and between *A* and all points on I_1 In particular, she would be indifferent when choosing between *A* and *B*, between *A* and C, and accordingly between *B* and *C*. But *B* is clearly preferred to *C*; therefore, indifference curves cannot cross.

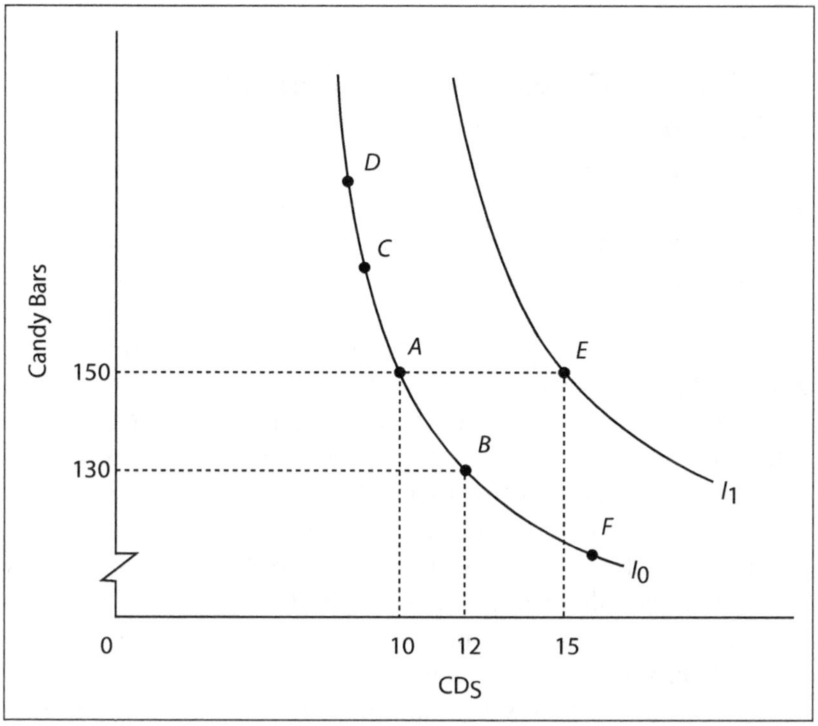

FIGURE 7-5

Indifference Curves

An indifference curve traces combinations of goods to which an individual is indifferent. Each reflects Fran's taste for CDs and for candy bars. She is just as well-off. (has an identical amount of utility) at all points on the indifference curve I_0: *A*, *B*, *C*, *D*, or *F*.

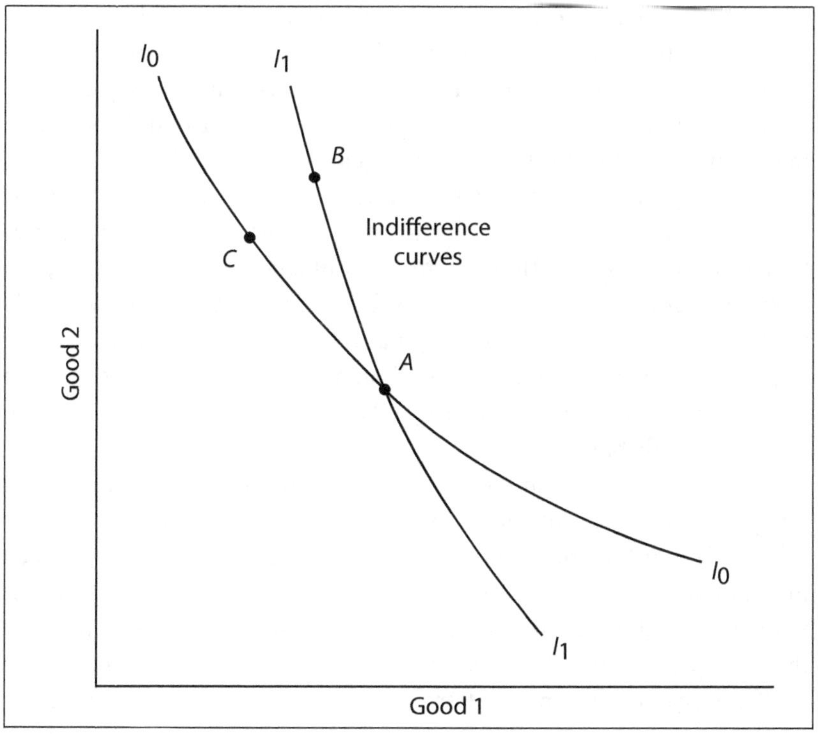

FIGURE 7-6

Why Indifference Curves Cannot Cross

If two indifference curves crossed, a logical contradiction would occur. If curves crossed at point *A*, then Fran would be indifferent between *A* and *B*, between *A* and *C*, and therefore between *B* and *C*. But since *B* involves higher consumption of both goods than *C*, *B* is clearly preferred to *C*.

Indifference Curves and Marginal Rates of Substitution

The slope of the indifference curve measures the number of candy bars that the individual is willing to give up to get another compact disc. The technical term for the slope of an indifference curve is the **marginal rate of substitution**. The marginal rate of substitution tells us how much of one good an individual is *willing* to give up in return for one more unit of another. The concept is quite distinct from the amount a consumer *must* give up, which is determined by the budget constraint and relative prices.

If Fran's marginal rate of substitution of candy bars for CDs is 15 to 1, this means that if she is given 1 more CD, she is willing to give up 15 candy bars. If she only had to give up 12 candy bars, she would be happier. If she had to give up 20, she would say, "That's too much-having one more CD isn't worth giving up twenty candy bars." Of course, Gary could have quite different attitudes toward CDs and candy bars. His marginal rate of substitution might be 25 to 1. He would be willing to give up 25 candy bars to get 1 more CD.

The marginal rate of substitution rises and falls according to how much of an item an individual already has. For example, consider point *F* back in Figure 7-5, where Fran has many CDs and few candy bars. In this case, Fran already has bought all her favorite CDs; the marginal CD she buys now will be something she likes but not something she is wild over. In other words, because she already has a large number of CDs, having an additional one is less important. She would rather have some candy bars instead. Her marginal rate of substitution of candy bars for CDs at *F* is very low; for the sake of illustration, let's say that she would be willing to give up the marginal CD for only 10 candy bars. Her marginal rate of substitution is 10 to 1 (candy bars per CD).

The opposite holds true when Fran has lots of candy bars and few CDs. Since she is eating several candy bars almost every day, the chance to have more is not worth much to her. But since she has few CDs, she does not yet own all of her favorites. The marginal value of another candy bar is relatively low, while the marginal value of another CD is relatively high. Accordingly, in this situation, Fran might insist on getting 30 extra candy bars before she gives up 1 CD. Her marginal rate of substitution is 30 to 1(candy bars per CD).

As we move along an indifference curve, we increase the amount of one good (like CDs) that an individual has. In Fran's case, she requires less and less of the other good (candy bars) to compensate her for each one-unit decrease in the quantity of the first good (CDs). This principle is known as the **diminishing marginal rate of substitution**. As a result of the principle of diminishing marginal rate of substitution, the slope of the indifference curve becomes flatter as we move from left to right along it.

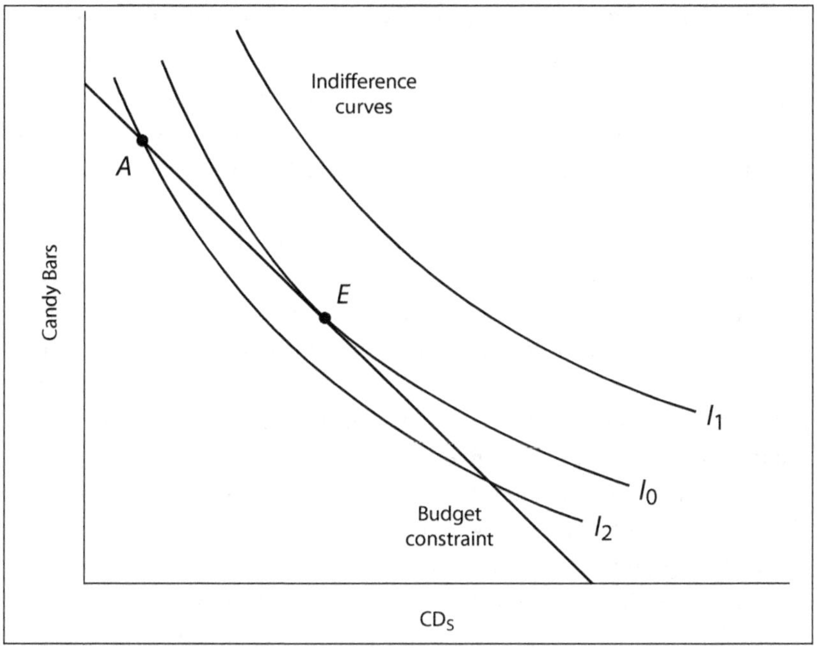

FIGURE 7-7

Indefference Curves and the Budget Constraint

The highest feasible indifference curve that can be reached is the one just tangent to the budget constraint, or indifference curve I_0 here. This individual's budget constraint does not permit her to reach I_1, nor would she want to choose point *A*, which would put her on I_2'since along I_2 she is worse off.

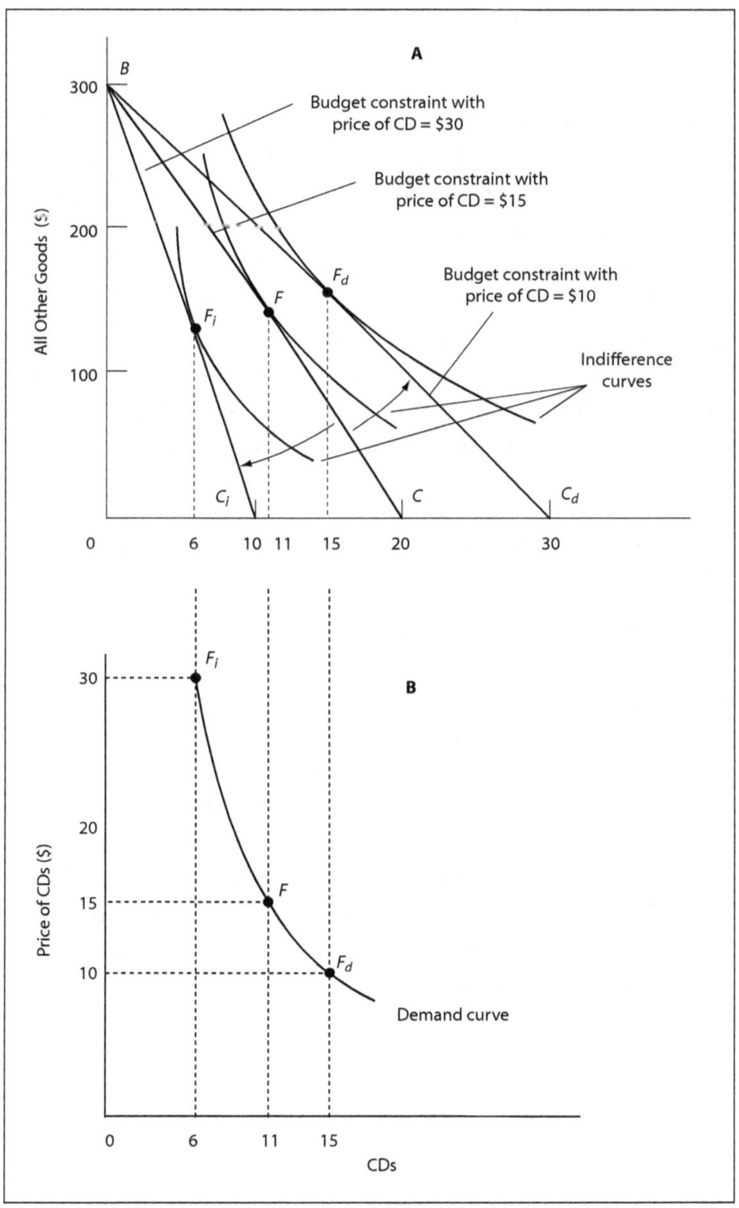

FIGURE 7-8

Deriving Demand Curves from Shifting Budget Constraints

In panel *A*, the budget constraint rotates down to the left as the price of CDs increases, leading Fran to change consumption from *F* to F_i.The budget constraint rotates to the right when the price of CDs decreases, and Fran moves from *F to* F_d. Panel B shows the corresponding demand curve for CDs, illustrating how the rising prices lead to a decline in the quantity consumed.

Using Indifference Curves to Illustrate Choices

By definition, an individual does not care where he sits on any *given* indifference curve. But he would prefer to be on the highest indifference curve possible. What pins him down is his budget constraint. As Figure 7-7 illustrates, the highest indifference curve that a person can attain is the one that just touches the budget constraint-that is, the indifference curve that is *tangent* to the budget constraint. The point of tangency (labeled *E*) is the point the individual will choose. Consider any other point on the budget constraint, say *A*. The indifference curve through *A* is below the curve through *E*; the individual is better off at *E* than at *A*. But consider an indifference curve above I_o-for instance, I_1 Since every point on I_1 lies above the budget constraint, there is no point on Il that the individual can purchase given his income.

When a curve is tangent to a line, the curve and line have the same slope at the point of tangency. Thus, the slope of the indifference curve equals the slope of the budget constraint at the point of tangency. The slope of the indifference curve is the marginal rate of substitution; the slope of the budget constraint is the relative price. This two-dimensional diagram therefore illustrates a basic principle of consumer choice: *individuals choose the point where the marginal rate of substitution equals the relative price.*

This principle makes sense. If the relative price of CDs and candy bars is 15 (CDs cost $15 and candy bars cost $1) and Fran's marginal rate of substitution is 20, Fran is willing to give up 20 candy bars to get 1 more CD, but only *has* to give up 15; it clearly pays her to buy more CDs and fewer candy bars. If her marginal rate of substitution is 10, she is willing to give up 1 CD for just 10 candy bars; but if she gives up 1 CD, she can get 15 candy bars. She will be better off buying more candy bars and fewer CDs. Thus, if the marginal rate of substitution exceeds the relative price, Fran is better off if she buys more CDs; if it is less, she is better off if she buys fewer CDs. When the marginal rate of substitution *equals* the relative price, it does not pay for her to either increase or decrease her purchases.

USING INDIFFERENCE CURVES TO DERIVE DEMAND CURVES

Indifference curves and budget constraints can be used to derive the demand curve, and thus to show what happens when prices increase. The analysis consists of two steps.

First, we identify what happens to the budget constraint as, say, the price of CDs increases. We did this earlier in Figure 5.6, but now we can add indifference curves to the analysis. In the budget constraint drawn in Figure 7-8, we find CDs on the horizontal axis and all other goods on the vertical axis. If Fran buys no CDs, she has $300 to spend on all other goods. At a CD price of $15, she can buy up to 20 CDs, producing the budget line running from point B to C. As the price of CDs increases, the budget constraint rotates in and becomes steeper. If she buys no CDs, she still has $300 to spend on other goods. But if she buys only CDs, the number of CDs she can buy falls as their price rises. If the price of CDs falls, the budget constraint rotates out and becomes flatter.

For each budget constraint, we find the point of tangency between the indifference curve and the budget constraint, here labeled F_i, F, and *Fd*. This shows the point chosen along each budget constraint. Looking at the horizontal axis, we see, at each price, the quantity of CDs purchased. Panel B then plots these quantities for each price. At the price of \$15, Fran chooses 11 CDs; at a price of \$30, she chooses to buy only 6.

CHAPTER 8
Profits, Production, and Cost Curves

8 Profits, Production, and Cost Curves

EDITOR'S NOTE

Profits and Costs

By David Moglen

The theory of profit maximizing behavior by firms is a basic economic assumption. It is not an absolute that claims firms always and everywhere profit-maximize, but it is true often enough that profits will determine the firm's behavior that models assuming profit maximization will usually be correct.

Costs are central to determine profits, since Revenue—Costs = Profit

Money paid directly to/for factors of production is a cost, including rental cost, wages, employee benefits, interest payments, and taxes. Any cost that involves money actually being spent to cover it is an explicit cost.

Implicit or imputed costs are costs to the firm that do not directly involve money spent. Imputed costs come in four basic categories for a firm.

Accountant's Version of Depreciation

The one imputed cost accountants subtract is depreciation. Capital (machines, computers, conveyor belts etc.) gets used up, and the extent that it loses value from wearing out and going obsolete (becoming a poorer production method in comparison to increasingly advancing technology) is called depreciation. The question is: how much should the firm estimate for the exact dollar figure of depreciation?

Firms often estimate the dollar cost of this wear-down and obsolescence using "straight-line depreciation." A more aggressive accounting option is to give their depreciation estimate based on "accelerated depreciation." The standard "net profits" calculated by accountants for public record, investor information, and tax purposes only include one imputed cost: the accountant's version of depreciation.

Total Revenue—Explicit Costs—Accountant's Version of Depreciation = Accounting Profits

Four Imputed Costs Subtracted by Economists

There are four categories of imputed costs that economists will want to subtract before they have arrived at Economic Profit.

1. Economist's Version of Depreciation:

D (Depreciation) = Capital (Machine) Value at the start of the year – Value at the end of the year

In other words, economists try to assess how much value the machine has actually lost on the existing resale market, and call that loss in value Depreciation, while accountants use a rule for that type of machine that puts them in compliance with the Generally Accepting Accounting Principles.

One rare case you should be aware of is that if the capital cannot be re-sold, D=0 because the opportunity cost of using the machine is zero. An example would be installed machinery in a car factory, where the resale value to any other buyer is negligible—basically nothing—because they have to remove it and install their own or modify the machines at a high cost.

2. Cost of using one's own funds for the business: the foregone earned interest. The opportunity cost for a firm choosing to invest $1 million to open a new retail store is the alternative investment in a risk-free asset like the Treasury Bill (the US government bond), with a guaranteed return of, say, 5%. This means the million will turn into $1,050,000 in one year by buying T-Bills. But that is a "certain" amount while the retail store's value at the end of the year is "uncertain."

3. Risk Premium: an example of an uncertainty adjustment would be to assume the risky investment has a 10% chance of failing. The cost of this risk is 10% of the investment amount: 10% $1 million = $100,000. The investment will not be economically beneficial unless it covers the cost of risk (also called the risk premium) and the lost interest that could have been earned from T-Bills.

   In this case, $100,000 + $50,000 (the required return) = 15% of $1 million=$150,000.

   In other words, you take these percentages given (in the example above, 5% for the interest rate—called yield—on the T-bill yield and 10% for the risk premium . . . totaling 5% + 10%=15%) and you simply multiply that total percent by the explicit costs, in the above example, one million dollars. You multiply by explicit costs because the money the firm actually had to spend throughout the year is exactly the money they could have invested in U.S. Government Bonds had they chosen not to spend it running the business.

4. Foregone IP (Intellectual Property) income—lost licensing income the firm could have earned from leasing out their patents, copyrights, and trademarks (including logos and brand names) to other firms.

All of these imputed costs are subtracted from revenue in the calculation of "Economic profits," in addition to the costs firms normally subtract to get "net profits" such as wages, interest payments, overhead (building rental payments, power/water/phone services) and other factor payments.

Total Revenue—Explicit Costs—Implicit Costs = Economic Profit

If firms in an industry make economic profits, that sends the signal for more firms to start producing in that industry. If there is an economic loss (negative profits) firms stop producing and exit the industry. If the firm makes zero economic profits, that is called normal profits and long-run equilibrium, indicating that the number of firms and output of the firm in question will both remain constant. Quantity produced will not change and there is no entry or exit.

Economic Profit	Called	Future Output of this One Firm will . . .	Future Number of Firms in this Industry will . . .
Positive	Economic Profit	Increase	Increase
Negative	Economic Loss	Decrease	Decrease
Zero	Normal Profits, Long-run Competitive Equilibrium	Remain the same	Remain the same, no entry or exit

Production, Input, Choice, and Cost with One Variable Input

By William Baumol

While all real businesses use many different inputs, we will begin our discussion with the unrealistic case where there is just a single variable input. In doing so, we are trying to replicate in our theoretical analysis what a physicist or a biologist does in the laboratory when she conducts *a controlled* experiment in which only one variable is permitted to change at a time. This is done in order to study the influence of that variable in isolation.

THE TOTAL, AVERAGE, AND MARGINAL PHYSICAL PRODUCTS OF AN INPUT

We begin the analysis with the first of our three topics: the relation between the quantity of production and the quantity of input utilized. Consider, as an example, the amount of corn that Ivana and Ivan feed to their chickens. Ultimately, they can vary all their input quantities: they can buy more baby chicks, they can feed them other grains, they can give the chickens larger (or smaller) quantities of growth hormone, they can buy more land and chicken coops, and so on. But suppose for the moment that Ivana and Ivan have purchased all the non-food inputs they need to grow their flock of chickens and all other types of chicken feed other than corn. Thus their only choice is how much corn to feed the flock.

Ivana and Ivan have studied the relationship between the quantity of corn **input** and the **output** of poultry meat. In doing so, they have learned that more corn leads to more output, at least up to a point. The relevant data are displayed in Table 8-1. The table begins by confirming the common sense observation that chickens cannot be raised without food. Thus the total physical product of zero corn input is zero (first entry in the second column). After that, the table shows the increase in chicken output that additional corn yields. For instance, with an input of four 20-kilo bags of corn per week, output is 50 kilos of chicken. Eventually, however, a saturation point is reached beyond which additional corn over-feeds the chickens and causes some to become ill. After 9 bags of corn per week, more corn actually reduces the chicken output (from 92.7 to 90 kilos). The data in Table 8-1 are portrayed graphically in Figure 8-2, which is called a **total physical product (TPP) curve.** This curve shows how much chicken Ivana and Ivan can produce with different quantities of corn, given the quantities of all nonfood inputs.

Two other physical product concepts are added in Table 8-2. **Average physical product (APP)** measures output per unit of input; it is simply total physical product divided by the quantity of variable input used. In our example, it is total chicken output divided by number of

The firm's **total physical product (TPP) curve** shows what happens to output when the firm changes the quantity of one of its inputs while holding all other input quantities constant.

The **average physical product (APP)** is the total physical product (TPP) divided by the quantity of input used. Thus, APP = TPP/X where X = the quantity of input.

The **marginal physical product (MPP)** of an input is the increase in total output that results from a one-unit increase in the input, holding the amounts of all other inputs constant.

TABLE 8-1

Ivana and Ivan's Total Physical Product Schedule

Data of the sort provided in this table table do not represent the farmer's subjective opinion. They are objective information of the sort a poultry scientists can and does supply from experimental evidence.

Corn Input (20-kilo bags)	Chicken Output (kilos)
0	0
1	7
2	18
3	33
4	50
5	65
6	78
7	87.5
8	92
9	92.7
10	90
11	82.5
12	72

bags of corn used. APP is shown in the next to last column of Table 8-2, in which the TPP schedule is reproduced for convenience. For example, since 4 bags of corn yield 50 kilos of chicken, the APP of 4 bags of corn is 50/4= 12.5 kilos per bag of corn.

If Ivana and Ivan are to decide how much corn to use, they must know how much *additional* chicken output they can expect from each *additional* bag of corn. This concept is known as **marginal physical product (MPP).** For example, the marginal physical product of the fourth bag of corn is the total output of chicken when four bags of corn are used *minus* the total output when three bags are used, or 50-33 = 17 kilos. The other MPP entries for I&I's farm, given in the third column of Table 8-2, are calculated from the total product data in exactly the

FIGURE 8-2

Total Physical Product with Different Quantities of Corn

This graph shows how Ivana and Ivan's chicken output varies as they use more and more corn. (Other inputs, such as labor, are held constant in this graph.)

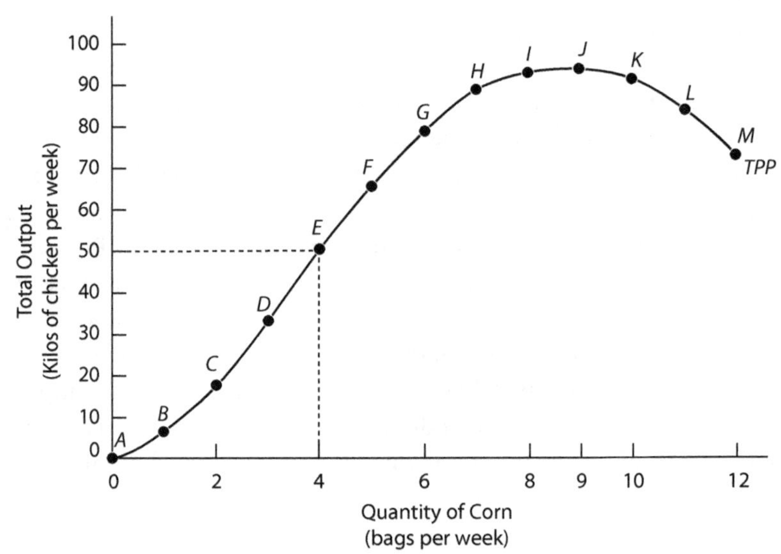

Corn Input (bags)	Total Physical Product (chicken output in kilos)	Marginal Physical Product (kilos per bag)	Average Physical Product (kilos per bag)	Marginal Revenue Product (dollars)
0	0.0			
1	7.0	7.0	7.0	10.15
2	18.0	11.0	9.0	15.95
3	33.0	15.0	11.0	21.75
4	50.0	17.0	12.5	24.65
5	65.0	15.0	13.0	21.75
6	78.0	13.0	13.0	18.85
7	87.5	9.5	12.5	13.78
8	92.0	4.5	11.5	6.53
9	92.7	0.7	10.3	1.02
10	90.0	−2.7	9.0	−3.92
11	82.5	−7.5	7.5	−10.88
12	72.0	−10.5	6.0	−15.23

TABLE 8-2
Ivana and Ivan's Schedules for Total Physical Product, Marginal Physical Product, Average Physical Product, and Marginal Revenue Product of Corn

same way. Figure 8-3 displays these numbers graphically in a marginal physical **product curve**.

THE "LAW" OF DIMINISHING MARGINAL RETURNS

The marginal physical product curve in Figure 8-3 shows a pattern that, will prove significant for our analysis. Until four bags of corn are used, the marginal physical product of corn is *increasing;* between four bags and nine bags it is *decreasing,* but still *positive;* and beyond nine bags the MPP of corn actually becomes *negative.* The graph has been divided into three zones to illustrate these three cases. The left zone is called

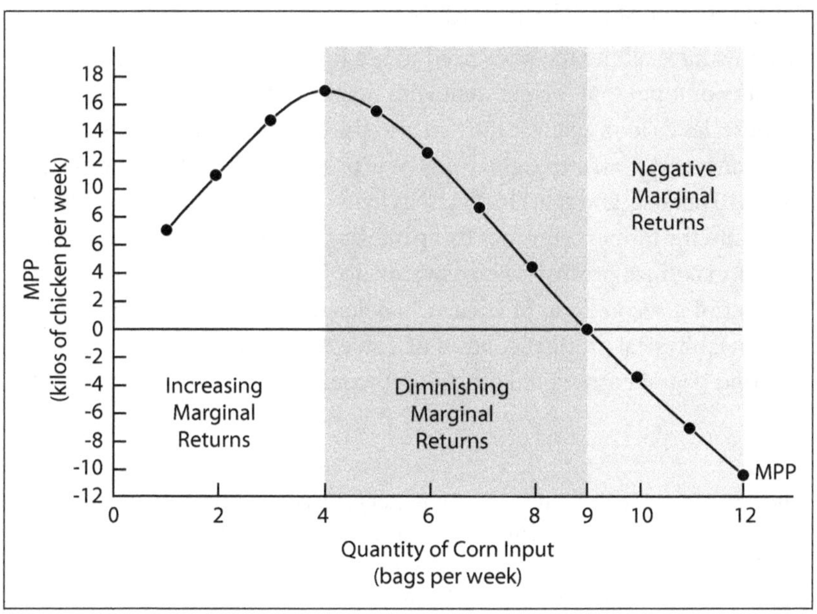

FIGURE 8-3
Ivana and Ivan's Marginal Physical Product (MPP) Curve This graph of marginal physical product (MPP) shows how much *additional* chicken Ivana and Ivan get from each application of an additional bag of corn.

the region of increasing marginal returns, the middle zone is the region of diminishing marginal returns, and the right zone is the region of negative marginal returns. In this graph, the marginal returns to corn increase at first and then diminish. This is the typical pattern.

In the increasing returns zone, each additional bag of corn adds more to TPP than the previous bag did. This corresponds to points *A* through *E* in Figure 8-2, where the curve is rising with increasing rapidity. In the diminishing returns area, each additional bag of corn adds less to TPP than the previous bag added. This corresponds to points *E* through *J*, where the TPP curve in Figure 8-2 is still rising, but at a diminishing rate. Finally, in the zone of negative marginal returns (input quantities greater than 9) additional corn actually reduces production by making the chickens ill.

The "law" of diminishing marginal returns, which has played a key role in economics for two centuries,[1] asserts that when we increase the amount of any one input, *holding-the amounts of all others constant*, the marginal returns to the expanding input ultimately begin to diminish. The so-called law is no more than an empirical regularity based on some observation of the facts; it is not a theorem deduced analytically.

The reason why returns to a single input are usually diminishing is straightforward. It is a consequence of what can be referred to as the "law" of variable input proportions. When we increase the quantity of one input while holding all others constant, the input whose quantity we are increasing gradually becomes more and more abundant compared with the others (for example, the proportion of corn to other foods increases). As Ivana and Ivan use more and more corn with their fixed quantities of other foods, the diet becomes unbalanced so that adding yet more corn does little good. Eventually the chickens eat so much corn that any further increase in the proportion of corn to other foods will actually harm them. At this point the marginal physical product of corn becomes *negative*.

THE OPTIMAL QUANTITY OF AN INPUT AND DIMINISHING RETURNS

We now have all the tools we need to see how the firm can decide on the quantity of input that is consistent with maximization of its profits. For this purpose, let us look again at the first and third columns of Table 8-2, showing Ivana and Ivan's marginal physical product schedule. Suppose corn costs $10 per bag, and that chicken sells for $1.45 per kilo ($14.50 per 10-kilo pack) and the farmers consider using one bag of corn. Is this optimal-that is, does it maximize profits? The answer is no, because the marginal physical product of a second bag of corn is 11 kilos of chicken (third entry in the marginal physical product column of Table 8-2). This means that although a second bag of corn would cost $10, it would yield an additional 11 kilos,

[1]The "law" is generally credited to Anne Robert Jacques Turgot (1727–1781), one of the great Comptrollers-General of France before the Revolution, whose liberal policies, it is said, represented the old regime's last chance to save itself. But, with characteristic foresight, the king fired him.

which at the price of $1.45 per kilo, would add $15.95 to revenue. Thus the farm comes out $15.95-$10 = $5.95 ahead if it adds a second bag of corn.

It is convenient to have a specific name for the additional *money revenue* that accrues to a firm when it increases the quantity of some input by one unit; we call that the input's **marginal revenue product.** So if Ivana and Ivan's chicken sells at a fixed price (say, $1.45 per kilo), the marginal revenue product (MRP) of the input equals its marginal physical product (MPP) multiplied by the price of the product:

The **marginal revenue product (MRP)** of an input is the additional revenue the producer earns from the increased sales when it uses an additional unit of the input.

$$\text{MRP} = \text{MPP} \times \text{Price of output.}$$

For example, we have just seen that the marginal revenue product of the second bag of corn to Ivana and Ivan is $15.95, which we obtained by multiplying the MPP of 11 kilos by the price of $1.45 per kilo. The other (MRP) entries in the last column of Table 8-2 are obtained in precisely the same way. The concept of MRP enables us to formulate a simple rule for the optimal use of any input. Specifically: When the marginal revenue product of an input exceeds its price, it pays the firm to use more of that input. Similarly, when the marginal revenue product of the input is less than its price, it pays the firm to use less.

Let us test this rule in the case of Ivana and Ivan's farm. We have observed that two bags of corn cannot be enough because the MRP of a second bag ($15.95) exceeds its price ($10). What about a third bag? Table 8-2 tells us that the MRP of the third bag ($21.75) also exceeds its price; thus, stopping at three bags also cannot be optimal. This is equally true of a seventh bag of corn whose MRP ($13.78) still exceeds the $10 price of a bag of corn. The same cannot be said of an eighth bag, however. An eighth bag is not a good idea because its MRP is only $6.53, which is clearly less than its $10 cost. Thus, the optimal quantity of corn for I&I to purchase each week is seven bags, yielding a total output of 87.5 kilos of chicken.[2]

Notice the crucial role of diminishing returns in this analysis. That is why the marginal *physical* product of corn eventually begins to decline. When marginal physical product declines we can also expect the money value of that product to fall; that is, the marginal revenue product will decrease as well. At the point where MRP falls below the price of corn, it is appropriate for Ivana and Ivan to stop increasing their corn purchases. In sum, it always pays the producer to expand input use until diminishing returns set in and reduce the MRP to the price of the input.

A common expression suggests that it does not pay to continue doing something "beyond the point of diminishing returns." As we see from this analysis, quite to the contrary, it normally *does* pay to do so! Only when the marginal revenue product of an input has been reduced (by diminishing returns) to the level of the input's price has the proper

[2] Some readers may notice that the profit-maximizing output of chicken that was determined in Chapter 5 is smaller than the figure obtained here. These two results are, however, not really comparable, because the calculation carried out at this point in the text is based on a number of temporary assumptions adopted to simplify the exposition-notably, the premise that the prices of all inputs other than corn are all zero (see below). Later in the chapter we will see what happens when this premise is dropped.

amount of the input been employed, because then the firm will be wasting no opportunity to *add* to its total profit. Thus, the optimal quantity of an input is that at which the MRP is equal to its price (P). In symbols,

$$\text{MRP} = \text{P of input.}$$

Notice that the logic of the analysis is exactly the same as in our discussion of marginal analysis. The farmers are trying to maximize the difference between the *total* revenue their corn input yields and the *total* cost of buying that input. To do so, they must increase their usage of corn up to the point where its *marginal* cost (the price of an additional bag) equals its marginal revenue product.

COST CURVES AND INPUT QUANTITIES

We turn now to the third of the three main topics of this chapter: How the firm's cost curves, are derived from the input decisions we have just studied. To do so, we use our two basic assumptions-that the price of corn is beyond the control of the firm and that the quantities of all inputs other than corn are fixed-to deduce the firm's total costs from its physical product schedule.

The method is simple: For each quantity of output, record from Table 8-1 or Figure 8-2 the amount of corn required to produce it. Then multiply that quantity of corn by its price. Here, it is critical to recognize that these additional costs must include the *opportunity costs* of any quantities of input the farmers contribute themselves-such as corn that they have grown themselves, and which they could have sold to other farmers instead of using it up themselves.

In addition to the cost of their corn, Ivana and Ivan must spend money on other inputs. But since, to keep the discussion from becoming too complex, we are focussing exclusively on corn input in this first part of the chapter, let us assume for the next several pages that all other inputs are free, so that corn is the only expense that needs to be considered. Later, we will see that we calculate the cost of each other input just

TABLE 8-3
A Portion of Ivana and Ivan's Total Cost Schedule
Obtained from the production data in Table 8-1, assuming corn is the only variable input.

Chicken Output (kilos per week	Corn Output (bags per week)	Total Cost (cost of corn, dollars per week)
7	1	10
18	2	20
33	3	30
50	4	40
65	5	50
78	6	60
87.5	7	70
92	8	80

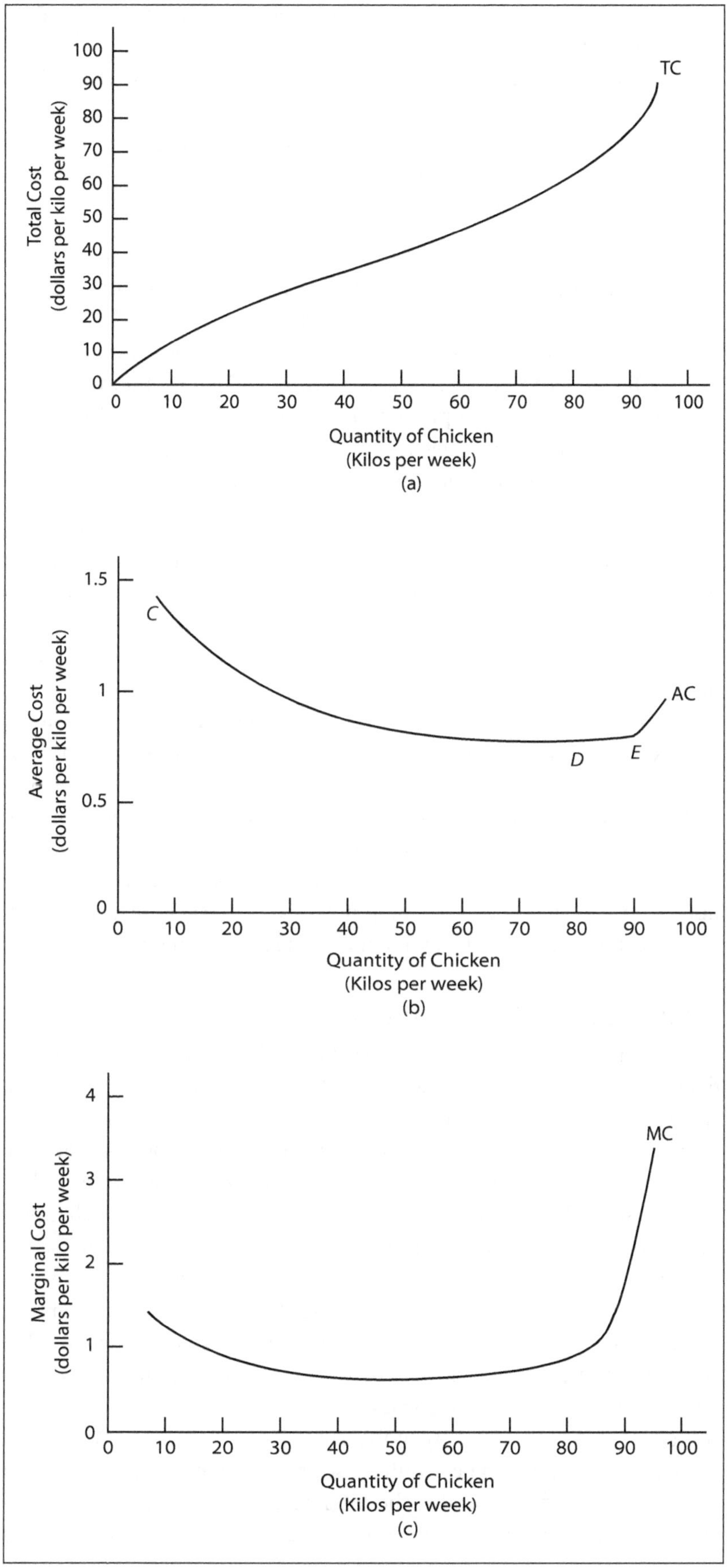

FIGURE 8-4
Total, Average, and Marginal Costs
Ivana and Ivan's costs are derived from the Total Cost schedule in Table 8-3. They are reproduced from Figure 8-3 in the preceding chapter.

as we do that of corn, by multiplying its quantity by its price, and adding the result to the farm's total cost number.

So, suppose, once more, that corn costs $10 per bag. Then, from Table 8-1, we have the table of total costs shown in Table 8-3. For example, to produce 33 kilos of chicken, we know from the fourth row of Table 8-1 that it requires 3 bags of corn at $10 per bag, which gives us the total cost, $30. The point of this exercise is that:

> The total product curve tells us the input quantities needed to produce any given output. And from those input quantities and the price of the inputs, we can determine the *total cost* (TC) of producing any level of output. This is the amount the firm spends on the inputs needed to produce the output, plus any opportunity costs that arise in that production activity. Thus, the relation of total cost to output is determined by the technological production relations between inputs and outputs, and by input prices.

The firm's other two cost curves-**average cost** and **marginal cost**-are calculated directly from the total cost curve which we have just determined. All three curves are shown here in Figure 8-4.

So far, by assuming that the price of every other input is zero, we have omitted from our calculations the costs of all of Ivana and Ivan's inputs other than corn, items we have held constant up to now in order to focus on the effect of changing the quantity of corn input. But this means that we have so far ignored the money that Ivan and Ivana must spend on those other inputs. Even if we had not assumed the prices of the other inputs to be zero, these costs would therefore have been treated as if they were constant in the present analysis; that is, the number of dollars spent on non-corn inputs is implicitly assumed, up to this point in the discussion, not to change when the farm's output varies. Since such unvarying costs are quite important in reality, it is appropriate to examine their properties.

A **fixed cost** is the cost of the inputs whose quantity does not rise when output goes up, and which are required to produce any output at all. The total cost of such indivisible inputs does not change when the output changes. Any other cost of the firm's operation is called a **variable cost**.

FIXED COSTS AND VARIABLE COSTS

Total, average, and marginal costs are often divided into two components: **fixed costs** and **variable costs**. *A fixed cost* is the cost of the smallest (least expensive) batch of inputs that the firm can buy if it is to be able to produce any output at all. These costs are called "fixed" because the total amount of money spent on the items in question does not increase when output rises, at least up to some point. That is, the total cost of such inputs remains the same whether output is five units or five hundred units.

Such fixed costs arise because there are some inputs whose quantities cannot be reduced, even if the firm's output is very small. For example, to run a taxi business one must have at least one automobile, and that cost is the same whether the cab driver finds only one rider per day or 50 riders. (Of course,-beyond some point, if the number of riders grows sufficiently large, the capacity of the cab will be exceeded, and a second automobile will have to be acquired, so that beyond that point the cost is no longer fixed). Naturally, the total cost of such an input does not change when the firm varies its output, at least within some range. Costs which are not fixed in this sense are called *variable* because they increase when the firm's output rises.

The difference between fixed costs and variable costs can be illustrated by comparing the cost of a railroad's fuel with that of its track construction. To operate between St. Louis and Kansas City, a railroad must lay a set of tracks. It cannot lay half a set of tracks or a quarter set of tracks. We therefore call such an input "indivisible."

We see that at any output *greater than zero* the firm has no choice but to pay the fixed cost of its track. Because the track is indivisible, its construction cost will be the same whether one train per month or five trains per day travel the route.[3] Thus, up to a point, track construction cost is unaffected by output size, that is, by the volume of traffic. On the other hand, the more trains that pass over those tracks, the higher the railroad's total fuel bill will be. We therefore say that its fuel costs are variable but its track-building cost is fixed.

Although variable costs are only part of total (fixed plus variable) costs, the variable costs of a firm exhibit patterns of behavior just like those shown in Table 8-3. However, the curves of *total fixed costs* (TFC) and *average fixed costs* (AFC) have very special.shapes, which are illustrated in Table 8-4 and Figure 8-5. We see that TFC remains the same whether the firm produces a lot or a little, so long as it produces anything at all.[4] As a result, any TFC curve, like the one in Figure 8-5(a), is horizontal-it has the same height at every output.

[3]Note, however, that an increase in traffic will increase annual maintenance and replacement cost, so that replacement and maintenance are variable costs. Note also that opportunity costs can be fixed, variable, or a combination of the two.

[4]Here we assume that the fixed costs are also what economists call "sunk," meaning that the firm has already spent the money in question or signed a contact to do so. Consequently, if the firm decides to go out of business (produce zero output), it must still spend the money.

Output per Period (10-kilo packages per week)	Total Fixed Cost (TFC) (dollars)	Average Fixed Cost (AFC) (dollars)
1	5	5.0
2	5	2.5
3	5	1.7
4	5	1.3
5	5	1.0
6	5	0.8
7	5	0.7
8	5	0.6

TABLE 8-4
Total and Average Fixed Costs on Ivana and Ivan's Chicken Farm

Average fixed cost, however, gets smaller and smaller as output increases because, with TFC constant, AFC = TFC/Q gets smaller and smaller as output (the denominator) increases. Business people typically put the point another way: any increase in output permits the fixed cost to be spread among more units, leaving less of it to be carried by any one unit. For example, suppose the fixed cost incurred by Ivana and Ivan is $5 per week. When only one ten-kilo package of chicken is sold, the entire $5 of fixed cost must be borne by that one unit of output. But if the farm produces two ten-kilo packages, each of them need only cover half the total-$2.5 each (Table 8-4).

Cost Minimization in Theory and Practice

Lest you be tempted to run out and open a business, confident that you now understand how to minimize costs, we should point out that decision making in business is a good deal harder than we have indicated here. Rare is the business executive who knows for sure what her production function looks like, or the exact shapes of her marginal physical product schedules, or the precise nature of her cost curves. No one can provide a cookbook for instant success in business. What we have presented here is, instead, a set of principles that constitutes a guide to good decision making.

Business management has been described as the art of making critical decisions on the basis of inadequate information, and in our complex and ever-changing world there is often no alternative to an educated guess. Actual business decisions will at best approximate the cost-minimizing ideal outlined in this chapter. Certainly, there will be mistakes. But when management does its job well and the market system functions smoothly, the approximation may prove amazingly good. While no system is perfect, inducing firms to produce at the lowest possible cost is undoubtedly one of the jobs the market system does best.

Summary

1. A firm's total cost curve shows the lowest possible cost of producing any given level of output. It is derived from the input combination used to produce any given output and the prices of the inputs.
2. The **marginal physical product** of an input is the increase in total output resulting from a one-unit increase in the use of that input, holding the quantities of all other inputs constant.
3. The **"law" of diminishing marginal returns** states that if we increase the amount of one input (holding all other input quantities constant), the marginal physical product of the expanding input will eventually begin to decline.
4. To maximize profits, a firm must purchase an input up to the point at which diminishing returns reduce the input's **marginal revenue product** to its price.

5. The **long run** is a period sufficiently long for the firm's plant to require replacement and for all its current contractual commitments to expire. The **short run** is any period briefer than that.
6. **Fixed costs** are costs whose total amounts do not vary when output increases. All other costs are called *variable.*
7. At all outputs the total fixed cost (TFC) curve is horizontal and the average fixed cost (AFC) curve declines toward the horizontal axis but never crosses it.
8. TC = TFC + TVC; AC = AFC + AVC.
9. A change in fixed cost will not change the profit-maximizing level of output.
10. It is normally possible to produce the same quantity of output in a variety of ways by substituting more of one input for less of another. Firms normally seek the least costly way to produce any given output.
11. A firm that wants to minimize costs will select input quantities at which the ratios of the **marginal physical product** of each input to its price-its MPP per dollar-are equal for all inputs.
12. The **production function** shows the relationship between inputs and output. It indicates the maximum quantity of output obtainable from any given combination of inputs.
13. If a doubling of all the firm's inputs *just* doubles its output, the firm is said to have **constant returns to scale**. If a doubling of all inputs leads *to more than* twice as much output, it has **increasing returns to scale** (or, **economies of scale**). If a doubling of inputs produces less *than* double the output, the firm has **decreasing returns to scale.**
14. With increasing returns to scale, the firm's long-run average costs are decreasing; constant returns to scale are associated with constant long-run average costs; and decreasing returns to scale are associated with increasing long-run average costs.
15. We cannot tell if there are economies of scale (increasing returns to scale) simply by inspecting a diagram of historical cost data. Only the underlying analytical cost curve' can supply this information.

Vocabulary Terms

Total physical product (TPP)
Average physical product (APP)
Marginal physical product (MPP)
Marginal revenue product (MRP)
"Law" of diminishing marginal returns
Fixed cost
Variable cost
Sunk Cost
Increasing (decreasing) average cost
Short and long runs
Substitutability of inputs
Cost minimization
Rule for optimal input use

Production function

Economies of scale (increasing returns to scale)

Constant returns to scale

Decreasing returns to scale

Historical versus analytical cost relationships

Review Questions

1. A firm's total fixed cost is $120,000. Construct a table of total and average fixed costs for this firm for output levels varying from 0 to 6 units. Draw the corresponding TFC and AFC curves.
2. With the following data, calculate the firm's AVC and MVC and draw the graphs for TVC, AVC, and MVC.

Quantity	Total Variable Costs (thousands of dollars
1	$80
2	160
3	240
4	352
5	480
6	720

3. From the figures in Questions 1 and 2, calculate TC and AC for each of the output levels from 1 to 6, and draw the two graphs.
4. If a firm's commitments in 1994 include machinery that will need replacement in five years, a factory building rented for 8 years, and a three-year union contract specifying how many workers it must employ, when, from its point of view in 1994, does the firm's long run begin?
5. If the marginal revenue product of a kilowatt hour of electric power is 8 cents and the marginal cost of a kilowatt hour is 12 cents, what can a firm do to increase its profits?
6. A firm hires two workers and rents 15 acres of land for a season. It produces 150,000 bushels of crop. If it had doubled its land and labor, production would have been 280,000 bushels. Does it have constant, decreasing, or increasing returns to scale?
7. Suppose wages are $20,000 per season and land rent per acre is $30000. Calculate the average cost of 280,000 bushels, using the figures in Question 6 above. (Note that average costs diminish when output increases.) What connection do these figures have with the firm's returns to scale?
8. Ivana and Ivan have bought a great deal of corn. Suppose they now buy more *land,* but not more corn, and spread the corn evenly over all this land. What is likely to happen to the marginal physical product of corn? What, therefore, is the role of input proportions in the determination of marginal physical product?

9. Labor costs $10 per hour. Nine workers produce 180 bushels of product per hour. Ten workers produce 196 bushels. Land rents for $1000 per acre per year. With ten acres worked by nine workers, the marginal physical product of an acre of land is 1400 bushels per year. Does the farmer minimize costs by hiring nine workers and renting ten acres of land? If not, which input should he use in larger relative quantity?
10. Suppose I&I's total costs are increased by $10 per week at every output level. Show in Table 8-2 how this affects their total and average costs.
11. In the wave of acquisitions of the 1980s, in which many firms bought other companies, many of the acquirers were left with heavy debts that amounted to huge additions to their fixed costs. Why did this not affect the output levels that maximized their profits?
12. (More difficult) A firm finds there is a sudden increase in the demand for its product. In the short run, it must operate longer hours and pay higher overtime wage rates. In the long run, however, the firm can install more machines instead of operating them for longer hours. Which do you think will be lower, the short-run or the long-run average cost of the increased output? How is your answer affected by the fact that the long-run average cost includes the new machines the firm buys, while the short-run average cost includes no machine purchase?

IN-CLASS PROJECT

Dell Group Work

By David Moglen

Directions

The following information is from a 2007 Associated Press article about the computer company Dell, Inc. The numbers that appear are given directly in the article. Calculate all the missing information.

The article says that revenue rose 10.5% to $15.99 billion in the 4th quarter of 2007.

Round to two digits after the decimal. Be careful to correctly identify numbers as in millions or billions.

4th Quarter 2006	4th Quarter 2007
Revenue (a.k.a. Sales):	Revenue (a.k.a. Sales): $15.99 billion
Profit (a.k.a. Earnings): $726 million	Profit (a.k.a. Earnings): $679 million
Costs (a.k.a. Expenses):	Costs (a.k.a. Expenses):
Profit Margin ((Profit/Revenue) *100):	Profit Margin ((Profit/Revenue) *100):

IN-CLASS PROJECT

Profits Group Work

By David Moglen

See directions and questions below this data.

Revenue is $50,000 in the year (Revenue and Costs could be thought of as all *in millions* of dollars for a more realistic company).
D=depreciation

Cost	Amount
Labor	$23,000
Land (rent, utilities)	$10,900
Insurance	$1,300
Supplies	$5,900
Lobbying	$20
Corporate Taxes; assume for simplicity this will be the fixed amount no matter what happens to depreciation)	$2,500
Accountant's Depreciation, version 1: Under straight-line depreciation:	$3,000
Accountant's Depreciation, version 2: Under accelerated depreciation	$5,000
Economist's Depreciation: Difference between purchase price and resale value of Capital Equipment	$4,000
Foregone income from renting out all intellectual property	$1,000
Foregone interest rate (current yield on the US Treasury Bond)	Add all explicit costs to find $ amount of investment to fund for the year; interest rate is 4%
Risk of the business	Add all explicit costs to find $ amount of investment to fund for the year; 6% chance of total loss

Directions

Form your usual group of up to five students. Half of the class answers questions #1 and #2, the other half answers #3 and #4. #5 is either bonus or required for everyone, at the teacher's discretion.

1. Calculate accounting profit under straight-line depreciation.

Also, draw a horizontal line to separate Explicit costs from Implicit costs in this list. Mark the first six costs listed as fixed (f) or variable (v) costs.

2. Calculate economic profit or loss.
    - Is the firm operating at economic profit, loss, or normal profits (0 economic profits)?
    - What does this imply for future output of the firm (will it increase or decrease), and if all firms in the industry are like this one, what is implied about future entrance or exit in the market (assuming no barriers to entry or exit)?

3. Calculate accounting profit under accelerated depreciation.

Also, draw a horizontal line to separate Explicit costs from Implicit costs in this list. Mark the first six costs listed as fixed (f) or variable (v) costs.

4. Replace the "Economist's Depreciation: Difference between purchase price and resale value of Capital Equipment" above with $7,900 and "Foregone income from renting out all intellectual property" with $450. Calculate economic profit or loss.
    - Is the firm operating at economic profit, loss, or normal profits (0 economic profits)?
    - What does this imply for future output of the firm (will it increase or decrease), and if all firms in the industry are like this one, what is implied about future entrance or exit in the market (assuming no barriers to entry or exit)?

*5. Calculate the economic profit or loss if the capital equipment has no resale value (there is no opportunity cost to the firm to using it).

*Note before you start: If you did #4, undo the changes to the costs #4 asks you to make. If you did not do #4, you can do #5 without having to restore costs back to their original values. In other words, just go back to the original data.

CHAPTER 9
The Firm in the Long Run

9 The Film in the Long Run

By Timothy Taylor

A business firm is a kind of social machine. It incurs costs as it combines the labor of workers, machinery or other tools, and supplies purchased from other businesses. The firm transforms these inputs into outputs of goods and services, and collects revenue from its sales.

When people think of business firms, often giants like Wal-Mart, General Electric, or IBM—which each have over 300,000 employees—come to mind. But firms come in all sizes, as shown in Exhibit 9-1. The U.S. Census Bureau counted 6 million firms with employees in the U.S. economy. Nearly half of all the workers in private firms are at one of the 18,000 large firms with more than 500 workers. But another 36% of workers in the U.S. economy are at firms with less than 100 workers. These small-scale businesses include everything from dentists and lawyers to businesses that mow lawns or clean houses. Indeed, Exhibit 9-1 doesn't include a separate category of millions of small "nonemployer" businesses where a single owner or a few partners are not official paid wages or a

Exhibit 9-1 U.S. Firms by Number of Employees in 2006

U.S. firms display a wide variety of sizes. Large firms with more than 500 employees hire about half of the labor force. Firms with fewer than 100 employees hire about 36% of the labor force.

	Firms (% of total firms)	Number of Paid Employees (% of total employment)
Total	6,022,000 (100%)	119.9 million (100%)
0–9 employees	4,731,000 (78.6%)	12.9 million (10.8%)
10–19 employees	647,000 (10.7%)	8.7 million (7.23%)
20–99 employees	536,000 (8.9%)	21.1 million (17.6%)
10–499 employees	91,000 (1.5%)	17.5 million (14.6%)
500 or more employees	18,000 (0.30%)	59.7 million (49.8%)

salary, but simply receive whatever they can earn. Each of these businesses, regardless of size or complexity, tries to earn a profit, where:

Profit = Total Revenue – Total Cost.

Total revenue is calculated by taking the quantity of everything that is sold and multiplying it by the sale price. Total costs include all spending on labor, machinery, tools, and supplies purchased from other firms.

The total revenue for a profit-seeking firm is determined by the price that a firm can charge and the quantity that it can sell, which in turn will be related to demand for its products and on the number of other firms that are selling similar or identical products. Exhibit 13-5 illustrates the range of different competitive conditions, which will be explored in the next three chapters. Chapter 10 examines **perfect competition**, in which each firm faces many competitors that sell identical products. Chapter 11 examines the opposite of perfect competition, which is the **monopoly** firm that faces no competitors. Chapter 12 examines two situations between perfect competition and monopoly: the case of **monopolistic competition** where many firms sell similar but different products and the case of **oligopoly** where a small number of firms sell a similar product but face no other competition.

perfect competition:
Each firm faces many competitors that sell identical products.

monopoly:
A firm that faces no competitors.

monopolistic competition:
Many firms competing to sell similar but differentiated products.

oligopoly:
When several large firms have all or most of the sales in an industry.

Regardless of what type of competition exists in a market, the definition of profit makes clear that a profit-maximizing firm will always attempt to produce its desired level of output at the lowest possible cost. After all, if any firm from a giant like Bank of America or Boeing down to the corner gas station can produce its desired level of production at a lower total cost, it will earn higher profits. This chapter begins by examining the costs of firms from a short-term perspective. In the short run, some types costs can be adjusted quickly, like hiring or firing workers, but other types of costs cannot be immediately changed, like building a large factory. The discussion then takes a longrun perspective on costs, when all costs can be adjusted. Firms can use this breakdown of their cost structure into what is adjustable in the short-term and what is adjustable in the long term both to understand the situation that they face in trying to earn profits and also to recognize the likely patterns of competition in their market.

The Structure of Costs in the Short Run

A list of the costs involved in producing cars will look very different from the costs involved in producing computer software or haircuts or fast-food meals. However, the cost structure of all firms can be broken down into some common underlying patterns. When a firm looks at its total costs of production in the short run, a useful starting point is to divide total costs into two categories: fixed costs that can't be changed in the short run and variable costs that can be.

FIXED AND VARIABLE COSTS

Fixed costs are expenditures that must be made before production starts and that do not change regardless of the level of production, at least not in the short run of weeks and months. Fixed costs can take many forms: for example, machinery or equipment, physical space for a retail or manufacturing business, research and development costs to develop new technology, even an expense like advertising to popularize a brand name. The level of fixed costs varies according to the specific line of business: for instance, manufacturing computer chips requires an expensive factory, but a local moving and hauling business can get by with almost no fixed costs at all if it rents trucks by the day when needed.

fixed costs: Expenditures that must be made before production starts and that do not change regardless of the level of production.

Variable costs, on the other hand, are incurred in the act of producing and will increase with the quantity produced. Labor is treated as a variable cost, since producing a greater quantity of a good or service typically requires more workers. But for many firms, variable costs would also include physical inputs, like the metal and plastic involved in manufacturing a car or the cloth for making shirts and trousers.

variable costs: Costs of production that increase with the quantity produced.

As a concrete example of fixed and variable costs, consider the barber shop called The Clip Joint shown in Exhibit 9-2. Fixed costs of operating the barber shop, like the space and equipment, are $160 per day. The fixed costs are represented in the exhibit as the point where the total cost curve touches the vertical axis; that is, they are the costs incurred even if output is zero.

Variable costs are the costs of hiring barbers, which is $80 per day. The first two columns of Exhibit 9-2 show the quantity of haircuts that the barbershop can produce as it hires additional barbers. The third column shows the fixed costs, which do not change regardless of the level of production. The fourth column shows the variable costs at each level of output; these are calculated by taking the amount of labor hired and multiplying by the wage. Adding together the fixed costs in the third column and the variable costs in the fourth column produces the total costs in the fifth column.

Once production starts, total costs and variable costs rise. Variable costs often show a pattern of **diminishing marginal returns**, which occurs when the marginal gain in output diminishes as each additional unit of input is added. In the figure, diminishing marginal returns is illustrated by the ever-steeper slope of the total cost curve—that is, the cost of producing each additional unit of output is rising. As the number of barbers increases from 0 to 1, the marginal gain in output is 16; as the number rises from 1 to 2, the output gain is 24—an increasing marginal output. From that point on, the marginal gain in output diminishes as each additional barber is added. To understand the reason behind this pattern, consider that a one-man barber shop is a very busy operation. The single barber needs to do everything: say hello to people entering, answer the phone, cut hair, sweep up, and run the cash register. A second barber reduces the level of disruption from jumping back and forth between these tasks, and allows a greater division of labor and specialization. The result can be greater increasing marginal returns. However, as

diminishing marginal returns: When the marginal gain in output diminishes as each additional unit of input is added.

Clearing It Up

What's the Difference Between Business and Economics?

There's a certain amount of tension between business and economics. Business people sometimes tend to view economists as smart but theoretical and naive, with no idea of what it actually takes to run a business. One economist recalled his childhood this way: "Economists always talked a lot about business but, to my father, economists bore about the same relationship to business and the general economy as stamp collecting did to the delivery of the mail." Economists, for their part, sometimes seem to think that business people are so wrapped up in day-to-day details of ordering paper clips and raking in executive bonuses that they have only a fuzzy perception of how the economic system as a whole works, or of their firm's place within that system.

Although both economists and business people think about business issues, they do so from different perspectives. One useful metaphor is that economists are to business people as mechanics are to chauffeurs. Both jobs involve cars. But the mechanic's view of how things are working under the hood is different from the driver's view of how to get to the destination. Economists typically have a better perspective on the market-oriented system as a whole and how it fits together. But business people have a wealth of detailed knowledge about specific products, human relations, management, accounting, new product launches, marketing, production, strategies of specific firms, and other issues that economists cannot match.

Exhibit 9-2 How Output Affects Total Costs

The first column shows the number of barbers hired. The second column shows the quantity of haircuts produced. The fixed costs of setting up the shop are $160, and these fixed costs do not change with the quantity of production. Fixes costs are shown by where the total cost line intersects the horizontal axis. The variable costs of hiring barbers are $80. Total costs are calculated by adding up the fixed and variable costs. Variable costs rise with production.

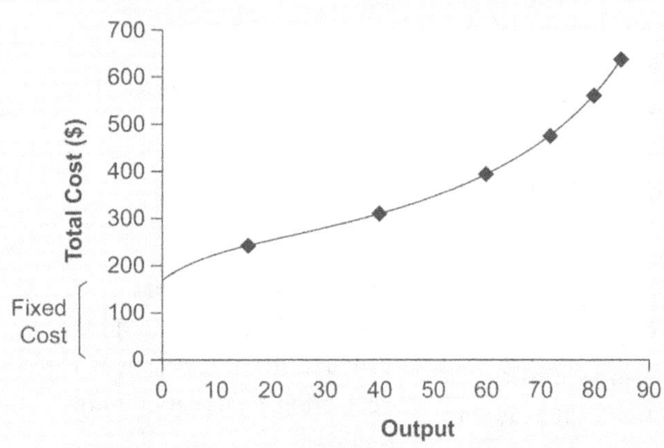

Labor	Quantity	Fixed Cost	Variable Cost	Total Cost
1	16	$160	$80	$240
2	40	$160	$160	$320
3	60	$160	$240	$400
4	72	$160	$320	$480
5	80	$160	$400	$560
6	84	$160	$480	$640

other barbers are added, at some point the additional barbers will begin bumping elbows and start to produce diminishing marginal returns. As a result, the total costs of production will begin to rise more rapidly as output increases.

This pattern of diminishing marginal returns is common in many industries. As another example, consider the problem of irrigating a crop on a farmer's field. The plot of land is the fixed factor of production, while the water that can be added to the land is the key variable cost. As the farmer adds water to the land, output increases. But adding more and more water brings smaller and smaller increases in output, until at some point the water floods the field and actually reduces output. Diminishing marginal returns occurs because given a certain level of fixed costs, marginal increases in output eventually require an ever-increasing number of inputs, and thus come at a higher cost.

Average Costs, Average Variable Costs, Marginal Costs

The breakdown of total costs into fixed and variable costs can provide a basis for other insights as well. The first five columns of Exhibit 9-3 duplicate the previous exhibit, but the last three columns offer additional calculations, where the costs are now analyzed not as a total, but on a per-unit basis. These additional calculations are also plotted on a graph.

average cost: Total cost divided by the quantity of output.

Average cost is calculated by dividing the total cost by the quantity of output. Thus, because the total cost of producing 40 haircuts is $320, the average cost for producing each of 40 haircuts is $320/40 = $8. A similar calculation is performed for each entry in the average cost column.

The average cost curve is U-shaped, as shown in Exhibit 9-3. It starts off relatively high, because at the far left end average cost is calculated including all of the fixed costs and relatively little output, so the denominator in the average cost calculation is close to zero. Average costs then decline, as the fixed costs are spread over an increasing quantity of output. In the average cost calculation, the rise in the numerator of total costs is relatively small compared to the rise in the denominator of quantity produced. But as output expands still further, the average cost begins to rise. At the right side of the average cost curve, total costs begin rising more rapidly as diminishing returns kick in.

average variable cost: Variable cost divided by the quantity of output.

Average variable cost is calculated by dividing the variable cost and by the quantity of output. For example, the variable cost of producing 80 haircuts is $400, so the average variable cost is $400/80 = $5. The average variable cost curve will always lie below the curve for average cost, as shown in Exhibit 9-3, because average cost includes fixed costs in the numerator of the calculation, and variable cost doesn't. However, as output becomes larger, fixed costs become relatively less important (since they don't rise with output), and so average variable cost sneaks closer to average cost.

marginal cost: The additional cost of producing one more unit.

Marginal cost is the additional cost of producing one more unit. Marginal cost can be calculated by taking the change in total cost (or the change in variable cost, because that will be the same amount) and dividing it by the change in quantity. For example, as quantity produced increases from 40 to 60, total costs rise by 80. Thus, the marginal cost for each of those marginal 20 units will be 80/20 = 4. A similar calculation is performed for each entry in the marginal cost column. The marginal cost curve is generally upward-sloping, because diminishing marginal returns implies that additional units are more costly to produce. A small zone of increasing marginal returns can be seen in the figure as a dip in the marginal cost curve before it starts rising. The marginal cost line intersects the average cost line exactly at the bottom of the average cost curve—which occurs at a quantity of 72 and costs of $6.60 in Exhibit 9-3. The reason why the intersection occurs at this point is built into the economic meaning of marginal and average costs. If the marginal cost of production is below the average cost for producing previous units, as it is for the points to the left of where MC crosses AC, then producing one more additional unit will reduce average costs overall—and the AC curve will be downward-sloping in this zone. Conversely, if the marginal cost of production for producing an additional unit is above the average cost for producing the earlier units, as it is for points to the right of where MC crosses AC, then producing a marginal unit will increase average costs overall—and the AC curve must be upward-sloping in this zone. The point of transition, between where MC is pulling AC down and where it is pulling it up, must occur at the minimum point of the AC curve. This idea of the marginal cost "pulling down" the average cost or "pulling up" the average cost may sound abstract, but think about it in terms of your own grades. If the score on the most recent quiz you take is lower than your average score on previous quizzes, then the marginal quiz pulls down your average. If your score on the most recent quiz is higher than the average on previous quizzes, the marginal quiz pulls up your average. In this same way, low marginal costs of production first pull down average costs and then higher marginal costs pull them up.

The numerical calculations behind average cost, average variable cost, and marginal cost will change from firm to firm. However, the general patterns of these curves, and the relationships and economic intuition behind them, will not change.

LESSONS TAUGHT BY ALTERNATIVE MEASURES OF COSTS

Breaking down total costs into fixed cost, marginal cost, average cost, and average variable cost is useful because each statistic offers its own insights for the firm.

Whatever the firm's quantity of production, total revenue must exceed total costs if it is to earn a profit. Fixed costs are important because at least in the short run, the firm cannot alter them. Fixed costs are sunk costs, to use a term introduced in Chapter 2. In thinking about what to do next, sunk costs should typically be ignored, since this spending has already been made and cannot be changed. However, variable costs can be changed, so they convey information about the firm's ability to cut costs in the present and the extent to which costs will increase if production rises. Average cost tells a firm whether it can earn profits given the price in the market. Rewrite the equation for profit to spell out that total revenues are the quantity produced multiplied by the price, and that total costs are the quantity produced multiplied by the average cost:

Profit = total revenue – total cost = (price) (quantity produced) – (average cost) (quantity produced)

Exhibit 9-3 Cost Curves at The Clip Joint

The information on total costs, fixed cost, and variable cost can also be presented on a per-unit basis. Average cost (AC) is calculated by dividing total cost by the total quantity produced. The average cost curve is typically U-shaped. Average variable cost (AVC) is calculated by dividing variable cost by the quantity produced. The average variable cost curve lies below the average cost curve and is typically U-shaped or upward-sloping. Marginal cost (MC) is calculated by taking the change in total cost between two levels of output and dividing by the change in output. The marginal cost curve is upward-sloping.

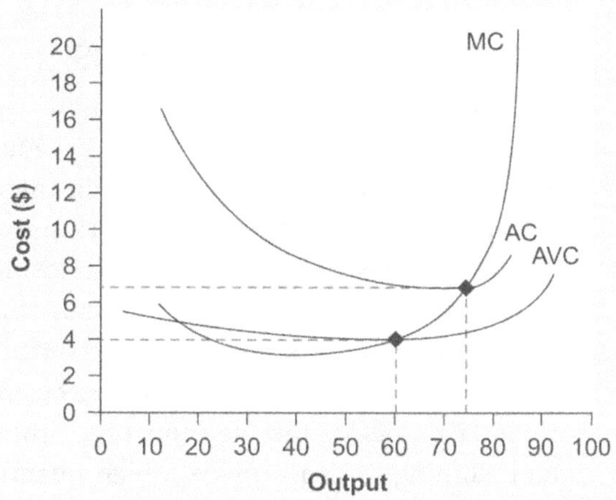

Labor	Quantity	Fixed Cost	Variable Cost	Total Cost	Marginal Cost	Average Cost	Average Variable Cost
1	16	160	80	240	5	15	5
2	40	160	160	320	3.3	8	4
3	60	160	240	400	4	6.6	4
4	72	160	320	480	6.6	6.6	4.4
5	80	160	400	560	10	7	5
6	84	160	480	640	20	7.6	5.7

This formula implies that if the market price exceeds average cost, profits will be positive; if price is below average cost, then profits will be negative.

The lesson to be learned from average variable cost is more subtle, but if a comparison between average cost and price reveals whether a firm is earning profits, then comparison between average variable cost and price reveals whether the firm is earning profit *if fixed costs are left out of the calculation*. In certain circumstances, discussed in more detail in the next chapter, this information may prove useful.

The marginal cost of producing an additional unit can be compared with the amount of revenue gained by selling that additional unit to reveal whether the marginal unit is adding to total profit—or not. Thus, marginal cost helps in how profits would be affected by increasing or reducing production.

Total cost, fixed cost, and variable cost are all add up certain costs of production over the entire quantity being produced. In contrast, marginal cost, average cost, and average variable cost are all calculated after dividing by the quantity being produced. Thus, it wouldn't be very practical to put all of these numbers on the same graph. If they were on the same graph, the lines for marginal cost, average cost and average variable cost would appear almost flat against the horizontal axis, compared to the values for total cost, fixed cost, and variable cost.

CLEARING IT UP

Why Total Cost and Average Cost Are Not on the Same Graph.

A VARIETY OF COST PATTERNS

The pattern of costs varies among industries and even among firms in the same industry. Some businesses have high fixed costs, but low marginal costs. Consider, for example, an Internet company that provides medical advice to customers. Such a company might be paid by health care consumers directly, or perhaps hospitals or health care practices might subscribe on behalf of their patients. Setting up the website, collecting the information, writing the content, and buying or leasing the computer space to handle the web traffic are all fixed costs that must be undertaken before the site can work. However, when the website is up and running, it can provide a high quantity of service with relatively low variable costs, like the cost of monitoring the system and updating the information. In this case, the total cost curve might start at a high level, because of the high fixed costs, but then might appear close to flat for a large quantity, reflecting the low variable costs of operation. However, if the website is popular, a large rise in the number of visitors will overwhelm the website, and increasing output further would require an additional purchase of computer space.

For other firms, fixed costs may be relatively low. For example, consider firms that rake leaves in the fall or shovel snow off sidewalks and driveways in the winter. For fixed costs, such firms may need little more than a car to transport workers to homes of customers and some rakes and shovels. Still other firms may find that diminishing marginal returns set in quite sharply. If a manufacturing plant tried to run 24 hours a day, seven days a week, then little time remains for routine maintenance of the equipment, and marginal costs can increase dramatically as the firm struggles to repair and replace overworked equipment.

Every firm can gain insight into its task of earning profits by dividing its total costs into fixed and variable costs, and then using these calculations as a basis for average cost, average variable cost, and marginal cost. However, making a final decision about the profit-maximizing quantity to produce and price to charge will require combining these perspectives on cost with an analysis of sales and revenue, which in turn requires looking at the competitive setting in which the firm finds itself. Before turning to the analysis of these competitive settings like perfect competition, monopolistic competition and monopoly in the next three chapters, let's analyze the firm's cost structure from a long-run perspective.

The Structure of Costs in the Long Run

No costs are fixed in the long-run. All costs are potentially variable over time. A firm can build new factories and purchase new machinery, or it can close existing facilities. In planning for the long-run, the firm will compare alternative **production technologies**, where the term "technology" doesn't refer to a specific new invention like the laser beam or the assembly line, but refers to any alternative methods of combining inputs to produce output. The firm will search for the production technology that allows producing the desired level of output at lowest cost. After all, lower costs lead to higher profits—at least if total revenues remain unchanged. Moreover, each firm must fear that if it does not seek out the low-cost methods of production, then it may lose sales to competitor firms who find a way to produce and sell for less.

production technologies: Alternative methods of combining inputs to produce output.

CHOICE OF PRODUCTION TECHNOLOGY

Many tasks can be performed with a range of combinations of labor and physical capital. For example, a firm can have human beings answering phones and taking messages, or it can invest in an automated voicemail system. A firm can hire file clerks and secretaries to manage a system of paper folders and file cabinets, or it can invest in a computerized record-keeping system that will require fewer employees. A firm can hire workers to push supplies around a factory on rolling carts, or it can invest in motorized vehicles, or it can invest in robots that carry materials without a driver. Firms often face a choice between buying a number of small machines, which need a worker to run each one, or buying one larger and more expensive machine, which only requires one or two workers to run it. In short, physical capital and labor can often substitute for each other.

Consider the example of a private firm that is hired by local governments to clean up public parks. Three different combinations of labor and physical capital for cleaning up a single average-sized park appear in Exhibit 9-4. The first production technology is heavy on workers and light on machines, while the next two technologies substitute machines for workers. Since all three of these production methods produce the same thing—one cleaned-up park—a profit-seeking firm will choose the production technology that is least expensive, given the prices of labor and machines.

In Exhibit 9-4, example A shows the firm's cost calculation when wages are $40 and machines cost $80. In this case, technology #1 is the low-cost production technology. In example B, wages rise to $70, while the cost of machines does not change, in which case technologies #2 and #3 are tied for being the low-cost production technology. If wages keep rising up to $90, while the cost of machines remains unchanged, then technology #3 clearly becomes the low-cost form of production, as shown in example C.

Exhibit 9-4 Three Ways to Clean a Park

Three production technologies

Production technology 1	10 workers	2 machines
Production technology 2	7 workers	4 machines
Production technology 3	3 workers	7 machines

All three technologies accomplish the same task; in this case, cleaning up one park. Production technology #1 uses the most labor and least machinery, while #3 uses the least labor and the most machinery. As the cost of labor rises from example A to B to C, the firm will choose to substitute away from labor and use more machinery.

Example A: Workers cost 40, machines cost 80

	Labor Cost	Machine Cost	Total Cost
Cost of technology #1	10 × 40 = 400	2 × 80 = 160	560
Cost of technology #2	7 × 40 = 280	4 × 80 = 320	600
Cost of technology #3	3 × 40 = 120	7 × 80 = 560	680

Example B: Workers cost 60, machines cost 80

	Labor Cost	Machine Cost	Total Cost
Cost of technology #1	10 × 60 = 600	2 × 80 = 160	760
Cost of technology #2	7 × 60 = 420	4 × 80 = 320	740
Cost of technology #3	3 × 60 = 180	7 × 80 = 560	740

Example C: Workers cost 90, machines cost 80

	Labor Cost	Machine Cost	Total Cost
Cost of technology #1	10 × 90 = 900	2 × 80 = 160	1600
Cost of technology #2	7 × 90 = 630	4 × 80 = 320	950
Cost of technology #3	3 × 90 = 270	7 × 80 = 560	830

This example illustrates that as an input becomes more expensive (in this case, the labor input), firms will attempt to conserve on using that input and will instead shift to other inputs that are now relatively less expensive. This pattern helps to explain why the demand curve for labor (or any input) slopes down; that is, as labor becomes relatively more expensive, profit-seeking firms will seek to substitute the use of other inputs. When a multinational employer like Coca-Cola or McDonald's sets up a bottling plant or a restaurant in a high-wage economy like the United States, Canada, Japan, or western Europe, it is likely to use production technologies that conserve on the number of workers and focuses more on machines. However, that same employer is likely to use production technologies with more workers and less machinery when producing in a lower wage country like Mexico, China, or South Africa.

economies of scale: When the average cost of producing each individual unit declines as total output increases.

ECONOMIES OF SCALE

Economies of scale refers to the situation where as the quantity of output—the "scale" of production—goes up, average cost of production falls. When economies of scale exist, doubling of all inputs will result in more than doubling output (or equivalently, doubling all inputs will result in producing at a lower average cost). In everyday language, a larger factory can produce at a lower average cost than a smaller factory. Exhibit 9-5 illustrates the idea of economies of scale (which was originally introduced in Chapter 1), showing the average cost of producing an alarm clock falling as the quantity of output rises. For a small-sized factory like S, with an output level of 1,000, the average cost of production is $12 per alarm clock. For a medium-sized factory like M, with an output level of 2,000, the average cost of production falls to $8 per alarm clock. For a large factory like L, with an output of 5,000, the average cost of production declines still further to $4 per alarm clock. The average cost curve in this economies of scale diagram may appear similar to the average cost curves presented earlier in this chapter, although it is downward-sloping rather than U-shaped. But there is one major difference. The economies-of-scale curve is a long-run average cost curve, because it allows all factors of production to change. The short-run average cost curves presented earlier in this chapter assumed the existence of fixed costs, and only variable costs were allowed to change. One prominent example of economies of scale occurs in the chemical industry. Chemical plants have a lot of pipes. The cost of the materials for producing a pipe is related to the circumference of the pipe and its length. However, the volume of gooky chemical stuff that can flow through a pipe is determined by the cross-section area of the pipe. The calculations in Exhibit 9-6 show that a pipe which uses twice as much

Exhibit 9-5 Economies of Scale

A small factory like S produces 1,000 alarm clocks at an average cost of $12 per clock. A medium factory like M produces 2,000 alarm clocks at a cost of $8 per clock. A large factory like L produces 5,000 alarm clocks at a cost of $4 per clock. Economies of scale exist because the larger scale of production leads to lower average costs.

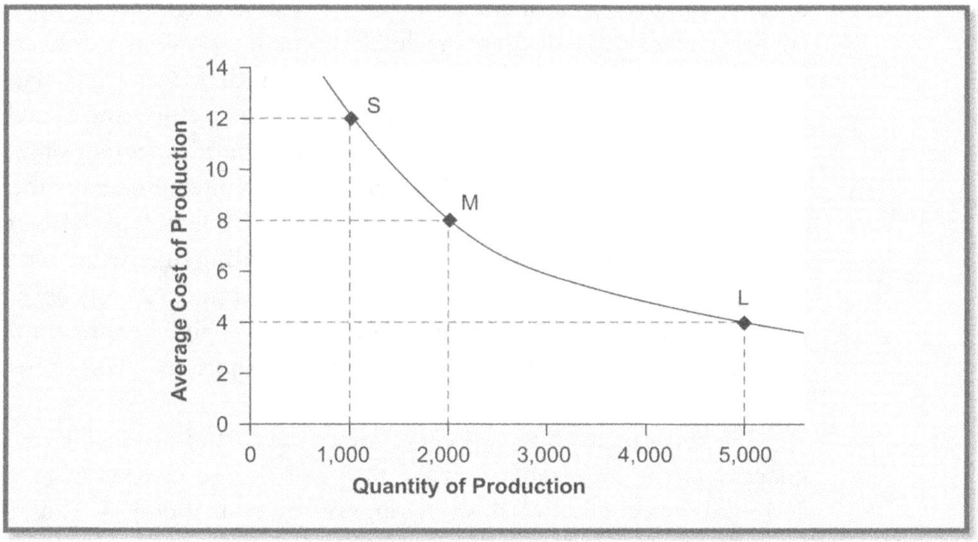

Exhibit 9-6 Comparing Pipes: Economies of Scale in the Chemical Industry

	Circumference ($\pi 2r$)	Area (πr^2)
4-inch pipe	12.5 inches	12.5 square inches
8-inch pipe	25.1 inches	50.2 square inches
16-inch pipe	50.2 inches	201.1 square inches

A circular pipe that is four inches in diameter will have a circumference of 12.5 inches. A circular pipe that is eight inches in diameter will have a circumference of 25.1 inches—so it will take twice as much material to make that pipe. However, although the pipe that is eight inches in diameter will take twice as much material to make, and thus cost roughly twice as much, it will carry four times as much, as can be seen in the area. The area of the cross-section of an eight-inch pipe is four times as great as the corresponding area of a four-inch pipe. Thus, a doubling of the cost of producing the pipe allows the chemical firm to process four times as much material. This pattern is a major reason why economies of scale in chemical production, which uses a large quantity of pipes.

material to make (as shown by the circumference of the pipe doubling) can actually carry four times the volume of chemicals (because the cross-section area of the pipe rises by a factor of four). Of course, economies of scale in a chemical plant are more complex than this simple calculation suggests. But the chemical engineers who design these plants have long used what they call the "six-tenths rule," a rule of thumb which holds that increasing the quantity produced in a chemical plant by a certain percentage will increase total cost by only six-tenths as much.

SHAPES OF LONG-RUN AVERAGE COST CURVES

The long-run average cost curve, where all costs are allowed to vary, is actually based on a group of different short-run average cost curves, each of which represents one specific level of fixed costs. Exhibit 9-7 shows how the long-run average cost curve is built up out of a group of short-run average cost curves. Five short-run-average cost or SRAC curves appear on the diagram. Each SRAC curve represents a different level of fixed costs. For example, you can imagine $SRAC_1$ as a small factory, $SRAC_2$ as a medium factory, $SRAC_3$ as a large factory, and $SRAC_4$ and $SRAC_5$ as very large and ultra-large. Although this diagram shows only five SRAC curves, presumably there are an infinite number of other SRAC curves between the ones that are shown. This family of shortrun average cost curves can be thought of as representing different choices for a firm, which is planning its level of investment in fixed costs physical capital—knowing that different choices about capital investment in the present will cause it to end up with different short-run average cost curves in the future.

The long-run average cost curve shows the cost of producing each quantity in the long-run, when the firm can choose its level of fixed costs and thus choose which short-run average costs it desires. Thus, if the firm plans to produce in the long run at an output of q_3, it should make the set of investments that will lead it to locate on $SRAC_3$, which allows producing q_3 at the lowest cost. A firm that intends to produce q_3 would be foolish to choose the level of fixed costs at $SRAC_2$ or $SRAC_4$. At $SRAC_2$ the level of fixed costs is too low for producing q3 at lowest possible cost, and producing q_3 would require adding a very high level of variable costs and make the average cost very high. At $SRAC_4$, the level of fixed costs is too high for producing q_3 at lowest possible cost, and again average costs would be very high as a result.

The shape of the long-run cost curve as drawn in Exhibit 9-7 is fairly common for many industries. The left-hand portion of the long-run average cost curve, where it is downward sloping from output levels q_1 to q_2 to q_3 illustrates the case of economies of scale, which is sometimes also referred to as **increasing returns to scale**. In this portion of the long-run average cost curve, larger scale leads to lower average costs. This pattern was illustrated earlier in Exhibit 9-5.

increasing returns to scale: When a larger-scale firm can produce at a lower cost than a smaller-scale firm, also called economies of scale.

In the middle portion of the long-run average cost curve, the flat portion of the curve around q_3, economies of scale have halted. In this situation allowing all inputs to expand does not much change the average cost of production, and it is called **constant returns to scale**. In this range of the LRAC curve, the average cost of production does not change much as scale rises or falls.

constant returns to scale: When expanding all inputs does not change the average cost of production.

Finally, the right-hand portion of the long-run average cost curve, running from output level q_4 to q_5, shows a situation where as the level of output and the scale rises, average costs rise as well. This situation is called **diseconomies of scale** or **decreasing returns to scale**. A firm or a factory can become so large that it becomes very difficult to manage, resulting in unnecessarily high costs as many layers of management try to communicate with workers and with each other, and as failures to communicate lead to disruptions in the flow of work and materials. Not many overly large factories are observed in the real world, because with their very high production costs, they are unable to compete for long against plants with lower average costs of production and so they go out of business. However, in some planned economies, like the economy of the old Soviet Union, plants that were so large as to be grossly inefficient were able to continue operating for a long time, because the government economic planners protected them from competition and assured that they would not make losses. Although economies of scale may be easiest

diseconomies of scale: Another term for decreasing returns to scale.

decreasing returns to scale: As the quantity of output rises, the average cost of production rises.

Clearing It Up

Economies of Scale vs. Diminishing Marginal Returns?

The concept of economies of scale, where average costs decline as production expands, might seem to conflict with the idea of diminishing marginal returns, where marginal costs rise as production expands. But diminishing marginal returns refers only to the short-run average cost curve, where one variable input (like labor) is increasing, but other inputs (like capital) are fixed. Economies of scale refers to the long-run average cost curve where all inputs are being allowed to increase together. Thus, it is quite possible and common to have an industry that has both diminishing marginal returns when only one input is allowed to change, and at the same time has increasing or constant returns to scale when all inputs change together to produce a larger-scale operation.

Exhibit 9-7 From Short-Run Average Cost Curves to Long-Run Average Cost Curves

The five different short-run average cost (SRAC) curves each represents a different level of fixed costs, from the low level of fixed costs at $SRAC_1$ to the high level of fixed costs at $SRAC_5$. Other SRAC curves, not shown in the diagram, lie between the ones that are shown here. The long-run average cost (LRAC) curve shows the lowest cost for producing each quantity of output when fixed costs can vary, and so it is formed by the bottom edge of the family of SRAC curves. If a firm wished to produce quantity q_3, it would choose the fixed costs associated with $SRAC_3$.

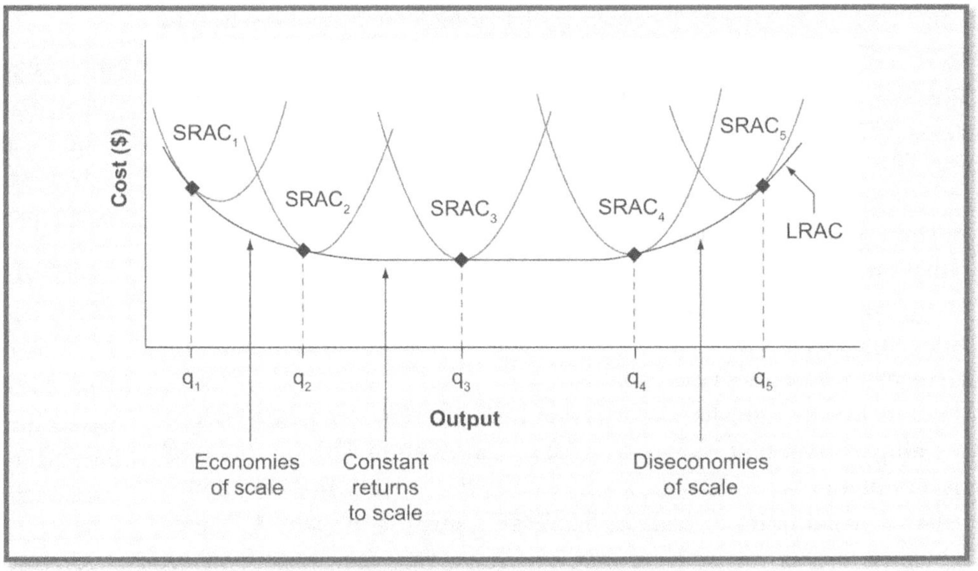

to visualize in terms of the size of manufacturing plants, the concept has many applications. In some cases, economies of scale may arise because doubling advertising or promotional expenses may expand sales more than proportionately, or because a larger retail space can expand sales more than proportionately, or because spreading the fixed costs of administration and recordkeeping over more customers (as in the banking or insurance industries, for example) can hold down average costs. In any industry where small firms have a difficult time competing because their average costs are too high, economies of scale offers one plausible explanation.

THE SIZE AND NUMBER OF FIRMS IN AN INDUSTRY

The shape of the long-run average cost curve has implications for how many firms will compete in an industry, and whether the firms in an industry have many different sizes, or tend to be the same size. For example, say that 1 million dishwashers are sold every year at a price of $500 each and the long-run average cost curve for dishwashers is shown in Exhibit 9-8a. In Exhibit 9-8a, the lowest point of the LRAC curve occurs at a quantity of 10,000 produced. Thus, the market for dishwashers will consist of 100 different manufacturing plants of this same size. If some firm built a plant that produced 5,000 dishwashers per year or 25,000 dishwashers per year, the average costs of production at such plants would be well above $500, and such firms would not be able to compete.

A more common case is illustrated in Exhibit 9-8b, where the LRAC curve has a flat-bottomed area of constant returns to scale. In this situation, any firm with a level of output between 5,000 and 20,000 will be able

Exhibit 9-8 The LRAC Curve and the Size and Number of Firms

(a) Low-cost firms will produce at output level R. When the LRAC curve has a clear minimum point, then any firm producing a different quantity will have higher costs. In this case, a firm producing at a quantity of 10,000 will produce at a lower average cost than a firm producing, say, 5,000 or 20,000 units.

(b) Low-cost firms will produce between output levels R and S. When the LRAC curve has a flat bottom, then firms producing at any quantity along this flat bottom can compete. In this case, any firm producing a quantity between 5,000 and 20,000 can compete effectively, although firms producing less than 5,000 or more than 20,000 would face higher average costs and be unable to compete.

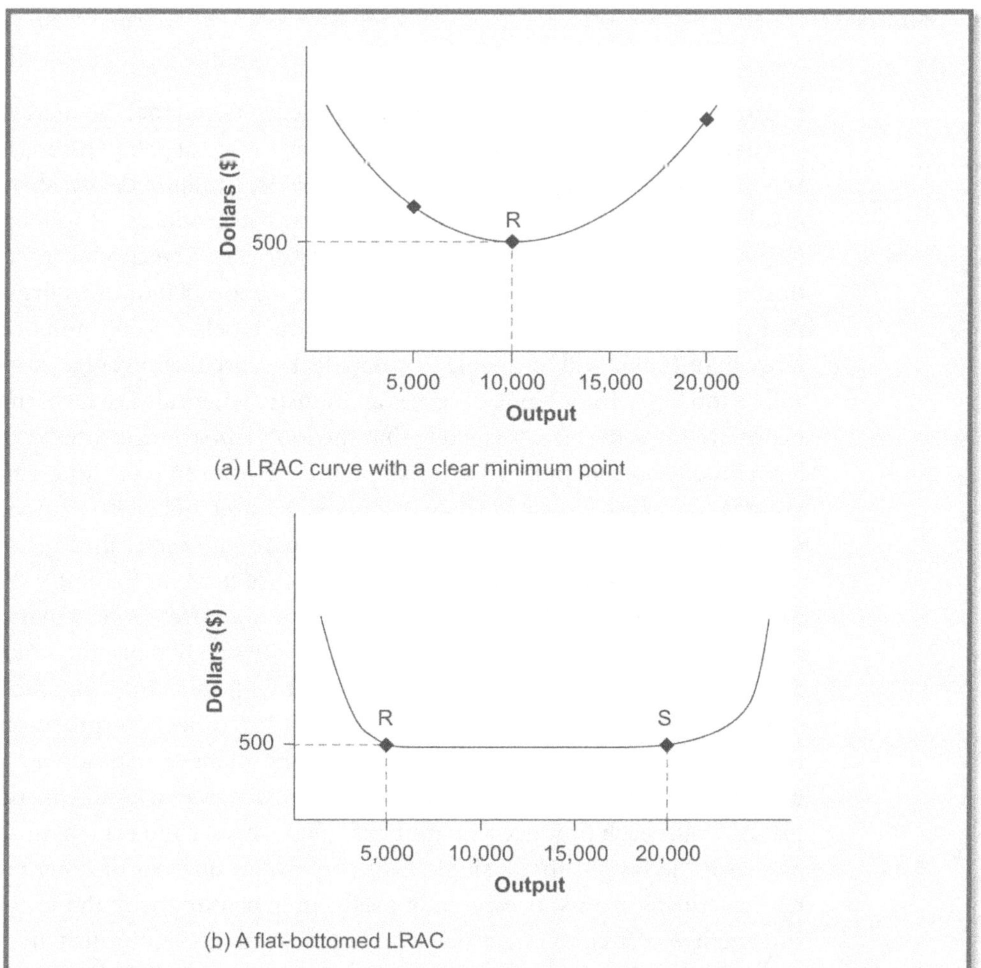

(a) LRAC curve with a clear minimum point

(b) A flat-bottomed LRAC

Cities as Economies of Scale

Why are people and economic activity concentrated in cities, rather than distributed evenly across a country? The fundamental reason must be related to the idea of economies of scale—that grouping economic activity together is more productive in many cases than spreading it out. For example, cities provide a large group of nearby customers, so that businesses can produce at an efficient economy of scale. They also provide a large group of workers and suppliers, so that business can hire easily and purchase whatever specialized inputs they need. Many of the attractions of cities, like sports stadiums and museums, can only operate if they can draw on a large nearby population base. Cities are big enough to offer a wide variety of products, which is what many shoppers are looking for.

These factors are not exactly economies of scale in the narrow sense of applying to the production function of a single firm, but they are related to growth in the overall size of population and market in an area. They are sometimes called "agglomeration economies."

These agglomeration factors help to explain why every economy, as it develops, has an increasing proportion of its population living in urban areas. In the United States, about 80% of the population now lives in metropolitan areas (which include the suburbs around cities), compared to just 40% in 1900. However, in poor nations of the world, including China, India, and much of Africa, the proportion of the population in urban areas is only about 30%. One of the great challenges for these countries as their economies grow will be to manage the growth of the great cities that will arise.

If cities offer economic advantages that are a form of economies of scale, then why don't all or most people live in one giant city? At some point, agglomeration economies must turn into diseconomies. For example, traffic congestion may reach a point where the gains from being geographically nearby are counterbalanced by how long it takes to travel. High densities of people, cars and factories can mean more garbage and air and water pollution. Facilities like parks or museums may become overcrowded. There may be economies of scale for negative activities like crime, because high densities of people and businesses, combined with the greater impersonality of cities, make it easier for illegal activities as well as legal ones. The future of cities, both in the United States and in other countries around the world, will be determined by their ability to benefit from the economies of agglomeration and to minimize or counterbalance the corresponding diseconomies.

to produce at about the same level of average cost. Given that the market will demand 1 million dishwashers per year at a price of $500, this market might have as many as 200 producers (that is, 1 million dishwashers divided by firms making 5,000 each) or as few as 50 producers (1 million dishwashers divided by firms making 20,000 each). The producers in this market will range in size from firms that make 5,000 units to firms that make 20,000 units. But firms that produce below 5,000 units or more than 20,000 will be unable to compete, because their average costs will be too high. Thus, if one observes an industry where almost all of the plants are the same size, it is likely that the long-run average cost curve has a unique bottom point like in Exhibit 9-8a. However, if the long-run average cost curve has a wide flat bottom like Exhibit 9-8b, then firms of a variety of different sizes will be able to compete with each other.

The flat section of the long-run average cost curve in Exhibit 9-8b can be interpreted in two different ways. One interpretation is that a single manufacturing plant producing a quantity of 5,000 has the same average costs as a single manufacturing plant with four times as much capacity that produces a quantity of 20,000. The other interpretation is that one firm owns a single manufacturing plant that produces a quantity of 5,000, while another firm owns four separate manufacturing plants, which each produce a quantity of 5,000. This second explanation, based on the insight that a single firm may own a number of different manufacturing plants, is especially useful in explaining why the long-run average cost curve often has a large flat segment—and thus why a seemingly smaller firm may be able to compete quite well with a larger firm. At some point, however, the task of coordinating and managing many different plants raises the cost of production sharply, and the long-run average cost curve slopes up as a result.

In the examples to this point, the quantity demanded in the market is quite large (1 million) compared with the quantity produced at the bottom of the long-run average cost curve (5,000, 10,000 or 20,000). In such a situation, the market is set for competition between many firms. But what if the bottom of the long-run average cost curve is at a quantity of 10,000 and the total market demand at that price is only slightly higher than that quantity—or even somewhat lower?

Return to Exhibit 9-8a, where the bottom of the long-run average cost curve is at 10,000, but now imagine that the total quantity of dishwashers demanded in the market at that price of $500 is only 30,000. In this situation, the total number of firms in the market would only be three. A small handful of firms in a market is called an "oligopoly," and Chapter 12 will discuss the range of competitive strategies that can occur when oligopolies compete.

Alternatively, consider a situation, again in the setting of Exhibit 9-8a, where the bottom of the long-run average cost curve is 10,000, but total demand for the product is only 5,000. (For simplicity, imagine that this demand is highly inelastic, so that it does not vary according to price.) In this situation, the market may well end up with a single firm—a monopoly—producing all 5,000 units. If any firm tried to challenge this monopoly while producing a quantity lower than 5,000 units, the prospective competitor firm would have a higher average cost, and so it wouldn't be able to compete in the longer term without losing money. A firm producing 10,000 units could produce at a lower average cost—but it could only sell 5,000 units, and so it would lose money as well. Chapter 11 discusses the situation of a monopoly firm in this situation.

Thus, the shape of the long-run average cost curve reveals whether competitors in the market will be different sizes. If the LRAC has a single point at the bottom, then the firms in the market will be about the same size, but if the LRAC has a flat-bottomed segment of constant returns to scale, then firms in the market may be a variety of different sizes.

The relationship between the quantity at the minimum of the long-run average cost curve and the quantity demanded in the market at that price will foretell how much competition is likely to exist in the market. If the quantity demanded in the market far exceeds the quantity at the minimum of the LRAC, then many firms will compete. If the quantity demanded in the market is only slightly higher than the quantity at the minimum of the LRAC, a few firms will compete. If the quantity demanded in the market is less than the quantity at the minimum of the LRAC, a single-producer monopoly is a likely outcome.

SHIFTING PATTERNS OF LONG-RUN AVERAGE COST

New developments in production technology can shift the long-run average cost curve in ways that can alter the size distribution of firms in an industry.

For much of the twentieth century, the most common change has been to see alterations in technology, like the assembly line or the large department store, where large-scale producers seemed to gain an advantage over smaller ones. In the long-run average cost curve, the downward-sloping economies of scale portion of the curve stretched over a larger quantity of output.

However, new production technologies do not inevitably lead to a greater average size for firms. For example, in recent years some new technologies for generating electricity at a smaller scale have risen to prominence. The traditional coal-burning electricity plants needed to produce 300-600 megawatts of power to exploit economies of scale fully. However, high-efficiency turbines to produce electricity from burning natural gas can produce electricity at a competitive price while producing the smaller quantity of 100 megawatts of electricity or less. These new technologies create the possibility for smaller companies or plants to generate electricity as efficiently as large ones. Another example of a technology-driven shift to smaller plants may be taking place in the tire industry. A traditional mid-size tire plant produces about 6 million tires per year. However, in 2000, the Italian company Pirelli introduced a new tire factory that uses many robots. The Pirelli tire plant produced only about one million tires per year, but did so at a lower average cost than a traditional mid-sized tire plant.

Controversy has simmered in recent years over whether the new information and communications technologies will lead to a larger or smaller size for firms. On one side, the new technology may make it easier for small firms to reach out beyond their local geographic area and find customers across a state, or the nation, or even across international boundaries. This factor might seem to predict a future with a larger number of small competitors. On the other side, perhaps the new information and communications technology will create "winner-take-all" markets where one large company will tend to command a large share of total sales, as Microsoft has done in the production of software for personal computers or Amazon has done in online bookselling. Moreover, improved information and communication technologies might make it easier to manage many different plants and operations across the country or around the world, and thus encourage larger firms. This ongoing battle between the forces of smallness and largeness will be of great interest to economists, businesspeople, and policymakers.

CONCLUSION

The cost structure of a firm reveals many useful lessons. From a short-run perspective, each firm should be thinking about what costs are fixed and what costs are variable, and comparing the market price to its average costs and marginal costs. In the long run, each firm should have an idea the extent of economies of scale in its industry, what the range of sizes is to produce at the lowest possible average cost in its industry, and how technological conditions may be shifting the long-run average cost curve over time.

While a careful examination of costs is vital, it is only half the story of the decision-making for any firm. Decisions about the profit-maximizing level of output must always include total revenues as well as total costs. Thus, the next three chapters consider the different market situations of perfect competition, monopoly, monopolistic competition, and oligopoly. In each of these setting, firms must combine their insights about total revenues and total costs, and thus reach a decision about the profit-maximizing price to charge and quantity of output to produce.

Cost Minimization

By William Baumol

The rules of profit maximization explain the behavior of firms in the factor market. These rules predict that firms will employ that level and combination of inputs that maximizes their profit. In the product market, firms produce that level of output (and charge the associated price) that maximizes their profit.

To maximize profit, it is necessary to minimize the cost of producing a given quantity of output. Thus far, we have explained how a firm selects the optimal level of *one* factor input. But firms produce output with cooperating factors. How will they know when they are combining *all* their inputs in a least-cost fashion? Suppose a firm has decided to produce 200 units of output and currently uses 15 labor hours and 25 machine hours to produce this output. The wage rate (the price of labor) is \$5 per hour, and the rental rate on the machinery is \$20 per hour. Thus, an extra hour of machine time costs four times as much as an extra hour of labor. The marginal physical product of capital is 30 units of output. The marginal physical product of labor is 10 units of output. Thus, an extra hour of machine time produces three times as much as an extra hour of labor. Is the firm using the optimal amount of labor and capital?

In this example, the firm is using too much capital and too little labor. If the firm were to substitute 3 hours of labor for 1 hour of capital, total output would not change, but costs would be reduced by \$5. One hour of capital (at the margin) is three times as productive as 1 hour of labor. Adding 3 units of labor increases output by 30, and subtracting 1 machine hour decreases output by 30; there is no net change in output. However, cutting back on 1 machine hour saves \$20, while hiring 3 more hours of labor costs \$15. Output remains the same, but costs fall by \$5.

To determine whether a substitution of this sort will increase profits, the firm will look at marginal physical product *per dollar of cost.* In this example, because an extra hour of labor increases output by 10 units and increases costs by \$5, an extra dollar spent on labor produces 2 units (10/\$5) of output. Because an extra machine hour increases output by 30 units and increases costs by \$20, an extra dollar spent on capital produces 1.5 units of output. In our example, a dollar spent on more labor is more effective than a dollar spent on more capital. (See Example 3.)

The marginal physical product per dollar of a factor is its marginal physical product divided by its price. The price-taking firm takes both the wage rate for labor (*W*) and the rental rate on capital (*R*) as given. As the preceding example shows, if the marginal physical product per dollar of labor is greater than the marginal physical product per dollar of capital, the firm is not combining inputs in a least-cost fashion. It can produce the same output at lower cost by substituting labor for capital until:

$$\frac{MPP_L}{W} = \frac{MPP_K}{R}$$

where MPP_K is the marginal physical product of capital.

According to the least-cost rule, the price-taking firm is producing at minimum cost only if the marginal physical products per dollar of the various factors are equal.

Example 3

ONE DOCTOR, TWO OFFICES

The least-cost rule states that the factors of production will be combined so that their marginal physical products per dollar are equal. Physicians, for example, produce medical services by combining their labor with capital. Your doctor practices in an office equipped with scales, lab equipment, and medical supplies. He or she combines labor, capital, and supplies so that medical services can be provided "efficiently."

Until recently, it was most efficient for a physician to practice out of one office. However, in the late 1980s and early 1990s, many physicians began to operate out of two or more offices in order to serve patients in the city as well as the suburbs.

This trend came about as the result of declining office rents, which were associated with the overbuilding of office space during that time. As rents declined, physicians saw that they were not allocating resources efficiently. They could provide more efficient" medical care if they rented an extra office. This use of more capital relative to labor allowed physicians to reach a new, efficient combination of labor and capital.

Key Concepts and Summary

By Timothy Taylor

1. Since profits are equal to total revenues minus total costs, every firm must consider its costs with care. Indeed, a profit-maximizing firm will always seek to produce its chosen level of output at the lowest possible cost.
2. At one end of the spectrum of competition is **perfect competition**, with many firms selling extremely similar products. At the other end is **monopoly**, where only one firm sells a particular product. In the middle are the cases of **monopolistic** competition, where many firms sell similar but clearly different products, and the case of **oligopoly**, where only a few firms sell a particular product.
3. In a short-run perspective, a firm's total costs can be divided into **fixed costs**, which a firm must incur before producing any output, and **variable costs**, which the firm incurs in the act of producing.
4. Fixed costs are sunk costs; that is, because they are in the past and cannot be altered, they should play no role in economic decisions about future production or pricing.
5. Variable costs typically show **diminishing marginal returns**, so that the marginal cost of producing higher levels of output rises.
6. **Marginal cost** is calculated by taking the change in total cost (or the change in variable cost, which will be the same thing) and dividing it by the change in output, for each possible change in output. Marginal costs are typically rising. A firm can compare marginal cost to the additional revenue it gains from selling another unit to find out whether its marginal unit is adding to profit.
7. **Average cost** is calculated by taking total cost and dividing by total output at each different level of output. Average costs are typically U-shaped on a graph. If a firm's average cost of production is lower than the market price, a firm will be earning profits.
8. **Average variable cost** is calculated by taking variable cost and dividing by the total output at each level of output. Average variable costs are typically U-shaped. If a firm's average variable cost of production is lower than the market price, then the firm would be earning profits if fixed costs are left out of the picture.
9. A **production technology** refers to a specific combination of labor, physical capital and technology that makes up a particular method of production.
10. In the long run, firms can choose their production technology, and so all costs become variable costs. In making this choice, firms will try to substitute relatively inexpensive inputs for relatively expensive inputs where possible, so as to produce at the lowest possible long-run average cost.

Timothy Taylor, "Cost and Industry Structure," Principles of Macroeconomics, pp. 169-184.

11. **Economies of scale** refers to a situation where as all inputs are allowed to increase at a certain rate, the quantity of output rises at a faster rate. For example, doubling all inputs might result in more than doubling output. **Constant returns to scale** refers to a situation where as all outputs are allowed to increase at a certain rate, the quantity of output rises at the same rate. **Diseconomies of scale** refers to a situation where as all inputs are allowed to increase at a certain rate, the quantity of output rises at a slower rate.
12. The long-run average cost curve shows the lowest possible average cost of production, allowing all the inputs to production to vary so that the firm is choosing its production technology. A downward-sloping LRAC shows economies of scale; a flat LRAC shows constant returns to scale; an upwardsloping LRAC shows diseconomies of scale.
13. If the long-run average cost curve has only one quantity produced that results in the lowest possible average cost, then all of the firms competing in an industry should be the same size. However, if the LRAC has a flat segment at the bottom, so that a range of different quantities can produce at lowest average cost, then the firms competing in the industry will display a range of sizes.
14. If the quantity demanded in the market of a certain product is much greater than the quantity found at the bottom of the long-run average cost curve, where the cost of production is lowest, the market will have many firms competing. If the quantity demanded in the market is only slightly greater than the quantity at the bottom of the LRAC, the market is likely to be an oligopoly. If the quantity demanded in the market is less than the quantity at the bottom of the LRAC, the result is likely to be a monopoly.

Vocabulary Terms

Long-Run Average Cost Curve (LRAC)
Minimum Efficient Scale (MES)
Economies of Scale
Returns to Scale
Scalability
Cost minimizing equation

Review Questions

1. How are total costs related to profits?
2. What is the difference between perfect competition, monopolistic competition, oligopoly, and monopoly?
3. What is the difference between fixed costs and variable costs?
4. Are there fixed costs in the long-run? What about in the short-run? Explain briefly.
5. Are fixed costs also sunk costs? Explain.

6. What are diminishing marginal returns?
7. Which costs are measured on per-unit basis: fixed costs, average cost, average variable cost, variable costs, and marginal cost?
8. How are each of the following calculated: marginal cost, average cost, average variable cost?
9. What shape would you generally expect each of the following to have on a cost-curve diagram: fixed costs, variable costs, marginal costs, average costs, and average variable costs?
10. What is a production technology?
11. In choosing a production technology, how will firms react if one input becomes relatively more expensive?
12. What is the difference between economies of scale, constant returns to scale, and diseconomies of scale?
13. What is a long-run average cost curve?
14. What shape of a long-run average cost curve illustrates economies of scale, constant returns to scale, and diseconomies of scale?
15. Why will firms in most markets be located at or close to the bottom of the long-run average cost curve?

IN-CLASS PROJECT

LRAC Group Work

By David Moglen

Directions

Form your usual group of up to five students. Half of the class will be working on even-numbered questions, and half will be assigned the odd-numbered questions.

Minimum average cost= minimum average total cost= minimum efficient scale (MES)

Draw the LRAC as a rounded, continuous curve. Label the average cost per unit produced (ATC) on the vertical axis and the output measured on the horizontal axis so that your labels make sense for the specific market in the question.

Show the point described as where the producer is currently operating and state whether this is economies of scale or diseconomies of scale (or exactly at the MES). Label where they currently operate as point A.

The graph should have estimated numbers or numbers given from the question for the following: the vertical/horizontal values of point A and the MES (the lowest vertical point on the LRAC—which should be labeled as MES).

For each scenario, start with a blank, unlabeled LRAC graph and then fill in the details: axes labels, numbers, point A and MES.

Draw the fixed factors as SRATC's (Short-Run Average Total Cost Curves). Wherever the lowest cost point, MES, is described as being, you can put the center SRATC with an equal number of SRATC's to its left and right (note that question two does not quite allow for this symmetrical result so just get as close as possible).

1. Fixed factor: restaurant
   Good: Meals/ month
   The business would minimize costs (down to $7 per meal on average) if they had three restaurants, although they currently only have two. Therefore costs are higher than would be ideal, at $11 per meal. With any number of restaurants, each restaurant is selling 10,000 meals per month.

2. Fixed factor: brand (aka the make of the car)
   Good: Cars/ year
   GM (General Motors) reduces their number of brands.
   GM had eight brands sold in the United ... until it sold three and liquidated one of those brands during bankruptcy,[1] leaving four (Chevrolet, Cadillac, GMC and Buick). Four brands gives GM the minimum cost per car, which is $18,000. Show point A as before they got rid of the Pontiac, Hummer, Saturn, and Oldsmobile brands. At either number of brands each brand is producing two million cars per year.

3. Fixed factor: Divisions
   Good: Books/ year
   Thomson Reuters, a publishing company, finds it most efficient to have five separate divisions, each selling an average of 15 million books per year, at which point their costs will be minimized at $5/book. However they had grown too large and are now halfway to their goal after having just sold off their health care publishing division. (Show point A as after they have completed this sale)

4. Fixed factor: (Drilling & Extraction) Rig
   Good: Natural gas in thousands of cubic meters
   Chesapeake is producing 4 Billion cubic meters of natural gas per year with six Drilling & Extraction "Rigs" (on land).

   Their minimum cost is $90 per thousand cubic meters, which will be reached when they shut down or sell off enough rigs that they have only four operating.

5. Fixed Factor: Factories
   Good: Electric Cars/ year
   Tesla Motors needs to sell six times as many cars as they currently do (1,000 cars per year), in order to reach their minimum cost of $35,000 per car. They currently have one factory (that is producing all 1,000 current annual cars sold) operating at 50% capacity of where even that one factory would reach its efficient output level.

6. Fixed Factor: Airplane
   Good: Tickets/ day
   The airline achieves minimum costs of $300 per passenger when their eight planes, which can carry 100 passengers each, are 70% full, the industry average. However the industry (including this firm) is in a slump and planes are only 60% full. Assume each plane makes one flight per day.

1 http://en.wikipedia.org/wiki/Effects_of_the_2008%E2%80%9310_automotive_industry_crisis_on_the_United_States#cite_note-31#cite_note-31

CHAPTER 10
Perfect Competition

10 Perfect Competition

By Timothy Taylor

Any firm must recognize two stark realities: no consumer is required to buy the goods that it produces, and even consumers who might want its goods may choose to buy from other firms instead. Firms in a situation of **perfect competition** sell their product in a market with other firms who produce identical or extremely similar products. As a result, if a firm in a perfectly competitive market raises the price of its product by so much as a penny, it will lose all of its sales to competitors. Perfectly competitive firms are sometimes known as **price takers,** because the pressure of other competing firms forces them to accept the prevailing price in the market as given. A related underlying assumption is that a perfectly competitive firm must be a relatively small player in the overall market, so that a perfectly competitive firm can increase or decrease its output without noticeably affecting the overall quantity supplied in the market.

perfect competition: Each firm faces many competitors that sell identical products.

price takers: A firm in a perfectly competitive market that must take the prevailing market price as given.

A perfectly competitive industry is a hypothetical extreme; after all, "perfect" is an extreme word. However, producers in a number of industries do face many competitor firms selling highly similar goods, in which case they must often act as price takers. For example, many farmers grow any given crop and crops grown by different farmers are largely interchangeable. In 2009, U.S. corn farmers were receiving about $3.70 per bushel and coffee (of the mild arabica variety) was selling for $1.80 a pound on world markets. A corn farmer who attempted to sell corn for $4.00 per bushel, or a coffee grower who attempted to sell for $2.00 a pound, would not have found any buyers. Similarly, gold was selling for $1,100 per ounce, which meant that sellers could not negotiate for $1,200 per ounce. Some manufactured products are similar enough that producers must sell at the price prevailing in the market. In the market for mid-sized color televisions, the quality differences are mostly not perceptible to the untrained eye, so price plays a major role in the decisions of purchasers. Gasoline is very similar between different gas stations. Blank CD-ROM disks are extremely similar regardless of the manufacturer. This chapter examines how profit-seeking firms make decisions about how much to produce in perfectly competitive industries. Such firms will analyze their costs as discussed in the previous chapter, using the concepts of total cost, fixed cost, variable cost, average cost, marginal cost, and average variable cost. In the short run, the perfectly competitive firm will seek out the quantity of output where profits are highest, or if profits are not possible, where losses are smallest. In the long run, the perfectly competitive firms will react to profits by increasing production further and to losses by reducing production or shutting down. Firms will tailor their decisions about the quantity of inputs like labor and physical capital to purchase according to what they need to produce the profit-maximizing quantity of output at the lowest possible average cost.

Quantity Produced by a Perfectly Competitive Firm

A perfectly competitive setting really has only one major choice to make: namely, what quantity to produce. To understand why this is so, consider a different way of writing out the basic definition of profit:

Profit = Total revenue – Total cost = (Price) (Quantity produced) – (Average cost) (Quantity produced)

Since a perfectly competitive firm must accept the price for its output as dictated by the forces of demand and supply, it cannot choose the price that it charges. Moreover, the perfectly competitive firm must also pay the market price for inputs to production like labor and physical capital, so it cannot control what it pays for the inputs that make up its costs of production. When the perfectly competitive firm chooses what quantity to produce, then this quantity—along with the prices prevailing in the market for output and inputs—will determine the firm's total revenue, total costs, and profits.

COMPARING TOTAL REVENUE AND TOTAL COST

As an example of how a perfectly competitive firm decides what quantity to produce, consider the case of the Disk Production Shoppe, which makes boxes of CD-ROM disks. Exhibit 10-1 shows total revenue and total costs for the firm. The horizontal axis of the figure shows the quantity of boxes of disks produced; the vertical axis shows both total revenue and total costs, measured in dollars.

A perfectly competitive firm can sell as large a quantity as it wishes, as long as it accepts the prevailing market price. Thus, the total revenue line slopes up at an angle, with the slope of the line determined by the price. In this example, a 10-pack of CDROM disks costs $3.50. Sales of one box will bring in $3.50, two boxes will be $7, three units will be $10.50, and so on.

The total costs for the Disk Production Shoppe, broken down into fixed and variable costs, are shown in the table that also appears in Exhibit 10-1. The total cost curve intersects with the vertical axis at a value that shows the level of fixed costs, and then slopes upward. (If it bothers you that these numbers don't seem more realistic, you may

Exhibit 10-1 Total Cost and Total Revenue at the Disk Production Shoppe

Total revenue for a perfectly competitive firm is a straight line sloping up. The slope is determined by the price of the good. Total cost also slopes up, but with some curvature. Total cost intersects the vertical axis at the level determined by fixed costs. At higher levels of output, total cost begins to slope upward more steeply because of diminishing marginal returns. At levels of output where total cost is higher than total revenue, like 10 or 20, the firm would suffer a loss. At levels of output where total revenue is higher than total costs, like 60 or 70, the firm would earn profits. The maximum profit will occur at the quantity where the gap of total revenue over total cost is largest.

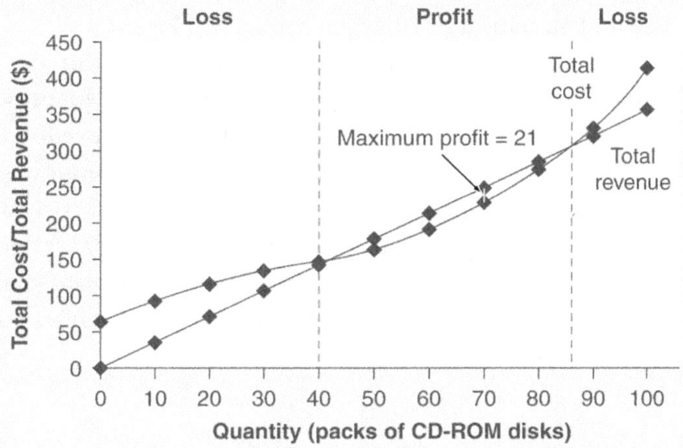

Quantity	Total Cost	Fixed Cost	Variable Cost	Total Revenue	Profit
0	62	62	—	0	–62
10	90	62	28	35	–55
20	110	62	48	70	–40
30	126	62	64	105	–21
40	144	62	82	140	–4
50	166	62	104	175	+9
60	192	62	130	210	+18
70	224	62	162	245	+21
80	264	62	202	280	+16
90	324	62	262	315	–9
100	404	62	342	350	–54

wish to imagine that these total cost and quantity figures represent thousands: that is, fixed costs of the plant are $62,000, and the total cost of producing 10,000 boxes of CD-ROM disks is $90,000. The shape of the total revenue and total cost picture does not change if both quantity and cost are expressed with the extra three zeros.)

Based on its total revenue and total cost curves, a perfectly competitive firm like the Disk Production Shoppe can calculate the quantity of output that will provide the highest level of profit. At any given quantity, total revenue minus total cost will equal profit. On the figure, the vertical gap between total revenue and total cost represents either profit (if total revenues are greater that total costs at a certain quantity) or losses (if total costs are greater that total revenues at a certain quantity). In this example, total costs will exceed total revenues at output levels from 0 to 40, and so over this range of output the firm will be making losses. At output levels from 50 to 80, total revenues exceed total costs, so the firm is earning profits. But then at an output of 90 or 100, total costs again exceed total revenues and the firm is making losses. Total profits appear in the final column of the table. The highest total profits in the table occur at an output of 70, when profits will be $21.

A higher price would mean a steeper slope for the total revenue curve, so that total revenue was higher for every quantity sold; a lower price would mean a flatter slope, so that total revenue was lower for every quantity sold. What happens if the price drops low enough so that the total revenue line is completely below the total cost curve; that is, at every level of output, total costs are higher than total revenues? Then the best that the firm can do is to suffer losses, but a profit-maximizing firm will prefer the quantity of output where total revenues come closest to total costs and thus where the losses are smallest.

COMPARING MARGINAL REVENUE AND MARGINAL COSTS

Firms often do not have the necessary data they would need to draw a complete total cost curve for all different levels of production. They can't be sure of what total costs would look like if they, say, doubled production or cut production in half, because they haven't tried it. Instead, firms experiment; that is, they produce a slightly greater or lower quantity and observe how profits are affected. In economic terms, this practical approach to maximizing profits means looking at how changes in production affect marginal revenue and marginal cost.

Exhibit 10-2 presents the marginal revenue and marginal cost curves based on the total revenue and total cost curves in Exhibit 10-1. The **marginal revenue** curve shows the additional revenue gained from selling one more unit. For a perfectly competitive firm, the marginal revenue curve is drawn as a flat line equal to the price level, which in this example is $3.50 per box of disks. The marginal revenue gained from selling one additional box of disks is just the price of that unit. Since a perfectly competitive firm is a price-taker, it can sell whatever quantity it wishes at the market-determined price. Marginal cost, the cost per additional unit sold, is calculated by dividing the change in total cost by the change in quantity. In this example, marginal cost at first declines as production increases from 10 to 20, which represents the area of increasing marginal returns that is not uncommon at low levels of production. But then marginal costs start to increase, displaying the typical pattern of diminishing marginal returns.

marginal revenue: The additional revenue gained from selling one more unit.

Exhibit 10-2 Marginal Revenues and Marginal Costs at the Disk Production Shoppe
For a perfectly competitive firm, the marginal revenue (MR) curve is a horizontal straight line because it is equal to the price of the good. Marginal cost (MC) is sometimes first downward-sloping, if there is a region of increasing marginal returns at low levels of output, but is eventually upward-sloping at higher levels of output as diminishing marginal returns kick in. If the firm is producing at a quantity where MR > MC, like 40 or 50, then it can increase profit by increasing output because the marginal revenue is exceeding the marginal cost. If the firm is producing at a quantity where MC > MR, like 90 or 100, then it can increase profit by reducing output because the reductions in marginal cost will exceed the reductions in marginal revenue. The firm's profit-maximizing choice of output will occur where MR = MC (or at a choice close to that point).

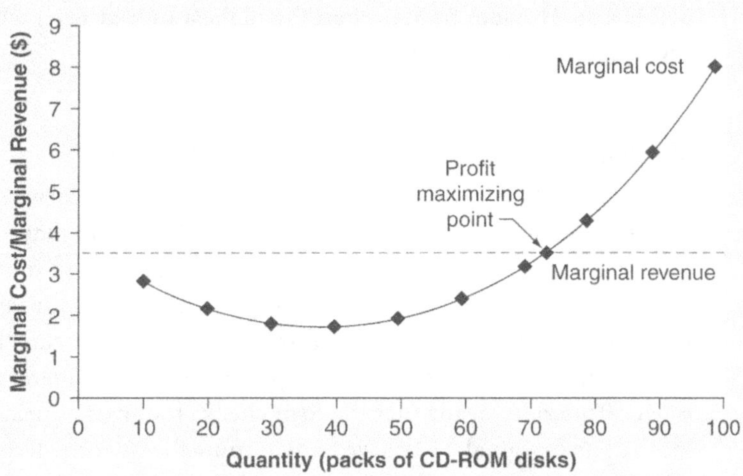

Quantity	Total Cost	Fixed Cost	Variable Cost	Marginal Cost	Total Revenue	Marginal Revenue
0	$62	$62		—	—	—
10	$90	$62	$28	$2.80	$35	$3.50
20	$110	$62	$48	$2.00	$70	$3.50
30	$126	$62	$64	$1.60	$105	$3.50
40	$144	$62	$82	$1.80	$140	$3.50
50	$166	$62	$104	$2.20	$175	$3.50
60	$192	$62	$130	$2.60	$210	$3.50
70	$224	$62	$162	$3.20	$245	$3.50
80	$264	$62	$202	$4.00	$280	$3.50
90	$324	$62	$262	$6.00	$315	$3.50
100	$404	$62	$342	$8.00	$350	$3.50

In this example, the marginal revenue and marginal cost curves cross at a price of $3.50 and a quantity between 70 and 80 produced. If the firm started out producing at a level of 60, and then experimented with increasing production to 70, marginal revenues from the increase in production would exceed marginal costs—and so profits would rise. However, if the firm then experimented further with increasing production from 70 to 80, it would find that marginal costs from the increase in production are greater than marginal revenues, and so profits would decline.

The profit-maximizing choice for a perfectly competitive firm will occur at the point where marginal revenue is equal to marginal cost—that is, where MR = MC. A profit-seeking firm should keep expanding production as long as MR > MC. But at the level of output where MR = MC, the firm should recognize that it has achieved the highest possible level of profits and that expanding production into the zone where MR < MC will only reduce profits. Because the marginal revenue received by a perfectly competitive firm is equal to the price P, so that P = MR, the profit-maximizing rule for a perfectly competitive firm can also be written as a recommendation to produce at the quantity where P = MC. (If the firm's choices for quantity of output don't include a choice where MR is exactly equal to MC, then the highest output level where MR > MC will be the profit-maximizing choice.)

MARGINAL COST AND THE SUPPLY CURVE

For a perfectly competitive firm, the marginal cost curve is identical to the firm's supply curve. To understand why this perhaps surprising insight holds true, first think about what the supply curve means. A firm checks the market price and then looks at its supply curve to decide what quantity to produce. Now think about what it means to say that a firm will maximize its profits by producing at the quantity where P = MC. This rule means that the firm checks the market price and then looks at its marginal cost curve to determine the quantity to produce. In other words, the marginal cost curve and the firm's supply curve contain the same information—that is, they both tell the firm what quantity to produce, given the market price.

As discussed back in Chapter 4, many of the reasons that supply curves shift relate to underlying changes in costs. For example, a lower price of key inputs or new technologies that reduce production costs cause supply to shift to the right; in contrast, lousy weather or added government regulations can add to costs of certain goods in a way that causes supply to shift to the left. These shifts in the firm's supply curve can also be interpreted as shifts of the marginal cost curve. A shift in costs of production that increases marginal costs at all levels of output—and shifts MC to the left—will cause a perfectly competitive firm to produce less at any given market price. Conversely, a shift in costs of production that decreases marginal costs at all levels of output will shift MC to the right and as a result, a competitive firm will choose to expand its level of output at any given price.

PROFITS AND LOSSES WITH THE AVERAGE COST CURVE

If the price that a firm charges is higher than its average cost of production for that quantity produced, then the firm will earn profits. Conversely, if the price that a firm charges is lower than its average cost of production, the firm will suffer losses. Exhibit 10-3 illustrates three situations: (a) where price intersects marginal cost at a level above the average cost curve, (b) where price intersects marginal cost at a level equal to the average cost curve, and (c) where price intersects marginal cost at a level below the average cost curve.

First consider a situation where the price is equal to $4 for a box of disks. The rule for a profit-maximizing perfectly competitive firm is to produce the level of output where P = MR = MC, so the Disk Production Shoppe will produce a quantity of 80, which is labeled as q in Exhibit 10-3a. The firm's total revenue at this price will be shown by the large shaded rectangle, which represents a price of $4 per box and a quantity of 80. Total costs will be the quantity of 80 times the average cost of $3.30, which is shown by the lightly shaded rectangle. Thus, profits will be the heavily shaded rectangle which represents the large rectangle of total revenues minus the rectangle of total costs. It would be calculated as:

Profit = Total revenue – Total cost
$56 = (80) ($4.00) – (80) ($3.30)

Now consider Exhibit 10-3b, where the price has fallen to $3.20 for a box of CDROM disks. Again, the perfectly competitive firm will choose the level of output where P = MR = MC, but in this case, the quantity will be 70. At this price and output level, where the marginal cost curve is crossing the average cost curve, the price received by the firm is exactly equal to its average cost of production. Thus, the total revenue of the firm is exactly equal to the total costs of the firm, so that the firm is making zero profit.

In Exhibit 10-3c, the market price has fallen still further to $2.20 for a box of CDROM disks. Again, the perfectly competitive firm will choose the level of output where P = MR = MC, and in this case the firm will choose to produce a quantity of 50. At this price and output level, the price level received by the firm is below the average cost of production. The total costs for the firm will be $166 (that is, the average cost of $3.32 multiplied by a quantity of 50), which appear as the large rectangle. Total revenue will be $110 (price of $2.20 multiplied by a quantity of 50), which is the smaller shaded rectangle. The firm's losses of $56 are shown by the rectangle created by subtracting the total revenue rectangle from the total cost rectangle.

If the market price received by a perfectly competitive firm leads it to produce at a quantity where the price is greater than average cost, the firm will earn profits. If the price received by the firm causes it to produce at a quantity where price equals marginal cost, at the point where the MC curve crosses the AC curve, then the firm earns zero profits. Finally, if the price received by the firm leads it to produce at a quantity where the price is less than average cost, the firm will earn losses.

Exhibit 10-3 Price and Average Cost at the Disk Production Shoppe

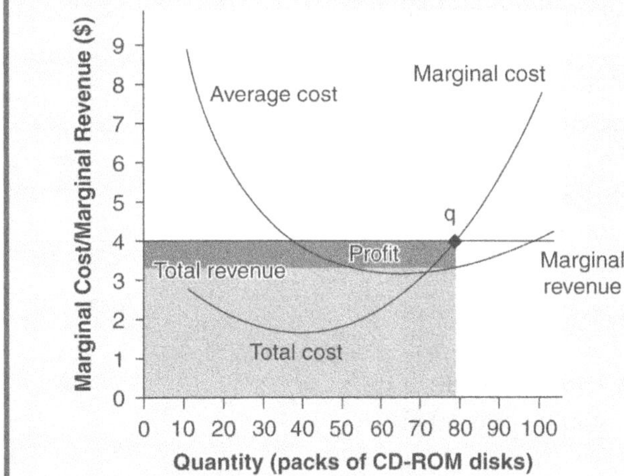

(a) Price is above average cost. Price is at a level where producing at the quantity where P = MC leads to a price that is above average cost. In this case, the firm is earning a profit. Total revenue is the quantity of 80 times the price of $4, or $320, shown by the overall shaded box. Total cost is the quantity of 80 times an average cost of $3.30, or $264, shown by the bottom shaded box. The leftover rectangle where total revenue exceeds total cost is the profit earned.

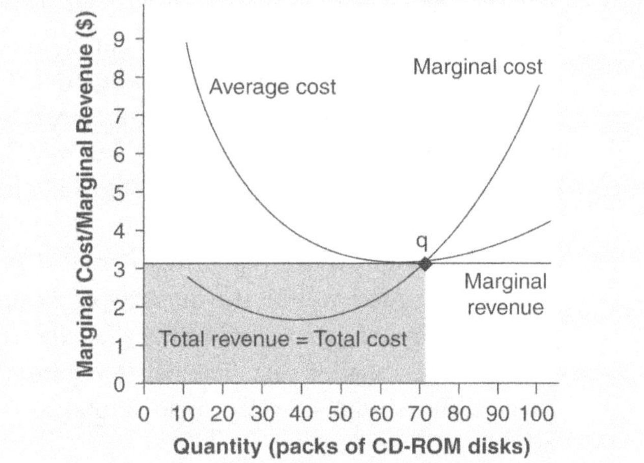

(b) Price equals average cost. The price is now at a level where producing at the quantity where P = MC leads to a price that is equal to the average cost. Total revenue is now a quantity of 70 times a price of $3.20. Total cost is the same: a quantity of 70 times an average cost of $3.20. Zero profit is being earned in this situation.

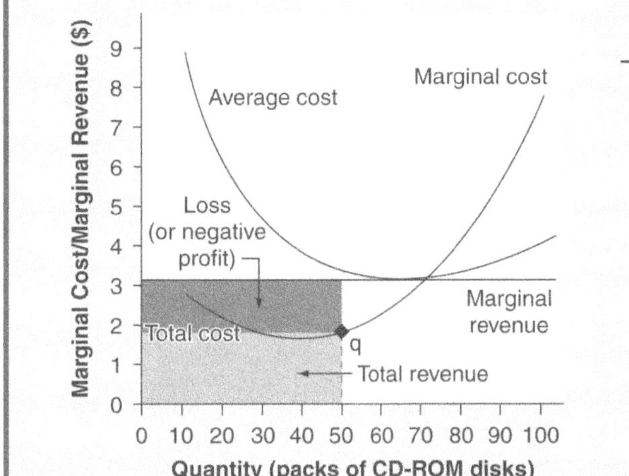

(c) Price is lower than average cost. At a price of $2.20, when the firm produces at a quantity where P = MC, the price is below average cost. Here, the firm is suffering losses. Total costs are the large rectangle with a quantity of 50 and a price of $3.32, for total costs of $166. Total revenues are a quantity of 50 and a price of $2.20, or $110, shown by the smaller shaded box. The leftover rectangle on top thus shows the losses; that is, the amount that total cost exceeds total revenue.

Quantity	Total Cost	Fixed Cost	Variable Cost	Marginal Cost	Average Cost
0	$62	$62	—	—	—
10	$90	$62	$28	$2.80	$9.00
20	$110	$62	$48	$2.00	$5.50
30	$126	$62	$64	$1.60	$4.20
40	$144	$62	$82	$1.80	$3.60
50	$166	$62	$104	$2.20	$3.32
60	$192	$62	$130	$2.60	$3.20
70	$224	$62	$162	$3.20	$3.20
80	$264	$62	$202	$4.00	$3.30
90	$324	$62	$262	$6.00	$3.60
100	$404	$62	$342	$8.00	$4.04

Exhibit 10-4 Should the Yoga Center Shut Down Now or Later?

Scenario 1

The firm shuts down now, so revenues are zero but the firm must pay fixed costs of $10,000.

$$\text{Total revenue} - (\text{fixed cost} + \text{variable cost}) = \text{profit}$$

$$0 - 10{,}000 = -10{,}000$$

Scenario 2

The firm keeps operating, variable costs are $15,000 and revenues are $10,000.

$$\text{Total revenue} - (\text{fixed cost} + \text{variable cost}) = \text{profit}$$

$$10{,}000 - (10{,}000 + 15{,}000) = -15{,}000$$

Conclusion: The firm should shut down now.

Scenario 3

The firm keeps operating, variable costs are $15,000 and revenues are $20,000.

$$\text{Total revenue} - (\text{fixed cost} + \text{variable cost}) = \text{profit}$$

$$20{,}000 - (10{,}000 + 15{,}000) = -5{,}000$$

Conclusion: The firm should shut down later.

THE SHUTDOWN POINT

The possibility that a firm may earn losses raises a question: Why can't the firm avoid losses by shutting down and not producing at all? The answer is that shutting down can reduce variable costs to zero, but in the short run, shutting down does not reduce fixed costs. As a result, if the firm produces a quantity of zero, it would still make losses because it would still need to pay for its fixed costs. Thus, when a firm is experiencing losses it must face a question: will its losses increase or decrease if it shuts down?

As an example of this decision, consider the situation of the Yoga Center, which has signed a contract to rent space that costs $10,000 per month. If the firm continues to operate, its marginal costs for hiring yoga teachers is $15,000 for the month. If the firm shuts down, it must still pay the rent, but it would not need to hire labor. Exhibit 10-4 shows three possible scenarios. In the first scenario, the Yoga Center shuts down, in which case it faces losses of $10,000. In the second scenario, the Yoga Center remains open, earns revenues of $10,000 for the month, and experiences losses of $15,000. In the third scenario, the Yoga Center remains open and earns revenues of $20,000 for the month, and experiences losses of $5,000. In all three cases, the Yoga Center loses money. In all three cases, when the rental contract expires in the long run, the store should exit this business. But in the short run, in scenario 2, the store's losses increase because it remains open, so the store should shut down immediately. In contrast, in scenario 3 the revenue that the firm can earn is high enough that the store's losses diminish when it remains open, so the store should remain open in the short run.

This example suggests that the key factor is whether the firm can at least cover its variable costs by remaining open. Exhibit 10-5 illustrates this lesson for the example of the Disk Production Shoppe, by adding the average variable cost curve to the marginal cost and average cost curves. At a price of $2.20 per box, shown in Exhibit 10-5a, the firm produces at a level of 50. It is making losses of $56 (as explained earlier), but price is above average variable cost and so the firm continues to operate. However, if the price declined to $1.80 per box, as shown in Exhibit 10-5b, if the firm applied its rule of producing where P = MR = MC, it would produce a quantity of 40. This price is below average variable cost for this level of output. At this price and output, total revenues would be $72 (quantity of 40 times price of $1.80) and total cost would be $144, for overall losses of $72. If the firm shuts down its must only pay its fixed costs of $62, so shutting down is preferable to selling at a price of $1.80 per box.

The intersection of the average variable cost curve and the marginal cost curve, which shows the price where firm lacks enough revenue to cover its variable costs, is called the **shutdown point**. If the perfectly competitive firm can charge a price above the shutdown point, then the firm is at least covering its average variable costs, and it should limp ahead even if it is making losses in the short run, since at least those losses will be smaller than if the firm shuts down immediately. However, if the firm is receiving a price below the price at the shutdown point, then the firm is not even covering its variable costs. In this case, staying open is making the firm's losses larger, and it should shut down immediately.

shutdown point:
When the revenue a firm receives does not cover its average variable costs, the firm should shut down immediately; the point where the marginal cost curve crosses the average variable cost curve.

SHORT-RUN OUTCOMES FOR PERFECTLY COMPETITIVE FIRMS

The average cost and average variable cost curves divide the marginal cost curve into three segments, as shown in Exhibit 10-6. At the market price, which the perfectly competitive firm accepts as given, the

Exhibit 10-5 The Shutdown Point for the Disk Production Shoppe

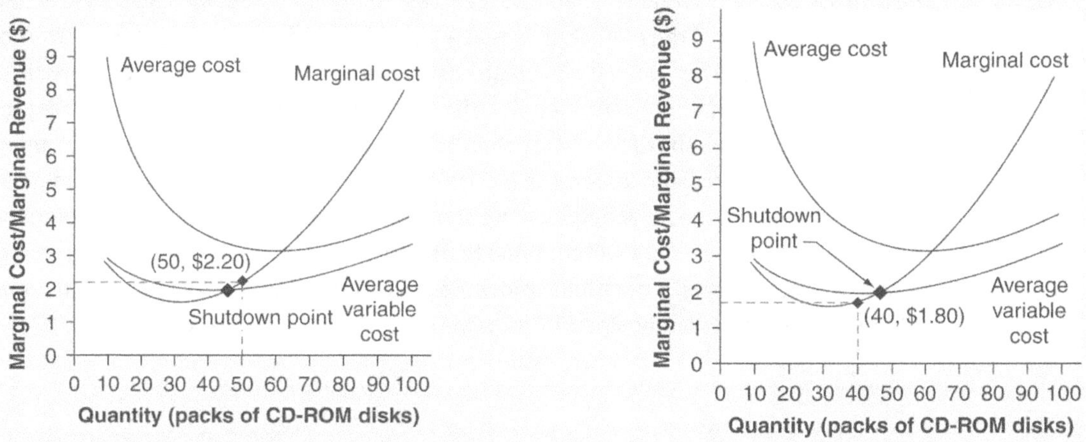

(a) Price is above shutdown point. The price is $2.20. Producing at the quantity where P = MC leads to a situation where price is below average cost but above average variable cost. Thus, the firm is suffering losses, but because it is covering its variable costs, it will continue to operate.

(b) Price is below shutdown point. Price drops to $1.80, which leads to a quantity of output where price is less than average variable cost. Because the firm is now not even covering its variable costs, it will shut down immediately. The point where MC crosses AVC is called the shutdown point.

Quantity	Total Cost	Fixed Cost	Variable Cost	Marginal Cost	Average Cost	Average Variable Cost
0	$62	$62	—	—	—	—
10	$90	$62	$28	$2.80	$9.00	$2.80
20	$110	$62	$48	$2.00	$5.50	$2.40
30	$126	$62	$64	$1.60	$4.20	$2.13
40	$144	$62	$82	$1.80	$3.60	$2.05
50	$166	$62	$104	$2.20	$3.32	$2.08
60	$192	$62	$130	$2.60	$3.20	$2.16
70	$224	$62	$162	$3.20	$3.20	$2.31
80	$264	$62	$202	$4.00	$3.30	$2.52
90	$324	$62	$262	$6.00	$3.60	$2.91
100	$404	$62	$342	$8.00	$4.04	$3.42

profit-maximizing firm chooses the output level where price or marginal revenue, which are the same thing for a perfectly competitive firm, is equal to marginal cost: P = MR = MC.

First consider the upper zone, where prices are above the level where marginal cost MC crosses AC at the zero profit point. At any price above that level, the firm will earn profits in the short run. If the price falls exactly on the zero profit point where MC and AC curves cross, then the firm earns zero profits. Next consider a price which falls into the zone between the zero profit point where MC crosses AC and the shutdown point where MC crosses AVC. In this case, the firm will be making losses in the short run—but since the firm is more than covering its variable costs, the losses are smaller than if the firm shut down immediately. Finally, consider a price below the shutdown point where MC crosses

Exhibit 10-6 Profit, Loss, Shutdown

The marginal cost curve can be divided into three zones, based on where it is crossed by the average cost and average variable cost curves. The point where MC crosses AC is called the zero-profit point. If the market price is at a level higher than the price at the zero-profit point, then price will be above the average cost curve and the firm is earning profits. If the price is exactly at the zero-profit point, then the firm is making zero profits. If the price below the price at the shutdown point, then price will fall below the average cost curve and the firm will be making losses. The point where MC crosses AVC is called the shutdown point. If price falls in the zone between the shutdown point and the zero-profit point, then the firm is making losses but will continue to operate in the short run, since it is covering its variable costs. However, if price falls below the price at the shutdown point, then the firm will shut down immediately, since it is not even covering its variable costs.

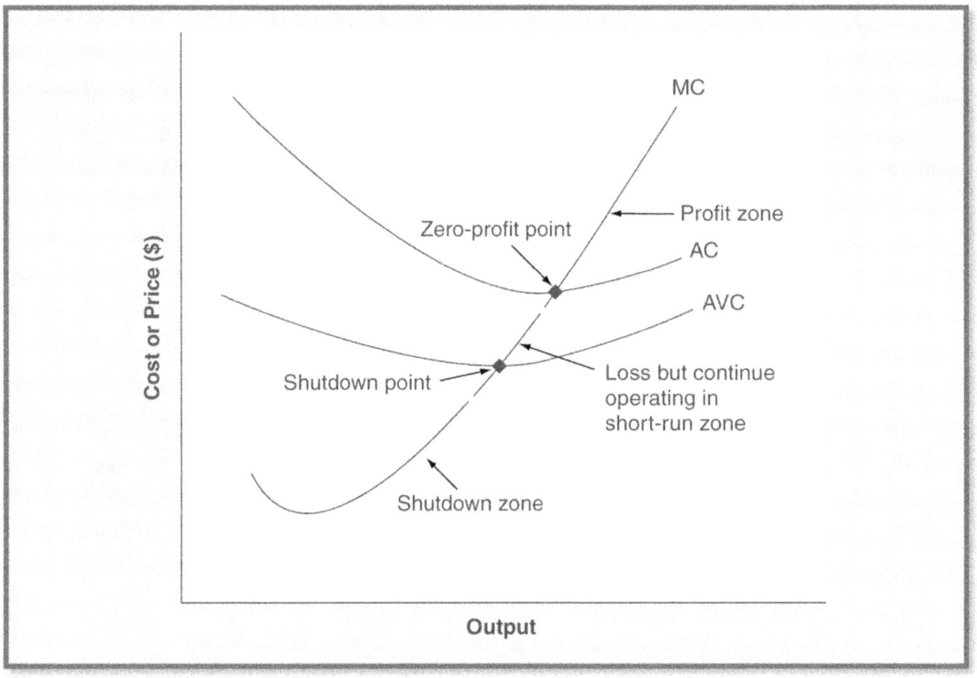

Business Failure

In the model of perfectly competitive firms, those that consistently can't make money will "exit," which is a nice bloodless word for a more painful process. When a business fails, after all, workers lose their jobs, investors lose their money, and owners and managers can lose their dreams, too. Many businesses fail. From 2005–2006, for example, 670,000 firms were born in the United States, but 599,000 firms died. About 95% of these business births and deaths involved small firms with fewer than 20 employees.

Sometimes a business fails because of poor management or workers, or because of tough domestic or foreign competition. Businesses also fail from a variety of causes that might best be summarized as bad luck. Conditions of demand and supply in the market shift in an unexpected way, so that the prices that can be charged for outputs fall or the prices that need to be paid for inputs rise. With millions of businesses in the U.S. economy, even a small fraction of them failing will affect many people—and business failures can be very hard on the workers and managers directly involved. But from the standpoint of the overall economic system, business deaths are sometimes a necessary evil if a market-oriented system is going to offer a flexible mechanism for satisfying customers, keeping costs low, and inventing new products.

AVC. At any price like this one, the firm will shut down immediately, because it cannot even cover its variable costs by operating.

Entry and Exit in the Long Run Output

The line between the short run and the long run can't be defined precisely with a stopwatch, or even with a calendar. It varies according to the specific business. But in the long run, the firm can adjust all factors of production.

In a competitive market, profits are a red cape that incites businesses to charge. If a business is making a profit in the short run, it has an incentive to expand existing factories or to build new ones. New firms may start production, as well. **Entry** is the long-run process of expanding production in response to a sustained pattern of profit opportunities.

entry:
The long-run process of firms beginning and expanding production in response to a sustained pattern of profits.

Losses are the black thundercloud that causes businesses to flee. If a business is making losses in the short run, it will either keep limping along or just shut down, depending on whether its revenues are covering its variable costs. But in the long run, firms that are facing losses will shut down at least some of their output, and some firms will cease production altogether. **Exit** is the long-run process of reducing production in response to a sustained pattern of losses.

exit:
The long-run process of firms reducing production and shutting down in response to a sustained pattern of losses.

HOW ENTRY AND EXIT LEAD TO ZERO PROFITS

No perfectly competitive firm acting alone can affect the market price. However, the combination of many firms entering or exiting the market will affect overall supply in the market. In turn, a shift in supply for the market as a whole will affect the market price. Entry and exit are the driving forces behind a process that, in the long run, pushes the price in a perfectly competitive market to be at the zero-profit point where the marginal cost curve crosses the average cost curve.

To understand how short-run profits for a perfectly competitive firm will evaporate in the long run, imagine that the market price starts at level where, when the perfectly competitive firm applies the rule P = MR = MC, it produces a quantity where price is above the average cost curve and the firm is earning profits. However, these profits attract entry. Entry of many firms causes the market supply curve to shift to the right, so that a greater quantity is produced at every market price. The shift of the supply curve to the right pushes down the market price. Entry will continue to shift supply to the right until the price is driven down to the zero-profit level, where no firm is earning profits.

Short-run losses will fade away by reversing this process. Now imagine that the market price starts at level where, when the perfectly competitive firm applies the rule P = MR = MC, it produces a quantity where price is below the average cost curve and the firm is experiencing losses. These losses lead some firms to exit. The process of exit by a number of firms causes the market supply curve to shift to the left, so that a lesser quantity is produced at every market price, and the market price rises. The process of exit will continue as long as firms are making losses, until the price rises to the zero-profit level, where firms are no longer suffering losses.

Thus, while a perfectly competitive firm can earn profits in the short run, in the long run the process of entry will push down prices until they reach the zero profit level. Conversely, while a perfectly competitive firm may earn losses in the short run, firms will not continually lose money. In the long run, firms making losses are able to escape from their fixed costs, and their exit from the market will push the price back up to the zero profit level. In the long run, this process of entry and exit will drive the price in perfectly competitive markets to the zero profit point at the bottom of the AC curve, where marginal cost crosses average cost.

ECONOMIC PROFIT VS. ACCOUNTING PROFIT

This talk of "zero profit" in the long run must worry anyone who is thinking about starting a business—or making a financial investment in one. But the conclusion that perfectly competitive firms end up with zero profits in the long run is less dire than it may sound, because profit means something different to economists than it does to businesses. The difference arises because economists insist on considering all the opportunity costs of production, including both explicit and implicit costs.

To understand the difference between the economic view of profit and the business or accounting view of profit, think about a business where the owner plunks down $1 million to pay for fixed costs, and at the end of a year, after total revenues and total costs are tallied, the owner has a business that is still worth $1 million and in the meantime has earned a return of $50,000, or 5% of the original investment. How large a profit has the owner earned? To a business owner and the accountant, the answer is clear: the profit is the 5% or $50,000 that was earned. To put it another way, the **accounting profit** is total revenues minus the firm's expenditures on explicit costs.

accounting profit: Total revenues minus the firm's costs, without taking opportunity cost into account.

economic profit: Total revenues minus all of the firm's costs, including opportunity costs.

To an economist, the question is more difficult, because the economist wants to take all opportunity costs, including both explicit and implicit costs, into account. Say that the business owner could have invested the money in another business, run by someone else, and it would have paid an 8% return. From the economic point of view, this implicit cost of how the financial capital could have been invested must be included as one of the firm's costs. Thus, **economic profit** is measured by total revenues minus all of the firm's opportunity costs, including both explicit expenditures and implicit costs of financial capital. From this perspective, the business owner has not experienced a gain of 5% for the year, but a loss of 3% (that is, 5% accounting profit minus 8% in implicit costs).

For the economy as a whole, financial investors earn an average or "normal" level of profit. That normal level of profit determines the opportunity cost of financial investments. Thus, an economist who says that perfectly competitive firms will earn "zero profit" in the long run really means "zero profit after all opportunity cost, including implicit costs, has been taken into account," or to put it differently, that the firm will earn a normal level of profit. When an economist says that a firm will earn positive profits, the economist really means that the profits will be above the normal level. Conversely, losses to an economist include both returns that are negative in an accounting sense and also returns that are slightly positive in an accounting sense, but that do not cover the implicit cost of financial capital.

Although perfectly competitive firms will earn zero economic profits—or a normal rate of profit—in the long run, it's important to remember that not all industries are perfectly competitive, and the long run, by definition, takes some time to arrive. In the real world, businesses will often earn economic profits or losses in the short run.

THE ECONOMIC FUNCTION OF PROFITS

In popular discussions, the term "profit" is sometimes pronounced as if the speaker is sucking on a lemon. But profits are not a dirty word, any more than "high prices" or "low prices" are dirty words. Profits have an economic rationale, which is built upon the incentives that they provide for entry and exit.

High profits are a messenger. They transmit the message that the willingness of people to pay for that good is higher than the average cost of production, and so society as a whole will benefit if more resources are allocated to production of that certain good or service. Losses are a messenger, too. They carry the message that fewer resources should be allocated to production of a certain good or service, because the benefits people are receiving from that production—as measured by their willingness to pay for it—is below the cost of the resources used in the production process.

Profits also serve as a messenger to businesses to seek out the most cost-effective methods of production. As profits lead to entry or losses lead to exit, perfectly competitive firms are pressured to seek out the minimum point of the average cost curve, which is the point where economic profits are zero and also the point where output is being produced at the lowest possible average cost.

Factors of Production in Perfectly Competitive Markets

A firm in a perfectly competitive market must accept the market price for its output, and must also pay the prevailing market price for its inputs like labor and physical capital. However, a perfectly competitive firm can decide what quantity of those inputs to use. The earlier discussion of how perfectly competitive firms make decisions about the quantity of output to produce was built on a distinction between short-run decisions, where certain inputs costs like physical capital investment were fixed, and long-run decisions where all inputs to production could vary. In the same spirit, let's first consider how a perfectly competitive firm will determine the quantity that it uses of a variable input like labor in the short run, and then how it will determine its quantity of physical capital and its overall method of production in the long run.

THE DERIVED DEMAND FOR LABOR

When a profit-maximizing firm considers how much labor to hire in the short run, it may first calculate the profit-maximizing quantity of output, and then figure out the quantity of labor needed to produce that quantity of output. For this reason, the demand for labor (and other inputs) is sometimes called a "derived demand"; that is, the demand for labor is derived from the firm's decision about how much to produce.

For an example of this decision process operates in the short run, consider the Cheep-Cheep Company in Exhibit 10-7, a firm in a perfectly competitive industry that hires workers to assemble birdhouses. Assume that the cost of hiring a worker is $100 per day and that fixed costs of the birdhouse workshop are $7,000. The quantity of output for a profit-seeking perfectly competitive firm will be determined by applying the rule that production up to the point where P = MC. Thus, if the price for a birdhouse is $6, then the profit-maximizing level of output (from the choices in the table) is 85, and the derived demand for labor to produce that desired level of output is 5 workers. If a surge in demand for birdhouses drives the market price up to $10, then the optimal level of output would become 96, and the derived demand for labor rises to six workers.

Thus, one way to determine what quantity of a variable input to hire is first to determine the profit-maximizing quantity to produce, and then to work backwards and determine what quantity of the input is needed.

THE MARGINAL REVENUE PRODUCT OF LABOR

Instead of calculating the amount of labor to hire based on the profit-maximizing quantity, an alternative approach is to compare the cost of hiring a worker to the value of what a worker produces.

The cost of hiring a worker is straightforward: it's the wage or compensation paid to the worker. To calculate the value of what a worker produces, find the quantity of production attributable to the marginal worker and multiply it by the price of that output. Exhibit 10-8 takes a different look at the basic cost information from Exhibit 10-7, focusing on the output of workers for workers at the Cheep-Cheep Birdhouse Company. The first column repeats information from Exhibit 10-7, showing different numbers of workers and what they produce. The third column of the figure shows **marginal physical product**, which is the quantity of goods produced by the marginal worker. The fourth column shows the **marginal revenue product (MRP)**, which reveals how much revenue a firm could receive from hiring an additional worker and selling the output of that worker. The MRP is calculated by multiplying the marginal physical product by the market price of $6. A second calculation of marginal revenue product, this one based on a market

marginal physical product:
The quantity of goods produced by the addition of an additional input (like an additional worker).

marginal revenue product (MRP):
Reveals how much revenue a firm could receive from hiring an additional worker and selling the output of that worker.

Exhibit 10-8 Marginal Revenue Product: The Cheep Cheep Example Continues

The wage is shown as a horizontal line, because it does not vary according to how many workers the firm hires. Marginal revenue product first slopes up, because of the increasing marginal returns at low levels of output in this example, and then slopes down because of diminishing marginal returns at higher levels of output. If a worker brings in more than enough marginal revenue to cover the wage of that worker, it will make sense to hire the worker. If the price of the birdhouse is $6, then the firm will hire five workers, because the marginal revenue product of the fifth worker is $102. If the price rises to $10 per birdhouse, then the value of what workers produce increases, and the firm will hire six workers. Finally, if the wage rises—in the diagram, imagine the horizontal line at a higher level—the firm will hire fewer workers, because fewer workers will have a high enough marginal revenue product to justify paying the higher wage.

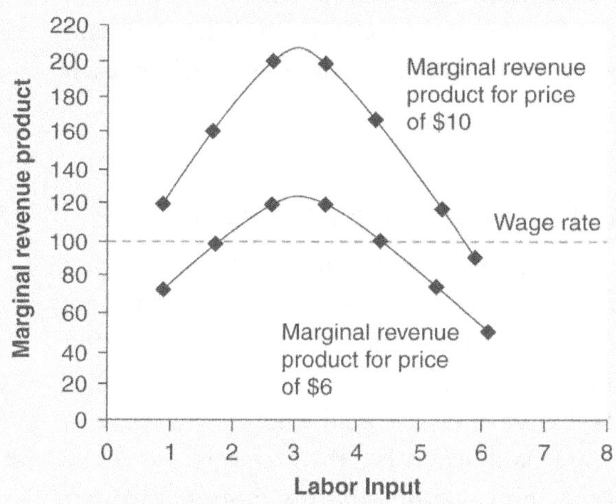

Labor	Output	Marginal Physical Product	Marginal Revenue Product (price $6)	Marginal Revenue Product (price $10)
0	0	—		—
1	12	12	$72	$120
2	28	16	$96	$160
3	48	20	$120	$200
4	68	20	$120	$200
5	85	17	$102	$170
6	96	11	$66	$110
7	105	9	$54	$90

price for birdhouses of $10, appears in the final column. The two different marginal revenue products, one based on a price for birdhouses of $6 and one based on a price of $10, are also shown in Exhibit 10-8. The marginal revenue product of hiring additional workers gradually declines because of diminishing marginal returns.

When a profit-seeking, price-taking perfectly competitive firm is thinking about the quantity of labor to hire, it will compare the input price with the marginal revenue product for that input. For example, say that the cost for Cheep Cheep of hiring a birdhouse maker is $100. At a market price of $6, Cheep Cheep will notice that hiring a third worker and the fourth worker will have a marginal revenue product of $120, but only cost $100. So it will clearly make sense to hire these workers. In fact, it makes sense to hire the fifth worker as well, since the marginal revenue product of that worker still exceeds the wage. But at a market price for birdhouses of $6, it won't make sense to hire the sixth or seventh worker, because the marginal revenue product of hiring a worker will be less than $100.

A higher market price for the output of birdhouses will encourage more hiring. If the market price for birdhouses increased to $10, then Cheep Cheep will wish to hire a sixth worker, with a marginal revenue product of $110, but not a seventh worker, since the marginal revenue product of that final worker would only be $90. The optimal quantity of labor to hire will be where the price of the input is equal to the marginal revenue product of that input.

The concept of the marginal revenue product of labor hired explains why the demand curve for labor slopes down. When the wage is lower, more workers will have a marginal revenue product above that wage, so that firms will be willing to hire them. Conversely, when the wage is higher, fewer workers will have a marginal revenue product above that wage, so firms will demand a lower quantity of workers.

The derived demand approach and the marginal revenue product approach to figuring out the quantity of labor to hire are just two different ways of using the same basic information on production functions, input costs, and output prices. The two approaches should always obtain the same answer; in fact, the two methods can be used to check on each other.

ARE WORKERS PAID AS MUCH AS THEY DESERVE?

Many workers strongly suspect that they are not being paid as much as they deserve. Is this complaint nothing more than self-interested people who desire some additional income? Or is there reason to believe that in a competitive labor market, workers are systematically paid too little? The argument here suggests that workers are paid what they deserve in the specific sense that they are paid according their marginal revenue product—that is, according to the value of what the marginal worker produces.

In the real economy, calculating the marginal revenue product may be nearly impossible for many workers. Imagine a company making refrigerators where workers perform many jobs: some work on the assembly line, some maintain and repair equipment, some do paperwork for paying workers and suppliers, some plan future investment in physical capital, some do sales and marketing, and some work on the shipping dock. How could any accountant disentangle exactly what each of these very different worker contributes to making a refrigerator?

However, even when firms cannot calculate marginal revenue product directly, the pressures of competition in the labor market will push pay toward the marginal revenue product of labor. After all, if a foolish employer consistently paid its workers more than the marginal revenue product of what the workers produced, then that employer would make losses, and such pay could not be sustained. On the other hand, if an employer tried to pay workers less than what they produce as measured by their marginal revenue product, then other employers will see an opportunity to hire away some of the marginal workers by offering them a modest increase over their current pay. With these competitive pressures in the labor market, wages are pushed in the direction of marginal revenue product. Of course, just as a market price is not always exactly at equilibrium, but only tending toward equilibrium, it will also be true that wages are not always exactly at the marginal revenue product, although they tend toward that level. Studies of labor markets over time, and between countries, show that differences in how much workers are paid are strongly linked to the market value of what workers produce.

If workers find it difficult or costly to switch between employers, and firms know that workers may be unable or unwilling to move to other jobs, then the employer will be able to pay those workers somewhat less than their marginal revenue product. For example, a worker in a rural area may have relatively few employment options that do not involve high monetary and emotional costs of moving. A recent immigrant may lack the information and the social network that would provide information and connections to other jobs. A society with widespread discrimination on the basis of race or gender may block people in certain groups from taking certain jobs. In any of these cases, employers may be able to pay certain workers less than the marginal revenue product of their labor.

PHYSICAL CAPITAL INVESTMENT AND THE HURDLE RATE

In the long term, a perfectly competitive firm can adjust all of its inputs, including its investments in physical capital like buildings and machinery. Such investments in physical capital, by their nature, involve thinking about a rate of return over time; that is, the firm purchases the inputs of physical capital in the present and then uses them for production over a period of time in the future.

Consider a firm making plans for investments in physical capital. Managers from all over the company submit proposals. Each proposal includes either an estimate of the marginal revenue product of this capital investment—that is, how much additional revenue will this investment generate, or alternatively, by how much will this investment reduce the costs of the current level of output. Higher-level managers collect these proposals and check them over, estimating the rate of return that can be realistically expected from each proposal. The rates of return for a hypothetical list of 25 projects, ranked from top to bottom, are illustrated by the bar graph in Exhibit 10-9. In deciding which project to carry out, the profit-seeking firm will obviously prefer projects with high rates of return rather than the project with low rates of return (as long as the risk of the projects is similar). But to determine how many investment projects the firm should undertake, the managers of the firm must compare the rates of return to the cost of financial capital.

Financial capital always comes at a cost. Sometimes the firm must pay this cost directly; for example, the firm may borrow financial capital from a bank, and thus need to pay an interest rate. However, even if the firm can use funds that it has earned from past profits, spending this money on an investment in physical capital still has an opportunity cost. After all, the firm's financial capital could have been invested in some other way that would have paid a rate of return. Thus, the cost of financial capital to the firm can be conceived of either as a rate of return or interest rate paid to others, or as an opportunity cost of a rate of return that was not received. The specific ways in which firms can raise money

Exhibit 10-9 Considering Investment Projects

When a firm makes plans for investments in physical capital, it compares the projected rates of return on these investments with the cost of financial capital to the firm. Often, this comparison will use a hurdle rate as the rate of return that must be exceeded to make the project worth undertaking. In this example, projects A to S do not exceed the hurdle rate. A lower cost of capital will result in more investment projects being undertaken (imagine the horizontal hurdle rate line moving down, so that more projects cross the hurdle). Conversely, a higher cost of financial capital will result in fewer physical capital investment projects being undertaken.

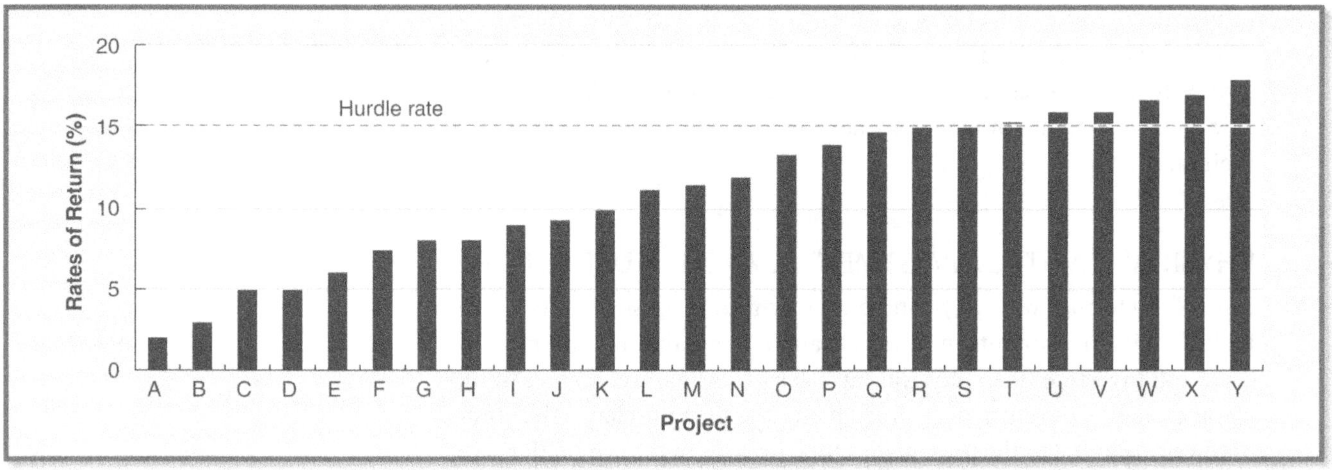

for investment—including reinvesting the profits that they earn or using bank loans, bonds, and stocks—will be discussed in Chapter 19.

Firms must also remember that any physical capital investment has some degree of risk. The business world is full of horror stories of factories that were constructed months or years late and cost much more than expected. In other cases, the costs may be estimated accurately, but the returns turn out to be lower than expected. When a company drills for oil, or decides to make a major investment in upgrading its Internet capabilities, it can't be certain of the results in advance.

Firms often take risk into account by using a "hurdle rate," which is an interest rate that is somewhat higher than the actual cost of financial capital to the firm. The intuitive meaning of the hurdle rate is the rate of return that proposed investment projects must cross before being approved. Estimates of typical hurdle rates, based on studies of the investment decisions that firms make, are often about 5–8 percentage points higher than the actual cost of financial capital, whether it is measured as the borrowing interest rate or the opportunity cost of capital. This higher hurdle interest rate can be thought of as a risk premium; that is, it's an adjustment for the risks involved and it gives the firm a margin for errors of bad luck and overly optimistic forecasts.

If a firm chooses a 15% hurdle rate for its physical capital investment, then such projects must pay an expected return of at least 15% to be worthwhile. A 15% rate of return is represented by the dashed line across Exhibit 10-9. If the cost of financial capital for the firm was higher, then fewer investment projects will make economic sense. Conversely, if the cost of financial capital declines, then a larger number of investment projects will make sense. This logic explains why the demand for financial capital is a downward-sloping curve; the downward slope means that a higher interest rate leads to a lower demand for financial capital, because fewer physical capital investments appear desirable.

PHYSICAL CAPITAL INVESTMENT AND LONG-RUN AVERAGE COST

In a perfectly competitive market, firms seek out the combination of variable inputs like labor and fixed inputs like physical capital investment inputs that will allow them to produce at the minimum of the long-run average cost curve. If a firm does not produce at the lowest possible average cost, then firms with a lower cost of production will be able to sell at a lower price. Thus, the pressure of competition between firms will shape both the specific kinds of machinery and equipment and the overall quantity of investment in physical capital.

Efficiency in Perfectly Competitive Markets

When profit-maximizing firms in perfectly competitive markets combine with utility-maximizing consumers, something remarkable happens: the resulting quantities of outputs of goods and services demonstrate both productive and allocative efficiency (terms that were first introduced back in Chapter 2).

Productive efficiency means producing without waste, so that the choice is on the frontier of the production possibility frontier. In the long run in a perfectly competitive market, because of the process of entry and exit, the price in the market is equal to the minimum of the long-run average cost curve. In other words, goods are being produced and sold at the lowest possible average cost. When the average cost of production is as low as possible, the economy will be operating on the production possibility frontier.

Allocative efficiency means that among the points on the production possibility frontier, the point that is chosen is socially preferred—at least in a particular and specific sense. In a perfectly competitive market, price will be equal to the marginal cost of production. Think about the price that is paid for a good as a measure of the social benefit received for that good; after all, the willingness to pay conveys what the good was worth to a buyer. Then think about the marginal cost of producing the good as representing not just the cost for the firm, but more broadly as the social cost of producing that good. When perfectly competitive firms follow the rule that profits are maximized by producing at the quantity where price is equal to marginal cost, they are thus ensuring that the social benefits received from producing a good are in line with the social costs of production.

To explore what is meant by allocative efficiency, it is useful to walk through an example of what allocative inefficiency would imply. Begin by assuming that the market for ordinary television sets is perfectly competitive, and so P = MC. Now consider what it would mean if firms in that market produced a lesser quantity of television sets. At a lesser quantity, marginal costs will not yet have increased as much, so that price will exceed marginal cost; that is, P > MC. In that situation, the benefit to society as a whole of producing additional goods, as measured by the willingness of consumers to pay for marginal units of a good, would be higher than the cost of the inputs of labor and physical capital needed to produce the marginal good. In other words, the gains to society as a whole from producing additional marginal units will be greater than the costs. Conversely, consider what it would mean if, compared to the level of output at the allocatively efficient choice when P = MC, firms produced a greater quantity of television sets. At a greater quantity, marginal costs of production will have increased so that P < MC. In that case, the marginal costs of producing additional television sets are greater than the benefit to society as measured by what people are willing to pay. For society as a whole, since the costs are outstripping the benefits, it will make sense to produce a lower quantity of such goods.

When perfectly competitive firms maximize their profits by producing the quantity where P = MC, they also assure that the benefits to consumers of what they are buying, as measured by the price they are willing to pay, equal to the costs to society of producing the marginal units, as measured by the marginal costs the firm must pay—and thus that allocative efficiency holds.

The statements that a perfectly competitive market in the long run will feature both productive and allocative efficiency do need to be taken with a few grains of salt. Remember, economists are using the concept of "efficiency" in a particular and specific sense, not as a synonym for "desirable in every way." Perfect competition in the long run is a hypothetical extreme. In other competitive situations discussed in the next two chapters, like monopoly, monopolistic competition, and oligopoly, firms will not always produce at the minimum of average cost, nor will they always set price equal to marginal cost. Thus, these other competitive situations will not produce productive and allocative efficiency. Moreover, real-world markets include many issues that are assumed away in the model of perfect competition, including pollution, inventions of new technology, poverty which may make some people unable to pay for basic necessities of life, government programs like national defense or education, discrimination in labor markets, and buyers and sellers who must deal with imperfect and unclear information. These issues are explored in later chapters of this book. However, the theoretical efficiency of perfect competition does provide a useful benchmark for comparing what issues arise from these real-world problems.

Conclusion

Extreme assumptions often provide a useful starting point for analysis. In a physics class, it may be useful to analyze gravity by assuming that a ball which is dropped from a tower experiences zero friction as it falls through the air.

This assumption of zero friction is not literally true. But if the amount of friction from the air is relatively small compared to the pull of gravity, then assuming zero friction may not make much difference to the results. If friction is significant, then calculations for the effects of friction can be added, once the basic no-friction example is understood. The assumption of perfect competition that firms are perfect price-takers, unable to raise their price by so much as a penny without losing all of their sales, is not literally true. But in a market with many competitors who have highly similar products, the assumption of perfect competition may provide a reasonable start for the analysis. In a highly competitive market—even if it is not strictly speaking perfectly competitive— firms will not lose all of their sales if they raise prices by a penny, but they might lose a large enough proportion of their sales to cripple the firm if they raise prices by 5%. In a highly competitive real world market, not all firms will be producing at the absolute bottom of the average cost curve at all times—but the firms will still face considerable pressure to keep average costs as low as possible. Firms in a highly competitive market may earn profits in the short run, but the entry of new firms or the expansion of existing firms means that such profits will not persist in the long run. Truly perfect competition is a hypothetical extreme, but many real-world producers face highly competitive markets every day.

Key Concepts and Summary

1. A perfectly competitive firm is a price taker, which means that it must accept the prices at which its sell goods and the prices at which it purchase inputs as determined in the market. If a perfectly competitive firm attempts to charge even a tiny amount more than the market price, it will be unable to make any sales.
2. As a perfectly competitive firm produces a greater quantity of output, its total revenue steadily increases at a constant rate determined by the given market price.
3. Profits will be highest (or losses will be smallest) at the quantity of output where total revenues exceed total costs by the greatest amount (or where total revenues fall short of total costs by the smallest amount). Alternatively, profits will be highest where marginal revenue, which is price for a perfectly competitive firm, is equal to marginal cost.
4. If the market price faced by a perfectly competitive firm is above average cost at the profit-maximizing quantity of output, then the firm is making profits. If the market price is below average cost at the profit-maximizing quantity of output, then the firm is making losses. If the market price is at average cost, at the profitmaximizing level of output, then the firm is making zero profits. The point where the marginal cost curve crosses the average cost curve, at the minimum of the average cost curve, is called the "zero profit point."

5. If the market price faced by a perfectly competitive firm is below average variable cost at the profit-maximizing quantity of output, then the firm should shut down operations immediately. If the market price faced by a perfectly competitive firm is above average variable cost, but below average cost, then the firm should continue producing in the short run, but exit in the long run. The point where the marginal cost curve crosses the average variable cost curve is called the shutdown point.
6. In the long run, firms will respond to profits through a process of entry, where existing firms expand output and new firms enter the market. Conversely, firms will react to losses in the long run through a process of exit, in which existing firms reduce output or cease production altogether.
7. Through the process of entry in response to profits and exit in response to losses, the price level in a perfectly competitive market will move toward the zero-profit point where the marginal cost curve crosses the AC curve, at the minimum of the average cost curve.
8. Accounting profit is measured by taking total revenues and subtracting expenditures. Economic profit is measured after taking total revenue, subtracting all expenditures, and also subtracting the opportunity cost of financial capital. Thus, zero economic profit actually means a normal accounting rate of profit.
9. A profit-maximizing firm will determine its optimal quantity of output, and then hire the amount of the variable input, like labor, needed to produce that quantity of output.
10. The marginal revenue product, the value of what is produced by an additional worker, is calculated by taking the quantity of output produced by the marginal worker and multiplying it by the price of that output. A profit-maximizing firm will hire workers as long as the marginal revenue product of what they produce exceeds the wage, up to the point where the marginal revenue product is equal to the wage.
11. If an employer paid wages that were higher than marginal revenue product—that is, higher than the value of what workers produced—the employer will tend to make losses and such wages cannot be continued. If one employer paid wages that were lower than the marginal revenue product, then other employers will see a profit opportunity in hiring those workers and paying them more. As long as workers can move freely between comparable alternative jobs, the pressures of the labor market will tend to push wages toward marginal revenue product.
12. Firms will invest as long as the expected returns of the investment exceed the cost of capital, where the cost of capital typically includes a "hurdle rate" to take account of the risk involved.
13. When perfectly competitive firms produce at the minimum of the long-run average cost curve, the market will show productive efficiency, since they are producing at the lowest possible average cost. When perfectly competitive firms produce at the quantity

where P = MC, the market will illustrate allocative efficiency, since each good is being produced up to the quantity where the amount that the good benefits society, as measured by the price people are willing to pay, is equal to the cost to society, as measured by the marginal cost of production.

Vocabulary Terms

Breakeven point
Entry
Exit
Marginal Physical Product
Marginal Revenue Product
Pure competition
Price takers
Shutdown point

Review Questions

1. How does a perfectly competitive firm decide what price to charge?
2. What prevents a perfectly competitive firm from seeking higher profits by increasing the price that it charges?
3. How does a perfectly competitive firm calculate total revenue?
4. Briefly explain the reason for the shape of a marginal revenue curve for a perfectly competitive firm.
5. What rule does a perfectly competitive firm apply to determine its profit-maximizing quantity of output?
6. How does the average cost curve help to show whether a firm is making profits or losses?
7. What two lines on a cost curve diagram intersect at the zero-profit point?
8. Should a firm shut down immediately if it is making losses?
9. How does the average variable cost curve help a firm know whether it should shut down immediately?
10. What two lines on a cost curve diagram intersect at the shutdown point?
11. Why does entry occur?
12. Why does exit occur?
13. Do entry and exit occur in the short run, the long run, both, or neither?
14. What price will a perfectly competitive firm end up charging in the long run? Why?
15. What's the difference between accounting profit and economic profit? Which one is higher?
16. Why is labor called a "derived demand"?
17. How can a perfectly competitive firm use derived demand to decide how much labor to hire?
18. How is the marginal revenue product of labor calculated?

19. How can a perfectly competitive firm use the marginal revenue product of labor to determine what quantity of labor to hire?
20. What is the "hurdle rate"?
21. How does a firm use the hurdle rate to decide which investments in physical capital to undertake?
22. Will a perfectly competitive industry display productive efficiency? Why or why not?
23. Will a perfectly competitive industry display allocative efficiency? Why or why not?

CHAPTER 11
Monopoly

11 Monopoly

By Timothy Taylor

There is a widespread belief that top executives at firms are the strongest supporters of market competition, but this belief is far from the truth. Think about it this way: If you very much wanted to win an Olympic gold medal, would you rather be far better than everyone else, or locked in competition with many athletes just as good as you are? Similarly, if you'd like to attain a very high level of profits, would you rather manage a business with little or no competition, or struggle against many tough competitors who are trying to sell to your customers? Competition can benefit society as a whole because it encourages firms to try their hardest to please customers. But for individual firms, a lesser degree of competition can seem very attractive.

Thus, the dreams of business managers rarely take place in a world of perfect competition, with many firms selling identical products. Instead, top executives salivate over the idea of **imperfect competition**, which involves either a smaller number of competing firms, or products that aren't identical, or both. Imperfect competition comes in several flavors: monopoly, oligopoly, and monopolistic competition. In the case of **monopoly**, one firm produces all or nearly all of the output in a market. In the case of **monopolistic competition**, a large number of firms compete, but their products differ somewhat from each other. In the case of **oligopoly**, a small number of firms—perhaps just two or three or four—sell all or nearly all of the output in a market. This chapter focuses on monopoly; the next chapter addresses the intermediate cases of monopolistic competition and oligopoly. One of the most-publicized U.S. monopolies in the last decade or so is the Microsoft Corporation, which sells (among other products) the Windows operating system for personal computers—that is, the background software that organizes and enables all the other programs on the computer. In the early 2000s, the Windows system ran on 90% or more of the most commonly sold type of personal computers. Most people deal with monopolies every day. The U.S. Postal Service has a monopoly on the delivery of first-class mail. Most people have only one firm from which they can purchase electricity or garbage collection. Some new drugs are produced by only one pharmaceutical firm—and no close substitutes for that drug may exist.

imperfect competition: Competition that does not fit the definition of perfect competition either because it involves a smaller number of firms or only one firm, or products that aren't identical.

monopoly: A firm that faces no competitors.

monopolistic competition: Many firms competing to sell similar but differentiated products.

oligopoly: When several large firms have all or most of the sales in an industry.

This chapter begins with the ways in which monopolies are protected from competition, including laws that prohibit competition, technological advantages, and certain configurations of demand and supply. The chapter then discusses how a monopoly will choose its profit-maximizing quantity to produce and what price to charge. While a monopoly must be concerned about whether consumers will purchase its products or spend their money on something altogether different, the monopolist need not worry about the actions of other competing firms. As a result, a monopoly is not a price-taker like a perfectly competitive firm, but instead exercises some power to choose its market price.

Barriers to Entry

Barriers to entry are the legal, technological, or market forces that may discourage or prevent potential competitors from entering a market. In some cases, barriers to entry may lead to pure monopoly; in other cases, they may limit competition to a few oligopoly firms. Barriers to entry will block entry even if the firm or firms currently in the market are earning profits. Thus, in markets with barriers to entry, it is not true that abnormally high profits will attract the entry of new firms, and that this entry of new firms will eventually cause the price to decline so that surviving firms earn only a normal level of profit in the long run.

barriers to entry: The legal, technological, or market forces that may discourage or prevent potential competitors from entering a market.

LEGAL RESTRICTIONS

In some cases, the government erects barriers to entry by prohibiting or limiting competitors. Under U.S. law, no organization but the U.S. Post Office is legally allowed to deliver first-class mail. Many states or cities have laws or regulations that allow households a choice of only one electrical company, one water company, and one company to pick up the garbage.

Government limitations on competition used to be even more common in the United States. For most of the twentieth century, only one phone company—AT&T—was legally allowed to provide local and long-distance service. From the 1930s up to the 1970s, one set of federal regulations limited which destinations airlines could choose to fly to and what fares they could charge; another set of regulations limited the interest rates that banks could pay to depositors; and yet another set specified what trucking firms could charge customers. However, a wave of **deregulation**, starting in the late 1970s and running into the 1990s, eliminated or reduced government restrictions on the firms that could enter, the prices that could be charged, and the quantities that could be produced in many industries, including telecommunications, airlines, trucking, banking, telecommunications, electricity and more. Around the world, from Europe to Latin America to Africa and Asia, many governments continue to control and limit competition in what those governments perceive to be key industries, including airlines, banks, steel companies, oil companies, telephone companies and others.

deregulation: Removing government controls over setting prices and quantities in certain industries.

CONTROL OF A PHYSICAL RESOURCE

If a company can control a scarce physical resource, then other firms may find it difficult to compete. In the U.S. economy, one historical example of this pattern occurred when ALCOA—which stood for Aluminum Company of America—controlled most of the supply of bauxite, a key mineral used in making aluminum, back in the 1930s. Today, two well-known arrangements for controlling a physical resource involve oil and diamonds. The Organization for Petroleum Exporting Countries, commonly known as OPEC, includes many of the world's leading petroleum-exporting countries, including Saudi Arabia and most of the Middle Eastern oil producers, along with Nigeria, Venezuela and Indonesia. When the OPEC countries make a decision to raise the price of oil, the effects can be dramatic. In one famous case, from 1973–1975, OPEC more than doubled the price of oil. The majority of global diamond production is controlled by DeBeer's, a South African firm that controls over 10 prolific African diamond mines and also directs the Central Selling Organization, which controls a majority of the world's distribution and resale of rough diamonds.

TECHNOLOGICAL SUPERIORITY

Technological capabilities may also discourage competitors. The Windows operating system sold only by Microsoft is one example; it is technologically difficult, although not impossible, for other firms to produce an equivalent product. Attempts to gain a technological advantage are widespread. Pharmaceutical companies strive to invent new drugs that only they know how to make. Software companies strive to write distinctive new programs.

In some cases, technological superiority may combine with the law to create a barrier to entry. The Constitution of the United States specifies in Article I, Section 8: "The Congress shall have Power . . . To Promote the Progress of Science and Useful Arts, by securing for limited Times to Authors and Inventors the Exclusive Right to their Writings and Discoveries." Congress used this power to create the U.S. Patent and Trademark Office, as well as the U.S. Copyright Office. A **patent** gives the inventor the exclusive legal right to make, use, or sell the invention for a limited time; in the United States, exclusive patent rights last for 20 years.

A **trademark** is a word, name, symbol or device that indicates the source of the goods, like Chiquita bananas, Chevrolet cars, or the Nike "swoosh" that appears on shoes and athletic gear. Roughly 800,000 trademarks are registered with the U.S. government. A firm can renew its trademarks over and over again, as long as it remains in active use.

A **copyright**, according the U.S. Copyright Office, " is a form of protection provided by the laws of the United States for 'original works of authorship' including literary, dramatic, musical, architectural,

patent:
A government rule that gives the inventor the exclusive legal right to make, use, or sell the invention for a limited time.

trademark:
A word, name, symbol or device that indicates the source of the goods and can only be used by the firm that registered that trademark.

copyright:
A form of legal protection to prevent copying for commercial purposes original works of authorship, including books and music.

Willy Wonka Trade Secrets

Roald Dahl wrote a book in 1964 called *Charlie and the Chocolate Factory* which has twice been made into a movie: the first time in a 1971 version starring Gene Wilder as the candy-maker Willy Wonka, and the second time in 2005 starring Johnny Depp. For economists, the story is about trying to steal candy industry trade secrets. Here's how Dahl tells it:

> "You see, Charlie, not so very long ago there used to be thousands of people working in Mr. Willy Wonka's factory. Then one day, all of a sudden, Mr. Wonka had to ask every single one of them to leave, to go home, never to come back."
>
> "But why?" asked Charlie.
>
> "Because of spies."
>
> "Spies?"
>
> "Yes. All the other chocolate makers, you see, had begun to grow jealous of the wonderful candies that Mr. Wonka was making, and they started sending in spies to steal his secret recipes. The spies took jobs in the Wonka factory, pretending they were ordinary workers, and while they were there, each one of them found out exactly how a certain special thing was made."

In fact, Dahl's story was rooted in common business practices of the candy industry during his childhood. The two biggest candy makers of that time, Cadbury and Rowntree, were famous for the number of spies they attempted to infiltrate into other companies. Other candy firms were known to hire detectives to investigate their own workers, and to require outside contractors to be blindfolded when they entered the factory. Dahl went to school not far from the Cadbury headquarters, where he and fellow students were sometimes brought in as taste testers for new kinds of chocolate bars in plain foil wrappings.

cartographic, choreographic, pantomimic, pictorial, graphic, sculptural, and audiovisual creations." No one can reproduce or display or perform a copyrighted work without permission of the author. Copyright protection ordinarily lasts for the life of the author plus 70 years.

Roughly speaking, patent law covers inventions and copyright protects books, songs, and art. But in certain areas, like the invention of new software, it has been unclear whether patent or copyright protection should apply. There is also a body of law known as **trade secrets**. Even if a company does not have a patent on an invention, competing firms are not allowed to break into their factories and files and steal their secrets. One famous trade secret is the formula for Coca Cola, which is not protected under copyright or patent law, but is simply kept secret by the company.

trade secrets: Methods of production kept secret by the producing firm.

Taken together, this combination of patents, trademarks, copyrights, and trade secret law is called **intellectual property**, because it implies ownership over an idea or concept or image, not a physical piece of property like house or a car. Countries around the world have enacted laws to protect intellectual property, although the time periods and exact provisions of such laws vary across countries. There are ongoing negotiations, both through the World Intellectual Property Organization (WIPO) and through international treaties, to bring greater harmony to the intellectual property laws of different countries, to determine the extent to which patents and copyrights in one country will be respected in other countries.

intellectual property: The body of law including patents, trademarks, copyrights, and trade secret law that protect the right of inventors to produce and sell their inventions.

Exhibit 11-1 Economies of Scale and Natural Monopoly

In this market, the demand curve intersects the long-run average cost curve in the downward-sloping part of the LRAC curve. Imagine the situation where a monopoly is producing 6,000 units at a price of p_1. If a potential competitor tried to produce a smaller quantity, then its average costs would be too high to compete. If a potential competitor tried to produce a larger quantity, like 8,000 or 20,000, then it could produce at a lower average cost—but it could not sell the additional units because of a lack of demand in the market. Thus, a natural monopoly occurs when the quantity demanded is less than the minimum quantity it takes to be at the bottom of the long-run average cost curve.

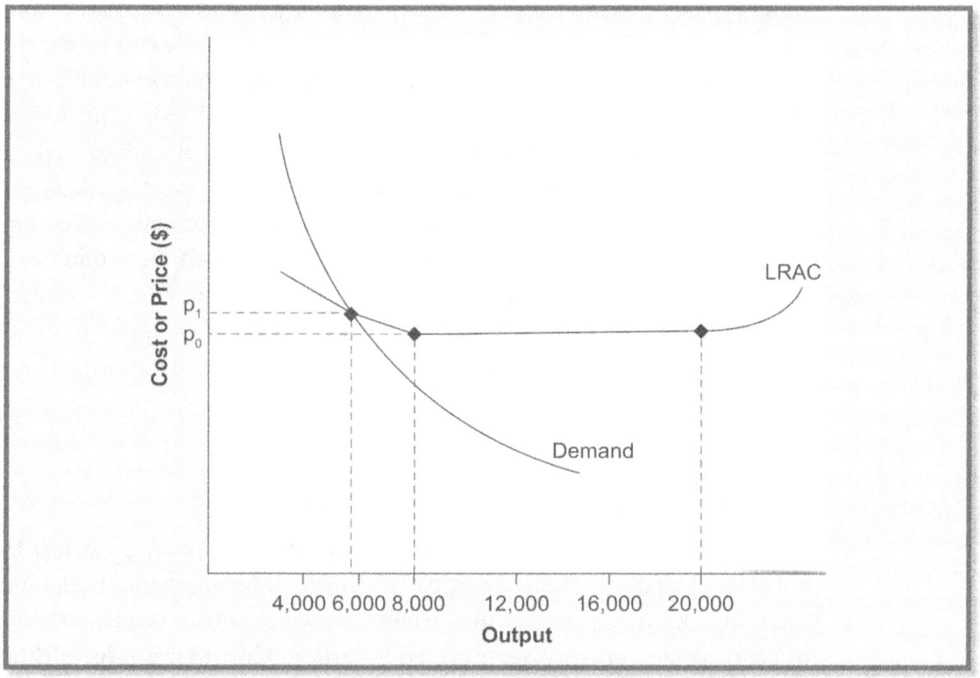

NATURAL MONOPOLY

Economies of scale can combine with the size of the market to limit competition. (This theme was introduced in Chapter 9.) Exhibit 11-1 presents a long-run average cost curve for the airplane manufacturing industry. The long-run average cost curve shows economies of scale up to an output of 8,000 planes per year and a price of p_0, then constant returns to scale from 8,000 to 20,000 planes per year, and diseconomies of scale at a quantity of production greater than 20,000 planes per year. Now consider the market demand curve in the diagram, which intersects the long-run average cost curve at an output level of 6,000 planes per year and at a price p_1 which is higher than p_0. In this situation, the market has room for only one producer. If a second firm attempts to enter the market at a smaller size, say by producing a quantity of 4,000 planes, then its average costs will be higher than the existing firm, and it will be unable to compete. If the second firm attempts to enter the market at a larger size, like 8,000 planes per year, then it could produce at a lower average cost—but it couldn't sell all 8,000 planes that it produced because of insufficient demand in the market.

natural monopoly: When the quantity demanded in the market is less than the quantity at the bottom of the long-run average cost curve.

This situation, when economies of scale are large relative to the quantity demanded in the market, is called a **natural monopoly**. Natural monopolies often arise in industries where the marginal cost of adding an additional customer are very low, once the fixed costs of the overall system are in place. Once the main water pipes are laid through a neighborhood, the marginal cost of providing water service to another home is fairly low. Once electricity lines are installed through a neighborhood, the marginal cost of providing additional electrical service to one more home is very low. It would be costly and duplicative for a second water company to enter the market and invest in a whole second set of main water pipes, or for a second electricity company to enter the market and invest in a whole new set of electrical wires. These industries offer an example where, because of economies of scale, one producer could serve the entire market more efficiently than a number of smaller producers that would have needed to make duplicative physical capital investments. A natural monopoly can also arise in smaller local markets for products that are difficult to transport. For example, cement production exhibits economies of scale, and the quantity of cement demanded in a local area may not be much larger than what a single plant can produce. Moreover, the costs of transporting cement overland are high, and so a cement plant in an area without access to water transportation may be a natural monopoly.

INTIMIDATING POTENTIAL COMPETITION

predatory pricing: When an existing firm uses sharp but temporary price cuts to discourage new competition.

Businesses have developed a number of schemes for creating barriers to entry by deterring potential competitors from entering the market. One method is known as **predatory pricing**, in which a firm uses the threat of sharp price cuts to discourage competition. Consider a large airline that provides most of the flights between two particular cities. A new, small start-up airline decides to offer service between these two cities. The large airline immediately slashes prices on this route to the bone, so that the new entrant can't make any money. After the new entrant has gone out of business, the incumbent firm can raise prices again. After this pattern is repeated once or twice, potential new entrants may decide that it isn't wise to try to compete. Small airlines often accuse larger airlines of predatory pricing: in the early 2000s, for example, ValuJet accused Delta of predatory pricing, Frontier accused United, and Reno Air accused Northwest. In late 2009, the American Booksellers Association, which represents independently owned and often smaller bookstores, accused Amazon, Wal-Mart and Target of predatory pricing for selling new hardcover best-sellers at low prices. In some cases, large advertising budgets can also act as a way of discouraging the competition. If the only way to launch a successful new national cola drink is to spend more than the promotional budgets of Coca Cola and Pepsi Cola, not too many companies will try. A firmly established brand name can be difficult to dislodge.

Exhibit 11-2 Barriers to Entry

Barrier to Entry	Government Role?	Example
Laws against entry or price changes	Yes	Post office, past regulation of airlines and trucking
Control of a physical resource	No	OPEC for oil, DeBeer's for diamonds
Technological advantage	Yes, through protection of intellectual property	New drugs or software
Natural monopoly	Government often responds with regulation	Water and electricity companies
Intimidating potential competitors	No	Predatory pricing; well-known brand names

SUMMING UP BARRIERS TO ENTRY

Exhibit 11-2 lists the barriers to entry that have been discussed here. This list should not be viewed as exhaustive, since firms in many industries have proven to be highly creative in inventing business practices that discourage competition. When barriers to entry exist, perfect competition is no longer a reasonable description of how an industry works. When barriers to entry are high enough, monopoly can result.

How a Profit-Maximizing Monopoly Chooses Output and Price

Consider a monopoly firm, comfortably surrounded by barriers to entry so that it need not fear competition from other producers. How will this monopoly choose its profit-maximizing quantity of output and what price will it charge? Profits for the monopolist, like any firm, will be equal to total revenues minus total costs. The pattern of costs for the monopoly can be analyzed within the same framework as the costs of a perfectly competitive firm—that is, by using total cost, fixed cost, variable cost, marginal cost, average cost, and average variable cost. However, because a monopoly faces no competition, its situation and its decision process will differ from that of a perfectly competitive firm.

DEMAND CURVES PERCEIVED BY A PERFECTLY COMPETITIVE FIRM AND BY A MONOPOLY

A perfectly competitive firm acts as a price taker, so its calculation of total revenue is made by taking the given market price and multiplying it by the quantity of output that the firm chooses. The demand curve *as it is perceived by a perfectly competitive firm* appears in Exhibit 11-3a. The flat perceived demand curve means that, from the viewpoint of the perfectly competitive firm, it could sell either a relatively low quantity like q_L or a relatively high quantity like q_H at the market price p^*.

What Is the Market?

A monopoly is a firm that sells all or nearly all of the goods and services in a given market. But what defines a "market"?

In a famous 1947 case, the federal government accused the DuPont company of having a monopoly in the cellophane market, pointing out that DuPont produced 75% of the cellophane in the United States. DuPont countered that even though it had 75% market share in cellophane, it had less than 20% of the "flexible packaging materials," which includes all other moisture-proof papers, films, and foils. In 1956, after years of legal appeals, the U.S. Supreme Court held that the broader market definition was more appropriate, and the case against DuPont was dismissed.

Questions over how to define the market continue today. True, Microsoft in the 1990s had a dominant share of the software for computer operating systems, but in the total market for all computer software and services, including everything from games to scientific programs, the Microsoft share was only about 16% in 2000. The Greyhound bus company may have a near-monopoly on the market for intercity bus transportation, but it is only a small share of the market for intercity transportation if that market includes private cars, airplanes, and railroad service. DeBeer's has a monopoly in diamonds, but it is a much smaller share of the total market for precious gemstones and an even smaller share of the total market for jewelry. A small town in the country may have only one gas station: is this gas station a "monopoly" or does it compete with gas stations that might be five or ten or 50 miles away?

In general, if a firm produces a product without close substitutes, then the firm can be considered a monopoly producer in a single market, but if buyers have a range of similar—even if not identical—options available from other firms, then the firm is not a monopoly. But arguments over whether substitutes are close or not close can be controversial.

Exhibit 11-3 The Perceived Demand Curve for a Perfect Competitor and a Monopolist

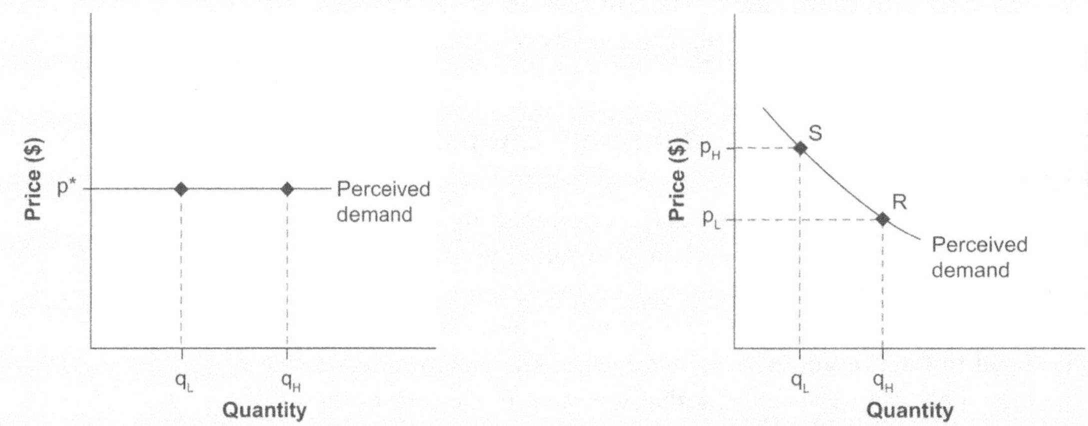

(a) Perceived demand for a perfect competitor. A perfectly competitive firm perceives the demand curve that it faces to be flat. The flat shape means that the firm can sell either a low quantity q_L or a high quantity q_H at exactly the same price p*.

(b) Perceived demand for a monopolist. A monopolist perceives the demand curve that it faces to be the same as the market demand curve, which for most goods is downward-sloping. Thus, if the monopolist chooses a high level of output q_H, it can charge only a relatively low price p_L; conversely, if the monopolist chooses a low level of output q_L, it can then charge a higher price p_H. The challenge for the monopolist is to choose the combination of price and quantity that maximizes profits.

No monopolist, even one who is thoroughly protected by high barriers to entry from other competing firms, can require consumers to purchase its product. The demand curve for the monopolist's products *as it is perceived by a monopolist* is exactly the same as the market demand curve—because the monopolist is the only firm in the market. Because demand for most products is neither completely elastic nor

Clearing It Up

Perceived Demand and Market Demand

The demand curve as perceived by a perfectly competitive firm is not the overall market demand curve for that product. However, the firm's demand curve as perceived by a monopoly is the same as the market demand curve. The reason for the difference is that each perfectly competitive firm perceives the demand for its products in a market that includes many other firms; in effect, the demand curve perceived by a perfectly competitive firm is a tiny slice of the entire market demand curve. In contrast, a monopoly perceives demand for its product in a market where the monopoly is the only producer.

completely inelastic, an in between case is drawn in Exhibit 11-3b. The monopolist can either choose a point like R with a low price p_L and high quantity q_H, or a point like S with a high price p_H and a low quantity q_L, or some intermediate point. Setting the price too high will result in a low quantity sold, and thus won't bring in much revenue. Conversely, setting the price too low may result in a high quantity sold, but because of the low price it won't bring in much revenue either. The challenge of the monopolist is to strike a profit-maximizing balance between the price it charges and the quantity that it sells.

TOTAL AND MARGINAL REVENUE FOR A MONOPOLIST

Profits for a monopolist can be illustrated with a graph of total revenues and total costs, as shown with the example of the hypothetical HealthPill firm in Exhibit 11-4. The total cost curve has its typical shape; that is, total costs rise and grow steeper as output increases.

To calculate total revenue for a monopolist, start with the demand curve perceived by the monopolist. The table shows quantities along the demand curve, the price at each quantity demanded, and then calculates total revenue by multiplying price times quantity at each level of output. (In this example, the output is given as 1, 2, 3, 4, and the like, for the sake of simplicity. If you prefer a dash of greater realism, you can imagine that these output levels and the corresponding prices are measured per 1,000 or 10,000 pills.) As the exhibit illustrates, total revenue for a monopolist rises, flattens out, and then falls. In this example, total revenue is highest at a quantity of 6 or 7. Clearly, the total revenue for a monopolist is not a straight upward-sloping line, in the way that total revenue was for a perfectly competitive firm. The different total revenue pattern for a monopolist occurs because the quantity that a monopolist chooses to produce affects the market price, which was not true for a perfectly competitive firm. If the monopolist charges a very high price, then quantity demanded drops, and so total revenue is very low. If the monopolist charges a very low price, then even if quantity demanded is very high, total revenue won't add up to much. At some intermediate level, total revenue will be highest.

However, the monopolist is not seeking to maximize revenue, but instead to earn the highest possible profit. Profits are calculated in the final row of the table. In the HealthPill example in Exhibit 11-4, the highest profit will occur at the quantity where total revenue is the

Exhibit 11-4 Total Revenue and Total Cost for the HealthPill Monopoly

Total revenue for the monopoly firm called HealthPill first rises, then falls. Low levels of output bring in relatively little total revenue, because the quantity is low. High levels of output bring in relatively less revenue, because the high quantity pushes down the market price. The total cost curve is upward-sloping. Profits will be highest at the quantity of output where total revenue is most above total cost; of the choices in the table, the highest profits happen at an output of 4. The profit-maximizing level of output is not the same as the revenue-maximizing level of output, which should make sense, because profits take costs into account and revenues don't.

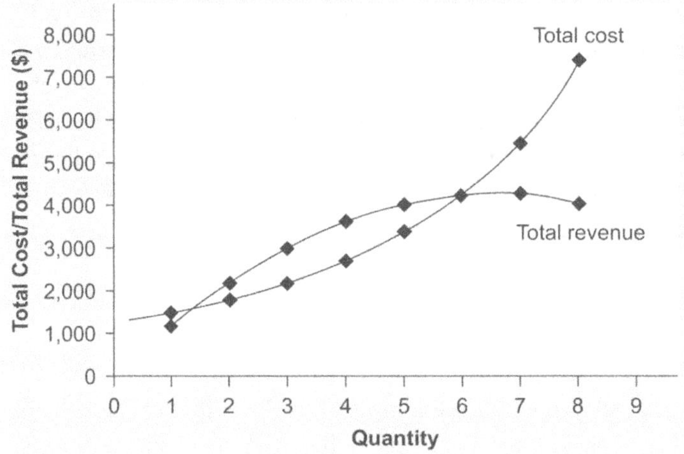

Quantity	Total Cost	Quantity	Price	Total Revenue	Profit = Total Revenue – Total Cost
1	1,500	1	1,200	1,200	–300
2	1,800	2	1,100	2,200	400
3	2,200	3	1,000	3,000	800
4	2,700	4	900	3,600	900
5	3,300	5	800	4,000	700
6	4,200	6	700	4,200	0
7	5,400	7	600	4,200	–1,200
8	7,200	8	500	4,000	–3,200

farthest above total cost. Of the choices given in the table, the highest profits occur at an output of 4, where profit is 900.

MARGINAL REVENUE AND MARGINAL COST FOR A MONOPOLIST

In the real world, a monopolist often does not have enough information to analyze its entire total revenues or total costs curves; after all, the firm doesn't know exactly what would happen if it was to alter production dramatically. But a monopoly often has fairly reliable information about how changing output by small or moderate amounts will affect its marginal revenues and marginal costs, because it has had experience with such changes over time and because modest changes are easier to

Exhibit 11-5 Marginal Revenue and Marginal Cost for the HealthPill Monopoly

For a monopoly like HealthPill, marginal revenue decreases as additional units are sold. The reason is that each additional unit sold causes a decrease in the price for all units. Marginal revenue can even be zero, as at an output of 7, or negative, as at an output of 8. The marginal cost curve is upward-sloping. The profit-maximizing choice for the monopoly will be to produce at the quantity where marginal revenue is equal to marginal cost: that is, MR = MC. If the monopoly produces a lower quantity, then MR > MC at those levels of output, and the firm can make higher profits by expanding output. If the firm produces at a greater quantity, then MC > MR, and the firm can make higher profits by reducing its quantity of output.

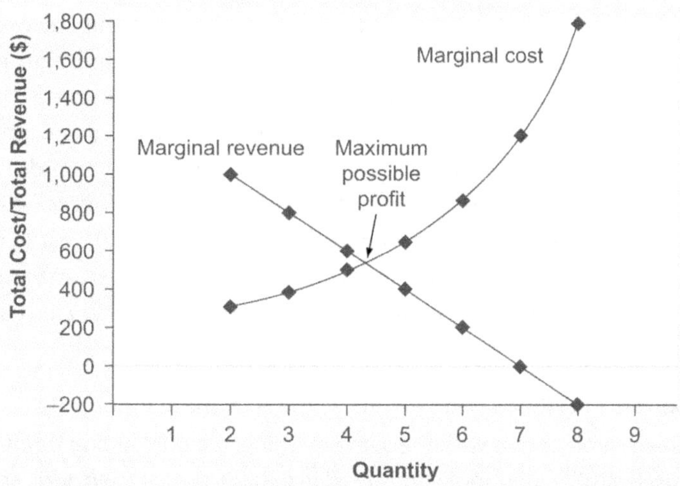

Cost Information				Revenue Information			
Quantity	Total Cost	Marginal Cost	Average Cost	Quantity	Price	Total Revenue	Marginal Revenue
1	1,500	—	1,500	1	1,200	1,200	—
2	1,800	300	900	2	1,100	2,200	1,000
3	2,200	400	733	3	1,000	3,000	800
4	2,700	500	675	4	900	3,600	600
5	3,300	600	660	5	800	4,000	400
6	4,200	900	700	6	700	4,200	200
7	5,400	1,200	771	7	600	4,200	0
8	7,200	1,800	900	8	500	4,000	–200

extrapolate from current experience. A monopolist can use information on marginal revenue and marginal cost to seek out the profit-maximizing combination of quantity and price.

The first four columns of Exhibit 11-5 use the numbers on total cost from the HealthPill example in the previous exhibit and calculate marginal cost and average cost. This monopoly faces a typical U-shaped average cost curve and upward-sloping marginal cost curve. The second four columns use the total revenue information from the previous exhibit and calculate marginal revenue. Notice that marginal revenue is zero at a quantity of 7, and turns negative at quantities higher than 7. It may seem counter-intuitive that marginal revenue could ever be zero or negative: after all, doesn't an increase in quantity sold always mean more revenue? For a perfect competitor, each additional unit sold brought a positive marginal revenue, because marginal revenue was equal to the given market price. But a monopolist can sell a larger quantity and see a decline in total revenue. When a monopolist increases sales by one unit, it gains some marginal revenue from selling that extra unit, but also loses some marginal revenue because every other unit must now be sold at a lower price. As the quantity sold becomes higher, the drop in price affects a greater quantity of sales, eventually causing a situation where more sales cause marginal revenue to be negative.

A monopolist can determine its profit-maximizing price and quantity by analyzing the marginal revenue and marginal costs of producing an extra unit. If the marginal revenue exceeds the marginal cost, then the firm should produce the extra unit. For example, at an output of 2 in the example, marginal revenue is 1,000 and marginal cost is 300, so producing this unit will clearly add to overall profits. At an output of 4, marginal revenue is 600 and marginal cost is 500, so producing this unit still adds to overall profits. However, expanding output from 4 to 5 would involve a marginal revenue of 400 and a marginal cost of 600,

Exhibit 11-6 Illustrating Profits at the HealthPill Monopoly

This exhibit begins with the same marginal revenue and marginal cost curves from the HealthPill monopoly presented in Exhibit 11-5. It then adds an average cost curve and the demand curve faced by the monopolist. The HealthPill firm first chooses the quantity where MR = MC; in this example, four is the highest level of output before this occurs (although the intersection of MR and MC actually happens at a slightly higher level of output). The monopolist then decides what price to charge by looking at the demand curve it faces. The large box, with quantity on the horizontal size and price on the vertical side, shows total revenue for the firm. Total costs for the firm are shown by the darkershaded box, which is quantity on the horizontal axis and average cost of production on the vertical axis. The large total revenue box minus the smaller total cost box leaves the lightly shaded box that shows total profits. Since the price charged is above average cost, the firm is earning positive profits.

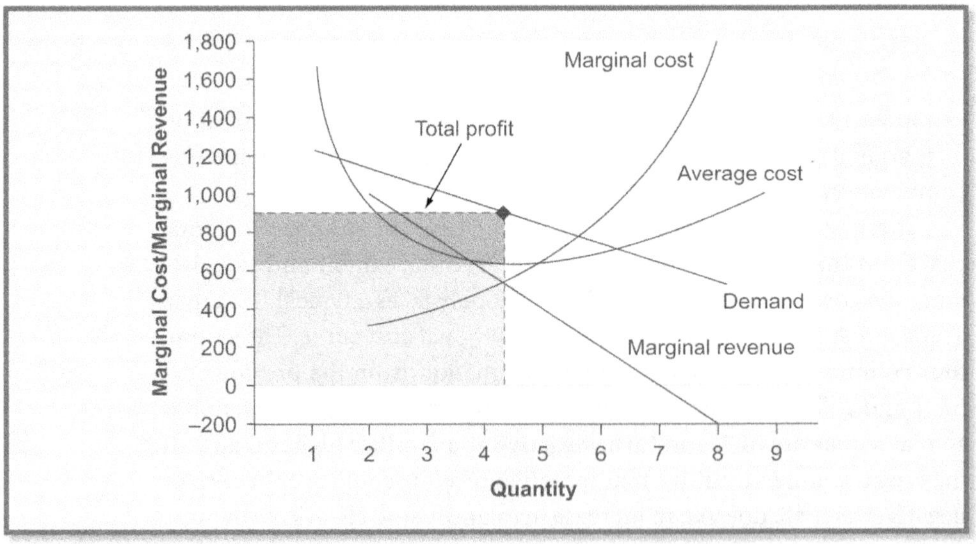

so that fifth unit would actually reduce profits. Thus, the monopoly can tell from the marginal revenue and marginal cost that of the choices given in the table, the profit-maximizing level of output is 4. Indeed, the monopoly could seek out the profit-maximizing level of output by increasing quantity by a small amount, calculating marginal revenue and marginal cost, and then either increasing output as long as marginal revenue exceeds marginal cost or reducing output if marginal cost exceeds marginal revenue. This process works without any need to calculate total revenue and total cost. Thus, a profit-maximizing monopoly should follow the rule of producing up to the quantity where marginal revenue is equal to marginal cost—that is, MR = MC. A perfectly competitive firm will also find its profit-maximizing level of output where MR = MC. The key difference with a perfectly competitive firm is that in the case of perfect competition, marginal revenue is equal to price (MR = P), while for a monopolist, marginal revenue is not equal to the price, because changes in monopoly quantity of output affect the price.

ILLUSTRATING MONOPOLY PROFITS

It is straightforward to calculate profits if given numbers for total revenue and total cost. However, the size of monopoly profits can also be illustrated graphically with Exhibit 11-6, which takes the marginal cost and marginal revenue curves from the previous exhibit and adds an average cost curve and the monopolist's perceived demand curve. This diagram can also illustrate the three-step process where a monopolist: (1) selects the profit-maximizing quantity to produce; (2) decides what price to charge; (3) determines total revenue, total cost, and profit.

STEP 1: THE MONOPOLIST DETERMINES ITS PROFIT-MAXIMIZING LEVEL OF OUTPUT

The firm can use the points on the demand curve D to calculate total revenue, and then based on total revenue it can calculate its marginal revenue curve. The profit-maximizing quantity will occur where MR = MC—or at the last possible point before marginal costs start exceeding marginal revenue. On this figure, the closest possible point to MR = MC occurs at an output of 4.

STEP 2: THE MONOPOLIST DECIDES WHAT PRICE TO CHARGE

The monopolist will charge what the market is willing to pay. A dotted line drawn straight up from the profit-maximizing quantity to the demand curve shows the profit-maximizing price. This price is above the average cost curve, which shows that the firm is earning profits.

Clearing It Up

Why Is a Monopolist's Marginal Revenue Under the Demand Curve?

The marginal revenue curve for a monopolist always lies beneath the market demand curve. To understand why, think about increasing the quantity along the demand curve by one unit, so that you take one step down the demand curve to a slightly higher quantity but a slightly lower price. This step affects marginal revenue in two ways. First, it adds one additional unit sold at the new market price. Second, it means that all the previous units, which used to be sold at the higher price, now sell for less. Because of the lower price on all units sold, the marginal revenue of selling a unit is less than the price of that unit—and the marginal revenue curve is below the demand curve.

STEP 3: CALCULATE TOTAL REVENUE, TOTAL COST, AND PROFIT

Total revenue is the overall shaded box, where the width of the box is the quantity being sold and the height is the price. The bottom part of the shaded box, which is shaded more lightly, shows total costs; that is, quantity on the horizontal axis multiplied by average cost on the vertical axis. The larger box of total revenues minus the smaller box of total costs will equal profits, which is shown by the darkly shaded box.

In a perfectly competitive market, the forces of entry would erode this profit away in the long-run. But a monopolist is protected by barriers to entry. In fact, one telltale sign of a possible monopoly is when a firm earns profits year after year, while doing more or less the same thing, without ever seeing those profits eroded by increased competition.

THE INEFFICIENCY OF MONOPOLY

To understand why a monopoly is inefficient, it is useful to compare it with the benchmark model of perfect competition.

In perfect competition, the process of entry and exit means that eventually the market price is driven down to the price at the minimum of the average cost curve. Productive efficiency occurs when goods are being produced at the lowest possible average cost. However, a monopoly does not need to worry about entry, nor does it need to produce at the bottom of the average cost curve. As a result, a monopoly will not display productive efficiency. The rule of profit-maximization in a world of perfect competition was for each firm to produce the quantity of output where P = MC, where the price P is a measure of how much buyers value the good and the marginal cost MC is a measure of what marginal units cost society to produce. Following this rule assures allocative efficiency. If P > MC, then the benefit to society as measured by P is greater than the marginal cost to society MC of producing additional units, and a greater quantity should be produced. But in the case of monopoly, price is always greater than marginal cost at the profit-maximizing level of output, as can be seen by looking back at Exhibit 11-6. Thus, consumers will suffer from a monopoly because a lower quantity will be sold in the market, at a higher price, than would have been the case in a perfectly competitive market.

Is a Diamond Monopoly Forever?

The DeBeer's diamond company is a South African firm that has organized a monopoly for selling diamonds around the world. The diamond monopoly works through a Central Selling Organization, which signs long-term exclusive contracts with diamonds mines around the world to purchase all of their diamonds. It then groups the diamonds by size, brilliance, and other characteristics, and then sells them to diamond cutters and dealers. At its peak in the 1970s and 1980s, the CSO controlled about 85% of the world's diamonds. Thus, DeBeer's could control the quantity sold in the market and keep the price high.

But in the 1990s, a group of Australian diamond producers pulled out of the CSO. Diamonds were discovered in Canada at the Ekati mine. Diamond producers in Russia threatened to leave the CSO. Diamond production increased in Angola—organized in part by Russian and Australian firms. By early in late 2000s, the CSO controlled only about 40% of the world's diamond market.

What's next? DeBeer's will negotiate with other producers, pointing out that if the Central Selling Organization doesn't control the quantity produced, prices and profits will be lower for diamond producers as a group. However, the other producers may feel that they individually can earn higher profits by remaining outside the CSO. Instead of the "Diamonds are forever" ad campaign that DeBeer's started in the 1940s, which applied to all diamonds, different diamond producers will try to make consumers believe that there is something particularly special about the diamonds produced by their firm.

Productive and allocative efficiency refer to the quantity and price at a point in time. The problem of inefficiency for monopolies often runs even deeper than these issues, and also involves incentives for efficiency over longer periods of time. There are counterbalancing incentives here. On one side, firms may strive for new inventions and new intellectual property because they want to become monopolies and earn high profits—at least for a few years until the competition catches up. In this way, monopolies may come to exist because of competitive pressures on firms. However, once a barrier to entry is in place, a monopoly that doesn't need to fear competition can just produce the same old products in the same old way—while still ringing up a healthy rate of profit. John Hicks, who won the Nobel Prize for economics in 1972, wrote back in 1935: "The best of all monopoly profits is a quiet life." He didn't mean the comment in a complimentary way. He meant that monopolies may bank their profits and slack off on trying to please their customers.

Until the early 1980s, for example, AT&T provided all of the local and long-distance phone service in the United States, along with manufacturing most of the phones. The payment plans and types of phones didn't change much. The old joke was that you could have any color phone you wanted, as long as it was black. But in 1982, AT&T was split up by government litigation into a number of local phone companies, a long-distance phone company and a phone equipment manufacturer. An explosion of innovation followed. Services like call waiting, caller ID, three-way calling, voice mail though the phone company, mobile phones, and wireless connections to the Internet all became available. A wide range of payment plans was offered, as well. It was no longer true that all phones were black; instead, phones came in a wild variety of shapes and colors. The end of the telephone monopoly brought lower prices, a greater quantity of services, and also a wave innovation aimed at attracting and pleasing customers.

Exhibit 11-7 How a Profit-Maximizing Monopoly Decides

In Step 1, the monopoly chooses the profit-maximizing level of output Q_1, by choosing the quantity where MR = MC. In Step 2, the monopoly decides how much to charge for output level Q_1 by drawing a line straight up from Q_1 to point R on its perceived demand curve. Thus, the monopoly will charge a price P_1. In Step 3, the monopoly identifies its profit. Total revenue will be Q_1 multiplied by P_1. Total cost will be Q_1 multiplied by the average cost of producing Q_1, which is shown by point S on the average cost curve to be P_2. Profits will be the total revenue rectangle minus the total cost rectangle, shown by the shaded zone in the figure.

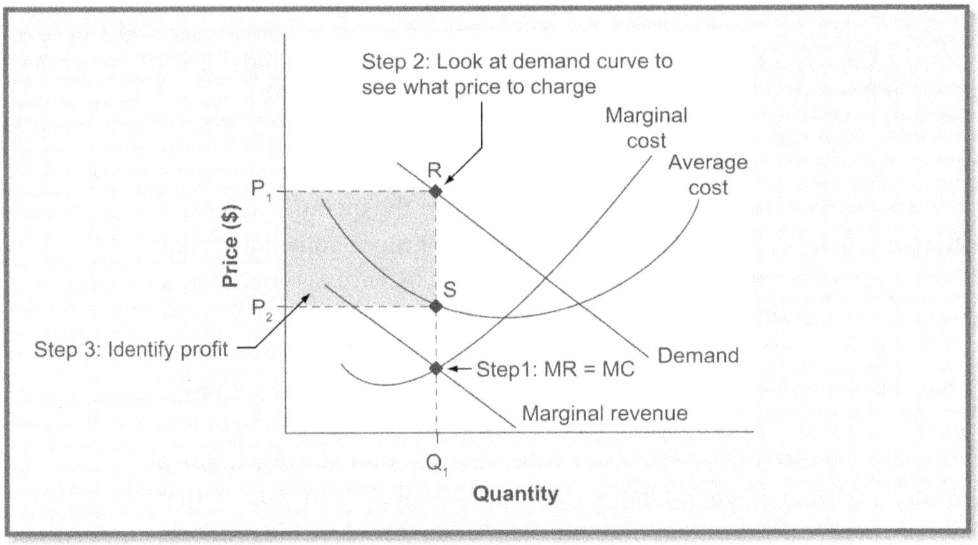

Conclusion

A monopolist can analyze its costs with the same analytic tools as other firms: total cost, marginal cost, and average cost. Monopolists will often face the U-shaped average cost curve and upward-sloping marginal cost curve as shown in Exhibit 11-7. To maximize profits, Step 1 for the monopolist is to choose the quantity q_M, where marginal costs and marginal revenues intersect. Step 2 is to sell that quantity at the price p_M, which is determined by point R on the demand curve. Step 3 is for the monopolist to determine its profits. As long as that monopoly price pM is above the average cost curve at the monopoly quantity q_M, the monopoly is earning profits, shown by the shaded rectangle with its corners at p_M, R, S, and T. Moreover, if the monopolist is protected by sufficiently high barriers to entry, it can earn those profits forever, without fear of competitor firms that would be willing to sell at a lower price. Chapter 13 will discuss how government policy may respond to monopolies that charge a higher price and produce a lower quantity than would a group of firms in a competitive industry. But before turning to the policy issues, Chapter 12 analyzes the profit-maximizing choices at two locations on the spectrum of competition between perfect competition and monopoly—that is, monopolistic competition and oligopoly.

Key Concepts and Summary

1. Perfect competition refers to an industry where many firms produce identical products. Conversely, **imperfect competition** refers to industries where either there are a small number of firms, or the firms don't sell an identical product, or both. There are three main varieties of imperfect competition: **monopoly**, which is the case of a single seller; **monopolistic competition**, where there are many sellers but their products are not identical; and **oligopoly**, which is the case of a small number of sellers.
2. **Barriers to entry** prevent or discourage competitors from entering the market. These barriers include legal restrictions on competition, control of a physical resource, technological superiority, economies of scale that lead to natural monopoly, and practices to intimidate the competition like **predatory pricing**.
3. **Intellectual property** refers to legally guaranteed ownership of an idea, rather than a physical item. The laws that protect intellectual property include **patents**, **trademarks**, **copyrights**, and **trade secrets**.
4. A **natural monopoly** arises when economies of scale persist over a large enough range of output that if one firm supplies the entire market, no second firm can enter without facing a cost disadvantage.
5. The demand curve perceived by a perfectly competitive firm is horizontal, which shows that such a firm is a price-taker, charging whatever price is determined in the market for the quantity that it sells. The demand curve perceived by a monopolist is the market demand curve, which is typically downward-sloping. A monopolist is not a price-taker, because when it decides what quantity to produce, it also determines the market price.
6. For a monopolist, total revenue is relatively low at low quantities of output, because not much is being sold. Total revenue is also relatively low at very high quantities of output, because a very high quantity will sell only at a low price. Thus, total revenue for a monopolist will start low, rise, and then decline.
7. The marginal revenue for a monopolist from selling additional units will decline. Each additional unit sold by a monopolist will push down the overall market price, and as more units are sold, this lower price applies to more and more units.
8. A monopolist can seek out the profit-maximizing quantity of output in two ways: it can choose the quantity where total revenue exceeds total cost by the highest amount, or it can choose the quantity where marginal revenue is equal to marginal cost.
9. The monopolist will select the profit-maximizing level of output where MR = MC, and then charge the price for that quantity of output as determined by the market demand curve. If that price is above average cost, the monopolist earns positive profits.
10. Monopolists are not productively efficient, because they do not produce at the minimum of the average cost curve. Monopolists are not allocatively efficient, because they do not produce at the quantity

where P = MC. As a result, monopolists produce less, at a higher average cost, and charge a higher price than would a combination of firms in a perfectly competitive industry. Monopolists also may lack incentives for innovation, because they need not fear entry.

Vocabulary Terms

Barriers to entry
Copyright
Intellectual property
Monopoly
Patent
Predatory pricing
Trade secrets
Trademark

Review Questions

1. How is a monopoly industry different from perfect competition?
2. How is monopolistic competition different from perfect competition?
3. How is oligopoly different from perfect competition?
4. What is a barrier to entry? Give some examples.
5. What is predatory pricing?
6. How is intellectual property different from other property?
7. By what legal mechanisms is intellectual property protected?
8. In what sense is a natural monopoly "natural"?
9. How is the demand curve perceived by a perfectly competitive firm different from the demand curve perceived by a monopolist?
10. How does the demand curve perceived by a monopolist compare with the market demand curve?
11. Is a monopolist a price-taker? Explain briefly.
12. What is the usual shape of a total revenue curve for a monopolist? Why?
13. What is the usual shape of a marginal revenue curve for a monopolist? Why?
14. How can a monopolist identify the profit-maximizing level of output if it knows its total revenue and total cost curves?
15. How can a monopolist identify the profit-maximizing level of output if it knows its marginal revenue and marginal costs?
16. When a monopolist identifies its profit-maximizing quantity of output, how does it decide what price to charge?
17. Is a monopolist productively efficient? Why or why not?
18. Is a monopolist allocatively efficient? Why or why not?
19. How does the quantity produced and price charged by a monopolist compare to that of a perfectly competitive industry?

CHAPTER 12
Oligopoly

12 Oligopoly

By Timothy Taylor

Oligopoly

Oligopoly arises when several large firms have all or most of the sales in an industry. Oligopolistic firms are like cats in a bag. They can either scratch each other to pieces or cuddle up and get comfortable with one another. If oligopolists compete hard against each other, the result may be that they end up acting very much like perfect competitors, driving down costs and leading to zero profits for all. But if oligopolists cooperate with each other, they may effectively act like a monopoly and succeed in pushing up prices and earning consistently high levels of profit. Analyzing the choices of oligopolistic firms about pricing and quantity produced involves thinking through these different choices.

oligopoly: When several large firms have all or most of the sales in an industry.

WHY DO OLIGOPOLIES EXIST?

A combination of the barriers to entry that create monopolies and the product differentiation that characterizes monopolistic competition can create the setting for an oligopoly. For example, when a government grants a patent for an invention to one firm, it may create a monopoly. But when the government grants patents to, say, three different pharmaceutical companies that each has its own drug for reducing high blood pressure, those three firms may become an oligopoly.

Similarly, a natural monopoly will arise when the size of the firm that is needed to operate at the minimum of the long-run average cost curve is large compared to the quantity demanded in the market. In such a setting, the market only has room for one firm, because no smaller firm can operate at a low enough average cost to compete, and no larger firm could sell what it produced given the quantity demanded in the market. But quantity demanded in the market may also be, say, two or three times the quantity needed to produce at the minimum of the average cost curve—which means that the market would have room for only two or three oligopoly firms. Again, smaller firms would have higher average costs and be unable to compete, while larger firms would produce such a high quantity that they would not be able to sell it at a profitable price. This combination of economies of scale and market demand probably explains the Boeing-Airbus oligopoly in making large passenger aircraft.

The product differentiation at the heart of monopolistic competition can also play a role in creating oligopoly. For example, firms may reach at least a certain minimum size before they are able to spend enough on advertising and marketing to create a recognizable brand name. The problem in competing with, say, Coca-Cola or Pepsi is not that producing fizzy drinks is technologically difficult, but rather that creating a brand name and marketing effort to equal Coke or Pepsi is an enormous task.

four-firm concentration ratio:
What percentage share of the total sales in the industry are accounted for by the largest four firms.

market share:
The percentage share of total sales in the market.

THE FOUR-FIRM CONCENTRATION RATIO

The **four-firm concentration ratio**, which measures what share of the total sales in the industry are accounted for by the largest four firms, is one numerical way to measure the extent of competition in an industry. Say that the market for replacing broken automobile windshields in a certain city has 16 firms with the **market shares** shown in Exhibit 12-1, where the market share is each firm's proportion of total sales in that market. The four-firm concentration ratio is calculated by adding the market shares of the four largest firms: in this case, 16 + 10 + 8 + 6 = 40.

Exhibit 12-1 Calculating Concentration Ratios from Market Shares

If the market shares in the market for replacing automobile windshields are:	
Smooth as Glass Repair Company	16% of the market
The Auto Glass Doctor Company	10% of the market
Your Car Shield Company	8% of the market
Seven firms that each have 6% of the market	42% of the market, combined
Eight firms that each have 3% of the market	24% of the market, combined
Then the four-firm concentration ratio is 16 + 10 + 8 + 6 = 40.	

Exhibit 12-2 Some Herfindahl-Hirschman Index Calculations

HHI for a monopoly	$100^2 = 10{,}000$
HHI for an industry with 100 firms that each have 1% of the market	$100(1^2) = 100$
HHI for the industry market share in Exhibit 13-2	$16^2 + 10^2 + 8^2 + 7(6^2) + 8(3^2) = 744$

This concentration ratio would not be considered especially high, because the largest four firms have less than half the market. The concentration ratio approach can help to clarify some of the fuzziness over deciding when a merger might affect competition. For example, if two of the smallest firms in the hypothetical market for repairing automobile windshields merged, the four-firm concentration ratio would not change—which implies that there isn't much worry that the degree of competition in the market has notably diminished. However, if the top two firms merged, then the four-firm concentration ratio would become 46 (that is, 26 + 8 + 6 + 6). While this concentration ratio is modestly higher, the four-firm concentration ratio would still be less than half, so such a proposed merger might barely raise an eyebrow among the antitrust regulators.

THE HERFINDAHL-HIRSHMAN INDEX

A four-firm concentration ratio is a simple tool, which may reveal only part of the story. For example, consider two industries that both have a four-firm concentration ratio of 80. However, in one industry five firms each control 20% of the market, while in the other industry, the top firm holds 77% of the market and all the other firms have 1% each. Although the four-firm concentration ratios are identical, it would be reasonable to worry more about the extent of competition in the second case—which is nearly a monopoly—than in the first.

Thus, another approach to measuring industry concentration which can distinguish between these two cases is called the **Herfindahl-Hirschman Index**. The HHI, as it is often called, is calculated by taking the market share of each firm in the industry, squaring it, and adding them up to get a total. Exhibit 12-2 gives examples of an HHI calculation. For a monopoly with a market share of 100%, the HHI would reach a maximum value of 10,000. For an extremely competitive industry, with dozens or hundreds of extremely small competitors, the value of the HHI might drop as low as 100 or even less.

Herfindahl-Hirschman Index (HHI):
Take the market share of each firm in the industry, square each one, and add them.

Exhibit 12-3 Some Examples of Concentration Ratios and HHIs in the U.S. Economy, 2009

U.S. Industry	Four-Firm Ratio	HHI
Wireless Largest five: Verizon, AT&T, Sprint Nextel, T-Mobile, MetroPCS	91	2,311
Automobiles Largest five: GM, Toyota, Ford, Honda, Chrysler	63	1,121
Computers Largest five: HP, Dell, Acer, Apple, Toshiba	74	1,737
Airlines Largest five: Southwest, American, Delta, United, U.S. Airways	44	536

The HHI gives greater weight to large firms. Consider the example given a moment ago, comparing one industry where five firms each have 20% of the market with an industry where one firm has 77% and the other 23 firms have 1% each. The two industries have the same four-firm concentration ratio of 80. But the HHI for the first industry is 5(202) = 2,000, while the HHI for the second industry is much higher at 772 + 23(12) = 5,952. The near-monopolist in the second industry drives up the HHI measure of industrial concentration. Exhibit 12-3 gives some examples of the four-firm concentration ratio and the HHI in various U.S. industries in 2009.

In the 1980s, the FTC followed guidelines that if a merger would result in an HHI of less than 1,000, the FTC would probably approve it. If a merger would result in an HHI of more than 1,800, the FTC would probably challenge it. If a merger would result in an HHI between 1,000 and 1,800, then the FTC it would scrutinize the plan and make a case-by-case decision. However, in the last 10–20 years the antitrust enforcement authorities have moved away from relying as heavily on measures of concentration ratios and HHIs to determine whether a merger will be allowed, and instead carried out more case-by-case analysis of the extent of competition different industries.

COLLUSION OR COMPETITION?

When oligopoly firms in a certain market decide what quantity to produce and what price to charge, they face a temptation to act as if they were a monopoly. By acting together like a monopoly, oligopolistic firms could then hold down output, charge a higher price, and divide up the monopoly level of profit amongst themselves. When firms act together in this way to reduce output and keep prices high, it is called **collusion**. A group of firms that collude to produce the monopoly output and sell at the monopoly price is called a **cartel**. The desire of businesses to avoid competing with each other, so that they can instead raise the prices that they charge and earn higher profits, has been well-understood by economists for a long time. Adam Smith wrote in *The Wealth of Nations* way back in 1776: "People of the same trade seldom meet together, even for merriment and diversion, but the conversation ends in a conspiracy against the public, or in some contrivance to raise prices."

collusion:
When firms act together to reduce output and keep prices high.

cartel:
A group of firms that collude to produce the monopoly output and sell at the monopoly price.

But even when oligopolists recognize that they would benefit as a group by acting like a monopoly, each individual oligopoly faces a private temptation to produce just a slightly higher quantity and earn slightly higher profit—while still counting on the other oligopolists to hold down their production and keep prices high. If at least some oligopolists give in to this temptation and start producing more, then the market price will fall. Indeed, a small handful of oligopoly firms may end up competing so fiercely that they all end up earning zero profits—as if they were perfect competitors.

THE PRISONER'S DILEMMA

To gain a deeper understanding of how oligopoly firms may either act together like a monopolist or competing with each other, economists use **game theory**, a branch of mathematics often used by economists that analyzes situations in which players must make decisions and then receive payoffs. Game theory has found widespread applications in the social sciences, as well as in business, law, and military strategy. The number of players, the range of choices available to them, the order in which they decide, the ways in which the players interact, the amount of the payoffs, and the amount of information available to the players can all differ from game to game. The **prisoner's dilemma** is a game in which the gains from cooperation are larger than the rewards from pursing self-interest, and which can be used to illustrate the possibilities for acting together faced by oligopolistic firms. Many games are named for a story that offers an intuitive understanding of the situation, and the story behind the prisoner's dilemma runs like this. Two prisoners are arrested. When they are taken to the police station, they refuse to

game theory:
A branch of mathematics often used by economists that analyzes situations in which players must make decisions and then receive payoffs.

prisoner's dilemma:
A game in which the gains from cooperation are larger than the rewards from pursuing self-interest.

Exhibit 12-4 The Prisoner's Dilemma Problem

		Prisoner B: Remain Silent (cooperate with other prisoner)	Prisoner B: Confess (don't cooperate with other prisoner)
Prisoner A	Remain Silent (cooperate with other prisoner)	A gets 2 years, B gets 2 years	B gets 1 year, A gets 8 years
	Confess (don't cooperate with other prisoner)	A gets 1 year, B gets 8 years	A gets 5 years, B gets 5 years

Exhibit 12-5 A Prisoner's Dilemma for Oligopolists

		Firm B: Holds Down Output (cooperates with other firm)	Firm B: Increase Output (don't cooperate with other firm)
Firm A	Holds Down Output (cooperates with other firm)	A gets \$1,000, B gets \$1,000	A gets \$200, B gets \$1,500
	Increase Output (don't cooperate with other firm)	A gets \$1,500, B gets \$200	A gets \$400, B gets \$400

say anything and are put in separate interrogation rooms. Eventually, a police officer enters the room where Prisoner A is being held and says: "You know what? Your partner in the other room is confessing. So your partner is going to get a light prison sentence of just one year, and because you're remaining silent, the judge is going to stick you with eight years in prison. Why don't you get smart? If you confess, too, we'll cut your jail time down to five years, and your partner will get five years, too." Over in the next room, another police officer is giving exactly the same speech to Prisoner B. What the police officers don't say is that if both prisoners remain silent, the evidence against them is not especially strong, and the prisoners will end up with only two years in jail each. The game theory situation facing the two prisoners is shown in Exhibit 12-4. To understand the dilemma, first consider the choices from Prisoner A's point of view. If A believes that his partner B will confess, then A ought to confess, too, so as to not get stuck with the eight years in prison. But if

The Lysine Cartel

Lysine, a $600 million-a-year industry, is an amino acid used by farmers as a feed additive to ensure the proper growth of swine and poultry. The primary U.S. producer of lysine is Archer Daniels Midland (ADM), but several other large European and Japanese firms are in this market. For a time in the first half of the 1990s, the world's major lysine producers met together in hotel conference rooms and decided together exactly how much each firm would sell and what it would charge. But the U.S. Federal Bureau of Investigation had learned of the cartel and bugged a number of their phone calls and meetings.

From FBI surveillance tapes, here's a comment that Terry Wilson, president of the corn processing division at ADM, made to the other lysine producers at a 1994 meeting in Mona, Hawaii:

> I wanna go back and I wanna say something very simple. If we're going to trust each other, okay, and if I'm assured that I'm gonna get 67,000 tons by the year's end, we're gonna sell it at the prices we agreed to . . . The only thing we need to talk about there because we are gonna get manipulated by these God damn buyers—they can be smarter than us if we let them be smarter. . . . They [the customers] are not your friend. They are not my friend. And we gotta have 'em, but they are not my friends. You are my friend. I wanna be closer to you than I am to any customer. Cause you can make us . . . money. . . . And all I wanna to tell you again is let's—let's put the prices on the board. Let's all agree that's what we're gonna do and then walk out of here and do it.

The price of lysine doubled while the cartel was in effect. Confronted by the FBI tapes, Archer Daniels Midland pled guilty in 1996 and paid a fine of $100 million. A number of top executives, both at ADM and other firms, later paid fines of up to $350,000 and were sentenced to 24–30 months in prison.

In another one of the FBI recordings, the president of Archer Daniels Midland told an executive from another competing firm that ADM had a slogan that, in his words, had "penetrated the whole company." The company president stated the slogan this way: "Our competitors are our friends. Our customers are the enemy." That slogan could stand as the motto of cartels everywhere.

A believes that B will not confess, then A will be tempted to act selfishly and confess, so as to serve only one year. The key point is that A has an incentive to confess regardless of what choice B makes! B faces the same set of choices, and thus will have an incentive to confess regardless of what choice A makes. The result is that if prisoners pursue their own self-interest, both are likely to confess, and end up doing a total of 10 years of jail time between them. But if the two prisoners had cooperated by both remaining silent, they would only have had to serve a total of four years of jail time between them. If the two prisoners can work out some way of cooperating so that neither one will confess, they will both be better off than if they each follow their own individual self-interest, which in this case leads straight into longer jail terms.

THE OLIGOPOLY VERSION OF THE PRISONER'S DILEMMA

duopoly: An oligopoly with only two firms.

The members of an oligopoly can face a prisoner's dilemma, too. If each of the oligopolists cooperates in holding down output, then high monopoly profits are possible. But each oligopolist must worry that while it is holding down output, other firms are taking advantage raising output and earning higher profits. Exhibit 12-5 shows the prisoner's dilemma for a two-firm oligopoly—known as a **duopoly**. If Firms A and B both agree to hold down output, they are acting together as a monopoly and will each earn $1,000 in profits. But can the two firms trust each other? Consider the situation of Firm A. If A thinks that B will cheat on their agreement and increase output, then A will increase output too, because

Exhibit 12-6 A Kinked Demand Curve

Consider a member firm in an oligopoly cartel that is supposed to produce a quantity of 10,000 and sell at a price of $500. The other members of the cartel can encourage this firm to honor its commitments by acting so that the firm perceives a kinked demand curve. If the oligopolist attempts to expand output and reduce price slightly, other firms also cut prices immediately—so if the firm expands output to 11,000, the price per unit falls dramatically, to $300. On the other side, if the oligopoly attempts to raise its price, other firms will not do so, so if the firm raises its price to $550, its sales decline sharply to 5,000. Thus, the members of a cartel can discipline each other to stick to the pre-agreed levels of quantity and price through a strategy of matching all price cuts but not matching any price increases.

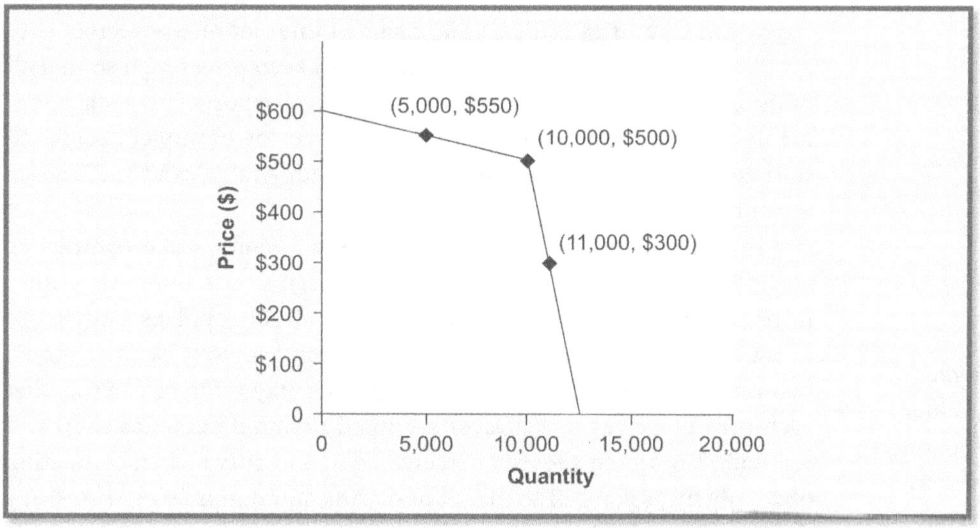

The kinked demand curve in this case is also creating a tacit collusion outcome.

for A the profit of $400 when both firms increase output (the bottom right-hand choice in the table) is better than a profit of only $200 if A keeps output low and B raises output (the upper right-hand choice in the table). But if A thinks that B will cooperate by holding down output, then A may seize the opportunity to earn higher profits by raising output. After all, if B is going to hold down output, then A can earn $1,500 in profits by expanding output (the bottom left-hand choice in the table) compared with only $1,000 by holding down output as well (the upper left-hand choice in the table). Thus, firm A will reason that it makes sense to expand output if B holds down output and that it also makes sense to expand output if B raises output. Again, B faces a parallel set of decisions. The result of this prisoner's dilemma is often that even though A and B could make the highest combined profits by cooperating in producing a lower level of output and acting like a monopolist, the two firms may well end up in a situation where they each increase output and earning only $400 each in profits.

HOW TO ENFORCE COOPERATION

How can parties who find themselves in a prisoner's dilemma situation avoid the undesired outcome and cooperate with each other? The way out of a prisoner's dilemma is to find a way to penalize those who do not cooperate. For example, prisoners who confess to the police and cause others to be convicted may face verbal and physical abuse from other criminals. Given that one oligopoly can't physically beat up another oligopoly, firms that find themselves in a prisoner's dilemma may try to seek other alternatives to create pressure for members to keep output down and prices up.

Perhaps the easiest approach for colluding oligopolists, you might imagine, would be to sign a contract with each other that they will hold output low and keep prices high. But if a group of U.S. companies signed such a contract, it would be illegal. Certain international organizations, like the nations that are members of the Organization of Petroleum Exporting Countries (OPEC), have signed international agreements to act like a monopoly, hold down output, and keep prices high so that all of the countries can make high profits from oil exports. But such agreements are not legally enforceable. If Nigeria, for example, decides to start cutting prices and selling more oil, Saudi Arabia can't sue Nigeria in court and force it to stop.

kinked demand curve: A perceived demand curve that arises when competing oligopoly firms commit to match price cuts, but not price increases.

Because oligopolists cannot sign a legally enforceable contract to act like a monopoly, the firms may instead keep close tabs on what other firms are producing and charging. Alternatively, oligopolists may choose to act in a way that generates pressure on each firm to stick to its agreed quantity of output. For example, oligopolists may act in such a way that each firm perceives that it faces a **kinked demand curve**, as shown in Exhibit 12-6, which shows a perceived demand curve when competing oligopoly firms commit to match price cuts, but not price increases. Say that an oligopoly airline has agreed with the rest of a cartel to provide a quantity of 10,000 seats on the New York-to-Los Angeles route, at a price of $500. This choice is right at the kink in the firm's perceived demand curve. The reason that the firm perceives a kink in its demand curve is because of how the other oligopolists react to changes in prices. If the oligopoly decides to produce more and cut its price, other oligopolists will immediately match any price cuts—and therefore, a lower price brings very little increase in quantity sold. For example, if the firm cuts price to $300, it will only be able to sell 11,000 seats. However, if the airline seeks to raise prices, the other oligopolists will not raise their prices, and so the firm that raised prices will lose a considerable share of sales. For example, if the firm raises its price to $550, its sales drop to 5,000 seats sold. Thus, if oligopolists always match price cuts by other firms in the cartel, but don't match price increases, then none of the oligopolists will have any incentive to change prices. This strategy can work like a silent form of cooperation, in which the cartel successfully manages to hold down output, increase price, and share a monopoly level of profits even without any legally enforceable agreement.

Many real-world oligopolies, prodded by economic changes, legal and political pressures, and the egos of their top executives, go through episodes of cooperation and competition. If oligopolies could sustain cooperation with each other on output and pricing, they can earn profits as if they were a single monopoly. But each firm in an oligopoly has an incentive to produce more and grab a bigger share of the overall market, and when oligopoly firms start behaving in this way, the market outcome in terms of prices and quantity can be similar to that of a highly competitive market.

Trade-offs of Imperfect Competition

Competition has many faces. For example, perfect competition displays both productive and allocative efficiency; that is, products are produced at the lowest possible average cost and the social benefits of products as measured by willingness to pay for them are balanced against the marginal cost of producing these products. But in the real world, perfect competition is rare. Firms in some industries are close to perfect competition, in the sense that they produce very similar products and must accept a market price as given. But very few markets for goods and services would meet the literal definition of perfect competition—that is, many firms selling near-identical products so that no firm can raise its price by even a penny.

Monopolistic competition among firms with differentiated products is probably the single most common form of competition in the U.S. economy. It provides useful incentives for innovation, as firms seek to earn profits in the short-run, while entry assures that firms do not earn profits in the long run. However, monopolistically competitive firms do not produce at the lowest point on their average cost curves. In addition, the endless search to impress consumers through product differentiation may lead to excessive social expenses on advertising and marketing.

Oligopoly and monopoly are well-known, too. When oligopolies and monopolies result from patented innovations or from taking advantage of economies of scale to produce at low average cost, they may provide considerable benefit to consumers. But monopolies and oligopolies often try to earn sustained profits over long periods of time by holding down output and increasing price. They typically do not produce at the minimum of their average cost curves. Because they lack vibrant competition, even though oligopolies at least have some competitors, they may lack incentives to provide innovative products and high quality service.

The task of public policy with regard to competition is to sort through these multiple realities, attempting to encourage firm behavior that is beneficial to the broader society and to discourage firm behavior that only adds to the profits of a few large companies with no corresponding benefit to consumers. The next chapter will discuss the delicate judgments that go into this task.

EDITOR'S NOTE

Three Types of Cartels with Examples

By David Moglen

1. Explicit and Overt Cartels

Explicit collusion means firms in the industry have an agreement to cooperate.

Overt collusion means that not only is there an agreement, but the consumers and general public have information on the agreement available to them.

Examples

OPEC, DeBeers, Sports Leagues (NFL, NHL, and NBA have partial antitrust exemptions, MLB has total antitrust exemption).[1]

2. Explicit and Covert Cartels[2]

Covert collusion means the price fixing/ quantity restricting agreement exists, but it was drawn up in secret between the firms. Not only does the public not know of the agreement (collusive behavior is illegal in the U.S.) but any strategic planning and meetings had to be done secretly. Hint: if there is a successful court case (antitrust prosecution) against a cartel, resulting in penalties, you can bet that cartel is one of explicit and covert collusion.

Examples

Note—in all examples, not all of the firms involved are necessarily listed here.

Vitamin Industry: Roche, BASF, and Sommer paid hundreds of millions in fines for price fixing.

Chocolate: Cadbury, Hershey's, Nestle, and Mars been fined for their price fixing cartel

Lysine: The market for the agricultural chemical was cartelized by Archer Daniels Midland (ADM) and Ajinomoto.

Dynamic Random Access Memory (DRAM) chips: Ten chipmakers paid hundreds of millions in fines for price fixing including: Samsung, Infineon, Hitachi, Toshiba, Mitsubishi, and NEC Electronics. US chip maker Micron Technology alerted authorities to the price fixing cartel and therefore escaped a fine.

Perfume: Companies/brands fined for price fixing include: LVMH (Louis Vuitton Moet Hennessy), L'Oréal, Chanel, Clinique, Estée Lauder, Shiseido, Procter & Gamble

LCD Panels: AU Optronics and LG

Air Cargo: numerous airlines colluded

Software engineers labor market: The Justice Department focused on Adobe, Apple, Google, Intel, Intuit, Lucasfilm and Pixar, but others were involved including Dell, IBM, eBay and Microsoft, to Comcast, Clear Channel, and Dreamworks.[3]

E-Books: Apple set up the cartel to prevent E-books from becoming too cheap, organizing all the major publishers in the US market, those being Penguin Group USA, Simon & Schuster, Harper Collins, Macmillan, and Hachette.[4]

LIBOR benchmark interest rates Cartel: Banks colluding to fix interest rates included Barclays, Deutsche Bank, RBS, Société Générale, Citigroup and JP Morgan. [5]

Car parts: Over 20 companies colluded including Denso, Yazaki Corp., and Bridgestone.

1 http://www.post-gazette.com/business/legal/2011/02/14/Antitrust-law-looms-over-sports-contracts-analysis/stories/201102140219

2 http://www.economist.com/news/business/21599799-trustbusters-have-got-better-detecting-cartels-and-bolder-punishing-them-incentives

3 http://pando.com/2014/03/22/revealed-apple-and-googles-wage-fixing-cartel-involved-dozens-more-companies-over-one-million-employees/

4 http://www.cnet.com/news/apple-e-book-trial-how-the-case-has-unfolded-so-far/

5 http://www.theguardian.com/business/2013/dec/04/banks-rate-rigging-libor-euribor-rbs-citigroup-jpmorgan

Railroad construction: Alstom and Siemens.

Auction houses: Sotheby's and Christie's.[6]

3. Tacit Collusion

Firms in the industry recognize, without communicating with each other, that it is in their mutual interest to reach the cooperative outcome. Profits are maximized in the industry when output is restricted, and firms may on their own engage in this strategic behavior with only tacit (literally, quiet) agreement. All of these examples are, intrinsically, alleged cartels.

Examples

Big Oil: Exxon-Mobil, Chevron-Texaco, BP/Arco, Conoco-Phillips, Royal Dutch Shell

Cereal: Post, General Mills, Kellogg's, Quaker

Bank monthly ATM fees: Chase, Bank of America, Wells Fargo

Airline tickets: see kinked demand curve in Exhibit 12-6.

6 http://www.theguardian.com/uk/2002/apr/20/andrewosborn

IN-CLASS PROJECT

OPEC's Reckless Ploy

Directions:

Recommended allocation of questions to groups: All groups do question 2, and you are told by the teacher if you are one of the following three group numbers: Group 1, Group 3, or Group 4. Your group number identifies the additional question you should answer. For example, group 4 will do question 4 in addition to question 2 that everyone is answering.

1. Explain, separately, how OPEC's action described in the article will affect supply in the market for oil, and why these changes will have an expected effect of "delaying if not derailing" the recovery. In other words, how will the shift in the oil market end up impacting markets for many other industries (you could give as examples two or three industries that will be affected or two or three ways many industries are likely to be affected by the shift in the oil market).

2.
   - Why is OPEC regarded as a "cartel," what are the effects of the presence of a cartel in the oil market, and what is meant by cartel members "cheating"?
   - Why do they have an incentive to do so and why has cheating been minimal?
   - In what ways does this current scenario of cartel members adhering closely to quotas have both economic and non-economic origins? (Alternative to last two sub-questions—on economic vs. non-economic causes—give reasons for adhering to quotas for these specific countries mentioned in the article: Indonesia, Venezuela, and Iraq.)

3. How does Saudi Arabia differ from the other OPEC members, and what position does this give it in the world oil market? Explain how Iraq's future oil exports affect Saudi Arabia's position.

4. From the perspective of a Multinational Corporation supplying oil to international consumers, explain the effect OPEC's recent move has on drilling projects in non-OPEC countries. What effect do these projects in places like Russia and Mexico have on expectations of future prices, and how would the expectations affect current market demand?

*5. Why would there be some expectation that OPEC's recent action may result in not only "reducing OPEC's market share and, ironically, reducing its long-term ability to control the global oil market," but reducing their OPEC's hold on the global *energy* market? Focus on changes in consumer behavior and energy producers' technology.

OPEC'S RECKLESS PLOY

By Thorsten Fischer

Septepmber 29, 2003

OPEC is flexing its muscles for now. However, once Iraq's oil exporting capabilities are back on line, OPEC's ability to manipulate global oil supplies, and thus, prices will require Iraq's participation.

With its latest decision to cut production quotas by 900,000 barrels per day or roughly 3.5%, the cartel has abandoned all pretenses that its interest is anything other than maximizing its own members' revenues. The cartel's reckless actions debunk the myth that OPEC is concerned about stable energy prices and adequate supplies. OPEC's mission is to extract as high as possible a price from oil importing nations.

OPEC's announcement came at a time when commercial crude oil stocks are critically low in the U.S. and throughout the industrialized world, and when the price for the basket of seven crudes is well within OPEC's target band.

Worse, OPEC decided to cut quotas as the U.S. economy is still in a fragile state, nursing a recovery that has yet to show that it is self-sustaining. In the end, the increase in revenues for OPEC will translate into the loss of disposable income and ultimately purchasing power in the U.S., potentially delaying if not derailing the nascent recovery. Moreover, without the U.S. economy leading the way, the global economy will remain in the doldrums as well. Thus, it is no exaggeration to suggest that OPEC risks the destruction of billions of dollars in economic growth for the sake of its own narrow interests.

The damage OPEC may be causing is real. The surprise move to cut quotas caused crude oil prices to rise markedly. The front month contract for the North American benchmark West Texas Intermediate jumped by more than $1 per barrel, and while prices have eased somewhat, crude defended most of these gains. On Thursday, the price for the basket of seven crudes jumped to $26.47.

Given OPEC's decision, it is useful to understand what might have prompted the cartel to disregard the West's interests so blatantly. To start with, current production estimates suggest that OPEC is adhering closely to official quotas with minimal excess supply, which is a departure from the usual cheating. The main reason is that many countries have no spare capacity and Venezuela and Indonesia have failed to even reach the targets assigned to them under the quota system.

In the case of Venezuela, production is well below its official quota because the Caribbean nation's state-controlled oil industry is in disrepair following the debilitating strike at state-owned PdVSA earlier in the year. Unrest and instability in Indonesia have likewise taken a toll on that country's oil industry.

Thus, OPEC's adherence to quotas is not so much due to new found discipline, but to the fact that some member countries are incapable of taking advantage of the prevailing higher prices.

The unfortunate position in which most OPEC member countries find themselves in has strengthened Saudi Arabia's position within the cartel. Saudi Arabia is the only member country with significant spare capacity, and therefore is able to pursue profit maximization without fear of excess production by other cartel members. Thus, Saudi Arabia is in the comfortable position of a monopolist, able to set quantity without any regard for a subsequent breakdown in cartel discipline, which could ultimately lead to a collapse in prices. It is not a stretch to conclude that OPEC's decision has been put forward by its most powerful member.

OPEC's strategy will pay for OPEC in the short term. A cut in output has already led to higher prices and OPEC stands to collect the windfall. However, OPEC's short-sightedness may come back to hurt the cartel. Higher oil prices, if they delay the global economic rebound, will also reduce consumption of crude oil, possibly reducing total revenue for the cartel. Moreover, high crude prices will stimulate production in countries outside OPEC, thereby reducing OPEC's market share and, ironically, reducing its long-term ability to control the global oil market.

This is already happening as the prolonged period of high crude prices has led to a pickup in drilling activity in the former Soviet Union, Mexico and the North Sea. The additional supplies, anticipated to materialize later this year and early next, prevented an even sharper increase in crude oil prices after OPEC's announcement.

While the additional production from non-OPEC sources is welcome news for oil importing countries, the big prize is Iraq. This is because OPEC's future hinges on its ability to discipline producers outside the cartel. Possession of the vast oilfields in the Middle East allows Saudi Arabia and other Gulf nations to threaten other producers with flooding global oil markets, bringing about a collapse in prices that would render most of the activity outside the Middle East unprofitable due to the immense difference in lifting costs.

The ability to generate extra capacity at low marginal costs already dampens investment outside OPEC, ensuring that OPEC maintains some control of global oil markets. Therefore, Saudi Arabia and other members of OPEC have a big stake in bringing Iraq back into the cartel. While Iraq's oil industry will contribute little to the global crude oil market until at least the spring of 2004, it has the potential to reshape the entire global petroleum market.

Representatives of the coalition should keep this in mind when planning for Iraq's future. Iraq will play an important role in determining our future energy costs, and may well determine the very existence of OPEC.

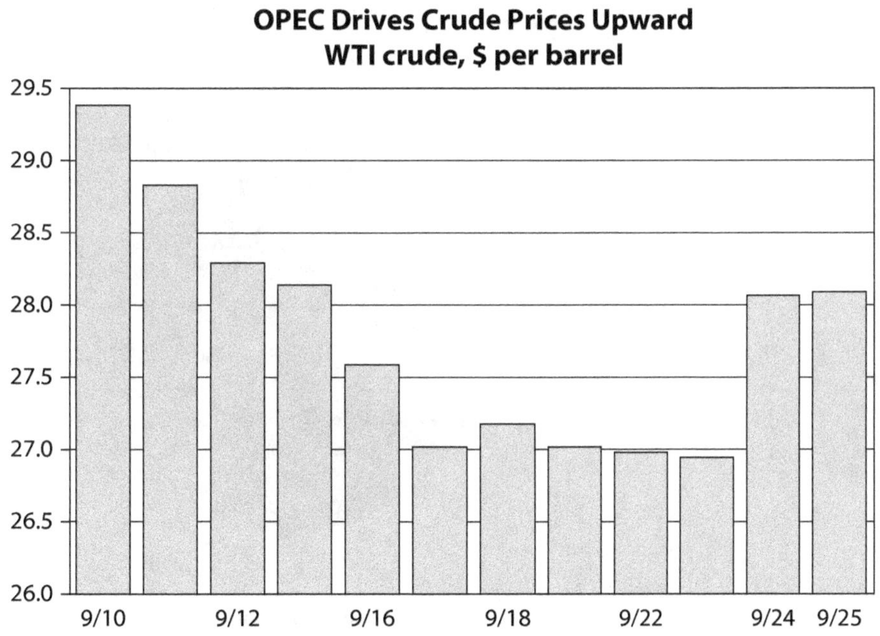

Table 1. Percentage of Sales for Four Largest Firms in Selected U.S. Retail Industries

Industry (NAICS code)	1992	1997	2002	2007
Food & beverage stores (445)	15.4	18.3	28.2	27.7
Health & personal care stores (446)	24.7	39.1	45.7	54.4
General merchandise stores (452)	47.3	55.9	65.6	73.2
Supermarkets (44511)	18.0	20.8	32.5	32.0
Book stores (451211)	41.3	54.1	65.6	71.0
Computer & software stores (443120)	26.2	34.9	52.5	73.1

Notes: The transition to the NAICS system means that 1992 cannot be strictly compared to later years (see Chart 1). However, the above industries were matched using "NAICS Concordances" provided by the U.S. Census Bureau.
Source: "Economic Census," 1992, 1997, 2002, and 2007, American FactFinder (U.S. Census Bureau, 2011).

Nielsen SoundScan reported that the big four accounted for 81.87% of the US music market in 2005:[21]

- Universal Music Group (USA based) — 31.71%
- Sony Music Entertainment (USA based) — 25.61%
- Independent labels — 18.13%
- Warner Music Group (USA based) — 15%
- EMI Group (UK based) — 9.55%

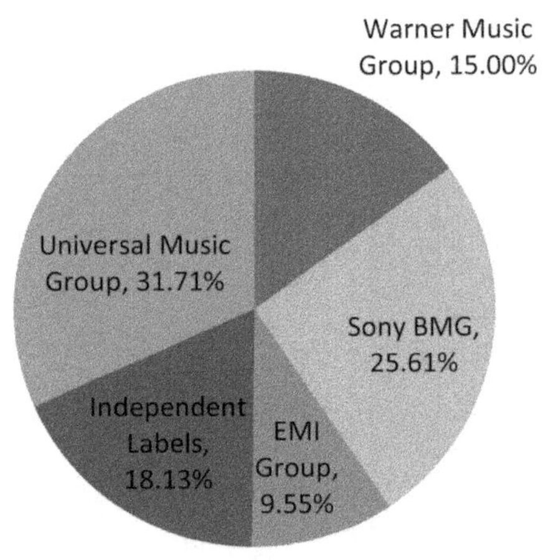

Source: (URL: http://en.wikipedia.org/wiki/Music_industry)

Key Concepts and Summary

1. An **oligopoly** is a situation where a few firms sell most or all of the goods in a market.
2. Oligopolists would earn their highest profits if they can band together as a **cartel** and act like a monopolist by reducing output and raising price. But since each member of the oligopoly can benefit individually from expanding output, such collusion often breaks down—especially since explicit collusion is illegal.
3. The **prisoner's dilemma** is an example of **game theory**. It shows how, in certain situations, all sides can benefit from cooperative behavior rather than self-interested behavior. However, the challenge for parties is to encourage cooperative behavior.
4. Competition has many faces. Perfect competition has powerful incentives for efficiency, flexibility, and responsiveness. But the profits to be derived from imperfect competition encourage variety and innovation, whether in the form of monopolistic competition, monopoly, or oligopoly. Moreover, there may be cases like natural monopoly where a monopolist or an oligopoly can produce at a lower price than competition.

Vocabulary Terms

Duopoly
Cartel
Collusion
Competitive fringe
Covert
Explicit collusion
Game theory
Oligopoly
OPEC
Overt
Price fixing
Tacit collusion

Review Questions

1. Will the firms in an oligopoly act more like a monopoly or more like competitors? Briefly explain.
2. What is a cartel?
3. What is collusion?
4. Does each individual in a prisoner's dilemma benefit more from cooperation or from pursuing self-interest? Explain briefly.
5. What is game theory?
6. Compare the advantages of perfect competition with those of monopolistic competition, and oligopoly.

CHAPTER 13

Monopolistic Competition and Product Differentiation

13 Monopolistic Competition and Product Differentiation

By Timothy Taylor

Perfect competition and monopoly stand at opposite ends of the spectrum of competition. A perfectly competitive market involves many firms selling identical products, who must all act as price-takers in the face of the competition. Monopoly arises when a single firm sells a product for which there are no close substitutes. But what about the in-between cases?

Many markets feature a large number of competing firms, but the products that they sell are not identical. In 2010, the Mall of America in Minnesota, the largest shopping mall in the United States, had 24 stores that sold women's "ready-to-wear" clothing (like Ann Taylor and Coldwater Creek), another 50 stores that sold clothing for both men and women (like Banana Republic, J. Crew, and Nordstrom's), plus 14 more stores that sold women's specialty clothing (like Motherhood Maternity and Victoria's Secret). These clothing stores, competing to sell similar but not identical products, engage in what economists call monopolistic competition. Other markets feature a small number of competing firms, which is called an oligopoly. One example of an oligopoly is Boeing and Airbus, the two major firms in the world that manufacture large passenger aircraft. Another example is the Coca-Cola Company and PepsiCo, Incorporated, the two firms that dominate sales in the U.S. soft drink market.

This chapter begins with a discussion of how monopolistic competition arises, and how monopolistically competitive firms will choose their profit-maximizing level of quantity and output. As the name "monopolistic competition" implies, a firm's decisions in this setting will in certain ways resemble monopoly and in other ways resemble perfect competition. Since a monopolistically competitive firm is not selling an identical product to other firms, it has a sort of mini-monopoly; for example, clothing stores in the Mall of America can have a monopoly on some of the specific brand names of clothing that they sell. However, monopolistic competitors must also expect a process of entry and exit, like perfectly competitive firms, so they cannot earn higher-than-normal profits in the long run. The chapter then turns to a discussion of oligopoly firms, which face two conflicting temptations. On one side, oligopoly firms will wish to cooperate as if they were a single monopoly, to make their decisions about the price to charge and quantity to produce accordingly, and then to divide up the monopoly profits. On the other side, each oligopoly firm acting individually may seek to gain profits by expanding its levels of output and cutting prices. Thus, the behavior of oligopoly firms can also take on elements both of monopoly and of perfect competition.

Monopolistic Competition

monopolistic competition: Many firms competing to sell similar but differentiated products.

Monopolistic competition involves many firms competing against each other, but selling products that are distinctive in some way. Examples include stores that sell different styles of clothing; restaurants or grocery stores that sell different kinds of food; and even products like golf balls or beer that that may be at least somewhat similar in fact, but differ in public perception because of advertising and brand names. When products are distinctive, each firm has a mini-monopoly on its particular style or flavor or brand name. However, firms producing such products must also compete with other styles and flavors and brand names. The term "monopolistic competition" captures this mixture of mini-monopoly and tough competition.

DIFFERENTIATED PRODUCTS

A firm can try to make its products different from those of its competitors in several ways: physical aspects of the product, location from which the product is sold, intangible aspects of the product, and perceptions of the product. Products that are distinctive in one of these ways are called **differentiated products**.

differentiated products: Products that are distinctive in a particular way.

Physical aspects of a product include all the phrases you hear in advertisements: unbreakable bottle, nonstick surface, freezer-to-microwave, non-shrink, extra spicy, newly redesigned for your comfort, and many others. The location of a firm can also create a difference between producers. For example, a gas station located at a heavily traveled intersection can probably sell more gas, because more cars drive by that corner. A supplier to an automobile manufacturer may find that it is an advantage to locate close to the car factory. Intangible aspects can differentiate a product, too. Some intangible aspects may be promises like a guarantee of satisfaction or money back, a reputation for high quality, services like free delivery, or offering a loan to purchase the product.

Finally, product differentiation may occur in the minds of buyers. For example, many people couldn't tell the difference in taste between common varieties of beer or cigarettes if they were blindfolded, but because of past habits and advertising, they have strong preferences for certain brands. Advertising can play a role in shaping these intangible preferences.

The concept of differentiated products is closely related to the degree of variety that is available. If everyone in the economy wore only blue jeans, ate only white bread, and drank only tap water, then the markets for clothing, food and drink would be much closer to perfectly

Exhibit 13-1 Perceived Demand for Firms in Different Competitive Settings

(a) Perfect competitor: Perceived demand as a price taker. If a perfectly competitive firm raises its price, the quantity demanded of its product falls to zero.

(b) Monopoly: Perceived demand is market demand. If a monopoly or a monopolistic competitor raises their prices, the quantity demanded will decline.

(c) Monopolistic competitor: Perceived demand is not a price taker but does take competitors into account. However, the decline in quantity demanded will be larger for a monopolistically competitive firm, because such a firm has competitors offering close substitutes for its products, which a monopolist does not.

competitive. The variety of styles, flavors, locations, and characteristics creates product differentiation and monopolistic competition.

PERCEIVED DEMAND FOR A MONOPOLISTIC COMPETITOR

A monopolistically competitive firm perceives a demand for its goods that is an intermediate case between monopoly and competition. Exhibit 13-1 offers a reminder that the demand curve as perceived by a perfectly competitive firm is flat, because the perfectly competitive firm can sell any quantity it wishes at the prevailing market price. In contrast, the demand curve as perceived by a monopolist is the market demand curve, since a monopolist is the only firm in the market.

The demand curve as perceived by a *monopolistic competitor* is not flat, but rather downward-sloping, which means that the monopolistic competitor can raise its price without losing all of its customers. However, the demand curve as perceived by the monopolistic competitor is flatter than the demand curve perceived by a monopolist. If a monopolist raises its price, some consumers will choose not to purchase its product—but they will then need to buy a completely different product. However, when a monopolistic competitor raises its price, some consumers will choose not to purchase the product at all but others will choose to buy a similar product from another firm. If a monopolistic competitor raises its price, it will not lose as many customers as would a perfectly competitive firm, but it will lose more customers than would a monopoly that raised its prices.

At a glance, the demand curves faced by a monopoly and by a monopolistic competitor look similar—that is, they both slope down. But

Golf Balls and Product Differentiation

The U.S. Golf Association runs a laboratory that tests 20,000 golf balls a year. There are strict rules for what makes a golf ball legal. The weight of a golf ball cannot exceed 1.620 ounces and its diameter cannot be less than 1.680 inches (which is a weight of 45.93 grams and 42.67 millimeters, in case you were wondering). The balls are also tested by being hit at different speeds. For example, the distance test involves having a mechanical golfer hit the ball with a titanium driver and a swing speed of 120 miles per hour. As the testing center explains: "The USGA system then uses an array of sensors that accurately measure the flight of a golf ball during a short, indoor trajectory from a ball launcher. From this flight data, a computer calculates the lift and drag forces that are generated by the speed, spin, and dimple pattern of the ball. . . . The distance limit is 317 yards."

Over 1800 golf balls made by more than 100 companies meet the USGA standards. The balls do differ in various ways, like the pattern of dimples on the ball, the types of plastic used on the cover and in the cores, and so on. But since all balls need to conform to the USGA tests, they are much more alike than different.

However, retail sales of golf balls are about $500 million per year, which means that a lot of large companies have a powerful incentive to persuade players that golf balls are highly differentiated and that it makes a huge difference which one you choose. Sure, Tiger Woods can tell the difference. But for the average duffer who plays a few times a summer—and who loses a lot of golf balls in the woods and the lake and needs to buy new ones—most golf balls are pretty much indistinguishable.

the underlying economic meaning of these perceived demand curves is different, because a monopolist faces the market demand curve and a monopolistic competitor does not.

HOW A MONOPOLISTIC COMPETITOR CHOOSES PRICE AND QUANTITY

The monopolistically competitive firm decides on its profit-maximizing quantity and price in much the same way as a monopolist. A monopolistic competitor, like a monopolist, faces a downward-sloping demand curve, and so it will choose some combination of price and quantity along its perceived demand curve.

As an example of a profit-maximizing monopolistic competitor, consider the Authentic Chinese Pizza store, which serves pizza with cheese, sweet and sour sauce, and your choice of vegetables and meats. Although Authentic Chinese Pizza must compete against other pizza businesses and restaurants, it has a differentiated product. The firm's perceived demand curve is downward sloping, as shown in the first two columns of the table in Exhibit 13-2 and on the graph. The combinations of price and quantity at each point on the demand curve can be multiplied to calculate the total revenue that the firm would receive, which is shown in the third column. The fourth column, marginal revenue, is calculated as the change in total revenue divided by the change in quantity. The final columns of the table show total cost, marginal cost, and average cost. As always, marginal cost is calculated by dividing the change in total cost by the change in quantity, while average cost is calculated by dividing total cost by quantity.

The process by which a monopolistic competitor chooses its profit-maximizing quantity and price resembles very closely how a monopoly makes these decisions, and can be summed up in the same three-step

Exhibit 13-2 How a Profit-Maximizing Monopolistic Competitor Decides What Price to Charge

Step 1: The monopolistically competitive firm determines the profit-maximizing quantity of output by applying the rule MR = MC. In this case, the profit-maximizing output is 40.

Step 2: The firm then decides how much to charge for this quantity by looking at its perceived demand curve. The vertical line up through a quantity of 40 hits the perceived demand curve at a price of $16.

Step 3: The firm calculates total revenue, total cost, and profit. Total revenue is the rectangle with quantity on the horizontal axis and price on the vertical axis. Total cost is the rectangle with quantity on the horizontal axis and average cost on the vertical axis. Profit is total revenue of $640 minus total cost of $580, or $60, which is the shaded area in the diagram.

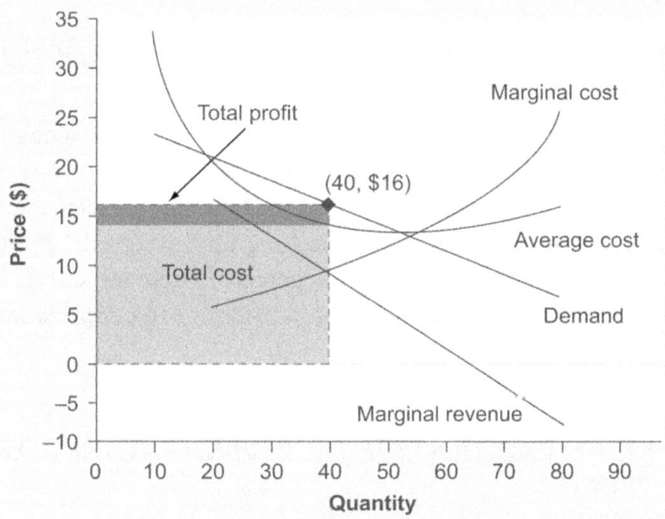

Quantity	Price	Total Revenue	Marginal Revenue	Total Cost	Marginal Cost	Average Cost
10	$23	$230	—	$340	—	$34
20	$20	$400	17	$400	6	$20
30	$18	$540	14	$480	8	$16
40	$16	$640	10	$580	10	$14½
50	$14	$700	6	$700	12	$14
60	$12	$720	2	$840	14	$14
70	$10	$700	–2	$1,020	18	$14 4/7
80	$8	$640	–6	$1,280	26	$16

process in which the firm: (1) selects the profit-maximizing quantity to produce; (2) decides what price to charge; (3) determines total revenue, total cost, and profit.

STEP 1: THE MONOPOLISTIC COMPETITOR DETERMINES ITS PROFIT-MAXIMIZING LEVEL OF OUTPUT

The Authentic Chinese Pizza company firm will determine the profit-maximizing quantity to produce by considering its marginal revenues and marginal costs. If the firm is producing at a quantity of output where marginal revenue exceeds marginal cost, then the firm should keep expanding production, because each marginal unit is adding to profit by bringing in more revenue than its cost. In this way, the firm will produce up to the quantity where MR = MC. If the firm is producing at a quantity where marginal costs exceed marginal revenue, then each marginal unit is costing more than the revenue it brings in, and the firm will increase its profits by reducing the quantity of output. In this example, MR and MC intersect at a quantity of 40, which is the profit-maximizing level of output for the firm.

STEP 2: THE MONOPOLISTIC COMPETITOR DECIDES WHAT PRICE TO CHARGE

When the firm has determined its profit-maximizing quantity of output, it can then look to its perceived demand curve to find out that what it can charge for that quantity of output. In graphical terms, this process can be shown as a vertical line reaching up through the profit-maximizing quantity until it hits the firms perceived demand curve. For Authentic Chinese Pizza, it should charge a price of $16 per pizza for a quantity of 40.

STEP 3: CALCULATE TOTAL REVENUE, TOTAL COST, AND PROFIT

At a quantity of 40, the price of $16 lies above the average cost curve, so the firm is making economic profits. From the table, at an output of 40, the firm's total revenue is $640 and its total cost are $580, so profits are $60. In Exhibit 13-2, the firm's total revenues are the rectangle with the quantity of 40 on the horizontal axis and the price of $16 on the vertical axis. The firm's total costs are the smaller rectangle with the same quantity of 40 on the horizontal axis but the average cost of $14.50 on the vertical axis. Profits are total revenues minus total costs, which is the shaded area above the average cost curve.

Although the process by which a monopolistic competitor makes decisions about quantity and price is similar to the way in which a monopolist makes such decisions, two differences are worth remembering. First, although both a monopolist and a monopolistic competitor face downward-sloping demand curves, the monopolist's perceived demand curve is the market demand curve, while the perceived demand curve for a monopolistic competitor is based on the extent of its product differentiation and how many competitors it faces. Second, a monopolist is surrounded by barriers to entry and need not fear entry, but a monopolistic competitor who earns profits must expect the entry of firms with similar, if differentiated, products.

MONOPOLISTIC COMPETITORS AND ENTRY

If one monopolistic competitor earns abnormally high profits, other firms will be tempted to enter the market. A gas station with a great location must worry that other gas stations might open across the street or down the road—and perhaps the new gas stations will also sell coffee or have a carwash or some other attraction for customers to drop by. A successful restaurant with a unique barbecue sauce must be concerned that other restaurants will try to copy the sauce and offer their own unique recipes, too. A laundry detergent with a great reputation for quality must be concerned that other competitors may seek to build their own reputations.

The entry of other firms into the same general market (like gas or restaurants or detergent) shifts the demand curve perceived by a monopolistically competitive firm. As more firms enter the market, the quantity demanded at a given price for any particular firm will decline, and the firm's perceived demand curve will shift to the left. As a firm's perceived demand curve shifts to the left, its marginal revenue curve will shift to the left, too. The shift in marginal revenue will change the profit-maximizing quantity that the firm chooses to produce, since marginal revenue will then equal marginal cost at a different point.

Exhibit 13-3a shows a situation where a monopolistic competitor was earning a profit with its original perceived demand curve D_0. The intersection of the marginal revenue curve MR_0 and marginal cost curve MC occurs at a quantity Q_0, which is associated on the demand curve at point T with price P_0. The combination of price P_0 and quantity Q_0 lies above the average cost curve, which shows that the firm is earning profits. However, after entry occurred, the firm's perceived demand curve shifts to the left from D_0 to D_1, and the associated marginal revenue curve shifts from MR_0 to MR_1. The new quantity of profit-maximizing output is Q_1, because the intersection of the MR_1 and MC now occurs at point U. Moving vertically up from that quantity, the optimal price/quantity choice on the demand curve occurs at point V where the firm's perceived demand curve touches the average cost curve. When price is equal to average cost, economic profits are zero. Thus, although a monopolistically competitive firm may earn abnormally high profits in the short term, the process of entry will drive those profits down to zero in the long run. Exhibit 13-3b shows the reverse situation, where a monopolistically competitive firm is originally earning losses. The intersection of the original marginal revenue curve MR_0 and the marginal cost curve MC occurs at point W, which represents a quantity of Q_0. The price associated with Q_0 at point X on the original demand curve D_0 is P_0. This price lies below the average cost curve, which shows that the firm is making losses. In the short run, firms may continue to produce, as long as the price covers their average variable costs (which for simplicity are not shown in this exhibit). But in the long run, some firms will

Exhibit 13-3 Monopolistic Competition, Entry and Exit

(a) The intersection of the original marginal revenue curve MR_0 and the marginal cost curve occurs at point S. Thus, the profit-maximizing quantity is Q_0 and the corresponding price on demand curve D_0 is P_0. The firm is earning a profit, because price is above average cost. Profit encourages entry. As a result, the firm's perceived demand curve shifts from D_0 to D_1, and the marginal revenue curve shifts from MR_0 to MR_1. The new intersection of MR_1 and MC is at U. Now, the profit-maximizing quantity is Q_1 and the profit-maximizing price on demand curve D_1 is P_1. Point V sits right on the average cost curve, so because of entry, the firm is now earning zero profit.

(b) The intersection of the original marginal revenue curve MR_0 and the marginal cost curve occurs at point W. Thus, the profit-maximizing quantity is Q_0 and the corresponding price on demand curve D_0 is P_0. The firm is suffering a loss, because price is below average cost. Loss leads to exit. As a result, the firm's perceived demand curve shifts from D_0 to D_1, and its marginal revenue curve shifts from MR_0 to MR_1. The new intersection of MR_1 and MC is at Y. Now, the profit-maximizing quantity is Q_1 and the profit-maximizing price on demand curve D_1 is P_1. Point Z sits right on the average cost curve, so because of exit, the firm is now earning zero profit.

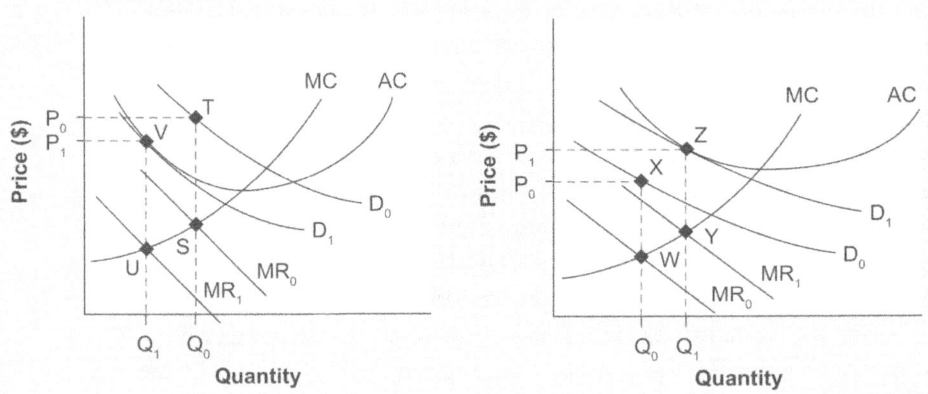

(a) Profit induces entry; shift to zero profit

(b) Loss induces exit; shift to zero profit

exit. When exit occurs, the perceived demand curve for the remaining firms will shift to the right from D_0 to D_1, because at any given price, each of the remaining firms will be able to sell a larger quantity. The associated marginal revenue curve will shift from MR_0 to MR_1. The new intersection of MR_1 and MC occurs at point Y, which is at the quantity Q_1. The price P_1 associated with Q_1 on the firm's new perceived demand curve D_1 now sits right on the average cost curve at point Z. Through the process of exit, the monopolistically competitive firms remaining in the market are no longer earning losses, but instead are earning zero economic profits.

Monopolistic competitors can make a profit or loss in the short-run, but in the long run, entry and exit will drive these firms toward a zero-profit outcome. However, the zero-profit outcome in monopolistic competition looks different from the zero-profit outcome in perfect

The combinations of price and quantity at each point on a firm's perceived demand curve are used to calculate total revenue for each combination of price and quantity. This information on total revenue is then used to calculate marginal revenue, which is the change in total revenue divided by the change in quantity. A change in perceived demand will change total revenue at every quantity of output and in turn, the change in total revenue will shift marginal revenue at each quantity of output. Thus, when entry occurs in a monopolistically competitive industry, the perceived demand curve for each firm will shift to the left, because a smaller quantity will be demanded at any given price—and the marginal revenue curve will shift to the left as well. Conversely, exit causes the perceived demand curve for a monopolistically competitive firm to shift to the right and the corresponding marginal revenue curve shift right, too.

Clearing It Up

Why Does a Shift in Perceived Demand Cause a Shift in Marginal Revenue?

Advertising and Monopolistic Competition

The U.S. economy was spending about $270 billion per year on advertising in the late 2000s. Roughly one-seventh of this was newspaper advertising, one-third was television advertising, and one-fifth was direct mail. The rest was divided up between magazines, radio, telephone directory yellow pages, billboards, Internet ads, and some other miscellaneous sources. More than 400,000 workers held jobs in the advertising industry.

Advertising is all about explaining to people, or making people believe, that the products of one firm are differentiated from the products of another firm. In the framework of monopolistic competition, there are two ways to conceive of how advertising works: either advertising causes a firm's perceived demand curve to become more inelastic (that is, it causes the perceived demand curve to become steeper); or advertising causes demand for the firm's product to increase (that is, it causes the firm's perceived demand curve to shift to the right). In either case, a successful advertising campaign may allow a firm to sell either a greater quantity or to charge a higher price, or both, and thus increase its profits.

However, economists and business owners have also long suspected that much of the advertising may only offset other advertising. Famous economist A. C. Pigou wrote all the way back in 1920:

> It may happen that expenditures on advertisement made by competing monopolists [that is, what we now call monopolistic competitors] will simply neutralise one another, and leave the industrial position exactly as it would have been if neither had expended anything. For, clearly, if each of two rivals makes equal efforts to attract the favour of the public away from the other, the total result is the same as it would have been if neither had made any effort at all.

competition in several ways relating both to efficiency and to variety in the market.

MONOPOLISTIC COMPETITION AND EFFICIENCY

The long-term result of entry and exit in a perfectly competitive market is that all firms end up selling at the price level determined by the lowest point on the average cost curve. This outcome is why perfect competition displays productive efficiency; goods are being produced at the lowest possible average cost. However, in monopolistic competition, the end result of entry and exist is that firms end up with a price that lies on the downward-sloping portion of the average cost curve, not at the very bottom of the AC curve. Thus, monopolistic competition will not be productively efficient.

In a perfectly competitive market, each firm produces at a quantity where price is set equal to marginal cost, both in the short run and in the long run. This outcome is why perfect competition displays allocative efficiency; the social benefits of additional production, as measured by the price that people are willing to pay, are in balance with the marginal costs to society of that production. But in a monopolistically competitive market, the rule for maximizing profit is to set MR = MC—and price is higher than marginal revenue, not equal to it. When P > MC, which is the outcome in a monopolistically competitive market, the benefits to society of providing additional quantity as measured by the price that people are willing to pay exceeds the marginal costs to society of producing those units. Thus, a monopolistically competitive industry will produce a lower quantity of a good and charge a higher price for it than would a perfectly competitive industry.

A monopolistically competitive industry does not display productive and allocative efficiency in either the short-run, when firms are making profits and losses, nor in the long-run, when firms are earning zero profits.

THE BENEFITS OF VARIETY AND PRODUCT DIFFERENTIATION

Even though monopolistic competition does not provide productive efficiency or allocative efficiency, it has benefits of its own. Product differentiation is based on variety and innovation. Many people would prefer to live in an economy with many kinds of clothes and foods and car styles, not a world of perfect competition where everyone will always wear blue jeans and white shirts, eat only spaghetti with plain red sauce, and drive an identical model of car. Many people would prefer to live in an economy where firms are struggling to figure out ways of attracting customers by methods like friendlier service, free delivery, guarantees of quality, variations on existing products, and a better shopping experience.

Economists have struggled, with only partial success, to address the question of whether a market-oriented economy produces the optimal amount of variety. Critics of market-oriented economies argue that society doesn't really need dozens of different athletic shoes or breakfast cereals or automobiles. They argue that much of the cost of creating such a high degree of product differentiation, and then of advertising and marketing this differentiation, is socially wasteful—that is, most people would be just as happy with a smaller range of differentiated products produced and sold at a lower price. Defenders of a market-oriented economy respond that if people don't want to buy differentiated products or highly advertised brand names, no one is forcing them to do so. Moreover, they argue that consumers benefit substantially when firms seek short-term profits by providing differentiated products. This controversy may never be fully resolved, in part because deciding on the optimal amount of variety is very difficult, and in part because the two sides often place different values on what variety means for consumers.

Equilibrium with Monopolistic Competition

By Joseph Stiglitz and Carl Walsh

In most industries there is some but limited competition. The number of firms in the industry is perhaps the most important determinant of the nature of competition. If the fixed costs are large-not so large as to result in a single firm but sufficiently large that there are only two, three, or four firms-then the outcome is a natural oligopoly. We discuss oligopolies in the next section; we here consider the case in which fixed costs are relatively small-sufficiently small that the numerous firms drive profits to zero, but sufficiently large that only a single firm produces any single product. However, because these products are *close* but not perfect substitutes, each firm faces a downward-sloping demand curve. This is the case of monopolistic competition, first analyzed by Edward Chamberlin of Harvard University in 1933.

The market for women's dress shoes is one such industry. The producers include Steve Madden, Bass, Diverse, Naturalizer, Bruno Magli, Nine West, and many more. No two firms produce exactly the same shoes, but the shoes made by the different companies are close substitutes. Each producer faces a downward-sloping demand curve, but each firm has a small portion of the overall market. The market for fine pens provides another example. There are many manufacturers (Montblanc, Parker, Cross, Aurora, Pelikan, etc.). Each produces pens that differ from the pens of the others, each has a downward-sloping demand curve, and each is small relative to the total market for fine writing instruments.

Figure 13-4 illustrates a market in which there is monopolistic competition. Assume initially that all firms are charging the same price, say p_1. If one firm were to charge a slightly lower price, it would steal some customers away from other businesses. And if it should raise its price above that of its rivals, it would lose customers to them. Each firm assumes that the prices charged by other firms will remain unchanged as it changes its price or the quantity it produces. The demand curve facing each firm is thus the one shown in the figure.

In deciding how much to produce, the firm sets marginal revenue equal to marginal cost. The market equilibrium is (p_1, Q_1), with marginal revenue equaling marginal cost. In the equilibrium depicted in the figure, price exceeds average costs. One can think of this situation as a sort of minimonopoly, where each firm has a monopoly on its own brand name or its own store location.

But if existing firms are earning monopoly profits, there is an incentive for new competitors to enter the market until profits are driven to zero, as in the perfectly competitive model. *This is the vital distinction between monopolies and firms in monopolistic competition.* In both cases, firms face downward-sloping demand curves. In both cases, they set marginal revenue equal to marginal cost. But monopolistic competition

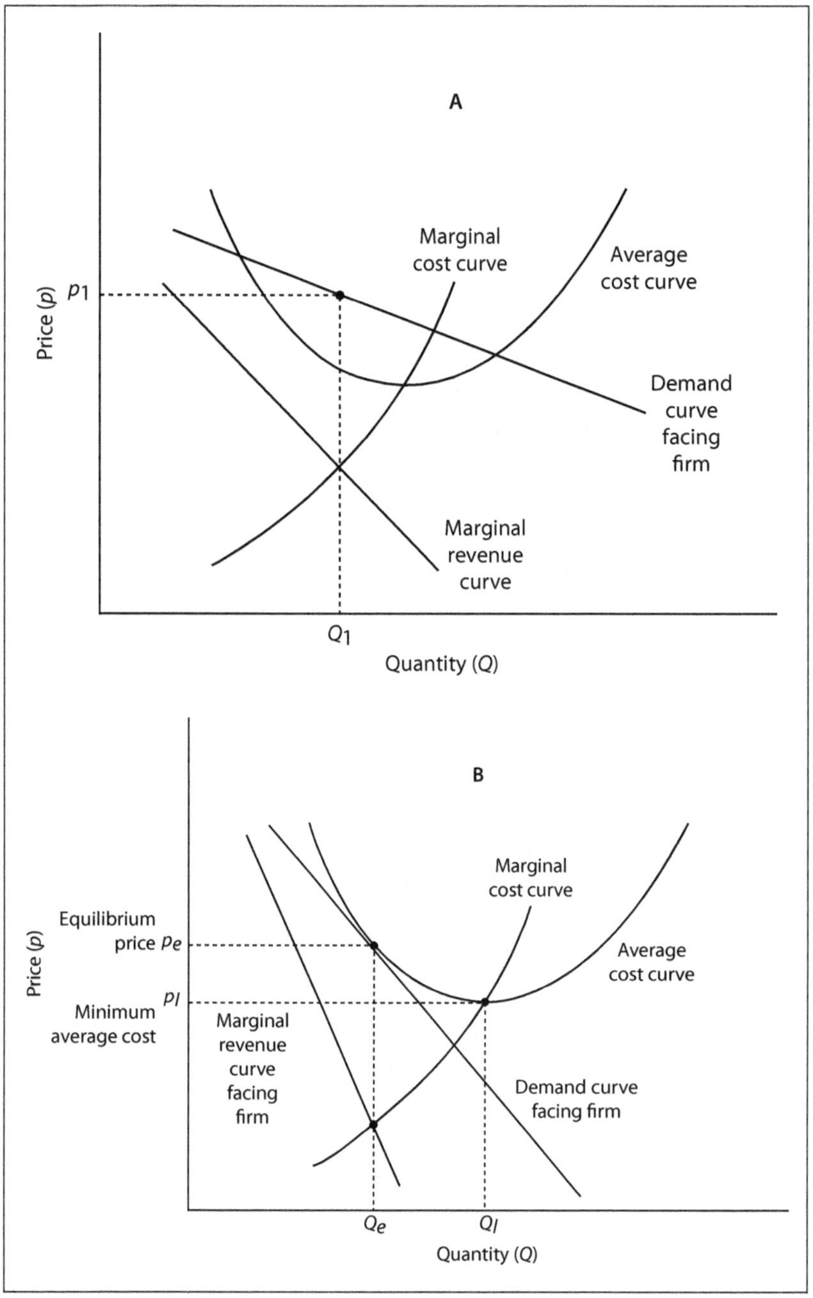

FIGURE 13-4

Profit Maximizing for a Monopolistic Competitor

A monopolistic competitor chooses the quantity it will produce by setting marginal revenue equal to marginal cost (Q_1), and then selling that quantity for the price given on its demand curve (p_1). In panel A, the price charged is above average cost, and the monopolistic competitor is making a profit, enticing other firms to enter the market. As firms enter, the share of the market demand of each firm is reduced, and the demand curve facing each firm shifts to the left. Entry continues until the demand curve just touches the average cost curve (panel B). When the firm produces the quantity Q_e, it just breaks even; there is no incentive for either entry or exit.

raises no barriers to entry, which continues so long as profits are positive. As firms enter, each firm's share of the industry demand is reduced. The demand curve of each firm thus shifts to the left, as depicted in panel B. This process continues until the demand curve just touches the average cost curve, at point (p_e, Q_e), where profits are zero.

The figure also shows the firm's marginal revenue and margin cost curves. As we have said, the firm sets its marginal revenue equal to its marginal cost. This equality occurs at exactly the level of output at which the demand curve is tangent to the average cost curve. At any other point, average costs exceed price, so profits are negative. Only at this point are profits zero. Accordingly, this is the profit-maximizing output.

The monopolistic competition equilibrium has some interesting characteristics. Note that in equilibrium, price and average costs exceed the minimum average costs at which the goods could be produced. *Less is produced at a higher price.* But there is a trade-off here. Whereas in the perfectly competitive market every product was a perfect substitute for every other one, the world of monopolistic competition offers variety in the products available. People value variety and are willing to pay a higher price to obtain it. Thus, that goods are sold at a price above the minimum average cost does not necessarily indicate that the economy is inefficient.

Exhibit 13-5 The Spectrum of Competition
Firms face different competitive situations. At one extreme—perfect competition—many firms are all trying to sell identical products. At the other extreme—monopoly—only one firm is selling a product, and this firm faces no competition. Monopolistic competition and oligopoly fall between the extremes of perfect competition and monopoly. Monopolistic competition is a situation with many firms selling similar, but not identical, products. Oligopoly is a situation with few firms that sell identical or similar products.

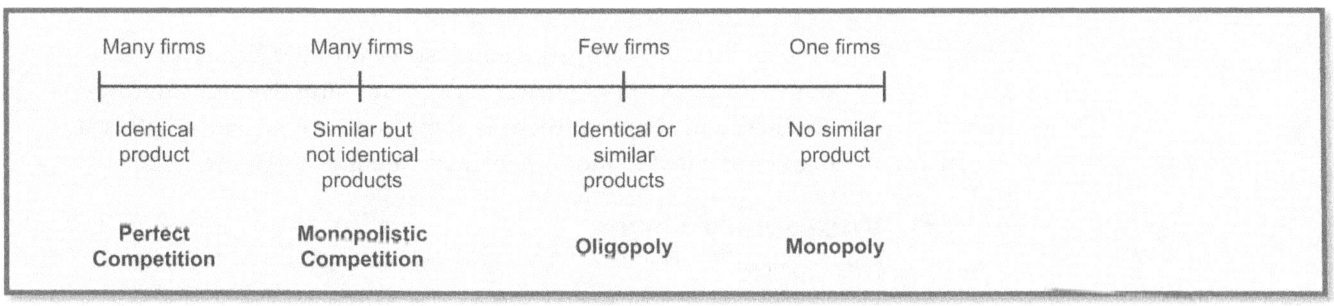

Key Concepts and Summary

1. Monopolistic competition refers to a market where many firms sell differentiated products. Differentiated products can arise from characteristics of the good or service, location from which the product is sold, intangible aspects of the product, and perceptions of the product.
2. The perceived demand curve for a monopolistically competitive firm is downward sloping, which shows that unlike a perfectly competitive firm with its flat perceived demand curve, a monopolistically competitive firm is not a price-taker, but rather chooses a combination of price and quantity. However, the perceived demand curve for a monopolistic competitor is flatter than the perceived demand curve for a monopolist, because if a monopolistic competitor

raises price it will lose some customers to the competition, while a monopolist does not face any competition.

3. A profit-maximizing monopolistic competitor will seek out the quantity where marginal revenue is equal to marginal cost. The monopolistic competitor will produce that level of output and charge the price that it can as determined by the market demand curve.
4. If the firms in a monopolistically competitive industry are earning economic profits, the industry will attract entry until profits are driven down to zero in the long run. If the firms in a monopolistically competitive industry are suffering losses, then the industry will experience exit until profits are driven up to zero in the long run.
5. A monopolistically competitive firm is not productively efficient, because it does not produce at the minimum of its average cost curve. A monopolistically competitive firm is not allocatively efficient, because it does not produce where P = MC, but instead produces where P > MC. Thus, a monopolistically competitive firm will tend to produce a lower quantity at a higher cost and to charge a higher price than a perfectly competitive firm.
6. Monopolistically competitive industries do offer benefits to consumers in the form of greater variety and incentives for improved products and services. There is some controversy over whether a market-oriented economy generates "too much" variety.

Vocabulary Terms

Differentiated

Equilibrium with monopolistic competition

Monopolistic competition

Spectrum of competition

Review Questions

1. What are some of the ways a product can be differentiated?
2. What is the relationship between product differentiation and monopolistic competition?
3. How is the perceived demand curve for a monopolistically competitive firm different from the perceived demand curve for a perfectly competitive firm?
4. How is the perceived demand curve for a monopolistically competitive firm different from the perceived demand curve for a monopoly?
5. How does a monopolistic competitor choose its profit-maximizing quantity of output?
6. When a monopolistic competitor has chosen its profit-maximizing quantity of output, how does it determine what price to charge?
7. How can a monopolistic competitor tell whether the price it is charging will cause the firm to earn profits or losses?
8. If the firms in a monopolistically competitive firm are earning economic profits in the short run, would you expect them to continue doing so in the long run? Why?

9. If the firms in a monopolistically competitive firm are earning losses in the short run, would you expect them to continue doing so in the long run? Why?
10. Is a monopolistically competitive firm productively efficient? Why or why not?
11. Is a monopolistically competitive firm allocatively efficient? Why or why not?
12. Explain how a monopolistically competitive industry may offer benefits of variety.

CHAPTER 14
The Financial Crisis

14 The Financial Crisis

By David Moglen

The Subprime Mortgage Meltdown and Credit Crunch

INTRODUCTION: THE CREDIT CRUNCH AS AN OBJECT LESSON FOR FINANCIAL CRISES

Rather than brief summaries of an array of historical financial crises, the focus of this chapter is an in-depth presentation of the Banking Crisis that is still ravaging the economy at this writing in 2010 through the ongoing Credit Crunch, widespread foreclosures, and lingering effects of the directly induced Great Recession which officially began in December of 2007. This approach will cover key elements of the Credit Crunch, and provide insights into financial crises past and future and how they impact your life. You will have to do your own research to learn about other crashes, but if you do, you may find their similarities to this crisis are striking. You could investigate the gas price bubble of 2004-2008, the Electric Power (Enron) bubble in California of 2000-2001, the Dot-Com Internet bubble of the 1990's, the Savings & Loan crisis of the 1980's, the bursting of the Japanese Real Estate bubble of the 1990's, or the Asian Financial Crises in that same decade.

The Myth of the Subprime Borrower

subprime (sbpram)—**adj.** (of a loan) made to a borrower with a poor credit rating, usually at a high rate of interest. *Collins English Dictionary*

> In finance, **subprime lending** (also referred to as **near-prime**, **non-prime**, and **second-chance lending**) means making loans that are in the riskiest category of consumer loans and are typically sold in a separate market from prime loans. The standards for determining risk categories refer to the size of the loan, "traditional" or "nontraditional" structure of the loan, borrower credit rating, ratio of borrower debt to income or assets, ratio of loan to value or collateral, and documentation provided on those loans which do not meet Fannie Mae or Freddie Mac underwriting guidelines for prime mortgages (are "non-conforming"). Although there is no single, standard definition, in the United States subprime loans are usually classified

UNLOCKING THE MYSTERIES

The Subprime Crisis

By David Moglen

It's not surprising that people who were offered mortgage loans with low payments, often by brokers who concealed the downside of the loans and the real estate market, would go ahead and sign such a mortgage to own a home and live the American Dream. A valid debate can occur regarding how much of the blame for the mortgage meltdown should be placed on these subprime borrowers. But regardless how much we decide the borrower is to blame, it should not hide the fact that a loan requires not only a borrower but also a willing lender. So why did lenders make these loans which in many cases had little to no chance of being fully repaid?

To illustrate the point, just look at what mortgage brokers and lenders like CountryWide and Ameriquist called their loans: No-Doc loans (no documentation of the borrower's qualifications), Liar loans, NINA loans (No Income, No Assets), or NINJA loans (No Income, No Job, No Assets). Now, if you were going to lend someone $300,000 for thirty years, wouldn't you want to verify some things about that borrower first? Sure, you would want to check their income, assets, job stability, and credit rating. It's called "underwriting." In the entire history of mortgage lending, anyone offering such a loan would carefully check all these vital statistics before they hand over the $300,000 loan. But, quite suddenly, banks, mortgage brokers, and lenders stopped checking this information and simply made the loan. Something quite fundamental changed in the mortgage industry.

That something was the rapid, widespread introduction of private- label MBS (Mortgage Backed Securities), also called CDOs (Collateralized Debt Obligations). This mortgage derivative is simply a large number of subprime loans pooled together, and then sliced into thousands of shares to be sold off to investors. While in the basic concept of a mortgage loan, a lender has to diligently screen all borrowers to be quite certain that person can and will repay this loan for the next thirty years, now we have entered a whole new world. Why should the lender care if the borrower can't pay for thirty years? The lender doesn't need to care if the borrower will fail to make even the first month's mortgage payment. The lender is repaid the entire loan amount (let's say, $300,000) immediately, or within a week of making the loan. That's because the loan was sold (by way of an Investment Bank's CDO) to an investor. It's their problem now. The only incentive for banks, lenders, and brokers became to earn fees and create volumes of subprime loans. Just make as many of these bad loans as possible, because the full amount is repaid immediately as far as they are concerned.

This goes towards explaining why about 55-61% of all subprime borrowers actually qualified for a "prime rate" loan, with lower interest rates, fees and risk. A large percentage of subprime borrowers actually had credit that wasn't that bad, and qualified for a lower-priced loan they could have paid off, but instead they were steered by brokers into the subprime loan which they would not be able to pay off. Why? Because a high-interest rate loan looked better in the CDO than trying to sell investors a CDO with a low-interest prime rate loan for that same borrower.

And why did lenders provide loans to people with little to no chance of fully repaying such a treacherous loan? Because the derivative, the CDO, allowed lenders to have literally no skin in the game. They were repaid the whole entire loan amount not in thirty years, the way it's supposed to work, but by the end of the week.

Now, in this transaction where brokers and bankers have much more knowledge and information about the Real Estate market and the fine print in these subprime loans than the borrower, it is not surprising that the borrower winds up belly-up: bankrupt and in foreclosure. But why did the titans of Wall Street also find themselves on the bullet train to bankruptcy, what with all their access to the most sophisticated financial experts on the planet? To understand why even the most established investment banks, from Bear Stearns to Lehman Brothers, Citigroup to JP Morgan Chase all found themselves on a fast track to extinction (only to survive due to government bailouts, if at all), one must dis-aggregate, one must separate, the company from the individual people who ran it. Sure, these century-old companies were on the brink of bankruptcy, but the executives who should have known better probably did know better and they made off like bandits, made very wealthy by their firms as they retired with their golden parachutes and left their storied company to die or grab the life raft of a government bailout.

as those where the borrower has a FICO score below 640. Subprime lending encompasses a variety of credit types, including mortgages, auto loans, and credit cards. The term was popularized by the media during the "credit crunch" of 2007.[1]

A subprime loan has higher a interest rate over the life (the term) of the loan. That interest rate might start low, but will increase – causing monthly mortgage payments to skyrocket. This variable rate is referred to as the loan's rate "reset." Subprime loans regularly have fees such as prepayment penalties. It is generally the loan - not the borrower - that is classified as subprime.

The widespread public belief is that subprime loans are so obviously worse than the prime rate loans that well-qualified borrowers receive due to the subprime borrowers' poor credit rating. In one of the most shocking findings in the subprime crisis, several sources and researchers (given below) cite evidence that 55-61% of subprime borrowers qualified for the more affordable prime rate loan. Had the broker been incentivized or compelled to get them the best loan for which they qualified, millions of households in foreclosure would have had a much better chance of avoiding losing their homes.

One explanation of the broker incentives leading to such an outcome is the yield-spread premium explained in the CNN Money article in Group 2 of the In-Class Project.

> "In 2005, the peak year of the subprime boom, the study says that borrowers with such credit scores got more than half — 55% — of all subprime mortgages that were ultimately packaged into securities for sale to investors, as most subprime loans are. The study by First American LoanPerformance, a San Francisco research firm, says the proportion rose even higher by the end of 2006, to 61%. The figure was just 41% in 2000, according to the study. Even a significant number of borrowers with top-notch credit signed up for expensive subprime loans, the firm's analysis found." ("Subprime Debacle Traps Even Very Credit-Worthy" by Rick Brooks and Ruth Simon in the Wall Street Journal, December 3, 2007).[2]

> "Economic and housing experts have estimated that 55 percent of subprime borrowers qualified for a prime loan with lower interest rates and no resets in the first place." ("Majority of Minnesotans with Subprime Loans had 'Good' Credit" by Molly Priesmeyer in the Minnesota Independent, April 7, 2008).[3]

1 http://en.wikipedia.org/wiki/subprime_lending

2 http://online.wsj.com/article/NA_WSJ_PUB:SB119662974358911035.html

"It's estimated that fully 55% of current subprime borrowers — particularly African Americans and Latinos — could have qualified for a prime loan at better rates and with better terms in the first place. Had these borrowers not been offered faulty products destined to fail, the subprime meltdown would not be the massive debacle that it is." ("Relief or a raw deal?" by Paul Leonard in the LA Times, March 27, 2008).[4]

"**Yield-spread premiums** (Ed. Note: see 2nd article under Group 2 in the in-class Project at the end of this chapter re: YSPs) ...YSPs distort competitive market forces by creating a reverse competition effect with brokers incented to shop for the best deal for them, not the best deal for the borrower. YSPs not only encouraged the steering of subprime borrowers into more costly and riskier loans, but also the steering of prime credit borrowers into subprime loans. **It is estimated that up to 60% of subprime borrowers could have qualified for prime loans** (emphasis added) or loans through FHA, Fannie Mae, or Freddie Mac that would have given them interest rates that were lower by 3% or more. Steering borrowers into worse and riskier loans than those for which they qualify is intrinsically linked to the issue of YSPs. As noted previously, compensation based on the terms or conditions of a credit transaction places the interests of brokers and borrowers at odds. Due to an informational asymmetry inherent in the broker-borrower relationship, the practice of steering is on its face an unfair and deceptive practice." ("Advanced Notice of Proposed Rule-Making: Mortgage Acts and Practices" by The Center for Responsible Lending July 30, 2009).[5]

In addition to steering borrowers into unaffordable subprime loans when so many qualified for prime rate loans, borrower lawsuits allege that they were told their loan had a fixed rate when in fact it had a rate that would later increase. "McCollum's complaint alleges many of the same things cited in Bennett's suit: Countrywide told customers interest rates were fixed when they were adjustable, misrepresented the length of teaser rates and long-term higher rates."[6] ("Saying They Were Tricked, Borrowers Fight Back With Lawsuits" by John Pacenti in the Daily Business Review July 10, 2008)

Financial Crisis Timeline[7]

Don't feel like you need to know every detail from this timeline. Just try to get the main ideas about the events and actions taking place at the time, and any specifics your teacher mentions.

3 http://minnesotaindependent.com/3570/majority-of-minnesotans-with-subprime-loans-had-good-credit

4 http://www.latimes.com/business/investing/la-op-leonard-thornberg-27mar27,0,187810.story

5 http://www.ftc.gov/os/comments/map/542308-00048.pdf

6 http://www.law.com/jsp/article.jsp?id=1202422873307

November 12, 1999: Key Deregulation – the Gramm-Leach-Bliley Act (GLB), also known as the Financial Services Modernization Act (FSMA) overturns the 1933 Glass-Steagall Act (GSA). The GSA was a law to keep Wall Street firms and activities such as securitizing, gambling and speculating separate from Main Street firms and activities such as deposits and home loans. While the 1999 GLB Act tore down that firewall between Wall Street and Main Street, which stood to protect the latter from the former for 66 Depression-free years, it did leave intact the GSA's other creation, the FDIC.

December 21, 2000: Key Deregulation – the Commodity Futures Modernization Act of 2000 ensured that derivatives (including CDS) would not be regulated by any direct federal or state rules, which included the elimination of capital requirements, transparency, and preemption of state laws that prohibited derivatives transactions as gambling or otherwise illegal. Part of the CFMA included the "Enron Loophole" deregulation which helped enable Enron's electricity speculating that caused blackouts and Californians' electric bills to multiply in the summers of 2000 and 2001.

August 2007: The market for mortgage derivatives dries up and becomes illiquid, meaning almost no one will buy the CDOs. New CDOs cannot be issued since existing CDOs are of unknown value or sharply reduced values. So the huge volume of subprime loans that had been issued abruptly slows to a trickle. With no investors to sell mortgage derivatives comprised of subprime loans, there was no more reason for Wall Street to continue subprime lending.

Dec. 31, 2007: By the end of 2007, 1.3 million homes are in foreclosure proceedings

March 11, 2008: The Federal Reserve (the "Fed") makes an early foray into backing major investment banks in what ultimately would represent their lending, guaranteeing, or buying assets in amounts that total several trillion. Most of that was loaned or guaranteed against possible losses and never had to be spent, but the Fed has expanded its balance sheet by a few trillion, most of which it should recover. The Term Securities Lending Facility (TSLF) program started in 2008 committed up to $200 billion in T-bills in a temporary swap for mortgage securities.

March 16, 2008: JP Morgan Chase agrees to buy Bear Stearns, one of the half-dozen major Wall Street investment banks (founded1923) for about a billion dollars. The Fed provided a $29 billion loan to cover the deal. Bear Stearns collapsed when "hedge funds" it owned were heavily invested in suddenly illiquid (thus temporarily worthless) CDOs.

7 Some timeline information is from http://money.cnn.com/news/storysupplement/economy/bailouttracker/

UNLOCKING THE MYSTERIES

Financial Derivatives

By David Moglen

What are financial derivatives? A financial derivative is a *bet* that an underlying asset will go *up* or *down*.

The underlying asset involves real production, and a real asset in the real economy. In other words, the underlying asset is on the "Main Street" side. The derivative, on the other hand, is largely meant to aid the Main Street economic activity, but it is a financial product (or security), so it is on the "Wall Street" side.

For example, a potato farmer would like to get a high price for his crop when he brings his potatoes to market, but he knows there is some possibility that the market price of potatoes at the time he is ready to sell may be low. So to protect himself from making too little revenue, he buys a large number of Short Potato Futures Contracts, which, as you see above (in the "any commodity" row), are simply bets that the price per pound of Potatoes will fall. So if the bad scenario occurs, and the potato price is low, while his main business of selling potatoes will receive a dismally low amount of revenue, his bets that this was going to happen will pay off big time, putting his total revenue (and profit) at a reasonable level. If, on the other hand, the price of potatoes is high, then his main business of selling potatoes will make plenty of money, and he will not be too worried that his side bet (the Futures Contract) did not pay off.

This is called hedging. Our potato farmer has hedged his main business of selling potatoes by owning a large number of bets that the price of potatoes will fall. The Futures Contract, like all derivatives, is meant to aid activity on the Main Street side (a farmer is considered Main Street, not Wall Street).

Another example is that of company employees who typically have a lot of their personal investment portfolio in their company's stock. They own a lot of their own company's stock because that, in part, is how they are paid, and the stock they own for their company has restrictions preventing them from selling it for years. So, to protect their retirement portfolio from losing value, our company employee buys a lot of put options on their own company's stock. If the stock goes up, they are happy, even though their bet the stock would go down (the put option) is not worth anything. If, on the other hand, the stock falls in value, or the company even goes bankrupt (the stock price falls to zero) then at least they have this side bet (the put option) which will now be worth a lot of

Underlying Asset	The Derivative for that Asset is called:	To Bet it will go UP (+), one would buy a:	To Bet it will go DOWN (–), one would buy a:
Any Commodity, e.g., Rice, Sugar, Steel, Oil, Cotton, Milk, Electricity, etc.	The (oil) futures contract	Long (oil) futures contract	Short (oil) futures contract
Any economic indicator, e.g., the Interest Rate or a Currency	The (dollar) futures contract	Long (dollar) futures contract	Short (dollar) futures contract
Any Stock	Stock option	Call option	Put option
Subprime Loans	**Mortgage backed security (MBS)**	**MBS or Collateralized debt obligation (CDO)**	**Credit default swap (CDS) or short MBS**

money, so their retirement account is not completely financially destroyed.

This is another example of hedging, and exemplifies how the derivative aids activity on the Main Street side. Unlike "genuine hedgers" who buy the appropriate derivative to offset what they fear will happen to the underlying asset they need or sell for their Main Street business activities, "speculators" only buy the derivative and have no role in the real economy, Main Street underlying asset related to that financial derivative.

Visualize a dog wagging its tail. The dog is the Main Street side, the underlying asset, and the tail is the Wall Street side, the derivative. The activity on the Main Street side is supposed to dictate what happens with the derivative – the dog is supposed to wag the tail. That is what happens in our examples of hedging. But what often happens – some would say, what inevitably happens – is that at some point the tail wags the dog. Wall Street investors – speculators – buy or sell the derivative in overwhelming numbers, and the Main Street underlying asset is severely impacted.

This is what happened in the oil market. In 2008 when gasoline was over four dollars per gallon, oil analysts like Fadel Gheit and Antonia Juhasz, and hedge fund managers like Michael Masters (not to mention the airlines, oil refineries, and trucking companies who set up the web site www.StopOilSpeculationNow.com) provide evidence that 50% or more of the price you were paying at the pump for gasoline was caused by speculators running up the price of the Oil Futures Contract. A bubble in the derivative due to Wall Street Investment activity severely impacted Main Street: how much you paid for gas at the gas station.

Something similar happened in the mortgage market: the sudden emergence of massive trading in Collateralized Debt Obligations (CDOs) created a massive increase in banks making subprime mortgage loans. Then the sudden near-total unwillingness on the part of investors to buy any CDOs starting in August 2007 brought an immediate end to banks making any more subprime loans. The tail wagged the dog. The activity with the derivatives (the CDOs) almost completely dictated the Main Street activity for the underlying asset – both the sudden, widespread availability of these new subprime loans, and the even more sudden almost complete disappearance of subprime loans from the mortgage market.

Note that the terms CDO and MBS are often, and quite rightly, used interchangeably. But you should also be aware that when one says MBS or "mortgage securities," they could be referring either to CDOs or credit default swaps (CDS: insurance against the failure of subprime mortgage derivatives) so you have to pay attention to the context and may want to use the terms CDO or CDS *only*, in order to avoid confusion when describing the mortgage meltdown.

July 11, 2008: FDIC seizes and shuts down insolvent bank IndyMac, supplying $10 billion to cover insured depositors. It is one of the first of about 80-100 banks per year over the next three years that the FDIC seizes and shuts down before the bank completely plunges into bankruptcy.

July 30, 2008: Help For Homeowners Act housing bill authorizing up to $300 billion in loan guarantees for a selected group of borrowers, at lender's option. Predicted actual cost at the time: $68 billion. (See footnote #6) To date: $20 billion actually spent.

Sept. 7, 2008: Treasury takes ownership of the GSEs (founded 1938, privatized in 1969 and 1984), committing up to $200 billion to back up their losses and ensure Fannie and Freddie bondholders will be paid off.

Sept. 13, 2008: Lehman Brothers, a major investment bank (founded 1850) is bankrupt due to credit default swaps and subprime investments. It is the one example in this crisis where a "Too Big to Fail" firm actually was allowed to fail, and many or most analysts say that inaction accelerated and needlessly worsened the crisis.

Sept. 14, 2008: After having already acquired ailing subprime lender CountryWide, Bank of America doubles down and buys Merill Lynch (founded 1914) for $50 billion before their eminent collapse due to investments in mortgage securities. Merill Lynch simultaneously pays executives $3.6 billion in bonuses.

Sept. 16, 2008: The Fed takes ownership of the collapsing insurance giant AIG (founded 1919) as it buckled under the payout demands required as a major provider of credit-default swaps. The $85 billion backstop at the time was later increased, when combined with other programs, to guarantee up to $182 billion, of which $127.4 billion was actually spent.

Sept. 26, 2008: Washington Mutual (founded 1889) is acquired by JP Morgan for about two billion dollars, despite the major deposit-taking bank having net assets with a nominal value of $240 billion on paper. Again, bad mortgage investments were the cause. The sixth largest bank in the country, WaMu saw over $16 billion withdrawn by depositors over a ten day period, amounting to almost 10% of its deposits before the FDIC blew the whistle and shut it down.

Oct. 3, 2008: The Treasury's TARP (Troubled Asset Relief Program) passes into law and offers up to $700 Billion to buy toxic mortgage securities. About half of that would be actually spent.

Oct. 3, 2008: Wachovia (founded 1906), the fourth-largest bank holding company in the nation, is bought by Wells Fargo for $15.1 billion as mounting mortgage losses were forcing them into bankruptcy.

Oct. 14, 2008: Treasury announces that instead of buying toxic assets, the TARP funds will be used to buy new stock shares (equity) in all major banks. Buying or temporarily swapping safe assets for toxic mortgage derivatives is mostly left to the Fed.

Nov. 23, 2008: Treasury increases its investment in Citigroup to $45 billion, to own about a third of the company, and Fed and FDIC agree to cover up to 90% of $306 billion in potential losses (Citigroup itself is responsible for the first $29 billion in losses), although the government has not had to pay on any of that. Government's ownership of the firm decreases to 18% by August 2010.

Dec. 31, 2008: By the end of 2008, 2.3 million homes are in foreclosure proceedings

Feb 18, 2009: Making Home Affordable Program is launched, which includes four programs to help borrowers.[8] The primary vehicle is called the Home Affordable Modification Program through which qualified borrowers have mortgage payments reduced to 31% of their income. While still offering a loan modification at the lender's option, the program reverses the incentive some middlemen (called loan servicers) had to collect more fees by pursuing foreclosure. The program pays $500, $1000, and $1,500 amounts to the loan servicers, lenders, or investors who make the loan modification happen. Initially stated cost: up to $75 billion. Amount actually invested, loaned, or spent as of late 2009: $350 million.[9] Permanent loan modifications completed through the program as of April 2010: 300,000[10]

Dec. 31, 2009: By the end of 2009, 2.8 million homes are in foreclosure proceedings. 870,000 foreclosure were finalized and the homes repossessed, about the same number as in 2008.

July 1, 2010: In the first six moths of 2010, 1.7 million homes are in foreclosure proceedings. Banks have repossessed about 528,000 homes over the period.

As I implied at the start of this timeline, this is information for your reference and to deepen your understanding of the Subprime Crisis and Credit Crunch, not something you need to memorize in detail.

Nevertheless, if you feel this is getting to be a bit too much information or too many numbers, you can skip the next two sections and go straight to the In-Class Project and Discussion Question Sets at the end of this chapter. You already have read enough to complete those activities. If you are ready for more context, read the last two segments.

Fannie Mae and Freddie Mac

The commonly used nickname for the Federal National Mortgage Association is Fannie Mae and the nickname for the Federal Home Loan Mortgage Corporation is Freddie Mac.

The two mortgage giants (also referred to as the GSEs - government sponsored enterprises) started by the Federal Government with specific "charters" directions as to how to operate and parameters around the loans they can own or insure, now totaling about half of all US mortgages. In other words, they have unique regulations that do not apply to other private sector financial institutions. Fannie Mae and Freddie Mac were privatized, with their shares traded in the stock market until they were re-nationalized and taken over by the Federal Government in September of 2008. It was widely perceived that these two shareholder-owned

8 http://makinghomeaffordable.gov/about.html

9 http://bailout.propublica.org/programs/6-making-home-affordable

10 http://makinghomeaffordable.gov/pr_05172010.html

private sector firms retained the implicit backing of the government. The perception was that the government would rescue them if they got in trouble. Before their nationalization, July 30, 2008[11] legislation added some confirmation to this perception.

That law authorized "the government until the end of 2009, to lend them emergency money or buy" stock in Fannie and Freddie. Without specific limits, this unlimited cushion rendered them even more quasi-public in an attempt to shore up the dwindling investor confidence that had cost both GSEs the majority of their stock's share value. The Treasury worked out a deal to cover up to $200 Billion in Fannie and Freddie losses in return for 80% ownership of the two mortgage giants.[12]

This summary of the early history of Fannie Mae and Freddie Mac describes what mortgage lending was like before the GSEs existed.[13]

MORTGAGES IN THE DEPRESSION ERA

Fannie and Freddie are the products of an earlier and larger mortgage meltdown. During the Great Depression, 50% of borrowers were late or in default on their mortgages (sound familiar?) and banks became dangerously strapped for cash. So President Franklin D. Roosevelt and Congress created the Federal National Mortgage Association (Fannie Mae) in 1938. The agency's mission was to buy mortgages from lenders, providing liquidity that could be used to make more loans.

Fannie Mae's creation allowed lenders to loan money to low- and middle-income buyers who otherwise might not have been considered creditworthy. According to the St. Louis Federal Reserve,[14] mortgage lending before Fannie Mae was very different from the way it is done today. Lenders typically required 50% down payments. Moreover, they usually structured their home loans with short terms — terms as brief as five years, after which the borrower had to come up with a "balloon payment" for the remaining balance. As a result, homeownership was out of reach for most American households.

Fannie Mae and Freddie Mac's charters specify roles that they should take in promoting homeownership affordability. If your parents own their homes, chances are it's because of Fannie Mae that they were able to finance their purchases.

FREDDIE MAC: FANNIE MAE'S YOUNGER BROTHER

Fannie Mae grew so large over the years that in 1968, with the pressures of the Vietnam War straining the national budget, President Lyndon

11 http://money.cnn.com/2008/07/30/news/economy/housing_bill_bush/index.html?postversion=2008073010, and http://money.cnn.com/2008/07/26/news/economy/housing_bill_senate

12 http://money.cnn.com/2008/09/07/news/companies/fannie_freddie/index.htm?postversion=2008090711

13 http://library.hsh.com/articles/government-programs/fannie-mae-freddie-mac-and-you.html

Johnson took Fannie Mae's debt portfolio off the government's balance sheet. Fannie Mae was converted into a publicly traded company owned by investors. Two years later, the Federal Home Loan Mortgage Corporation (Freddie Mac) was launched, mainly to keep Fannie Mae from functioning as a monopoly. Freddie went public in 1989. Freddie Mac's guidelines and pricing structure are almost identical to Fannie Mae's.

Also note that the GSEs "went public," meaning they now were owned not by the government but by shareholders who own their publicly traded shares. In other words, Fannie Mae was privatized in 1969 as was Freddie Mac in 1984, and both were re-nationalized in 2008.

Standard & Poor's (S&P) is a U.S. financial services company with a 150-plus year history. An S&P study[15] shows only 4% of GSE loans outstanding in late 2009 were to borrowers with credit scores below 620. Their research also shows that even for the lowest credit score loans (under 620), the default rate is 13-16% in late 2009, deep into the mortgage crisis. This rate, while historically high, is far lower than the rates for private-label securitized subprime loans.

A Chicago Federal Reserve study[16] shows that, after controlling for credit scores and many other variables, GSE loans defaulted at lower rates than non-GSE loans. While Fannie and Freddie had 13-16% default rates for sub-620 borrowers, 40-60% of subprime loans held outside of the GSEs were in default, a number that only increases as this crisis goes on.

More specifically, the Chicago Fed study shows that from 2004-2006, Lender Processing Servicing data (a lending research service) indicates that less than 5% of subprime loans were purchased by the GSEs. A higher percentage in 2007 is largely due to the shutdown of the subprime market; so the portion that GSEs purchased became a third of all subprime loans purchased, but the total number of subprime loans being made had sharply fallen. While some of these statistics may be cherrypicked data based on the dates, the totality of the evidence shows that the GSEs at most enabled the crisis and were clearly not the sole cause.

Finally, in an article[17] for McClatchy Newspapers on October 12, 2008 headlined "Private sector loans, not Fannie or Freddie, triggered crisis," David Goldstein and Kevin G. Hall write: "More than 84 percent of the subprime mortgages in 2006 were issued by private lending institutions." And: "In 2005 and 2006, the private sector securitized almost two thirds of all U.S. mortgages, supplanting Fannie and Freddie, according to a number of specialty publications that track this data." And: "Fueled by low interest rates and cheap credit, home prices between 2001 and 2007 galloped beyond anything ever seen, and that fueled demand for mortgage-backed securities, the technical term for mortgages that are sold to a company, usually an investment bank, which then pools and sells them into the secondary mortgage market. About 70 percent of all

---

14 http://www.stlouisfed.org/publications/cb/articles/?id=797

15 http://www2.standardandpoors.com/spf/pdf/fixedincome/Housing_GSEs.pdf (see page 9, table 3)

16 http://papers.ssrn.com/sol13/papers.cfm?abstract_id=1406594

U.S. mortgages are in this secondary mortgage market, according to the Federal Reserve."

In essence, a major cause (many would argue, the main cause) of the mortgage crisis was mortgage securities, aka derivatives, in this case known as the MBS, CDOs, and CDS. Yet the GSEs were essentially giant securitizers. So isn't the whole thing their fault? The question then becomes, how exactly did GSE-based government assistance in the mortgage market, which began in 1938, cause a subprime bubble from 2003-2007 and subsequent financial meltdown from 2007 to the date of this writing in 2010?

Did Government Cause the Crisis?

It is insightful to include the reasoning that government intervention caused the subprime bubble and mortgage crisis. As expressed in the flagship conservative magazine, National Review, the GSEs are secondarily responsible but the primary fault is with the mortgage interest tax exemption and other misplaced tax incentives to own and/or "flip" properties.

The following is excerpted from the National Review Article, "The Committee to Reinflate the Bubble" by Kevin D. Williamson published June 8, 2009:[18]

> Policies that encourage and reward homeownership are deeply embedded into our government and financial institutions, from the mortgage-interest deduction to the FHA loan. It's a case of the best of intentions producing the worst of economics.
>
> Consider the case of the government-sponsored enterprises (GSEs), Fannie Mae and Freddie Mac, which are at the center of the current meltdown. The GSEs created a market for poorly assessed real-estate securities based on mortgages implicitly guaranteed by the U.S. government, but doing this made it easier and cheaper for people to get mortgages, so nobody much bothered. Their mission was encouraged, and sometimes distorted, by political forces left and right. There was tremendous political pressure from Barack Obama's community-organizing gang to get banks and institutions to loosen lending standards. The most frequently cited example of this is the Community Reinvestment Act, the effects of which probably have been overstated, but there is no denying that for a decade Barney Frank labored furiously against Republican efforts at tightening Fannie oversight. At the same time, tax-cutting Republicans zealously defended the mortgage-interest deduction, which did much to encourage interest-only loans during the boom — and added a new tax break, the capital-gains tax exemption for home sales, the effects of which are only now becoming clear.

17 http://www.mcclatchydc.com/2008/10/12/53802/private-sector-loans-not-fannie.html

18 http://nrd.nationalreview.com/article/?q=YjU3ZTIyYjI5MTRkNjRiYWVhNTkzODU2NjVIYTmyMjc=

> The Taxpayer Relief Act of 1997 might well have been called the House Flippers' Enabling Act, and it put a lot of money into the pockets of a lot of realtors: The law exempts most home sellers from paying capital-gains taxes on houses, without requiring them to invest the profits in new houses. It created what might be called a literal tax shelter: an investment you could live in while escaping the 20 percent tax on capital gains. When the dot-com bubble burst, the lure of tax-free real assets attracted a lot of investors looking to ride out market turbulence in the comfort of their new, highly leveraged homes. Republicans love a capital-gains tax cut, and they should, but creating special tax breaks for particular investments inevitably will warp the market. Predictably, capital gushed out of dot-bomb and into the housing bubble.
>
> The result was the sort of thing that should offend every conservative's inner Puritan: Buyers stopped calculating whether they could afford the house, and instead calculated whether they could afford the mortgage. The more daring buyers took out interest-only mortgages, placing a counterintuitive bet that buying a house they couldn't afford would make them rich enough to afford it. That bet was hedged up by what is probably the most popular item in the U.S. tax code: the mortgage-interest deduction. That made interest-only loans a sweet deal indeed for the investors with good timing, which set off a rodeo of speculation: borrow the whole nut, pay nothing but interest (which, thanks to the work of Alan Greenspan, might be less than rent would have run), get a huge income-tax benefit in return thanks to the mortgage-interest deduction, sell the house at a profit, and pay no taxes on the capital gain. Place a losing bet and you end up bankrupt or in foreclosure.

So certain misplaced tax incentives and the GSEs, Fannie Mae and Freddie Mac, were to blame for the bubble. There is some causality between Mr. Williamson's targets and the crisis, but it is limited and, more importantly, presents some vital questions about what exactly are the policy implications of this narrative?

Regarding the GSEs, recall from the section on Fannie Mae and Freddie Mac above that they bought a minority percent of subprime loans, made only a tiny percentage (4%) of their loans to people with very poor credit, and have a much lower loan default rate than loans made or owned by private banks and investors.

Additionally, the loans they did buy from private investment banks had agreements that if the loans are found to have fraudulent borrower information, the banks have to repurchase (buy back) these bad loans from the GSEs. So, as always, much depends on enforcement, which

---

19 http://topics.nytimes.com/top/news/business/columns/fair_game/index.html?scp=1-spot&sq=fair%20game&st=cse

in this case means how aggressively the court cases are prosecuted to force banks to make good on their repurchase obligations. "Fannie and Freddie require lenders or loan servicers to sign contracts requiring those firms to repurchase loans that don't meet certain standards relating to borrower incomes, job status or assets. Loans that were extended fraudulently, or deemed to have been predatory, are also candidates for buybacks."[19]

But if we accept for argument's sake that the GSEs were to blame, recall what life was like before the GSE (see the section on Fannie Mae and Freddie Mac). Borrowers faced five or ten years to pay the mortgage off, a fifty percent down payment, huge balloon payments, and a reality where middle-class homeownership is virtually nonexistent and impossible under those conditions. If the policy proposal is removing the GSEs from the picture, where are borrowers to turn? Williamson's promotion of "tightening Fannie oversight" – increasing regulation of the GSEs – seems to make more sense than calls for their total elimination.

Regarding the mortgage interest tax deduction, which allows homeowners to receive thousands of dollars in tax refunds for interest paid each year on their home loan, Williamson may be right that it played a role in the crisis. But the policy implication to eliminate this fundamental tax benefit for homeowners would face an uphill battle finding political support or passing legislatively, to put it mildly. The Taxpayer Relief Act of 1997 which he criticizes may be easier politically to do something about, and even repeal, but it is striking to hear a generally anti-tax magazine argue convincingly against these two tax cuts.

In response to the charge that government involvement caused the subprime mortgage meltdown, the financial crisis, and the great recession, one might say that one part of that statement is correct: the subprime mortgage meltdown, the financial crisis, and the great recession are inextricably intertwined in just that sequence of causation. GSE Critics like Tom Lamalfa could point to a number of problems with GSEs. Lamalfa writes, "Fannie and Freddie formed a duopsony (in the mortgage insurance market)...a market with only two buyers but many sellers." He adds that these GSEs "appear to be nationalizing the mortgage market," hinder Fed policy, create moral hazard, distort the mortgage market into excessive risk.[20] The premise that the GSEs (Government Sponsored Enterprises) Fannie Mae and Freddie Mac were the key (or even a key) cause of the crisis is a great deal less axiomatic. As covered earlier in this chapter, Fannie Mae has been doing what they do since 1933. Only after the deregulations of 1999 and 2000 dismantled the Glass-Steagall Act and deregulated derivatives did we have the explosion in private-label MBS (mortgage backed securities), CDOs (collateralized debt obligations) and the poisonous insurance contract, the CDS (credit default swaps). It seems much easier to link a problematic subprime market from 2003 to its collapse in 2007 (when

20 http://www.housingrisk.org/alan-greenspan-fannie-mae-and-freddie-mac/

the MBS market became illiquid in August of that year) to major changes in 1999 and 2000 than to a law from 1933.

GSE critics abound and their critiques persist. Fannie and Freddie had to be bailed out, they say. Doesn't that prove they were bankrupt? Bankrupt and causing the crisis are two very different designations. In what may be the definitive book on the Financial Crisis, Bethany McClain and Joe Nocera go to great lengths in their research and details to ascribe exacting blame to a wide array of culprits in their seminal tome, "All the Devils are Here." In their section on the GSE's, they make it clear they were late in following the private banks into subprime, having an almost nonexistent presence early in the subprime bubble and a minority stake much later, near the very end of the bubble cycle.

GSEs have been like a big giant MBS since their founding. But only when private investment banks got in the game did we have a crisis soon thereafter. In the words of Jeff Madrick and Frank Partnoy, "The GSEs did generate large losses, but their bad investments in housing loans followed rather than led the crisis; most of those investments involved purchases or guarantees made well after the subprime and housing bubbles had been expanded by private loans and were almost about to burst." They continue, "the subprimes the GSEs bought in these years (the 2000s) were from the safer triple-A tranches of basic mortgage-backed securities, i.e., the highest quality of groups of mortgages rated by their risk of default. The GSEs never bought the far riskier collateralized debt obligations (CDOs) that were also rated triple-A and were the main source of the financial crisis. (The triple-A classifications of some of those CDOs were conferred on them very dubiously by the credit-rating agencies, Standard & Poor's and Moody's.) It turned out that subprimes accounted for only 5 percent of the GSEs' ultimate losses."[21]

"In fact, the rate of delinquencies for all GSE securities in 2004 was 4.3 percent, compared to a delinquency rate in private industry of 15.1 percent of mortgages. In 2005, the GSE rate was 7.8 percent compared to 28.7 percent, and in 2006 and 2007, the rates reached 13.2 and 14.9 percent in the GSEs and 45.1 and 42.3 percent in the private market. None of these figures are cited in *Reckless Endangerment*. In fact, losses as a proportion of mortgages guaranteed or bought by the GSEs were far lower than in private industry."

Still, despite acknowledging that default rates in the GSE loan portfolios were lower than those of the more purely private sector lenders, critics still conclude that "We all know how this ended…in tragedy, a tragedy for about seven millions families and households, and counting, and a Great Recession for the country. House prices plummeted, unemployment soared and pain aplenty spread across the country, affecting a majority of Americans. Looking back on the evolution of the tragedy, all of the concerns and risks I pointed out to Mr. Greenspan in 2000 proved to play a role. The GSEs market structure was and is wrong, especially

---

21 http://www.nybooks.com/articles/archives/2011/oct/27/did-fannie-cause-disaster/

juxtaposed against a perfectly competitive market of thousands of lenders, small and large."

Finally, any mortgage that the GSEs would buy or insure came with a "mortgage-putback clauses" meaning if any part of the mortgage was obtained fraudulently, that private issuer had to buy the mortgage back from the GSEs if the GSE had bought it or cover the GSE for losses if the GSE had insured the loan. So it is largely a question of whether our legal system is going to function and make the banks buy back all the junk mortgages they cut-and pasted at Ameriquist and all the undocumented loans they made at CountryWide and numerous other lenders. The closest analog to that ideal manifesting in reality is the roughly $100 Billion in settlement costs that banks have already agreed to. Sure, firms may settle to avoid a frivolous lawsuits, but 100 Billion dollars is starting to talk about some real money. Clearly the banks thought they would be worse off if they went to court and had to really be swayed by the evidence of their culpability to settle for such a large and increasing amount.

At the risk of being too idealist, just imagine if mortgage brokers had a fiduciary duty to get the borrower the best loan they could instead of being paid a legalized kickback bribe known as the yield-spread premium by investment banks for putting the borrower into a far worse loan than that for which they qualified; about 33% to 55% of the borrowers would have avoided difficulty repaying according to various studies cited earlier in this chapter.

Summary

Many different groups (homeowners, brokers, banks, etc.) and even social phenomena (greed, groupthink, deregulation, etc.) had a hand in the subprime crisis which induced the Great Recession, the longest and deepest downturn since the Great Depression. If any of the links in this chain had acted more prudently, the catastrophe could have been lessened or even stopped cold in its evolution. To most people, grasping the significance of this crisis requires new concepts and buzzwords like derivatives, mortgage securities, credit default swaps, and securitization. For economists, this crisis provides countless case studies of old concepts like bubbles, moral hazard, and too big to fail. It became a sounding board and test case for policy prescription. Forward-thinking economists like Robert Shiller and Dean Baker saw the crisis coming and proposed policies to proactively deal with the crash that was coming soon. Time will tell if policymakers and their advisors have learned enough that they can deal better with the next disaster that may threaten the communities, neighborhoods, and cities that comprise this nation.

Vocabulary Terms

Bailouts

CDO

CDS

Derivatives

GSEs
MBS
Securitization
Subprime lending
Yield-Spread Premium

DISCUSSION QUESTIONS

Financial Crisis: Set 1

By David Moglen

1. Who is to Blame?
   There is plenty of blame to go around in the subprime/financial/banking/mortgage crisis. Explain how each of these groups were to blame, and specify which were *primarily* to blame (can you argue for a number one, most at-fault group?) and which groups were *more peripheral* (only blameworthy in a narrow or limited sense) or fairly blameless.

   The groups to analyze (in no particular order) are:

   a. Mortgage borrowers
   b. Lenders
   c. Brokers
   d. Mortgage derivative investors/ derivatives themselves
   e. Investment banks ("securitizers")
   f. Ratings Agencies
   g. Banking and other Regulators including the Fed, SEC, OTS, Congress, and others
   h. Politicians
   i. Appraisers
   j. Fannie Mae and Freddie Mac (the GSEs)
   k. Anyone or anything else to blame?

2. To what extent is assigning blame simply a time-wasting blame-game, and to what extent does it give us useful insights in dealing with the current crisis and preventing future financial meltdowns?

3. Once the banks have received bailouts and other assistance from the federal government and the Federal Reserve, name several things taxpayers would like the banks to do with that money? What are several uses of that money taxpayers would least like for the banks to select? How can the government's response be designed so that taxpayers get what they want out of the banks in terms of how the bailout money is spent?

IN-CLASS PROJECT

Subprime Mortgage Meltdown / Banking Crisis

By David Moglen

Directions

Once you are assigned a group number from (from Group 1-7 below), take five to ten minutes to meet with your group, and begin planning how you will coordinate your responses. Then everyone should go read the links (articles) assigned to your group, and type your rough draft answers to the questions. When your group emails their rough answers to each other, start to synthesize the best parts of your members' contributions into one answer you are happy with for each question. **Alternatively**, you may want to lessen your workload by coordinating with your group so that question 1 assigned to your group (let's say you are Group 3 below, for instance) is done by person A, person B is responsible for question 2, etcetera. Your group should determine what is the most fair distribution of the questions for your members.

When you have your answers finalized, put all your names on the top of the first page and staple all your pages together. Your teacher will pick whatever questions they feel are most pertinent for your group to answer verbally, explaining your group's response to that question.

GROUP 1

http://www.counterpunch.org/toussaint01122008.html

1. What are the roots of the financial crisis according to the article?
2. What is a CDO and what is a CDS? How do CDOs figure into the current crisis? To answer this, you might want to think about what happened to subprime lending when the CDO market dried up (meaning the CDO became something no one would buy) as described in paragraph 15:

   The SIVs mentioned previously specialize in selling CDOs (Collateralized debt obligations) that many investors have been trying to get rid of since August 2007. As of mid-December 2007, default repayments of CDOs had reached a sum of 45 billion dollars . Since August 2007, the issuing of new CDOs has stopped as a result of the severity of the crisis.
3. How does the author describe risks and costs of the crisis will be shifted, i.e. who will bear the burden, and who should bear the burden?
4. Describe at least 2 of the financial "time bombs" for the economy mentioned in paragraph 20.

http://blogs.wsj.com/economics/2008/10/23/greenspan-testimony-on-sources-of-financial-crisis/

1. Why does Greenspan say, "I see no choice but to require that all securitizers retain a meaningful part of the securities they issue." Explain in terms that would make sense to someone who has never taken an economics class.

GROUP 2

The rent-to-own solution:
http://tpmcafe.talkingpointsmemo.com/2007/08/19/own_to_rent_the_way_to_save_su/

1. What is the own-to-rent solution? Who elects the option, and at what point? What if the bank sells the house?
2. How does this plan affect neighbor homeowners?
3. How is the current crisis a Wall Street vs. Main Street conflict?

http://money.cnn.com/2008/07/14/news/economy/fedrules/index.htm?cnn=yes

1. What did you think of the fact that a rule had to be passed against mortgage brokers "saying a rate is fixed when it can change"? How do mortgage brokers gain from the situation where they have been allowed to call a variable, adjustable rate mortgage "fixed"? How is the borrower impacted?
2. What did you think of the fact that "In a nod to the brokerage industry, the Fed withdrew a proposal requiring additional disclosure of the 'yield-spread premium,' which allows banks to pay brokers for steering homeowners into higher-priced loans"? What incentives do these payments create for brokers? Why should these payments be legal or illegal?

GROUP 3

http://www.nytimes.com/2007/12/06/washington/06cnd-debt.html

1. "Secretary Henry M. Paulson Jr. argued that lenders should try to work out new terms on a case-by-case basis. But Mr. Paulson and federal banking regulators became increasingly impatient with the industry's failure to produce a systematic, rapid approach to evaluating borrowers." Why is there a "but" in this quote? Is there a conflict between Sec Paulson's desire for a systematic resolution and his reluctance to regulate?
2. Explain why this is or is not a problem in the mortgage (home loan) market: "Some analysts say that more than a third of all subprime borrowers could have qualified for cheaper conventional loans at the outset."
3. President Bush said: "Some borrowers took out loans they knew they could not afford. And to compound the problem, many mortgages are packaged into securities and sold to investors around the world." It's clear enough how the first sentence says borrowers are partly to blame. Explain how the second sentence says someone else is also to blame.

Critique of December 2007 plan:
http://www.illinoisattorneygeneral.gov/pressroom/2007_12/20071206b.html

1. Illinois Attorney General Lisa Madigan on the Dec 07 law is critical of White House Plan – why is she critical?

2. Analyze how effective at least two of her proposals will be to address the crises.

Group 4

http://www.rollingstone.com/politics/story/29127316/the_great_american_bubble_machine (Editor's note: Make sure you click "next" to read all pages of the article.)

1. What are the bubbles that occurred and what was Goldman Sachs role in each (describe separately)?
2. How are these bubbles similar?
3. What is the next bubble Taibbi foresees and what is Goldman's role in that?
4. How did Goldman make money when the housing market collapsed and other financial institutions were taking massive losses?
5. Which activities during the Internet IPO craze and subprime housing boom were illegal enough that Goldman paid a fine or settled litigation with the claimants? What was the impact of these legal cases on Goldman's behavior?
6. What tax rate did Goldman pay and how does that compare to its CEO's pay and other employee compensation statistics?

GROUP 5

http://www.propublica.org/article/banks-favorite-toothless-regulator-1125 Esp. photograph, even just photo and caption if rights too much/too slow

1. What is the significance of this article's 2003 photo to banks and non-bank financial institutions like AIG and Countrywide?

   Be sure to describe the relevance of the following people (A and B specified below) to be posing in such a photo-op:

   "This photo from 2003 shows two regulators: **(A)** James Gilleran of the Office of Thrift Supervision (holding the chainsaw) and John Reich (then Vice Chairman of the FDIC and later at the OTS, second from right), along with **(B)** representatives of three banker trade associations. (FDIC/OTS file photo)
2. What is regulator shopping?
3. Explain how two specific actions by the Office of Thrift Supervision contributed to the subprime bubble. The two specific actions mentioned in the article were (1) with regard to appraisers and (2) when the "Office of the Comptroller of the Currency (OCC)...made a move to...make sure that borrowers could afford their monthly payments on adjustable-rate loans after the rate reset".

Opinion Survey:
http://www.gallup.com/poll/106114/Six-Oppose-Wall-Street-Bailouts.aspx

1. Do Americans lean toward helping banks or struggling homeowners? How is this poll asking a Wall Street vs. Main Street question?
2. What questions were asked in the poll? How would you respond to these questions, and why?
3. What is the "too big to fail" concept?

*4. What does this mean? "In fact, swooping in to rescue struggling homeowners could be crucial in offsetting consumer resentment toward the Fed over its Wall Street bailout."

GROUP 6

Fannie Mae bailout suggested by (Treasury Secretary) Paulson:
www.toprealtynews.com/realestatenews/id_48442.

1. What are Paulson's proposals and what is the argument for why they would help?
2. What does this mean? "If you have a squirt gun in your pocket, you may have to take it out," he said. "But if you've got a bazooka in your pocket, you may not have to take it out.""
3. What is naked short selling, why do some consider it a problem, and who temporarily banned the practice?

The Financial Reform Bill of 2010, a.k.a. the Dodd-Frank Act.
http://www.nytimes.com/2010/06/27/business/27gret.html?_r=1&ref=fair_game
http://www.economist.com/node/16481494

1. What are the three best parts of the Dodd-Frank Act and what are its three worst aspects? Use quotes and reasoning in your own words to support your answer.
2. "Much depends on how American regulators implement its provisions." What will be the main factors determining the effectiveness and enforcement of provisions in the Dodd-Frank Wall Street reform bill?

*3. Explain why you predict it will be effective reform or why/where do you think it will be (in the article's description) on the spectrum between "interpret(ing) the new rules in the friendliest possible way to Wall Street" and regulatory "overreach—stifling innovation"?

4. Which of these did the new Dodd-Frank Act do something to address (pick the best answer):
   a. Fannie Mae and Freddie Mac
   b. Too big to fail
   c. Exact implementation guidelines for affected agencies
   d. Securitizers are required to retain part of the securities they issue
5. Which of these did the new Dodd-Frank Act **fail** to address:
   a. Creating a Consumer Financial Protection Agency
   b. Creating a resolution authority–a system of orderly "winding down" of troubled financial firms
   c. GSEs
   d. Rules to make derivatives trading more transparent

GROUP 7

http://www.forbes.com/2008/09/26/wamu-morgan-deposits-oped-cx_lw_0926white.html

1. What accounts for the huge gap between "The net assets acquired by JP Morgan Chase had a nominal value of around $240 billion" and the $1.9 billion JP Morgan paid for WaMu's Assets?
2. How does having JP Morgan Chase take over WaMu have benefits and also pose threats to the economy? Hint: you might include how this and similar takeovers can worsen and improve the "too big to fail" problem. Propose another solution for Washington Mutual that would have been more ideal than the JP Morgan takeover.

http://www.bis.org/publ/work163.pdf (See pages 10–12)

A report about the Bond Rating Agencies including the concept of "Ratings Shopping,"

1. What is ratings shopping?
2. What is the concern or fear about what can happen when investment banks who create CDOs are allowed to decide which agency will rate the instrument?
3. Why isn't there the same fear (induced by the possibility of ratings shopping) you see with derivatives such as CDOs when it comes to the same agencies rating typical corporate bonds?

*4. Who are the three major credit rating agencies for Personal Credit–the ones who determine your credit rating?

*5. Why isn't there a possibility for rating shopping in the personal credit market? What would be the effects if there was that possibility?

*6. How would such a standard (the same one as for personal credit) work for rating derivatives such as CDOs?

DISCUSSION QUESTIONS

Financial Crisis: Set 2

By David Moglen

All group questions with a * above can be omitted from the small-group assignment and posed to the whole class, in addition to the overall queries listed below.

1. What insights can we learn from the subprime crisis/financial meltdown that apply to other crisis, and can help avoid future catastrophes?
2. Are there some ways in which the subprime crisis/financial meltdown are so unique that fixing the flaws that led to it will not prevent future crisis?
3. In what ways is the Financial Crisis of 2007 macroeconomic and how is it microeconomic?

CHAPTER 15
Antitrust

15 Antitrust

By Timothy Taylor

How much competition should society encourage? If an industry is perfectly competitive or monopolistically competitive, then the government has relatively little reason for concern about the extent of competition: after all, in these competitive settings, profits will lead firms to enter the market and losses will lead firms to exit, so the incentives for producing at low cost and coming up with new ways of pleasing customers are strong. But monopoly and oligopoly pose harder issues. On one side, the monopoly or oligopoly may have been created because a firm invented and patented a new product, or one or several large firms in an industry may be able to take advantage of economies of scale in a way that leads to lower production costs and potentially lower prices for consumers. On the other side, a monopoly or oligopoly may attempt to raise prices and reduce the quantity of output in a way that improves the firm's profits, but offers no corresponding benefits for consumers.

Government policy-makers often must decide how to balance the potential benefits of corporate size against the potential benefits of competition. For example, in 2006, AT&T and BellSouth, two telecommunications companies, wished to merge into a single firm. In the year before the merger, AT&T was the 121st largest company in the country when ranked by sales, with $44 billion in revenues and 190,000 employees. BellSouth was the 314th largest company in the country, with $21 billion in revenues and 63,000 employees. The two companies argued that the merger would benefit consumers, who would be able to purchase better telecommunications services at a cheaper price because the newly created firm would be able to produce more efficiently taking advantage of economies of scale and eliminating duplicative investments. However, a number of activist groups like the Consumer Federation of America and Public Knowledge expressed fears that the merger would reduce competition and lead to higher prices for consumers for decades to come. In December 2006, the federal government allowed the merger to proceed. By 2009, the new post-merger AT&T was the eighth largest company by revenues in the United States, and by that measure the largest telecommunications company in the world. Economists will spend years trying to determine whether the

Timothy Taylor, "Competition and Public Policy," *Principles of Macroeconomics*, pp. 241–258.

merger of AT&T and BellSouth, as well as other smaller mergers of telecommunications companies at about this time, helped consumers, hurt them, or didn't make much difference.

This chapter discusses public policy issues about competition. How can economists and governments analyze when mergers of large companies like AT&T and BellSouth should be allowed and when they should be blocked? The government also plays a role in policing anti-competitive behavior other than mergers, like prohibiting certain kinds of contracts that might restrict competition. In the case of natural monopoly, however, trying to preserve competition probably won't work very well, and so government will often resort to regulation of price and/or quantity of output. In recent decades, there has been a global trend toward less government intervention in the price and output decisions of businesses. In the United States, for example, the government regulated the price and quantity in many industries during the twentieth century, but has removed many of those regulations since the late 1970s. Similarly, many governments around the world owned firms directly during much of the twentieth century. However, in recent decades, many countries have sold off many of those formerly government-owned firms to private ownership.

Corporate Mergers

merger:
When two formerly separate firms combine to become a single firm; for practical purposes, often combined with acquisitions.

acquisition:
When one firm purchases another; for practical purposes, often combined with mergers.

A corporate **merger** occurs when two formerly separate firms combine to become a single firm. When one firm purchases another, it is called an **acquisition**. An acquisition may not look just like a merger, since the newly purchased firm may continue to be operated under its former company name. However, both mergers and acquisitions lead to two formerly separate firms being under common ownership, and so they are commonly grouped together.

REGULATIONS FOR APPROVING MERGERS

Since a merger combines two firms into one, it can reduce the extent of competition between firms. Therefore, when two U.S. firms announce a merger or acquisition where at least one of the firms is above a minimum size of sales (a threshold set that moves up gradually over time, and is at $63 million in 2008), or certain other conditions are met, they are required under law to notify the U.S. Federal Trade Commission. The left-hand panel of Exhibit 15-1 shows the number of mergers submitted for review to the FTC each year from 1999 to 2008. Mergers were very high in the late 1990s, diminished in the early 2000s, and then had rebounded somewhat by 2008. The right-hand panel of the exhibit shows the distribution of those mergers submitted for review in 2008 as measured by the size of the transaction. It's important to remember that this total leaves out many small mergers under $50 million, which only need to be reported in certain limited circumstances. But about a quarter of all reported merger and acquisition transactions in 2008 exceeded $500 million, while about 10 percent exceeded $1 billion.

Exhibit 15-1 Mergers and Acquisitions: Number and Size

In the early 2000s, the number of mergers and acquisitions declined from the levels at the tail end of the 1990s.

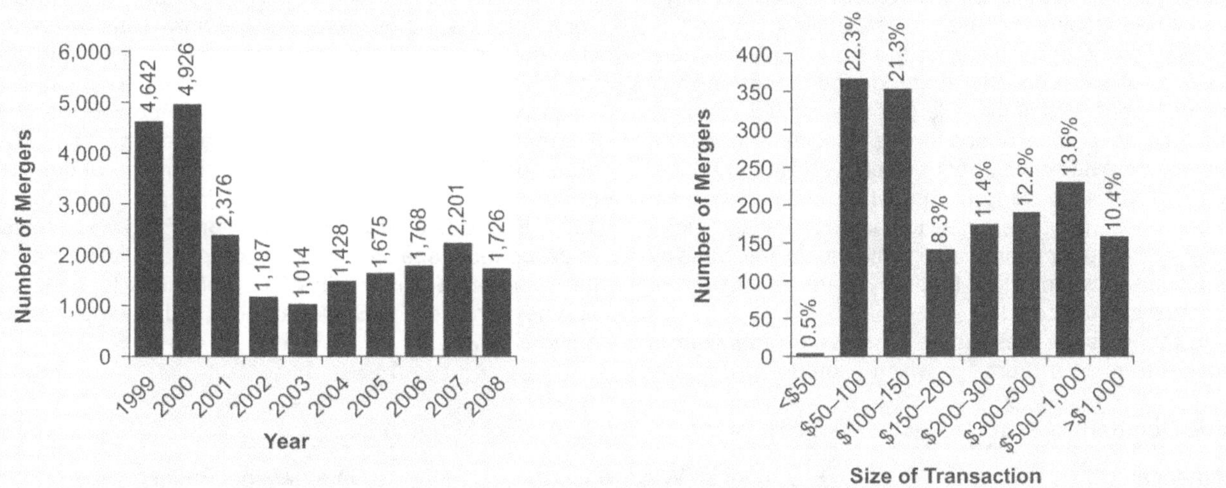

(a) Number of mergers submitted for review by the Federal Trade Commission, 1999–2008

(b) Size of transaction for mergers submitted for review in 2008 (in millions of dollars)

The laws that give government the power to block certain mergers, and even in some cases to break up large firms into smaller ones, are called **antitrust laws**. Before a large merger happens, the antitrust regulators at the FTC and the U.S. Department of Justice can either allow the merger, prohibit it, or allow it if certain conditions are met. One common condition is that the merger will be allowed if the firm agrees to sell off certain parts. For example, in 2006, Johnson & Johnson bought the Pfizer's "consumer health" division, which included well-known brands like Listerine mouthwash and Sudafed cold medicine. As a condition of allowing the merger, Johnson and Johnson was required to sell off six brands to other firms, including Zantac heartburn relief medication, Cortizone anti-itch cream, and Balmex diaper rash medication, to preserve a greater degree of competition in these markets.

antitrust laws: Laws that give government the power to block certain mergers, and even in some cases to break up large firms into smaller ones.

The government approves most proposed mergers. In a market-oriented economy, firms have the freedom to make their own choices. Private firms generally have the freedom to expand or reduce production; to set the price that they choose; to open new factories or sales facilities or to close them; to hire workers or to lay them off; and to start selling new products or stop selling existing ones. If the owners want to acquire a firm or be acquired, or to merge with another firm, this decision is just one of many decisions that firms are free to make. Yes, the managers of private firms will make mistakes sometimes. They may close down a factory which, it later turns out, would have been profitable. They may start selling a product that ends up losing money. A merger between two companies can sometimes lead to a clash of corporate personalities that makes both firms worse off. But the fundamental belief behind a market-oriented economy is that firms are in the best position to know

The Birth of Antitrust Law

In the closing decades of the nineteenth century, many industries in the U.S. economy were dominated by a single firm that had most of the sales for the entire country. The table lists some of the firms at this time that had more than 70% of sales for the entire United States in their industry. Supporters of these large firms argued that they could take advantage of economies of scale and careful planning to provide consumers with products at low prices. However, critics pointed out that when competition was reduced, these firms were free to charge more and make permanently higher profits, and that without the goad of competition, it wasn't clear that they were as efficient or innovative as they could be.

In many cases these large firms were organized in the legal form of a "trust," in which a group of formerly independent firms were consolidated together by mergers and purchases, and a group of "trustees" then ran the companies as if they were a single firm. Thus, when the U.S. government passed the Sherman Act in 1890 to limit the power of these trusts, it was called an "antitrust" law. In an early demonstration of the law's power, the U.S. Supreme Court in 1911 upheld the government's right to break up Standard Oil, which had controlled about 90% of the country's oil refining, into 34 independent firms. In 1914, the Federal Trade Commission (FTC) was created to define more specifically what competition was unfair. In the twenty-first century, the FTC continues to work with attorneys from the U.S. Department of Justice to enforce antitrust laws.

Single Companies That Had More Than 70% of the Total U.S. Market about 1900

- American Can
- American Fork and Hoe
- American Hide and Leather
- American Ice
- American Locomotive
- American School Furniture
- American Window Glass
- American Writing Paper
- Corn Products
- DuPont
- Eastman Kodak
- International Harvester
- International Paper
- National Asphalt
- Otis Elevator
- Union Box Board and Paper
- United Shoe Machinery
- United States Envelope

if their actions will lead to attract more customers or let them produce more efficiently.

Indeed, government regulators agree that most mergers are beneficial to consumers. As the Federal Trade Commission has noted on its website: "Most mergers actually benefit competition and consumers by allowing firms to operate more efficiently." But the FTC continues: "Some [mergers] are likely to lessen competition. That, in turn, can lead to higher prices, reduced availability of goods or services, lower quality of products, and less innovation. Indeed, some mergers create a concentrated market, while others enable a single firm to raise prices." Thus, the challenge for the antitrust regulators at the FTC and the U.S. Department of Justice is to figure out when a merger may hinder competition. This decision involves both numerical tools and some judgments that are difficult to quantify.

NEW DIRECTIONS FOR ANTITRUST

Both the four-firm concentration ratio and the Herfindahl-Hirschman index share some weaknesses. First, they begin from the assumption that the "market" under discussion is well-defined, and the only question is measuring how sales are divided in that market. Second, they are based on an implicit assumption that competitive conditions across industries are similar enough that a broad measure of concentration in the market is enough to make a decision about the effects of a merger. In response to these two problems, the antitrust regulators been changing their approach in the last decade or two.

Defining a market is often controversial. For example, Microsoft in early 2000s had a dominant share of the software for computer operating systems. However, in the total market for all computer software and services, including everything from games to scientific programs, the Microsoft share was only about 16% in 2000. A narrowly defined market will tend to make concentration appear higher, while a broadly defined market will tend to make it appear smaller.

There are two especially important shifts in how markets are defined in recent decades: one involves technology and the other involves globalization. With the vast improvement in communications technologies, including the development of the Internet, a consumer can order books or pet supplies from all over the country or the world. As a result, the degree of competition faced by many local retail businesses has increased. The same effect may operate even more strongly in markets for business supplies, where so-called "business-to-business" websites can allow buyers and suppliers from anywhere in the world to find each other.

The effect of globalization has changed the boundaries of markets as well. As recently as the 1970s, it was common for measurements of concentration ratios and HHIs to stop at national borders. Now, many industries find that their competition comes from the global market. A few decades ago, three companies, General Motors, Ford, and Chrysler, dominated the U.S. auto market. By 2007, however, these three firms were making less than half of U.S. auto sales, and facing competition from well-known car manufacturers as Toyota, Honda, Nissan, Volkswagen, Mitsubishi, and Mazda. When HHIs are calculated on a global perspective, concentration in most major industries—including cars—is lower in the early 2000s than it was several decades ago. Because attempting to define a particular market can be difficult and controversial the Federal Trade Commission has begun to look less at market share and more at the data on actual competition between businesses. For example, in February 2007, Whole Foods Market and Wild Oats Market announced that they wished to merge. These were the two largest companies in the market that the government defined as "premium natural and organic supermarket chains." However, one could also argue that they were two relatively small companies in the broader market for all stores that sell groceries or specialty food products. Thus, rather than relying on a market definition, the government antitrust regulators looked at detailed evidence on profits and prices for specific stores in different cities, both before and after other competitive stores entered or exited. Based on that evidence, the Federal Trade Commission decided to block the merger. After two years of legal battles, the merger was eventually allowed in 2009 under the conditions that Whole Foods sell off the Wild Oats brand name and a number of individual stores—to preserve competition in certain local markets.

This new approach to antitrust regulation involves detailed analysis of specific markets and companies, instead of defining a market and counting up total sales. A common starting point is for antitrust regulators to use statistical tools and real-world evidence to estimate the demand and supply curves faced by the firms that are proposing the merger. A second step is to specify how competition occurs in this specific industry: some possibilities include competing to cut prices, raise to output, to build a brand name, through advertising, and to build a reputation for good service or high quality. With these pieces of the puzzle in place, it's then possible to build a statistical model which estimated the likely outcome for consumers if the two firms are allowed to merge. Of course, these models do require some degree of subjective judgment, and so they can become the subject of legal disputes between the antitrust authorities and the companies that wish to merge.

Regulating Anticompetitive Behavior

The U.S. antitrust laws reach beyond blocking mergers that would reduce competition to include a wide array of anticompetitive practices. For example, it is illegal for competitors to collude together and make pricing and output decisions, as if they were a monopoly firm. The Federal Trade Commission and the U.S. Department of Justice have guidelines stating firms will be forbidden to agree to fix prices or output, rig bids, or share or divide markets by allocating customers, suppliers, territories, or lines of commerce. In the late 1990s, for example, the antitrust regulators prosecuted an international cartel of vitamin manufacturers, including the Swiss firm Hoffman-La Roche, the German firm BASF, and the French firm Rhone-Poulenc. These firms reached agreements on how much to produce, how much to charge, and which firm would sell to which customers. The highpriced vitamins were then bought by firms like General Mills, Kellogg, Purina-Mills, and Proctor and Gamble, which pushed up the prices of products for people and animals. Hoffman-La Roche, for example, pleaded guilty in May 1999 and agreed both to pay a fine of $500 million and to have at least one top executive serve four months of jail time.

Under the U.S. antitrust laws, monopoly itself is not illegal. If a firm has a monopoly because of a newly patented invention, for example, the law explicitly allows a firm to earn higher-than-normal profits for a time as a reward for innovation. If a firm achieves a large share of the market by producing a better product at a lower price, such behavior is not prohibited by antitrust law.

RESTRICTIVE PRACTICES

restrictive practices: Practices that reduce competition but that do not involve outright agreements between firms to raise price.

Antitrust law includes rules against **restrictive practices**—practices that do not involve outright agreements to raise price or to reduce the quantity produced, but that might have the effect of reducing competition. Antitrust cases involving restrictive practices are often controversial, because they delve into specific contracts or agreements between firms that are allowed in some cases but not in others.

For example, if a product manufacturer is selling to a group of dealers who then sell to the general public, it is illegal for the manufacturer to demand a **minimum resale price maintenance agreement,** which would require the dealers to sell for at least a certain minimum price. A minimum price contract is illegal because it would restrict competition among dealers. However, the manufacturer is legally allowed to "suggest" minimum prices and to stop selling to dealers who regularly undercut the suggested price. If you think this rule sounds like a fairly subtle distinction, you're right.

minimum resale price maintenance agreement: An agreement that requires a dealer who buys from a manufacturer to sell for at least a certain minimum price.

An **exclusive dealing** agreement between a manufacturer and a dealer, which requires that the dealer sell only products from one manufacturer, can be legal or illegal. It is legal if the purpose of the contract is to encourage competition between dealers; for example, it is legal for the Ford Motor Company to sell its cars only to Ford dealers, for General Motors to sell only to GM dealers, and so on. However, exclusive deals may also limit competition. For example, if one large retailer obtained the exclusive rights to be the sole distributor of televisions, computers and audio equipment made by a number of companies, then this exclusive contract would have an anticompetitive effect on other retailers.

exclusive dealing: An agreement that a dealer will sell only products from one manufacturer.

Tie-in sales refer to a situation where a customer is allowed to buy one product only if the customer also buys a second product. Tie-in sales may sometimes be illegal. For example, suppose that in order to purchase a popular CD, the store required that you also purchase two other CDs of your choice. However, in other cases tie-in sales, or **bundling** as it is sometimes called because it wraps together several products, may be legal and even common. It is common for people to purchase season tickets to a sports team or a set of concerts so that they can be guaranteed tickets to the few contests or shows that are most popular and likely to sell out. Computer software may often bundle together a number of different programs, even when the buyer only actually wants a few of the programs.

tie-in sales: A situation where a customer is allowed to buy one product only if the customer also buys another product; also called "bundling."

bundling: A situation where a customer is allowed to buy one product only if the customer also buys another product; also called "tie-in sales."

Predatory pricing occurs when the existing firm (or firms) reacts to a new firm by dropping prices very low for a short time, until the new firm is driven out of the market, and then raising prices again. This pattern of pricing is aimed at deterring the entry of new firms into the market. But in practice, it can be hard to figure out when pricing should be considered predatory. Say that American Airlines is flying between two cities, and a new airline starts flying between the same two cities, at a lower price. If American Airlines cuts its price to match the new entrant, is this predatory pricing? Or is it just market competition at work? A commonly proposed rule is that if a firm is selling for less than its average variable cost—that is, at a price where it should be shutting down—then there is evidence for predatory pricing. But calculating in the real world what costs are variable and what costs are fixed is often not obvious, either.

predatory pricing: When an existing firm uses sharp but temporary price cuts to discourage new competition.

THE MICROSOFT® CASE

The most famous restrictive practices case of the last several decades involved a series of lawsuits by the U.S. government against Microsoft—lawsuits which were encouraged by some of Microsoft's competitors. All sides admitted that Microsoft's Windows program had a near-monopoly position in the market for the software used in general computer operating systems. All sides agreed that the software had many satisfied customers. All sides agreed that the capabilities of computer software that was compatible with Windows—both software produced by Microsoft and that produced by other companies—had expanded dramatically in the 1990s. Having a monopoly or a near-monopoly is not necessarily illegal in and of itself, but in cases where one company controls a great deal of the market, antitrust regulators look at any allegations of restrictive practices with special care.

The antitrust regulators argued that Microsoft had gone beyond profiting from its software innovations and its dominant position in the software market for operating systems, and had tried to use its market power in operating systems software to take over other parts of the software industry. For example, the government argued that Microsoft had engaged in an anticompetitive form of exclusive dealing by threatening computer makers that, if they didn't leave another firm's software off their machines (specifically, Netscape's Internet browser), then Microsoft wouldn't sell them its operating system software. Microsoft was accused by the government antitrust regulators of tying together its Windows operating system software, where it had a monopoly, with its Internet Explorer browser software, where it did not have a monopoly, and thus using this bundling as an anticompetitive tool. Microsoft was also accused of a form of predatory pricing; namely, giving away certain additional software products for free as part of Windows, as a way of driving out the competition from other makers of software.

In April 2000, a federal court held that Microsoft's behavior had crossed the line into unfair competition, and recommended that the company be broken into two competing firms. However, that penalty was overturned on appeal, and in November 2002 Microsoft reached a settlement with the government that it would end its restrictive practices.

AN EVOLVING SET OF STANDARDS

The concept of restrictive practices is continually evolving, as firms seek out new ways to earn profits and government regulators define what is permissible and what is not. A situation where the law is evolving and changing is always somewhat troublesome, since laws are most useful and fair when firms know what they are in advance. In addition, since the law is open to interpretation, competitors who are losing out in the market can accuse successful firms of anticompetitive restrictive practices, and try to win through government regulation what they have failed to accomplish in the market. Officials at the Federal Trade

Commission and the Department of Justice are of course aware of these issues, but there is no easy way to address them.

Exhibit 15-2 Regulatory Choices in Dealing with Natural Monopoly

A natural monopoly will maximize profits by producing at the quantity where MR = MC and by then looking to the market demand curve to see what price to charge for this quantity. This monopoly will produce at point A, with quantity of 4 and a price of 9.3. If antitrust regulators split this company exactly in half, then each half would produce at point B, with average costs of 9.75 and output of 2. Over time, these two firms might expand production, but with a downward-sloping AC curve, average costs for two smaller firms will always be higher than average costs for one large firm. The regulators might require the firm to produce where marginal cost crosses the market demand curve at point C. However, if the firm is required to produce at a quantity of 8 and sell at a price of 3.5, the firm will suffer from losses, because the price is below average cost for this quantity of output. The most likely choice is point F, where the firm is required to produce a quantity of 6 and charge a price of 6.5. Because price is equal to average cost, the firm is able to continue operating but does not make an abnormally high profit.

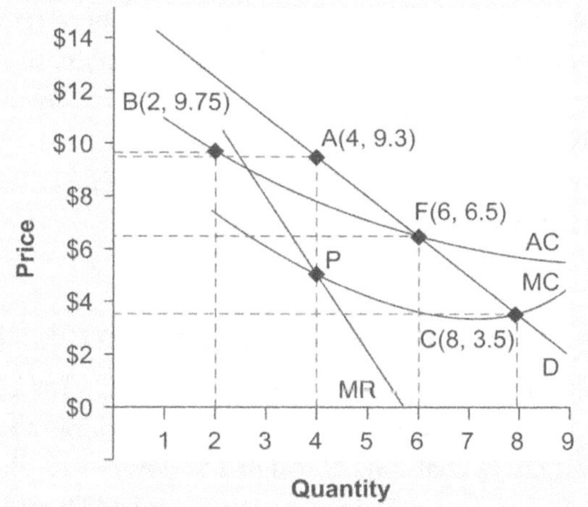

Quantity	Price	Total Revenue	Marginal Revenue	Total Cost	Marginal Cost	Average Cost
1	14.7	14.7	—	11	—	11
2	12.4	24.7	10	19.5	7.5	9.75
3	10.6	31.7	7	25.5	6	8.5
4	9.3	37.2	5.5	31	5.5	7.75
5	8	40	2.8	35	4	7
6	6.5	39	−1	39	4	6.5
7	5	35	−4	42	3	6
8	3.5	28	−7	45.5	3.5	5.7
9	2	18	−10	49.5	4	5.5

When Breaking Up Is Hard to Do: Regulating Natural Monopolies

The case of natural monopoly poses a difficult challenge for competition policy, because the structure of costs and demand seems to make competition unlikely or costly. A natural monopoly arises when average costs are declining over the range of production that satisfies market demand. As a result, one firm is able to supply the total quantity demanded in the market at lower cost than two or more firms—so splitting up the natural monopoly would raise the average cost of production and force customers to pay more. Public utilities, the companies that have traditionally provided water and electrical service across much of the United States, are leading examples of natural monopoly. It would make little sense to argue that, say, a local water company should be broken up into several competing companies, each with its own separate set of pipes and water supplies. Installing four or five identical sets of pipes under a city, one for each water company, so that each household could choose its own provider of water, would be terribly costly. The same argument applies to the idea of having many competing companies for delivering electricity to homes, each with its own set of wires. Before the advent of wireless phones, the argument also applied to the idea of many different phone companies, each with its own set of phone wires running through the neighborhood.

The Choices in Regulating a Natural Monopoly

What is the appropriate competition policy for a natural monopoly? Exhibit 15-2 illustrates the case of natural monopoly, with a market demand curve that cuts through the downward-sloping portion of the average cost curve. Points A, B, C, and F illustrate four of the main choices for regulators possibilities.

The first possibility is to leave the natural monopoly alone. In this case, the monopoly will follow its normal approach to maximizing profits. It determines the quantity where MR = MC, which happens at point P at a quantity of 4. The firm then looks to point A on the demand curve to find that it can charge a price of 9.3 for that profit-maximizing quantity. Since the price is above the average cost curve, the natural monopoly would earn economic profits.

A second outcome arises if antitrust authorities decide to divide the company, so that the new firms can compete with each other. As a simple example, imagine that the company is cut in half. Thus, instead of one large firm producing a quantity of 4, two half-size firms each produce a quantity of 2. Because of the declining average cost curve, the average cost of production for each of the half-size companies each producing 2, as shown at point B, would be 9.75, while the average cost of production for a larger firm producing 4 would only be 7.75. Thus, the economy would become less productively efficient, since the good is being produced at a higher average cost. In a situation with a downward-sloping average cost curve, two smaller firms will always have higher average costs of production than one larger firm for any quantity of total output. In addition, the antitrust authorities must worry that splitting the natural monopoly into pieces may be only the start of their problems. If one of the two firms grows larger than the other, it will have lower average costs and may be able to drive its competitor out of the market. Alternatively, two firms in a market may discover subtle ways of coordinating their behavior and keeping prices high. Either way, the result will not be the greater competition that was desired.

A third alternative is that regulators may decide to set prices and quantities produced for this industry. The regulators will try to choose a point along the market demand curve that benefits both consumers and the broader social interest. Point C illustrates one tempting choice: the regulator requires that the firm produce the quantity of output where marginal cost crosses the demand curve at an output of 8, and charge the price of 3.5, which is equal to marginal cost at that point. This rule is appealing because it requires price to be set equal to marginal cost, which is what would occur in a perfectly competitive market, and it would assure consumers a higher quantity and lower price than at the monopoly choice A. But attempting to bring about point C through force of regulation runs into a severe difficulty. At point C, with an output of 8, a price of 3.5 is below the average cost of production which is 5.7, and so at if the firm charges a price of 3.5, it will be suffering losses. Unless the regulators or the government offer the firm an ongoing public subsidy (and there are numerous political problems with that option), the firm will lose money and need to go out of business.

Perhaps the most plausible option for the regulator is point F; that is, to set the price where AC crosses the demand curve at an output of 6 and a price of 6.5. This plan makes some sense at an intuitive level: let the natural monopoly charge enough to cover its average costs and earn a normal rate of profit, so that it can continue operating, but prevent the firm from raising prices and earning abnormally high monopoly profits, as it would at the monopoly choice A. Of course, determining this level of output and price with the political pressures, time constraints, and limited information of the real world is much harder than identifying the point on a graph.

COST-PLUS VERSUS PRICE CAP REGULATION

Indeed, regulators of public utilities for many decades followed the general approach of attempting to choose a point like F in Exhibit 15-2. They calculated the average cost of production for the water or electricity companies, including an adjustment for the normal rate of profit the firm should expect to earn, and set the price for consumers accordingly. This method was known as **cost-plus regulation**. But cost-plus regulation raises difficulties of its own. If producers are reimbursed for their costs, plus a bit more, then at a minimum, producers have less reason to be concerned with high costs—because they can just pass those costs along in higher prices. Worse, firms under cost-plus regulation even have an incentive to generate high costs by building huge factories or

cost-plus regulation: When regulators permitted a regulated firm to cover its costs and to make a normal level of profit.

employing lots of staff, because what they can charge is linked to the costs they incur.

price cap regulation: When the regulator sets a price that a firm cannot exceed over the next few years.

Thus, in the 1980s and 1990s, some regulators of public utilities began to use **price cap regulation**, where the regulator sets a price that the firm can charge over the next few years. A common pattern was to require a price that declined slightly over time. If the firm can find ways of reducing its costs more quickly than the price caps, it can make a high level of profits. On the other hand, if the firm can't keep up with the price caps or suffers bad luck in the market, it may suffer losses. A few years down the road, the regulators will then set a new series of price caps based on the firm's performance.

Price cap regulation requires delicacy. It won't work if the price regulators set the price cap unrealistically low. It may not work if the market changes dramatically so that the firm is doomed to incurring losses no matter what it does—say, if energy prices rise dramatically on world markets, then the company selling natural gas or heating oil to homes may not be able to meet price caps that seemed reasonable a year or two ago. But if the regulators compare the prices with producers of the same good in other areas, they can in effect pressure a natural monopoly in one area to compete with the prices being charged in other areas. Moreover, the possibility of earning greater profits or experiencing losses—instead of having an average rate of profit locked in every year by cost-plus regulation—can provide the natural monopoly with incentives for efficiency and innovation.

Natural monopoly presents a situation where market competition is unlikely to take root, and so if consumers are not to suffer the high prices and restricted output of an unrestricted monopoly, government regulation will need to play a role. But in attempting to design a system of price cap regulation with flexibility and incentive, government regulators do not have an easy task, either.

The Great Deregulation Experiment

Governments across the United States have regulated the prices in a wide range of industries. In some cases, like water and electricity that have natural monopoly characteristics, there is some justification in economic theory for such regulation. But once politicians are given a basis to intervene in markets and to choose prices and quantities, it's hard to know where to stop.

DOUBTS ABOUT REGULATION OF PRICES AND QUANTITIES

In the years before wireless phones, when telephone technology required having a wire running to every home, it seemed plausible that telephone service had diminishing average costs and might need to be regulated like a natural monopoly. For most of the twentieth century, the national U.S. phone company was AT&T, and the company functioned as a regulated monopoly. A number of transportation-related industries

Airline Deregulation

In the early days of air travel, no airline could make a profit just by flying passengers. Airlines needed something else to carry. And so the first U.S. government regulation of the airline industry happened through the postal service, when in 1926 the postmaster general began giving airlines permission to fly certain routes based on the needs of mail delivery—and the airlines took some passengers along for the ride. In 1934, the postmaster general was charged by the antitrust authorities with colluding with the major airlines of that day to monopolize the nation's airways. In 1938, the Civil Aeronautics Board (CAB) was created to regulate airfares and routes instead. For 40 years, from 1938 to 1978, the CAB regulated the industry with a heavy hand. It approved all fares, controlled all entry and exit, and specified who could fly which routes. There was zero entry of new airlines on the main routes across the country for 40 years, because the CAB didn't think it was necessary.

In 1978, Airline Deregulation Act took the government out of the business of determining airfares and schedules. The new law shook up the industry. Famous old airlines like Pan American, Eastern, and Braniff went bankrupt and disappeared. Some new airlines like People Express were created—and then vanished.

But the greater competition from deregulation reduced airfares by about one-third over the next two decades, saving consumers billions of dollars a year. The average flight used to take off with just half its seats full; now it is two-thirds full, which is far more efficient. Airlines have also developed hub-and-spoke systems, where planes all fly into a central hub city at a certain time and then depart. As a result, one can fly between any of the spoke-cities with just one connection—and there is greater service to more cities than before deregulation. With lower fares and more service, the number of air passengers doubled from the late 1970s to the start of the 2000s—an increase that in turn doubled the number of jobs in the airline industry. Meanwhile, with the watchful oversight of government safety inspectors, commercial air travel has continued to get safer over time.

The U.S. airline industry is far from perfect: for example, a string of mergers in recent years has raised concerns over how competition might be strengthened. But it provides a better deal for consumers after deregulation than it did before.

may have declining marginal costs, in the sense that once a network of railroads or trucks or planes or buses was set up, the marginal cost of adding an extra passenger was low. Thus, for much of the twentieth century, the federal government had laws setting prices for the airline, railroad, bus, and trucking industries. Natural gas was shipped over pipelines, and since the fear of duplicate pipes could imply a natural monopoly, natural gas prices were regulated. In the United States until the late 1970s, banks were limited in the rate of interest they could pay to depositors. The argument was that if banks competed to pay higher rates of interest, they might also compete to make riskier loans, potentially imperiling the safety of the banking system.

However, by the 1970s, it became clear to policymakers of all political leanings that the widespread price regulation in all of these industries wasn't working especially well. The United States carried out a great policy experiment in **deregulation**, removing government controls over prices and quantities produced in airlines, railroads, trucking, intercity bus travel, natural gas, and bank interest rates.

deregulation: Removing government controls over setting prices and quantities in certain industries.

One difficulty with government price regulation is what economists call **regulatory capture**, in which the firms supposedly being regulated end up playing a large role in setting the regulations that they will follow. When the airline industry was being regulated, for example, the airline industry will suggest appointees to the regulatory board, attend every meeting of the board, send lobbyists to argue with the board, provide most of the information on which the board makes decisions, and offer

regulatory capture: When the firms supposedly being regulated end up playing a large role in setting the regulations that they will follow.

well-paid jobs to at least some of the people leaving the board. In comparison, consumers can easily end up not being very well represented by the regulators. The result of regulatory capture is that government price regulation can often become a way for existing competitors to work together to reduce output, keep prices high, and limit competition.

THE EFFECTS OF DEREGULATION

Deregulation, both of airlines and of other industries, has not been an unmixed blessing. The greater pressure of competition led to entry and exit. When firms went bankrupt or contracted substantially in size, they laid off workers who had to find other jobs. Market competition is a full-contact sport.

But the bottom line is that after deregulation, firms found ways to make innovations in their management, operations, marketing, and technology. They offered more flexible arrangements to consumers and cut their costs substantially. For example, airline deregulation led to planes flying with two-thirds of the seats filled on average, compared to about half the seats filled before deregulation. In turn, fuller planes led to lower costs and to consumer prices that are one-third lower. Since trucking prices were deregulated, trucks now drive many fewer empty miles, and the costs to shippers have fallen by 35%. When railroads were deregulated they shut down a lot of track that was barely being used and prices to shippers fell by 50%. Bottom line: by the start of the 2000s, the United States' great deregulation experiment of the 1970s and 1980s was saving consumers more than $50 billion per year in lower prices.

FRONTIERS OF DEREGULATION

The overall success of the United States' great deregulation experiment in airlines, banking, trucking, and other industries has encouraged deregulators to push further and to think about injecting competition into industries where the arguments for deregulation are not as obvious. In the electricity and the telecommunications industry, for example, the challenge is to combine competition where possible with regulation where necessary.

Electricity had long been thought of as a natural monopoly. However, the argument that electricity is a natural monopoly focuses on the grid of wires that bring electricity to homes. It does not focus on how the electrical power is generated. Thus, a deregulation movement has grown up in which the electrical grid would continue to be publicly owned or regulated, but the business of producing electrical energy would become competitive. Since 1989, the United Kingdom has tried out various market arrangements for having electricity generators compete with each other. A number of U.S. states have also experimented with electricity deregulation, some with considerable success (Pennsylvania) and some with near-disastrous consequences (California). Many other states have been holding back on electricity deregulation, waiting to learn from the experience of the pioneers what methods work better or worse.

Another frontier for deregulation is the telecommunications industry. In 1982, the AT&T telephone monopoly that had served the United States for decades reached an agreement with the government antitrust lawyers to split itself up into several pieces: AT&T, which competed in the market for long-distance phone service; Bell Labs, the laboratory research arm and phone equipment maker, which later changed its name to Lucent Technologies; and seven local phone companies nicknamed the "Baby Bells" that each provided local phone service to a different geographic region of the United States. Since then, long-distance phone service has been a battleground for AT&T, Sprint, MCI, Worldcom, Internet firms that provide phone calls through a computer, and others. This situation evolved considerably over the last decade, with mergers like the AT&T and BellSouth deal discussed at the start of the chapter, and seems likely to evolve further. At least in theory, a variety of companies and technologies could provide local phone service, including existing regional "Baby Bell" phone companies, wireless phone companies, and cable TV companies that could use their cables to deliver phone service. In many areas, electricity or water companies own fiber optic cables that, at least in theory, could be used to provide phone service. In addition, the Internet is bringing a rising demand for high-speed computer connections, which can also carry telephone calls. As the degree of competition in telephone markets has risen, so has the level of innovation, from cheaper long-distance to wireless telephones that can access the Internet.

Deregulation does not eliminate all forms of government regulation. A deregulated airline industry, for example, still has government inspectors looking at airplane safety and counting the number of on-time departures. A deregulated banking system still has government bank inspectors making sure that banks are solvent and not taking crazy risks with depositor's money. A deregulated electrical system still has government regulation of the electrical grid that delivers power. While deregulation expands the role of prices and incentives in production, market forces do rely on a foundation of laws and institutional arrangements to operate at their best.

Around the World: From Nationalization to Privatization

While the U.S. economy has had considerable experience with regulating the prices and output of various industries—airlines, water, electrical, telephones, trucking, and banking—**nationalization**, which is the outright ownership of firms by the government has been relatively rare in the United States. However, other countries around the world have often had public ownership of a broad range of industries including defense contracting, banking, airlines, energy production, auto manufacturing. In many European countries in the 1990s, 8–10% of the economy consisted of government-owned production. In poorer countries of the world, including some nations in Latin America and Asia, the government-owned share of the economy was often larger, at perhaps

nationalization: When government takes over ownership of firms.

10–12% and in Africa, the government-run share of the economy often reached 14%.

Nationalization of an industry has many of the same problems as government regulation of prices charged and quantities produced. In theory, an industry is nationalized to serve the citizens of the country, but often it turns out that the nationalized industry can act as a monopoly, charging high prices and reducing the quantity of output. When nationalized industries suffer losses, they turn to taxpayers for a bailout. When a nationalized industry lacks competition, it also lacks incentives for productive efficiency and for innovation.

privatization: When a government-owned firm becomes privately owned.

Thus, recent decades have seen a trend in which formerly government-owned firms are turned back into private companies. The world leader in **privatization**, whereby a government-owned firm becomes privately owned, was the United Kingdom in the 1980s, under the leadership of Prime Minister Margaret Thatcher. Firms run by the British government constituted about 10% of Britain's economy in mid-1970s, similar to the European average. But by the mid-1990s, after privatizing BritOil, British Steel, British Gas, British Telecom, British Aerospace, a national water company, a national electricity company, and others, government-run firms made up only about 2% of Britain's economy.

After Britain led the way, a global wave of privatization followed in the 1990s and into the 2000s. More than 100 countries have privatization efforts in effect in the 2000s. Some of the most prominent cases have involved the shift of Russia and countries of Eastern Europe from communism to a more market-oriented society, but a great deal of privatization has also happened in Latin America and Western Europe. As governments worldwide have sold off firms to the private sector, they received more than $100 billion annually in the late 1990s and early 2000s. However, during the grim economic conditions in 2008 and 2009, governments of many countries found themselves owning part or all of banks and other firms that could otherwise have gone bankrupt. For example, the U.S. government ended up for a time owning the majority of the General Motors and Chrysler auto companies.

The main public argument for privatization often revolves around the amount of money it could raise for the government when the government sells off firms to private owners. But as economists are quick to point out, if Harriet the Homeowner sells her house, she doesn't get any richer. Instead of owning a house, which has a certain value, she now has money of that same value. Similarly, when the government sells a company, the government then has cash instead of a physical asset. The change in the form of the asset, from property to cash, doesn't make the government any richer. Instead, the deeper argument for privatization is that government regulators often aren't too good at quick reactions and innovation in an ever-changing marketplace, and that a private firm that can't rely on government bailouts will be exposed to incentives for efficiency and innovation.

Advocates of privatization often cite this motto: "Government should steer, not row." In other words, government should set the conditions and general direction of competition, but not try to micromanage the details of production. Although this motto is usually applied to privatization, it also conveys an appropriate government policy toward competition as a whole. All market-based economies operate against a background of laws and regulations, including laws about enforcing contracts; collecting taxes, and protecting health and the environment. The government competition policies discussed in this chapter—like blocking certain anticompetitive mergers, ending restrictive practices, imposing price cap regulation on natural monopolies, and deregulation—are not about eliminating government, but about shaping and reshaping the role of government to strengthen the incentives that come with a greater degree of competition.

Limiting Market Domination

By Joseph Stiglitz and Carl Walsh

In this section, we look at how government tries to limit economic power. In the decades following the Civil War, entrepreneurs in several industries attempted to form **trusts.** These were organizations that controlled a market. One individual had a controlling interest in a firm, which in turn had a controlling interest in all the other firms in the industry. Through the addition of more layers—firms that controlled firms that controlled firms, and so on—a relatively small ownership stake could be leveraged into enormous economic power.

Among the most famous of the nineteenth-century trusts was the oil industry trust; John D. Rockefeller and his partners eventually controlled 90 percent of all oil sold in America between 1870 and 1899. In the early 1900s, Andrew Carnegie and J. P. Morgan merged many smaller steel companies to form U.S. Steel, which in its heyday sold 65 percent of all American steel.

Concern about these so-called robber barons led to passage of the Sherman Antitrust Act of 1890, which outlaws "every contract, combination in the form of a trust or otherwise, or conspiracy in restraint of trade or commerce." Further, "every person who shall monopolize, or attempt to monopolize, or combine or conspire with any other person or persons, to monopolize any part of the trade or commerce among the several States, or with foreign nations, shall be deemed guilty of a mis demeanor." (A 1974 amendment made violations felonies.) Two important decisions based on the Sherman Act led to the breakups of Standard Oil and American Tobacco in 1911, each of which had dominated its respective industry.

The Sherman Act was supplemented by the Clayton Act in 1914, which forbade any firm to acquire shares of a competing firm when that purchase would substantially reduce competition. The act also outlawed interlocking directorates (in which the same individuals serve as directors of several firms) among firms that were supposedly in competition.

These antimerger provisions were further strengthened in 1950 by the Celler-Kefauver Antimerger Act.

The government does not care about absolute size itself. In the 1960s, huge firms called *conglomerates* were formed that brought together such disparate enterprises as a steel company, an oil company, and a company making films. For example, United Airlines for a few years owned Hertz rental cars and Westin Hotels (both sold in the late 1980s). But while large, these conglomerates generally did not have a dominant position in any one market, and thus the antitrust laws were not concerned with them. The early antitrust laws were particularly concerned with **horizontal mergers**, and thus with competition within a market. These are distinguished from **vertical mergers**, in which a firm buys a supplier or a distributor, thereby amalgamating the various stages in the production process within a firm. Thus, Ford made its own steel, and General Motors bought out Fisher Body (the maker of GM's car bodies), as well as many of the specialized firms that produced batteries, spark plugs, and other components.

Under current court interpretations, market power per se is also not a primary concern. To be convicted of an antitrust violation, the firm must be shown to have acquired its market position by anticompetitive practices or to have used its market power to engage in anticompetitive practices.

DEFINING MARKETS

We have seen that the extent to which a firm's demand curve is downward sloping, enabling it to raise its price without losing all its customers—its market power—is related to the number of firms in the industry and the extent of product differentiation. Both factors are important for purposes of antitrust enforcement, since the government must first define "the market" before it can determine whether a firm dominates its market.

Market Bounds and Globalization

Over the past two hundred years, the geographical scope of markets has grown enormously. Technological improvements in transportation, from steam-powered ships to railroads to airplanes, have lowered the cost of transportation and expanded the boundaries of markets. As a market expands, it may become more competitive—as happened in the U.S. auto industry during the 1980s and 1990s, when the big three domestic firms (Ford, General Motors, and Chrysler) faced increasing competition from Japanese, European, and Korean manufacturers. Today, the degree of competition in a market must be judged by a global assessment rather than by a simple examination of how many firms produce a good in the United States. Because of the Internet, many markets have enlarged even more. Twenty years ago, a local bookstore might have been the only bookseller in a town; now that same business must face competition from online vendors such as Amazon.com and Borders.com.

Product Differentiation

All firms that produce the same good and sell in the same location are clearly in the same market, but definitions become more ambiguous when goods produced by different firms are imperfect substitutes. What, for example, is the market for beer? Those in the industry might claim that premium beers and discount beers really constitute two different markets, as relatively few customers cross over from one to the other. In the 1950s, DuPont had a virtual monopoly on the market for clear wrapping paper, but it fought off charges of monopoly by arguing that its product was one among several "wrapping materials." It claimed that brown paper was a good, though not perfect, substitute for clear wrapping paper, and that DuPont did not have a particularly large share of this larger market.

Legal Criteria

Today, the courts look at two criteria in defining a market and market power. First, they consider the extent to which a change in price for one product affects the demand for another If an increase in the price of

TABLE 15-1
Major Antitrust Legislation and Landmark Cases

Legislation	Result
Sherman Antitrust Act, 1890	Made acts in restraint of trade illegal.
Standard Oil and American Tobacco cases, 1911	Broke up both firms (each of which accounted for more than 90% of its industry) into smaller companies.
Clayton Act, 1914	Outlawed unfair trade practices. Restricted mergers that would substantially reduce competition.
Establishment of the Federal Trade Commission, 1914	Established to investigate unfair practices and issue order to "cease and desist."
Robinson-Patman Act, 1936	Strengthened provisions of the Clayton Act, outlawing price discrimination.
Alcoa case, 1945	Alcoa, controlling 90% of the aluminum market, was found to be in violation of the Sherman Act.
Tobacco case, 1946	The tobacco industry, a concentrated oligopoly, was found guilty of violation of the Sherman Act on the basis of tacit collusion.
Celler-Kefauver Antimerger Act, 1950	Placed further restrictions on mergers that would reduce competition.
DuPont Cellophane case, 1956	Broadened the definition of market. Ruled that a 20% market share was insufficient to established market power.

aluminum has a large positive effect on the demand for steel, then steel and aluminum may be considered to be in the same market—the market for metals. Second, if a firm can raise its price, say by 5 percent, and lose only a relatively small fraction of its sales, then it is "large"-that is, it has market power.

Before one large company can acquire or merge with a competitor, it must convince the government that the acquisition would not seriously interfere with the overall competitiveness of the market.

CURBING RESTRICTIVE PRACTICES

In addition to promoting competition by limiting the degree of concentration within an industry, the government works to limit restrictive practices. The history here begins with the 1914 Federal Trade Commission Act. The first ten words of the act read: "Unfair methods of competition in commerce are hereby declared unlawful." President Woodrow Wilson defined the purpose of the new commission as being to "plead the voiceless consumer's case." Since then, a number of laws have been passed by Congress to specify what is "unfair."

> **Internet Connection**
>
> U.S. DEPARTMENT OF JUSTICE AND ANTI-TRUST LAW
>
> At http://www.justice.gov/atr/about/index.html, the Department of Justice explains the mission of its Antitrust Division and its role in preventing monopolies from depriving consumers of the benefits of competition.

Many of the restrictive practices targeted by the government involve the relations between a firm and its distributors and suppliers. Such practices include tie-ins, exclusive dealing, and price discrimination. Tie-ins require a consumer to purchase additional items when she buys a product. In exclusive dealing, a producer says to a firm that wants to sell its product, "If you sell my product, you cannot sell that of my rival." Price discrimination entails charging different customers different prices on grounds unrelated to the costs of serving those customers. The Robinson-Patman Act of 1936 strengthened the provisions outlawing price discrimination, making it easier to convict firms engaged in the practice.

The precise definition of an illegal restrictive practice has changed over time with varying court interpretations of the antitrust laws. Some practices are illegal per se-firms conspiring to fix prices, for example. In 1961, General Electric, Westinghouse, and other producers of electrical equipment were found guilty of such conspiracy. More recently, several huge price-fixing cases were prosecuted successfully, most notably one against ADM (Archer Daniel Midland) involving lysine, citric acid, and high-fructose corn syrup. The corporations paid more than $100 million in fines, and some of their officials went to prison. Most practices, however, are not so clear-cut, and today a "rule of reason" prevails: they are acceptable if they can be shown to be reasonable business procedures, designed to promote economic efficiency. The efficiency gains are balanced against the higher prices resulting from the reduced competition.

Consider the example of Budweiser beer, which delivers its product through distributors. In any area, there is only one distributor, and the distributors are not allowed to compete against one another. The New York attorney general has argued that this system, by restricting competition, raises prices. Anheuser-Busch has replied that the system of exclusive territories enhances the efficiency with which beer is delivered and is necessary to ensure that customers receive fresh beer. They have maintained that their distribution system satisfies the rule of reason, and thus far their view has prevailed in the courts.

States have also been accused of adopting laws that restrict competition in ways designed to favor in-state firms. In December 2004, the U.S. Supreme Court heard arguments brought by a small Virginia winery against New York's laws restricting direct sales by out-of-state wineries to residents of New York. A challenge to a similar law in Michigan was also heard by the courts. The states argued that they were given regulatory power over the sale of alcoholic beverages by the Twenty-first Amendment to the Constitution, adopted to repeal Prohibition in 1933. However, because the New York and Michigan restrictions apply only to out-of-state producers while allowing in-state producers to ship directly to consumers, the laws have the effect of limiting competition. In May 2005, the Supreme Court ruled in favor of the Virginia winery and struck down the New York and Michigan laws that had restricted sales by out-of-state wineries.

ENFORCING THE ANTITRUST LAWS

Today antitrust laws are on the books at both state and federal levels, and they are enforced by both criminal and civil courts. The government takes action not only to break up existing monopolies but also to prevent firms from obtaining excessive market power.

The Federal Trade Commission (FTC) and the Antitrust Division of the Department of Justice are at the center of the government's efforts to promote competition. The FTC works like a law enforcement agency, investigating complaints it receives. It can provide advisory opinions on how an individual business should interpret the law, provide guidelines for entire industries, and even issue specific rules and regulations that businesses must follow. When necessary, the FTC enforces these decisions in court.

One interesting and controversial aspect of the antitrust laws is the use they make of *private* law enforcement. Any firm that believes it has been injured by the anticompetitive practices of another firm can sue; if successful, it can receive three times the dollar value of the damages and attorney fees incurred. The treble damages provision helps encourage private firms to call violations to the attention of the government. For example, in 1974 MCI sued AT&T, claiming that the latter had used unfair trade practices to hurt MCI in its attempt to enter the long-distance telephone business. In 1982, the jury estimated that MCI had, as a result of AT&T's activities, lost $600 million in profits, and ordered AT&T to pay triple that amount$1.8 billion-in damages to MCI. The award was subsequently reduced on appeal to higher courts.

Two arguments favor private enforcement of antitrust laws. First, those who are injured by anticompetitive practices are in the best position to detect a violation of the law. Second, government may be lax in the enforcement of these laws because cartels and dominant firms may wield a great deal of political influence.

On the other side of the argument are concerns about the rising costs of antitrust litigation-the number of private suits doubled between the 1960s and the 1970s. And many worry that businesses use the threat of an antitrust suit as a way of raising a rival's costs. Thus, Chrysler charged General Motors with an antitrust violation when GM proposed a joint venture with a Japanese firm, only to drop the action when it found a Japanese partner for its own joint venture.

Thinking Like an Economist

INCENTIVES AND THE REMEDY TO THE MICROSOFT MONOPOLY PROBLEM

In 1999, Judge Thomas Penfield Jackson found Microsoft guilty of violating U.S. antitrust laws. He then was faced with a difficult problem: what remedy to impose. Jackson was keenly aware of the *incentives* that Microsoft faced; its profitability depended on its ability to preserve its market power, and it therefore had strong incentives to stifle innovations that might reduce that market power. For instance, Sun Microsystems had developed a language, Java, that would enable programmers to develop applications to run not just on Microsoft's Windows operating system but on other operating systems as well. One of the reasons why Microsoft's operating system was so dominant was that rivals started with a marked disadvantage-a lack of applications to run on their operating systems. By changing all of that, Java would result in real competition in the market for operating systems. Microsoft similarly worried that Netscape might serve as a platform through which competition in the operating system might be enhanced, and it sought to quash this threat by bundling its own browser, Internet Explorer, free with the Windows operating system. Microsoft had done what comes naturally to monopolists-it simply sought to maximize its long-run profits by reducing the threat of competition. The judge worried that no matter how he scolded Microsoft, or what fines he imposed, Microsoft had every incentive to continue these anticompetitive practices. Moreover, he was aware of how difficult detecting and proving anticompetitive behavior can be, and Microsoft had already demonstrated its willingness to face risks of antitrust prosecution. Hence, the only way to alter behavior was to alter incentives, and doing so entailed changing the structure of the enterprise. The Department of Justice proposed splitting Microsoft into two, with one company focusing on applications and the other focusing on the operating system. The application company would have every incentive to ensure that its applications could be used on as many operating systems as possible. The hope was that Microsoft Word might then be written to work on more operating systems, like Linux, so that demand for them would increase. And restraining the operating system company from writing applications would at least prevent a repeat of what had happened with Netscape and the browser market.

Some critics thought the judge, in approving the Justice Department's recommendations in 2000, went too far; others thought he did not go far enough. Those in the former camp worried that he overlooked important economies of scope—efficiencies that arose from the close interaction between those writing the operating system and those developing applications. These advantages, they contended, more than offset the disadvantages from the loss in competition. Moreover, they believed that Microsoft's monopoly power was temporary; within a few years, surely competition would erode its dominant position. Already, Linux was rapidly growing as an alternative operating system. They argued that Microsoft had achieved its dominant position by strong innovation, and it was wrong to punish this success now by breaking the company up.

But critics on the other side said that at least a significant part of Microsoft's success was due to its ruthless business practices, and such behavior should not go unpunished. And more was at stake: Microsoft represented a threat to innovation. Few would invest in innovation if they believed that any innovation threatening Microsoft's competitive position would be suppressed by Microsoft. Many Silicon Valley firms shared this fear.

These critics worried that the Microsoft application company still might not write programs for other operating systems, that there might be sweetheart deals between the two companies; they argued for other approaches to changes Microsoft's incentives. For instance, some suggested limiting intellectual property protection-and requiring the disclosure of the code-for operating systems of a firm with a dominant position (like Microsoft) to, say, three to five years. Doing so would automatically create a competitor to, say, Windows XP-the freely available Windows 2000. Only if Windows XP were markedly better than Windows 2000 would people pay anything for it. This approach would enhance Microsoft's incentives to innovate. Meanwhile, application programmers would have an incentive to write programs that worked better and better with the freely available 2000 operating system. The hope was that out of this competition, consumers would benefit not only from lower prices hut also from innovations, possibly leading to programs that crash less often and are tailored better to the needs of particular groups of users, that run faster, and that perform new tasks.

Wrap-up

ANTITRUST POLICIES

Antitrust policies are designed to ensure competition in the marketplace by

- Limiting market dominance
- Curbing restrictive trade practices

The problems faced in designing and enforcing antitrust policies include

- The problem of defining the market
- Determining how to deal with firm practices that may *both* reduce competition *and* enhance efficiency

Enforcement of antitrust regulations can involve criminal or civil penalties.

Case in Point

COKE AND PEPSI PLAY MERGER

The Coca-Cola Company and PepsiCo, Inc., dominate the market for carbonated soft drinks. Early in 1986, each proposed to grow larger through acquisition. In January, PepsiCo proposed buying 7-Up, the fourth-largest soft drink manufacturer, for $380 million. In February, Coca-Cola proposed buying Dr. Pepper, the third largest, for $470 million.

The mergers would have made the big even bigger. Coca-Cola and PepsiCo already held 39 percent and 28 percent of the market, respectively, while Dr. Pepper had 7 percent and 7-Up had 6 percent. The next largest firm in the market after 7-Up was R. J. Reynolds (known for Canada Dry and Sunkist), which held 5 percent of the soft drink market.

The Federal Trade Commission announced that it would oppose the mergers. To assess the impact on competition in such cases, the government often uses what is called the Herfindahl-Hirschman index

TABLE 15-5
Herfindahl-Hirschman Index

Level of HH1	Policy Recommendation
Less than 1,000 unconcentrated	Mergers allowed without government challenge
Less than 1,000 and 1,800 moderately concentrated	Mergers challenged if they raise the industry HHI by more than 100 points
Above 1,800 concentrated	Mergers challenged if they raise the industry HHI by more than 50 points

(HHI). The HHI is calculated by summing the squares of the market shares. If the industry consists of a single firm, then the HHI is $(100)^2 = 10{,}000$. If the industry consists of 1,000 firms, each with 0.1 percent of the market, then the HHI is $(0.1)^2 \times 1{,}000 = 10$. Thus, higher values of the HHI indicate less competitive industries.

Merger guidelines used by the federal government divide markets into three categories, with different policy recommendations. The divisions and policy recommendations are given in Table 15-5.

Before the mergers, assuming that the 15 percent of the market not accounted for by the big five was divided equally among fifteen small producers, a somewhat simplified HHI for the soft drink industry was

$$HHI = 39^2+28^2+7^2+6^2+5^2+15\,(1)^2 = 2{,}430.$$

If we plug in the 34 percent share that PepsiCo would have after acquiring 7-Up, the PepsiCo-7-Up merger would raise the HHI to 2,766. The two proposed mergers together would raise the HHI to 3,312.

After the FTC announced its opposition, PepsiCo immediately gave up on purchasing 7-Up. Coca-Cola pushed ahead with its plan to buy Dr. Pepper until a federal judge ruled that it was a "stark, unvarnished" attempt to eliminate competition that "totally [lacked] any apparent redeeming feature."

The court case did bring a secret to the surface, however. The trial disclosed certain Coca-Cola company memos written after PepsiCo's offer for 7-Up had been made. In the memos, Coca-Cola executives expressed fear that the FTC might allow the PepsiCo merger, despite the agency's guidelines. By announcing plans to buy Dr. Pepper, Coca-Cola hoped that the FTC would step in and block *both* mergers, as it did, thereby preventing PepsiCo from using a merger to catch up in size to Coca-Cola.[5]

Restrictive Practices

If members of an oligopoly could easily get together and collude, they would. Their joint profits would increase. We have seen, however, that there are significant impediments to collusion. As a result, oligopolists typically resort to other ways of increasing profits. One approach is to restrict competition.

Firms engage in a number of restrictive practices to limit competition. Some were made illegal by the Federal Trade Commission Act of 1914. While these practices may not increase profits for the firms quite as successfully as the collusive arrangements discussed above, they do raise prices. In some cases, consumers may be even worse off than under outright collusion. Many restrictive practices are aimed at the wholesalers and retailers who sell a producer's goods. When one firm buys or sells the products of another, the two companies are said to have a "vertical" relationship. Such restrictive practices are called *vertical restrictions,* in distinction to the price-fixing arrangements among producers or among wholesalers selling in the same market, which are referred to as *horizontal restrictions.*

One example of a vertical restriction is the use of *exclusive territories:* a producer gives a wholesaler or retailer the exclusive right to sell a good within a certain region. Beer and soft drink producers, for instance, typically give their distributors exclusive territories. Coca-Cola manufactures its own syrup, which it then sells to bottlers who add the soda water. Coca-Cola gives these bottlers exclusive territories, so the supermarkets in a particular area can buy Coke from only one place. A store in Michigan cannot buy the soft drink from Coca-Cola bottlers in New Jersey, even if the price in New Jersey is lower. In 1979, Indiana passed a law prohibiting exclusive territories for beer within the state. As a result, beer prices there are substantially lower (adjusting for other differences) than in other states.

Another restrictive practice is *exclusive dealing:* a producer insists that any firm selling its products not sell those of its rivals. When you go into an Exxon gas station, for instance, you can be sure you are buying gas refined by the Exxon Corporation, not Texaco or Sunoco. Like most refiners, Exxon requires stations that want to sell Exxon to sell only its brand of gasoline.

A third example of a restrictive practice is *tie-ins,* which force a customer who buys one product to buy another. Mortgage companies, for example, used to insist that those who obtained mortgages from them purchase fire insurance as well. Nintendo designs its console so that it can be used with only Nintendo games. In effect, it forces a tie-in sale between the console and the software. In the early days of computers, IBM designed its computers so that they could be used only with IBM "peripherals," such as printers.

A final example is *resale price maintenance.* Under this restrictive practice, a producer insists that any retailer selling his product must sell it at the "list" price. Like exclusive territories, it is designed to reduce competitive pressures at the retail level.

Consequences of Restrictive Practices

Firms engaging in restrictive practices *claim* they are doing so not because they wish to restrict competition but because they want to enhance economic efficiency. Exclusive territories, they argue, provide companies with a better incentive to "cultivate" their territory. Exclusive dealing contracts, they say, provide incentives for firms to focus their attention on one producer's goods.

Despite these claims, restrictive practices often reduce economic efficiency. Exclusive territories for beer, for example, have limited the ability of *very* large firms, with stores in many different territories, to set up a central warehouse and distribute beer to their stores more efficiently. And regardless of whether they enhance or hurt efficiency, restrictive practices may lead to higher prices by limiting competitive pressures.

Some restrictive practices work by increasing the costs of, or otherwise impeding, one's rivals. In the 1980s, several major airlines developed computer reservation systems that they sold at very attractive prices to travel agents. If the primary goal of these systems had been to serve consumers, they would have been designed to display all the departures near the time the passenger desired. Instead, each airline's system provided a quick display for only its own flights—United's, for instance, focused on United flights—although with additional work, the travel agent could find out the flights of other airlines. Airlines benefited from these computer systems not because they best met the needs of the consumer, but because they put competitors at a disadvantage and thereby reduced the effectiveness of competition.

An exclusive dealing contract between a producer and a distributor also exemplifies how one firm may benefit from hurting its rivals. The contract might force a rival producer to set up its own distribution system, at great cost, when the already-existing distributor might have been able to undertake the distribution of the second product at relatively low incremental cost. The exclusive dealing contract increases total resources spent on distribution.

Courts have responded inconsistently to these and similar practices—in some circumstances ruling that they are illegal because they reduce competition, while in others allowing them, having been persuaded that they represent reasonable business practices.

---

[5]See the following *Wall Street Journal* articles: Timothy K. Smith and Scott Kilman, "Coke to Acquire Dr. Pepper Co. for $470 Million," February 21,1986, p. 2; Andy Pasztor and Timothy K. Smith, "FTC Opposes Purchase Plans by Coke, Pepsi," June 23,1986, p. 2; Pasztor and Smith, "Coke Launched Dr. Pepper Bid to Scuttle Plans by PepsiCo, Documents Indicate," July 29, 1986, p. 3; Pasztor and Smith, "Coke's Plan to Buy Dr. Pepper Is Blocked by U.S. Judge, Pending Decision by FTC," August 1, 1986, p. 3.

Wrap-Up

FORMS OF RESTRICTIVE PRACTICES

Exclusive territories
Exclusive dealing
Tie-ins
Resale price maintenance

Key Concepts and Summary

1. A corporate merger involves two private firms joining together. An acquisition refers to one firm buying another firm. In either case, two formerly independent firms become one firm.
2. Antitrust laws seek to ensure active competition in markets, sometimes by preventing large firms from forming through mergers and acquisitions, sometimes by regulating business practices that might restrict competition, and sometimes by breaking up large firms into smaller competitors.
3. A four-firm concentration ratio is one way of measuring the extent of competition in a market. It is calculated by adding the market shares—that is, the percentage of total sales—of the four largest firms in the market.
4. A Herfindahl-Hirschman Index (HHI) is another way of measuring the extent of competition in a market. It is calculated by taking the market shares of all firms in the market, squaring them, and then summing the total.
5. The forces of globalization and new communications and information technology have increased the level of competition faced by many firms by increasing the amount of competition from other regions and countries.
6. Because firms are blocked by antitrust authorities from openly colluding to form a cartel that will reduce output and raise prices, many antitrust cases involve restrictive practices that can reduce competition in certain circumstances, like (also called bundling), and predatory pricing.
7. In case of a natural monopoly, market competition will not work well, and so rather than allowing an unregulated monopoly to raise price and reduce output, the government may wish to regulate price and/or output. Common examples of regulation are public utilities, the regulated firms that often provide electricity and water service.
8. Cost-plus regulation refers to government regulation of a firm which sets the price that a firm can charge over a period of time like a year by looking at the firm's accounting costs and then adding a normal rate of profit. Price cap regulation refers to government regulation of a firm where the government sets a price level several years in advance, and the firm can either make high profits by producing at lower costs or selling a higher quantity than expected or suffer

low profits or losses by producing at higher costs or selling a lower quantity than expected.

9. The U.S. economy experienced a wave of deregulation in the late 1970s and early 1980s, when a number of government regulations that had set prices and quantities produced in a number of industries were eliminated. There are current efforts to deregulate telecommunications and electricity—areas that were once thought to be natural monopolies.
10. Regulatory capture occurs when the industries being regulated end up having a strong influence over what regulations exist.
11. Privatization can increase the level of market competition and efficiency through the selling of previously nationalized assets to private owners. However, if privatization is to work well, it must provide incentives for a firm to be operated more efficiently, not just replace government ownership with an unregulated private monopoly.

Vocabulary Terms

Antitrust
Bundling
Deregulation
Exclusive dealing
Exclusive territories
Nationalization
Natural Monopoly
Predatory Pricing
Privatization
Regulatory Capture
Resale Price Maintenance
Restrictive Practices
Tie-Ins
Trusts

Review Questions

1. What is a corporate merger? What is an acquisition?
2. What is the goal of antitrust policies?
3. How is a four-firm concentration ratio measured? What does a high measure mean about the extent of competition?
4. How is a Herfindahl-Hirshman Index measured? What does a low measure mean about the extent of competition?
5. Why can it be difficult to decide what a "market" is for purposes of measuring competition?
6. What is a minimum resale price maintenance agreement? How might it reduce competition and when might it be acceptable?

7. What is exclusive dealing? How might it reduce competition and when might it be acceptable?
8. What is a tie-in sale? How might it reduce competition and when might it be acceptable?
9. What is predatory pricing? How might it reduce competition, and why might it be difficult to tell when it should be illegal?
10. If public utilities are a natural monopoly, what would be the danger in deregulating them?
11. If public utilities are a natural monopoly, what would be the danger in splitting them up into a number of separate competing firms?
12. What is cost-plus regulation?
13. What is price-cap regulation?
14. What is deregulation? Name some industries that have been deregulated in the United States.
15. What is regulatory capture?
16. Why does regulatory capture reduce the persuasiveness of the case for regulating industries for the benefit of consumers?
17. Who owns a nationalized firm?
18. Who owns a privatized firm?

CHAPTER 16
Labor Markets

16 Labor Markets

By Paul Wonnacott and Ronald Wonnacott

> *You must offer the American working man bread and* butter *in the here* and *now, instead of pie in* the sky in the *sweet bye and bye.*
>
> —The philosophy of early labor leader Samuel Gompers (as described by Charles Killingworth)

Like Rodney Dangerfield, baseball players sometimes "don't get no respect." Ted Turner, owner of the Atlanta Braves, has been quoted as saying, "I don't understand why grown men play this game anyhow. They ought to be lawyers or garbage men. Games should be left for kids." By 1990, players could laugh about these comments all the way to the bank. It was no longer unusual for a star to get over $2 million a year. Twenty years before, things were different. Players got only a small fraction of their present-day salaries. This chapter will show why.

The broad objective of this chapter is to describe departures from perfect competition in labor markets. Specifically, it covers:

- Imperfect competition on the supply side of the labor market, when unions acquire the market power to bargain for a higher wage.
- Imperfect competition on the demand side, when employers acquire the market power to keep wages down.
- Imperfect competition on both sides of the market, in the special circumstances of bilateral monopoly.
- The effect of strikes and measures to prevent or resolve them.
- A review of why wage differences exist.

Labor Unions: The Benefits to Labor of Collective Action

A union is established so that workers—the suppliers of labor—can bargain with "one voice." They collectively negotiate for higher wages rather than take the wage rate as given. Once they form a union, the labor market is no longer perfectly competitive, because they exercise market power in order to influence price (their wage).

In addition to bargaining for higher wages, unions have other important roles as well, such as helping workers to maintain their stake in their jobs and providing them with a collective voice in setting the conditions of their employment.[1] With the backing of unions, workers are protected from arbitrary dismissal or changes in the "rules of the game" by management. Because of these assurances, workers get a stake in their jobs and are able to commit themselves to an occupation more completely than they could in an impersonal, perfectly competitive market with "no memory and no future."

COLLECTIVE BARGAINING

Collective bargaining is any negotiation between a union and management over wages, fringe benefits, hiring policies, job security, or working conditions.

Workers in a union who speak with a collective voice overcome three disadvantages of standing alone: (1) A single worker may have difficulty even getting management to listen to a grievance, let alone negotiate to remove it. (2) Management may retaliate personally against an individual who is complaining, but it generally cannot against workers acting collectively. (3) Even if an individual could negotiate a change, it is unlikely to be worth the effort, because most of the benefits would go to other workers. In this sense, the resolution of a labor grievance is a public good; all workers benefit, regardless of who bargains for it. Therefore bargaining is undertaken collectively—by a union.

HOW UNIONS RAISE WAGES

In addition to raising wages by negotiating higher pay rates, unions may attempt to raise wages indirectly by negotiating other terms of employment. For example, unions may:

1. Negotiate a shorter work week and early retirement. Such changes reduce the supply of labor and thus put upward pressure on wages.
2. Negotiate with employers to hire only union members, and then limit union membership by imposing barriers to entry such as high initiation fees or long periods of apprenticeship. This approach also restricts the supply of labor and thus raises wage rates.

In such negotiations, a union may, of course, have other objectives than just raising wages. For example, a shorter work week may be desired for its own sake, and apprenticeship may be a way of screening bumbling amateurs out of dangerous occupations. Not surprisingly, motives are sometimes mixed. The charge has been made that the American Medical Association—the association of U.S. doctors—used to act like a union. Before its change in policy about 25 years ago, the association used its power to limit the number of medical schools and the number of students admitted to these schools. Although the stated reason for

[1]This chapter, in particular the discussion of labor's voice, draws heavily on Richard B. Freeman and James L. Medoff, *What Do Unions Do*? (New York: Basic Books,1984)

this tough policy was to improve the quality of medical service, it also restricted the supply of graduating doctors and thus increased the incomes of the members of the association.

OTHER OBJECTIVES OF UNIONS

Unions also try to negotiate reasonably pleasant physical conditions and establish seniority rules to protect those who have been on the job longest and who have the most to lose if they are discharged.

Without seniority rules, older workers might be in a vulnerable position. Because of their declining productivity, they might be the first to be laid off.

Seniority rules typically ensure that those who have been longest on the job will be laid off last and rehired first.

Unions also seek to negotiate job security, sometimes even in preference to a wage increase. For example, in 1984 the United Auto Workers (UAW) successfully negotiated to get General Motors to agree to spend up to $1 billion to keep displaced workers on its payroll. Moreover, in its 1987 negotiations with Ford and GM, the UAW allowed the companies to relax some union work rules (and thereby introduce Japanese-style production innovations) in exchange for

Example 1

THE CONFLICTING OBJECTIVES OF COMPASSION AND EFFICIENCY

Two centuries ago, at the beginning of the Industrial Revolution in Britain, labor-saving machinery was introduced into the textile industry. Displaced workers in those days had much bleaker prospects than today: It was harder to find another job. Without a job, a worker's family faced severe malnutrition, or worse. Consequently, there were riots in which workers (the Luddites) broke into the factories and destroyed the new labor-saving machines. While recognizing their plight, we might ask: What if they had succeeded? What if labor-saving machinery had been banned and primitive handcrafting jobs guaranteed? If the Luddites and their heirs had been successful in thwarting technological change, wouldn't our situation today be very much like theirs two centuries ago? If so, what progress would we have made against the problem that concerned them most: poverty?

Although labor-saving machinery may create transitional unemployment, it creates far better jobs in the long run. When bulldozers are introduced, whole armies of workers with shovels lose their jobs. But in the long run, this is beneficial not only for society but also, in most cases, for the workers who initially lose their jobs. This is not only true of the ditch-diggers who get high-productivity and high-paying jobs driving the bulldozers. It is also true of other ditch-diggers who get high-productivity jobs in new, growing industries such as electronics and aircraft. These jobs exist because the introduction of bulldozers and other machines increases our ability to produce and therefore raises our income and purchasing power. This in turn means that we can afford to buy products that did not exist before.

In brief, society benefits because the labor force is engaged in more productive activities than ditch-digging. Because machines now perform menial jobs, we produce more. The resulting increase in our income allows us to afford more compassion-that is, we are able to ensure people against the extremes of poverty that had to be faced in earlier, less productive eras. The point is a simple one: In protecting people against severe economic adversity, it is important not to use methods that thwart progress by locking in inefficiency.

a guarantee that current workers would not lose their jobs for any reason except reduced car sales.

Protecting jobs is a way of introducing compassion into an often impersonal economic system. However, it may be far from the best way to do it, especially if it goes beyond ensuring jobs for those individuals who now have them, to ensuring that *their jobs will continue* even after they have retired or gone elsewhere. For example, when an industry gets long-term protection from imports, it is not just the workers at that time whose jobs are protected. The jobs themselves continue to exist as long as protection remains. When new people, perhaps now studying in high school, take these low-productivity jobs, the cost, in terms of reduced efficiency, can extend far into the future. (For more on the relation between compassion and efficiency, see BoxExample 1.)

WILL UNIONS SEEK BROADER AREAS OF INFLUENCE?

Will unions seek a voice in the nation's boardrooms? West Germany is experimenting with co-determination which provides labor with the same number of seats as management on the board of directors, with the owners making the decision in the event of a tie. In the United States, Douglas Fraser, UAW president in 1980, became the first union leader to get a seat on the board of a major U.S. corporation-Chrysler. This was not so much the result of a change in any underlying philosophy of management-labor relations as an act of desperation to save a near-bankrupt company: The UAW got a seat on Chrysler's board in exchange for deferring several hundred million dollars in wages and benefits. Pan American and a number of other companies also introduced this innovation. Although such experiments may have improved communications between labor and management, some rank-and-file workers fear that their leaders may begin to think like managers and soften their demands for higher wages and better working conditions.

Unions, with their wide variety of objectives, faced a long struggle in becoming established in, the United States.

Labor Unions: Their Historical Development

Trade unionism is not socialism. It is the capitalism of the proletariat.
—George Bernard Shaw

The beginning of the American union movement dates back to an era in which a relatively powerless labor force lived in poverty, or near it. In the last third of the nineteenth century, the Knights of Labor emerged, hoping to become the one great organization that might speak for all labor. Like the labor movement in England and a number of other European countries, the organization sought to make labor a unified force for radical political change.

However, American workers have never been sympathetic to such an overt political objective. The Knights disappeared, to be replaced in the 1880s by the American Federation of Labor (AFL), led by Samuel Gompers

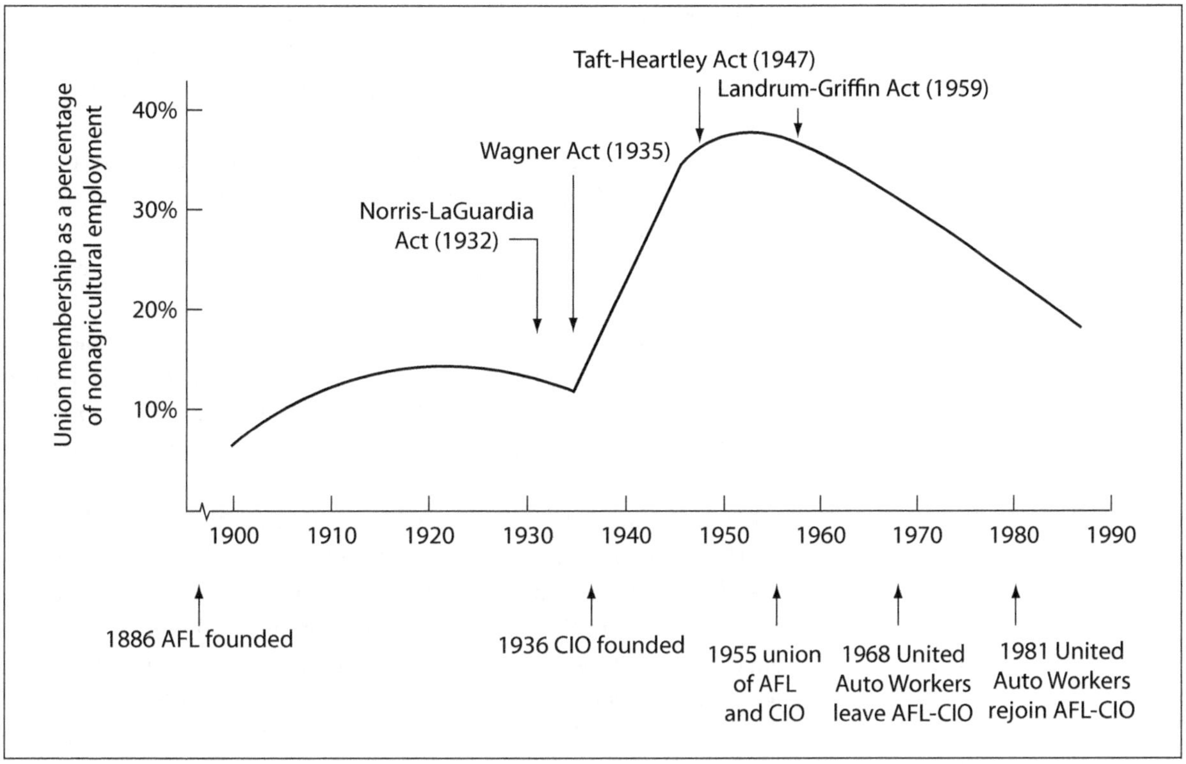

FIGURE 16-1
Major trends in U.S. union membership, 1900–1986
American union membership remained low until the mid-1930s, then rose rapidly until the end of World War II. After a postwar decade of little or no growth, union membership has fallen as a proportion of the labor force. *(Sources:* These data are only approximations. They are based on U.S. Department of Labor figures and data in the two articles by R. B. Freeman and M. W. Reder in the *Journal of Economic Perspectives,* Spring 1988, pp. 63–110. The Freeman and Reder articles are drawn on heavily throughout this chapter.)

and devoted to the bread and-butter issues of improving wages and working conditions, rather than a "pie-in-the-sky" political class struggle.

The bread-and-butter approach remains an important characteristic of American labor. While unions sometimes support Democratic candidates, they often remain uncommitted and sometimes support Republicans. Thus American labor has not followed the common pattern in Britain and some other European countries of formal, close association with one political party.

There are two kinds of unions in the United States:

1. **Industrial unions**, such as the United Auto Workers, which draw on all workers in a specific industry or group of industries, regardless of the workers' skills.
2. **Craft unions**, such as the plumbers' or carpenters' unions, which draw their members from any industry, provided the workers have a common skill.

The history of American unions can be divided into the three periods sketched in Figure 16-1: (1) an initial low-membership period until the mid1930s, (2) rapid growth for the next decade, and (3) a period of decline since World War II.

THE PERIOD BEFORE THE GREAT DEPRESSION

Until the early 1930s, unions developed in a hostile climate. On the one hand, business executives strongly resisted any attempts to unionize their firms and would frequently retaliate against prounion workers by firing them and then blacklisting them with other potential employers. They would also sometimes use so-called yellow-dog contracts which specified that a worker getting a job had first to sign a commitment not to join a union.

An important question was how the courts would treat labor-management disputes. In particular, in light of the Sherman and Clayton antitrust acts, would the courts view unions as restraints on trade? Judgments either for or against unions seemed possible. On the one hand, a union could be viewed as a restraint on trade, since it is a combination of workers seeking to raise wages, just as a collusive oligopoly is a combination of sellers seeking to raise price. On the other hand, the Clayton Act seemed to exclude unions by stating that "labor is not an article of commerce." By and large, the courts' judgments during this early period did not favor labor.

For several reasons, union growth was thwarted during the 1920s and early 1930s. The AFL lost ground because it remained firmly committed to the idea of craft unionism on which it was founded. Therefore it did not adequately appeal to the increasing number of unskilled workers in mass-production industries, such as steel and autos. Moreover, there was growth in employer resistance to unionism. Employers introduced paternalistic schemes providing labor with relatively generous benefits in an attempt to demonstrate that workers would do better without a union. As a result of growing court hostility toward unions, employers were allowed to use injunctions (court orders) to prevent unions from picketing, striking, or pursuing almost any other activity judged threatening to business. Sometimes the courts issued injunctions without even hearing the union case.

THE PERIOD OF RAPID UNION GROWTH: THE EARLY 1930S TO 1945

In the depths of the depression in the 1930s, Congress passed several laws that improved the climate for unions. The first was the Norris-LaGuardia Act of 1932 which limited employers' use of what had become a prime weapon in the struggle against unions: the injunction. Court intervention in a labor dispute was to be limited to protecting property and preventing violence.

In 1935, the Wagner Act (the National Labor Relations Act) moved the government from a position of neutrality to one that favored labor. This act had three key provisions:

1. It declared the legal right of workers to form unions.
2. It prohibited employers from using a number of unfair labor practices, such as firing or blacklisting pro-union workers.
3. It established the National Labor Relations Board (NLRB) to control unfair labor practices by employers and to resolve disputes among unions. For example, the NLRB is empowered to hold elections in which workers decide which of two or more competing unions will represent them.

The Wagner Act achieved its objective of removing barriers to the growth of unions. During the decade that followed, the proportion of the labor force that belonged to unions almost tripled. There was another important reason for this growth. In 1936, several union leaders, led by John L. Lewis, split away from the AFL because of its concentration on craft unions. They formed the Congress of Industrial Organizations (CIO), a collection of industrial unions. Between 1936 and 1945, the CIO had great success in unionizing the auto, steel, and other mass-production industries. (In 1955, the two unions resolved their differences and rejoined forces in the new AFL-CIO.)

THE PERIOD SINCE WORLD WAR II

After a period of little growth in the first postwar decade, the percentage of workers in unions has steadily declined. Reasons cited include the relative decline in employment in heavy industry, where union membership has been most heavily concentrated, and the shift in industrial jobs to the south, where unionism is weaker than in the north.

The popularity of unions began to decline during World War II when unions may have overplayed their hand. During the early years of the war, unions had added muscle in the form of a rapidly increasing membership. By 1944 they were flexing that muscle in a series of strikes that were viewed by many as damaging to the war effort. The feeling that unions were becoming too powerful contributed to the passage of the Taft-Hartley Act in the face of stiff union opposition.

The Taft-Hartley Act (1947)

Just as the Wagner Act 12 years earlier had dealt with unfair employer practices, the Taft-Hartley Act now attempted to outlaw unfair union practices. For example, it prohibited **closed shops** in industries engaged in interstate commerce. (Since only union members could be hired in a closed shop, it provided a union with veto power over who could be hired.) The Taft-Hartley Act also prohibited jurisdictional strikes—strikes arising from conflicts between unions over whose members will do specific jobs. It also forbade the "check off" of union dues unless workers agree to it in writing. (With a check-off, employers collect dues for the union by deducting them from workers' paychecks.) In addition, the Taft-Hartley Act included provisions to increase the financial responsibility of union leaders. For example, it required pension funds to be kept separate from other union funds, and it required union leaders to provide both their own membership and the National Labor Relations Board with detailed information on how union funds were to be spent. The act also contained a provision to delay strikes that "imperil the national health or safety." Specifically, the U.S. president was empowered to seek a court injunction in such circumstances to require strikers to return to work for an 80-day cooling-off period.

A **closed shop** means that a firm can hire only workers who are already union members.

The most controversial provision of the Taft-Hartley Act is its famous section 14(b). This recognizes the right of states to enact

A right-to-work law outlaws the closed shop and the union shop in favor of the *open shop,* in which there can not be a requirement to join a union.

A union shop permits the hiring of nonunion members but requires workers who are not yet members to join the union within a specified period, such as 30 days.

right-to-work laws that make the **closed shop** and the **union shop** illegal. In states with such laws, workers cannot be required to join a union. By 1963, 20 states-more than half in the south-had passed right-to-work laws. Union leaders consider section 14(b) to be overtly antiunion. They argue that, if membership in a union is not compulsory, workers can be free riders, participating in the benefits provided by a union without being members. Moreover, if many workers choose not to be members, it weakens the union's bargaining position.

Although the precise impact of right-to-work laws is still controversial, one estimate suggests that union membership has been reduced by 5 or 10% in states that have enacted these laws.[2]

The Landrum-Griffin Act (1959)

The Landrum-Griffin Act was passed by a Congress that was concerned over union corruption and wished to increase the restraints on union leaders. Among other stipulations, union officials were prohibited from borrowing more than $2,000 of union funds, the embezzlement of union funds became a federal offense, and restrictions were placed on ex-convicts seeking union offices. This act also sought to make union decisions more democratic by strengthening the power of members to challenge their leaders through the ballot box. It required regularly scheduled elections of union officers by secret ballot, with every member being eligible to vote. A member's right to participate in union meetings was also guaranteed, and any member was given the right to sue a union that tried to withhold any of these privileges.

It is difficult to judge how effective this legislation has been in limiting union corruption, but it is clear that it has not completely solved the problem. For example, in the Teamsters, the largest and most powerful union in the United States, four recent presidents have been in trouble with the law. Three spent time in jail, and charges against the fourth were dropped because he was dying. U.S. workers have found that their labor leader, as well as their boss, may end up in jail. (A sample of white-collar crime by management was provided back in Example 1).

THE 1980S: UNIONS UNDER PRESSURE

During the 1980s unions came under a great deal of pressure. In August 1981, in response to an illegal strike by air-traffic controllers, President Reagan fired the striking workers. In a number of industries, unions have been unable to prevent a decline in real wages. In the airline industry, deregulation has meant a much more competitive environment. To survive, the airline companies have put pressure on employees to accept lower wages. In an extreme case, Texas Air declared bankruptcy in order to nullify its union contract and pay its workers less. In the construction industry, some unions were forced to accept lower real wages during the severe recession

---

[2]David T. Ellwood and Glenn Fine, "The Impact of Rightto-Work laws on Union Organizing," *Journal of Political Economy,* April 1987, pp. 250–273.

of 1981–1982. In autos and steel, the unions made substantial wage concessions in the early 1980s because of intense foreign competition. A number of unions found their bargaining power weakened when firms threatened to move to the less unionized Sunbelt or abroad. Between 1982 and 1984, over one-third of non-government workers under major newly negotiated union contracts accepted a wage freeze or cut.[3]

Management opposition to unions has become stronger. By 1980, the number of charges of unfair labor practices against management had reached a level three times as high as the pre-1970 average. Moreover, in 1980, the National Labor Relations Board judged that 15,000 workers had been illegally fired for union activities; the penalty for those who were caught was not high enough to discourage the practice. As an example of how embattled and defensive the unions had become, some of the members of the United Food and Commercial Workers International Union took a 25% cut in hourly wages, while others lost their jobs altogether and were replaced by nonunion workers at a 50% lower wage. Economic pressures forced a number of unions to accept such two-tiered wage contracts under which new workers could be hired at substantially lower wages than old workers. As the economic recovery continued into the late 1980s, wage concessions became less frequent. However, it wasn't clear that the unions would be able to recapture their earlier position of power.

Labor Unions: The Exercise of Market Power

While the fortunes of U.S. workers-union and nonunion alike-have ebbed and flowed, statistical studies indicate that unions have succeeded in their major task of raising wages. Union members earn an average of 10% to 25% more than nonunion workers in comparable activities. However, some of this higher wage can be explained by the fact that union workers are different; for example, unionized firms are able to hire more productive workers who could be earning a higher wage, whether or not they were in a union. This means that, for workers with the same productivity and other characteristics, a union is able to raise wages by an estimated average of about 10 to 15%.[4]

EFFECTS OF A HIGHER UNION WAGE: A FIRST APPROXIMATION

Figure 16-2 illustrates a perfectly competitive labor market, with equilibrium at El. Employers have no market power and take the wage

[3]Daniel J.B. Mitchell, "Shifting Norms in Wage Determination," in *Brookings Papers on Economic Activity 2* (1985), pp. 576–577.

[4]See H. Gregg Lewis, *Union Relative* Wage *Effects: A Survey*-(Chicago: University of Chicago Press,-1986), Ch. 9; and Gopa Chowdhury and Stephen Nickell, "Hourly Earnings in the United States," *Journal of Labor Economics*, January 1985, p. 62. In addition, Peter Linneman and Michael L. Wachter provide evidence of how widely the 1984 union versus nonunion wage dfferential varied among industries in "Rising Union Premiums and the Declining Boundaries Among Noncompeting Groups," *American Economic Review Proceedings*, May 1986, pp. 105, 106.

FIGURE 16-2

The effects of unionizing an industry in a previously competitive labor market

When a union is formed and raises the wage rate from $10 to $12, equilibrium moves from the perfectly competitive point E_1 to E_2; that is, employers respond by reducing employment from N_1 to N_2. The result of "too little employment," first described in Figure 21-6c, is the red efficiency loss 4 + 1. This arises because N_2N_1 workers don't have jobs in this industry where their productivity would be high, as shown by the height of the demand curve *D*. Instead they have to take jobs elsewhere with lower productivity shown by the height of the marginal cost for labor curve MC_L. The higher wage also results in a transfer to labor from other factors of production, as shown by the arrow on the left.

rate as given. Workers have no market power and also take the wage rate as given.

Now suppose that the workers who supply labor form a union that raises the wage rate from, say, $10 to $12 per hour. The enforcement of this higher wage requires "union discipline"; members must not be allowed to offer their labor services for less than $12. Faced with this wage, employers react by moving up their demand curve from E_1 to E2. Because the union has raised wages, employment is reduced from N_1 to N_2.

Transfer Effects

Capital and other nonlabor factors of production lose area 3 + 4. (As explained back in Figure 16-4, they earned 6 + 3 + 4 at initial equilibrium E_1. After the union is formed and equilibrium moves to E_2, they earn only area 6, for a net loss of 3 + 4.) Of this loss, 3 is a transfer to the N_2 workers who retain their jobs in this industry and enjoy a wage increase of $2. This is the reason why they formed a union: to acquire area 3 of income that the owners of capital and other factors of production would otherwise receive. However, while these N_2 workers in the industry gain, there is a loss to the workers between N_2 and N_1 who would like to work in this industry but who must instead take

Efficiency Effect

The standard deadweight efficiency loss is shown by the red triangle. This loss occurs because employment has been reduced from its perfectly competitive, efficient amount at N_1 to N_2. Displaced workers have had to move elsewhere, to industries where their productivity is lower, and the nation's output is consequently reduced.

Figure 16-2 illustrates the similarity of the markets for labor and goods. Specifically, note how a union's monopolization of a labor market in Figure 16-2 is similar to the monopolization of a product

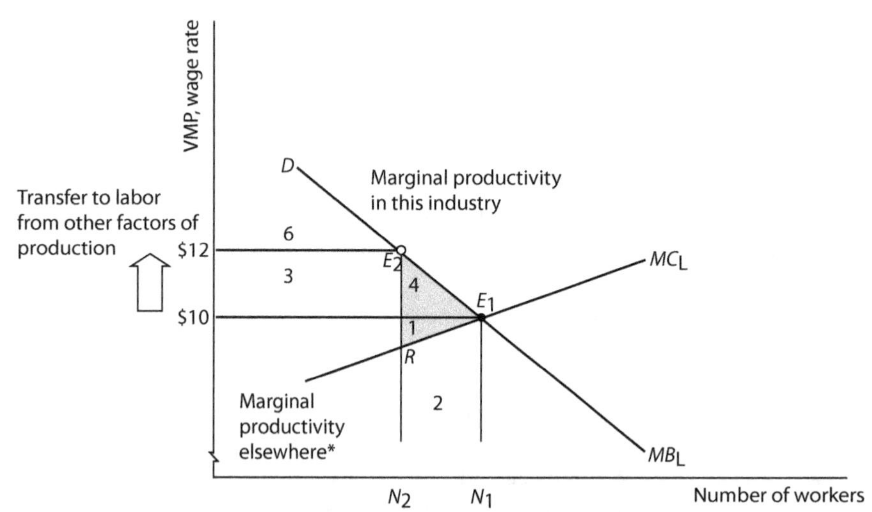

* If there is a monopoly—in this case a union—then this curve ceases to be a supply curve. (Remember: a monopoly has no supply curve.)

market in Figure 16-5 except, of course, that the union's actions affect the wage and employment of labor rather than the price and quantity of a product.[5]

How Unions Increase Efficiency

A union may also have favorable effects on efficiency.[6]

1. Unions may set up grievance procedures and improve the morale of the work force, thus improving communication between workers and management.
2. By providing workers with a collective voice, a union makes it possible for them to improve their working conditions rather than quitting. Because unions reduce quit-rates and labor turnover, there is less disruption in the workplace.
3. If market power is held by employers on the other side of the market, then the formation of a union may be a counterbalance that increases efficiency.

Monopsony: Market Power on the Employers' Side of the Labor Market

Employers typically quote the wage rate they will pay. In doing so, they frequently do not act like perfect competitors who take a market wage as given. Instead, they exercise a degree of market power. In particular, any firm that employs a large fraction of a local labor force may influence the wage rate, or even be able to set it.

To analyze this situation in Figure 16-3, initially assume a perfectly competitive labor market with equilibrium at El. But now, instead of introducing monopoly (a single seller, in the form of a union), introduce *monopoly—a* single buyer, in the form of a single employer of labor. What happens if this single employer quotes a lower wage rate, while workers on the other side of the market act as perfect competitors, taking the wage rate as given? Specifically, suppose that the employer quotes a

---

[5]There is an important reason why monopoly cannot be analyzed in a labor market in exactly the same *way* as in a product market. In a product market, a monopoly firm will take into account any loss of sales (reduction in output) that results from its high price. However, in a labor market, it is not clear how fully a union will take into account any reduced employment that results from its high wage-especially if the industry is growing and the high wage reduces only the number of new workers coming into the industry, rather than the number of current union members. This difficulty prevents us from applying the standard analysis of monopoly to determine precisely how high the union will try to push up the wage rate.

[6]For evidence that unions may increase efficiency, perhaps by raising the performance of management, see Robert N. Mefford, "The Effect of Unions on Productivity in a Multinational Manufacturing Firm," *Industrial and Labor Relations Review,* October 1986, p. 114. For a more skeptical view, see Barry T. Hirsch and John T. Addison, *Economic Analysis of* Labor Unions-New A*pproaches and Evidence* (Boston: George Allen and Unwin, 1986).

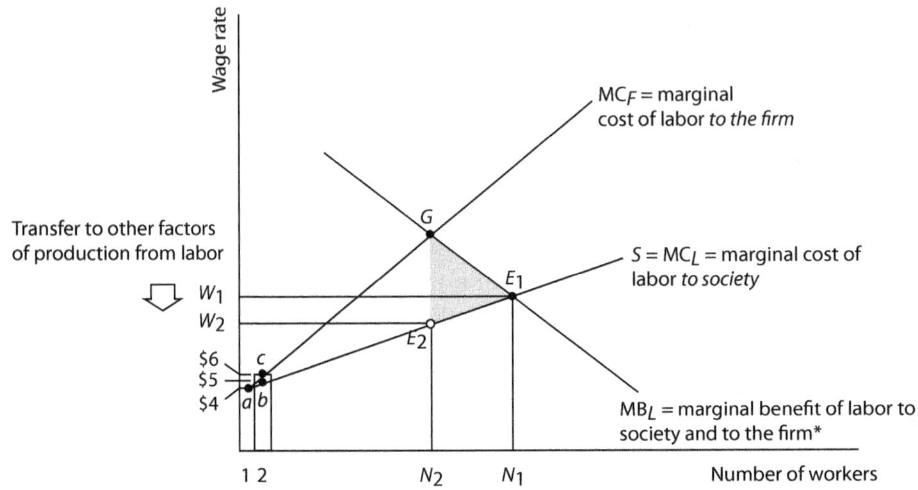

* If monopsony exists, them MB_L ceases to be a lobor demand curve. (A monopsonis has no demand curve for the same sort of reason that a monopolist has no supply curve.)

FIGURE 16-3
Effects when a perfectly competitive labor market is monopsonized.
When a monopsony is formed, equilibrium moves from the perfectly competitive point E_1 to E_2. (Because the monopsonist quotes lower wage W_2, fewer workers offer their labor services and employment falls from N_1 to N_2.) Because too few workers are employed in this industry, there is the efficiency loss shown by the red triangle. The lower wage also results in a transfer from labor to other factors of production, as shown by the white arrow.

wage of W_2, which is well below the perfectly competitive wage of W_1. In response to wage W_2, some workers leave the industry for other jobs that are now more attractive. In other words, the workers in this industry move down their supply curve from E_1 to a new equilibrium at E_2. The result is the red triangular efficiency loss because employment at N_2 is less than the perfectly competitive amount at N_1. Workers being paid W_2 are getting (the less than their marginal benefit to society height of G).

At the same time, the reduction in the wage paid by the employer results in the transfer shown by the white arrow. This transfer is from workers who receive the lower wage, to other factors of production who benefit because there is more of the firm's income left for them. (Further details on how a monopsonist may lower wages are given in Example 2.)

Here we see another example of how Adam Smith's invisible hand may go astray. The monopsonistic employer's pursuit of private benefit does not lead to public benefit. Quite the contrary: It leads to the triangular efficiency loss in Figure 16-3.

In reality, there are few cases in which monopsony occurs in its pure form with only one buyer.

One-company towns and coal mines have been cited as examples, but they are very rare. There is more likely to be a small group of employers, that is, an oligopsony with a few buyers. Although each firm has some latitude in quoting a wage rate, it is influenced by the wages quoted by competing firms. On the one hand, competition among these firms may leave each with very little influence over the wage it can quote. In this case, the wage may be close to the competitive level W_1. On the other hand, if the few oligopsonists collude, perhaps in some covert way, they may together lower the wage rate well below W_1 toward the W_2 that a monopsonist would choose. Although monopsony rarely occurs in its pure form, with only one buyer, there has been a notable example: the monopsony power a baseball club used to have in buying the services of its players.

MONOPSONY AND BASEBALL SALARIES

Before 1976, a "reserve clause" made each major league baseball team a monopsony, because a player could not sign a contract with any other team. This meant that the typical star was paid less than his value to the club. However, beginning in 1976, a player in certain circumstances could become a free agent and negotiate with other clubs.

Figure 16-4 shows what happened to a few of the players who became free agents. These before and after comparisons showing how much free agency raised salaries indicate the remarkable way that the monopsony power of the reserve clause had previously depressed salaries. Since 1976 confirming evidence has continued to accumulate. In 1980, the baseball world was astonished when the New York Yankees signed free agent Dave Winfield for an estimated \$1.5 million to \$2 million per year for 10 years. Compare this with his \$350,000 salary in San Diego the previous year before his escape, as a free agent, from the monopsony power of the reserve clause. To get some idea of Winfield's "before and-after"

Box Example 2

HOW FAR DOES A MONOPSONIST TRY TO REDUCE THE WAGE RATE?

To choose the wage rate that will maximize its profits, the monopsony firm first calculates its marginal cost of hiring labor MCF from the supply of labor S. This calculation is illustrated in the lower left-hand corner of Figure 16-3: From the S curve we see that the firm must pay \$4 an hour at point a to hire one worker and \$5 an hour at point b to hire two. However, the firm's marginal cost MC_F of hiring the second worker is not \$5 but \$6-the \$5 x 2 = \$10 it costs to hire the two workers less the \$4 it costs to hire one. Thus MC_F, the marginal cost of labor to the monopsony firm, lies above the supply curve of labor S.

To maximize profit, this firm hires labor to point G, where its marginal cost of hiring labor MC_F is equal to MB_L, the marginal benefit it receives from hiring labor. With its desired employment thus being *N2*, what is the lowest wage it can quote? The answer is W_2. At this wage rate, the labor supply curve S indicates that just exactly the desired number of workers N_2 will offer their services to this firm.

Finally, Figure 16-3 provides another view of why a red efficiency loss arises from an employment level of N_2:

The private firm equates the marginal benefit of labor MB_L not to *society's* marginal cost MC_L, but instead to its *own* marginal cost MC_F. Since the marginal benefit and cost of labor to society are not equated, the outcome is not efficient.

As a final note, consider the monopsony firm that has already used its market power to depress the wage rate of its entire labor force from W_1 to W_2. It may go one step further and reduce even more the wage paid to a specific subset of its workers, such as a minority group. The firm may discriminate in this way for the same reason that the dentist who was a monopolist in a small town discriminated by charging different fees. In either case, discrimination is a way of increasing profit. However, in other respects, the two cases are different. The action of the dentist who discriminated between patients on the basis of their income was efficient since it left everyone better off. It also was equitable because it made incomes (after dental expenses) more equal. On the other hand, discrimination based on race or sex cannot be justified, since it *reduces* efficiency, (as we will confirm later), makes incomes *less* equal, and is objectionable for noneconomic reasons.

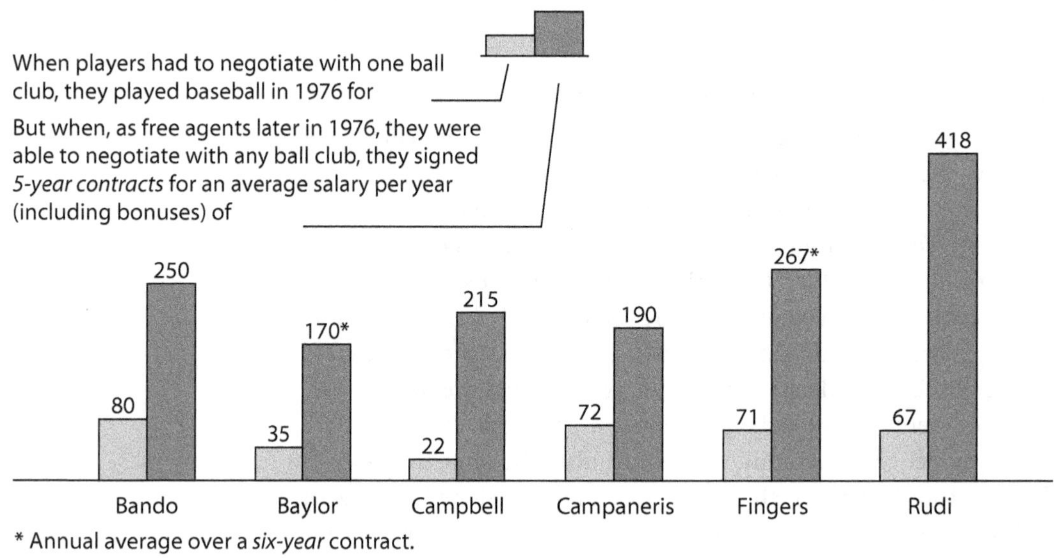

FIGURE 16-4

How monopsony (the reserve clause) depressed baseball salaries. (Figures in $000s, rounded)

situation, just increase the height of both bars for Baylor in Figure 16-4 by *ten times.* But even these numbers are no longer surprising; by 1990, salaries of over $2 million per year are no longer uncommon. (Whereas recent before-and-after salary figures confirm the importance of free agency in raising salaries, they don't do nearly as accurate a job as Figure 16-4 in estimating its precise effect. The reason is that free agency now raises salaries both before and after it happens; owners today often increase the pay of players well before they become free agents in order to reduce their incentive to choose this option.)

THE EFFECTS OF UNIONS RECONSIDERED

Suppose that the monopsony firm in Figure 16-5 has lowered the wage rate from the $10 competitive level to $8, and perfectly competitive workers have taken this wage rate as given. At this lower wage, fewer workers have been offering their labor services to this industry. Therefore employment has been reduced from N to N_1—that is, equilibrium has moved from E to E_1—with a consequent efficiency loss of areas 1 + 2. If a union is now formed and raises the wage rate from $8 to $9moving the equilibrium from E_1 to E_2—the efficiency loss is reduced from areas 1 + 2 to just area 2. In other words, the formation of this union results in an efficiency *gain* of area 1. Thus a union that reduced efficiency in a perfectly

[7]This diagram can be used to illustrate another example of the theory of the second best, first encountered in Example 1. If there is only a single firm in a small town, it will be able to exercise monopsony influence over the wage rate, driving it down toward $8. The economist's "first best" efficient solution-with perfect competition on both sides of the market is simply not possible, no matter how desirable it might be. However, there is a good second-best solution-namely, for workers to form a union in order to raise wages. If they roughly counterbalance the power that the monopsonist already enjoys on the other side of the market, the outcome may be close to the perfectly competitive $10 price and efficient employment of N.

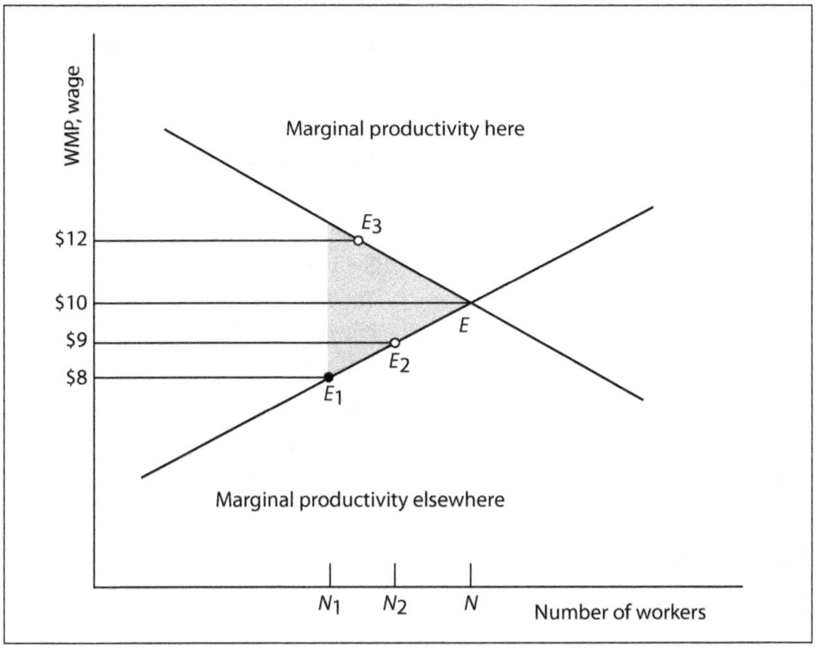

FIGURE 16-5

How inefficiency may be reduced if a union raises wages in a monopsonized labor market

Before the union, the monopsonist set the wage rate at $8. With equilibrium at E_1, there was an efficiency loss of 1 + 2. When the unon is formed, it raises the wage to $9. Equilibrium moves from E_1 to E_2, some employment is restored, and the efficiency loss is reduced to area 2. Consequently, the union increases efficiency by area 1.

competitive labor market *increases* efficiency in the monopsonized labor market in Figure 16-5.[7] Of course, the union in this diagram also benefits union members by recapturing some of the income previously lost to the monopsonist.

If the union gets very strong and pushes the wage up beyond $10 toward $12, equilibrium will shift away from E toward E_3, and efficiency will once again be reduced.

Bilateral Monopoly in a Labor Market

When both sides have market power as in Figure 16-5, they push in opposite directions. While the employer tries to keep the wage rate down close to $8, the union tries to push it up close to, say, $12. The outcome in this case of **bilateral monopoly** depends on the bargaining power of the two sides. An examination of the two curves in this diagram will not indicate precisely where the final solution will be.

Bilateral monopoly is a market in which there is only one buyer and one seller.

WHICH SIDE HAS THE STRONGER BARGAINING POSITION?

To see the importance of bargaining power, suppose that there is only one company in a mining town and that it faces an ineffective union representing only a few workers. In this case, the company will be in a good position to keep the wage low. On the other hand, if there is a single, strong union facing a number of employers, the union will have the stronger bargaining position.

An outcome close to the efficient outcome E requires that the market power of the two sides be in rough balance. If labor has all the market power, the outcome will be the inefficient E_3. If management has all the market power, the outcome will be the inefficient E_1.

TABLE 16-1
Union Member as a Percentage of the Labor Force Source: *The World Factbook 1990*

Country	Percentage	Country	Percentage
Israel	90%	Canada	31%
Sweden	90	Netherlands	29
Finland	80	Japan	29
Belgium	70	France	20
Norway	66	Switzerland	20
Denmark	65	Taiwan	18
Austria	62	Singapore	17
Italy	42	Hong Kong	15
United Kingdom	37	United States	14
Ireland	36	South Korea	10
Germany	34		

Wage Differentials

By Joseph Stiglitz and Carl Walsh

The basic competitive model suggests that if the goods being sold are the same, prices will also be the same. Wages are the price in the labor market; but even in the absence of unions, similar types of workers performing similar types of jobs are sometimes paid quite different wages. For example, some secretaries are paid twice as much as others. How can economists explain differences like these?

An understanding of wage differentials begins with the observation that although different jobs may have the same title, they can be quite different. Some are less pleasant, require more overtime, and are in a less convenient location. These are **nonpecuniary attributes** of a job. Other nonpecuniary attributes include the degree of autonomy provided the worker (that is, the closeness with which her actions are supervised) and the risk she must bear, whether from physical hazard or from variability in income. Economists expect wages to adjust to reflect the attractiveness or unattractiveness of these nonpecuniary characteristics. **Compensating wage differentials** arise because firms have to compensate their workers for the negative aspects of a job.

Other differences are accounted for by differences in the productivity of workers. These are *productivity wage differentials.* Some workers are much more productive than others, even those with the same experience and education.

Compensating and productivity wage differentials fall within the realm of the basic competitive model analysis. But other wage differentials are due to imperfect information. It takes time to search out different job opportunities. Just as one store may sell the same object for a higher price than another store, one firm may hire labor for a lower wage than another firm. The worker who accepts a lower-paying job

Joseph Stiglitz and Carl Walsh from *Principles of Microeconomics*, pp. 362–364. Published by W.W. Norton & Company, Inc.

simply because he did not know about the higher-paying one down the street illustrates an *information-based differential.*

Limited information has important implications for firms. First, in the standard competitive model, firms face a horizontal supply curve for labor. If they raise wages slightly above the "market" wage, they can obtain as much labor as they want. In practice, mobility is more limited. Even if workers at other firms knew about the higher wage offer, they might be reluctant to switch. They *may worry* that they are not well matched for the job, or that the employer is offering high wages because the work is unattractive.

Second, firms worry about the quality of their workforce. If an employer offers a higher wage to someone working for another firm and the worker accepts, the employer might worry about the signal the acceptance sends about the worker's quality. Did his current employer—who presumably knows a lot about the worker's productivity—fail to match the job offer because his productivity does not warrant the higher wage? Does the worker's willingness to leave demonstrate a "lack of loyalty," or an "unsettled nature"-in which case, he may not stick with the new firm long enough to make his training worthwhile? These concerns again impede labor mobility, leading employers to prefer to keep their existing labor force even when there are lower-paid workers with similar credentials whom they might recruit at a lower wage.

Different groups of individuals may differ in their mobility. For instance, older workers may be much more reluctant to move than younger workers. Sometimes, firms take advantage of these differences to cut their own costs. Knowing that older workers will not leave even if their wages fail to keep pace with inflation, employers may hold back raises from them. Their lack of mobility provides a rationale for employers to engage in age discrimination.

DISCRIMINATION

Discrimination is said to occur if two workers of seemingly similar *work-related* characteristics are treated differently. Paying higher wages to better-educated workers is not discrimination, as long as the higher level of education is related to higher productivity. If older workers are less productive, then paying them lower wages is not discrimination. But if they are just as productive as younger workers, then taking advantage of their lower mobility to pay them less is discrimination.

Forty years ago, there was open and outright discrimination in the labor market. Some employers simply refused to hire African Americans. Today much of the discrimination that occurs is more subtle. Firms seek to hire the best workers they can for each job at the lowest cost possible, operating with imperfect information. In making predictions about future performance, employers use whatever information they have available. Employers may have found that those receiving a degree from a well-established school are more productive, on average, than those receiving a degree from a less-established college. Of the African Americans and Hispanics who are college graduates, more may have gone to less-prestigious schools. Screening the applicant pool to pick those with degrees from well-established colleges effectively excludes many African Americans and Hispanics. This more subtle form of discrimination is called **statistical discrimination.**

Some discrimination reflects neither old-fashioned prejudice nor statistics. Employers may just feel more comfortable dealing with people with whom they have dealt in the past. Highly uncertain about who is a good worker, and knowing that a bad worker can do enormous damage, top management may rely on certain trusted employees for recommendations. And such judgments are inevitably affected by friendships and other ties. Many claim that if discrimination is to be eliminated, this associative form, based on "old boy networks," has to be broken.

When firms pay lower wages to, say, women or minorities, they are practicing **wage discrimination**. Today, wage discrimination is perhaps less common than **job discrimination**, the denial to disadvantaged groups of equal access to better-paying jobs. Women are often said to face a "glass ceiling": they can climb up to middle management jobs but can't get beyond that level to reach top management.

Some market forces tend to limit the extent of discrimination. If a woman earns less than a man of comparable productivity, it pays a firm to hire her. Not to do so costs the firm profits. To put it another way, the firm pays a price for discriminating. If there are enough firms that put profits above prejudice, then the wages of women will be bid up toward the level of men of comparable productivity.

Beginning in the 1960s, the government has taken an active stance in combating discrimination. In 1964, Congress passed the Civil Rights Act, which banned employment discrimination and set up the Equal Employment Opportunity Commission to prosecute cases of discrimination. The reach of these laws was extended in 1975 when the government prohibited age discrimination; in 1990, job discrimination against qualified individuals with disabilities was barred.

Beyond this, the federal government has required its contractors to undertake **affirmative action**. They must actively seek out minorities and women for jobs, and actively seek to promote them to better-paying positions. Affirmative action has occasionally taken the form of quotas that specify that a certain number or fraction of positions be reserved for minorities or women. Critics claim that quotas are discriminatory-they imply that a minority individual would be chosen over a more qualified white male. One of the objectives of antidiscrimination laws was to discourage thinking in racial or gender terms. Courts have reaffirmed this aim, allowing quotas only in special circumstances such as redressing the effects of specific instances of past discrimination.

Wrap-Up

EXPLANATIONS OF WAGE DIFFERENTIALS

Unions
Unions may succeed in obtaining higher wages for their workers. Compensating differentials: Wage differences may correspond to differences in the nature of the job.

Productivity differentials
Wage differences may correspond to differences in the productivity between workers.

Information-based differentials
Wage differences may be a reflection of workers' not having perfect information about the opportunities available in the market, and employers' not viewing all workers as perfect substitutes for one another.

Imperfect labor mobility
Differentials are preserved because of the reluctance of individuals to move between jobs.

Discrimination
Wage differentials and hiring and promotion decisions can sometimes be traced to nothing more than differences of race or sex.

SUMMARY

By Paul Wonnacott and Ronald Wonnacott

1. Labor markets are often imperfect. Workers form unions to exercise monopoly power on the supply side of the market. On the other side of the market, employers may exercise monopsony power. Examples include a government that hires public service employees, and a private firm that is the only major employer in a small town.
2. Unions provide labor with a collective voice. In collective bargaining, unions promote the interests of their workers by pressing for such improvements as (a) better working conditions, (b) seniority rules to protect long-time workers, and (c) higher wages.
3. If a union is formed in a perfectly competitive labor market without externalities and uses its market power to raise the wage rate, there is an overall efficiency loss. The reason is that some workers are not hired in this industry even though they would be more productive here than elsewhere. There is also a transfer: by raising the wage rate, the union transfers income to labor from other factors of production.

Paul Wonnacott and Ronald Wonnacott from *Microeconomics*, pp. 406–407. Published by John Wiley & Sons, Inc.

4. On the other side of the market, if employers acquire monopsony power and lower the wage below its perfectly competitive level, there will be the same sort of efficiency loss. But while the efficiency effects of monopoly and monopsony will be similar, their transfer effects will be in opposite directions. When a monopsonist lowers wages, the transfer is from labor to other factors of production.
5. If a labor market is already monopsonized by a single employer, it no longer necessarily follows that efficiency will be reduced if a union is formed to raise the wage rate. In fact, if the union's market power is used only to offset the market power of the employer, efficiency will be increased.
6. A union may increase efficiency in other ways, too. By providing workers with a collective voice, it may improve their performance and reduce costly turnover of the labor force. A union may increase productivity by improving morale and communication between labor and management.
7. Bilateral monopoly occurs when market power exists on both sides of the market: Unions with monopoly power bargain with employers with monopsony power. The wage that results will fall between the high wage an unopposed union would seek and the low wage an unopposed monopsonist would offer. But, within these limits, it is impossible to predict precisely where the wage rate will be set. However, it will be heavily influenced by the bargaining power of each side. For example, a large union strike fund will increase the union's bargaining power, whereas a large inventory of finished goods will increase the bargaining power of management. Bargaining is also affected by the negotiating expertise of labor and management. An incompetent negotiator who won't provide the other side with a face—saving compromise may prevent an agreement from being reached.
8. Membership in public service unions has grown rapidly in recent years. Such a union may have a strong bargaining position, particularly if it provides an essential service. To avoid a strike, a government employer may be willing to tax or borrow to meet a wage claim that would drive a private employer out of business. An important policy issue is whether public employees should have the right to strike.

KEY CONCEPTS

industrial union
craft union
collective bargaining
seniority rules
codetermination
closed shop
union shop
open shop
right-to-work law

transfer and efficiency effects of a union
transfer and efficiency effects of monopoly
bilateral monopoly
spillover costs of a strike mediation
mediation
arbitration
final-offer arbitration
dynamic wages differential
compensating wage differential

PROBLEMS

1. Before deregulation, the Civil Aeronautics Board allowed the airlines to charge high fares, with some of the resulting profit being absorbed by high wage and salary payments. In such circumstances, would you expect that the deregulation that has made the airlines more competitive in setting their fares has affected their labor contracts as well? If so, how? What, in fact, did happen to the wages and salaries of employees when the airlines were deregulated?
2. "Monopsony in the labor market may have exactly the same effect on efficiency as a union." Is this possible? Explain. Would the transfer effects be the same in the two cases? (show how the two cases in the present example can involve identical efficiency effects but entirely different transfer effects.) Explain.
3. In the case of monopsony, which efficiency condition in Figure 21-7 has been violated?
4. In Figure 16-5, suppose that the initial wage rate in a unionized labor market is $12. If employers form a bargaining association and successfully negotiate a lower wage rate, show how efficiency is affected. Consider two cases: What happens if the association negotiates the wage down to $9? Down to $8?
5. Do you think that, as capital accumulates, the bargaining power of workers vis-à-vis management increases or decreases? Which workers can more effectively threaten to strike: Workers who would be leaving bulldozers idle? Or workers who would be laying down their shovels?
6. Which union in each of the following pairs has the greater bargaining power? In each case, explain why. (a) A union of workers on the New York subway or a union of workers who build the trains. (b) A firefighters' union or a public school teachers' union. (c) A public school teachers' union or a university professors' union.
7. "Tying wage increases in the public sector to wage increases in private industry will not necessarily equalize wages. All it will do is keep them the same if they start out equal. If public sector wages are initially less than private sector wages, tying wages in this way only guarantees that inequities will be preserved." Do you agree? Do you think it is fair to pay both public and private employees the same wage if public employees have greater job security? If not, explain why, and give an estimate of the differential you consider fair.
8. Use a diagram to show how the theory of the second best applies to labor forming a union in a market that is already monopsonized.

EXPERIMENT

Labor Market

By David Moglen

Supplies needed: 3 x 5 Cards – half one color (let's say green) and half another color (we'll say purple). The number of cards you need, in total, should be equal to the number of students in the class or slightly more.

Directions

From the stack of green 3 x 5 cards, write the number "3" on the first card, "4" on the second green card, etc., up to "22" on the twentieth green card.

Next, from the stack of purple 3 x 5 cards, write the number "30" on the first card, "29" on the second purple card, etc, counting down to "21" on the twentieth purple card.

Purple cardholders are employers and Green Cardholders are employees. There are multiple rounds so everyone will have plenty of chances to experience both roles.

Give the green stack of 3 x 5 cards to a student on the left side of the class, and the purple stack to a student on the right side and ask them to shuffle. (Any student should shuffle the cards before each round). Ask the shuffler to hold the stack face down and pass out one card to each person on their side of the room. An employee, for instance, with a green card that says "7" has a willingness to work at any wage above or equal to seven dollars per hour. To use the economic term, $7 is their "transfer earnings." If they can get an employer (purple cardholder) to agree to pay them $16 per hour, they are receiving a net bonus ("economic rent") of $16-$7=$9.

For the employer, let's say you have a purple card that says $27. This is the most you are willing to pay your employee. So if you agree to hire the above-mentioned employee at $16 per hour, your **net gain** is $27-$16=$11.

Round one will last three minutes. Future rounds will be timed to last two minutes.

Once the time is up, all employee and employer pairs will be clearly visible standing next to each other. Not all students will find a job or an employee in every round. The teacher or their delegate will keep track of the **top three net gainers on both employees' side and employers' side**. The board in front of the room will simply read, for example:

Round

1	2	3	4	5	etc.
Jones 10	Simpson 9	etc.	etc.	etc.	
Smith 9	Varney 8				
Brown 9	Keel 6				
Dennehy 11	Gellman 10				
Crown 10	Jones 8				
Bones 9	Smith 6				

Those are my examples of student names for the **top three net gainers in each round, followed by their net gain**. Notice you don't need to keep track of who was employer vs. employee. Jones and Smith apparently did quite well, winning in round one and round two.

The first round is the free market. They pair off at any wage rate that makes sense for both parties. i.e., if you have an employer who's purple card says that the most they will pay is $25 and they agree to pay someone $40, their deal is not valid and neither party's net gain will count or get written on the board. You can't have a negative net gain. Similarly, an employee with a minimum acceptable wage of $12 cannot accept a wage of, say, $3, or even $11. $12 would be the absolute minimum acceptable wage if that is what their green card says. The top three net gains are recorded on the board.

continued

For the second round, the left half of class collects and hands over green cards to the right half of class, and receives the stack of purple cards in exchange. **A repeat of the free market** experiment starts, and in two minutes the round ends and the winners and their scores are recorded on the board.

The third round has a union: green card holders will get two minutes to decide collectively what wage they will accept. This is the one single wage rate that all hirings will pay in this round. Let's say it's $15. Notice some employees will inevitably be unable to work at the wage since they need a minimum of, say, $18 to work. When the union has decided their wage (cents are okay too, e.g., $15.50) then the round begins and employers/employees have two minutes to agree to any hiring. The top three net gainers from the workers and the top three from the bosses are recorded.

In the fourth round, students will **simply trade roles** and the other half of class will now have green cards and agree upon one **union** wage while the employers remain competitive and non-collluding.

In the fifth round, employers form a **monopsony (single buyer)** in the labor market and decide on one single wage to pay, while workers are non-unionized. Optional Additional Round: switch roles and let the other half of class be a monopsony.

In the sixth round you experience a **"bilateral monopoly:"** both employers and employees get their two minutes to collude with their own side. Employees, in a union, then state their agreed-upon, ideal wage, and employers state their agreed-upon, ideal wage they would like to pay. A delegation of three union-selected representatives will meet for one to two minutes with the three-member delegation from the employers' side. These six students will agree to one wage that will be the only wage rate in the round. If they cannot agree, the teacher (who should be listening in on these six-student negotiations) will announce that the wage is halfway between the lowest stated wage proposed by the union and the highest stated wage proposed by the employers' monopsony. As before, the scores of the top net gainers are recorded on the board. Optional Additional Round: switch roles and simulate the bilateral monopoly again.

Winners: Add up your score for each round you were a top-three net gainer with your name on the board. The top three overall totals should be rewarded a few extra points.

Notes

www.ingramcontent.com/pod-product-compliance
Lightning Source LLC
LaVergne TN
LVHW080629011026
849160LV00014B/1163
* 9 7 8 1 6 3 4 8 7 0 1 1 5 *